KW-743-790

The Rural Landscape
of the Welsh Borderland

By the same author

MAP AND LANDSCAPE
(with Geoffrey Nulty)

THE HISTORICAL ATLAS OF CHESHIRE

170 14

© Dorothy Sylvester 1969

First published 1969 by
MACMILLAN AND CO LTD
Little Essex Street London WC2
and also at Bombay Calcutta and Madras
Macmillan South Africa (Publishers) Pty Ltd Johannesburg
The Macmillan Company of Australia Pty Ltd Melbourne
The Macmillan Company of Canada Ltd Toronto
Gill and Macmillan Ltd Dublin

Printed in Great Britain by
ROBERT MACLEHOSE AND CO LTD
The University Press Glasgow

The Rural Landscape of the Welsh Borderland

A Study in Historical Geography

Dorothy Sylvester

PEMBROKESHIRE · UNIV LIBRARY

MACMILLAN
London · Melbourne · Toronto

To Professor E. G. Bowen

Contents

8 CONTENTS

List of Plates

List of Maps

List of Tables

Preface

IN 1953 Professor E. G. Bowen of Aberystwyth suggested that
I should incorporate and extend the work I had already published
in papers on the rural landscape of the Welsh Borderland in a
book covering the whole area, and the present volume is the
result. No part of Britain is more varied and few are more beautiful than this border country where the past haunts both the present
scene and the long memory of its people. Two thousand years of
conflict and adjustment have gone into the making of a land
where natural wealth and poverty co-exist, and on this geographical stage the differences between rural communities and
the questions that these differences pose to the student of
human and historical geography are challenging indeed. There is
a poetry in the search for historical rhythm and an excitement
in the analysis of contributory data which may be sensed not
only by the geographer and the historian but by all who are
aware of the world around them and of the part that environment plays in the slow shaping of village and hamlet, of field and
farm.

This study is based on the essential familiarity with geography
in the field and a wide range of published material, but such
claims as it may have to originality depend primarily on the
application of the methods of historical geography to the sifting
and mapping of data culled from tens of thousands of documents.
These range in date from the Domesday Book to the Tithe Survey
and the Enclosure Awards, and a great number of them have
here been used for the first time in the context of rural geography.
Many of the documents which together have provided the most
significant distributions, such as are depicted on the map of open
arable and common meadow lands (Fig. 23), are brief minor
deeds in estate collections. At the other end of the scale are major
surveys. Some of these, like the *Survey of the Honour of Denbigh* and

the *First Extent of Bromfield and Yale*, long since published, have here been integrated into the evolving pattern of the rural land-scape of north-east Wales and of the Borderland as a whole. The documentary sources now available are so abundant that one volume is only sufficient to provide a summary illustrated by selected areas and examples. For this reason the distribution map – one of the shorthand devices most useful to the geographer – has been freely used.

Numerous papers and a number of books have been written on rural settlement and its associated land patterns but comparatively few of these are studies in the round. Still fewer cover sizeable areas with the detailed distribution maps which I believe are fundamental to the full interpretation of the historical geography of the rural scene. The present work covering a critical border zone is a modest attempt to contribute to the knowledge and understanding of the patterns which are slowly emerging, to the methodology of the subject, and to the solution of some at least of the teasing problems which still bedevil the study of settlement in Britain from the Dark Ages onwards.

It is impossible to acknowledge by name the many people to whom I am indebted in such a variety of ways for help in the preparation of this volume, but none is forgotten and the assistance of all is warmly appreciated. There are, however, some to whom specific acknowledgement must be made and first among these is Professor E. G. Bowen to whom the book is dedicated in gratitude. He not only suggested that it should be written, but on many occasions gave me the benefit of his own particular brand of stimulating discussion and read the script at various stages. Many of his suggestions have been followed. To Professor P. R. Crowe I am indebted for the facilities he made available in the Department of Geography in the University of Manchester. One of my major debts is to the National Library of Wales where, thanks to the courtesy of its librarian, Mr E. D. Jones, C.B.E., I have enjoyed the many facilities that it offers. In particular, I would express my gratitude for the untiring help of Miss Megan Ellis, head of the Department of Prints, Drawings, and Maps, and of her staff, and of Mr B. G. Owens, head of the Department of Manuscripts and Records. In the Public Record Office, the headquarters of the

Historical Manuscripts Commission, the John Rylands Library, Manchester, the library of the University College of North Wales, Chester and Hereford City Libraries, Shrewsbury Public Library, Radnorshire County Library Headquarters, and the County Record Offices of Cheshire, Shropshire, Herefordshire, Monmouthshire, and Flintshire I have been accorded similar facilities, and to these must be added a large number of parish churches and the Diocesan Record Office of Chester where tithe documents and other parish records were readily made available.

Of the maps and plans in this book the frontispiece and Figures 1, 3–12, 15, 16, 18–23, 37–39 and 42–44, are wholly or in large part original. The material incorporated in Figure 13 is used by courtesy of Professor William Rees. For the compilation of Figure 14 I am most grateful to Mr D. F. Renn. Similarly, I am happy to acknowledge the right to reproduce part or all of Figure 17 by courtesy of His Grace the Duke of Beaufort and Mr H. Noel Jerman, Figures 24, 45 and 46 by courtesy of the Librarian, Hereford City Library. Figure 26 was adapted from a re-drawing of a map in the Downton Castle Estate Office and is included by courtesy of Major H. Kincaid Lennox and of Mr D. G. Bayliss, who re-drew it. Figure 30 based on the Leeke Collection is included by courtesy of Lady Wakeman. In addition, a number of plans are reproduced from originals in the National Library of Wales by courtesy of the Librarian. These are Figure 31 from the Glynne of Hawarden Family Papers and Documents, Figure 33 from the Glansevern Collection, Figure 53 from the Ashburnham Deposit and Figure 56 from the Longueville Deposit. Figure 58 is based on maps in the National Library of Wales Collection. Figures 8 and 29 have previously been published in my papers in the *Transactions of the Historic Society of Lancashire and Cheshire* (**114**, 1962, and **108**, 1956), Figure 31 in the *Transactions of the Flintshire Historical Society* (1954–5), and Figure 28 in the *Agricultural History Review* (**6**, 1958).

Apart from Figures 28, 49 and 50 drawn by her predecessor Mrs Thelma Morgan, the draughting of all the maps and plans in this book has been done by Miss E. Anne Lowcock, senior cartographer in the Department of Geography in the University of Manchester. To her excellent and untiring work I owe much of the presentation both of my original maps and of the many others that she has adapted and re-drawn, and I gratefully acknowledge the invaluable help that she has afforded me.

In the compilation of the Glossary, the checking of the orthography and definition of the Welsh words and elements was carried out by Mr R. J. Thomas and Mr Elfyn Jenkins, editor and assistant editor respectively of the University of Wales Dictionary, and I am greatly indebted to them. My thanks are also due to Mrs Margaret J. C. Steele and Mrs Patricia Spriggs, secretary and former assistant secretary in the Department of Geography in the University of Manchester, and to Mrs Jean Bennett, who between them typed most of the final copy of the script; to Mrs Grace Corbett, who has read the book in proof; and to Mr William Taylor, whose proof-reading has been the culminating task in long years of filing, of general help, and unfailing support and encouragement. Last, I must include my many past students in the Universities of Durham and Manchester who, consciously or unconsciously, by their work, their discussions, and their interest, have contributed to the building up of a methodology in rural landscape studies which I have tried to demonstrate in the chapters which follow.

Wistaston,   D. S.
Cheshire
1967

Acknowledgements

In addition to acknowledgements made in the Preface, the author would also like to thank the following for permission to use photographs:

Aerofilms, Plates I, II, V, VI, VII, IX, X, XI, XIV, XV and XVII; Manchester Airviews, Plates XII, XX and XXI; Reece Winstone, Plates III, IV, VIII and XIX; H. Tempest, Plates XIII, XVI and XVIII

Figure 47 is reproduced by permission of the Ordnance Survey

LIST OF ABBREVIATIONS

A. *Used in Part IV and in Chapter 9*

Habitation Grouping
A Nucleated village
B Hamlet
C Semi-dispersed settlement
D Dispersed settlement
E Park-estate type
F Farm type
U Small town or country town

Location
L   Lowland
V   Vale
Lv Valley in lowland area
Hv Narrow valley in upland area
H   Hill (excluding hill location in lowland)
Lh Hill site in lowland
W   Site in post-Conquest woodland
J   Junction of upland and lowland
Jw Junction of woodland and open country

Other settlement features
p   parochial settlement
(p) late-formed parish
m   market
(m) former market
c   castle
(c) former castle
b   motte and bailey
l   head or former head of lordship

Subsidiary and late settlement elements
e late enclosure hamlet
i industrial settlement
o orchard settlement
q mining and/or quarrying settlement
r chapel hamlet
s suburban or residential settlement
t road, rail or canal side settlement
w squatting settlement on the waste

B. *Other abbreviations*

Agric. Hist. Rev.	*Agricultural History Review*
Archaeol. Camb.	*Archaeologia Cambrensis*
Br.	Brythonic
Brec.	Breconshire
Bull. Bd Celtic Stud.	*Bulletin of the Board of Celtic Studies*
C.B.	County Borough

Ch.	Cheshire
D.B.	Domesday Book
Denb.	Denbighshire
Fl.	Flintshire
Geog.	*Geography*
Geogrl J.	*Geographical Journal*
Gl.	Gloucestershire
Glam.	Glamorgan
Glam. R.O.	Glamorgan Record Office
He.	Herefordshire
Her. Cath. Lib.	Hereford Cathedral Library
Her. City Lib.	Hereford City Library
Jl Geol.	*Journal of Geology*
Jl R. Anthrop. Inst.	*Journal of the Royal Anthropological Institute*
Jl R. Soc. Antiquaries of Ireland	*Journal of the Royal Society of Antiquaries of Ireland*
La.	Lancashire
Lat.	Latin
Mon.	Monmouthshire
Mont.	Montgomeryshire
M.W.	Medieval Welsh
N.L.W.	National Library of Wales
Norm.Fr.	Norman French
O.D.	Ordnance Datum
O.Dan.	Old Danish
O.E.	Old English
O.N.	Old Norse
O.S.	Ordnance Survey
O.Sc.	Old Scandinavian
O.W.	Old Welsh
P.R.O.	Public Record Office
Rad.	Radnorshire
Sa.	Shropshire
Sa.R.O.	Shropshire Record Office
S.A.S.	Shropshire Archaeological Society
Soc. Rev.	*Sociological Review*
Trans. Anglesey Antiq. Soc.	*Transactions of the Anglesey Antiquarian Society*
Trans. Cymmrod. Soc.	*Transactions of the Cymmrodorion Society*
Trans. Fl. Hist. Soc.	*Transactions of the Flintshire Historical Society*
Trans. Hist. Soc. Lancs. and Cheshire	*Transactions of the Historic Society of Lancashire and Cheshire*

Trans. Inst. Br. Geogr.	*Transactions of the Institute of British Geographers*
Trans. Lancs. and Ches. Antiq. Soc.	*Transactions of the Lancashire and Cheshire Antiquarian Society*
Trans. Rad. Soc.	*Transactions of the Radnorshire Society*
Trans. R. Hist. Soc.	*Transactions of the Royal Historical Society*
Trans. Shrops. Archaeol. Soc.	*Transactions of the Shropshire Archaeological Society*
Trans. Woolhope Nat. Fld Club	*Transactions of the Woolhope Naturalists' Field Club*
T.R.E.	Tempore regis Edwardi
T.R.W.	Tempore regis Wilhelmi
U.C.N.W.	University College of North Wales
W.	Welsh
Wo.	Worcestershire

Introduction

THE Welsh Borderland is a contact area. Here the ancient Cambrian uplands adjoin the newer rocks of the English lowlands. Here Welsh and English people and cultures meet and mingle, and the result, as in so many cases of hybridisation, is not a weaker but a more robust product. During the centuries of conflict prior to the Union of England and Wales and in the quieter and more prosperous centuries which have followed, this Borderland has evolved a personality of its own and yet has conserved numerous strands from the several cultures and periods which have helped to make it what it is today.

Its area is incapable of easy definition, though its axis lies indubitably in a zone triply marked by the Roman roads which linked Deva (Chester) and Isca (Caerleon), the less devious line of Offa's Dyke which for the Welsh still symbolises the division between *Cymru* and *Saeson,* and the political boundary between the Principality and England. Before the coming of the Romans, however, and for a brief period after their withdrawal, all Britain was Celtic, and the north–south edge of the Welsh hills – die-straight except for the promontory of the south Shropshire hills – had no significance as a frontier. Its strategic possibilities, though they were made use of locally by the hill-fort builders of the Early Iron Age, were first envisaged as a through line by the Romans who used it as a base from which to launch their campaigns against the Welsh Upland. As an ethnic frontier, it dates only from the seventh century when the late tide of Anglo-Saxon advance lapped gently up to the hill edge. In the late eighth century Offa's Dyke set a sort of seal on this ethnic function of the physical border which Welshmen at least have never since forgotten. It was during the Mercian period that the broad carpet of Celtic settlement and place-names became partially overlaid by Anglo-Saxon occupation and Anglo-Saxon names, and its peoples

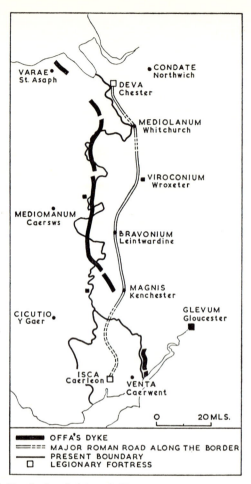

VARAE● St. Asaph

●CONDATE Northwich

☐ DEVA Chester

MEDIOLANUM Whitchurch

VIROCONIUM Wroxeter

MEDIOMANUM Caersws

BRAVONIUM Leintwardine

MAGNIS Kenchester

GLEVUM Gloucester

CICUTIO● Y Gaer

ISCA Caerleon ☐

VENTA Caerwent

0   20 MLS.

███ OFFA'S DYKE
===== MAJOR ROMAN ROAD ALONG THE BORDER
───── PRESENT BOUNDARY
☐   LEGIONARY FORTRESS

1. The Welsh Borderland: historic lines associated with its definition

mingled, though in what proportions is still a vexed question. Apart from a narrow fringe, however, the Cambrian Uplands remained almost inviolate until after 1066 when, with the setting up of Norman manors and the founding of the great belt of marcher lordships, the wide zone of the Marches was pressed into eastern Wales and across South Wales, the Norman lords using the valleys which break up the hill edge as their main lines of advance. Where the Romans built military roads and an occasional fortress, Mercians and Anglo-Normans made genuine settlements, modified some of the existing hamlets, and made significant and widespread changes in land use and territorial patterns.

For well over 1500 years prior to the Union of England and Wales, the Welsh Borderland had a troubled history of intermittent war and raiding, and it is unique in Britain, not in the fact that it is a border country in both the ethnic and the strategic sense, but in the scale of its strategic building. There is an equally clear ethnic frontier between Cornwall and Devon, and the Scottish Borderland is renowned in history and legend on account of its centuries of war and forays, but neither compares in length or depth, nor in the multiplicity of its defensive works, with the Welsh Borderland. Here, Early Iron Age forts, Roman camps and military roads, Anglo-Saxon dykes, Norman mottes, innumerable little castles and defended manor houses, and – most impressive of all – the great medieval castles such as Ludlow and Shrewsbury, Powys and Chirk, Raglan and Chepstow, exist in numbers in a deep belt across the Welsh Border. To this day, its people cannot but remember the past, and the echo of battles long ago, by a strange twist of history, has been a factor in welding a frontier zone into a human province. That many of the battles fought here were of national significance needs no underlining. The Yorkist defeat of the Lancastrians at Mortimer's Cross a few miles north-west of Leominster put Edward IV on the throne. The Mortimers' involvement in the struggle for power, meant that many campaigns in the long Wars of the Roses were fought out here, but the ultimate outcome which put Henry Tudor on the throne in 1485 was to prove the economic salvation of this troubled countryside in that his son, Henry VIII, brought about the Union of the two countries in 1536 and the end – apart from the Civil Wars – of centuries of ravaging a fair and productive land.

From that time onwards, a common economic and political history has undoubtedly operated towards the expunging of some of the many differences. In terms of rural pattern, the most important of these changes have perhaps been a moderate growth of population and the consequent expansion of villages, hamlets and country towns, the increasing prosperity of agriculture, and the widespread results of the Great Enclosure movement. Yet despite the changes of the past four centuries, the conservatism of country ways of life has tended to preserve a high proportion of the earlier forms, and the old patterns of village and hamlet, manor house and farm have remained remarkably and blessedly stable in this extensive province of the Borderland, and only at its termini and in the small Shropshire coalfield have there been experienced to any degree the metamorphoses wrought by wide-scale urban expansion.

What is now recognised as a joint field of study of historical geographers and economic historians, was long considered the province of historians. Two notable early contributions to the elucidation of the English village as an institution were made by Sir Henry Sumner Maine in *Village Communities in the East and West* (1871) and Frederic Seebohm in *The English Village Community: an essay in economic history* (1883). These were followed by George Laurence Gomme's *The Village Community* in 1890. Maine's work was largely an essay in jurisprudence and made comparison between the village communities of Europe and India, but Seebohm and Gomme got right down to field plans of British townships though Gomme was also concerned with Indian comparisons. In 1897 was published Frederic William Maitland's classic and scholarly work *Domesday Book and Beyond* applying his knowledge of early and medieval English laws and customs to society and land in town and country. This was followed by Paul Vinogradoff's *Growth of the Manor* in 1904, embodying a not dissimilar approach by a professor of jurisprudence. Meantime, the interest in field systems was growing, together with a wider enquiry into other forms of land use,[1] of which H. L. Gray's *English Field Systems* (1915) and G. Slater's *The English Peasantry and the Enclosure of the Common Fields* (1907) have remained as standard works of great value. In 1922, Harold Peake published *The English Village* as an anthropological study, but it was rapidly adopted by geographers as providing the first overall approach to the study of English rural landscape with a firm foot on the soil

---

[1] For example, G. Shaw Lefèvre, *English Commons and Forests* (1894); A. N. Palmer and E. Owen, *The History of Ancient Tenures of Land in North Wales and the Marches* (1910); and F. Seebohm, *Customary Acres and their Historical Importance* (1914).

and a geographical basis of classification. Written largely from the agricultural angle, C. S. and C. S. Orwin's *The Open Fields* (1938) is a more recent specialist volume contributing to the whole question of English field systems and their historical modes of working, but more broadly based and of considerable value as a reference volume is the *Report of the Royal Commission on Common Lands*, 1955–8. Of the general studies which link the work of the historian and the geographer, the most recent are that of W. G. Hoskins, *The Making of the English Landscape* (1955), a delightful book which offers a broadly comprehensive introduction to the story of both town and village in relation to their geographical setting, and M. W. Beresford and J. K. S. St Joseph's *Medieval England* (1958) based on aerial survey and old maps.

Organised geographical studies of rural forms and distributions began some forty to fifty years ago with the setting up of a Commission on Rural Habitat by the International Geographical Congress and since then, although numbers of papers have been published, the analysis of rural geography in this country from the point of view of origins, development, and patterns has proceeded all too slowly and no single volume has been published by a geographer dealing solely with this subject in relation to the country as a whole or to a major area. If, as I believe, the geographer has a distinctive contribution to make in this field, it is on the grounds of his bias as an environmentalist, on the avowed aim of the historical geographer to think 'in the round' and four-dimensionally, and – not least – in the use of maps, not simply in an illustrative sense though that is of self-evident importance, but of distributional maps as a research tool. These last, by amassing a large amount of information on a single sheet, both summarise data and point the way to interrelationships of spatial, ethnic, historical, and economic interest and significance. They thus become not only a means of recording and setting out information, but a source of discovery and a pointer to new and possible lines of enquiry.

All research work aims at pressing outwards the bounds of knowledge and is, therefore, of its nature likely to be amplified if not superseded as time goes on. During the past half-century, enormous strides have been made in archaeology on which we are so dependent for the elucidation of the early stages of human settlement, but only a small number of excavations of direct relevance to the origins of the village have so far been made in the Welsh Borderland, though recently there have been an increasing number of digs and of related field surveys in Flintshire and the English border counties which, if continued, promise much. For the present, however, widely based distributional studies of relevance begin principally with the Iron Age hill forts and with place-names. From the Dark Ages, data of one sort and another become steadily more abundant and varied. Documentation which is exceedingly thin prior to the Norman Conquest then increases, and from the Domesday Book onwards territorial facts are available in greater and greater volume, but maps and plans of direct use in connection with this study hardly exist prior to the Tudor period, and become really abundant only in the eighteenth and nineteenth centuries. Further, most local boundaries changed only slowly if at all prior to the Local Government Acts of the nineteenth century, and although the twentieth-century evidence is of high utility, the early nineteenth century serves for many purposes as a valuable datum line in relation to rural settlement, few of the ancient parishes having then been altered and the tithe survey becoming available from the late 1830s. During the Second World War and afterwards, a wealth of private and public documents came into public archives and this has revolutionised work in this field. As more and more local studies are made available, it becomes increasingly clear that what is needed is a country-wide series of distributional analyses of such basic elements as nucleated and dispersed settlement, open arable fields and common meadows, early place-names, early churches, manor houses at various dates and so on. Only with the help of such factual, geographical and historical studies correlated over extensive areas can unsubstantiated generalisation be replaced by firm and informed interpretations of the character, origin, development, and interrelationships of rural settlements and other elements in the rural landscape. Not least, the physical basis, that inescapable backcloth of the human drama and the essential source of daily living, must be seen like the settlements and fields themselves, the roads, the streams, and every other item in the topographical complex, through field study on the ground and, where possible, with the help of aerial photographs, as adjuncts to the use of maps of many types.

It is now many years since Dr Maitland said: 'We are learning from the ordnance map (that marvellous palimpsest, which under Dr Meitzen's guidance we are beginning to decipher) that in all probability we must keep at least two types before our minds. On the one hand, there is what we might call the true village or the nucleated village. . . . On the other hand we may easily find a country in which there are few villages of this character. The houses which lie within the boundary of the parish are scattered about in small clusters. . . . The outlines of our nucleated villages may have been drawn for us by Germanic settlers, whereas in the land of hamlets and scattered steads old Celtic arrangements may never have been thoroughly effaced.'[1] The forty years that have elapsed since this was written have served to show, as a result of various regional studies, that the simplicity of Meitzen's distinction between Germanic nucleated and Celtic dispersed settlement cannot by any means be maintained. But this early thesis was valuable first in that it underlined the primary distinction between nucleated and dispersed settlement which remains fundamental, and secondly in that it stimulated research along an exceedingly fruitful line. Further, Maitland's expression 'that marvellous palimpsest' was inspired and has often been quoted in and out of context, and it remains one of the central aims of the settlement geographer to explain the rural landscape in terms of existing realities and of the vanished yet living past which, as in a palimpsest, has so often been partly erased and constantly over-written. This is in line with the concept of the landscape as a moving picture in which innumerable images, each slightly different from the last, appear only to give place to others. As the landscape slowly changes, different geographies in part replace each other, but none is wholly different from the previous ones.

The term 'rural landscape' as used in the present study is the rural scene and its various components as it is adapted and added to by Man, and extended to include the associated invisible and cultural elements. These are shown in the Frontispiece. For some time, the term 'rural settlement' was used in this comprehensive sense, but 'rural landscape' is now the preferred description of this field of work, and 'rural settlement' is used *sensu stricto* for

[1] F. W. Maitland, *Domesday Book and Beyond*, 3rd impression (1921), p. 15.

habitations and other constructions rather than for the land and its divisions. These settlements, varied in form and content, may be put into the main categories of village, hamlet, manor-house, farm, dispersed and semi-dispersed communities, but they reflect, alas, the inadequacy of both English and Welsh settlement vocabularies. The original village was a settlement of co-cultivators, pastoralists and coparceners and represented a stage of social development beyond tribalism. It was, and has increasingly become, a settlement of moderate size, smaller than a town and lacking urban functions, but this unspecific use of the word has led to its wider application to such diverse communities as lapsed market-towns, mining and quarrying villages, modern seaside resorts, and the core of suburban districts. While recognising that even in rural areas the village is varied in character and size, the basic meaning is a medium-sized community in, and dependent upon, its rural surroundings, especially on agriculture. A hamlet is more easily defined as the smallest grouped community in a country setting, though in this case also there is no hard and fast definition in terms either of population or numbers of houses other than a subjective one. A family group such as was the basis of medieval Welsh tribal society might expand into a hamlet or it might shrink back to a single farmhouse. This is just one of the social distinctions which may lie between dispersed settlements and the nucleated English village, and it is only part of a far more complicated story. Dispersal of habitations may be total with no two houses adjacent, or partial with two or three to be found in minor groupings but insufficiently large to be called a hamlet. All types of intermediate arrangement are to be found in the Welsh Borderland including semi-hamleted townships in which dispersed dwellings and one or more hamlets are mixed.

The English township and its equivalent the Welsh *tref* are confusing terms. In rural study they are simply the basic territorial unit associated with a group of people who work their land in common. From 1066, the Normans substituted the manor for the township with *nulle terre sans seigneur* as the guiding principle instead of joint ownership by the commoners, but the older institution of the township revived and became the basis of most of the civil parishes which were created in England and Wales by the Local Government Act of 1894. Since this Act, the word 'parish' has to do double duty and it is now necessary to specify an ecclesiastical or a civil parish. Despite the inevitable variations certain territorial patterns in the layout of individual townships repeated themselves, and the concept of pattern, both local and regional, is the thread running through every geographer's attempts to interpret spatially.

One of the difficulties of research today into the many aspects of rural landscape is the handling and systematising of the vast amounts of material evidence available. A glance at the list of primary sources in the appended bibliography will make evident the fact that no single volume can do more than contain a summary of information from the documentary sources alone, and partly for this reason use has been made of distribution maps, tables, and lists. Far more justice can be done to the detail of the rural landscape in more restricted local studies, but the significance of interrelationships can only be brought out by presenting them in a broader setting. The area here included has been taken, for convenience, as the counties immediately adjoining the boundary of the Principality – Flintshire, Denbighshire, Montgomeryshire, Radnorshire, and Breconshire on the Welsh side, together with Monmouthshire, and on the English side Cheshire, Shropshire and Herefordshire. For the purposes of mapping, Gloucestershire west of the Severn has been added, and for some statistical summaries the whole of Gloucestershire where a breakdown was not readily obtainable. Within this area, however, physical geography and human and historical factors combine to indicate a narrower definition of the Borderland and part of the purpose of this study is the search for a true Border Zone as revealed by its rural patterns. The Welsh Borderland is one of the critical areas in connection with the whole study of Britain's rural landscape and the many associated questions of origin and development. It had, for example, long been supposed by earlier workers that the nucleated village and the two- and three-field system were linked as part of a traditional pattern of Anglo-Saxon origin; that primary dispersal and the absence of an arable field system were basic features of the Welsh landscape. Both are now recognised as being only partial truths. Indeed Welsh dispersal is known to be secondary and not primary in many instances. In an area like the Welsh Borderland where Celt, Angle and Norman were the main contributors to the basic settlement patterns, the truth or falsity of many such preconceptions can be tested. Why, for instance, is the distribution of the nucleated villages of south Shropshire and Herefordshire not continuous with those of the counties to the east as one would expect, but found in a western belt beyond the hamleted and dispersed areas of the centre and east of these two counties? Why is the principal area of the two- and three-field arable system in the Borderland to be found in Herefordshire and south-east Shropshire where the nucleated village is almost entirely absent? Why is the northern Borderland divided into large multi-township parishes and the southern part into single-township parishes? What part has ecclesiastical geography to play in rural pattern as cause or effect? What light can the distribution of place-names throw on the question of ethnic distributions in the early Borderland and these in turn on early settlement history? These and many other questions indicate the sort of problems in the historical geography of the Welsh Border-land which challenge the student of rural landscape, and they point the way to comparable problems in relation to the country as a whole.

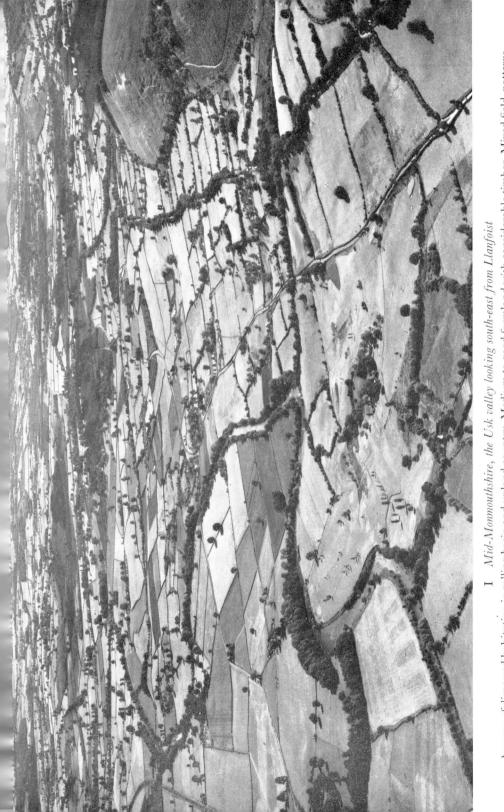

I *Mid-Monmouthshire, the Usk valley looking south-east from Llanfoist*

An area of dispersed habitation in rolling basin and upland country. Medium to good farmland with considerable timber. Mixed field patterns. Edge of the Welsh plateau on the right, Wentwood in the far distance.

II *The Black Mountains, looking north-north-west from Abergavenny*

The minor valleys towards the left are largely areas of Welsh settlement. To the right, as the width and fertility increase, the valleys offered routes for Anglo-Norman ingress and settlement.

III and IV   *The Horseshoe Pass and Eglwyseg Mountain, Denbighshire*

A nearer and a more distant view, showing (*a*) the barren Carboniferous Limestone heights of Eglwyseg Mountain offering poor rough grazing, (*b*) upland holdings of the 'croft' type, marginal in every sense, (*c*) the better land of the Eglwyseg valley.

V   Above: *Nercwys, Flintshire, from the south-east*

Dispersed farmsteads at 600 feet on the Flintshire plateau, many of them representing ancient *tyddynod*. Originally in Mold parish, the church dates only from 1844. Note shelter belts to west of farmhouses.

VI   Below: *Gwernymynydd, Flintshire, from the south-west*

The basic settlement pattern is the same as at Nercwys, two miles to the south-east, but the cross-road has become the focus of a late hamlet.

VII   Above: *Warmingham, Cheshire*

An -*ingaham* settlement in a typical valley site (river Wheelock) that failed to grow to
more than a hamlet. Church, inn, mill, two or three farms and a few cottages.

VIII   Below: *Eardisland, Herefordshire*

A medium-sized village in northern Herefordshire, also based on a stream. Half-timbered
farmhouses and cottages are characteristic of much of the border lowlands.

IX   *Tarvin, Cheshire, from the west*

A strongly nucleated T-junction village west of the Central Cheshire Ridge. It has a Celtic name, avoids Holme Street, a Roman road here

XV   *Holt, Denbighshire, and Farndon, Cheshire, linked by the Dee bridge seen from the north*

'Lyons' with a castle and market was the only borough in the lordship of Bromfield and Yale in the fourteenth century, but was even then being overtaken by Wrexham, and today is the mere village of Holt. Farndon, on the opposite bank of the Dee, is now considerably more extensive, though it was, and is, a purely agricultural village.

XVI *Raglan castle and village, Monmouthshire, from the north*

A perfect example of a fortress representing the might of the Norman conquerors, and symbolically set above, and at a distance from, the village of Raglan which grew in its shadow.

XIII   *Grosmont, Monmouthshire*

An Anglo-Norman borough based on a castle and market which decayed during the
nineteenth century and is now only a hamlet.

XIV   *Clun, Shropshire, from the north*

An Anglo-Norman borough dominated by castle and market. The castle ruins, a high
motte formerly surmounted by a keep with a bailey whose traces are still visible in the
adjoining field, dominate the western side of the small town in which the market hall
(market now defunct) is situated in the wide main street. The bridge across the river Clun
leads to the parish church (top right corner), the position of which suggests a different
and earlier origin. It is the centre of Shropshire's largest ancient parish.

XII *Church Stretton, Shropshire, from the south*

A minor defensive site, a country market town until recently, and now a tourist and residential centre, Church Stretton occupies the full width of the Dale. The main north–south railway and the Roman Watling Street, modernised to form the new line of the main road on the east side of the valley, show its significance in communications.

XI *Stretton Dale, Shropshire, from the south*

Dale settlement between intervening ridges, so characteristic of south Shropshire, is here illustrated by Stretton Dale between the Longmynd on the left and Ragleth Hill on the right. Little Stretton lies along the road.

X *Alveley, eastern Shropshire*

A village more characteristic of the English Plain than of the Borderland. Strongly nucleated with clear evidence of former open arable fields. Celtic and early Anglo-Saxon roots are claimed for it.

XVII *New Radnor, Radnorshire, looking south-east from above Castle Hill*

Another medieval borough of Anglo-Norman origin once dominated by the castle, the site of which makes evident its former strength. Its decline was delayed until the nineteenth century when it lost its status of borough and county town, and its markets and courts were lost to Presteigne. Note the grid plan of the village which is little changed from the seventeenth century.

XVIII   *Rhuddlan, Flintshire, looking north-north-east*

An early motte near the bottom right-hand corner of the photograph was succeeded by the thirteenth-century castle which controlled the crossing of the river Clwyd. The small town grew adjacent to it, but today is yet another example of a former borough which is now a mere village.

XIX   Above: *Ludlow castle, and Ludford bridge over the river Teme, looking north-west*

XX   Below: *Ludlow castle and town from the west*

Unlike most of the previous examples, Ludlow, controlling the important routes from the middle Borderland into mid-Wales, retained its role as a market and route centre and remains a town. Sited on a meander core (*cf.* Shrewsbury), it had a strong defensive position.

XXI *Ironbridge, Shropshire, from the east*

Ironbridge represents the late urbanisation of a rural area, its growth springing from the development of the small Shropshire coalfield from the middle eighteenth century when the Darbys were ironmasters in nearby Coalbrookdale. The cooling-towers at Buildwas are a further evidence of de-ruralisation, but on the left the wooded slopes of Wenlock Edge remain unaffected.

PART ONE

The Rural Picture

1 The Settlement Scene

Highland and Lowland

THE bold contrast of upland and lowland affords the most striking feature of the canvas on which the settlement picture of the Welsh Borderland must first be drawn. The hills of eastern Wales rise sharply above the gentle contours of the plains in a hard north–south line except where the blunt promontory of the south Shropshire uplands breaks the continuity of the marcher lowlands. Sir Cyril Fox defined the Highland Zone geologically, using the edge of the Primary rocks as the boundary, and from near Chester to the neighbourhood of Bewdley his boundary corresponds closely with that based on relief. From the eastern side of the Clee Hills, however, the boundary of the Primary rock region continues southwards but the edge of the uplands swings west towards north-west Herefordshire where it again turns south under the shadow of Radnor and Colwyn Forests, the Black Mountains, and the South Wales coalfield. Thus, as Figure 2 depicts, Herefordshire and Monmouthshire, except for their western margins, lie geologically in the Highland Zone but in terms of relief in the Lowland Zone. Elsewhere, the coincidence of the two is remarkably close.[1]

The south Shropshire ridges and vales break the continuity of the Lowland Zone on the English side of the border, but the nearly north–south trend of these vales means that, from the Roman period onwards, there has been no break in the through

[1] The fundamental significance of the Highland and Lowland Zones in British geography first put forward by Sir Halford Mackinder in *Britain and the British Seas* in 1902, was followed by Sir Cyril Fox in *The Personality of Britain* in 1932 when he applied the concept to explain the distribution of certain early cultures. In the present study, as already indicated, the Borderland is regarded as a contact zone and although the concept of the two zones is accepted as a useful physical basis, its modification in terms of human and historical geography to include an intermediate zone is the theme of much of what follows.

'Corridor' which has afforded the main line of communication
down the Borderland for nearly two thousand years. From the
Dee estuary to the mouth of the Usk or the Wye or, further east,
to the head of the Severn estuary the main roads of this Corridor
have traversed the Border country, extending north across
Lancashire and Shap into western Scotland and south around the
Somerset marshes to the south-western peninsula. A glance at
Figure 2 will underline the narrowness of the Midland Gate
where the Pennines swing towards the Shropshire hills partially
isolating the Cheshire–Shropshire lowland from the rest of the
Midland Plain.

These more northerly lowlands of the Borderland are distinguished from those of Herefordshire and Monmouthshire in a
number of ways. The south Shropshire hills in pre-glacial times
were the main watershed of the Border lowlands, and during the
Quaternary Ice Age halted the movement of the ice sheets moving
south from the Irish Sea and the Lake District. The southern
lowlands were affected only by valley glaciers coming down the
Wye and Usk valleys and some lesser ones. Consequently,
glacial drift in the south of the area is nowhere deep and is limited
to the western parts of the Herefordshire and Monmouthshire
lowlands. Sedentary soils predominate elsewhere and the relief
is varied by low hills. By contrast, the northern lowlands are
gently rolling. Deep glacial drift masks the whole of their width
and Secondary rocks emerge at the surface only along the line of
the narrow scarped hills which extend from Frodsham in the
north to Nesscliff in the south. All rural settlement in the northern
part of the Corridor is conditioned by the relief, soils and drainage
of a largely drift-covered region. The southern lowlands, by contrast, have little glacial drift other than the limited tongues
associated with Welsh valley ice.

In addition to the basic contrasts between highland and lowland, a third feature of the physical setting is provided by the
great vales which gash the eastern highland edge, making breaks
in the harsh upland environment, but also offering historic gateways into Welsh territory which invaders have been quick to
utilise. Dee, Vyrnwy, Severn, Wye and Usk have afforded entry
points only less significant in Welsh history than the northern and
southern coastal routes. Nor can it be forgotten that, in turn, each

2 (*opposite*). The Welsh Borderland:
Highland and Lowland

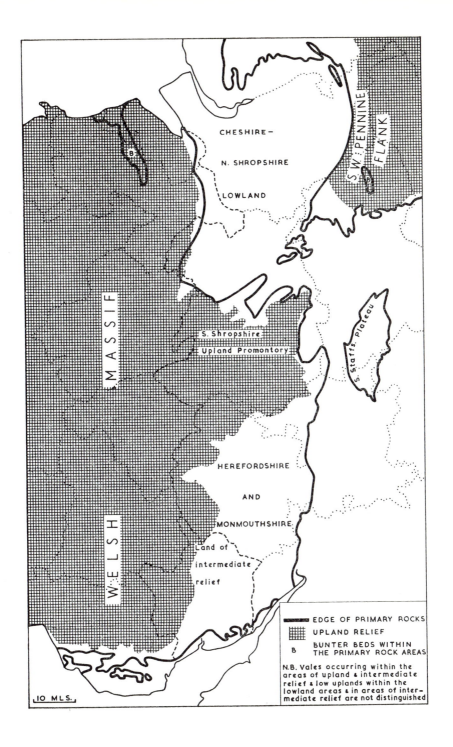

CHESHIRE—

N. SHROPSHIRE

LOWLAND

S.W. PENNINE FLANK

B.

MASSIF

WELSH

S. Shropshire
Upland Promontory

S. Staffs. Plateau

HEREFORDSHIRE

AND

MONMOUTHSHIRE

Land of

intermediate

relief

EDGE OF PRIMARY ROCKS
UPLAND RELIEF
B   BUNTER BEDS WITHIN
THE PRIMARY ROCK AREAS

N.B. Vales occurring within the
areas of upland & intermediate
relief & low uplands within the
lowland areas & in areas of intermediate relief are not distinguished

10 MLS.

has brought Welsh people and Welsh culture down into the plains.

The hill country is in general economically poor and has remained so except for the development of mining and industry in Flintshire, Denbighshire and Monmouthshire. Altitude and slope, thin soils, exposure to wind and high rainfall, have been among the factors which have combined throughout its history to limit agricultural activity to animal farming with a modicum of crop growing on lands which, at best, have a low potential. But these same hills inured their inhabitants to hardship, and offered perfect conditions for defence by scattering in times of invasion and a perfect refuge from lowland invaders. At the same time, ancient cultural characteristics were preserved so that to this day an unbroken continuity can be claimed from the Celtic roots on which Welsh life, language, traditions and settlement patterns are based, while the lowlands, because of their richer and more attractive environment, have been the scene of successive incursions. To what extent and in what ways physical conditions and historical geography have become interwoven to produce differing settlement and land-use forms in this human borderland is the theme of the present study.

The Rural Pattern

That the Welsh Borderland is a complex area from the point of view of the rural settlement geographer needs no stressing. Sitting astride both a physical and a cultural boundary, it provides one of the critical areas of Britain in relation to rural landscape features and their origin, causation and development. Yet if a common history gave in the course of the centuries a sense of unity, then this same Borderland must be expected to display convergent characteristics and a degree of hybridisation in the elements which make up its human geography. If the interpretation of the rural landscape has any meaning in this respect it should point the way to the definition of the Borderland as a geographical zone and help to define its limits. The term 'Marches' has long indicated the existence of such a belt on the eastern flanks of the Welsh Uplands, and though marcher lordships spread far across South Wales as well as extending north and south along the Border, the term Marches is today regarded as applicable only to the Border country, though historically this is inaccurate usage.

West of the marcher zone lies poor, pastoral upland, part of the Welsh massif, and a region of sparse population and predominantly dispersed and scanty settlement. The upland, however, is ribboned by vales where greater fertility and more favourable settlement conditions result in a closer distribution of population. There are occasional villages, related in many cases to a history of Norman penetration though at best these valley nucleations are few and small and from many valleys are entirely absent. To the east of the highland line, conditions are far more favourable to agriculture and a denser distribution of population, and the almost wholly dispersed habitation pattern of the Welsh Uplands is replaced on the English side by a mixed settlement belt stretching from Cheshire in the north to Monmouthshire and western Gloucestershire in the south. It extends without any real break eastward into the Midland Forest triangle which persisted as a comparatively dense woodland area until the late Middle Ages. Beyond this in turn lies the village region of middle England spreading from south Durham through Yorkshire, north Lincolnshire and the east Midland counties to Dorset, Buckinghamshire and north Hampshire. The correspondence of the belt of nucleated villages with H. L. Gray's Midland field system is so close that the tradition of linking the two has seemed deceptively and dangerously obvious. East of this belt again is to be found a second mixed settlement area, that of East Anglia and the south-east of England between Kent and south Hampshire. The relationships of these two mixed settlement belts pose one of the major problems of rural settlement history and origins in Britain. In both, the field systems of the Middle Ages differed from that of the Midland system, but this common characteristic may or may not yield comparable detail, much less can they be assumed to share a history of parallel development. In one important respect it is evident at the outset that the rural landscape of the Welsh borderland differs from that of the south-east, that is, that it gives place westwards to the dispersed Welsh settlement zone in which there

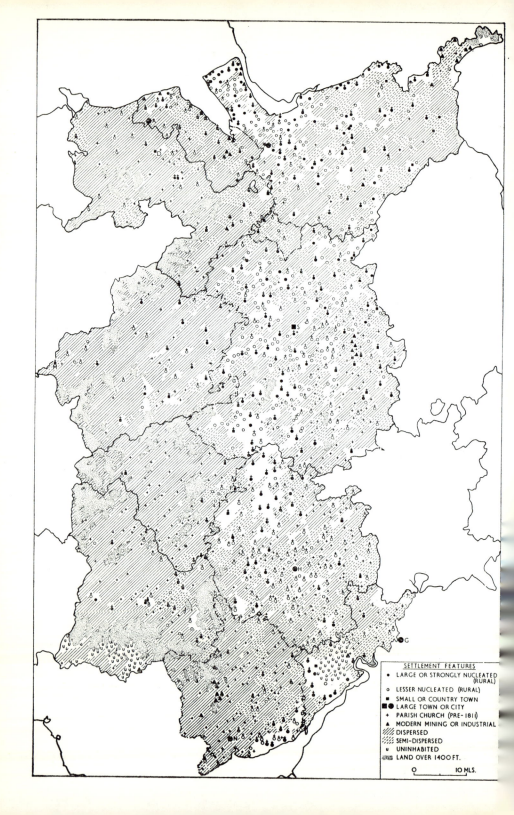

SETTLEMENT FEATURES
- • LARGE OR STRONGLY NUCLEATED (RURAL)
- ○ LESSER NUCLEATED (RURAL)
- ■ SMALL OR COUNTRY TOWN
- ■● LARGE TOWN OR CITY
- + PARISH CHURCH (PRE-1811)
- ▲ MODERN MINING OR INDUSTRIAL
- ░ DISPERSED
- ▒ SEMI-DISPERSED
- u UNINHABITED
- ▨ LAND OVER 1400 FT.

0   10 MLS.

has been a marked degree of cultural and ethnic continuity. Indeed, it is the hybrid settlement zone *par excellence* in all Britain, lying as it does between the nucleated village area on the east and the zone of Welsh dispersal on the west.

In the Welsh Borderland are to be found great stretches of country without a single village, areas characterised by hamlets both early and late, by villages clustered in the rather formless tradition of the border country, small market towns and ex-market villages which long worked their own open arable fields and which are but thinly divided from the villages proper, and by patches of semi-dispersal where scattered cottages cluster or separate in every degree of part-dispersal, and mingle with the hamlets. Here are relict open field systems, both arable and meadow, varying from the two- and three-field system of the Midlands to the multi-field system of much of the English side of the border on the one hand and to the small Welsh sharelands and scattered ploughing strips on the other, but with a tendency for a single *Town Field* or *Maes y Dre* to survive in the nineteenth century as the sole representative of the dying custom of communal agriculture apart from the common pastures.

Strategic geography has resulted in the embroidering of a third pattern corresponding, not with the two sides of the highland line, but sitting uncompromisingly across it. So impressive are the visual remains of the Iron Age camps and the medieval defences, and so vital the Roman routes, that they give an easily accepted impression of the unity of the Marcher zone. But under the flaunted Norman rule, the Welsh west and the English east, though merged politically, long kept their separate cultural character, and the Marches display in their settlement both separate Welsh and English features and hybrid Anglo-Celtic-Norman characteristics. Although Anglo-Norman influence on the agronomy may have been less widespread and less deeply planted than either Welsh or English, it was none the less real and persistent in many of the *capita*[1] of the Marcher lordships such as Talgarth, Hawarden and Caldicot.

On the Welsh side of the border the four counties of Denbigh, Montgomery, Radnor and Brecon resemble each other in that

[1] The *caput* of a lordship was its principal settlement, the seat of the marcher lord, and the *capita* ranged in size from villages to towns.

3 (*opposite*). The Welsh Borderland: nucleated and dispersed settlement based on maps of the mid-nineteenth century

they are part of a predominantly dispersed rural settlement belt. Hamlets are rare, villages still more rare, and the majority of the parish churches are solitary or associated with only a minor habitation group – a *ty'n llan* (parsonage), a farm and a cottage or two. The *tyddyn* or family steading is the most characteristic unit in the settlement scene and over vast areas its dispersed distribution is unbroken by any form of clustering. The major breaks in this dispersal pattern occur in the broader vales. For example in the vale of Clwyd there are small, irregular villages such as Bodfari and Tremeirchion; in the Vyrnwy valley Llansant-ffraid-ym-Mechain and Meifod; in the vale of Welshpool, Ber-riew; in the Wye valley where it forms the boundary between Radnorshire and Breconshire, Llyswen and Glasbury; in the wider part of the valley of the Breconshire Usk, Llangynidr and Llangattock and further downstream in Monmouthshire, Caer-leon. Each has a different history, but each is in size a village. Each is a rare example in its area and, apart from the Clwyd villages, each is in a valley pointing outwards to the border lowlands.

In both Flintshire and Monmouthshire the character of the upland settlements is similar to those in mid-border counties, but both have a larger number of villages, hamlets and small towns. In Flintshire they occur principally along the marine and estuarine coastal strips. They include Rhuddlan, St Asaph, Newmarket, Flint, Holywell and Hawarden all of which have a partially urban history, as well as such agricultural settlements as Northop, Gwaenysgor, Halkyn and Dyserth. In Monmouthshire, the main area of nucleated settlement is on or near the 'Moors' or coastal flats between the mouths of the Usk and the Wye. Above Chep-stow the only villages are St Arvans and Trelleck, but between Chepstow and Newport is a considerable group of nucleations, clean-cut with hardly any intervening scatter, though there are occasional hamlets. The villages include Bishton (Llangadwaladr), Magor, Undy, Crick and Caldicot, all on the Moors, and Shire-newton on the 'upland' (or solid land) above them. Occasional small nucleations also occur further north on the 'upland' such as Llanfair Discoed, Raglan and Llangattock-juxta-Caerleon.

On the English side of the border begins the major mixed settlement zone of the eastern Borderland, extending through

Cheshire, Shropshire, Herefordshire and western Gloucestershire, but the dividing-line on the west by no means corresponds with the political boundary. In all four counties there are nucleated villages set cleanly amid fields and commons which were long innocent of dispersed dwellings. But throughout the belt are also areas of hamlets, dispersed and semi-dispersed dwellings in clear stretches or intermingled. Such was the settlement map in the mid-nineteenth century, and in the greater part of the Borderland the pattern remains virtually unaltered today. Two thousand years of invasion and conquest, of ethnic separatism and inter-penetration have left their many marks. Yet if hybridisation is the keynote in this eastern belt, it by no means excludes distinctive types showing little or no sign of mixing. The major riddle of Borderland settlement is the degree and character of the influence of Celt, English and Anglo-Norman, and the extent to which the four hundred-odd years since the Union of England and Wales have applied a similar colour-wash over the whole.

In this belt, the nucleated village is an example of the way in which outlines have in many cases become blurred. Rarely is it sizeable in comparison with the villages of, say, the Cotswolds. Rarely is it built on a regular plan, but has about it a formless, ragged, casual look as if it were uncertain or uncaring about whether it is a village or a hamlet. In some cases it is completely self-contained and surrounded by fields and pastures unbroken by other habitation-units. More often it is surrounded by an irregular grouping of hamlets and dispersed farmsteads and cottages, with few remaining indications of its former communal arrangements. This confusion of pattern is to be found both in the large parishes of the north and in the small parishes of the south of the belt, though the details are different.

In Cheshire, the settlement scene consists mainly of scattered farmsteads and cottages but with widely spaced villages and hamlets across the entire width of the plain. The original market-towns were set at relatively small intervals, and many of these are now only large villages. In west Cheshire – in Wirral, the Gowy and lower Dee Valleys – the pattern of hamlets and villages becomes denser. It is in fact the most closely nucleated part of the Border-land, and the intervening areas of dispersal are very minor. Most, though not all, Cheshire villages are parochial as are a number of hamlets, but the solitary church occurs at not infrequent intervals.

The northern plain of Shropshire to a considerable extent continues the Cheshire pattern, but its aspect is kinder and more southerly, and in the western half its border character is marked by castles which are rare in Cheshire whose marcher defences lay in what is now Flintshire and Denbighshire. Nucleated villages are similarly spaced, but the hamlets are more numerous notably increasing in number towards the middle belt of the county. In eastern Shropshire sizeable villages are comparatively few except in and near the Worfe basin where are situated rather large villages such as Beckbury, Worfield and Claverley. But in the west the nucleated villages occur regularly, generally at the centre of large parishes as in the cases of Pontesbury, Westbury, Worthen and Chirbury. By contrast, the small parishes of the south-east centre on solitary churches or small church-hamlets.

In Herefordshire large villages cleanly set in open country are characteristic of the north-west and mid-west. Elsewhere in the county, villages are few and generally small and the characteristic settlement pattern is dispersal and semi-dispersal mixed with hamleting except in the Welsh districts of Ewyas and Archenfield in the south where the hamlet is found only rarely and settlement is sparser.

Western Gloucestershire is dominated by the Forest of Dean, much of which was uninhabited in the mid-nineteenth century and is still largely a virgin area as regards settlement. A line of strongly nucleated villages – Staunton, Newland and St Briavels – lies along its western edge near the lower Wye valley, and is continued along the shore of the Severn estuary in Alvington, Aylburton, Blakeney and Newnham. The northern edge of Dean continues the Herefordshire settlement pattern, but across the Severn the nucleated village again holds sway.

2 The Geography Behind Settlement

AT least 95 per cent of the rural communities of the Borderland are agricultural and prior to the Industrial Revolution the proportion was even higher. Mineral wealth and timber have their place in rural economy, but the basic needs of the traditional countryman are potable water and land which he can farm. It is, of course, true that with the centuries rural settlements have changed. The nomad became a transhumant; the transhumant became a transpastoralist. Farming techniques and the standard of rural living have slowly demanded better land and equipment and improved housing. Siting has altered, hill locations steadily becoming less favoured, and lowlands and valleys once cleared of woodland attracting an increasing proportion of the rural population. That economic advantage can both be differently interpreted and be overruled by ethnic tradition or historical necessity, is one of the major axioms of the historical geographer. So in turn Celt, Anglo-Saxon and Anglo-Norman made differing use of the Border countryside. Nevertheless, looking back, changes have on the whole been slow, and in seeking the geography behind rural settlement one has to recognise that the early editions of the One-inch Ordnance Survey maps delineated settlement distributions which, with few and minor exceptions, had persisted basically unchanged from the early Middle Ages and in many cases had originated long before that. It is with the geography behind this quasi-permanent rural settlement picture that we are now concerned before considering the mode of its evolution.

The Physical Basis

There is no question that in searching for the physical basis of rural settlement, the prime distinction is that between upland and lowland. Within these two major divisions there are many lesser ones which prove the exceptions to the general rule that the hills offer fewer advantages than the plains: upland vales are both fertile and sheltered, peat mosses in Cheshire and Shropshire deterred settlers for centuries after the Bronze Age, thin droughty soils in the lowland heaths were only late in being drawn into the neighbouring farmlands. But by and large the rule is applicable on economic grounds: less so on grounds of strategy and ethnic preference.

The fundamental human needs, water, food and shelter, dictate a different choice of sites in upland than in lowland. From a variety of sites which are chosen, two types are repeated innumerable times – hillsides with high insolation values, and favourable valleys. Where hill pasture is the basis of farming, the benefits of a hillside site are numerous, and springs or minor hillside rills are rarely lacking. During the centuries of war and raiding, their remoteness gave added security, and there was generally some small patch of earth where a few oats or vegetables could be raised to relieve the monotony of a diet of animal flesh and milk products. Rather larger communities, however, have been drawn of necessity to the better water supplies and more fertile ground of the valleys. Many minor valleys in the hills of mid-eastern Wales are seen to shelter a single farmhouse, but hamlets and larger nucleations are forced to settle by larger streams and in wider valleys, where soils are deeper and communications easier. This distinction between the single farmstead on the hillside or in a minor valley and the parochial centre in the larger upland valleys or in the vales is illustrated perfectly in Radnorshire where small parochial clusters are sited in valleys in Colwyn and Radnor Forests as at Betws Diserth, Rhulen, Glascwm and Llanbadarn y Garreg, and the larger in the Wye valley as at Glasbury, Llyswen and Clyro. Further north, where broken and even rugged hill country gives place to broad plateau surfaces in western Denbighshire and in Flintshire, there is level ground both for grazing and crop raising, and sites such as Halkyn and Caerwys occupy at medium altitudes are far from unfavourable. Nearby, at the foot of the Clwydian Heights hamlets and minor villages have the dual advantage of nearness to hill pastures and to the rich, well watered land of the Vale of Clwyd.

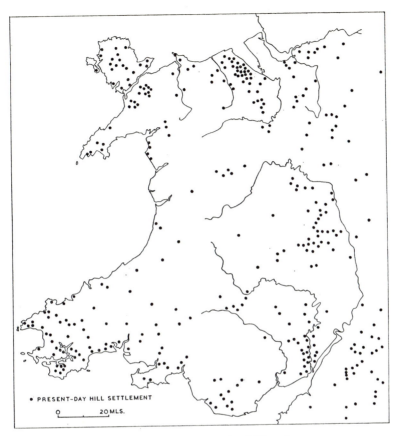

• PRESENT-DAY HILL SETTLEMENT

O   20 MLS.

4. Wales and the Borderland: present-day hill settlements

A wider view over the country as a whole, reveals that hill sites have not only been sought in the past, but continuously occupied by hamlets and even by sizeable villages and towns to the present day. In some cases they suffer anything but disadvantage, as on broad plateau surfaces or on hillsides above valleys subject to flooding, but many more cannot be explained so simply. Ten villages in England and Wales stand at over 1000 feet above sea level and apart from Hutton Roof in Cumberland, all are in the Welsh Borderland or the southern Pennines. A larger group at between 800 and 1000 feet is only a little more widely dispersed, and the major concentration of these high villages is between the mouths of the Clwyd, the Towy, the Derbyshire Derwent and the Severn with extensions into the Cotswolds and Devon. In addition there are numerous hill-top villages at lower altitudes which would appear to be at a physical disadvantage, for which traditional hill settlement, and religious and strategic causes must be invoked. So strong, it would seem, is the traditional association of early churches with an elevated site that the church itself is in many villages so placed even where the houses themselves are on low ground.[1] (Fig. 4.)

There were few alternatives to upland grazing as the basis of life in the hills apart from rare examples of communities which came to depend on mineral wealth. As time has gone on, mining, quarrying, and forestry have increasingly supplemented pastoralism, but still it is mountain grazing which is the basis of hill economy in eastern, as in the rest of upland Wales. In the border counties which lie on the Welsh Massif, 8 per cent of the total area is rough grazing as compared with the Corridor counties which have only 2·8 per cent of their total area classed as this type of land and most of this is either in the South Shropshire Hills or on the flanks of the Welsh Hills.

Water is a prime essential for any settlement, not only for man but for beasts: potable water, and water for innumerable other purposes, among which fishing is by no means the least valuable. Until the twentieth century, few rural districts had piped water and much of the rural Borderland depends to this day on springs and wells and, in fewer cases, even on surface water for human consumption. This is a national rather than a regional problem and since the passing of the 1934 Act which reduced the rural population out of reach of piped water in England and Wales to 30 per cent, vast strides have been made, yet in the 1946 *National Farm Survey of England and Wales* it was stated that 47 per cent of farmhouses had no piped water and 37 per cent of farmholdings had none in their buildings. Some 55,000 holdings suffered from seasonal water shortage. The modern problem of supplying piped water is greatest in areas of dispersed farmhouses and the greater part of Wales and much of the Borderland suffers disproportionately as a result. Piped water has freed one of the most rigid

[1] Dorothy Sylvester, 'The Hill Villages of England and Wales', *Geogrl J.* cx (1947), pp. 76–93.

physical controls of siting, but it still operates mainly in relation to urban and suburban areas and has had virtually no effect as yet on the map of rural house distribution which is geared to more primitive water sources. A typical position for a farmhouse on the hills is on slopes on a fault or on an outcrop of aquiferous rocks. Hill-tops require the sinking of deep wells, and the water supply of hill-top villages is among the first to become desperate in periods of drought. Millstone Grits, Coal Measures sandstones, the Pennant Grits and the Devonian and Triassic sandstones provide the purest and most ample water. All but the hardest limestones give copious but harder and less pure supplies. In Monmouthshire, there are innumerable points in the coalfield valleys where springs arise from the Pennant Grits, though some are too strongly chalybeate to be palatable.[1] The upper beds of the Old Red Sandstone in western Monmouthshire and the Dittonian and Brownstone Beds in Herefordshire provide good spring water and so do the Holdgate and Downton Castle sandstones in the Downtonian areas. In the northern plains, where Keuper Marls provide the impermeable base of the Wilmslow–Prees syncline, wells are sunk through the overlying sandstones or drift deposits, or water is taken from natural springs at the junction of clays or marls and sands. Faults, as in Stretton Dale, provide spring water in many parts of the hill country. Most of the drift-covered lowlands depend on shallow wells in glacial sands underlain by clays with the disadvantage that, being shallow, they are liable to fail in drought. Wells and springs in the sandstones and conglomerates are far more reliable, and Clive and Grinshill are well situated in this respect, as is Stanton on Hine Heath which derives spring water from a fault in the Pebble Beds. These, however, are rare examples, for most places on the drift use shallow well water from sands or alluvium.

Dependence on surface streams for potable water is rare except on impermeable rocks, and such sources are used mainly in the mountains where there is less likely to be pollution. Most of the Lower Primary rocks are hard and impermeable and surface water is in general use for men and animals, but exceptions occur on the limestones and sandstones of the Ordovician and Silurian

---

[1] Aubrey Strahan, *The Country around Newport*, Geol. Survey Memoir, Sheet 249, 1909.

as in north-west Shropshire, on Wenlock Edge, and in north-west Herefordshire. The cost of well-sinking is high, but it is essential if the effects of prolonged drought such as that of 1959 are to be avoided. As a result of the experiences of that year, the Minister of Housing and Local Government asked all water undertakings to review their resources, and among the new water supply schemes which were listed to be undertaken were those by Llan-fyllin Rural Council using the river Vyrnwy and Llanidloes Rural Council rebuilding the Van reservoir, both in typically dispersed and thinly populated Border upland areas.

An excess of water associated with seasonal and occasional flooding is a particularly serious hazard in the valleys of the Borderland and on the coastal flats of Monmouthshire. Melting snow, heavy rain, or a combination of both causes a rapid rise in the level of all the major rivers flowing into the Corridor counties from the Welsh Uplands. The Severn in flood soon converts the plain of Shrewsbury and the tributary Rea valley between the Long Mountain and the Stiperstones into one vast lake, and the riverside villages which are not above flood level become at such times the 'God help us' villages like Melverley on the Severn and Glasbury on the Wye. The advantages normally reaped by farmers in these rich vales can be wiped out in a night by severe losses of stock and crops, but land and houses are not lightly abandoned and rural siting is affected by such disasters barely if at all.

At least equal hazards are faced by the population of the coastal flats of southern Monmouthshire on the so-called Moors or Levels. Here, a combination of high spring tides and onshore winds with heavy rain and full drains and pills can bring the most spectacular disasters to which any part of the Border counties is subject. The floods of 1606 affected 26 of the small Levels parishes, reputedly causing 2000 deaths, drowning hundreds of cattle, carrying away corn and hay ricks, damaging houses and barns and causing overall losses estimated at £100,000. On the bitter January morning when the flood waters reached their greatest height, the tide swept breast-high into the churches and houses of coastal villages such as Goldcliff.

The related needs of flood control and piped water supply can surely need no underlining in view of facts such as these, which serve also in the present context to stress the point that neither all the advantages nor all the disadvantages are to be found in any one type of region. Nevertheless, the most important single consideration is the capacity of the land to produce rich returns or, at worst, sufficient to eke out a livelihood; for the real country-man, over the centuries which have made the rural settlement map, has always been first and foremost a farmer.

The Agricultural Basis

Soil, altitude, slope, aspect, climate and weather are the signifi-cant factors on which farming is based. But from the humblest squatter who scuffs out a rood or two of rough heath or a clearing in deep woodland to the farmer with over a thousand rich acres, the labour, the available capital, the implements and the neces-sary seeds, stock, fertilisers and techniques are equally indispens-able. The results, both in terms of produce and income on the one hand, and in their contribution to rural pattern and popu-lation density on the other, are dependent on both sets of factors. The physical factors, except for the changing composition of the soil, have altered little through the historic period, but economic factors, tenurial patterns, modes of dividing and cultivating the arable and meadow land, the organisation and science of farming, the available labour, and the extent of farmed land have undergone very marked change during the various phases of agricultural history in Britain. These factors, physical and non-physical, have combined to impose patterns on the vast acres of countryside surrounding village, hamlet, and farmstead, and what we see today in the shape of barren sweeps of rugged mountain, great stretches of upland grazing, woodland and copse, parkland, fields, paddocks, and gardens is the immediate 'end product' of all of these. The history of their evolution is the concern of later chapters, but the analysis of the seemingly simple patchwork of field and farm, heath and meadow can only be realistically approached with the recognition that underlying occupancy patterns exist almost universally in the farmlands of today.

The physical complex which is the initial consideration in

relation to farming potential may be illustrated from the central part of the plain of north Shropshire which, alone in the Borderland as yet, is covered by solid, drift and soil survey maps.[1] Over some 250 square miles covered by these surveys, the blanket of drift is widespread except where Triassic sandstones and marls emerge along the line of escarpments from Hawkstone to Nesscliff, in the lowlying heathlands further east, and where the sandstones of the Middle Lias emerge around Prees. The Bunter sandstones break down characteristically into brown earths; neighbouring Keuper deposits bear brown earths on their thin sandstones and gley soils on the Marls. The remaining area carries a complicated distribution of boulder clay giving gley soils; glacial sands and gravels bearing brown earths, patches of peat and ribbons of alluvium. The brown earths have numerous advantages such as yielding more easily to the plough, being more favourable to crop raising, and giving a warmer soil and better sites for homesteads, both on account of their relative permeability and because shallow wells can be sunk. By contrast, the gley soils are heavy and ill-drained, become sour without lime, and have consequently tended to be avoided in the earlier stages of settlement. Today they are incorporated in the large dairy farms which are now so important a feature of Cheshire and Shropshire, and long leys tend to replace permanent pasture, but the earlier village communities avoided them. Approximately 60 per cent of the villages and hamlets in the district covered by the Wem sheets are located on the sands and sandstones, though they only occur over a quarter to a third of the area. Such ancient parochial centres as are not on these sandy sites are to be found at the junction of sands and clays or sands and peat and constitute a further 15 per cent. Some of these last, like Clive and Grinshill, are on solid sandstone, but most, like Moreton Corbet, Shawbury and Welshampton lie on brown earths. Others are at the contact line of sands and clays where the resulting loam is the most useful of all soil types to the mixed farmer. The agricultural value of the sands, however, depends on their texture. Coarse sands and gravels, such as are found on the wide hungry heathlands near the river Tern, were useless except to provide thin common pasture in the Middle Ages, later becoming the sites of a number of late enclosure

[1] The Wem Sheets, scale one inch to the mile, no. 138.

hamlets. Among these are Prees Green, Wytheford Heath and Poynton Green whose smallholders and cottagers either wrung a marginal living from their inadequate acres or served as farm labourers for the large-scale farms which increased both in size and number in the Great Enclosure period.

Only 25 per cent of the nucleated settlements on the Wem sheet are situated on the clays and none of these is an old parochial centre. The clays are for the most part naturally wooded, bearing damp oakwood over much of their surface, and they were in general the last to be cleared for expanding settlement. In the Middle Ages, some of these too constituted the waste or common pasture of townships centred on the sands; some became absorbed into park-estates, and yet others became the sites of hamlets, though many were already in existence by 1086. Today, the solitary farmhouse dating from the late eighteenth or early nineteenth century is found widely over the clays, basing its farming economy on large-scale dairy farming, varied by crop raising with the emphasis on fodder as the leys are in turn broken up.

The peat mosses offer a further distinctive type of farming. From their desertion after the Bronze Age, they were usually avoided except in so far as they afforded common grazing and could be used for cutting peat turves for fuel. Their ill-drained state ensured their remaining as common land and being avoided by roads and settlements. When, as in the case of Whixall Moss on the boundary of Shropshire and Maelor Saesneg, they began to be drained by Dutchmen in the seventeenth century, they became the site of mossmen's cottages, and today with the rapidly increasing demand for peat as a fertiliser, peat cutting has been transformed into a commercial venture. Nevertheless, the moss remains open for the most part, one of the few examples in these northern plains of a primitive landscape almost unaltered vegetationally. In Cheshire, many of the mosses have been drained and used for early cropping and for more intensive ventures such as market and nursery gardening.

In agriculture, as in physical geography, the essential distinction lies, however, between the lowlands and the uplands. The Welsh counties with their high proportion of poor mountain land include 86 per cent of all the rough grazing of the ten counties of the Borderland. Only in Flintshire (10 per cent) and

Monmouthshire (19·4 per cent) does this fall to a comparatively low proportion of the total farmed land. The mid-Welsh counties on the border – Montgomeryshire, Radnorshire and Breconshire – all have more than two-fifths of their area in this category, the Brecon figure rising to over three-fifths.[1] A further significant feature of these three counties' land use is that their rough grazing acreage exceeds their permanent pasture, but in the remaining three east Welsh counties, permanent pasture is in excess of rough grazing. In all six, arable land accounts for less than one-third of the total farmed land, falling in Breconshire to under one-seventh. As on the English side of the border, a large part of the ploughed-up area is given over to fodder crops, but in even greater proportion, for wheat and barley are of negligible importance in eastern Wales.

The contrast between the rich farmlands of the English lowlands and the natural poverty of the upland holdings remains marked despite the reclamation of many favourable hill slopes by seeding with new strains of hill grasses bred at the Plant Breeding Station at Aberystwyth. In Wales as in England farming is becoming a more prosperous industry and farms are increasing in size, often at the expense of uneconomic smallholdings, but farms are largest in the poorest land except where an individual estate owner or a large farmer has the capital to extend and develop. In most of the hill farms rough grazing and limited in-land are the basis of hard won returns and it is only in the broader vales that farming can be compared with the more prosperous activities across the border. On the hills, abandoned steadings and stone built farmhouses are set sparsely on hill slopes amid mile upon mile of mountain and upland pasture. The physique of the hill lands is such that vast areas are either uncultivable or on the margins of cultivation. Until the twentieth century, the margins ebbed and advanced as dictated by population growth and decline or by political and economic exigencies. From the time of the Tudors, hill grazings were extensively reclaimed and enclosed in the interests of the woolmen, but enormous stretches still

[1] In 1956 Breconshire ranked third of the counties of all England and Wales in its acreage under common rough grazing, following the North Riding of Yorkshire and Devon, though the North Riding is nearly three times as large in total area, and Devon more than three times. Data from the *Report of the Royal Commission on Common Land, 1955–1958* (1958), pp. 25–6.

remained open. It was only in the period of the Great Enclosures, from the late eighteenth until after the mid-nineteenth century, that the major reclamations were effected. Over Wales as a whole, the commons were reduced by over a million acres between 1795 and 1895, and of this total 600,000 acres lay in the east Welsh counties. As in the more limited hill enclosures in England, a new pattern of large rectangular fields resulted, immediately recognisable on the ground or on the map. A number became associated with new steadings, but the majority were added to existing farms or incorporated in demesne land.

The tendency during this phase was to overextend the in-land and to establish additional smallholdings on the common allotments and thus to force the squatting population, hitherto straggling around the edge, into new enclosure hamlets, many of which disappeared because of their inability to compete with the larger landholders. The tiny cottages fell into decay and their rough field boundaries became indistinguishable, except from the air, as they became part of the larger fields of their new owners. In general, this tendency to increase the in-land at the expense of rough grazing has continued, especially during the past forty years with the introduction of modern machinery to supplement the falling labour supply, but there are exceptions as in the case of Monmouthshire where 33,700 acres were returned as common land in 1958 as against 27,000 in 1895. The coalfield is no doubt responsible for this in large part, but in many instances, the ebb and flow is affected by war. All these changes influence not only the farming régime and the land pattern, but are eventually reflected in the number and distribution of habitations, and thus in the entire settlement pattern: so much so, that much of the rural geography of upland counties like Radnorshire hinges on the character and use of the upland pastures as much as on any other single factor.

In recent centuries, the entire Borderland has been an area in which pastoralism was of major importance. On the hills this was a physical compulsion. In the lower lands the turnover of the open arable fields and the enclosure of open pasture was in part due to the rising wool trade, and in part to the climate which favoured grass rather than cereals. As a result, the patterning usually associated with the Great Enclosure period affected the Borderland both earlier and more gradually, though the retention of a single open field or of remnants of two or more open arable fields was far more widespread a custom than was formerly assumed. In Cheshire today, well over half the arable acreage is under rotation grasses, clover and oats for animal feed. In Shropshire, the proportion is under half but still considerable. Further south, the shortened winters and the reduced incidence of May frosts increasingly favour wheat and fruit growing, the wheat acreage increasing from under one-tenth of the total farmed land in Cheshire to over one-seventh in Shropshire and Herefordshire. Fruit growing has played a major role in the economy of rural Herefordshire and neighbouring parts of Shropshire, and has had a sharp impact on the tenurial and habitation pattern of the principal orcharding areas from the seventeenth century onwards. But in Herefordshire, arable farming has declined at the expense of pastoralism, centring in particular on beefstock in contrast with the dairy farming of the northern lowlands.

From mid-Cheshire to the south Shropshire hills, the country is one vast stretch of greensward – excellent cattle pasture broken only by parkland and occasional villages and hamlets, by rare heaths and by peat mosses. Its dairy farms with their herds of Friesians and Shorthorns are unsurpassed in Britain, and the farms bring a higher price per acre than those of any other part of the Borderland.

The south Shropshire hill country breaks into this lowland corridor in sudden contrast, for although the broader vales are good cattle country the higher hills are for the most part sheep run, and their barrenness repeats in miniature the patterns of the Welsh uplands. In southern Herefordshire and Monmouthshire, once again the level or rolling lowlands of the north give place to broken hill and basin country of greater average height and lower fertility, but except in a few areas such as the Black Mountains and the coalfield uplands of western Monmouthshire, farming remains relatively good.

One further factor must be mentioned which affected this part of Britain especially – the long history of border raids and the resulting retardation of economic progress in many of the parts which were worst affected. Even in 1086, many manors were returned in the border districts as 'wasted' and were without recorded population. This was to repeat itself not only during

TABLE I. *Total farmed land and percentage use, 1958*

County	Total farmed land %	Total farmed land (000 ac.)	arable %	arable (000 ac.)	perm. grass %	perm. grass (000 ac.)	rough grazing %	rough grazing (000 ac.)	common %	common (000 ac.)
Cheshire		498	42·7	213	50·9	253	6·4	32	0·29	1·8
Shropshire		742	44·9	333	48·5	360	6·6	49	1·64	14·0
Herefordshire		459	46·4	213	49·1	225	4·5	21	1·02	5·5
Gloucestershire		627	47·5	298	48·5	304	4·0	25	1·75	14·0
	45	2326	73·0	1057	60·0	1142	14·0	127		
Flintshire		130	30·8	40	59·2	77	10·0	13	1·3	2·1
Denbighshire		376	23·7	89	41·5	156	34·8	131	9·8	41·8
Montgomeryshire		454	17·8	81	39·0	177	43·2	196	1·6	8·2
Radnorshire		270	23·7	64	31·8	86	44·5	120	15·8	47·6
Breconshire		423	13·7	58	24·8	104	61·5	261	28·9	135·5
Monmouthshire		258	22·1	57	58·5	151	19·4	50	9·7	33·9
	55	1911	37·0	389	42·0	751	86·0	771		
	100	4237	100·0	1446	100·0	1893	100·0	898		

[1] From *Agricultural Statistics, 1958/9* (Ministry of Agriculture and Fisheries).

TABLE II. *Reduction in area of Common Land in Welsh Counties of the Border*[1]

Area in ooos acres

County	1795	1895
Flintshire	40	4
Denbighshire	102	48
Montgomeryshire	250	109
Radnorshire	200	67
Breconshire	256	142
Monmouthshire	67	27
Wales	1696	693

[1] From David Thomas, *Cau'r Tiroedd Comin* (1952).

much of the Marcher period, but in the Wars of the Roses and the Civil Wars, when villages which lay across the route of marching armies lay devastated, not simply for a season, but for many years to come. Relative remoteness, the proportion of poor land, and the past incidence of war and raiding are among the factors which have brought about the retardation of population growth or its actual decline not only in the Welsh counties, but in Herefordshire, and the point was well made by J. N.

TABLE III. *Area of Common Land, c. 1958*[1]

County	ooos acres	% total area
Cheshire	1·8	0·29
Shropshire	14·0	1·64
Herefordshire	5·5	1·02
Gloucestershire	14·0	1·75
Flintshire	2·1	1·3
Denbighshire	41·8	9·8
Montgomeryshire	8·2	1·6
Radnorshire	47·6	15·8
Breconshire	135·5	28·9
Monmouthshire	33·7	9·7

[1] From the *Report of the Royal Commission on Common Land* (1958).

Jackson that Herefordshire has the lowest population density of any county in lowland Britain. This is the more significant in view of its having been described by the West Midland Planning Group as including 'the highest proportion and largest absolute area of first-class land of any of the West Midland counties.'[1]

The Distribution of Population

The area of the nine administrative counties of the Borderland (i.e. excluding Gloucestershire) in 1951 was just under 6600 square miles and the average population density 301 per square mile.[2] The addition of Gloucestershire gives an almost unaltered density of 299 per square mile. Taken county by county the position is very different and varies from as little as 42·5 per square mile in Radnorshire to 575 in Flintshire and 602 in Monmouthshire on the Welsh side of the border, the two last figures now inflated by high urban and mining and industrial densities. On the English side, Cheshire ranks highest for similar reasons and the average density in Cheshire was 837 per square mile. Gloucestershire came next with 355, Shropshire third with 214 and Herefordshire lowest with only 151. In the six Welsh counties included in this study the average density in 1951 was 219, in the three main English counties it was 391 per square mile.

A more detailed picture is afforded by isolinear or dot maps of population distribution.[3] Maps of the first type show that rural densities vary from nought in the higher parts of the Welsh Uplands through increasing, but still low, densities only rarely and locally rising to as much as 100 in any part of the Welsh rural areas. Similarly low densities are also found in the south Shropshire hill country, and in the heaths, peat mosses, and woodlands on the English side. Indeed, a 'good rural' population averaging 200 to 400 per square mile only occurs in the rich dairying and mixed

[1] 'Thoughts upon the distribution of the rural population in Herefordshire at the beginning of the nineteenth century', *Trans. Woolhope Nat. Fld Club* (1954).
[2] All figures quoted in this section refer to the administrative counties if for 1951, to the counties minus their town population if for 1801.
[3] Such maps are readily consulted in any good atlas. The Ten-Mile series of population maps published by the Ordnance Survey for 1931 and 1951 are particularly useful.

agricultural lowlands of central Cheshire, parts of north and east Shropshire, the Shrewsbury Plain and the more fertile vales of Herefordshire, Monmouthshire and western Gloucestershire.

In 1801, when the first *Census of Population* was taken, the population of the mid-border Welsh uplands was little different from that of the present day. In 1951 it was, in fact, hardly higher in Radnorshire than in 1801, for in the intervening 150 years it had increased by fewer than 1000 or approximately 5 per cent. In the same period, Montgomeryshire has suffered a loss of approximately 2000 or 4 per cent – figures which highlight the long historical background and the seriousness of the present problems of that county. The remaining four eastern Welsh counties all experienced appreciable overall gains largely on account of the development of their mineral resources and related industries. The increase in Monmouthshire was as high as 609 per cent, and in Flintshire 272 per cent, but the true rural growth can only be calculated by examining separate agricultural parishes. That this rural growth was real can be quickly confirmed, the early increase being due to expanding agricultural production to meet the needs of the coalfield populations.

Of the English border counties, only Cheshire's rising growth rate can be compared with the Welsh coalfield counties. Though its coal resources were small, it experienced a rapid economic expansion along the Mersey and in the saltfields, while the increasing road and rail traffic of Chester, and the rapid growth of Crewe as a rail centre swelled numbers in those two detached towns. The population of the administrative county of Chester increased more than four times (330 per cent) in the 150 years and this had, and is still having, a profound effect on rural patterns in many areas.[1]

In the administrative county of Gloucestershire, the 1801–1951 increase in population was only 71 per cent, in Shropshire 64 per cent, and in Herefordshire 42 per cent, figures which were characteristic of English agricultural districts during that period.

These increase figures also indicate the reliability of the present-day picture as a guide to conditions at the turn of the eighteenth century. In other words, the rural settlement pattern is little changed in Montgomeryshire and Radnorshire as compared with that of 1800.

[1] See pp. 282–3.

TABLE IV. *Population of the Border Counties, 1801 and 1951*

County	1801 Total pop.[1] (ooos)	1801 Density per sq. mile[1]	1951 Total pop. (ooos)	1951 Density per sq. mile	1801–1951 % increase	1951 Area adm. co. sq. miles	1801 Inhab'd houses (ooos)	1801 Pop. emp. in agric. (ooos)	1801 Houses per sq. mile	1801 Houses: agric. pop.
Cheshire	191	196	824	837	336	972	34	38	35	1:1·12
Shropshire	167	124	289	214	72	1345	31	45	23	1:1·45
Herefordshire	89	106	127	151	42	840	17	31	20	1:1·82
Gloucestershire	250	198	429	355	71	1205	46	49	38	1:1·06
								av. 29	av. 24	
Total English counties	c.697		c.1669			4362				
Flintshire	39	154	145	575	272	252	7	10	27	1:1·43
Denbighshire	60	90	170	255	183	667	12	21	18	1:1·75
Montgomeryshire	47	59	45	56·5	-4	797	8	13	10	1:1·62
Radnorshire	19	40	20	42·5	5	470	3	8	6	1:2·66
Breconshire	31	43	56	78	81	720	6	14	8	1:2·33
Monmouthshire	45	85	319	602	609	530	8	12	15	1:1·5
								av. 13	av. 8	
Total Welsh counties	c.241		c.754			3436		Average for 10 counties:	22	
Grand total	c.940		c.2424			7798				

[1] Calculated on the total population of the county minus that of the towns. The 1951 figures are those for the administrative counties. The comparability for the two dates is thus limited.

TABLE V. *Population of Wales*[1]

Year	Est. total[2] (000s)	Est. density per sq. mile[2]
1536	258	35
1570	301	41
1600	351	47
1630	375	51
1670	378	51
1700	391	52
1750	450	60
1801	541	73

[1] From David Williams, 'A Note on the Population of Wales, 1536–1801', *Bull. Bd. Celtic Stud.*, viii (1937), pp. 359–63.
[2] Except 1801 for which the figures are from the Census.

In Breconshire, apart from the southern fringe where it touches the South Wales coalfield, the same is substantially true, as it is in the remoter upland areas of Denbighshire and Flintshire, and to a lesser degree in central and eastern Monmouthshire. In the English border counties, the rural map has changed little in Herefordshire and in Gloucestershire west of the Severn, moderately only in Shropshire, but appreciably in considerable parts of Cheshire, Flintshire, Denbighshire and Monmouthshire.

From the 1801 returns, there can also be calculated the housing density prior to the varying regional growth rates of the succeeding

TABLE VI. *Population Densities per square mile, 1801 and 1951*

	1801	1951	Total area in sq. miles admin. cos.
3 English counties	141	391	3157
6 Welsh counties	72	219	3436
9 Border counties	116	301	6593
10 Border counties	120	299	7798

century and a half. Averaged for the whole area, there were 22 houses per square mile in the ten counties, 29 in the four English and just under 13 in the six Welsh. County by county, the figures are even more revealing, highlighting the fundamental contrast between the mid-Welsh border counties with their exceptionally low housing density of 6 to the square mile in Radnorshire, 8 in Breconshire and 10 in Montgomeryshire. True, mining and some industrialisation had already affected the two northern counties of eastern Wales as well as Monmouthshire but apart from this there is a somewhat greater natural fertility in Flintshire and Monmouthshire which is also reflected in the housing densities for those two counties.

On the English side of the Border something must be allowed for developments already beginning in north Cheshire, but the high figure for Gloucestershire is almost entirely a reflection of the superior agricultural and climatic conditions, not in western Gloucestershire, but in the area which is outside the Borderland to the east of the Severn. The figures 20 and 23 to the square mile for Herefordshire and Shropshire respectively are probably fair indications of the rural housing density for the greater part of the English border counties about 1800. For the three main border counties (Cheshire, Shropshire and Herefordshire) the average of 24 gives a fair idea – just about double the housing density for the entire Welsh group and three times that for the mid-border counties of Montgomeryshire, Radnorshire and Breconshire.

The proportion of houses to agricultural workers at the same date may, with a certain amount of caution, also be of some value as an economic social index. It is highest for Gloucestershire (1:1·06), second highest for Cheshire (1:1·12). It is lowest for Radnorshire (1:2·66) and Breconshire (1:2·33), but Hereford-shire then breaks into the Welsh list with 1:1·82), followed by Denbighshire (1:1·75) and Montgomeryshire (1 : 1·62). Assuming that the agricultural workers included the main breadwinner and an average of perhaps one in three of the children, the figures of houses per agricultural worker may indicate overcrowding in the lower-proportioned counties or larger families or more child labour – in any case, a lower standard of living in those areas.

PART TWO

The Evolution of the Rural Landscape

3 The Celtic Foundations
and the Roman Intrusion

TO introduce the story of rural settlement at the Celtic phase is not to suggest that the Bronze Age was unimportant. It was particularly notable as a period in which trade routes were opened up, as for example between Anglesey and the middle Severn valley.[1] The bases of pastoralism and even, perhaps, of primitive cultivation were being laid or strengthened, though this area has as yet yielded no examples of Bronze Age corn plots. Burial-sites are widely distributed over the Borderland in both upland and lowland sites, and numerous cultural features continued without a break from the Bronze into the Early Iron Age in Wales and the Borderland. There are even certain place-names, for example *Ewyas*, which are unrelated to any known Celtic element and which, it is thought, may pre-date the Iron Age. To this extent, the Bronze Age was directly ancestral to the Celtic period and it lingered long in remote areas such as the Welsh hills. Yet, as E. G. Bowen wrote: 'It is only when we come to the pre-Roman Iron Age that we encounter an important formative period in the life of Wales.'[2] This might be said with equal truth of the rural settlements of the entire Borderland.

The Pre-Roman Iron Age

An Early Iron Age culture became fully established in south-eastern Britain about 500 B.C., but in Wales and the West generally, its introduction was delayed. Iron-using folk from Brittany came up through Cornwall about the end of the fifth or the beginning of the fourth century B.C. bringing with them duck-motif

[1] Sir Cyril Fox, *A Find of the Early Iron Age from Llyn Cerrig Bach, Anglesey* (1946).
[2] *Wales* (1957), p. 136.

pottery. Through Dorset and Somerset they moved up the valleys of the Severn and the Wye, and thence into North Wales and other parts of the bordering lowlands, bringing a preponderantly Iron Age B culture.[1]

W. F. Grimes has pointed out that the normal sequence of settlement in south-eastern England from open sites to simple camps and then to multi-rampart sites may have been followed in Wales, but that in most cases it was likely to include only the last two. By early Christian times Celtic tribes were established throughout Wales especially in hill settlements adjacent to lowlands such as coastal plains, river valleys, and inland plains.[2] The early Celts were predominantly pastoral, but used sloping land terraced into lynchets for cultivation.[3]

However remote in time and however piecemeal, the settlements and simple agriculture of these Celtic tribes represent the beginnings of the evolution of the rural landscape as we know it today, and it is still impossible to say whether or not there has been in some cases actual continuity of site.

The Roman Occupation

The light of written history shone first on these islands as a result of the Roman conquest and occupation of Britain, and classical writers referred to a number of Celtic tribes who spoke a Brythonic language. Reaching Britain in A.D. 43, the Romans were approaching the Welsh Border by A.D. 47, but Wales remained throughout the occupation part of the military zone of Britain. It was, in fact, their failure to settle in the highland zone as they did in the

---

[1] Large multi-vallate camps distinguished the B areas but an earlier A layer has been found in some, e.g. Ffridd Faldwyn (Mont.), and Titterstone Clee and Old Oswestry (Sa.).

[2] W. F. Grimes in *A Hundred Years of Welsh Archaeology, Centenary Vol.*, Camb. Arhaeol. Assoc. (1946), pp. 72–7.

[3] Numerous ancient fields are known in Wales near deserted hut groups but their prehistoric date has yet not been established. (W. F. Grimes, loc. cit.). The same difficulty is encountered in the English border areas. In Cheshire, J. D. Bu'Lock believes there may be Celtic fields near Kelsall ('Possible Remains of Celtic Fields near Kelsall in Cheshire', *Trans. Lancs. and Ches. Antiq. Soc.*, lxiv, 1954, pp. 24–6), and Celtic fields have been identified by Miss Lily F. Chitty on Longmynd (Sa.) (*Trans. Shrops. Archaeol. Soc.*, lvi, 1957–8, p. 5) but these remain rare examples.

lowland zone, which first distinguished a Welsh Borderland as such, and in the first century of the Christian era the highland edge assumed a strategic importance which it was to retain for fifteen hundred years.

From the Roman fortress of Viroconium (Wroxeter, Sa.) the Deceangli of North Wales were conquered between A.D. 47 and 52. The Silures of South Wales were eventually overcome only after A.D. 74, but by the year 79 Wales had capitulated and the creation of a frontier system of roads and forts followed. A series of roads was made to link the legionary fortresses of Deva (Chester) and Isca (Caerleon), and V. E. Nash-Williams estimated that the Deva Command had a military establishment of 12–13,000 men, and the Isca Command of between 13,000 and 16,000.[1] The road which linked them, though not very direct, was the precursor of later roads down the Marches and of the railway which today links Chester and Newport, and it is deemed by I. D. Margary to have been planned as a single strategic line between Chester and Chepstow.[2] Lesser roads diverged westwards into Wales, and those into mid-Wales were relatively minor, but the north and south coast roads were of considerable importance. The roads were protected by occasional small forts of varying size, and today a number of them have inhabited villages on or adjacent to their site. Thus tiny Wroxeter adjoins Viroconium, Kenchester Magnis and Leintwardine Bravonium. Caerwys, Caersws and Caerwent, all sizeable villages, lie actually within the lines of the Roman fortresses but there is no proof of continuous occupation in any one of them. On a minor scale, were small forts such as those near Abergavenny, Usk, Llanfair Caereinion and Forden. During the first century of Roman rule it seems that a number of the Celtic hill-forts were strengthened, for example, Bickerton (Ch.), and Dinorben (Fl.), while Moel Fenlli (Denb.) was first fortified at that time. Later, the two peoples lived peacefully side by side. There were a few Roman mines in the Borderland as at Shelve (Sa.) and Coleford (Glam.), but the villas which represent the spread of the Romans from the towns during the third century have few representatives in this part of Britain, having been found only near Castle Tump and Portskewett Hill (Mon.), Llantwit

[1] *The Roman Frontier in Wales* (1954).
[2] *Roman Roads in Britain*, ii (1957), p. 49.

Major and Oystermouth near Ely (Glam.), Acton Scott, Lea, and Cruckton (Sa.), Bishopstone (He.), and Woolaston (Gl.). Their influence on the Celtic people and on their economy can at best have been slight.

Deva and Isca became the major settlements of the Roman March and, in addition to their military strength, they housed very considerable civil populations. Chester, despite a period of desertion which, according to the *Anglo-Saxon Chronicle*, lasted for five hundred years[1] had its foundations as a town, a port and a road centre well and truly laid by the Romans, and the present-day street plan and the line of the walls, apart from the medieval extension southward and westward, follow the Roman plan. The civil settlement outside the walls was of considerable size.[2] Like Deva, Isca was at the hinge of the border road and that which led west along the coast into Wales, but despite the importance of the southern hinge, and the great size of Roman Isca, no later town succeeded it on the site. Caerleon today is only a big village, and Isca's real successor at the mouth of the Usk is Newport.[3] Dr Nash-Williams estimated that the total population of Isca, including the civilians, was probably 18,000 at its height.[4]

In the cases of both Chester and Caerleon, there was probably a very considerable population left after the withdrawal of the legions in the early fifth century and, deserting the urban sites, these former town-dwellers must have swollen the rural populations of many nearby settlements. They may even have initiated some of the villages and hamlets of west Cheshire and southern Monmouthshire. It is known that the Romans were the first to attempt to drain the Monmouthshire Moors, and both there and in west Cheshire the population density in the Dark Ages seems to have been appreciably greater than in other parts of those counties.[5]

With these exceptions, interesting and important though they are, the Roman occupation probably had an almost negligible

---

[1] Under the year 893, it was described as 'a deserted Roman site in Wirral'. Under the year 907, the *Chronicle* records that 'in this year Chester was rebuilt'.
[2] F. H. Thompson, *Deva, Roman Chester* (1959).
[3] Probably because of changing tidal conditions.   [4] In conversation in 1955.
[5] Dr Nash-Williams discussed the possibility of a sub-Roman contribution to settlements around the Monmouthshire Roman stations in a paper on Redwick: 'Note on a new Roman Site at Redwick, near Magor, Mon.', *Bull. Bd Celtic Stud.*, xiv (1951), pp. 254–5.

effect on the rural settlement of the Borderland, except through the influence of roads which, prior to the turnpike era, in many cases provided the main through routes for several centuries, and a number of villages were subsequently sited on them, notably the several Strettons in the Borderland.

The Roman net was thin except in areas immediately around the legionary fortresses, and for the most part the Celtic farmer went on very much as before, increasing in numbers and advancing in culture and techniques with the passage of time and not solely because of Roman influence.

The effects of the Roman occupation on the Brythons was like a slow ferment, and it was only in the later years of the occupation and in the centuries following the withdrawal, that the romanisation of Celtic culture and the seeds of the Christian faith produced more spectacular results.

The Sub-Roman Period

The sub-Roman period was one of migration and there were four major directions of movement which affected the Brythonic world:

(i) Irish Goidels were moving into and settling much of western Wales, especially the south-western area between the Ystwyth, the south-coast, and Brecon, and to a lesser extent Anglesey and parts of the northern mainland.

(ii) Cunedda, Cyndeyrn and other Strathclyde Britons were using the great corridor of lowland and the passes which made movement easy between Strathclyde, the Solway, Wales and the Border, and the plains of Somerset and the south-western peninsula (Fig. 5).

(iii) Goidelic pressure is deemed responsible for a southward migration from South Wales, and later from Devon and Cornwall to Brittany when Saxon pressure was exerted against south-western Britain.

(iv) Most significant of all was the Anglo-Saxon advance westwards across the English plains towards the Highland

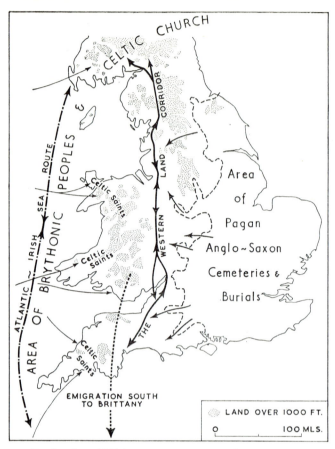

5. England and Wales, *c.* A.D. 600

Zone, and the consequent transferred thrust of Brythonic people westwards, or their subjection and absorption into conquered Anglo-Saxon territory.

But when this last push began to be felt in the Borderland, the Dark Ages may be said to have begun in this area, and the sub-Roman period to have ended.

From the fifth to the seventh century the Borderland enjoyed, with the rest of Celtic Britain, one of the greatest eras of cultural resurgence in the history of this country. From A.D. 400 until after

600, linguistic and archaeological evidences point to a single major culture province extending from the Clyde–Forth line to Brittany. Communication was doubly facilitated by the western sea route and the great land corridor from the Clyde through what is now western England but was, before 600, the eastern flank of Brythonic territory. The Welsh Borderland sat midway athwart that vital land line which, by the late sixth century, had been effectively hemmed in by the advancing Anglo-Saxons. H. N. Savory has published archaeological evidence[1] which bears out the significance of this corridor as an area of free movement and cultural interchange in the sub-Roman period. He has postulated close links between the Votadini of Strathclyde and the Cornovii of the northern Welsh Borderland, and while this corridor remained open – as it did until Ceawlin captured Gloucester, Cirencester and Bath – Savory has shown that it was a relatively prosperous area of sub-Romano-British culture. One of the bases of this prosperity was the trading of metalwork which was made and sold in quantity (especially penannular brooches showing Irish influence) to the Angles in the Midlands, profoundly influencing Anglian craftsmanship as a result. In presenting the Borderland at this time as an area in which, he suggests, Celtic and Anglo-Saxon settlers interpenetrated, and as a territory where Anglo-Saxon settlers perhaps remained as vassals after re-conquest by Arthur, he offers a radically different picture from that painted by earlier historians, and one fraught with significance in relation to the history of settlement.[2]

The Celtic renaissance became evident in many aspects of contemporary life – craftsmanship, bardic poetry, growing political power, and the rise and spread of Christianity in and through the Celtic Church. The increasing political definition of the Celtic tribal groups of west Britain from the fourth to the seventh century seems in part to have been initiated by the devolution of power in the late Roman period, in part by increasing Roman dependence on British aid to repel invaders, but not least by the upwelling of Celtic vigour. Freedom from Roman overlordship increased the speed of territorial and political

[1] 'Some sub-Romano-British Brooches from South Wales', in *Dark Age Britain*, ed. D. B. Harden (1956), pp. 41–58.
[2] See Ch. 4.

evolution. Tribal territories became kingdoms. Strathclyde and Rheged emerged in southern Scotland and north-west England, Elmet in the Pennines, and Gwynedd in north-west Wales during this period. Powys took shape as the 'middle kingdom' of Wales, a roughly triangular area with its apex on the Dyfi estuary, but with its long side flung far beyond the highland edge to embrace considerable portions of the west Cheshire and north Shropshire lowlands, its traditional capitals at various times including Mathrafal in the Vyrnwy valley, Pengwern in the middle Severn valley and Chester. In the southern Borderland, the upper Usk became the focus of Brychan's kingdom, Brycheiniog, at times including and at times excluding Buellt, which corresponded roughly with modern Radnorshire. Despite the series of Roman roads which centred on Y Gaer near modern Brecon, Brycheiniog tended to be influenced rather by west Wales than by the Border-land, while to the south the great wall of the Brecon Beacons isolated it from the south-eastern Welsh kingdom of Glwysing. From Glwysing there sprang Morgannwg and Gwent, probably in the late sixth or early seventh century, the first roughly cover-ing modern Glamorgan, the latter modern Monmouthshire, though Gwent proper lay between the Usk, the Wye and the Monnow. To what extent these divisions went their separate ways as regards settlement and economy is obscure, but their separa-tism is fraught with significance both in this late period of Celtic independence and in succeeding centuries. So, too, is the close association of the Cheshire and Shropshire lowlands with Powys, a westward link which, in the case of Cheshire particularly, was to be perpetuated until 1284 in political form and, in both coun-ties, far longer culturally. Each kingdom also evolved its own laws, its own field systems and its own land measurements.

The third aspect of the Celtic renaissance which was relevant to settlement geography was the spread of Celtic Christianity during these two hundred years. This was closely linked to, and reflected by the movements between Ireland and Wales, Wales and Brittany, and south-west Scotland and Wales during this period. Many North Welsh saints claimed descent from Cunedda, 'Dux Britannorum', who came down from Strathclyde reputedly in the late Roman period to subdue or expel Irish Goidels settled there. In the fifth century, the territories of his sons extended across the entire width of Wales from the Dee in the north-east to the Teifi in the south-west. From the mists of the Cunedda myths, Melville Richards concludes that the Strathclyde Brythons whom Cunedda led south at least represent 'a Brythonic surge which involved a clash with the existing Goidelic colonies and settlements'.[1] Richards considers it certain that Goidelic colonists from Ireland had planted their settlements along British shores from Argyll to Devon and Cornwall. Basing his conclusions largely on the evidence of Ogam stones and place-names, he has shown that they settled most closely between the Rheidol, St. David's and the Towy valley where an Irish dynasty remained in power until the tenth century. From there, Brychan, the founder of Brycheiniog, who was partly Irish, was considerably influenced by Goidelic culture and Irish Christianity, a further differentiating factor between Breconshire and the rest of the Borderland. In other parts of Wales there were far fewer settlements. They were fairly numerous in Anglesey, but fewer in number on the north Welsh mainland, while in the northern Border they are represented only by the one place-name of Knockin, and by two Ogams in mid-Denbighshire.

The derivation of Christianity in North Wales from northern sources continued with the coming of Cyndeyrn or St Kentigern to the Clwyd valley in the mid-sixth century from Strathclyde and the founding of St Asaph, named after his pupil. E. G. Bowen has shown that there are Kentigern associations with two north Welsh foci, Anglesey and the Clwyd valley, and that there were two distinctive cultural provinces in Wales during the age of the Celtic saints, a northern and a southern.[2] Breconshire tended throughout this period to be orientated south and west, while Radnorshire though looking south where its drainage was to the Wye, in its poorly populated northern districts was associated with Powys.

Bowen has also distinguished the south-eastern cults of the early Christian period from those of south-western Wales, emphasising the distinctiveness of Monmouthshire and southern

[1] 'The Irish Settlements in South-West Wales', *Jl R. Soc. Antiquaries of Ireland*, xc, ii (1960), p. 138.
[2] *The Settlements of the Celtic Saints in Wales*, ch. 1 and maps on pp. 18, 24, 26 and 73.

Herefordshire.[1] Early Christian monuments of the fifth to the seventh centuries are found predominantly in north-west Wales and in South Wales from Pembrokeshire and southern Cardiganshire across to Glamorgan and Breconshire, as is consistent with the western points of entry which Nash-Williams has proved. They are notably absent from Monmouthshire, and it is known that this southern part of the Border was associated with Romano-British Christianity.[2]

During the fifth and sixth centuries the Celtic Church extended over the whole of Highland Britain, including the south-west peninsula of what is now England, and from southern Scotland it had spread to include Northumbria, and perhaps much more of northern England. After the seventh century, Hodgkin shows that a territorially restricted British Church covered the old Brythonic territory of Strathclyde, Wales and Dumnonia.[3] To trace its eastward extension across the Welsh Borderland is less easy and largely conjectural. Many formerly Celtic churches were rededicated when they passed to the Roman Church and the original dedications forgotten. A few survived, such as those in southern Herefordshire, while others are perhaps indicated by place–names including the *llan* and the *eccles* element. Bowen's map of Celtic dedications in Wales takes them well across the border,[4] but there still remains a gap between them and the westward limit of Anglo-Saxon pagan cemeteries (i.e. cemeteries earlier than the mid-seventh century),[5] which lie within a line drawn irregularly from Poole in Dorset to a point a few miles east of Gloucester, thence irregularly again to the Stafford district, across the south-western Pennines, back to Nottingham, north to a point a few miles south-west of the head of the Humber, back along the Pennine foothills and so to the head of the Tees estuary. But as the Anglo-Saxons had advanced far west of this line by 650, either they had become converts of the British Church, or were present in insufficient numbers to affect the custom of Christian burial which that Church may long previously have established there. If the entire Borderland was at one time within the territory of the British Church, one would expect to find many solitary

---

[1] Ibid. ch. 2.   [2] *The Early Christian Monuments of Wales* (1950).
[3] R. H. Hodgkin, *History of the Anglo-Saxons* (1935), vol. i, end map.
[4] Op. cit. p. 105.
[5] This line is shown in Fig. 5 and based on Thurlow Leeds's distribution.

churches there, since the Celtic missionaries, not 'of the blood' and frequently hermits, were always set apart from the lay community. Figure 3 shows that, in fact, the distribution of isolated churches in the Borderland covers not only the Welsh area proper but extends from Monmouthshire over the greater part of Herefordshire and south Shropshire, thinning out towards north Shropshire and Cheshire. If from these solitary churches are subtracted those of known manorial origin the numbers are still considerable.

Ecclesiastical, political and cultural provinces were so often and so significantly co-terminous in early history, that these regional distributions cannot be ignored in a study of settlement.

The Evidence of Celtic Place-Names

The *Pax Romana* and later the upsurge of British political power, were associated with a movement into lowlands and valleys, and presumably with an increase of population which, together with the migration from the hills, must have given rise to new settlements. Roman roads had opened up a number of areas, and the larger Roman towns, such as Chester and Caerleon in the Borderland, encouraged trade and agriculture before themselves falling into ruin after the withdrawal and leaving a temporarily homeless Romano-British people ready to colonise the surrounding countryside.

In proportion to the density of their settlements, Brythonic names were correspondingly widespread in the Borderland prior to the battle of Deorham in 577 and the battle of Chester *circa* 615. The remarkable prevalence of Anglo-Saxon names in the English border counties, however, long deceived place-name etymologists and historians into supposing that the proportional importance of the Celtic and the Anglo-Saxon settlements was approximately indicated by the relative numbers of place-names incorporating the two groups of elements. Unfortunately in this connection, Teutonists have been more numerous among the ranks of place-name etymologists than Celticists. Yet as early as 1915, J. B.

Johnston listed numerous Celtic place-names in England.[1] In 1921, Max Förster suggested Celtic roots for many place-name elements which had long been accepted as English,[2] and in 1923 Allen Mawer wrote in his introduction to Bowcock's *Shropshire Place-Names*:[3]

There are few counties whose place-names offer as many problems as does Shropshire. . . . Its place-names abound in Celtic elements and there is no doubt that here, as in many other of the border counties, there has been an anglicising of Celtic names and a celticising of Anglian names.

Even in 1916, Bannister had already offered a boldly Welsh origin for many place-names in the English parts of Herefordshire.[4]

In 1953, Kenneth Jackson divided the English Plain into three areas each with more Celtic river names than the one to the east of it, and culminating in Area III which included most of the west of England, but stopped short at Cheshire.[5] Eilert Ekwall saw Celtic roots in innumerable river names in England[6] but was very cautious about attributing a Celtic origin to place-names, even in the Welsh Border counties.[7] Kenneth Cameron exercises a comparable reluctance to extend the accepted basis of many English place-names to include Celtic sources,[8] and as regards his interpretation of Derbyshire names,[9] R. W. P. Cockerton has joined issue with him on the matter of Celtic roots.[10] For Staffordshire names, W. H. Duignan, as early as 1902, had found a liberal supply of Celtic roots,[11] yet Simeon Potter in 1954 accepted only 26 places in Cheshire as having names of Celtic origin.[12]

A plot of Ekwall's Celtic-derived place-names for the English

[1] *The Place-Names of England and Wales* (1915).
[2] 'Celtisches Wortgut im Englischen' in *Texte und Forschungen zur Englischen Kulturgeschichte. Festgabe für Felix Liebermann* (1921).
[3] E. W. Bowcock, *Shropshire Place-Names* (1923), introduction, pp. 5–6.
[4] A. T. Bannister, *Place-Names of Herefordshire* (1916).
[5] *Language and History in Early Britain* (1953), pp. 220–3.
[6] *English River-Names* (1928).
[7] *A Concise Oxford Dictionary of English Place-Names* (1936), 4th ed. (1960).
[8] *English Place-Names* (1961).
[9] *The Place-Names of Derbyshire*, 3 vols (1959).
[10] 'Celtic Influence in Derbyshire Place-Names', *Derbys. Archaeol. Soc.*, lxxix (1959), and a rejoinder by K. Cameron in the same vol.: 'A Note on Celtic Elements in English Place-Names'.
[11] *Notes on Staffordshire Place-Names*.
[12] 'Cheshire Place-Names', *Trans. Hist. Soc. Lancs. and Ches.*, cvi (1954), p. 4.

6 (*opposite*). Shropshire: evidences of Celtic occupation in place-names

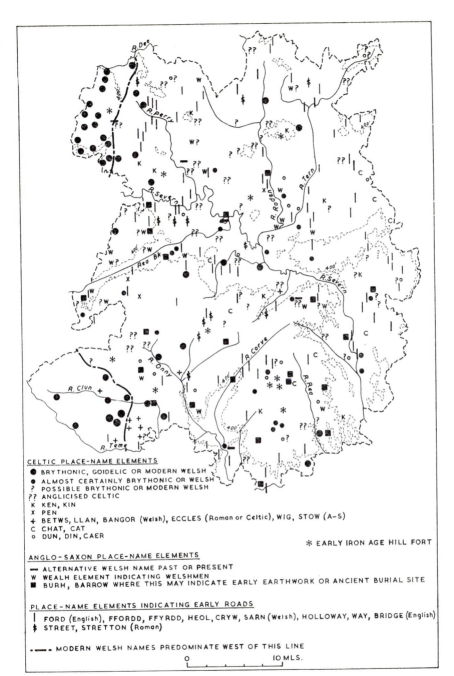

CELTIC PLACE-NAME ELEMENTS

● BRYTHONIC, GOIDELIC OR MODERN WELSH
● ALMOST CERTAINLY BRYTHONIC OR WELSH
? POSSIBLE BRYTHONIC OR MODERN WELSH
?? ANGLICISED CELTIC
K KEN, KIN
X PEN
+ BETWS, LLAN, BANGOR (Welsh), ECCLES (Roman or Celtic), WIG, STOW (A-S)
C CHAT, CAT
o DUN, DIN, CAER

✳ EARLY IRON AGE HILL FORT

ANGLO-SAXON PLACE-NAME ELEMENTS

— ALTERNATIVE WELSH NAME PAST OR PRESENT
W WEALH ELEMENT INDICATING WELSHMEN
■ BURH, BARROW WHERE THIS MAY INDICATE EARLY EARTHWORK OR ANCIENT BURIAL SITE

PLACE-NAME ELEMENTS INDICATING EARLY ROADS

| FORD (English), FFORDD, FFYRDD, HEOL, CRYW, SARN (Welsh), HOLLOWAY, WAY, BRIDGE (English)
$ STREET, STRETTON (Roman)

▪—▪— MODERN WELSH NAMES PREDOMINATE WEST OF THIS LINE

0 _____ 10 MLS.

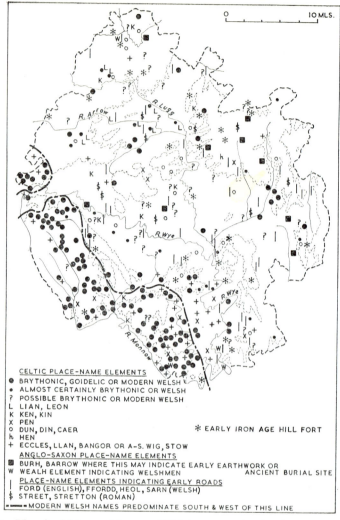

0   10 MLS.

CELTIC PLACE-NAME ELEMENTS
- ● BRYTHONIC, GOIDELIC OR MODERN WELSH
- • ALMOST CERTAINLY BRYTHONIC OR WELSH
- ? POSSIBLE BRYTHONIC OR MODERN WELSH
- L LIAN, LEON
- K KEN, KIN
- X PEN
- o DUN, DIN, CAER   ✳ EARLY IRON AGE HILL FORT
- h HEN
- + ECCLES, LLAN, BANGOR OR A-S. WIG, STOW

ANGLO-SAXON PLACE-NAME ELEMENTS
- ▣ BURH, BARROW WHERE THIS MAY INDICATE EARLY EARTHWORK OR
- W WEALH ELEMENT INDICATING WELSHMEN   ANCIENT BURIAL SITE

PLACE-NAME ELEMENTS INDICATING EARLY ROADS
- | FORD (ENGLISH), FFORDD, HEOL, SARN (WELSH)
- $ STREET, STRETTON (ROMAN)
- ■━━━ MODERN WELSH NAMES PREDOMINATE SOUTH & WEST OF THIS LINE

7. Herefordshire: evidences of Celtic occupation in place-names

border counties gives a very thin distribution. Moreover, for no apparent reason Ekwall deriving the suffix *-trey* or *-try* sometimes from *tref* (W.) and in other cases from *treu* (O.E. tree), other sources were consulted. B. G. Charles[1] and Bannister[2] went much

[1] 'The Welsh, their language and place-names in Archenfield and Oswestry', in *Angles and Britons*, O'Donnell Lectures (1962).
[2] Op. cit.

further in the matter of Celtic origins for the place-names of Herefordshire. Consequently maps were made on the basis not only of the virtually certain Celtic names, but on all probable and possible Celtic names that could be traced. The resulting distributions (Figs 6, 7 and 8) show that, with remarkably few exceptions, the whole set of these names occur within the areas which had been settled by the end of the early phases of Anglian colonisation in the now English parts of the Borderland (cf. Figs 9, 10 and 11). In other words, it establishes the strong probability that it was the Celtic folk who had first cleared the woodlands, in areas of early Mercian settlement and the Mercians who moved in and established overlordship and renamed the old settlements, in the already cleared border districts. This does not rule out the possibility that the Mercians initiated villages and hamlets additionally. In most of Herefordshire and Shropshire, the early cleared land was in the major river valleys, and this was the case also in central and eastern Cheshire. But in west Cheshire the entire area of Wirral, the Gowy valley and the lower Dee valley was cleared by the eighth century with the exception only of very minor patches which survived until Domesday. This was the most Romanised part of Cheshire. It also had strong evidence of Celtic settlement in sites such as Meols, of early Celtic churches in the place-names Landican and Eccleston, and in the nearby Celtic ecclesiastical centres of St Asaph and Bangor on Dee. In addition, there are numerous other names in this area which had a possible Celtic origin. The name Tarvin immediately west of the central Cheshire ridge, and on the edge of this early cleared lowland is generally believed to derive from *terfyn* (W. boundary) which suggests that this western lowland may have been a distinct province. To this day, the ecclesiastical parishes are small in the western area bounded until the Middle Ages by the great central forests of Delamere and Mondrem, and large to the east of it.[1]

If the Celtic folk indeed settled this area closely before the coming of the Mercians, it is probable that they did so in increasing numbers during and after the Roman occupation, moving down

[1] Dorothy Sylvester, 'Cheshire in the Dark Ages', *Trans. Hist. Soc. Lancs. and Ches.*, cxiv (1962). The evidence for these arguments is discussed in more detail in this paper.

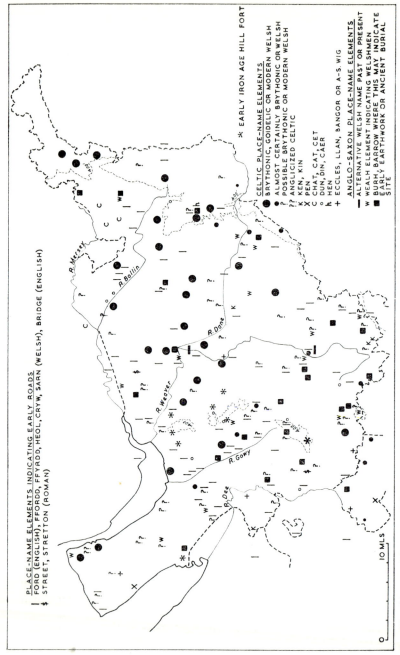

PLACE-NAME ELEMENTS INDICATING EARLY ROADS
FORD (ENGLISH), FFORDD, FFYRDD, HEOL, CRYW, SARN (WELSH), BRIDGE (ENGLISH)
§ STREET, STRETTON (ROMAN)

* EARLY IRON AGE HILL FORT

CELTIC PLACE-NAME ELEMENTS
BRYTHONIC, GOIDELIC OR MODERN WELSH
● ALMOST CERTAINLY BRYTHONIC OR WELSH
?● POSSIBLE BRYTHONIC OR MODERN WELSH
?? ANGLICIZED CELTIC
K KEN, KIN
X PEN
C CHAT, CAT, CET
o DUN, DIN, CAER
h HEN
+ ECCLES, LLAN, BANGOR OR A-S. WIG

ANGLO-SAXON PLACE-NAME ELEMENTS
— ALTERNATIVE WELSH NAME PAST OR PRESENT
W WEALH ELEMENT INDICATING WELSHMEN
■ BURH, BARROW WHERE THIS MAY INDICATE EARLY EARTHWORK OR ANCIENT BURIAL SITE

R.Mersey
R.Bollin
R.Dane
R.Weaver
R.Gowy
R.Dee

0   10 MLS

8. Cheshire: evidences of Celtic occupation in place-names

into the lowlands from the hill forts which crowned the central
ridge of Cheshire, and in from the west across the lower Dee and
the Dee estuary from the Flintshire plateau, and – not least –
spreading out into the country districts from the deserted City of
the Legions. In pre-Roman times this area was occupied by the
Cornovii, a Brythonic people, and their hold on the area according
to discoveries by Myrddyn Bevan-Evans[1] supports the assumption
that Celtic people were on Moel Hiraddug in northern Flintshire
by 300 B.C. The early history of Chester is shrouded in mystery,
and legends that it was the capital of the mythical King Lear have
no foundation in fact. Its growth in Roman times, however, not
only made it a town of appreciable size and with a considerable
civil population, but established its importance as a road centre.
At an undetermined date, Powys developed as a Welsh kingdom,
and in the words of William Rees: 'How far eastwards the boundaries of Powys ran we shall probably never know – doubtless well
into Cheshire and Shropshire even as far as the Severn. . . .'[2] If
this western province stretched as far as a north-south line through
Tarvin or to the hills immediately to the east of this, and was
closely settled before the coming of the Angles, then in turn proved
attractive to them and to the Irish-Norse, one would expect to
find a different and a denser settlement pattern in west Cheshire
than in the centre and east which so long remained wooded, and
was so slowly colonised apart from the attractive Weaver valley.
The facts support this assumption.[3]

The most numerous place-names in the three English counties
which may incorporate anglicisations of Brythonic or later Welsh
elements are those linked with roads, especially *heol* and the rather
difficult *ford* or *ffordd*. In plotting these on Figs 6, 7 and 8,
strata or *street* has been added as being relevant both to the period
and the roads in question, so has the rare *port* element together with
way and *bridge* where their incorporation was evidently datable to
routes used in the Dark Ages or earlier. But of these elements
giving possible clues to Celtic or Roman roads, *heol* and *ford* or
ffordd are by far the most numerous, the others except for *street* or
strata (with a Roman connotation), occurring very rarely indeed.

[1] During excavations in the summer of 1964.
[2] *An Historical Atlas of Wales* (1951), p. 18.
[3] See Chs 4 and 11.

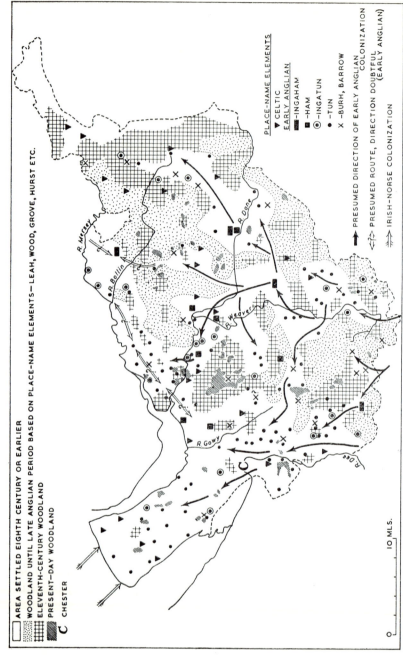

AREA SETTLED EIGHTH CENTURY OR EARLIER

WOODLAND UNTIL LATE ANGLIAN PERIOD BASED ON PLACE-NAME ELEMENTS—LEAH, WOOD, GROVE, HURST ETC.

ELEVENTH-CENTURY WOODLAND

PRESENT-DAY WOODLAND

C CHESTER

PLACE-NAME ELEMENTS

▼ CELTIC
EARLY ANGLIAN
▣ —INGAHAM
✚ —HAM
◉ —INGATUN
● —TUN
X —BURH, BARROW

➡ PRESUMED DIRECTION OF EARLY ANGLIAN COLONIZATION
⟵?⟶ PRESUMED ROUTE, DIRECTION DOUBTFUL (EARLY ANGLIAN)
⟹ IRISH-NORSE COLONIZATION

R. Mersey
R. Bollin
R. Dane
R. Weaver
R. Gowy
R. Dee

0   10 MLS.

9. Cheshire: woodland recession and the advance of settlement

The problem concerning *ford* is that, according to **T. H. Parry-Williams**,[1] it is an Old English word from which the Welsh *ffordd* was derived, and is cognate with the Old High German *furt* and the latin *portus*. In general it has come to mean a crossing-place, more specifically the crossing of a river, but in place-names the element *ford* has been widely associated also with a position on a Roman road. When it occurs in place-names which are remote from streams, it may therefore be assumed to have this less specific meaning. The fact that in Welsh, *ffordd* still means a road, may point to later Welsh influence in the English border counties, or mean that in the Dark Ages, *ford* had this wider meaning. The Longford, a stretch of Roman road crossing north-east Shropshire is a clear example of the use of the element. In plotting *ford* and *heol* elements, the principle of selection has been partly topographical, i.e. these elements have been recorded when it was extremely unlikely or incapable of proof that they could have other meanings. It must be stressed that they occur suggestively in linear distributions, and that between the lines they seem to form, there is an extraordinary dearth of names with even a suggestion of these elements (Figs 6, 7 and 8).

The first and most striking fact about the *ford* and *heol* place-names is that they occur along many known or presumed Roman roads. This in itself is valuable evidence of their use and meaning, but does not *per se* give them a precise date. They may be pre-Roman, Roman, or post-Roman in date, but the large number of possible *heol* elements along Roman roads or in similar linear distribution strongly suggests a Brythonic association with, or use of, these routeways, and the *fords* occur regularly intermixed along these lines which give so strong a suggestion of early roads. A physical difficulty is that only the Romans built and paved their roads, and so left causeways with some degree of permanence. A historical difficulty is that roads have long powers of survival, and this very continuity adds to the problem of dating. It is clear that the Cornovii of the northern Borderland used Roman roads as did their Anglian successors. With their shift from the hills to the lowlands in the Christian era, new tracks must have been made both for purposes of trade and to link the new (and

---

[1] *The English Element in Welsh* (1923), p. 34.

old) settlements. Many of these settlements must be presumed to have become permanently occupied sites, at least from the sub-Roman era, and the present inter-village roads may in many cases be laid down along these ancient lines. There must be some which are lost or survive only as tracks. Not only the road names, but other surviving Celtic and Roman names, are relevant in trying to use this information for the reconstruction of pre-Anglian roads, which linked up both civil settlements and forts.

It has often been assumed that the people of the post-Roman era made constant use of Roman roads. The opposite, however, may also be true – that the Romans made use of existing lines of Celtic roads, or built straighter roads nearby. This is supported by the fact that so many *ford–heol* lines run close to Roman roads, parallel to them, or diverge from them in loops. It is strikingly the case between Chester and Warrington where Hoole, Mickle Trafford, Bridge Trafford, Hapsford and Helsby lie along or very near the line of the Roman road, but Hoole village, Wimbolds Trafford, Halton and (across the Mersey) Hale, lie along a slightly different line. Again, between Roman roads in mid-Cheshire lie lines of *ford–heol* names, notably the long line from Latchford, near Warrington, through Cogshall, Hartford, Winsford, Darnhall, Wettenhall, Henhull, to Broomhall, which is continued southwards across Shropshire, still between the lines of Roman roads through Broughall, Calverhall, Sleapford, Wappenshall, the Ercall, Benthall and Posenhall along the east and south sides of the Clees by Sidnall, Redford, Hartall and Little Hereford to Gosford, and so into Herefordshire. Some lines, like this one, are long and continuous; others appear to die out after a certain distance. In nearly every case, they keep to the country which was cleared at an early date (cf. with Figs 9, 10 and 11). Many cross the major Roman road directions and suggestive strings of *heol–ford* names and of other names of Celtic origin cross east Cheshire towards Derbyshire, and in Shropshire appear to have connected the Rea–Camlad valley with a route midway across the northern plain by Walford, Milford, Besford, and Lostford to Longford (on the Longford). In 1960, A. W. J. Houghton linked *Yr Hen Ffordd*, a Bronze Age tradeway located by Miss L. F. Chitty in 1954 from Evesham over the Clees to Clungunford, Clun and

Kerry,[1] with a Roman road which he has traced from Droitwich through Greensforge to Bridgnorth, Aston Eyre, through Corvedale and by the gap south of Wenlock Edge to Halford (?*heol–ford*), thence north of Clun Forest by Edgton to Forden and Caersws.[2] Along this route, especially closely spaced north of the Clees and in Corvedale, occur the names Sidnall, Ruthall, Holdgate, Tugford, Holloway, Beambridge, Milford, Halford, Basford, Alport, Sidnal, Blackford, Rhyd-y-Groes and Forden itself.

History and archaeology have very little to say about Celtic settlements during the Roman and sub-Roman periods, and concerning individual places in the Borderland we know painfully little. It is for this reason that place-names, nebulous though the information can prove in individual cases, are so valuable when mapped over the whole area. In Figures 6, 7 and 8 the Celtic interpretation has purposely been stretched to the limit, but even so, it may not mirror the position as it was in the early seventh century on the eve of the Anglian inroads – indeed, it can be taken as an *a priori* fact that innumerable Celtic place-names have been expunged for ever from the map of Britain. What is important, is the way in which the Celtic and presumed Celtic place-names in the English border counties mass up in the areas where the earliest Anglo-Saxon place-names are also found, and spread over the whole of those areas. In other words, the conclusion is difficult to avoid that the Angles first settled in those parts of the Borderland where the initial work of clearing the primitive woodlands had already been done by the Brythonic tribes, and that these Brythons were sufficiently advanced beyond the stage of nomadic pastoralism to have considerable numbers of permanent or, at worst, winter quarters in the lowlands. It is clear that by this time they were already lowlanders where opportunity allowed, as it did in the border plains and valleys, and it is a fair assumption that they practised some crop growing. Both the Roman and their own roads and trackways seem to have been opened up widely, and trade was carried on along them, and communication maintained through the great Corridor of the area we now call a Borderland but which then was a vital and axial region in the

[1] *Archaeol. Camb.*, civ, pp. 193–5. See also 'The Clun–Clee Ridgway' in *Culture and Environment*, ed. I. Ll. Foster and L. Alcock (1963).
[2] 'The Roman Road from Greensforge through the Central Welsh March', *Trans. Shrops. Archaeol. Soc.*, lvi (1960).

Brythonic world. Like the place-names, it is reasonably certain that numerous Celtic churches were lost as such, but the western limit of pagan cemeteries and certain church sites and place-names give ground for assuming that they were once found well to the east of their present distribution area.

4 The Dark Ages
Britons and Angles

Offa's Dyke . . . is . . . among gentle and simple alike, the symbolic frontier – the 'boundary line of Cymru', because there is a natural limit to the territory of a highland people like the Welsh, and the Dyke is the only visible and historic structure which corresponds reasonably well to that fundamental reality: heolden for sippan Engle and Cumbran swa hit Offa geslog.

Sir Cyril Fox in *Offa's Dyke*, 1955

ABOUT a century and a half after their settlement in south-eastern England, the Anglo-Saxons began to press their conquest westwards into the Borderland and across to the highland edge of eastern Wales. In A.D. 600, according to Kenneth Jackson, the Anglo-Saxon advance had reached a line running along the eastern foothills of the Pennines, across the Peak District and thence along what are approximately the present-day eastern boundaries of Cheshire and Shropshire, and down the Severn valley to the head of its estuary. In the south-west, the land west of the Mendips and the Dorset Stour had fallen into their hands after the battle of Dyrham in 577. Some fifty to seventy years later, after the battles of Chester in *circa* 615 and Oswestry in 641, Mercia had reached the highland edge along the northern and middle border, and the Wye marked the limit of their conquests in the south. Thus the area of what are now the English border counties fell into Mercian hands during the first half of the seventh century except for what are still known as the Welsh districts of southern Herefordshire.[1] Only two other phases in Borderland history approached this half-century in importance – the years of the Norman conquest in the late 1060s, and the years following the Union of England and Wales which had achieved the final

---

[1] Kenneth Jackson, op. cit., map on pp. 208–9.

pacification of the border in 1536. The three together brought the most significant of all changes to the border scene and to its people.

The Mercian Conquest of the Borderland

The English advance on the Borderland came from three directions. From the south-east the Hwicce are thought by Jackson to have reached the Warwick Avon by the early part of the sixth century, but to have been halted by the dense woodland barrier of Morfe, Kinver and Wyre until after A.D. 600, for in 603, at St Augustine's conference with the British bishops, the Severn was still regarded as the boundary between the Anglo-Saxons and the British.

The second attempt to occupy the Borderland, in this case the northern part, took the form of a Northumbrian attempt to annex it perhaps from across the Mersey. Although they were successful in overcoming the British at the battle of Chester, and went on to fight – and lose – the battle of Oswestry in 641 against the Mercians, the Northumbrians' attempts at a settlement appear to have been ill timed, and the question of how far they settled south Lancashire and the Cheshire side of the Mersey valley is problematic.

The third, and successful invasion of the Borderland was by the Mercians. From the Humber, they had pushed up the Trent valley by the mid-sixth century, and occupied the area between Newark and Burton, a base which led them into the thinly settled woodland country of the great Midland forests. The slowness of their advance was due less to human opposition than to the immensity of the task of clearing a way through the dense growth of damp oakwood which clothed the heavy lowland clays of the region. As the century advanced, the Mercians moved up the Trent and the Tame valleys, and in the latter and in one of its small tributary valleys, were set up Tamworth and Lichfield. Eventually these two were to become the administrative and ecclesiastical centres respectively of early Mercia, but not for something like another century. Lichfield diocese was only created in 656 by which time the entire Borderland was probably in

Mercian hands up to the highland edge, and only twenty years later Hereford stemmed off as the south Mercian diocese.

When the Mercians pushed forward in the sixth century, they were still pagan, and Wednesbury and Wednesfield in Staffordshire, both within ten miles of the Shropshire boundary, were named in honour of the pagan god Woden. Later, there is documentary mention of the Tamsaetan, who dwelt in the Tame valley, of the Wroecensaetan, who advanced west to the foot of the Wrekin and thence into the northern plains of Shropshire, and of the Magonsaetan, who settled in the vales and lowlands between the middle Severn and the middle Wye. A more northerly movement, perhaps from the direction of the Humber, peopled the Peak District with a group who consequently became known as the Pecsaetan. By the mid-seventh century Penda of Mercia had advanced to the hill edge of Wales, and achieved the unification of the Angles and Saxons within his realm, the last including the 'under-kingdom of the Hwicce' which Stenton thinks was then brought under Mercian control.[1]

The Early Place-Name Evidence

Such, in essence, is the historical information available on the Mercian conquest of the Borderland. Apart from Offa's Dyke archaeological evidence is on the whole scanty and the main source of detail is place-names. One of the most useful approaches to the interpretation of Anglo-Saxon place-names is through the accepted phasing of the common suffixes. Of these, the *ingas* and *ingaham* elements are the earliest, the *ham* and *ingatun* endings represent the next phase, followed by the *tun* element, and later the suffixes which marked the advance into woodland such as *leah, hurst, graf, fyrð, rydding, rod, wald, weald, worðign* and *wudu*, all of which indicate either some form of woodland or clearing. It has already been seen that the early Anglian settlements in the Borderland corresponded with land which was apparently cleared by the British. Therefore, in theory, the earliest settlements should

[1] F. M. Stenton, *Anglo-Saxon England*, 2nd ed. (1947), p. 45.

be along a key river or land route, and these in turn should be followed up by *ingatun* settlements in the nearby area, these again by *tuns* and later still by those which marked the advance into woodland.

The *ingaham* settlements of the Borderland are significantly, though thinly distributed. As compared with six *ingas* and four *ingaham* settlements in Lancashire, there are only four *ingahams* in Cheshire, two in Shropshire and two in Herefordshire. Sir Frank Stenton has argued that there were enough early Anglo-Saxon place-names between the Mersey and the Solway by the end of the sixth century to prove that all Cumbria and the present area of Lancashire were in Æthelfrith's hands before the battle of Chester. This being so, he could have attacked with ease from the Mersey valley.[1] Jackson, on the contrary, believes that the *ingas* and *ingaham* elements which are associated with the earliest Anglo-Saxon settlements must be given a relatively, rather than a positively, early dating. He considers that the Northumbrian occupation of the north-west probably began nearer 670, for during the reign of Ecgfrith (670–85) land at Cartmel was granted to St Cuthbert also giving him *omnes Britannos cum eo*.[2]

This argument is directly related to the problems of early Anglian settlement in Cheshire. Of the four *ingahams*, three lie in south and south-east Cheshire, the fourth in the north. Of the three, Tushingham is on low ground which could be reached quite easily from the Roden valley across the gently undulating Ellesmere moraine, and in turn it gives access to the fertile lower Dee valley which was so important in the Roman and the sub-Roman periods. Warmingham and Kermincham lie, the one near the Weaver, the other near the Dane, in positions which suggest an approach from either the Roden to the south or from across the Midland Gap on the Staffordshire side. They are so near each other that they could have been colonised by a single group moving from one to the other, or – as the names themselves imply – by two separate groups in which case they may well have been converging from the two different directions. To the north of them were forests which appear to have formed an appreciable barrier cutting them off from the Mersey valley where lay Altrincham, the fourth Cheshire *ingaham*. There seems little

[1] Ibid. p. 78.   [2] Op. cit. pp. 216–17.

reason to doubt that the three southerly *ingahams* were colonised by Mercians from the south. There is little evidence to link Altrincham more convincingly with a northern than a southern approach or *vice versa*. It has been cogently argued that the Northumbrians attacked Chester in *circa* 615 from a base in the Mersey valley, but Jackson maintains that until the end of the sixth century Bernicia was no more than a coastal state and was too weak to expand across the Pennines. He believes that there is no proof of the occupation of north-west England by Northumbria prior to the death of Æthelfrith.[1] Hunter Blair thinks Northumbria was only established permanently west of the Aire Gap about 650–70.[2]

The Mercians were not on the scene at the battle of Chester, but when the Northumbrians conquered Anglesey and invaded North Wales – perhaps from the sea, perhaps from the landward side – Penda of Mercia allied himself with the British against them. After their defeat at Hatfield Chase in 632, or at latest from the defeat of Oswald at Oswestry in 641, Northumbria's minor role in the Borderland was probably played out, and the way up to the Mersey valley was open to Mercia. The Mersey was significantly so named as the 'boundary river', but whether Altrincham pre-dates or post-dates the Mercian occupation of north Cheshire remains problematical.

The Mercians' establishment of friendly relations with the British in the reign of Penda, who died in 655, makes it probable that they began to filter into Cheshire in the 640s or, at latest, the early 650s, and possibly much sooner. The alliance also implies that this settlement may have been by mutual agreement rather than by enforcement, and there is a growing body of opinion that by the time the Mercians reached this late stage of their expansion, the colonisation was appreciably thinner than had been that of the earlier phase prior to 600. If so, then there is every reason to expect truly hybrid settlement features such as would only be possible if there were an appreciable survival of both British inhabitants and British settlements.

In the middle and southern part of the Borderland there are only three *ingaham* elements which can be confirmed: two in Shropshire and one in Herefordshire. The Shropshire examples

---

[1] Ibid. p. 216.   [2] *Archaeologia Aeliana*, 4th series, pp. 123 ff.

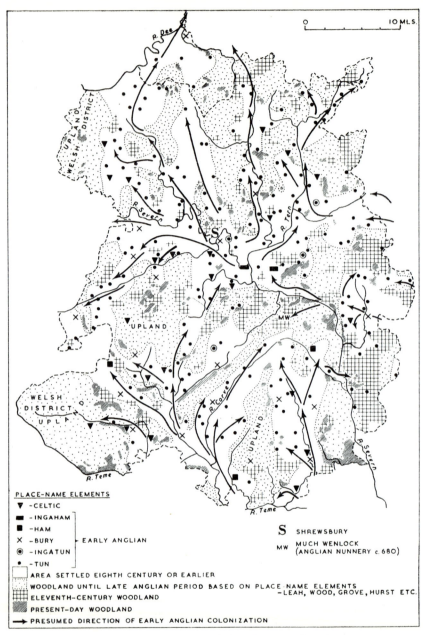

PLACE-NAME ELEMENTS

▼ -CELTIC
■ -INGAHAM
■ -HAM
✕ -BURY   ⎫ EARLY ANGLIAN
◉ -INGATUN   ⎬
• -TUN   ⎭

S   SHREWSBURY
MW MUCH WENLOCK
    (ANGLIAN NUNNERY c. 680)

☐ AREA SETTLED EIGHTH CENTURY OR EARLIER
▦ WOODLAND UNTIL LATE ANGLIAN PERIOD BASED ON PLACE-NAME ELEMENTS
  ─LEAH, WOOD, GROVE, HURST ETC.
▩ ELEVENTH-CENTURY WOODLAND
▨ PRESENT-DAY WOODLAND
➜ PRESUMED DIRECTION OF EARLY ANGLIAN COLONIZATION

10. Shropshire: woodland recession and the advance of settlement

are Uppington, which was originally Uppingham,[1] and Atcham which was Attingham. Both lie near the Severn in the trumpet-shaped lowland immediately west of the Severn Gorge, and it seems reasonable to suppose that the Wroecensaetan reached here from Pattingham in nearby Staffordshire and thence spread west and north into the plains of north Shropshire. This is rendered the more probable by the great woodland barrier which lay across the Severn valley between the Gorge and Kidderminster. In the Middle Ages much of it became incorporated in the Forest of Wyre, but the unbroken woodland cover of the Dark Ages was so extensive that it was known to the British simply as *Y Coed*. Place-name evidence suggests (Fig. 10) that what later became Brewood and the Long Forest were probably continuous with it, and so poses problems as to the settling of the great dales to the south.

In Herefordshire the two-*ingaham* suffixes occur in Ballingham and Bullingham[2] both in the middle Wye basin below Hereford. These could be approached by low gaps south of the Malverns, whence the Leadon and the Frome offer access to the middle Wye (Fig. 11). Arlingham east of the tidal Severn and opposite Newnham could be reached by the banks of the estuarine Severn and it is at one of the most ancient crossing places below Gloucester. The land between the middle Wye and the middle Severn may have been settled either from the north or the south, but the weight of both place-name evidence and reconstructed woodland distribution tends to support the latter. The strong possibility is that a further stream of migrants entered by the lower Severn and the Teme valleys, moving thence up the dales of south-east Shropshire. But the Worfe, further north, could have afforded a route leading into the area north of the Clees, and from some such direction presumably came the founders of Milburga's nunnery.[3] This was established at Much Wenlock (known to the British as Llan Meilien) by approximately 680, and its founding presupposes already peaceful conditions. The initial *ingaham* phase was presumably over, and the *ham* and *ingatun* settlements were

---

[1] Birch, *Cartularium Saxonicum*, no. 1315. H. P. R. Finberg, 'Three Anglo-Saxon Boundaries', *Shrops. Archaeol. Soc.*, LVI (i) (1957–8), p. 33.

[2] A medieval name-pedigree exists for Ballingham but not for Bullingham, but as the two lie in the same area, the geographical argument is not affected.

[3] See Ch. 14, p. 321.

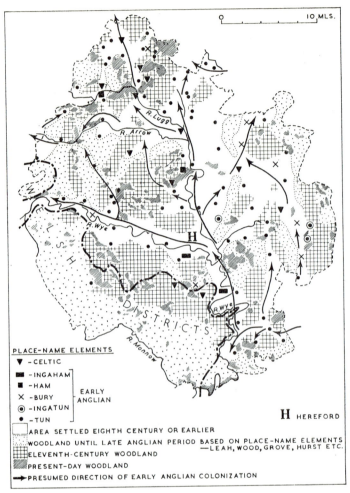

PLACE-NAME ELEMENTS
▼ – CELTIC
▆ – INGAHAM ⎤
■ – HAM ⎥ EARLY
✕ – BURY ⎥ ANGLIAN
◉ – INGATUN ⎥
● – TUN ⎦

☐ AREA SETTLED EIGHTH CENTURY OR EARLIER
▒ WOODLAND UNTIL LATE ANGLIAN PERIOD BASED ON PLACE-NAME ELEMENTS
⊞ ELEVENTH-CENTURY WOODLAND —LEAH, WOOD, GROVE, HURST ETC.
▨ PRESENT-DAY WOODLAND
➝ PRESUMED DIRECTION OF EARLY ANGLIAN COLONIZATION

H HEREFORD

11. Herefordshire: woodland recession and the advance of settlement

doubtless growing up around the original nuclei. They spread in the
next hundred years or so into a wide area of the existing clearings
in the main valleys, and the *tuns* in turn extended the area occupied
by the first Anglian settlement groups in the Borderland. Practically all these place-name elements lie in land which was cleared
of woodland before the *leah* or late phase of Mercian expansion,
and it is a fair assumption that, on account of their coincidence in
area with the Celtic place-names, Mercians were content in the

early stages to take over land already occupied, infiltrating peacefully among the pre-existing British settlements.

In Cheshire, the route from Tushingham into the Dee valley is marked by two *ingatuns*, Duckington and Coddington (Fig. 9). Further north in west Cheshire, two *hams*, Frodsham and Dunham on the Hill, mark out the area west of the Gowy valley as one of relatively early Anglian penetration, and a string of *tuns* links them all with Tushingham. The absence of *ham* and *ingatun* suffixes from Wirral suggests that expansion into this presumed Celtic stronghold was somewhat later than that into the Dee and Gowy valleys. The Weaver and some of its tributary valleys were highly favoured by early Mercian settlers and the only remaining *hams* and *ingatuns* in Cheshire are to be found there. Swettenham lies immediately south of Kermincham in the Dane valley but there seems to have been little attempt to colonise it further and apart from a few scattered *tuns* there is no evidence of this phase of Anglian settlement in the whole of east Cheshire which, to this day, is singularly devoid of villages other than the *burhs* (Astbury, Prestbury, etc.), and these, as has already been suggested, were at least equally likely to have been taken over from the British. The picture in the Weaver basin is quite different. Warmingham lies on the banks of the Wheelock Brook, and to the south-west, some four miles from Celtic-named Wheelock, lies Shavington between Wheelock Brook and the Weaver. Doddington and Baddington are some five miles away to the south-west and south, the latter actually in the Weaver valley. All these last three *ingatuns* occupy a pocket of lowland which, in approximately the late eighth century witnessed the growth of some nine *tuns*. Two lesser pockets of early settlement succeeded this downstream, and by the lower Weaver below Davenham, there was located one of the major 'second-early' settlement areas of Mercian Cheshire. It includes three *hams*, one of which – Weaverham – was to become an important manor in Norman Cheshire, and four *ingatuns* all within a distance of ten miles. In all these woodland pockets, most of them centred on a valley and all within fertile lowland clearings, there were earlier Celtic settlements. Hardly any of the *tuns* and none of the earlier names occurred far from Celtic centres, and it is doubtful whether the Mercians began to clear the woodlands during this early phase.

D

In Shropshire and Herefordshire, too, early Mercian place-names are associated with the pattern of cleared valleys where *tuns* surrounded *hams* and *ingatuns*, and where there was evidence of still earlier Celtic occupation. But wider cleared lands on the scale of those in west Cheshire are repeated nowhere else in the Borderland in the seventh and eighth centuries. In Shropshire, the pattern of valleys is related to the two master-streams of the Severn and the Teme. Apart from the Worfe and the streams draining the eastern slopes of the Clee Hills, all the major tributaries of the middle Severn join it in or near the Shrewsbury Plain. But even the Worfe permits access to the middle Severn lowlands via or north of the Gorge. Beyond the South Shropshire Hills, apart from the Clee drainage, all rivers similarly converge on the Teme in or near the Ludlow basin, and there is a comparable pattern of valley pockets within woodland, and again, in case after case, an initial Celtic-named settlement can be found. It is, however, noticeable that no *ingahams* occur except in the Shrewsbury Plain and that, to the north of it, there are no *hams* in Shropshire and only two *ingatuns* (Wellington and Cherrington). In the valleys which join the middle Severn from the south, the only early Mercian name is Cardington, but there is a *ham* (Aldenham) north of the Clees in the drainage basin of Mor Brook. The early Mercian phase is represented in the valleys which open to the Teme by only two *hams*, Lydham near the Montgomeryshire border and Caynham three miles east-south-east of Ludlow. The *tun* names are widespread in the cleared areas.

The only early names of the Mercian settlement in Hereford-shire are the two *ingahams* already referred to, two *hams* and three *ingatuns*. These last are Kinsham in the Lugg valley near the Radnorshire border, Bodenham midway between Leominster and Hereford (also in the Lugg valley), Withington four miles north-east of Hereford, and Coddington and Wellington in the Leadon basin near the Worcestershire border. The scatter of *tuns* is very significantly thinner than in either Shropshire or Cheshire; the distribution of Celtic and possibly Celtic names much heavier.

Mercian Expansion in the Borderland

The valleyward movement of the British was followed up by Mercian expansion into the areas already cleared by the British, and it took place during a period when power swayed backward and forward between Mercia and Northumbria. But by 731 Æthelbald of Mercia was the acknowledged overlord not only of his Mercian domains, but of all England south of the Humber. His successors, the two Offas, consolidating Mercian power, made possible first, the extension of Mercian settlement for a limited distance into the Welsh hills; and, secondly, the advance of Mercian settlers into hitherto untamed woodlands most of which lay on the interfluves between the main valleys already settled in the early phase.

The great dyke built by Offa I and Offa II between 757 and 796 was constructed from near Prestatyn in Flintshire to a point opposite Chepstow at the mouth of the Wye, and its significance, which can never to any real degree have been military, was that it defined the then accepted bounds of Mercian conquest, representing in some stretches an actual regression from the limit of the full tide of Anglian advance. Its course, broken for very considerable stretches, has been largely reconstructed by Sir Cyril Fox,[1] over a total length of 140 miles, a low earthen rampart supplemented by rivers and stretches of difficult hill terrain, and he considers its main function to have been that of a boundary.

With its steep side always facing Wales, its course begins high on the Flintshire plateau, well to the west of the 1284 boundary of Flintshire. Continuing across eastern Denbighshire, it drops to the hill edge behind Wrexham, continuing south to Ruabon and Llanymynech, whence it traverses the Long Mountain to Forden. In this northern stretch, a large group of Old English place-names lie to the east of the Dyke but within present-day Wales, most of

---

[1] (1955). Fox discards the view that Wat's Dyke was built either during the latter part of the seventh or the early part of the eighth century to mark the western boundary of Mercia at that time. He considers its workmanship comparable to that of Offa's Dyke, and therefore dates it as either 700–50 or 800–50.

Jackson believes that the Dyke merely established 'a situation which had existed along the whole Welsh border for over a hundred years'. (Op. cit. p. 211.)

them occurring in the valley of the lowland Dee or along its estuarine shores. Some, like Prestatyn (D.B., Prestetone, thirteenth century Prestaulton), have now been gallicised but most retain their English names as in the cases of Whitford, Northop, Coleshill, Overton, Bettisfield, Bronington and a large group in Denbighshire from Gresford to Eyton where occur such common English names as Sutton, Ridley, Burton, Broughton, Acton, Dutton and Moreton. All those mentioned in Flintshire have a name-pedigree which goes back to Domesday Book. Of the south-east Denbighshire group only Allington, Erbistock, Eyton, Gresford,[1] and Sutton were recorded in 1086. The number incorporating the *tun* element is remarkable. B. G. Charles argues that these stem from genuine Mercian plantation.[2] Their range of suffixes suggests that, like those in the English areas to the east, they may be the result of phased colonisations going back to the early eighth century, if not before, in the case of the *tuns*. They constitute the first of four such groups of non-Celtic names lying near the Anglo-Welsh boundary. The second group lies in Montgomeryshire, about one-third of the English names to the east and two-thirds to the west of the Dyke, but all in wide vales which open into Shropshire, or on nearby slopes of the Long Mountain. These include Forden, Buttington, Church Stoke, Leighton and Edderton. B. G. Charles thinks that perhaps the bulk of them date from a post-Offan settlement and that those west of the Dyke belong to a later period of Mercian ascendancy.[3] but one wonders whether it is, in fact, possible to date them separately from their Shropshire neighbours, and whether they were not part of the westward expansion which Kenneth Jackson believes reached the hill edge by the mid-seventh century[4] and from which initial settlement the rest steadily proliferated.

From the Long Mountain, Offa's Dyke cuts south across the more westerly part of Clun Forest to Knighton in the Teme valley, and hence a little to the west of Presteigne. From Radnorshire it passes, in broken stretches, across the plain of Herefordshire and, keeping to the English bank of the Wye, follows that river to its mouth. In Clun Forest, the Dyke crosses a district of largely

---

[1] Gresford is probably an anglicised form of Croesffordd.
[2] *Non-Celtic Place-Names in Wales* (1938), pp. xxii–xxiv.
[3] Ibid. p. xxvi.   [4] Op. cit., map on pp. 208–9.

Welsh names, with a scatter of English, but south of Clun a third group of English names lies to the west of the present boundary of Wales from Knighton to Glasbury. This is moderately elevated land on the lower flanks of Radnor Forest, and although the English names occur in valleys, they are comparatively narrow ones, and the settlements lie characteristically at heights of 400–700 feet above sea level.

The fourth and most southerly group of English names near the border is found west of the Dyke, in southern Monmouth-shire. But the history of Anglo-Saxon penetration across the Wye is obscure, for though for a time at least Gwent was subject to the English kings, nothing is known historically of this early settle-ment. Nash, Goldcliff, Itton and Ifton are among the few which may be pre-medieval. They may represent a genuinely earlier settlement, perhaps from the Hwiccan territory across the Severn which was detached from the West Saxons in 628.

The second Mercian expansion in the Borderland was made from the early valley settlements to the interfluves, and from the open country into the unbroken woodlands which covered vast stretches of land in eastern Shropshire and Herefordshire, in central Monmouthshire, and in central and eastern Cheshire. Compared with the great forests of the counties to the east, those of the Borderland were of only moderate size, but they played a significant role in the history of border settlement providing an outlet for the surplus population of older settlements from the Dark Ages until well after the end of the Middle Ages. On the fringes of *Y Coed*, the great woodland of the Midland Triangle, forests such as Wyre, Shirlott, Morfe, the Long Forest, Mara and Mon-drem, and Macclesfield Forest offered sites for new hamlets and new farmlands from the period of the *leahs* of the later Anglian colonisation to the emparkments by manorial lords from the Conquest to the eighteenth century. New parishes were carved out from Delamere as late as 1812.[1]

The most frequently recurring place-name element in the Borderland dating from the late Anglian colonisation of the wood-lands is *leah*, generally represented in the modern place-name in the form of the suffix *-ley*. *Hurst* is rare, *worthen* or its variants

[1] These were Oakmere and Delamere, created at that date by the Act of Enclosure of Delamere Forest.

such as *wardine* are comparatively numerous in Shropshire and north-west Herefordshire. The later topographical form *wood* is comparatively common but may also be medieval or later. By plotting the elements which indicate late Anglian woodland settlements, the areas of secondary expansion have been traced in the three English counties (Figs, 9, 10 and 11). When these woods had been cut down, residual, but still large virgin woodlands were left in some parts at the time of the Domesday Survey. In Cheshire the stipple (Fig. 9) shows that late Anglian settlement continued on an appreciable scale between the Weaver and the medieval bounds of Macclesfield Forest, on the south-eastern flanks of the county, and in parts of the south-west between the upper Weaver and the Dee above Chester. But there is no such belt around Delamere, nor were large parts of the sub-Pennine belt touched, which suggests that both these medieval forests may have been preserved for centuries before the Normans as hunting-grounds for the Mercian earls.

In Shropshire, the phase of woodland clearing in the late Anglian period seems to have been more thorough than in Cheshire. By Domesday, the northern plain was carrying few woods except for occasional patches in the Cheswardine area and near Whitchurch. On the northern hills of the south Shropshire hill country the Long Forest included some stretches of woodland in 1086, but the only great woodlands surviving were those of the southeast – Brewood, Shirlott, Morfe and Wyre. It is evident that, except in these last, settlement was very active in the *leah* phase in Shropshire as the frequency of this and other place-name elements with a comparable topographical connotation indicates.

In Herefordshire, on the other hand, there was nothing comparable to the colonising fervour displayed in Cheshire and Shropshire in this phase. The stippled areas of the Welsh Districts (Fig. 11) can be excluded from Anglian settlement activity, and in the rest of the county the extensive eleventh-century woodlands in most cases either abutted direct on to the earlier cleared lowlands or were separated from them only by a narrow fringe of this later Mercian occupation. The elements *leah* and *wood* are correspondingly rare.

The Scandinavians in the Borderland

The Scandinavian invaders played a comparatively minor role in the history of border settlement except in Cheshire. Lamby in Monmouthshire is the only place-name which bears witness to Norse incursions on the shores of that county. Axton in Flintshire is of Norse origin, and Wigdale (Hawarden), Hopedale and Moldsdale, also in that county, include the Scandinavian element *dale*.

But in Cheshire, north Wirral experienced a comparatively dense Irish-Norse settlement, similar to that on the adjoining coastlands of south Lancashire, and east Cheshire had a relatively thin extension of the Danish occupation of south-east Lancashire. The Norse, who came to Wirral on being expelled from Dublin, are known to have received a grant of land from Æthelflaed, the lady of the Mercians, in 902[1], and no doubt there were others during the first fifteen years of the tenth century. Today a group of Norse place-names including Greasby, Irby, Frankby, Meols, Arrowe, Thingwall, West Kirby, Caldy, Ness and Thurstaston, is mingled with earlier Celtic and Anglian names. F. T. Wainwright thought the Danes might have wintered in Chester in 893–4, and then settled in a few places in the east of Cheshire where there is a group of *hulme* names; Church Hulme (now Holmes Chapel), Cheadle Hulme, Hulme Walfield, Kettleshulme and Hulme Hall. Wainwright added Toft and Knutsford to the list of Danish names there together with what he considers to be Scandinavianised names – Croxton and Rostherne, and possibly Swanscoe and Handforth as well as the minor names Chadkirk, Kirkleyditch, Bowstonegate and Drakecar. Yet, as he pointed out, there is a total absence of -*by* names such as are commonly indicative of close Danish settlement.[2] Wainwright maintained that the Norse settlement of Wirral was, by contrast, dense and that the invaders included Danes and native Irish as well as Norse, though these last predominated. Danes continued to raid north Welsh coasts, possibly from Wirral bases, and these raids may have given rise to the *dale*

[1] W. G. Collingwood, *Scandinavian Britain* (1908), p. 191.
[2] 'North-west Mercia', *Trans. Hist. Soc. Lancs. and Ches.* (1942), pp. 3–56.

element in Flintshire names. Wirral field-names also bear ample witness to the Scandinavian settlement.

In the rest of the Borderland the Scandinavians exercised only an indirect influence by raids and threats of raids. Æthelflaed mounted a formidable campaign against the Danish threat to advance westwards, and built ten fortresses in the years following 910 or 911. These included Runcorn, Eddisbury (a refortification of the Early Iron Age camp), Chirbury,[1] and Bridgnorth in the border counties. This period of defensive building may have given rise to the naming of more *burhs*, but this place-name element is applied to so many different and differently dated fortifications that identification of tenth-century places so named is all but impossible. The proportion of Scandinavians in the population of Cheshire is unlikely to have been impressive, yet their influence was far from negligible. In 1086, the Cheshire portion of the Domesday Book included forty-one Scandinavian as compared with forty-five Anglo-Saxon personal names[2] and Scandinavian moneyers were important in the city of Chester.

The Anglo-Celtic Distribution Pattern

Although the process of Anglo-Celtic movement and adjustment was to continue long after the Dark Ages, the basic features of their territorial relationships were largely limned out before the Norman Conquest. This is most surely indicated by place-name evidence, but the theme runs through many other aspects of the historical geography of the Borderland: language, customs and the physical characteristics of the population among them.

For many centuries after the coming of the Anglo-Saxons, the country east of Offa remained as closely linked to Wales as to England in many respects. The establishment of the marcher lordships which persisted as political entities until 1536, part neither of England nor of Wales, further helped to blur a division

---

[1] F. T. Wainwright excavated the castle at Chirbury and in a preliminary report in the *Shropshire Newsletter*, no. 10 (Feb. 1960) wrote: 'it is possible to conclude that the so-called "castle" at Chirbury is in all probability the fortress built by Æthelflaed *aet Cyricbyrig* in 915.'

[2] Wainwright, loc. cit. (1942), pp. 31–5.

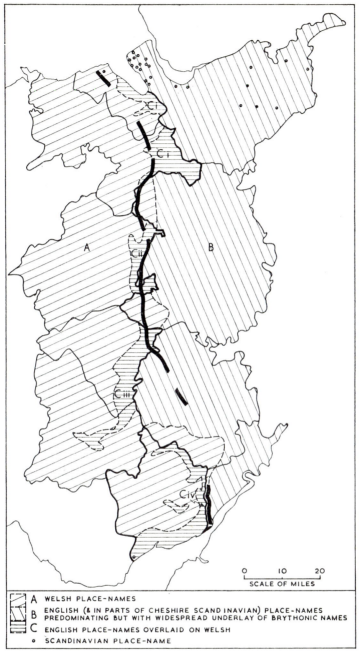

A WELSH PLACE-NAMES
B ENGLISH (& IN PARTS OF CHESHIRE SCANDINAVIAN) PLACE-NAMES
   PREDOMINATING BUT WITH WIDESPREAD UNDERLAY OF BRYTHONIC NAMES
C ENGLISH PLACE-NAMES OVERLAID ON WELSH
○ SCANDINAVIAN PLACE-NAME

SCALE OF MILES
0   10   20

12. The Welsh Borderland: place-name regions

S.R.L.W.B.

which was so long unreal. The decline of Welsh as a spoken language in the Marches was slow and by no means related either to Offa's Dyke or to the Anglo-Welsh political boundary. Modern Welsh, derived from the Brythonic of the Ordovices, gradually replaced Brythonic speech not only in South Wales but also in Ewyas and Archenfield. The Welsh hill districts of Shropshire were conquered and occupied by the Mercians and are believed by B. G. Charles to have experienced a re-invasion dating from before Domesday which brought Welsh speech, Welsh place-names and many Welsh customs which spread into the adjoining low-lands as opportunity permitted. In Herefordshire, the Welsh districts occupy the greater part of the country south of the fertile Wye lowlands, extending to within ten miles of the south-east corner of the county, and its Welsh place-names are older than those of north-west Shropshire.[1] Hereford itself has been claimed as Welsh by the Welsh, even to the present day. The Welsh language is now in retreat across the borders of South and mid-Wales, notably in Radnorshire which is almost entirely English speaking, but in the Oswestry area it is still the common speech of the country people, and one hears Welsh spoken almost as often as English. This was true in Shrewsbury for many centuries and in the early eighteenth century Edward Lhwyd referred to 'Shropshire Welsh' as a language.

On the basis of place-names of Celtic and English origin (Fig. 12), three belts may be distinguished in border counties: (*a*) the eastern Welsh area with an almost unbroken cover of Welsh place-names; (*b*) the greater part of the English border counties where English names predominate but overlie an impor-tant foundation of Brythonic names; and (*c*) a discontinuous narrow border zone where English place-names are mingled with modern Welsh. These two maps are not only of etymological but of ethnic and cultural significance, and offer one of the more important keys to the interpretation of rural settlement in this border zone.

Racially, Mediterranean and predominantly Nordic and Nordic-Alpine types represent broadly the pre-English and English populations. The short, dark inhabitants who are in the

---

[1] B. G. Charles, 'The Welsh, their language and place-names in Archenfield and Oswestry' in *Angles and Britons* (O'Donnell Lectures) (1963), p. 110.

majority in many parts of Wales are also to be found widely in Cheshire, Shropshire and Herefordshire, but the populations of the last three counties are notably more hybrid than those of the Welsh counties. Recently, I. Morgan Watkin made investigations into the ABO blood group frequencies of western Shropshire. He found that the O gene frequency is much lower in western Shropshire than in the Vale of Welshpool, but higher than in the industrial Midlands, and that the west Shropshire folk with Welsh surnames are lower in O and B than a similar group in east Montgomeryshire, lower in B than south Denbighshire folk, and higher in both O and B than the people of east Radnorshire. He submits that the blood group frequencies of the Welsh element in west Shropshire may, therefore, represent a mixture of people drawn in varying degrees from neighbouring parts of Wales.[1]

Important additions and modifications had still to be made to the population, settlements and culture of the Borderland, but there is no doubt that by the end of the Dark Ages the three major zones had already taken shape and were to be of abiding significance.

[1] 'English and Welsh Racial Elements in Western Shropshire and the adjacent Welsh Borderland: ABO Blood Group Evidence', *Jl R. Anthrop. Inst.*, 94 (1963), pp. 60–5.

5 The Marcher Period

THE occupation of the Borderland by the Normans[1] was swift
and thorough. A mixed group, in fact, of Normans, Bretons and
Flemings, they were in control of its entire length by 1071. Well
before the end of the twelfth century they had pressed their alien
settlements on to the hill flanks of eastern Wales, and organised
in depth the strategic zone of the Marches. Their comparatively
modest numbers bore no relationship to their strength and
effectiveness as conquerors and rulers, nor were the new settlements they founded great in number. But the mark they left in the
form of defensive works, abbeys, churches, manor houses, and
vigorously growing towns was sufficiently impressive to count
as among the most visually effective contributions ever made to
Borderland settlement. It was they who initiated the unbroken
centuries of town growth which have largely led to the present
urban pattern, and who developed English medieval town life
with its major functions of civil and ecclesiastical administration,
defence and trade and industry. It was they who built a wide
spatter of manor houses, large and small, and who introduced the
motte and bailey, the stone castle, and numerous other military
features into the settlement picture on so large a scale, and in no
part of England was the massing of medieval defensive works
comparable with that in the Welsh Borderland. Not least, it was
they who, by creating a marcher belt in depth, made the Borderland a triple instead of a dual cultural and settlement zone – a
Welsh west, a marcher middle and an Anglo-Norman-Celtic
eastern zone.

[1] Known at the Conquest as Normans, by the twelfth century they were self-styled
Anglo-Normans, but John was the first of the royal house to call himself *Rex Angliae* –
an indication of the growing mergence of Norman and English.

The Welsh and the Normans

Prior to their coming, the Welsh kingdoms and principalities had been emerging with some vigour from the lesser tribal divisions of the early phase. Gwynedd was centred on Snowdonia and Môn, and from time to time extended south and east. Powys, of which the long boundary was coincident with the Mercian frontier, stretched across mid-Wales to an apex on the Dyfi estuary, sometimes including the present Denbighshire and Radnorshire, long embracing Flintshire, but always with its heartland in Montgomeryshire. Deheubarth, the large south-western kingdom extended across modern Pembrokeshire, Cardiganshire and Carmarthenshire, sometimes taking in Brycheiniog and more rarely Radnorshire, but with a fatal tendency to break up into component regions – Dyfed, Ceridigion, Ystrad Towy and Brycheiniog. In the south-east, Glwysing or Morganwg and Gwent were sometimes under the rule of Deheubarth, sometimes separate. All were in some way and at some time involved in border history – Powys and Gwent as part of it, Deheubarth and Glwysing in their involvement with Gwent and Brycheiniog, and Gwynedd in its expansionist phases, and in its close relationship with Powys and Cheshire.

Isolated for centuries behind the Mercian border, Wales seemed built as a retreat, and when the Welsh were beaten or when they were harried by the English they could take flight into the mountains of Gwynedd or across the narrow waters of the Menai Straits into Anglesey. From time to time, however, a great leader would arise, and under his banner the Welsh would break out in a wave of national fervour which carried them not only towards the goal of national unity, but across the edge of the Welsh hills into the English plains. Unity was nearly achieved in the ninth century under Rhodri Mawr, in the tenth century under Hywel Dda, and in the eleventh century under Gruffydd ap Llewelyn. When Gruffydd ascended the throne of Gwynedd, the Normans were already softening up parts of England for conquest, notably Herefordshire. Already practically master of Wales, Gruffydd turned against the Normans, capturing Hereford castle in 1055, and in alliance with Mercia, burning and looting the city and the newly built cathedral. As a result of Gruffydd's campaigns in the Borderland, the country was ravaged, and the English settlements which Mercia had established beyond Offa's Dyke were abandoned to the Welsh. It is said that the country was made desolate from Rhuddlan to Gwent. Once the hills were left behind, movement into the plains was as easy as the rise of flood water – but only so long as the defences were weak and the Welsh armies remained strong and united.

In the reverse direction, the position strategically was very different. The hills opposed the would-be conqueror in a solid wall. Only a few wide vales and a number of narrower valleys, difficult to negotiate and offering no through route, lead into the Cambrian plateau. Moreover, the Welsh tactics of scattering in the face of enemy advance, meant the virtual melting away of a foe which to the pursuing Normans became incapable of pursuit. The only means of conquering Wales and the Welsh was by slow advance up the major valleys which break up the eastern hill edge and by the coastal routes which outflank the hills. Only thus could a hold be established militarily on the upland core itself. The fact that the final union of the two countries took almost five centuries, despite the wealth and might of the Anglo-Normans, bears witness to the intractability of the Welsh hill country and its defenders. Despite the military advantage of downhill movement, the Welsh flood rarely descended far into the English plain after the campaigns of Gruffydd ap Llewelyn, except under Owain Glyndwr immediately after 1400, yet despite the disadvantages of a strategy designed for advance into difficult hill country by a limited number of lowland routes, the Normans were able to cling by sheer weight of arms and men and wealth to the Border and, slowly and with immense odds against them, to build up the great belt of marcher lordships which defended that Border in depth and from which were launched expeditions against the Welsh with a view to their eventual subjugation. The vales of Usk, of Wye, of Vyrnwy, Severn and Dee formed the geographical spearheads of the Norman occupation of eastern Wales, and in these, and along the coasts and in the vale of Clwyd, are the major evidences of Norman occupation and settlement in eastern Wales. The entire length of eastern Wales was eventually included in the marcher belt, and Normanisation of the eastern slopes and the wider, more fertile vales which opened into the English lowlands left its mark in settlement features. But in most lordships there was a Welshry in which tribal life went on as by custom, and west of the marcher zone the pattern of Welsh life and economy continued along its ancient, traditional lines.

The Marcher Belt

The Normans established what today would be termed a fifth column in parts of England years before the final conquest of 1066. Herefordshire was one of these areas, and J. E. Lloyd maintained that they were there from 1052.[1] Richards Castle on the border of Herefordshire and Shropshire was one of only two pre-Conquest castles in England, and from the first the Normans showed a peculiar predilection for this rich and pleasant lowland with its gentle hills breaking into the smooth levels of the plain. They had established themselves at Chepstow (then Strigoil) by 1067, and they built the castle on the Welsh bank to secure the crossing. Other early Norman castles in the Borderland were those at Wigmore, Clifford, Ewyas Harold, Monmouth, Rhuddlan (where, contrary to general rule, the castle succeeded a Mercian stronghold on the near bank), Deganwy and Caus. Very little later were built Montgomery, Bridgnorth and Bronllys.

Three palatinate earldoms were created along the Border. The first of the three was Hereford, set up in 1066, but it was also the shortest lived, lapsing with the death of the second earl in 1075. Shropshire and Cheshire proved less tractable, and Chester was the goal of the Conqueror's advance across Cheshire following on his midwinter march over the Pennines in 1070–1. On its subjugation in 1071, the palatine earldom of Chester was created. Shrewsbury was threatening rebellion at the time but, on the town's prior surrender, William's march tailed off before much wasting was done in Shropshire, and in the same year the earldom of Shrewsbury was formed. This too survived as a palatinate for

[1] *A History of Wales*, ii, 2nd ed. (1912), p. 363.

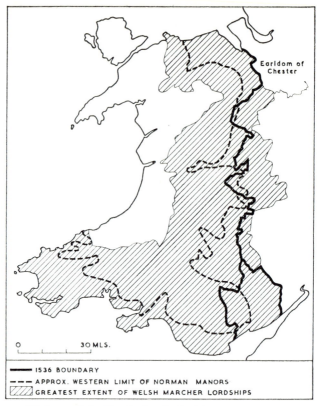

1536 BOUNDARY
APPROX. WESTERN LIMIT OF NORMAN MANORS
GREATEST EXTENT OF WELSH MARCHER LORDSHIPS

13. Wales and the Borderland: the Norman occupation

only two tenures, lapsing in 1102. The palatine earldom of Chester, however, survived throughout the marcher period, becoming part of the English realm only in 1536. Until 1284, Cheshire included what then became Flintshire and parts of what later was to be made into Denbighshire, and marcher lordships on the northern border were for this reason to be found only to the west of the River Dee. Further south, when the palatinates of Shropshire and Herefordshire lapsed, marcher lordships were set up for some distance on the English side of what is now the boundary of the Principality, and across the Dyke the giant pendulum of war swung back and to throughout the Middle Ages, but mainly prior to the Welsh Revolt of 1294–5.

The earliest lordships in the Marches were centred on a line of

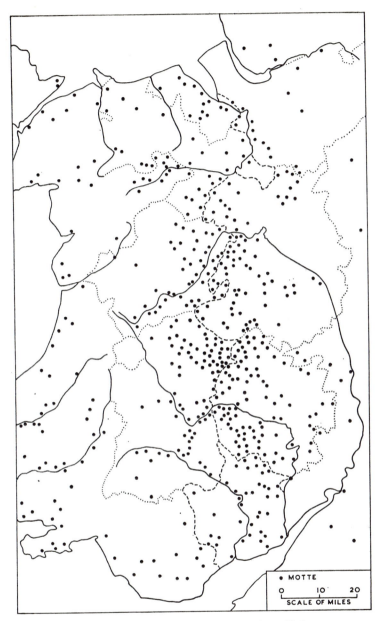

14. Wales and the Borderland: the distribution of Mottes

castles which were designed to secure the southern border –
Wigmore, Clifford, Ewyas Harold, Monmouth and Chepstow.
Chartered boroughs were created at Wigmore and Clifford.
Rather later, the northern border was fortified at points such as
Chester, Rhuddlan, Hawarden, Whittington and Oswestry. The
last years of the eleventh century saw the height of the early
Norman struggle to subjugate Wales, and very slowly the lordships were extended as the Norman grasp became firmer, and
eventually the great marcher zone extended deep across the
border and swung west across South Wales (Fig. 13). Within the
lordships, the marcher lords exercised feudal power in military,
judicial, economic and social spheres, their power absolute except
in that they owed fealty to the King and could not go to war
against him nor make treaties with foreign powers. In that age
of personal power, the old, relatively democratic communities
became subjected to the feudal ideas of the Middle Ages in which
hierarchical concepts of society were basic and were applied equally
in the state, the church and the army. The lordship or the manor
dominated rural structure, socially, economically and tenurially,
established its own new settlement features in many cases and
modified the old forms in others. Since these ideas were nowhere
applied more rigidly than in the Welsh Borderland, it added a
further ethnic and cultural element to the already hybrid Anglo-
Welsh border zone of the Dark Ages, and, furthermore, converted a relatively narrow belt of Mercian-Welsh contact into a
zone forty to fifty miles deep in which Anglo-Norman elements
became mingled in varying combinations with Welsh to the west,
Mercian and Welsh in the centre, and Mercian (or, more broadly,
Anglo-Saxon) in the eastern lowlands.   Three and a half centuries
of this Marcher régime left an indelible stamp on the settlement
geography of the Borderland.

Among the earliest defences were some of the mottes which D. F.
Renn thinks continued to be built over several centuries. His
map showing mottes for the whole of England and Wales[1] demonstrates, as perhaps nothing else could, the relative importance of
the Welsh Borderland militarily during the Middle Ages. On
natural or artificial mounds or mottes were usually erected, at
first, simple timber towers and palisades, and around the motte

[1] In 'Mottes: a Classification', *Antiquity* (1959), pp. 106–12.

or at one side of it was a fenced enclosure forming the ward or
bailey, the whole typically enclosed by a defending ditch. The
pattern varied in detail. On some of the more important mottes
the early defences were replaced later by stone shell keeps. Some
of the less important were abandoned; still others were supplemented by a newer and more elaborate stone castle. Most are
still recognisable on the ground, and in the Borderland they total
several hundred to be found over the main defensive belt of the
Marches in a wide zone varying from ten to forty miles in depth.
From Flintshire and the westernmost parts of Cheshire, they
extend through east Denbighshire and Montgomeryshire, western
Shropshire, most of Herefordshire and Radnorshire into Monmouthshire and mid-Brecon, but with many scattered outliers on
either side of the main belt. They are thickest on the ground from
the Vale of Welshpool and adjoining parts of south-west Shropshire to south-west Herefordshire and nearby parts of northern
Monmouthshire (Fig. 14).[1] The stone castles which date mainly
from the Norman and Edwardian phases are more thinly distributed over a similar area. The mottes and baileys had little
permanent influence on the settlement landscape, and the link
between the stone castles and later settlement was as varied as it
could be. Some castles became the central growth point of
boroughs which have survived and flourished until today, as in
the case of Shrewsbury, Hereford, Ludlow (Plates XIX and XX),
Monmouth and many more small border towns; others are
situated in and near what are now mere villages or hamlets, as
at Whittington, Chirk, Acton Burnell, Richards Castle and St
Briavels; while the once proud fortresses of Dinas Bran, Wattlesborough, Caus and Bwlch y Dinas now stand deserted and alone.
Nevertheless, the influence of the defensive aspect of the Marches
in the Middle Ages on rural settlement was considerable, especially
south of the Middle Severn, for until the Act of Union the
Marches remained a vast armed camp, ready at all times for
defensive or aggressive campaigns.

Many of the border castles were early Norman, but a second
phase of castle building associated with the Edwardian campaigns of 1272–84 caused some to be rebuilt or extended and new
ones to be erected in Flint, Conway, further west in North Wales,

[1] Based on a map of border mottes specially prepared by D. F. Renn.

and in many places in the Borderland. The Treaty of Rhuddlan created Flintshire as well as the counties of west Wales from Anglesey to Carmarthen, but left all the rest of eastern Wales in the Marches. Four new lordships were made in Perfeddwlad by this same treaty – Denbigh, Ruthin (or Dyffryn Clwyd), Bromfield and Yale, and Chirk – which in 1536 were to be combined to form Denbighshire. Marcher rule continued in the lordships, while southern Powys remained under Welsh rule but was subject to the English Crown.

The boundaries and even the names of the marcher lordships changed frequently during the three and a half centuries of their existence. Their maximum extent as a marcher zone is shown in Figure 13, and may with advantage be compared with William Rees's map of the 'manors' in his *Historical Atlas of Wales*.[1] The total number of separate lordships which had been created over these centuries has been variously estimated. Rees thinks the usual estimate of 143 too great,[2] and in any case, the total must have fluctuated from one century to another by division, absorption, conquest and marriage. Together, they constituted the greatest defensive system and achieved the greatest length and depth of any that Britain has known at any time in her history. In the early centuries they were dominated by the great Marcher families who have left their names on the place-name map – the Mortimers, the Says, the Bohuns, the Corbets, the Lacys, the Clares, the Bigods, the FitzAlans and many others. In the Act of Union, 136 lordships were mentioned and of these forty-one were Crown lordships; in addition, eleven not mentioned were Duchy of Lancaster lordships.[3] Many of the old Marcher families had by then sunk into insignificance or been replaced.

The lordships were divided into Englishries and Welshries. In the Englishry, the typical set-up was centred on the castle where the lord resided together with such of his retainers as were not housed in an adjoining bailey, and around it was usually a town where dwelt the burgesses (English in the early centuries) and which usually included one or more churches, sometimes an abbey. Most of them were chartered towns, privileged to hold a

[1] 1st ed. (1951), plate 47.
[2] *The Union of England and Wales* (1948), p. 33.
[3] It is thought that some were mentioned twice under different names, hence Rees's assumption that the total was probably less than 143.

market and fairs and generally conduct trade for the profit in the first instance of the castle or the church. Here too were held various courts, but their urban character was modified in that they also had open fields in which the lord, the church and the burgesses held shares. Similarly, they had rights in the open pastures beyond the town fields. Walls and dykes were used as boundaries for town and fields, and the limits of both were clearly set. This picture was repeated scores of times in the Borderland, though comparatively few of the medieval castle-towns have survived as such, and many have shrunk to the status of minor country towns or to villages. Among the lesser marcher towns of the period which have remained viable are Flint, Mold, Ruthin, Denbigh, Oswestry, Welshpool, Ludlow, Brecon, Abergavenny, Monmouth and Newport. Others like Ellesmere, Hawarden, Montgomery, Bishop's Castle, Clun, Hay, Talgarth and Raglan (Plate XVI), are now only small market or ex-market villages, but the influence of Anglo-Norman occupation on their form and character is clearly stamped to this day. The Normans built not only the military town, but the militarised village, compact and strongly sited, right across the Borderland.[1]

Outside the Englishries Anglo-Norman control was in the main limited to a vague overlordship which included the demand of tribute but otherwise left a tribal society very much as it had been except for the necessary forfeiture of lands to create an Englishry. In the Welshries, tribal society was slowly changing, but many of the old customs long remained, with the blood bond as the basis of society, and with the deeply rooted Celtic concept of land, economy and tribe still surviving, despite the deep geographical inroads of the Norman conquerors. There, dispersed *tyddynod* replaced the English village, and town and castle were alike absent. Pastoralism was the dominant economy. Common fields, if they existed at all, were small, and more often there were scattered ploughing strips or crofts enclosing a few *erwau*, since the principle of co-aration was more important than the sharing of a field in country where land suitable for the plough was limited, and where in the lordships the best land in any case had been included in the Englishry. Under the Welsh system, whether in

[1] The structure of the marcher lordships is described at length in Professor William Rees's book *South Wales and the March 1284–1415* (1924).

the Welshries or in free Wales, tribal principles of tenure prevailed – a tribe made up of family groups. In North Wales
especially, the *gwely* owned the patrimony or collective property
which consisted of land, stock and rights in woodland and pasture. On the death of the family head, the sons divided the
patrimony equally, their sons in turn inheriting equally at their
death and each in turn taking his share (the *gafael* in North Wales),
with the resultant morcellation of holdings, but with common
rights and practices little affected, and the common woodlands
and pasture remaining undivided. Little by little, English influence
seeped in, but common ownership and tribal customs in general
remained through much of the Middle Ages.

As parts of the Marches proper had already been subjected to
Mercian settlement, the Norman plantation succeeded in making
this the most hybrid settlement zone not only of the Borderland
but of the whole of south Britain. The Welsh hills, the Norman
valleys and the Norman-Mercian-Celtic lowlands still form the
basic pattern of settlement in this zone.

East of the Marches

East of the Marches, the Norman-Mercian-Celtic pattern was
continued but with the important difference that, apart from
Cheshire, it was part of the English realm and was not concerned primarily with the conquest of Wales. In this latter sense
it was comparable with the rest of England, but the Celtic
basis of settlement was far stronger than in the counties to the
east.

The unique value of the Domesday Book makes possible the
virtual reconstruction of the map of England of 1086 and, for some
features, of 1066. It was designed to cover the Conqueror's
realm as it was in 1086, hence Radnorshire, Breconshire and
Montgomeryshire were largely omitted except for a few border
manors. For Monmouthshire there is but the slightest mention
of a small number of places. In the northern Border, however,
Flintshire and much of Denbighshire were surveyed at some
length as they were part of Cheshire.

The extent of woodland (Figs 9, 10 and 11) can be reconstructed with remarkable accuracy. Widespread new settlement in the *leah* phase of Anglian expansion in Cheshire had reduced the Cheshire woodlands to the three major areas of Delamere Forest (the medieval Mara and Mondrem), a more southerly woodland between the Beeston Gap and Maelor Saesneg, and the great foothill zone of Macclesfield Forest. Apart from these, there only remained relatively isolated, small stretches in 1086. A still more wholesale clearance had taken place in Shropshire leaving the eastern fringe between Newport and Bewdley as the only area of great woodlands, with lesser patches on the northern slopes of the south Shropshire hills. In Herefordshire, however, where the *leah* settlement phase was of much lesser importance, extensive areas of both hill and plain remained wooded in 1086, especially in the west and south of the county. The Domesday woodlands fulfilled two major roles: first, they provided hunting grounds, pasture, pannage, and timber for the manorial lords; and secondly they were available for expanding settlement and cultivation. The Normans manorialised virtually all the territory they conquered in England and some in Wales, but, as in the case of the Anglo-Saxons, their later expansion was into the virgin woodlands, and it was in these that their most characteristic settlements were often to be found.

The inclusive term 'waste' covered land of three types: land which was uncultivated such as rough pasture or unused hill land and heath; land which had fallen out of cultivation; and land which had been devastated by William's armies or, on the border, by raiding Welshmen during border skirmishes. It reached an enormous total in Domesday Cheshire largely as the result of 'wasting' by William's armies in 1070–1. It trailed off in north Shropshire presumably because the threatened march on Shrewsbury was called off, but was found in some parts of western Shropshire. In Herefordshire it was at a minimum, for not only was much of the county wooded, but it was the most favoured by the Normans.

In the areas free of woodland and waste lay the ploughland and meadow and the Domesday settlements themselves. In status, most of the Old English townships had become manors under a lord, and many of the lords were Normans. But by 1086 the settlements can have grown little, nor could many new ones have been initiated since 1066. Norman wasting had caused considerable depopulation in eastern Cheshire together with a temporary abandonment or reduction of the cultivated area. To a lesser extent this was true of parts of central Cheshire, and to a minor extent of a few manors in north-east Shropshire but, allowing for this, the distribution of population and settlement in 1086 was late Old English rather than Norman, with perhaps some greater allowance for Norman influence in the boroughs. In Cheshire, there were two principal areas of development at this time, the first in west Cheshire, the earliest cleared and settled on a wide scale of any part of the county; the second in the Weaver basin which maps of Domesday population, ploughland, meadow and industries reveal as having advanced appreciably from the days of the early Mercian settlement.[1] In Shropshire, the northern plain declined in value even where it was not actually 'wasted' between 1066 and 1086, so although its widespread woodland clearance implies that it carried a large population in 1066 as compared with much of the south, by 1086 this was no longer so. It was not only outstripped by the plain of Shrewsbury, but by many of the richer manors of the southern vales. An axis of prosperity was developing across the wide, fertile valley of the middle Severn which was paralleled by a similar concentration in the middle Wye valley. Shrewsbury became the centre of the one, Hereford of the other, a characteristic which was to be further highlighted by future developments, both Norman and post-Norman. Geography and history lent themselves to a rather more even scatter of settlement and population, however, in Herefordshire in 1086 than in either of the two counties further north, and except for the low densities in the hill fringe to the south – then as now Welsh districts – no great area in any part of the county at that time was without a fair sprinkling of agricultural communities.[2]

The additions made to the settlement map by the Normans and the areas favoured by them for settlement can be judged better from later evidence than that in the Domesday Book. The manor

[1] Sylvester and Nulty, op. cit. pp. 18–23 (text and maps).
[2] Dorothy Sylvester, 'Rural Settlement in Domesday Shropshire', *Sociological Review* (1933); Emrys J. Howell, *Land Utilisation Survey of Shropshire* (1941), pp. 278–82; Atkin, 'Herefordshire,' in *The Domesday Geography of Midland England*, ed. H. C. Darby (1954).

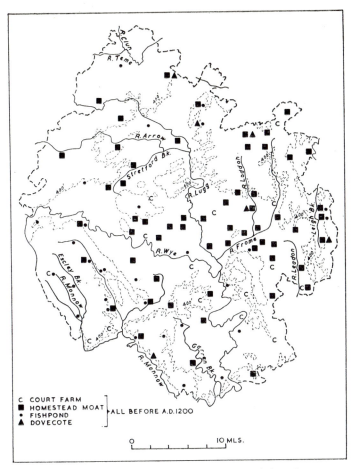

15. Herefordshire: features of Norman manorial settlement

was everywhere of superior importance to the community which it took over, and many of the great houses with their demesnes including gardens and ornamental grounds, their mills and dovecotes, their churches or private chapels, developed in time to grandiose proportions. The area and extent of Anglo-Norman settlement in the Borderland can be estimated by various features including churches of Norman foundation or with Norman work, Norman place-name elements and other early medieval affixes, courts and court farms, early homestead moats, fishponds and dovecotes.[1] In Herefordshire, they were largely complementary to the predominantly defensive mottes and border castles occurring principally in the plain of Hereford, extending across the lower Lugg valley towards the Malverns and the Bromyard plateau and thence more thinly into the southern hills. In western Herefordshire where castles and mottes are numerous, the evidences of non-military settlement are correspondingly sparse.

Church and state went hand in hand in Norman England and churches and religious houses were established very soon after the first planting of castles and mottes in any area the Normans occupied. The English Church was reorganised to bring it into line with the Church in Western Europe and, as the conquest spread westward into Wales, measures were taken which were calculated to bring it into subjection to Canterbury. Although nominally under the cloak of Rome, the Welsh Church had largely retained its national character and, in particular, had remained non-territorial in organisation. Before the middle of the twelfth century, the Church in Wales had acknowledged the authority of Canterbury and the country was divided into dioceses which in turn were subdivided into parishes. It is uncertain how far the parochialisation of England had gone prior to 1066 but to the Norman mind, territorial division into dioceses and parishes was as essential in the ecclesiastical sphere as was that into counties and manors in political and tenurial organisation. Parishes were increased in number in England and Wales until virtually all the land was parochialised, this being done in Wales west of the Marches through the Church's influence despite the fact that it remained outside the Norman political realm.

The replacement of Welsh dedications was only partial, but it was sufficiently thorough in the Marches and the country to the east to wipe out most of the evidence of the former eastward extension of the Celtic Church. Everywhere in the Norman realm churches were founded, some by religious houses and cathedrals, some by lay lords; and where there were already churches in existence, they were in many cases rebuilt or extended. As elsewhere in rural Britain, the overwhelming majority of parish churches in the Borderland counties are Norman, Early English,

[1] The last four groups are listed for Herefordshire in the *Historical Monuments Commission Survey* of Herefordshire and are mapped in Figure 15.

Decorated or Perpendicular or have replaced buildings of medieval date. Domesday returns are inadequate in this field, but the *Taxation of Pope Nicholas IV, circa* 1291 makes clear the extent to which the parish and the parish church had spread during the early Middle Ages.

Religious houses were no new feature either, but their number was enormously increased by the Normans, and today their ruins or the churches in which they have become incorporated are as impressive as the castles, though less numerous. Some, like the Benedictine houses of St Werburgh's (Chester), Shrewsbury Abbey and Monmouth, and the Augustinian Canons at Strigoil (Chepstow) pre-date 1100. The Cistercians, who were only first established in England in 1128, had houses in the Borderland soon after that date (Tintern, 1131; Combermere, 1133) and Cistercian communities continued to be founded in the twelfth and thirteenth centuries in both Wales and the Borderland. Some had comparatively little effect on the neighbouring lay settlements, but in other cases they were pioneers in extending agriculture, initiating open arable fields, and fostering the extension of hamlets through assarting. Further, their records, which in a number of cases go back to the twelfth and thirteenth centuries, are invaluable in providing concrete and detailed evidence of the establishment of cells, granges, daughter churches and of new fields and pastures.[1]

The Normanisation of place-names, though sporadic, gives some indication of the influence of the new overlords and examples are, as would be expected, particularly numerous in Herefordshire and Shropshire, less so in Cheshire, and rare beyond the boundary of the Principality. In Herefordshire, the addition of Norman surnames to pre-existing place-names is common especially in the centre and east of the county, for example, Acton Beauchamp, Brampton Bryan and Ewyas Harold. Many were used to distinguish split manors as in the cases of Edvin Loach and Edvin Ralph, Tedstone Wafre and Tedstone Delamere, and Mansell Gamage and Mansell Lacy. Other medieval affixes were added in names such as Grendon Bishop, Canon Pyon, King's Caple, Much Dewchurch and Little Birch. In Shropshire too, Normanised

---

[1] For example, *The Chartulary of the Abbey of St. Werburgh, Chester*, ed., James Tait, Chetham Soc. (1920), which includes documents going back to the twelfth century, and *The Hereford Cathedral Muniments*, calendared N.L.W., similarly dating from the twelfth century.

place-names were principally in the centre and east of the county (e.g. Child's Ercall, Stanton Lacy, Cleobury Mortimer, Hopesay, Moreton Say, Hope Bagot, Monkhopton, Middleton Priors, Much Wenlock and Little Wenlock, Market Drayton, Church Pulverbatch, etc.). Churches and religious houses of Norman foundation or re-foundation were widespread, but in Shropshire as in Herefordshire were predominantly in the central and eastern districts. In Cheshire, the great palatine earldom, castles and mottes are relatively few as the main defensive zone lay on and across the Dee to the west. The amount of Norman work in its churches is only moderate and the Normanisation of place-names less common than in the two southerly counties. Most of the surnames added to Cheshire place-names occur in the west of the county especially in the neighbourhood of Chester (e.g. Bruen Stapleford, Foulk Stapleford, Golborne Bellew, Golborne David, Cotton Edmunds). Distinguishing affixes such as Great and Little, Church, Monks, Over and Nether are more widespread. Purely Norman names in the Borderland are few but include Caus, Montgomery, two examples of Malpas, and a number of Belmonts.

The Norman settlement, apart from the all-important urban plantations, was mainly an infilling in the area to the east of the Marches. Woodlands in particular were cleared and gave rise to typically Norman park-estates and to some new scattered or hamleted communities. But the great period of rural colonisation was over, and the veneer of manorialisation was to wear very thin in areas where villages and hamlets had previously become well established, though in the more sparsely populated parts of the Borderland it was to add a spectacular element in the shape of great and lesser manor houses and their demesnes. Everywhere except in the late woodlands the stronger ground pattern of Celtic and Anglian settlement remained dominant.

The Later Middle Ages

The twelve-eighties were to prove a genuine watershed in the development of Wales and the Borderland. The Treaty of Rhuddlan brought about a general pacification of the area and, on the

16. Shropshire: markets past and present

whole, anti-English feeling had died down by the fourteenth century. A Welsh squirearchy was rising which was to become of increasing significance as the period of Union was approached, and the Borderland as a whole could at last turn to economic advancement. The early growth of the wool trade in the southern and middle Borderland was evidence of this and, together with the commutation of dues and renders in kind to money rents in the late thirteenth and early fourteenth centuries, encouraged the setting up or expansion of markets and fairs. From Shrewsbury and Bridgnorth southwards, the wool trade based on the improving breeds of Shropshire and Herefordshire (Ryelands) sheep, and associated with some of the numerous religious houses of the southern Borderland, experienced a period of expansion in the late thirteenth and early fourteenth centuries.

Of sixty-six markets in Shropshire, sixty were chartered before 1330, most of them in the reigns of Henry III and the first two Edwards, though some of these had an earlier existence. That far too many markets were set up, here as in other counties, is shewn by the fact that only nine are now extant, forty-four having become extinct by the eighteenth century. This over-proliferation was due to the anxiety on the part of every lay and ecclesiastical lord and every borough to share in the growing prosperity and the greater availability of money. Consequently many markets were sited at geographically and economically unsuitable points and not unnaturally were short-lived. Some today are mere hamlets, but a number have served to swell villages and to create small country towns which still retain or bear, as ex-market villages, the mark of their former status. A similar position obtained in Herefordshire and Cheshire, though the absence of the wool trade in the northern Borderland resulted in there being fewer medieval markets.

Chartered boroughs of royal or seignorial origin which are of earlier date in the southern Marches, were now introduced into the northern parts of Wales and into Cheshire. Flint was among the north Welsh boroughs founded in the late thirteenth century, while in Cheshire a number of seignorial boroughs including Frodsham, Knutsford and Tarporley were created and became market towns.[1] In Cheshire the salt trade, replacing the wool

[1] Ed. Joan Varley, *A Middlewich Chartulary*, pt. II, Chetham Soc. (1944), Introduction by James Tait.

trade in importance, led to the growing economic activity of the Weaver valley. As in the southern Marches, the boroughs became the nodal points around which agriculture and the adjacent rural settlements expanded. No better picture could be drawn of the southern Borderland at this time than that which is portrayed in the remarkable and detailed series of four maps of *South Wales and the Border in the XIVth Century* by William Rees,[1] showing administrative, military, ecclesiastical, economic and settlement features on the scale of half an inch to the mile.

The mid-fourteenth and the dawn of the fifteenth centuries were, however, to halt the growing prosperity first through the Black Death in 1349 and later years, and secondly through the Owain Glyndwr rebellions, the first in common with the whole of England, the latter bringing economic retrogression to Wales and a wide area of western England from Chester to Gloucester between 1400 and 1403. These years of war and pestilence brought about a shrinking of the population which may be estimated at anything from 25–40 per cent. Many clergy died, leaving vacant tenancies, and the period was associated with a sharp decrease in the documents referring to open field holdings. Throughout the Borderland, the Black Death hastened the break-up of community cultivation, or brought about a definite reduction in the number or size of the open arable fields. In Cheshire, the small and the newer communities were most affected economically, for example the Vale Royal Abbey manors on the edge of Delamere Forest where there had been a multiplication of arable fields in the thirteenth and early fourteenth centuries, but where widespread shrinkage followed so that by 1475 only one of the earlier (1334) field-names survived of some twenty-three mentioned in eight manors, though new names may have been given to others. However, the overall reduction in communal tillage is left in no doubt.[2]

It is easier to assume than to prove that villages were deserted at this time in the Borderland as in many other parts of England, but

[1] Published together with a handbook, by the Ordnance Survey, 1932.
[2] Ed. R. Stewart Browne, *Accounts of the Chamberlains and other officers of the County of Chester, 1301–60*, Record Soc. Lancs. and Ches., lix (1910), nos. 16, 17, 19, 23. In Drakelowe alone, 57 tenancies were vacant by the death of their holders in 1350–1. Ed. John Brownbill, *The Ledger Book of Vale Royal Abbey*, Record Soc. Lancs. and Ches. lxviii (1914). Dorothy Sylvester, 'The Open Fields of Cheshire', *Trans. Hist. Soc. Lancs. and Ches.*, cviii (1956).

they must certainly have shrunk. It is possible that many evidences of this on the ground were later erased when, in Tudor and Stuart times, the wool trade expanded in the middle and southern Borderland.

No new manors were created after 1300, and from that time they began to turn eventually into one of two courses: expansion especially of the park and estate with a corresponding growth in local influence; or decline and in many cases extinction, particularly where there were strong village communities. In many manors decay only threatened seriously from Tudor times, coinciding roughly with the Dissolution of monastic estates and their transference, decline or division. Rees, however, dates the beginning of the decay of the Norman manors in the southern Marches and South Wales from the late fourteenth century, relating their decline not only to the Black Death, but to absenteeism, the increased letting of land and the growth of individualism and commercialism in agriculture.[1] and T. Jones-Pierce has linked with this period the emergence of new estates from the consolidation of vacant holdings in Wales by a rising middle-class element who bought lesser holdings for this purpose and so turned hamlets into consolidated farms, especially in the belt adjoining the marcher lordships.[2]

Medieval changes in the rural landscape were thus considerable, but they were a matter of developing and changing function, of new elements and the ebb and flow of economic and military tides rather than of basic geography. Except in the extent and character of fields and woods and pastures, the essential rural distributions changed less than could have been expected, but gradually the condition of the peasants improved and by the end of the period there came at last better housing for the commoners. The first cottages to survive until today date from the end of the Middle Ages.

[1] William Rees, *South Wales and the March, 1284–1415* (1924), p. 258.
[2] 'The Social Scene in the Fourteenth Century', in *Wales through the Ages*, vol. i, ed. A. J. Roderick (1959).

6 From Medieval to Modern

The Union of England and Wales to the Nineteenth Century

THE later Middle Ages saw no modification of the petty wars and raiding which had for so long ravaged the Borderland. Owain Glyndwr's campaigns had left Wales and the Border a widespread legacy of devastation. During the first half of the fifteenth century, there were constant raids from the hills into the richer plains. Roads were unsafe, and border uplands such as Radnor Forest were a refuge for bandits and robbers. If the Wars of the Roses temporarily absorbed some of the more lawless element into the Yorkist armies, the pendulum swung back again afterwards, and men from the disbanded forces were sheltered from justice by the marcher lords. In such conditions there could be progress neither in settlement growth nor in land use.

The beginning of a better era, however, was at hand, heralded first perhaps by Edward IV's measure 'to restrain the wild Welchmanne' by no less an institution than the Council of the Marches. Under the early Tudors this was formed into a court of regular jurisdiction which, especially under Bishop Roland Lee's presidency, went far towards exterminating robbers and restraining the gypsies, restricting the powers of the lords marcher, and in fact paving the way to the Act of Union. Except for the period of the Civil Wars, peace and security had come to the Borderland at last.

The two Welsh Acts popularly known as the Acts of Union (1536 and 1542) were framed with the aim of absorbing Wales into the English realm and applying the English political, administrative and judicial systems to the government of Wales. They brought to an end the power of the marcher lords as independent rulers and henceforth the king's writ ran throughout England and Wales. The lordships remained as great estates, but the authority

E   S.R.L.W.B.

of their lords was in future to be seignorial only. The last seven Welsh counties came into being, including all the Welsh border counties other than Flintshire, but instead of the Quarter Sessional courts, Wales was given a system of Great Sessions. Monmouth was not included in this but was attached to an English circuit, hence the later distinction which has persisted between Wales and Monmouth. Most important of all, perhaps, from the angle of the settlement geographer was the extinction politically of the triple division between the Principality, the Marches and England which had persisted throughout the Middle Ages. From the Union there was to be, not uniformity, not even convergence in all aspects of development, but a marked similarity of trends in many matters. Trade, agriculture, prosperity, a slowly rising standard of living, the extension of physical amenities and certain social and cultural advances were by no means evenly shared as between the two countries, but the hard edges of difference were progressively softened. Nevertheless the contrasts in the landscape, soils and climate on the one hand and in the culture – and notably the language – of each were sufficiently strong to ensure the perpetuation of many of the settlement and cultural features which had evolved prior to 1536.

No longer divided politically, administrative and economic history henceforth ran largely parallel throughout the two countries and for the first time since the seventh century the Borderland entered on a phase of unification. Welsh commotes and cantrefs were replaced by English hundreds within the newly formed shires. The Great Sessions were held at the shire towns contributing, permanently or temporarily, to their growth. The Petty Sessional courts were attached to the new hundredal divisions as in England, but manorial courts continued in the countryside until they were abolished by the County Court Act of 1867.[1] Their continued power to deal with many offences such as encroachment on the commons and the common fields has made their records of long and continuous value. The replacement of the hundreds by rural districts in 1894 in bringing a new form of local government to the rural areas similarly brought

[1] In Radnorshire, where New Radnor was the first county town, this added function failed to save it from early decline to village status. The name 'Hundred House' occurs twice in this county, near Bleddfa in Radnor Forest where the Cefnllys sessions were held and at Llansantffraid formerly used for the Colwyn Division. Both remained rural.

some added importance to occasional settlements, e.g. Overton on Dee the centre of the rural district of Maelor Saesneg, but more often a central market town has gained rather than a village.

The old Welsh *trefydd* became townships on the English plan for administrative purposes, being converted in due course to civil parishes (also in 1894). But in much of Wales, for example Montgomeryshire, the position as regards the smallest units, i.e. townships and parishes, was still in a state of flux until the Parish Acts and the Local Government Acts of the nineteenth century sorted them out officially. Turbulent conditions, the prevalence of dispersed settlement and the extensive nature of common pasture all contributed to rural boundaries being without the usual English neatness or, in some cases, being non-existent or ill-defined. Parish boundaries which, until 1894, were ecclesiastical only, were similarly subject to change, especially in the three north-eastern Welsh counties where large, multi-township parishes were the rule as in Shropshire and Cheshire.[1] The result was that the administrative boundary map of Wales became at best complex, at worst inchoate.

The marcher lordships as such no longer existed. Many passed to the Crown. Many of the largest survived as large estates, as in the case of Badminton and Powys Castle, but simply with the status of great estates. The substitution of primogeniture for gavelkind brought to an end the morcellation of Welsh properties by divided inheritance and many other factors such as the increasing use of money, the ambition of newly arising landlords, and – from the seventeenth century especially – the more democratic temper of the country, made possible the appearance of entirely new estates especially in the former Marches and in Wales where the whole land position was rendered more fluid by the long centuries of border warfare. Thus everywhere in the English and Welsh countryside and not least in the Borderland, the Tudor period was marked by the rising prosperity of the squirearchy who built and re-built their manor houses in great numbers at that time and who, henceforth, became the core of that ill-defined but nonetheless real class, the gentry.[2] In England

---

[1] See Ch. 8.

[2] Penry Williams, 'The Tudor Gentry', in *Wales through the Ages*, ed. A. J. Roderick, vol. ii (1960).

the Tudor squires represented a more or less continuous series of manorial families whose claims went back to the Middle Ages. In Wales the antecedents of the Tudor gentry were harder to trace and still harder to prove or disprove, but while some were originally English or Anglo-Norman an increasing number were Welsh or Anglo-Welsh as was inevitable in so mixed an ethnic zone as the Marches. The newly created magistracy was recruited wholly from the landowning class and in both countries their comparative wealth combined with their political and juridical powers were to serve for up to three centuries more to set them apart socially. It was not only blood but well-arranged marriages, the acquiring of money and status through the professions (especially that of the law), successful capitalist farming and land purchase, and chance inheritance which were the making of some landowners while ill-luck or the inability to compete successfully in new and keener economic conditions broke others. No new manors could be created, but many new landed estates arose from the sixteenth to the nineteenth century throughout the two countries. After the high peak of their fortunes as a class in Tudor times a great many manorial lords ceased to exercise their powers as such and numerous lesser manor houses became farmhouses from the time of the Commonwealth onwards. The Civil Wars brought ruin to many estates, and the Restoration saw the numbers of the squirearchy appreciably reduced and those of the successful yeoman farmers increased. The fortunes of the manors have been traced in detail with some degree of accuracy period by period from Domesday to Georgian times in Cheshire[1] showing both continuity and failure to survive in different parts of the county. From Jacobean times onwards their numbers declined, but new soi-disant 'gentlemen's seats' made their appearance in the late eighteenth and the nineteenth centuries, many in Cheshire being built by successful manufacturers and business men. On the whole it was the lesser lords in the smaller manors who were squeezed out and whose houses are today farmhouses. By contrast, emptier areas which had long been woodland and common, offered opportunities for extending estates and dominating the settlement pattern. As a result, many hundreds of acres

[1] Dorothy Sylvester, 'The Manor and the Cheshire Landscape', *Trans. Lancs. and Ches. Antiq. Soc.*, lxx (1960).

had been absorbed into parks surrounding great houses by the early nineteenth century.[1] The parks expanded by various means and at various dates, deer parks becoming fashionable in both countries from Tudor times, but the great landscaping period was the eighteenth century when a further wave of building accompanied the laying-out of ornamental parks and many of the greater houses were re-built or added to.

From the seventeenth century in particular, the extent to which the park-estate dominated the immediate rural settlement pattern varied increasingly from district to district and from township to township. In some parts the old village communities regained their former significance at the expense of the lord of the manor as in the lower Dee valley (apart from the great Grosvenor estates). In others, as at Gwysaney (Fl.) and Doddington (Ch.), former open field land was absorbed into the parks. The wealthier lords were able to build new 'estate villages' for their workers, some compact, others semi-compact or dispersed. Lodges at the park gates, home farms, and workmen's cottages were erected in numbers in the eighteenth and nineteenth centuries around or at the gates of the park and in many estate townships were the only houses other than the manor house as at Bostock and Doddington (Ch.).

Although they failed to rise to the status of 'the quality', many yeoman farmers, especially those of Roundhead sympathies, seized the increasing opportunities to better their fortunes during and after the time of the Commonwealth. The farm in the modern sense, i.e. land cultivated in severalty by a single owner and generally though not necessarily compact, emerged at different dates in different parts of the country. In Montgomeryshire, one of the first times the word was used in this way was in 1735.[2] It was perhaps easier to achieve the status of an independent farmer in Wales where the *tyddynod* had a tradition of family farming behind them and where the *gwely* lands were for the most part grouped around a separate and dispersed *tyddyn*. The evolution of independent

---

[1] Ibid. pp. 13–15. The tracing and mapping of manor houses at successive periods for an entire county is a long and laborious task and has, consequently been completed only for Cheshire. Parallel conditions certainly obtained in Shropshire and other border counties. A list of Breconshire mansions in 1700 is appended in the *Atlas Brycheiniog* (1960), p. 118, and there are many similar late lists.

[2] *Coleman Deeds*, N.L.W., no. 669.

farm units in a compact pattern was facilitated in areas of dispersed dwellings, but rendered late in counties such as Herefordshire where, despite the prevalence of dispersal in the centre and east, disparate holdings in arable and meadow land were the rule over a wide area until as late as the eighteenth century. Around the villages, the decay of the open fields continued, gaining impetus in the sixteenth century as a result of the enclosures of which the main object was to advance sheep rearing for the wool trade. Both open fields and open common pasture were affected, for example in many south Shropshire townships,[1] and in some areas such enclosures led to rioting and the destruction of the newly made boundaries. Common ploughing was not necessarily abandoned, but in many townships it continued on a smaller scale. The open fields were reduced in number and size and the Town Field, single relic of two or more common fields in a formerly more extensive arable system, began to make its appearance, often to survive into the period of the Great Enclosures.

The increasing prosperity of the sixteenth and seventeenth centuries was associated with a rise in the population and a greater demand for land and houses, yet the growth of landed estates and the rise of ambitious yeomen farmers militated against the agrarian expansion of the rank and file. As a result, illegal enclosure or squatting became a feature of these centuries, and the tiny earthen and rough stone huts, and the small irregular enclosures around them combined, where land was scarce, to form a ragged edge to open commons as around the Clee Hills in south Shropshire where many remain to this day on Titterstone Clee, though on Brown Clee they have characteristically been engrossed into larger farms and estates. In Wales the parallel *ty un nos* came later, squatting on the waste only getting under way in Wales with the Great Enclosure movement.

Improved farming and breeding methods, the impetus of the growing demand for wool, the expansion of wool markets and cloth manufacture, had long contributed to the growing importance of the Borderland. Bridgnorth was a centre of weaving from as early as the thirteenth century. In the fourteenth century wool from the English border counties of Shropshire and Herefordshire

[1] W. E. Tate, 'A Hand List of English Enclosure Acts and Awards', *Trans. Shrops. Archaeol. Soc.*, LII, i (1947), pp. 1–29. See also Ch. 10.

was noted for its fine quality and in 1343 the highest priced wool was grown in Shropshire and Lincolnshire.[1] Wool from Abbey Dore in the Golden Vale (He.) was also of very high quality[2] and as early as the late thirteenth century Tintern had a flock of 2364.[3] Short-woolled Ryeland sheep were already emerging as a good breed, the wool from which had a good felting capacity.[4] In 1341 Welsh wools were described as of the poorest quality,[5] but were nevertheless exported in considerable quantity. Home weaving was carried on throughout upland Wales and in the fifteenth century the export of wool from Wales declined in favour of that of Welsh-produced russet cloths. Most of the larger border towns already had a considerable trade in wool and cloth before the end of the Middle Ages. In the fifteenth and sixteenth centuries Oswestry was the staple town for this trade, and the Shrewsbury drapers continued to buy their cloth there until 1621 when the staple passed to Shrewsbury. For any inland town to have the staple was a rare distinction and is some measure of the importance of the Borderland in the wool and cloth trade.

Although much of the credit for the early rise of the wool industry is due to the Cistercian houses, by Tudor times their decline and the rise of lay breeders on an ever increasing scale had clearly altered the position. During Tudor and Stuart times, weaving became of even greater importance in upland Wales, not only in cottage and farmhouse but by organised weavers in town and country, and the cloth was fulled in the numerous fulling mills (Welsh *pandy*, pl. *pandau*) found along Welsh and Borderland streams. The woollen industry was symptomatic of the increasing economic integration of the two countries from the time of the Union, large amounts of Welsh wool and cloth being sold in border markets, especially in the great market of Oswestry which sent as much as a hundred tons of cloth per annum to London in the sixteenth century.[6] Shrewsbury and, after 1582, Chester were other important markets, with many lesser ones on either side of the border. Welsh cloth was sold in English markets

[1] R. A. Pelham, 'Fourteenth Century England', in H. C. Darby, *The Historical Geography of England before 1800* (1936), p. 242.
[2] Ibid. p. 244, footnote 2.
[3] Ibid. p. 242, footnote 4, qu. *Pope Nicholas IV Taxation of 1291*.
[4] Ibid. p. 244.
[5] D. T. Williams, 'Medieval Trade: Western Ports' also in Darby, op. cit. p. 290.
[6] G. Dyfnallt Owen, *Elizabethan Wales* (1962), p. 148.

for clothing for the less well-to-do and although English cloth outmatched it in quality, wool and cloth brought increased prosperity to most parts of Wales during the sixteenth, seventeenth and eighteenth centuries.

Though Wales is poor in so many ways, Welsh pastoralism is rich and it was not only sheep but cattle which brought increased trade and wealth especially to Welsh drovers and cattlemen during those same centuries. Welsh drovers took their cattle in large numbers to London and other English towns along drovers' routes which are still incompletely traced. They went, of necessity, over open pasture as far as possible and thus over the hills, but knotted up at fords and bridging points many of which are marked by the hostelries they used such as the Drovers' Arms at Builth and Howey in Radnorshire, and inns bearing names such as the Black Ox.[1] In Shropshire small fields named 'Little London Field' were often to be found near villages and hamlets on the drovers' routes, used for impounding the cattle at night on their journeys to market. Not dissimilar from the drovers' roads, though probably more ancient, were the Cheshire saltways which centred on the 'wiches' and extended into Wales on the one side, down the Welsh border and eastward into Derbyshire. Lesser saltways focused on Droitwich in Worcestershire, crossing the border counties to Wales. Some of the salters' ways can be traced by names such as Saltersford and Salters' Lane which survive to this day. Many followed old Roman and perhaps Celtic routes and in Cheshire linked up with drovers' roads. Welsh drovers coming into Nantwich came by the street still known as Welsh Row, driving their cattle in and returning with the precious salt, so essential for the winter preservation of meat and for the seasoning of food.[2]

The compacting of holdings through enclosure and exchange was increasingly a feature of the agricultural landscape, but the countryside by no means necessarily became tidier as a result and in one respect in particular the Tudor period barely began to deal with one of its major defects – that of atrocious roads and communications. When, in 1555, an Act was passed which made

[1] Many of the known routes are mapped by Dr Margaret Davies in *Wales in Maps* (1951), p. 70.
[2] For a fuller account of the saltways see W. B. Crump, 'Saltways from the Cheshire Wiches', *Trans. Lancs. and Ches. Antiq. Soc.*, liv (1939).

each parish responsible for the upkeep of the highways within its boundaries, a beginning was made but it proved both minor and uneven, and the roads continued to be rutted and dangerous. They were quagmires in winter and wet weather, their courses changing and uncertain. Bridges, where they existed at all, were typically built of wood and liable to be broken by heavy traffic or washed away by floods, and more roads used fords than bridges.

Although each community was to a large degree self-supporting trade was increasing steadily both in the local markets and through the ports, creating a growing need for good main roads. Some parishes carried out their duties conscientiously, and occasional landowners were pioneers in road building and maintenance, but in most parts of the Borderland, and especially in the more remote areas, communications remained in a disgraceful state until the mid-eighteenth century. In many cases, the roads were in worse condition by the eighteenth century than in the Middle Ages, for trade was increasing everywhere, not only on account of the improvement in agricultural output, but because of the increase in mining and quarrying activities. Coal was mined and quarried in Flintshire and in South Wales; lead was mined in increasing quantities in Cardiganshire and Flintshire; iron was widely extracted, and some related industries were set up. For example, the first smelting mill for lead was established at Holywell in 1589, and a wireworks at Tintern in 1558.[1] These mineral-based industries and the consequent trade increased the need for better through-roads. So too did the increasing specialisation in the cloth trade and even in relatively minor trades. For example, it is noted by William Harrison that in the eighteenth century Nantwich shoemakers took their wares every Friday to Shude Hill market in Manchester.[2] Yet most roads, including those routes which were distinguished as the king's highway, remained either roughly paved or cobbled, or at best indifferently patched.

Part of the reason for the bad state of the roads was the almost total lack of wheeled traffic. Travellers generally went on foot or in the saddle. Wool and less bulky commodities were carried on packhorses and mules and, comparable to some degree with the

[1] G. Dyfnallt Owen, op. cit. pp. 155 and 162.
[2] 'Pre-Turnpike Highways in Lancashire and Cheshire', *Trans. Lancs. and Ches. Antiq. Soc.*, ix (1891), p. 129.

drovers' routes, most districts had their horseways and the comparatively rare stone bridges were increasingly designed to accommodate the packhorses. Even farm carts were not always wheeled but fitted with runners. Sledges often replaced carts in Radnorshire Forest, some remaining in use in the twentieth century.[1] Coaches were only introduced into England in 1564 and it was their increasing popularity and number in the seventeenth century, together with expanding trade and markets, which eventually led to a growing consciousness of the country's needs in this respect. The early road books were compiled towards the end of the seventeenth century following the Act which, in 1663, had empowered the formation of turnpike trusts.

Although there was a considerable network of these toll roads by 1820 in the English border counties, many were laid down later. From 1750, Acts were passed which led to the improvement of roads across the Border. A trust was created for the Shrewsbury–Wrexham road in 1752, and for those from Chester to Wrexham and Mold in 1756. The important North Wales coastal route was covered by trusts before 1759, and the movement spread in general from the English border counties into Wales. A comprehensive trust was created for Montgomeryshire in 1769, and for Radnorshire in 1767.[2] Many of the turnpike roads followed the line of earlier inter-village roads and were consequently winding and indirect and have remained so to this day. Others were largely new routes, especially those designed as through roads between major towns and those which served important ports. This was particularly true of the early nineteenth-century roads and notably the ones designed by Thomas Telford. The old Holyhead road, for example, entered Cheshire at Bridgemere, going thence by Nantwich, Tarporley, Tarvin, Chester, Mold and Denbigh, but the new Holyhead road, authorised in 1815, followed an entirely different route crossing eastern Shropshire by Wellington, going via Shrewsbury to Whittington (thus by-passing Oswestry), and on to Chirk, Llangollen, Corwen, across the Denbighshire Moors to Betws-y-coed, and thence by the hitherto isolated Nant Ffrancon to the Menai Bridge (completed in 1826) and so to Holyhead. These newer, straighter roads meant

[1] W. H. Howse, *Radnorshire* (1949), p. 229.
[2] A. H. Dodd, *The Industrial Revolution in North Wales*, 2nd ed. (1951), p. 92.

the desertion of the older post roads by the royal mail and by a certain amount of other traffic, giving a fillip to one place and depressing another. Turnpiked roads continued to be built or reconditioned for coaching traffic after 1820, but most of these were subsidiary routes and link roads[1] and within twenty to thirty years road traffic had begun its steep decline in favour of the railways.

The use of navigable waterways in the Borderland has always been limited and in the sixteenth century the only inland navigation of any note was on the Severn from its mouth at Gloucester to Shrewsbury. Rivers were, on the whole, far more important as barriers to communication in the Borderland than as aids with this major exception and, with the coming of the canal era, communication in this area was only increased in a relatively limited part, notably in Cheshire and north Shropshire, and on the edge of the south Welsh coalfield in western Monmouthshire. From the authorisation of the Bridgewater Canal in 1759, the canal-building period extended until the date of construction of the earliest railways. In Cheshire, the last canal to be built was the Macclesfield, authorised in 1827 and ten years later the first railway line was opened in Cheshire – part of the Grand Junction which linked Warrington to Birmingham via Crewe. Except for short lines in Wirral and north-east Cheshire, all the county's railway routes were laid down by 1875 and, as in the case of canals, its development and trade and industry were more affected by them than those of any other of the border counties, a reflection of its commercial advancement and locational importance.

Apart from the north and south Welsh coastal lines, and links between the Midlands and Shrewsbury, Oswestry and Chester, there were few other railways built in the border counties until after 1850. The main line through Shrewsbury down the border was completed in the early 1850s, and the line across Central Wales to Aberystwyth in 1864. Lesser lines, some of which were never to carry much traffic, were built in the 1860s and 1870s, one of the most abortive perhaps being the extension from Kington to New Radnor which failed to save either New Radnor's market or its status as a borough. Many of the railways of the border

[1] As for example in Cheshire. See the map of 'Turnpike Roads in Cheshire' by Elizabeth E. Beazley in Sylvester and Nulty, *The Historical Atlas of Cheshire*, p. 55.

counties have fallen out of use or are scheduled for closing under the Beeching axe, but not before making their impact on the settlement map.

The Changing Settlement Map

Although in 1800 England and Wales were still predominantly rural, a noticeable degree of regional differentiation had set in by that date and was to become more striking during the succeeding fifty to one hundred years. Once the least attractive to settlement of the three English border counties, Cheshire's economic advancement as part of the north-western industrial belt, and that of north-east and south-east Wales and Monmouthshire around their coalfields was marked, while the small Shropshire coalfield experienced a parallel economic revolution though on a much more restricted geographical scale.

Changing regional, much less changing national fortunes, are by no means evenly spread, and of the factors which led to the growth of some and the decline of other settlements after Union, none was more influential than mining and quarrying, industry, and communications, each linked in their various ways with expanding trade in the favoured areas, the attraction of population and the corresponding decline, relative or positive, of more remote districts. Growth and decay, function of all living things and not least of human communities, can be demonstrated widely in the Borderland, but most of the more spectacular growth in the towns and villages has taken place on the major coalfields, in the expanding industrial areas of Cheshire, and around Shrewsbury and the Shropshire coalfield. Examples of such communities, most of which are in the category of nineteenth- and twentieth-century urban expansion are familiar enough, but to see the physical growth of the lesser market towns and the villages, hamlets and scattered farms correctly it is essential to go back to the Tudor period when there took place the long overdue revolution in housing which laid the architectural basis of so many country places as we now know them, only the churches, the castles, and a very small number of dwelling-houses pre-dating 1485. Few parts of Britain benefited more than the Borderland from this improvement in economy and living conditions. The English border counties reaped the harvest of pacification after the long centuries of border warfare. The Welsh districts benefited both from peace and a vastly improving economy. As the castles and town walls ceased to be functional, many were used as quarries from which the common people built their houses. For the first time the cottages of the poor became reasonably habitable and permanent, and in many of the villages which have remained fairly stable in population the bulk of the houses to this day date between 1500 and 1700. In addition, the numbers of inns increased in the towns, the villages, and (from the initiation of the coaching era) on the open highway. The English border markets expanded and many built new stone or half-timbered market halls in the Tudor period, e.g. Shrewsbury, Ross on Wye, Market Drayton. Market towns as such sprang up in native Wales, some of these, like Llanidloes, also building market halls on the English model. The reigns of Edward VI and Elizabeth I in particular were noted for the founding of grammar schools in both town and village, their most characteristic siting being in or adjacent to the churchyard in the first instance, as at Nantwich and Great Budworth (Ch.). Almshouses were liberally endowed by the growing number of charities which were a feature of the sixteenth and later centuries. At the same time, the medieval gilds were losing their power and some gild halls disappeared, while others became town halls or remained as lesser halls with diverse functions, some at least being used for the sittings of the Sessional and other courts as is the Guildhall at Much Wenlock to the present day.

Comparatively few churches were built during the Tudor and Stuart periods in the Borderland, though some were restored and added to, but the compulsory keeping of parish registers from 1538, the greater care of churchyards, and the increasing number of funerary monuments and brasses, were features dating from the Reformation, and the church remained the social as well as the religious centre of the rural communities. In England it had long been the visible core of the nucleated village. Where nucleations were found, some on the sites of ancient *maerdrefi*, some as the new market centres arising in native Wales from this time, it was usually around the old churches as at Gwaenysgor (Fl.), Llanfwrog

(Denb.), Eglwys-Fach (Denb.), Llanbrynmair (Mont.), and Llanwddyn (Mont.). Where a tribal settlement is associated with a Celtic Church, it is now termed a *treflan*.

The best-placed markets, some new, some old, grew apace in the Tudor period, while many which had fulfilled a primarily strategic role declined. Among the last were a number whose situation lacked centrality or accessibility such as the 'Three Castles' of northern Monmouthshire (Grosmont, Skenfrith and White Castle) which are now mere villages. Caus on the Long Mountain, a walled market town in the early Tudor period, has vanished completely except for the fragmentary ruins of its once proud fortress. Talgarth and Hay on Wye in northern Breconshire failed to make the grade as 'new towns'[1] though Hay has remained a small market town. Some continued a modest expansion and later shrank. Such was the case in Ellesmere (Sa.), once the *caput* of a marcher lordship, and subsequently a considerable market town. Its population increased from a figure of 5909 in 1801 to 7080 in 1841, yet by the year 1931 had fallen to 1872, and in April 1967 it ceased to be an urban district and became absorbed into north Shropshire rural district. Others among the *capita* of former lordships continued to grow in the new role of shire town, for example Denbigh which is estimated to have had a population of approximately 3000 in the time of Elizabeth I, and Brecon which, at the junction of many ancient routes, mustered 1000 during that reign.[2] Today, their populations number *circa* 8000 and 5000 respectively, and this comparatively small rate of growth depends largely on their function as county towns and regional centres in thinly populated country, for their industries are in both cases few and small. Bishop's Castle, once a seat of the bishop of Hereford, has a population total which has hovered between 1300 and 1800 for a century and a half and is now back at the lower figure. It is a minor market town but nevertheless fought for the continuance of its status as an ancient borough. Ruthin had 395 houses in 1700[3] but only 243 in 1801. Recently it has resumed its growth as a small regional market and shopping centre with a population of approximately 3000. St Asaph's claim to the status of 'city'

[1] G. Dyfnallt Owen, op. cit. p. 194.
[2] Ibid.
[3] Edward Lhwyd, 'Parochialia' (1909–11 edition), I, p. 147.

solely on the basis of its rank as a cathedral settlement has been maintained with singular slenderness, for in 1700 it had 10 houses,[1] in 1801, 272, and still has a population of barely 2000 though a hospital, new industries, and a growing residential population promise increased numbers in future.

The causes of settlement expansion are occasionally simple, but more often complex and may rise and vanish with the centuries. In this the Borderland is no exception, but it is nevertheless true that where regional population is more stable, change in rural settlement patterns is less likely. Population itself, however, is only a partial guide to this, for family size, periods of plague, emigration and depression, are not always reflected in the number and pattern of the dwellings in any given township. For example, Radnorshire, which has suffered all these changes, still shows the same widespread dispersal pattern as it has done for several hundred years and with the decrease in size of families and numbers of farm labourers the ratio of houses to population is higher. Nevertheless there are now many 'gone down' houses and W. H. Howse quotes the case of two square miles of land on which there are now but two houses where the local farmer himself remembered thirteen.[2] Confronted with the thinly scattered population of the higher Welsh uplands, and with a paucity of early documents such as would be needed to reconstruct the settlement map in the Middle Ages, one is left with the problem of how, when, and in what density the dispersed farmhouses and cottages of upland Breconshire, Radnorshire and Montgomeryshire came into being, and what differences those 'gone down' houses have made to this pattern. The fluidity of territorial units – so easy in a dispersed community made up of separate *tyddynod* – only complicates the problem, the more so as houses rebuilt or built in simple styles in stone are difficult to date and early maps and evidence are scarce. Yet, apart from some fluctuation in numbers, it is clear that thin dispersal has been the characteristic of these overwhelmingly pastoral and farming hill communities throughout the modern period.

Beyond the hill edge and in the more fertile valleys which penetrate it, a more active economy and a greater density of population are associated with more varied settlement patterns

[1] Ibid. I, pp. 56–8.   [2] *Radnorshire*, p. 93.

and with a greater number of nucleations, though nucleated villages are by no means characteristic of the border country. Greater market activity and improving communications (mainly from the eighteenth century) wielded their selective influence on the older, and brought into being some newer units in the rural areas as was the case with the urban centres. For the greater part, the Borderland villages and hamlets were, and remain, predominantly agricultural and it was they which showed the most static form. But if the period after Union can be said to have contributed significantly to rural settlement pattern in the border countryside, it has been first through enclosure and secondly through non-agricultural economic developments.

Although the Great Enclosure movement was of comparable importance agriculturally in both upland and plain, its effect on settlement was unquestionably greater in the lowlands. In these last, land was scarcer and people more numerous and numbers of 'Green' hamlets either originated or expanded on the former common pastures of Cheshire, Shropshire and Herefordshire in particular, and on a smaller scale in the lowland Welsh fringe-belt. These characteristically took the names of the former 'waste' or common, hence the rise of the Cheshire hamlets of Gosland Green, Woodworth Green, Haughton Moss, Gradeley Green, Larden Green, Chorley Green, Oldcastle Heath; the Shropshire hamlets of Ightfield Heath, Preesgreen, Hodnetheath, Paddolgreen, Barkersgreen; the Herefordshire examples of Walkers Green, Paradise Green, Withington Marsh, Sutton Marsh and Winnal Common; Burton Green and Waters Green in Flintshire and many, many more. In some cases, these eighteenth- and nineteenth-century hamlets constituted the first (and in many the only) nucleations as at Willaston near Nantwich (Ch.) which was, until the mid-nineteenth century, a small township with only a few scattered farmsteads and a small manor house (Willaston Hall). The tithe map (1845) showed the nucleus of a new community on the recently enclosed common in the north-east of the township, and the opening of a railway station here in 1858, and the contemporary expansion of the Grand Junction railway works at nearby Crewe, soon after enclosure, gave the second impetus to growth which resulted in a large, compact non-parochial village.

Mining, quarrying and isolated industries gave a spurt to

innumerable new or swiftly expanded settlements in the Flintshire, Denbighshire and Monmouthshire countryside and on the small Shropshire coalfield (Plate 21), most of them becoming semi-urban and a few developing into full-scale towns, though in cases like Buckley (Fl.), a tile and brick making centre, the country often remained literally at their back door.

Far more rural though only at best partially agricultural, were the many minor settlements which clustered round tollgates, tollhouses, and coaching inns on the improved highways. These too can be exemplified in numbers throughout the Borderland, especially on the more important routes. Few compare with the large nucleations which grew along the post road across Anglesey and the later parallel A5, but lesser examples like Crossgates (near Llandrindod Wells, Rad.), Queen's Head (near West Felton, Sa., on the A5), Red Bull and Lawtongate (a new hamlet at an ancient entry point) near the Cheshire–Staffordshire boundary are typical examples of late road hamlets. Canals and railways more rarely gave rise to new rural hamlets, but they provided new elements in the form of lockhouses, stations, and such like, in remote areas, whilst major examples of railway growth in the direct sense are afforded by Crewe and Craven Arms. Along all these communications lines, the development of pre-existing villages tended to be stimulated, or new annexes to older settlements (for example the now appreciable industrial village of Elworth near Sandbach, Ch.) were encouraged by the new facilities.

The Nonconformist churches by using remote situations for many of their meeting places and chapels, added a further stimulus to hamlet growth (and sometimes provided a prime nucleus) and chapel hamlets are to be found throughout the Borderland as in many other parts of Britain,[1] many of the Quaker and Baptist chapels going back to the seventeenth and eighteenth centuries, many more to the nineteenth. Not dissimilar, but later, are the small nucleations which are found occasionally around hospitals, sanatoria, schools, colleges and modern hotels. Last must be added the twentieth-century extension into the countryside of adventitious elements associated particularly with the suburban-residential movement. These are far less conspicuous in the

[1] These are discussed more fully in Ch. 8.

Borderland than in the Midlands and metropolitan England, but nevertheless are a feature of expanding urban environs round the medium and larger towns such as Newport (Mon.), Shrewsbury, Chester and those of the Shropshire coalfield.

Apart from the enclosure hamlets and the isolated farms of the same date, it will be appreciated that virtually all the new settlements of the modern period are related to non-agricultural activities. The old order of community agriculture has been breaking down from the time of the Black Death, and it is evident that the twentieth century has done more to de-ruralise the countryside than any that has preceded it. Whether anything positive will be built up in its place is one of the major problems of country life today.

PART THREE

The Anatomy of Rural Geography

7 Administrative Units
Township, Manor, and Lordship

> . . . manorial and fiscal geography interferes with physical and villar geography.
>
> Maitland in *Domesday Book and Beyond*

THE smallest units of rural administration were for centuries the township, the manor and the parish. The last of these was solely an ecclesiastical division until 1894 when, under the Local Government Act of that year, the township was done away with and it was replaced by a unit with the unfortunate name of civil parish, so that it is now necessary to distinguish the original parishes by the term ecclesiastical parish.[1]

The township and the manor were basically economic units with important tenurial functions. The manor, additionally, held its own courts and administered justice. The nearest equivalent power in the parish was exercised by the vestry. In the township, there was no corresponding judicial or legislative body, but the commoners managed their own affairs in relation to communal agriculture where the township was not superseded by the manor. In both township and the manor, the main concern was agriculture.

Had Maitland said that manorial geography cut across parochial and township geography he would have expressed exactly the relationships which existed between the three units. Ecclesiastical parish boundaries almost invariably lay along township boundaries, though they might include one, two, or many more townships. The manor might coincide geographically with either or neither. It was not infrequently disparate, and was contained within complex and intricate boundaries. Something of their history is implicit in these facts: township preceded parish, but the two

---

[1] The ecclesiastical parishes, like the townships, are shown with their boundaries on the first three editions of the Ordnance Survey One-Inch maps.

units were closely related; manor succeeded township, but their boundaries might be coincident or completely at variance. The manor was essentially, though not exclusively, a Norman institution. The township goes back in name to the Anglo-Saxons, but the division itself, like the Welsh *tref* which in the old Laws was its equivalent, almost certainly goes back to the Early Iron Age or, in certain cases, perhaps even to the Bronze Age. The formation of parishes straddles the Conquest, dating back to the Conversion and continuing mainly until the twelfth and thirteenth centuries, although new parishes have continued to be formed, especially in the northern half of the country.

These three, the ultimate subdivisions for local administration prior to 1894, had an important role to play in rural geography, and were universal. In the Welsh Borderland, the lordship also was particularly well developed, reaching its extreme development in fact in the Marches. The marcher lordship followed a characteristic pattern, in which a *caput* or head manor which normally gave its name to the lordship was surrounded by lesser manors or townships. In this area, they were usually distinguished as belonging to either the Englishry or the Welshry, and their population, economic and tenurial arrangements varied accordingly. This arrangement of a head manor with satellites was not dissimilar from that of a parochial township with its satellites in the large parishes of the north.[1] Differential development was implicit. Thus, both ecclesiastical and tenurial factors helped to give individual townships their character and to produce a range of township types within a lordship as within a parish. In the more thinly populated Welsh areas, however, the parish came late. Where Norman influence was negligible or absent, the tradition of dispersal had, by that time, developed so far that the focal importance of the parochial township only became evident at a late date, if at all.

In that the township held no courts and usually had no lord (except when it was also a manor) township records as such are rarely come by. But the manor and the lordship, like the Church, kept records faithfully from the Conquest onwards, and it is to them that posterity owes the greatest debt for the information which has thus been preserved with regard to their character,

[1] See Ch. 8, pp. 167–71.

organisation, personnel, economy and many other aspects of these basic institutions of British rural life. Manorial and baronial court records are abundant, and many estates in addition kept all their records, personal, organisational, fiscal, as well as judicial, from a very early date. The same was true of the monasteries until the Dissolution, and of the cathedral churches and many parish churches, with the result that the history of a considerable number of estates and lesser properties can be followed without a break for centuries. In the Welsh Borderland, for example, the records of St Werburgh's Abbey (later the Cathedral), Chester, Hereford Cathedral, Lichfield Cathedral and Pitchford Hall (Sa.) date from the twelfth century; those of Badminton, Bodrhyddan, Gwysaney, Hawarden Castle, Llangibby Castle, Plas Yolyn, Dieulacres Abbey, Haughmond Abbey, Wombridge Abbey to the thirteenth; and Baker Gabb, Bridgwater, Legh of Booths, Milborne, Plymouth, St Pierre, Tabley House and Vale Royal Abbey to the fourteenth.[1] Research in the early history of rural settlement is dependent to a very great degree on such documents.

THE TOWNSHIP

The township stood at the bottom of the rural administrative scale. It was in essence a rural community, agriculturally interdependent, and its lands. The fundamental economic link was naturally expressed also in the kinship and social ties of the closely knit small group of people who ploughed their fields, regulated their common meadows, and depastured their animals together in wood and moorland. The commoners of any township were, in fact, an agricultural, tenurial, social and kinship group with a territorial ring round them. This ring might extend beyond the township for certain purposes, as in the case of a multi-township parish, or when several townships, like those around the Longmynd, shared the common pasture, but the township remained the smallest unit into which the Anglo-Saxon folk or the Celtic tribe and its lands was originally divided.

There is every reason to suppose that the township or its near-equivalent arose not later than the Early Iron Age all over Britain,

[1] See Bibliography, pp. 517-22.

and that the Welsh *tref* was its direct descendant. The Anglo-Saxons took it over and re-named it from the *tun* which represented the English unit of settlement, but the extent to which they altered it must have varied with circumstances. In the more sparsely populated parts of the Borderland, they probably established no more than a nominal overlordship in many of the old Celtic areas, changing the mode of life and the methods of cultivation hardly at all. Where the English were settled in strength, they would introduce their own type of nucleated settlement and their two common fields, and in the Borderland it is probable that this only occurred in a comparatively small proportion of the townships, so that the English and the old British pattern would continue side by side. The continuation of these contrasting types is still evident in the Borderland today. The Normans introduced the term *vill* to cover the township, but later the Old English name re-established itself and persisted until 1894 when many of the new civil parishes which were created were nothing more nor less than the old townships under another name.

As an agricultural unit, the people of the township needed a variety of types of land: ploughland, meadowland, rough pasture, woodland and, if it were available, mossland. The result was a striving after inclusiveness and an agricultural patchwork which tended to be repeated in township after township throughout a similar physical area or where traditional usage was similar, or both. Equally, a break in physique or in ethnic and economic tradition could result in a break in local patterns of land use.

The tumbled topography of the border hills rarely lends the same regularity to township geography as is found, say, in the scarplands of southern England, but streams and water partings regularly acted as boundaries, and in southern Shropshire in particular there are some striking examples of boundary drawing in relation to relief. The two parallel escarpments of Wenlock Edge and View Edge divided by Hopedale, and with consequent valleys carving up the dip slope of the lower, eastern escarpment afford an ideal basis for regular township units. Hardly less regular is the sharing out of the slopes of both Brown Clee and Titterstone Clee, which are similarly divided into townships shaped like slices of cake centring on the summit areas of the two Clee Hill masses. A third example of hill-orientated townships is the group which shares the slopes of the Longmynd and whose upper boundary is the prehistoric Portway, a ridge road following the high, bare watershed of this ancient upland. A certain pattern is also discernible in the groups of valley townships which follow most of the main streams of the Borderland and either sit astride the stream or use it as one line of delimitation. Thus the middle Severn in the plain of Shrewsbury, the middle Wye in the plain of Hereford, the Lugg, the Tern, the Weaver and many other streams are fringed by valley-orientated townships (Fig. 42). Not least significant is the fact that along much of its course, Offa's Dyke also serves as a boundary line between townships.

The areal extent of the townships differed widely. In the Welsh Borderland it decreased northwards in eastern Welsh counties from Breconshire to Flintshire, and eastwards to the English plain, except for Cheshire which was on average characterised by larger townships than both Flintshire and Shropshire.[1]

1811   Average Size of townships in square miles

Flintshire	1·69	2·08	Cheshire
Denbighshire	2·3	1·74	Shropshire
Montgomeryshire	3·48	2·83	Herefordshire
Radnorshire	5·46	3·22	Monmouthshire
Breconshire	6·66		

As regards population in 1811 the diagrammatic relationship was not directly opposite, but showed decreases towards the middle latitudes in both England and Wales, but a consistent increase from Wales to England as would be expected.

1811   Average Population per township[2]

Flintshire	323	453	Cheshire
Denbighshire	233	254	Shropshire
Montgomeryshire	215	309	Herefordshire
Radnorshire	268	403	Monmouthshire
Breconshire	333		

Within each county the variation was appreciable but the averages nevertheless have a broad regional significance.

---

[1] For comparison, Devonshire townships at the same date averaged 7·45 sq. miles, Sussex 6·9, Huntingdonshire 3·64, Leicestershire 2·58.

[2] Urban populations have not been extracted, but the growth of towns had not been marked by that date. Their inclusion however to some extent accounts for the higher figures in Flintshire, Cheshire and Monmouthshire.

The shape of the townships was also variable, though compact-ness characterised most of them. The line of a river or of a hill crest gave regularity to certain groups, as in the case of those on Wenlock Edge or along the Severn and Wye and many lesser streams, but in every case inclusion of a varied selection of arable, meadow and pastureland was aimed at together with woodland and mossland where possible. This was by no means always achieved. Cases of extreme poverty in one type of land might be compensated by inter-commoning with a neighbouring township, and this was frequently done in the case of the rough pasture with the result that boundaries might remain undefined for centuries as on some of the high Welsh hills, for example the boun-daries of the townships of Garthbeibio, Llanerfyl and Cemmaes are shown on the One-Inch Tithe Edition (1836) as discon-tinued on the slopes of Mynydd Llyn Coch-Lwyad and Mynydd Cemmaes.

Another common way of breaking the regularity and continency of the township in the Middle Ages was the result of tenurial changes, especially those brought about by exchanges, purchase, inheritance and seizure of land between and by lords of the manors. These might be small or large, but the most characteristic are those which clearly follow the boundaries of fields or field strips within a neighbouring township or along the boundary of the township concerned. This is often a reflection of the strength of the feudal system in the area and it is therefore not surprising to find that there are numerous examples of detached portions of townships in Herefordshire and in the former marcher lordships throughout the Borderland. The Church was also granted rights in many townships and the strips they held might pass eventually to a nearby landowner, for example, at the Dissolution, and pro-duce a similar result. In the case of Welshampton in north Shrop-shire, a former marcher lordship, a large group of field strips of earlier age are seen on the O.S. One-Inch LXXIII SW and NW of 1833 as detached portions of the township of Hampton Wood; and in 1831 a group of townships in eastern Herefordshire had cross-related holdings within one another's boundaries, but most of these were larger. (O.S. One-Inch Sheet XLIII NE.)

A feature of the township boundary in some parts of Welsh Wales was its fluidity. In Montgomeryshire, for example, the number and even the names of constituent townships appear to have been liable to change within an appreciable number of parishes. This may have been due to the dispersed nature of habitation or to a period of consolidation of holdings or both, but cannot be attributed to economic changes such as caused wholesale alterations in the boundaries of some Flintshire townships when they were converted to civil parishes in the late nineteenth century.

By 1894, the community within the old township had for most purposes ceased to practise communal agriculture. The arable fields were enclosed, and at best the common pasture might remain open, wholly or in part. Severalty farming had become the rule and even when the new civil parishes created in that year coincided in area with the former townships, they acknowledged the continuance of the community as a settlement group not as an economically knit territorial unit.

THE MANOR

The manor in 1086 was little more than the township by a different name – a name almost universally bestowed on the old English townships as a mark of Norman feudalisation. As time went on, however, manorialism made its impact on the townships through the establishment of the lord as the pivot of territorial organisation. A manor house was built and set significantly apart from the dwellings of the peasantry. In the more important manors it came to be enclosed in time within a park. In some cases, the community was sufficiently strong to struggle free, and the lord was engulfed by the community or the family died out. In other areas, where settlement was sparse, the Normans carried on active colonisation by means of manorialism, creating new manors from the waste or enclosing an almost uninhabited stretch of land to form a new manor. It was in such areas that the new image of the manor could best come into being, with the manor house as the sole focus of the new unit, and with the park occupying the greater part of its area. In due course, scattered or hamleted dwellings of the estate workers formed a distinctive community, quite different from that of the old democratic townships. A miller, a huntsman, a forester, a bailiff and a number of cottagers – all primarily estate workers – lived at or near the park gates, and places such as Calveley, Bostock and Doddington (Ch.) are the direct descendants of such medieval and later manorial communities. Between the two extremes of the free community surviving from pre-Conquest times and the highly manorialised townships in which all were subservient to the lord and the manorial family, lay every gradation of manor–township relationship. It is a testimony to the strength of the English communal tradition that by the later Middle Ages, the term township was freely back in use and the word manor had become specialised in its applicability only to the holdings of a manorial lord, but in the early Middle Ages, feudalism was so strong that the central concept of *nulle terre sans seigneur* had all but universal application in the Conqueror's realm.

In the Welsh Borderland, the military-feudal idea flourished throughout the years 1070–1485. There, where the advancing and maintenance of English power was the prime objective, Anglo-Norman feudalism was amply demonstrated as a working régime and, artificially fostered by the strategic importance of the Marches, it persisted long and late. It was grafted not only on to the English townships but on to the Welsh *trefydd*. Many of the soi-disant English townships were similar grafts on older Celtic communities, hence this became the zone of settlement hybrids *par excellence*. In Wirral, this same process had previously involved yet another element – the Irish-Norse.

In both the eastern belt of Shropshire and Herefordshire which bordered the great Midland forests, and Cheshire which lay on the northern edge of the better settled English lands, there was ample room for expansion. This took place in country which still awaited colonisation, or which had been but thinly populated in the Old English period or, perhaps, devastated as in the case of east Cheshire by the work of the Conqueror's armies during their mid-winter march of 1070–1. In such lands, the park-estate type of manor took root, and it continued to grow and flourish until the eighteenth and nineteenth centuries. By contrast, the older villages and the better populated areas of the pre-Conquest period such as the lower Dee valley gave only poor soil for the rooting of manorialism, and it wilted and largely disappeared from the Dee valley communities except in the case of the Grosvenor estates.[1] As time went on, this principle was demonstrated in many parts of the Borderland, and any large-scale map, particularly of nineteenth-century date, shows a preponderance of large parks in well wooded country such as east Shropshire, and 'upland' (i.e. central) Monmouthshire. By the same date, they had shrunk and become far fewer in number in the lands where the villages and larger hamlets flourished.

With manorial overlordship were associated numerous rights and privileges, but also many duties. These last included the *trinoda necessitas*; to accompany the king on military expeditions taking with him his quota of armed men from his manors; to give help in building castles; and to maintain bridges. The burdens of estate management, the responsibility for tenants and their dwellings, the maintenance of roads within the manor, and the dispensing of justice in the manorial courts were further additions to the tasks of overlordship. But there were privileges and rights which more than compensated for these – rights associated with multure, with pannage and pasture, with hunting, fishing, fowling, with the taking of timber, turves and building stone, with the claims on various dues and renders from all the tenants, with the rents which later replaced these, with the working and harvesting of the common lands, with servile labour, with the collecting of the rectorial or vicarial tithes and the patronage of livings, and not least the reward of a position of unchallenged social superiority. In the case of the greater lords, many of them earls and barons, went the further privileges, especially in the Marcher lordships, of founding seignorial boroughs and of chartering markets and fairs.

Among the benefits which manorialism brought to the community was the advance of cultivation and pastoralism in reclaimed woodlands and wastes. This altered the ground pattern of the woodland and moorland fringes once again, and led to increases in population which continued unabated until the tragedy of the Black Death. But although the commoners benefited the lords gained an increasing hold over the disposition and use of the woods and commons for which, according to the Statute of Merton (1235) they were only trustees. Yet by the mid-nineteenth century hardly a woodland remained in England which was not

[1] Dorothy Sylvester, 'The Manor and the Cheshire Landscape', *Trans. Lancs. and Ches. Antiq. Soc.* lxx (1960), pp. 1–15.

owned by the gentry, and the exceptions in Wales were by then very few in number.[1] Most had passed into private hands by the seventeenth or, at latest, by the eighteenth century. This close control of the common pastures and woodlands by the lords of the manors helped to bring about their early enclosure in the Borderland, and in the period of the Great Enclosures allowed them the major say in their allotment and letting. It led to new farmsteads and small holdings growing up and being added to the rent rolls of the larger estates.[2]

Although the manorial boundaries were generally those of the older townships, this was by no means invariably so. Townships were cut up or combined to form new manors and, especially as time went on, their boundaries might include many disparate portions acquired through marriage, inheritance, or purchase, or by less legal means. Some of these irregularities were perpetuated as late as the nineteenth century in township and parish boundaries in Shropshire and Herefordshire. Further complications arose as the result of subinfeudations which were numerous by the reign of Henry III, and which often caused extreme morcellation. This was checked in the same reign by a provision of the Great Charter of Henry III 'that no man should grant or sell land without reserving sufficient to answer the demands of his lord'. The Statute *Quia Emptores* of 18 Edw. I enacted that 'in all sales and enfeoffments of land the feoffee shall hold the same not of the immediate feoffer but of the chief lord of the fee'. This in effect ended the subdivision of manors and no new manors were created after 1300.

The Church also owned many manors but, apart from the absence of a great house and park, their manors were not dissimilar from those of the lay lord, and the Church was at least equally zealous in the extension of arable land. For example, the abbey of St Werburgh reclaimed 270 acres of Cranage Heath in mid-Cheshire in 1287–91,[3] and the abbey of Vale Royal had added

[1] A rare example of late-surviving English common woodland was recorded as existing at Daresbury in Cheshire in 1615. *Ches. Inquisitions Post-Mortem*, ed. R. Stewart Browne (Lancs. and Ches. Record Soc., 84), file 91, no. 3, 150.

[2] *The Abergavenny Deeds*, for example, include numerous documents referring to such new, rented holdings on the former commons in the eighteenth and nineteenth centuries.

[3] *The Chartulary of the Abbey of St Werburgh*, Chester, II, ed. J. Tait, Chetham Soc., lxxxii, no. 747, p. 405.

many new open fields to the community lands fringing eastern Delamere Forest by 1334.[1]

A few new elements such as dovecotes, barns, byres, mills and new chapels were added to the settlement landscape by ecclesiastical as well as by lay lords, but it was these last who were largely responsible for the great houses and deer parks with their ornamental waters – features which were to reach their peak expression in the eighteenth-century landscaping movement and the contemporary rebuilding of great houses. Some of the rural abbots also built on a grand scale, and a number of these estates, for instance that of Vale Royal Abbey, have been preserved by private owners since the Dissolution.

THE LORDSHIP

The lordship was a characteristically feudal administrative unit generally under a noble, and in some cases under the Crown. It was by no means confined to the Marches, but in the Marches achieved near-independence under lords of semi-regal power, so that its characteristics were exaggerated in proportion as the power of the lords was enhanced. It might consist of a single unit, but the typical marcher lordship was multi-unit. Amid the wide range of possible combinations of component units within a lordship, a certain degree of parallelism was discernible, and in all of them except the most minor, the growth of the *caput*, the dependence of the remaining manors or townships which had the relationships of satellites, and the differentiation between the Anglo-Norman inhabitants on the one hand and the Welsh on the other were type features. But there were also more complex associations in which lesser lordships were included within a greater, notably as a result of conquest or intermarriage, and the hierarchy was correspondingly raised at the upper end.

The *lordship of Hawarden* offers a fairly straightforward example of an important, yet not too extensive marcher lordship, which was often known after Union as the manor of Hawarden. It centred first on an early Norman motte, the site of which is in

[1] *The Ledger Book of Vale Royal Abbey*, ed. J. Brownbill, Lancs. and Ches. Record Soc., lxviii (1914), pp. 92–113. The 1334 rental is analysed in 'The Open Fields of Cheshire' by Dorothy Sylvester, *Trans. Hist. Soc. Lancs. and Ches.*, cviii, pp. 21–5.

dispute. This was succeeded by a stone keep whose site in a mound dominates that of the later medieval castle, the latter in turn overlooking the eighteenth-century house of the Glynnes and later the Gladstones. The last three stand within the wide expanse of a deer park of which the earliest extant map can be dated 1651 or immediately afterwards,[1] and at its gates lies the small town of Hawarden with its early Celtic-foundation church of St Deiniol and the wide street which was the scene of a medieval market. The most northerly stronghold in the line of the hill-edge castles of the Borderland, Hawarden commanded the Cheshire plain at its foot, the low Flintshire plateau behind and the estuarine marshes to the north. Its constituent townships, some from time to time referred to also as manors, extended into all three physical divisions. The townships were sixteen in number and included units as diverse as the street-nucleation of Bretton with its former open fields, the scattered communities of Aston and Shotton with their shared open fields,[2] Broad Lane which was almost certainly a late subdivision of Hawarden township itself, the estuarine townships of Sealand and Rake and Manor, Pentrobin a Welsh upland community and Bannel a late pastoral group arising on the common pasture of the plateau.[3] The convenience of intercommoning in any type of land led to close mutual economic arrangements, and the link between them all was doubly secured through the lordship and through the parish which was geographically coincident with it.

The *lordship of Ruyton*[4] was smaller and strategically of much less importance lying, as it did, well within the plain of north Shropshire astride the Perry valley (Fig. 41). The medieval lordship embraced the eleven townships which gave the place its name of Ruyton XI Towns, but at Domesday it consisted not of one, but of the three manors of Wykey, West Felton and Ruyton. Parochially the same eleven townships were divided between West Felton and Ruyton. Ruyton alone attained the status of a borough with a castle and an early market. It grew into a small country town but

---

[1] Dorothy Sylvester, 'Settlement Patterns in Rural Flintshire', *Trans. Fl. Hist. Soc.* (1954–5), pp. 25–6. The map referred to is the Hawarden Estate map, N.L.W.
[2] Ibid. figs 7, 8 and 9, and pp. 25–6, based on evidence from the *Hawarden Deeds* and the maps referred to above together with eighteenth-century enclosure agreements, and the tithe maps. See also Ch. 10, pp. 243–5.
[3] Ibid. fig. 10. This map dates Bannel Green as early seventeenth century at the latest.
[4] See Ch. 13, pp. 311–12.

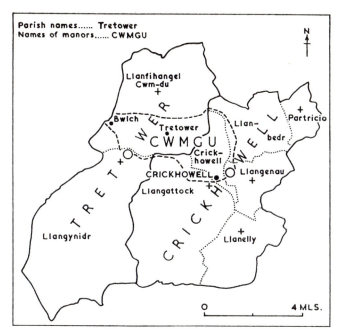

Llanfihangel
Cwm-du
+

Bwlch
Tretower
C W M G U
Crick-
howell
Llan-
bedr
Partricio
+

CRICKHOWELL
Llangenau
+

Llangattock

Llangynidr

Llanelly
+

0   4 MLS.

17. The lordship of Crickhowell, Breconshire

after the extinction of its market declined to a large village. West
Felton remains a tiny village round a church which is contained
within the ditches of a medieval motte and bailey. One or two
other townships have small hamlets, as in Edstaston and Wykey,
but most of them comprise only scattered farms.

In the *lordship of Frodsham* the whole position was different. It
was not a marcher lordship but an estate held at Domesday by the
earl of Chester. The seignorial borough of Frodsham was created
by Earl Randolf III in the mid-thirteenth century and its charter
granted a market, which still survives, and two fairs. Early in the
seventeenth century the manor was separated from the earldom,
leaving within it what became known in the lordship as a third
division of Frodsham. This included disparate holdings on
Frodsham Marsh and a considerable part of the wooded country
on the low plateau behind Overton, much of it now held by the
Marquess of Cholmondeley. The parish was the widest combination of these administrative units including in the nineteenth century the township and lordship of Frodsham and the townships

of Helsby, Kingsley, Manley, Newton and Norley. In 1841 the lordship contained 2593 acres as compared with the 2256 acres of the township of Frodsham, and over 13,000 acres in the parish of Frodsham.

The complexities of arrangements within any multiple administrative unit in Britain are in part historical, hence terms may be interchanged or have their meanings modified as is shown by comparing the above with Crickhowell. The *lordship of Crickhowell* in Breconshire was originally held by the lord of Blaenllyfni and included the manors of Crickhowell and Tretower, together with the borough of Crickhowell. After several changes it passed to the earls of Worcester and when the third marquess became the duke of Beaufort, to the Badminton estates. The *Badminton Manorial Records* include, in addition to court rolls, a number of rental surveys and custumals. A 1561 Survey of Crickhowell manor recorded a characteristic list of tenants: 79 free tenants in the town and borough of Crickhowell; 64 free tenants (in charge of an English reeve) and 2 customary tenants in the manor of Crickhowell; 40 free tenants in Llanbedr (of which 23 were in the charge of a Welsh bedell); 24 free and 27 customary tenants in Llangenny; 33 free and 23 customary tenants in Llangattock; 40 free tenants in Llanelly and 38 leaseholders; 12 free tenants in Patrishow; five farms of bailiwicks and bedellaries in the parishes of Llanelly, Llangenny, Llanbedr, Llangattock and Crickhowell and 138 Welsh tenants in 'le Kedi'. Englishry and Welshry are revealed by these figures, as is the existence of parishes within the manor.[1] An 1863–4 map of the manors shows Crickhowell embracing the parishes of Llanbedr, Patrishow, Llangenny, Llangattock, Llanelly and the town of Crickhowell; while Tretower manor covered the parishes of Llanfihangel Cwm Du, Llangynidr and the township of Tretower. A manor called Cwmgu cut across both and appeared to have no precise boundaries, while a number of the parishes were further cut into 'parcels' which appear in other lists as townships.[2] Within the park of Crickhowell a custumal of the latter part of the reign of Henry VIII describes 'liberties' in which free tenants had certain rights.[3] Similar though

[1] *Badminton Manorial Records*, I, no. 382 (1561).
[2] Ibid. frontispiece. See Fig. 17.
[3] Ibid. no. 380.

more extensive liberties were associated with towns, e.g. Shrewsbury.

The distinction between the greater manors and the lordships was a fine one, and often purely nominal, as the example of Hawarden illustrates. It was largely a difference of degree, and many large composite manors were lordships in all but name as in the case of *Leominster*. There, the borough and the manor together were ancient demesne lands of the Crown, allotted by Edward the Confessor to Queen Edith. In 1086 this manor had 16 members. It was given to Reading Abbey by Henry I and from that time was governed under the abbot of Reading's charter by the Priory of Leominster until the Dissolution when it reverted to the Crown. In the time of Edward I a survey revealed Leominster as one of the richest priories in England owning numerous manors with many open fields, meadows, mills, pastures, herds and woods. It is described sometimes as a manor, sometimes as a lordship.[1]

The *lordship of Denbigh* was described more usually as an honour, a term which was roughly equivalent in meaning with lordship but used only rarely. Britain is rich in such alternative terms for lordly holdings, but there is rather less variety in relation to divisions where the community was mainly concerned. Among those to be met with in the Welsh Borderland in the former group, are *bedellary*, an area under the charge of a beadle or bedell; a *hardwick* and its sister-type the *berewick*, the former by the Middle Ages a pastoral township attached to and serving a castle or manor-house in a great lordship, and the latter similarly given over for the same purpose to cultivation, but the derivation of both names suggesting a pre-Conquest origin. Outside a borough or lordship were the *liberties* where burghers and freemen had certain rights, for example of pasture and pannage. Larger groupings of townships were, in England, the *hundred*, a term of disputed origin which is variously thought to have been based originally on a hundred families, a hundred townships, or on the area capable of providing a hundred fighting men; and in Wales the *cantref*, literally a hundred townships, and its subdivision the *cwmwd* or *commote* which has no equivalent in English administrative divisions. The interrelationships of these numerous local units have done much to complicate the geography of administrative boundaries.

[1] John Price, *An Historical and Topographical Account of Leominster* (1795).

8 Church and Countryside

THE Church has had an intimate and significant part to play in the evolution of the rural scene and the development of administrative patterns, in part causal, in part reflective of rural conditions. In England particularly, the parish church has acted as a nucleating factor for village and hamlet, and has remained architecturally dominant in the characteristic English village. Much later, the Nonconformist chapel fulfilled a parallel though lesser function in relation to the chapel hamlets many of which arose after the religious revivals of the eighteenth and nineteenth centuries.

As a focal point for religious life, the Church also became to some extent a focus of community life, and as time went on took an increasing part in administration either directly or through the administrative unit of the parish. Indeed, the parish which began simply as an area in which a priest could carry out his pastoral duties, became entangled with the township – the area in which the communal rural unit carried on its agricultural activities – probably at a very early date in its history. Its link with the manor was close and in many parishes the incumbent was a member of the manorial family. Administration and defence in numerous villages became associated with Church as well as manor, and through his sharing of agricultural land and activities the parson became part too of the economic structure of the rural group. By the time of Elizabeth, two frankly civil tasks were added officially to those of the Vestry – the administration of the new Poor Laws, and the surveillance of the highways. Thus by Tudor times, the parish had accepted both religious and civil duties and functioned as an administrative unit in both spheres. This approximate status remained until the Local Government Act of 1894 under which the civil functions of the ecclesiastical parish passed to the newly created civil parishes.

From that date onwards, the ecclesiastical parish became functionally separate. Yet from its inception it had been geographically identical with the township or with a group of townships. In the majority of cases, the township boundaries were adopted unchanged as civil parish boundaries after the 1894 Act, but in districts where population changes were considerable, the old townships might be represented neither by shape nor name in the newly drawn civil parish map. This was notably true, for example, in the Flintshire coalfield where population had increased sharply with the industrialisation of the eighteenth and nineteenth centuries. Where such changes occurred the pattern of the ancient local divisions can only be found in maps which pre-date 1894.[1] The civil interdependence of the townships in a single parish was also lost when each became a separate unit with its own parish council. In most cases the disappearance of community agriculture had already destroyed the economic meaning of the townships. But in the pre-enclosure period, the pattern of parish and township was fundamental to the interpretation of the ancient rural geography of Britain. Over the greater part of south-eastern England, township and parish were co-terminous, and the characteristic focus of the single-township parish was the village nucleated about its church, and set in the midst of its common fields. The simplicity of this typically English pattern is absent, however, from the greater part of northern and north-western England and north-eastern Wales where large, multi-township parishes are the rule. In such parishes there may be only one village, and that the centre of the parochial township, the other townships being characterised by lesser settlements, and in Wales and even in the English border counties there may be only a church hamlet or a near-solitary church even in the parochial township. These two patterns represent basic contrasts in British rural settlement.

[1] For this purpose, the first and second editions of the One-Inch Ordnance Survey maps are the most useful, but for many parts of the Borderland there are, even on these, occasional parishes which are shown without the constituent township boundaries, e.g. Berriew in Montgomeryshire, Church Stretton in Shropshire and Hope in Flintshire. Occasionally, large-scale county maps printed privately supply this deficiency, but the only certain sources of the township boundaries are the Tithe Maps.

Parish–Township structure in England and Wales

In the Welsh Borderland both types of parish–township structure are to be found. The northern part (including Cheshire, north Shropshire, Flintshire, Denbighshire and Montgomeryshire) is an area of multi-township parishes. The southern counties (Hereford-shire, Monmouthshire, Radnorshire, Breconshire and western Gloucestershire) average fewer than two townships per parish, though in fact south-east Shropshire, Radnorshire and Brecon-shire lie across the boundary zone between the single- and multi-township parish and both types mingle there. The division of the Welsh Borderland into two major areas on the basis of parish–township structure raises immediate difficulties, for the division is not, as might have been anticipated, a division between English and Welsh or between Highland and Lowland Zone, but one which cuts right across both. It is not in fact a division which originates in the Borderland but one which stems from factors of much wider geographical significance. To see it truly and in perspective it must be extended to the whole of England and Wales. The lack of pre-nineteenth century parish–township maps and the difficulty and complexity of assembling earlier data enforce the use of early nineteenth-century material, but as most of the ancient parishes were little altered before 1811, the *Census of Population* of that date and the first and second editions of the One-Inch Ordnance Survey maps have been used for maps depicting parish–township geography (Figs 18 and 19). In many parts of Britain the picture had changed little during six or seven hundred years,[1] and such new parishes as had been created by that date brought only minor change to the ancient pattern.

The chief regional differences in England and Wales have been summarised in Figure 18. This shows two major geographical divisions in parochial structure:

[1] G. H. Tupling has estimated that of the 59 parish churches in Lancashire in 1600, only three had been created within the previous three hundred years and only five others between 1201 and 1250. ('The Pre-Reformation Parishes and Chapelries of Lancashire', *Trans. Lancs. and Ches. Antiq. Soc.*, lxvii, 1957, pp. 1–16.) In 1811, there were 74 parishes in Lancashire.

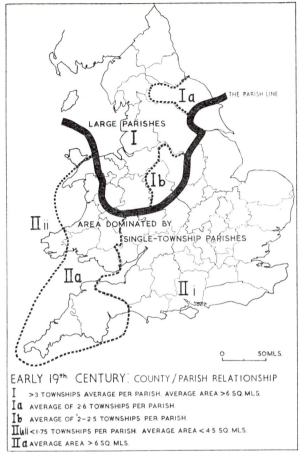

THE PARISH LINE

LARGE PARISHES

I

Ia

Ib

IIii

AREA DOMINATED BY
SINGLE-TOWNSHIP PARISHES

IIa

IIi

0   50 MLS.

EARLY 19th CENTURY: COUNTY / PARISH RELATIONSHIP
I   >3 TOWNSHIPS AVERAGE PER PARISH. AVERAGE AREA >6 SQ.MLS.
Ia   AVERAGE OF 2·6 TOWNSHIPS PER PARISH.
Ib   AVERAGE OF 2–2·5 TOWNSHIPS PER PARISH.
IIi&ii <1·75 TOWNSHIPS PER PARISH. AVERAGE AREA < 4·5 SQ. MLS.
IIa AVERAGE AREA >6 SQ. MLS.

18. England and Wales: the Parish Line

(1) *a northern division* of large parishes in which the parish has in
     every county an average of more than three townships and
     an average area of more than six square miles except in
     the North Riding, Derbyshire and Nottinghamshire which
     have lower average numbers of townships (2–2·6),

(2) *a southern division* dominated by single-township parishes,
     with an average everywhere of fewer than 1·75 townships
     per parish and an average area generally of under 4·5
     square miles except in south-west England and much of
     Wales which have together been shown as one of the three

sub-areas of this southern division. The sub-areas are: (*a*) south-eastern England (the major area), (*b*) south-western England and Wales excluding Anglesey, Pembrokeshire and the three north-eastern counties, (*c*) Anglesey and Pembrokeshire. These last, although numerically comparable to (*a*) are geographically distinctive.

The boundary between the two major divisions has necessarily been drawn somewhat arbitrarily, for the map has been constructed on the basis of county figures, but even these bring out the fact that there is no sharp boundary line. Had the maps been made for England only, the explanation of these contrasts might have appeared at first sight deceptively simple, corresponding approximately to areas of nucleated villages and mixed nucleated/

TABLE VII. *Parish–township Statistics for Welsh Border and near-by counties. Early nineteenth century*

	Area in sq. miles 1811	No. parishes¹	Average area per parish in sq. miles	Population 1811 (in thousands)	Average population per parish	% single-township parishes²	Average no. townships per parish²	% parishes with more than 7 townships²
E. Group								
N. Group — Lancashire	1766	74 (+2)	23·2	828	10,898	31	6·4	31
Cheshire	1052	84 (+6)	11·6	227	2522	20	6·0	27
Shropshire	1343	213 (+6)	6·1	194	887	53	3·6	13
S. Group — Herefordshire	863	211 (+5)	4·0	94	439	78	1·4	0·9
Monmouthshire	496	125	3·9	62	496	81	1·2	—
Gloucestershire	1258	318 (+28)	3·7	285	825	85	1·3	0·3
W. Group								
N. Group — Flintshire	244	28	8·7	46	1660	18	5·1	26
Denbighshire	633	60	10·5	64	1070	18	4·6	21
Montgomeryshire	839	53	15·8	51	979	10	4·5	26
S. Group — Radnorshire	426	47	9·0	20	444	74	1·5	—
Breconshire	754	64 (+3)	11·2	37	562	98	1·7	—
Glamorganshire	792	127	6·2	85	669	79	1·5	1·5

¹ The first figure excludes *towns* with more than one parish in the town itself. The figure in brackets represents the additional number of parishes in these towns.
² These figures are based on the rural parishes, i.e. they exclude the parishes numbered in the bracket in column 2.

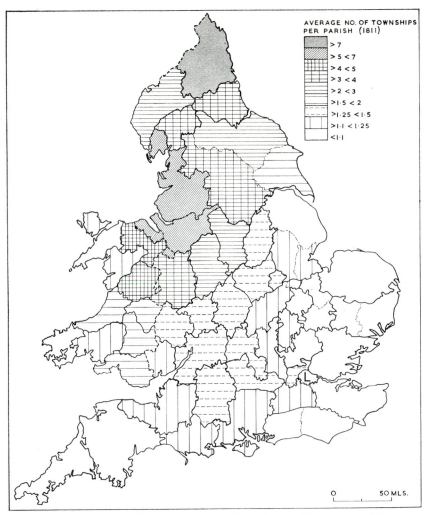

AVERAGE NO. OF TOWNSHIPS
PER PARISH (1811)

> 7
> 5 < 7
> 4 < 5
> 3 < 4
> 2 < 3
> 1·5 < 2
> 1·25 < 1·5
> 1·1 < 1·25
< 1·1

0 ____ 50 MLS.

19. England and Wales: average number of townships per parish (by counties) in 1811

dispersed settlement. But the extension to Wales immediately vitiates such a conclusion and makes it clear that though settlement geography may well have been an important factor in the limning of parishes, it cannot be invoked to explain the divisions within Wales or the similarity of the averages for south-eastern England and West Wales.

F2   S.R.L.W.B.

In an area south of a line drawn from the Humber to south Breconshire and west of a line enclosing Breconshire and the four remaining counties of mid- and north-east Wales, more than 70 per cent of all the rural parishes had only one township in 1811. But the really large parish does not begin abruptly to the north and west of this line. There is instead a transitional zone, very clearly marked in the diagonal belt across the English Midlands, where the average number of townships rises from 1·5 to over 3. The highest average and absolute number of townships per parish is to be found in two areas:

(a) Lancashire, Cheshire and Shropshire with an extension into Flintshire and Denbighshire; and (b) Northumberland. The lowest averages are in eastern England south of the Humber, south-western England (Devon and Cornwall) and the western peninsulas of Wales (Caernarvonshire and Pembrokeshire) all of which have an average of under 1·1 townships per parish. But south of a line drawn from the Humber to Herefordshire and Monmouthshire no county in southern England has more than 1·5 townships per parish. In the Welsh Borderland, from Cheshire to Monmouthshire, there is a fairly sharp gradation from the area with the second largest average number in the country to the second smallest average (see Table VII). On the basis of large parishes of more than 7 townships, the distribution is very similar. The county with the highest percentage of these is Northumberland (42·2 per cent) while Lancashire (31 per cent) and Cheshire, Flintshire, Denbighshire and Montgomeryshire (all 20–30 per cent) come second. Such large parishes are virtually non-existent in the southern division.

The inclusion of south-western England and of west and south Wales with southern England in this southern division renders void at the outset any simple, indeed any single, explanation of these two major subdivisions of England and Wales on the basis of parochial geography. Settlement patterns, the contrast between the Highland and Lowland Zone, between Celtic and Anglicised areas, between the English and the old Celtic Church areas, are all inapplicable to some part of the two main divisions, otherwise there would be a simple contrast between the parts of the country which have predominantly nucleated and predominantly dispersed or mixed settlement types, between the Highland Zone on the one hand and the Lowland Zone on the other, between the Celtic survival areas and those which became anglicised, or between parts of the country converted by and through the Augustinian mission from Rome and those parts which became part of the sphere of the Celtic Church in the period of the Conversion and afterwards. Nor do size and population density provide a complete answer, for on the basis of size most of Wales would go with northern England, and the whole of the south and the south-east would form a distinct area, with the addition of Anglesey and parts of southern Wales and Herefordshire (Fig. 18). As regards population, the earliest figures available (and those which are, therefore, nearest in date to the period of parish formation) are afforded by the Domesday Book and have been mapped for England by H. C. Darby.[1] Although contemporary Welsh figures are unavailable, the English returns certainly show a relationship to the parochial geography outlined above. Were the Welsh population returns available for that date, however, it is clearly unlikely that west and south Wales would compare with southern England, and thus population density is also insufficient to provide a complete explanation of the existence of two such strongly contrasted types of parish structure.

The Historical Geography of the Parish in England and Wales

All too little is known of the history of parish formation, but the difficulties of making clear geographical correlations render necessary a search for historical factors of another order. There is no certainty that even a handful of churches survive from the period of the Roman occupation. The earliest which are known to have existed in Britain are traceable to the period of the Conversion when, from the fifth century, Celtic missionaries brought the Christian faith to the west and north of the country. From the first, the Celtic Church was essentially a missionary Church accomplishing its work through the early Celtic 'saints' who wandered over most of the Highland Zone setting up primitive churches and hermit cells. During the fifth and sixth centuries,

[1] *An Historical Geography of England before 1800* (1936), p. 209 (fig. 25).

this Church spread over Ireland, Dumnonia, Wales, Scotland and Northumbria, but in the seventh century it divided to form an Irish-Scottish Church which stretched across Ireland and into the Highlands and eastern Lowlands of Scotland, and a British Church of which the territorial domain was Strathclyde, Wales and Dumnonia. By the end of the seventh century all Scotland, northern Ireland, northern England and the north Midlands were within the Irish-Scottish Church, leaving only Wales and Dumnonia in the British Church.

The Augustinian Mission sent by the Church of Rome to England began its work in Kent in A.D. 597, and by 660 southern England from Dorset to the lower Thames, together with Norfolk and Suffolk, was converted, leaving Essex, Bedfordshire and the south Midlands heathen. Although there is little positive evidence, the westward limit of Anglo-Saxon pagan cemeteries suggests that Celtic Christianity extended east in a line from Exeter to Cumbria, including the English side of the Welsh Border.

EARLY DIOCESAN INFLUENCE

The differences in organisation between the Celtic Churches and the early English Church were very considerable. Whereas in the Celtic Church territorial arrangements were at best of subsidiary interest, in the English Church they were from the beginning an outstanding feature. The earliest dioceses originated in the time of Augustine (597–668) and the earliest parishes have often been ascribed to his successor, Theodore of Tarsus (668–90). From the time of St Augustine, the policy was to consecrate bishops and to organise the country into dioceses under their care. The original plan was that St Augustine should consecrate twelve bishops and send another to York as a second metropolitan to create a further twelve for a northern province but this was never carried out in the form intended.[1] In the Welsh Border, Lichfield was created the centre of a see in 656, Hereford in 676 and Worcester in 680. In every case, the early dioceses were territorially linked with the kingdoms, Lichfield and Hereford serving Mercia, and Worcester

---

[1] Leicester, the twelfth southern diocese was only created in 737, and a permanent archbishopric came into being at York in 735 with Hexham, Lindisfarne and Whithorn as suffragan sees. These were afterwards reduced, though later Wilfred became bishop of Ripon serving western Deira.

the Hwicce, and since it is reasonable to suppose that early parochial organisation may have differed from the northern to the southern province and from diocese to diocese, the extent of the early English dioceses and kingdoms must be taken into consideration in relation to parish structure. Unfortunately for this argument both dioceses and Kingdoms suffered changes during the five or six hundred years preceding the Norman conquest and there were few stable boundaries during this period of political and ecclesiastical evolution.

The suggestion that parish structure varied in part with the diocese has a certain body of evidence to support it, but there are also difficulties. One of the most evident exceptions is the East Riding which, although it appears never to have been in the Southern Province, is more closely related in this matter to the south than the north, a fact which points to geographical influences such as the large number of villages, the comparative prosperity and the comparatively large density of population during the period of parish formation. Conversely, Lichfield is related in type to the north, although it belonged to the southern province and, in turn, St Asaph is of the northern type, though all the remaining early dioceses of Wales had small parishes.

There are and long have been many and diverse links between north-eastern Wales, the north-west of England and the north-west Midlands. In the seventh century Strathclyde, Wales, south-west England and – if the Celtic Church embraced the entire Welsh Borderland – probably mid-western England were within the fold of the British Church. Thomas[1] and many others have assumed that St Asaph or Llanelwy monastery was founded by Cyndeyrn or St Kentigern, bishop of Strathclyde, presumably having reached north-east Wales by the lowland of north-western England part of which was adjacent to if not included in his diocese. This ancient link would fit well with the similarity of parochial structure in the Welsh extension of the northern division though the story of Kentigern at St Asaph is shown by Kenneth Jackson to be less well supported by historical sources than by legend, and even to merit the epithet 'spurious'. But Jackson in a footnote mentions the mooting of a bishopric of St Asaph with the

[1] D. R. Thomas, *St. Asaph*, Diocesan History Series (London, 1888), ch. 1.

proposal that it should be under York, not Canterbury.[1] Whatever the historical detail, the ecclesiastical link between the diocese of St Asaph and the northern province seems to be of long standing.

As regards Lichfield, there are a number of interesting points to be noticed. Although Lichfield and Hereford dioceses both originated in the Anglian kingdom of Mercia, their parishes are contrasted in type, those of Lichfield belonging to the northern and those of Hereford to the southern division. The parishes of north Shropshire are generally multi-township, and about the line of the mid-Severn the small parish generally takes its place. There are of course exceptions on both sides of the Lichfield–Hereford boundary, for example the wide parish of Much Wenlock which arose from the subdivision of its extensive monastic estates, and in the north a number of single-township parishes which were consequential on manorial arrangements, some of which went back to the late eleventh century.[2] The boundary between the dioceses of Lichfield and Hereford corresponds approximately with that between the northern and southern divisions, and they cannot therefore have arisen as a result of political boundaries for both dioceses were Mercian.

Historically there was a close link between the Northumbrian Church and Lichfield going back to the seventh century when Diuma was made bishop of a see comprising Mercia, Mid-Anglia and Lindsey. Before 663 this see was divided into three dioceses which for a time at least seem to have been associated with Lindisfarne, not Canterbury. The Northumbrian mission to central England is still reflected in early dedications to Saints Oswald, Chad, Cuthbert and Wilfred.[3] Apart from one in Shropshire and one in Herefordshire, all lie on the English side of the Severn.

[1] 'The Sources for the Life of St. Kentigern' in *Studies in the Early British Church* (1958).

[2] The principle of distributing land among the barons in Domesday Shropshire was to give each a block of land across a strategic routeway and one or more manors in the more fertile land of the north Shropshire plain. Ford, a single-township parish in the north, was one of the isolated northern manors of Earl Roger. See Dorothy Sylvester, 'Rural Settlement in Domesday Shropshire', *Sociological Review* (1933).

[3] Of these early dedications, there are 4 to St Chad in Cheshire, 6 in Shropshire and 5 in Lancashire; 4 to St Wilfred in Cheshire and 5 in Lancashire; 4 to St Oswald in Cheshire, 1 in Lancashire, 1 in Shropshire; 1 to St Cuthbert in Shropshire (and possibly a second), 4 in Lancashire, and 1 in Herefordshire. The only ones in Wales are at Hanmer and Holt (both St Chad). Hanmer originated as a dependency of Haughmond abbey and its church was dedicated in the fifteenth century to the missionary who brought Christianity to this area.

The separateness of Lichfield was also demonstrated in the late eighth century when, for a few years, it became an archbishopric. Hill's view is that the pallium was bestowed for political rather than religious reasons,[1] but it is possible that its northern religious affinities were not altogether without influence, and even after the Lichfield metropolitan had lapsed (i.e. by A.D. 803) the quarrel with Canterbury continued.

In Wales in the Norman period the lack of a centralised authority proved as fatal to the independence of the Welsh Church as it did politically to the country. Before the eleventh century came to a close the Normans had begun to take measures to subject the Church in Wales to Canterbury. Llandaff, long linked with Hereford, Gloucester and Bristol, offered little resistance, and by 1107 it was subordinate to Canterbury, to be followed by St David's in 1115. Lloyd thinks that the diocese of St Asaph, which was in abeyance during this period, was divided, Tegeingl probably treated as part of the diocese of north-west Mercia (Chester for a brief period, then Lichfield and Coventry), and southern Powys perhaps attached for a time to St David's. Attempts to restore peace between York and Canterbury in 1125 brought the proposal to transfer the sees of Chester, Bangor and the dormant see of St Asaph to York. Lloyd interprets this as indicative of strong Normanisation in north-east Wales in religious matters,[2] and again the link was eastward and northward. By contrast the southern Borderland and the diocese of Hereford were more closely associated with the Welsh dioceses of Llandaff and St David's and their archdiocesan associations were always with Canterbury.

THE EARLY PARISHES

The early parishes were almost certainly large and ill-defined. The Latin *parochia* like the Greek *paroikia* indicated a primary unit and signified first a Christian community living in one place. It is even maintained by some writers that the original *parochia* was the equivalent of the later diocese, and that the latter was first known in the Roman Church as *provincia*, a term which in England was adopted for the primary archdiocesan division of the country.

[1] Geoffrey Hill, *English Dioceses* (1900), pp. 169–80.
[2] J. E. Lloyd, op. cit. ii, pp. 456–7.

The assumption that the early dioceses were first subdivided into large districts under minster churches from which the work of conversion was directed, and that in due course these gave rise to lesser areas under the care of parish churches (*ecclesiae* of the Middle Ages) and chapels (*capellae*) has much to commend it. During both the seventh and the eighth centuries and perhaps for much longer many parishes must have resembled the early townships in that they were bounded imprecisely by unoccupied land or by an area inhabited by the unconverted.[1]

Stenton distinguishes between head minsters or cathedral churches (i.e. with a bishop) and old minsters.[2] The first are known because of their historical importance and many have survived to this day, but the lesser minsters played a role which often went unrecorded, and they eventually subsided into the humbler role of parish church. Stenton takes the view that the O.E. *mynster* was a form of monastery if not identical with it.[3] A considerable number must have survived in the roles of 'mother church' (*matrix ecclesia*) and collegiate church a point which in some instances gives a possible clue to their identity, but many others not only lost status but disappeared. In the early eleventh century, Leominster, Pershore, Gloucester and Berkeley survived as monasteries; St Werburgh and St John (Chester) St Alkmund and St Chad (Shrewsbury), Wenlock, Morville, Bromfield and St Guthlac (Hereford) as secular monasteries, while Hereford alone in the Border counties proper was a cathedral minster.[4] Earlier minsters in some cases are suggested by their names (cf. Leominster), and in the Borderland there are also Minsterley, Shropshire (later submerged), Oswestry, Shropshire (Blancminster), Whitchurch, Shropshire (Album Monasterium) and Emstrey, Herefordshire (Eyminster).

Hunter Blair puts the old minsters and the lesser churches into separate categories.[5] The last had graveyards in contradistinction from the 'field churches' which had no graveyard and which may be compared with the later chapels which had no parochial status.

---

[1] The term 'heathen' originated from this very fact. They were the people of the heath.
[2] So called by the Old English code of law of 1014.
[3] *Anglo-Saxon England*, pp. 147–8.
[4] Stenton, op. cit. lists these as being in existence *circa* 1035 (p. 449).
[5] P. Hunter Blair, *An Introduction to Anglo-Saxon England* (1959), pp. 156–7.

Some of the field churches may have arisen on the site of ancient crosses. In Cheshire, the location of the pre-Norman crosses is of particular significance in relation to parish formation. The Mercian crosses (*c*. 750–900) were all on or near the sites of parish churches (e.g. Over, Sandbach, Chester); the late Mercian crosses were located near the Pennine Edge, but of these only Astbury and Cheadle were near parish churches; of the miscellaneous crosses all were on or near sacred sites, most of which are now parochial. The same is true of the Anglo-Norse crosses in Wirral.[1]

In the area of the Celtic Church in Wales and the Borderland, the three main types of religious foundation were (1) large monasteries, e.g. Bangor Is-coed, (2) *clas* churches corresponding approximately to the mother churches in England and collegiate in character, e.g. Llanynys (Denb.), Meifod (Mont.), Glascwm (Rad.), Caerwent (Mon.),[2] (3) lesser churches and hermit cells, corresponding to the English *ecclesiae* and *capellae* but without a parochial territory until Norman times. Both the Celtic and the English Churches were concerned with the extension of the Christian faith over the countryside, but whereas the English Church was from the first preoccupied with diocesan and parochial organisation, the Celtic Church long considered this a minor matter.

The theory of parish formation by subdivision of diocesan and minster territories probably accounts for the rise of the greater number of pre-Conquest parishes, though great lay landowners including kings must also have played their part in building churches on their lands in the Old English state. Stenton takes the view that most ancient minsters and their territories were tribal or folk divisions of the larger diocesan area which corresponded with an ancient kingdom or some other major political area, and that their eventual breakdown into parishes corresponded with the village communities and their (township) lands. This system applies perfectly to the southern division of the country, especially to Wessex where the original see broke up into dioceses which were at one time whole counties, and in them virtually every village

[1] Ed. Dorothy Sylvester and Geoffrey Nulty, op. cit. map and description of 'Pre-Norman Crosses' by Arthur Oakes, pp. 14–15.

[2] William Rees, *A Historical Atlas of Wales*. Plate 27 maps the mother churches of Wales.

became the centre of a parochial township. In much of the High-land Zone, by contrast, a naturally poor environment, a smaller population, and a settlement pattern in which the village was either occasional or absent, militated against the formation of numerous small parishes each neatly centred on a nucleated settlement. Like the northern diocese, the northern parish was tardy in origin, for territorial organisation was long in a state of flux, and the Welsh Church was simply not interested in parish formation.

The religious houses and the great collegiate churches continued to play their part in establishing chapels and churches in the coutryside, and comparatively distant parish churches were appropriated to them both before and after the Conquest. For example the abbey of St Werburgh in Chester, later the cathedral, eventually had over twenty churches in various parts of Cheshire, while prior to the Conquest as the Church of the Secular Canons, Neston church was linked with it.[1]

But whereas in England and in the marcher lordships the number of churches was greatly increased during the Middle Ages, in Wales the great spread of churches associated with the work of the Celtic saints during the Conversion was decelerated except where the estate of a monastery or a lay lord gave rise to new foundations and this happened more rarely in Wales than in England. Ecclesiastical organisation in Wales during this period was concerned to a large degree with hitching parishes to pre-existing churches of which in some parts there were large numbers, in others comparatively few. They were particularly numerous in Anglesey and Lleyn, in south-west Wales and in south-east Wales. Known Celtic dedications are fewer in the present-day counties of Flintshire, Denbighshire and Montgomeryshire, even in country likely to support a comparable density of population.[2] Unfortunately for this argument, it is the very area, as Bowen points out, where normanisation resulted in the changing of dedications. In the southern Borderland surviving Celtic dedications are more numerous though normanisation was at least as intensive, and it remains a possibility that the Celtic saints did in

[1] Sylvester and Nulty, op. cit. map and text 'Medieval Religious Houses' by Maurice Ridgway, pp. 24–5.
[2] E. G. Bowen, *The Settlements of the Celtic Saints in Wales*, ch. 6 and fig. 28.

fact leave a sparser distribution of churches in the northern than in the southern flank of eastern Wales.

The Domesday Book, which should offer a check on the pre-Norman parish churches, is sadly incomplete even when priests are added to the list. The number of places in Cheshire mentioned in Domesday as having either a church or a priest was twenty-five, in Shropshire fifty-three, in Herefordshire thirty-four. Traces of Saxon work in other churches and early dedications add to the number, but many Saxon churches must have been built of very impermanent material and left no tangible trace, while numerous early dedications have been lost. Even in stone country which is extensive along the Welsh Border, few pre-Norman churches survived either on the Welsh or English side without rebuilding (Fig. 43). The greatest period of church building was the Middle Ages, and from the Conquest great landowners, whether lay or religious, founded and built churches and chapels and extended and crystallised the parish system. Many parish churches in heavily normanised counties such as Herefordshire originated as private chapels. Where there was no village or where the lord's estate was large, they were in many cases built within or adjacent to the demesne so becoming, like the Celtic churches, solitary and separate from the community even though they eventually ranked as parochial. Nether Alderley in Cheshire, Adderley and Kinlet in Shropshire, Kentchurch in Herefordshire, Penhow in Monmouthshire are only a few of the many examples of such siting. In addition there were considerable numbers of domestic chapels which generally retained this status or went out of use. Leycester listed seventeen of these as existing in Cheshire in 1669 or but recently disused.[1] Occasionally monastic churches became parish churches at the Dissolution as was the case at Leominster where a considerable part of the parish church is monastic in origin. The Dissolution was also a period of re-formation of parishes as well as dioceses. Whitegate and Brereton parishes in Cheshire were both created in the time of Henry VIII, Whitegate from the lands of Vale Royal Abbey. The latter has a church which was built by the Brereton family near Brereton Hall in the time of Richard I and was first a chapel in Astbury parish.

[1] Sir Peter Leycester, *Historical Antiquities* (1673), pp. 192–7.

CONTRASTS IN THE PAROCHIAL GEOGRAPHY AND
HISTORY OF CHESHIRE AND HEREFORDSHIRE

Cheshire and Herefordshire lying one in the northern and one in
the southern division of the country illustrate a number of contrasts in parochial geography. Apart from Whalley in Lancashire
with forty-four, Cheshire included the two largest parishes in
England in terms of numbers of townships: Great Budworth with
thirty-five and Prestbury with thirty-two at the tithe commutation
period. Both were divided into three parts including in each case
two dependent chapelries. In the Middle Ages, Prestbury was
even larger, before the later parishes of Nether Alderley and
Gawsworth were taken from it, but even in the middle nineteenth
century it was reckoned the most extensive parish in Cheshire in
terms of acreage (60,378). The majority of Cheshire parishes included a number of townships, the average for the county being
six per parish. Despite having an area nearly 200 square miles
larger than that of Herefordshire, the total number of ecclesiastical
parishes in the tithe commutation period was only 90 including
six in Chester. A few one-township parishes are ancient, for
example Church Lawton which was a manor of the abbey of St
Werburgh (Chester) and Baddiley whose church was built by
the Praers family and given by them to the abbey of Combermere
in the mid-fourteenth century. Of the remaining thirteen single-
township parishes in Cheshire, most broke away from larger ones
at comparatively early dates.

In Herefordshire parish-township structure is completely
different. Of its 211 rural parishes in the early nineteenth century
165 were single townships, 26 had two townships, 12 had three
and only 8 had more than three, the largest being Leintwardine
with twelve and Leominster with ten. The single-township dominated Herefordshire parochial geography and the multi-township
parish was a comparative rarity. The average Herefordshire
parish had only a little more than one-third of the area and two-
fifths of the population of the average Cheshire parish in 1811.

The reasons for this contrast can be hazarded on lines already
followed, and are related to the periods at which they developed.
In *circa* 1291, the taxation returns of Pope Nicholas IV provided

lists of parish churches and chapels for the whole of England and Wales arranged under dioceses in turn divided into diaconates.[1] For Cheshire another list is available for 1669 in Leycester's *History*.[2] The following table summarises their growth:

		Cheshire (*1052 sq. m.*) (*excluding Chester*)	Herefordshire (*863 sq. m.*) (*excluding Hereford*)
Domesday (1086)	(Places with churches and/ or priests)	24	33
Pope Nicholas IV (1291)		54	198
Leycester (Cheshire only) (1669)		73	
Tithe Commutation (c. 1840)		84	211

From this it seems that 93·8 per cent of Herefordshire's rural parishes of the tithe commutation period were in existence by 1291 but only 64·3 per cent of those of Cheshire. In other words, the task of parish formation was all but complete in Herefordshire before the end of the thirteenth century, whereas in Cheshire, it continued by division, only 86·9 per cent of the early nineteenth-century parishes being numbered even in the 1669 lists, and only 64·2 per cent in the *Lincoln Taxation*.

In 1086, Cheshire was one of the poorest counties in the Norman realm with a population so small that only Middlesex and Rutland (to use present areas and boundaries) counted fewer inhabitants. Herefordshire, by contrast, was both rich and intensively normanised, and if 5–6 people are allowed for every person enumerated in Domesday, Herefordshire's population density at that time was approximately 30 per square mile as compared with Cheshire's 10. Norman predilection for Herefordshire showed itself not only in the building of numerous castles, minor defences and manor-houses, but in a spate of church building, and over seventy of its country or small town churches have Norman work in them. Many more are of Norman or earlier foundation. This

---

[1] *Taxatio Ecclesiastica Angliae et Walliae, auctoritate P. Nicholai IV, circa A.D. 1291*, Record Commission, 1802. Also known as the *Lincoln Taxation*. The 1254 Taxation is distinguished as the *Norwich Taxation*. The *Valor Ecclesiasticus* of 1534 provides a third list.

[2] Op. cit. pp. 190–9.

sudden springing to full stature in Norman times is very characteristic of Herefordshire, whereas Cheshire developed only slowly.
But by 1811 the population figures for the two counties had been
reversed, Cheshire leading with a density of 215 per square mile,
nearly double the Herefordshire density of 109. The parish geography, however, had long since crystallised and although some
new parishes were created in Cheshire during the nineteenth
century, as in other areas of vigorous growth, the rural pattern of
multi-township parishes remained.

THE PAROCHIAL GEOGRAPHY OF THE EAST WELSH COUNTIES

The change from a northern to a southern pattern is repeated
from Flintshire southward to Monmouthshire, and its origins
may possibly go back to the days of the Celtic saints, or may be
medieval, or both. There is no reliable Domesday check, for only
portions of the Welsh counties were assessed, and in any case the
parish system had still to be introduced into the greater part of
the country. In the *Taxation of Pope Nicholas IV* there were listed
more than 110 churches in the diocese of St Asaph as compared
with 90 in 1254.[1] In the meantime, sixteen deaneries had replaced
the eight of 1254, and some twenty churches had been raised to
the status of *ecclesia* (or their omission from the 1254 lists put
right). During the years of the Owain Glyndwr revolt, the Church
in Wales suffered. Owain burnt the cathedral and the bishop's
and canon's houses at St Asaph, and the Cathedral and palace
stood in ruins for eighty and a hundred years respectively. During
the latter part of the eighteenth century, the Church suffered
losses on account of the rise of Nonconformity, but the formation
of the Diocesan Church Building Society in St Asaph in 1834
began an era of expansion – the most important since the thirteenth century. Even allowing for a net loss of twenty-eight
churches to other dioceses in 1862, the diocese of St Asaph included 207 benefices in 1888 as compared with 131 in 1835,[2] most
of the new ones representing a response to the growing needs of
an expanding mining and industrial population.

[1] *Taxation of Pope Innocent IV* or the *Vetus Valor* or *Norwich Taxation*, Cottonian Coll.,
Vitellius, cx, reproduced in *Mont. Coll.* (1887), pp. 331 ff.
[2] Thomas, op. cit. (1888), pp. 47–66 and 96–111.

Apart from the creation of new parishes during the industrial period, the northern counties of eastern Wales retained the multi-township pattern and the ancient parishes of Flintshire, Denbighshire and Montgomeryshire showed a preponderance of large, spreading parishes with a scattered population and numerous dependent townships. In Flintshire, the largest number of townships in any one parish was in Hawarden whose boundaries followed those of the old marcher lordship and included sixteen townships. The average for the county was over five. In Denbighshire, the largest was Llanarmon-yn-Iâl with fourteen townships, though Llanrhaeadr-ym-Mochnant counted sixteen of which ten only were in Denbighshire and six in Montgomeryshire, while in Montgomeryshire Kerry had nineteen. The average number for the two counties was 4·6 and 4·5 respectively.

Those parts of the Welsh Border counties in Llandaff and St David's followed the southern pattern with a preponderance of one-township parishes, a characteristic most strongly marked in Monmouthshire where the average per parish was as low as 1·2 in the early nineteenth century, and only nine parishes had as many as three townships.

LATER PAROCHIAL DEVELOPMENTS

The earliest phase of parish formation appears to go back to the seventh century, and there was probably no break in the slow progress of dividing up the dioceses throughout the Old English period. Indeterminate boundaries were an early feature but even on the first and second editions of the Ordnance Survey One-Inch maps of the Welsh counties there are examples of parish boundaries not being drawn in across mountainous country. The medieval expansion of the parish system continued vigorously from the Conquest to the late thirteenth century in southern England, and then probably almost ceased until, at the Reformation, changes followed the dissolution of the monasteries. In many cases the archdeaconries, rural deaneries and parishes differed little in the *Taxation of Pope Nicholas IV*, the *Valor Ecclesiasticus* of 1534–5, and in the period preceding changes initiated by the Reform Parliaments of 1832 onwards. In Herefordshire there was no further need for subdivision after the thirteenth century for the ultimate pattern of small single-township parishes had already been reached by that date, as was probably the case in almost the whole of the southern division. But where large parishes existed and their population increased, occasional legislation was brought in to cover their division as for example after the Restoration when an Act of 14 Car. II (1662) made partitioning possible where a vill or hamlet existed in a dependent township.[1] This Act relating to Cheshire, Yorkshire, Derbyshire, Lancashire, Cumberland, Westmorland, Northumberland and Durham made implicit recognition of part of the northern division discussed here, but it could be made to refer to other counties where necessary. Unions were also allowed, mainly in the towns, by Acts passed during the eighteenth and nineteenth centuries, and the division of parishes was again provided for following on the unprecedented growth of population in the middle and later nineteenth century.[2]

In the diocese of St Asaph which included Flintshire, Denbighshire, Montgomeryshire and part of north-west Shropshire, twenty-three new churches were built between 1836 and 1894[3] and from 1817 to 1902 approximately sixty new parishes were formed,[4] principally in the coalfield, along Deeside and in the area of the rapidly growing North Wales resorts. Some developing rural areas were also affected where the large rural parishes were unwieldly, but for the most part the ecclesiastical parishes have kept their age-old shape and their numerous dependent townships.

The effects of Nonconformity on the countryside

In terms of its influence on settlement, Nonconformity has passed through three phases: itinerancy, worship in licensed meeting houses and the building of chapels. The first of these was negative; in the second it was usual to make use of existing cottage kitchens or farmhouses, and in itself was uninfluential, but it laid the

---

[1] W. E. Tate in *The Parish Chest* points out that in fact this operated where a township had a constable (Cambridge, 1951), p. 11.

[2] For example the Division of Parishes Act, 1882.

[3] D. R. Thomas, *The History of the Diocese of St. Asaph*, 3 vols. (1906–13), vol. i, p. 207.   [4] Ibid. vols ii and iii.

foundations of the chapel building phase and in many cases established the approximate location of the chapels.

The beginnings of the dissenting movement in the Welsh Borderland go back to 1639 when a church was organised on the Puritan model at Llanvaches in Monmouthshire, and at about the same time separatists appeared in the remote Olchon valley in the Black Mountains in Welsh speaking Herefordshire, followers of the London Baptists. Among early dissenters' churches were those set up by Baptists at Hay and Abergavenny.[1]

When the Toleration Act in 1689 allowed dissenters freedom to worship if their meeting houses were licensed, the way was open for the slow growth of a movement which was eventually to have considerable influence on the face of rural Britain, and not least on the Borderland. Discontent with the clergy and the state of the Church was rife in Wales, pluralism was common, and many churches were either rarely or never used. The way was thus open for the rise of the numerous dissenting societies which arose, at first slowly, then rapidly, especially from the 1730s. Baptists and Methodists, both Calvinist and Wesleyan, were the most numerous among the early dissenting groups, but many were known simply as independent or presbyterian. The eventual distinction between Methodism organised in 'circuits' and the remaining Nonconformist churches which developed as separate societies was to be of importance, for the last were independent congregations eventually with their own minister and became in terms of physical settlement a chapel-manse group, the manse typically adjoining the chapel. By contrast, the English Methodist Churches, notably the Primitive and Wesleyan, were organised in circuits, with the ministers and the head churches normally located in the towns and leaving the country chapels as single elements (or perhaps chapel-schoolroom) as contrasted with the congregational chapel-manse pair of buildings. The circuits of the English Methodist Church extend into Wales, especially along the eastern border, but on the whole the chapel-manse pair predominates on the Welsh side of the boundary, the chapel alone in rural areas on the English side.

[1] Quakerism was brought to Radnorshire and Montgomeryshire in the late 1650s but decayed following emigration due to persecution. A similar fate befell the Arminian Baptists in 1683.

Although dissent first spread during the seventeenth century the physical pattern of settlement was barely affected until the eighteenth when the Baptist and Calvinist movements gathered way, and Wesleyan Methodism began its widespread activities. Welsh Methodism under Howell Harris extended rapidly after 1735. The first building was erected at Dygoedydd, near Caerphilly in 1742, but there were other early centres in the Borderland proper at Oswestry and Pontypool. In 1743, the first Wesleyan chapel in Wales opened at Cardiff. But in all the churches, the three stages of itinerancy, cottage or farmhouse meetings, and finally chapel building succeeded each other, and where the chapel was associated with an adjoining manse, there was often the need for stabling for the horses of both preacher and congregation.[1]

The spread of Wesleyan Methodism in the Borderland and nearby areas during the early phase (eighteenth and early nineteenth centuries) brings out some interesting geographical relationships and gaps. At this time, cultural movements took place principally along the increasingly numerous turnpike roads, by no means all of which followed the ancient valley and upland ways. The cultural contact areas of the period are reflected in the major routes followed by the extension of Methodism. Its rural extension only gathered way from the middle of the nineteenth century, and already by that time there were many Baptist and Presbyterian churches in the villages and hamlets especially in the southern Borderland.[2] Spreading from the towns where it became established and active at comparatively early dates, the Wesleyan movement in the Borderland expanded from Cardiff over Glamorgan and Monmouthsire. From Brecon it covered much of the upland edge, southwards into the South Wales coalfield and northwards as far as Wrexham where it mingled with the southerly extension from Ruthin, the third main centre of dispersal along the eastern edge of the Welsh massif. Another centre stemming from Brecon was Kington from which the movement spread to Leominster, here meeting the expansion up the Severn valley from Gloucester, Worcester, Birmingham and Stourport which affected Herefordshire and south Shropshire.

[1] Leslie F. Church, *The Early Methodist People* (1948), p. 73.

[2] Hywel D. Emanuel, 'Dissent in the Counties of Glamorgan and Monmouth', *N.L.W. Journal* (1954 and 1955). When they were established many of these congregations described themselves simply as protestant or independent.

The Cheshire movement was linked with Wrexham, Manchester, Liverpool and to a lesser extent Chester, and from the Wrexham and Macclesfield centres south Cheshire and north Shropshire were brought in. The gaps at this period lay from west to east between Whitchurch and Shrewsbury, and south of Hereford, and the map makes clear that the east–west Anglo-Welsh links were closer than those from north to south.

During the latter half of the nineteenth century country chapels belonging to one or other of the English Methodist Churches sprang up in a great number of country villages and hamlets and in country where scattered dwellings were characteristic. The membership of the Wesleyan Church alone rose from 90,000 in 1800 to 358,000 in 1850 (mainly accounted for by the town congregations) and by 1906 reached 498,000,[1] an appreciable part of the later increase being a result of the expansion in small country towns and the rural areas beyond. In the towns and larger villages, the influence of the chapel on the physical plan was negligible, but in the extensive areas which carried only hamlets or dispersed dwellings, it became a significant nucleating force, as well as an expression of the increasing divergence of opinion between squire and tenantry. Yeoman farmers and cottagers alike contributed to the building funds which made possible the erection of huge numbers of Nonconformist chapels during the nineteenth century, until they became far more numerous than the parish churches, especially in the northern Borderland with its large, multi-township parishes. Fervour no doubt overran discretion in many cases, and sectional rivalry was a further powerful factor impelling the spate of building which took place from the 1850s until early this century.

It would be a formidable task to attempt to trace the effect, hamlet by hamlet, of the chapels as a nucleating factor. Many hamlets existed already, but it is undoubtedly the case that the chapels provided a centre around which new cottages sprang up. The rural areas have nothing to show which compares with the mining and quarrying districts where large urbanised villages and even towns arose round the nuclei of Nonconformist chapels,[2]

---

[1] *Hall's Circuits and Ministers*, 4th ed., pp. 607–9.

[2] The classic examples are places such as the slate-quarrying centres of Bethesda and Ebenezer in Caernarvonshire which were named after their chapels, but the chapel exercised its nucleating influence in many other places of nineteenth-century growth.

but the parallel is none the less valid. In south Cheshire and the adjoining parts of north Shropshire, examples of chapel hamlets are particularly numerous within the lines of early expansion between Wrexham and Macclesfield.[1] Associated particularly with the founders of Primitive Methodism are Mow Cop, primarily a quarrying centre and Englesea Brook, a small but compact rural hamlet consisting of late nineteenth-century cottages grouped round a Primitive Methodist chapel and its graveyard.[2] Many of the chapel hamlets are on settlement sites which long pre-date the chapels as their names and ancient records testify, but as in the cases of Blakenhall and Shavington the chapels provided a new centre of local growth and it was fortunate for the chapels that their founding corresponded with a period of increasing population and was aided by miscellaneous economic factors. For example, Shavington near Crewe is an ancient manor which in 1830 consisted only of a handful of scattered farms and cottages. The opening of railway lines centring on Crewe between 1837 and 1858 led to railway workers taking up residence in a number of outlying country places and between 1851 and 1901 the population of Shavington doubled. After a period of cottage meetings the Wesleyan Methodists built a chapel here in 1826, to be followed by a second built by the Warrenites in 1837 (later a United Methodist church and now the headquarters of Toc H in Shavington). A third (no longer in use as a place of worship) was built by the Independent Methodists, and a fourth on the outskirts by the Primitive Methodists. This is an extreme example, but by no means unique.[3]

Ecclesiastical influence on the countryside is thus varied and far-reaching. The Church of England and the Church of Wales throughout their long history have provided the dominant architectural feature of most English country parishes, part of the church–parsonage–glebe–churchyard–tithe-barn–church hall complex which is characteristic and which in much of England is

[1] For example, Wettenhall, Winterley, Oakhanger, Blakenhall, Buerton, Hankelow, Hatherton, Faddiley, Coxbank, Shavington, Englesea Brook, Burleydam, Aston near Wrenbury, Bradfield Green near Crewe, Barbridge, Hall Green and Mow Cop.

[2] Mow Cop is the site of annual camp meetings commemorating the founding of the Primitive Methodist movement. Hugh Bourne is buried in the graveyard at Englesea Brook.

[3] The history of this hamlet including its Nonconformist activities is described by Geoffrey Nulty in *Shavington, the Story of a South Cheshire Village* (1959).

the focal point of a nucleated village. Although its nucleating influence was lacking or negligible until the eighteenth century in most of Wales and much of the Borderland, the Welsh Church provided nonetheless the most permanent feature of the architectural scene and most Welsh parishes took their name from the patron saints. With the expansion of trade and communications from the late seventeenth century, some villages arose to provide markets and other facilities for scattered Welsh and Border districts, and in many cases the focus of the new centre was the church. The later Nonconformist chapels, though less ancient and less influential in the villages, have proved one of the most important foci of hamlets of nineteenth-century growth, and in many of them the chapel-manse, the chapel-school, or the chapel alone stands significantly as the only public building-complex among its late cottages and houses.

9 Nucleation and Dispersal

FROM the publication of Meitzen's *Siedelung und Agrarwesen der Westgermanen und Ostgermanen* in Berlin in 1895, much of the interest of students of rural settlement has revolved round the question of nucleation and dispersal. Meitzen's *haufendorf* or agglomerated village and his *einzelhof* or solitary dwelling have become the universal standards of assessment from which this study begins. The happy simplicity, however, of the concept that associated nucleation and the open field system with the Teutonic people, and dispersal and individual cultivation with the Celtic, has slowly been forced to give way before more intensive research in a number of countries. Celtic dispersal in Britain is now recognised to be secondary rather than primary, and many other causes of nucleation can be added to the tradition of nucleated villages associated with Teutonic folk.

Classification of settlements as nucleated or dispersed is not rendered easier by the numerous intermediate arrangements which are immediately encountered on any large-scale map. Villages large and small, hamlets, semi-dispersal and dispersal may appear to be self-explanatory terms but classification necessarily remains to some degree subjective. There is no agreed standard of division between them based on size or form. Nor does the number of houses and their grouping of necessity remain unaltered from century to century. The early and middle part of the nineteenth century has been taken for various reasons as the standard period for the mapping of nucleation and dispersal as seen in Figs 3, 20 and 21.[1]

As the village of the Borderland is rarely large, it has been so classified on these maps on the basis of comparative size or

[1] Nucleation and dispersal in these maps has been based on the One-inch tithe edition of the O.S. supplemented where necessary from the tithe maps themselves. This series varies in date from about 1830 to 1860 in the Borderland. The township has been adopted as the unit and, with certain exceptions, nucleation, dispersal, etc., have been mapped within these township boundaries.

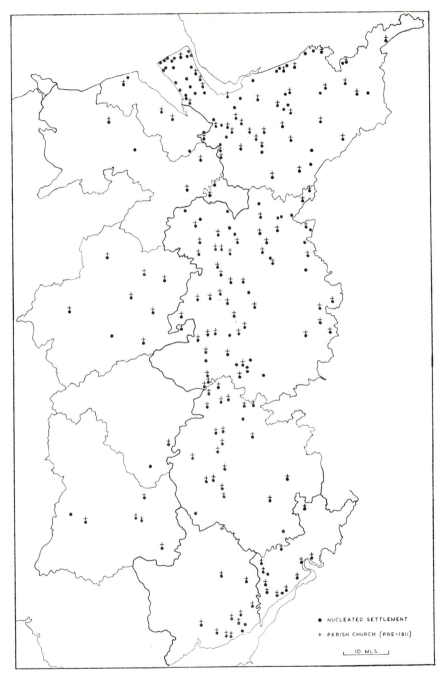

NUCLEATED SETTLEMENT

+ PARISH CHURCH (PRE-1811)

10 MLS.

20. The Welsh Borderland: nucleated villages (mid-nineteenth century).

marked nucleation or both. A hamlet has in general been taken as a minor nucleation of at least six to ten houses. Where nucleation is absolute, the white space around it corresponds to the uninhabited environs, usually but not always running up to the township boundary. Although there are self-evident limits to the historical value of early nineteenth-century maps for this purpose, there is no doubt that they are superior to the modern map in that they usually pre-date urban and suburban expansion associated with the mining and industrial ventures of the Industrial Period, and no earlier period yields a universal cover of large-scale maps and associated statistical information such as the early volumes of the Censuses of Population. In most of the Borderland, change has been remarkably slow, and it is probable that the settlements and administrative boundaries of the early nineteenth century were very similar for some centuries previously.

Factors affecting Nucleation and Dispersal

NUCLEATION

The reasons for, and the advantages of, nucleation spring to mind more readily than those for dispersal. Physically, the clustering of dwellings is usually on sites which are locally incomparable. These may include a spring or bourne; a river bank at a point of special advantage such as a ford, a bridging point, or a place above flood level but with the advantages of the alluvial belt for well water and the watering and depasturing of cattle; a hill top in a strategically commanding position; low plateaux suitable for the plough in dissected terrain where valley sides and valley bottoms are less accessible than upland; sites well placed for production and trade at the junction of unlike zones; a confluence point; the edge of woodland; or a place difficult of access in time of war and pillage. Most of these can be exemplified time and again in the Borderland.

The sites of springs and the junction of unlike zones account physically for the sites of hamlets at the foot of Wenlock Edge. The three Strettons in Shropshire are on a spring line in a fertile vale with all the advantages of alluvial land, water for cattle and nearby pasture on the hills. Most of the larger streams of the

Borderland are strung with settlements, for example the Wye, the Lugg, the Usk, the Severn, the Tern, the Perry and the Weaver in their lowland courses. Despite the disadvantages of gradient, poor soils and difficult water supply Prees and Wentnor and other hill villages still survive on hill tops, and in Cheshire on marsh-island sites or on low hills near marshes as in the cases of Dunham on the Hill and Barrow. Not only physical, but strategic and religious factors are usually involved in such siting. Even as late, however, as the nineteenth century, quarrying gave rise to the not inconsiderable village of Mow Cop[1] on the steep, knife-like sandstone edge which marks the boundary between Cheshire and Staffordshire. Settlements on the woodland fringe have already been seen to be part of the normal advance of colonisation, and they are numerous in the Borderland in all four English border counties. Confluence points of minor importance are occupied by villages or hamlets as at Worfield and Clun (Sa.) while vanished Caus is a monument to the former advantages of a commanding but inaccessible position which, because of its inaccessibility, failed to survive after the Tudors had brought peace to the Borderland.

In a community where the agricultural tradition leaned towards cultivation, and especially where the open-field system was followed, a centrally placed and clustered group of dwellings offered all the commoners equal advantages of access to the common fields. Such a pattern was ideal in lowlands and even in fertile vales, but in hill country ploughland is scarce and may only be found in small patches. In the seventeenth century land hunger could be assuaged by allotting not less than four acres of common field on which to build a new house. Records of this practice in the Wardens' Accounts of Bunbury (Ch.) explain the rise of a second (and now larger) nucleation, Lower Bunbury, on the edge of the old Town Field.[2] The process was still incomplete at the time of the tithe survey, but has continued into the present century with the result that Lower Bunbury is now a large and flourishing village.

Socially, the clustering of houses in a village has much to commend it, and this applies particularly to women and children

---

[1] Mow Cop exemplified the religious associations of hill sites in reverse. It became the rallying point in the early nineteenth century for Primitive Methodism.
[2] Fred H. Crossley, *Cheshire* (1949), pp. 245–6.

who, in a dispersed community may be out of touch with their neighbours for days, especially in winter in the Welsh mountains and where, as formerly, communication was only by tracks. That this is regarded differently by the Celt and the Anglo-Saxon, however, is abundantly evident. The focus of nucleation by the Middle Ages was characteristically the church, in both the morphological and the social sense. In most nucleated English villages the site of the church is central or dominant and the site of an ancient church is often indicative of the origin of the community. Thus a mound church suggests a group with hill traditions, a valley church a valley community and a hill church with the village below it, as in Pontesbury (Sa.), is strongly suggestive of a downhill movement of population. In Wales and the area served by the early Celtic Church the tradition was quite different, for the priest was 'not of the blood' and the solitary church was to be found everywhere. Its distribution over much of the English Border-land offers a key to Celtic influence. The isolation of Anglo-Norman churches, from a very different social motive, can in many cases, though not all, be distinguished from that of early Celtic sites.

As the centuries passed, various local factors operated to give rise to new clustered villages. Some, like Lower Bunbury, developed away from the old parochial centre. In Wales, the erstwhile solitary church site where the *ty'n llan* had perhaps been the only house, might become the focus at last of a small village. The occasional earlier Welsh nucleations were typically in a *maerdref*; more rarely at especially favourable sites. Among the commonest causes of the growth of villages after the Norman Conquest was the rise of a market or of new strategic centres. If they were well placed in relation to communications, a town might develop. But remoter markets such as abounded in south Shropshire, south Monmouthshire and other parts of the Marches, lapsed and, like the lesser defensive sites, settled back to village status. Some, like Caus (Sa.) vanished completely. Others, like Montgomery, New Radnor and Whittington sank back to the status of minor settlements.

Every county in England has its lapsed markets, but in the Marches, where the marcher lords almost automatically set up their market and castle in the place they selected as the *caput* of the lordship, and where in Tudor and Stuart times the wool trade in many areas continued to give a *raison d'être* for their continuance, they are particularly numerous. By the mid-Tudor period the decreasing need for castles and for many of the over-numerous markets had led to the decline of many boroughs and market centres. By the industrial period when the wool trade was also in decline, still more became redundant. In Shropshire, where sixty markets were established in the thirteenth century and only fourteen of these still functioned by 1950, Clun since then has tried to stage a revival, Wem is in difficulties because of the opposition of local tradespeople, and Much Wenlock has attempted but failed to revive its own market.[1] Over the county, ex-market centres range in size from tiny Holdgate in Corvedale which is now not even a hamlet, to Hodnet where the small market-place still offers proof of a market which had lapsed by the eighteenth century, and Acton Burnell where the castle was of major importance and the market which was established by the Burnells was only of minor importance, and so died out.

Civil administrative functions attached mainly to the county towns, but courts of various types, and merchant and trade gilds existed in many lesser centres from the Norman period in particular. These served to enhance the centralising functions of places which otherwise might never have reached more than village status. Some, like Overton (Fl.) have now become the administrative centres of rural districts or are themselves small centres of urban districts, like Much Wenlock (Sa.), though in size and character many are only villages.

As travel increased mainly from the Stuart period, first the stage coaches and in turn railways and modern road travel created new foci and resulted in a spurt of growth in many lesser old hamlets and villages. Where accurate large-scale maps are not available, it is not always easy to trace these by direct means. Indirectly, proof can often be found, as, for example, by comparing Edward Lhwyd's accounts collected during the years 1696–1701 of Welsh places which he visited or from which he elicited answers to his questionnaires, with Census of Population figures for the period from 1801 onwards.[2] Northop (Fl.) according to Lhwyd had '*deg a deigein o dai . . . wrth yr eglwys*' (50 houses near the church) and was the parochial village for five townships and four

---

[1] Fig. 16, p. 125.

[2] Ed. Rupert H. Morris, Edward Lhwyd's *Parochialia, Archaeol. Camb. Supplement* (1909–11).

'*pentrevydh*' (*pentrefydd* or hamlets).[1] Lying on what was to become
the post road to Holyhead prior to the building of the present A5
road in the early nineteenth century, Northop grew and in 1801
had a population of 2212 and 381 houses. Similarly Lhwyd records
that Bangor on Dee had 26 houses in the village,[2] and its dependency Alrhey '8 scattering houses', while of Pickhill in the same
parish he wrote 'Pickhill scatters much'. Bangor on Dee township
had a population of 560 in 1801, living in 115 houses.

DISPERSAL

Dispersal appears to be associated primarily with pastoralism
and with allodial land-holding, but whatever the cause, by its
very nature emphasis is laid on the individual household and the
family. In Wales, this state of affairs appears to have predominated
by the early Middle Ages, but then the loose clusters were still
associated by kinship and inheritance with the original *gwely*.
After Union, the end of gavelkind and increased compacting of
holdings brought about a truer and thinner dispersion. Yet the
contrast with the typical mid-English position where the village
by that time was the key to social links, did not necessarily mean a
weakening in social relationships since the tribal basis of society
still remained strong in that country, and blood ties, rather than
locational ties, were the cement of Welsh rural society – as indeed
they still are today. The community link only appears weaker to
English eyes because dispersed *tyddynod* and inter-aration in
scattered ploughing strips replaced the clustered houses and the
adjoining common arable fields of the more familiar English village.

The factors which shaped Welsh settlement patterns were, like
the patterns themselves, frequently different from those which
moulded the English village. Pastoralism rather than cultivation
dominated the agricultural régime. The need for defence which
drove the Anglo-Normans into compact settlements sent the
Welsh scattering into the hills. Nucleation broke down in favour
of dispersal. But dispersal appeared in England also under the
Anglo-Normans. Manorialism, where it took root in virgin territory, produced numerous scattered communities in east Cheshire
and east Shropshire, in much of Herefordshire and parts of Mon-

[1] Ibid. 1, pp. 86–9.   [2] Ibid. 1, pp. 134–5.

mouthshire. These park-estate communities, dominated by the manor-house, were especially characteristic of woodland which had survived the Anglo-Saxon inroads. The late Anglo-Saxon *leah* settlements have also survived in most cases as small hamlets only or as dispersed communities.

When, by Tudor times, Britain had recovered from the loss of population consequent on the Black Death, one of the solutions of expanded numbers in the old villages was to allow squatting on the heaths, the moorland edges, and the fringes of the woodlands. If a cottage could be erected sufficiently between sunset and sunrise to allow smoke to come out of its chimney at dawn, a claim could be made by custom on the land on which it stood. The *ty un nos*[1] was the exact equivalent in Wales. Their denizens were automatically excluded from sharing the open arable fields and became semi-individual holders in loosely dispersed or semi-dispersed squatting groups untidily set around the commons. Later, legalised commons enclosure resulted in a pattern of new, often large, dispersed farms difficult to distinguish by habitation pattern alone from the earlier Celtic *tyddynod* of the old *trefydd* and rendering difficult the problem of whether many of these lonely farmsteads in Wales and the Border were Celtic in origin, enclosure period, or a mixture of both.

With the less intensive land use of pastoralism and with the onset of severalty farming, the advantages of dispersal were unexpectedly underlined, but basic physical necessities such as a good water-supply, good building-sites, material supplies, and the means of communication to render them accessible and reasonably cheap, and now the added problems of piped water, gas, and electricity, telephonic and postal communication exaggerate the disadvantages. Socially too, many modern Welsh tend to see the advantages of centrality, but for the natural solitary it is still a drawback. The shepherd is a solitary, and so, often, is the farmer. But if isolation came to be preferred by the Celt and eschewed by the Anglo-Saxon, it is essential to remember the strength of the blood tie as a balancing factor. The English village also had close blood links, but the English thought primarily, not in terms of the tribe or the blood, but of a village society and its constituent links.

Any large-scale enterprise is hindered in a countryside of

[1] Literally 'house in one night'.

scattered population. Today, solutions such as the occasional market or cattle fair and the labour camp are employed to offset the difficulties resulting on non-centralised community life, which cars, buses, trains and telephones do something to relieve. Of the few villages in Welsh Wales, some at least appear to have arisen late as a response to such requirements. Nevertheless, in the pre-modern days, when need arose, the scattered families had their own means of communication, and long before the telephone was introduced, shepherds from miles apart would converge simultaneously on the high mountains in times of storm and difficulty to save their own and their neighbours' flocks.

HAMLETING

Numerically intermediate between the nucleations and the single steads of dispersed areas, the factors underlying hamleting are by no means intermediate. In some ways, the origin of the hamlet poses more difficult problems than that of either the nucleated village or of dispersal. Hamlets fall, however, more easily into dated groups, and the late hamlets can immediately be separated out and explained, leaving the more problematic earlier ones. In fact a hamlet may be a comparatively modern settlement growing in a definable period, a shrinking village, or a relatively stable community dating back to a pre-Conquest origin, Welsh or English. Again the difficulty arises that there is no hard and fast line between the hamlet and the village, and the non-parochial villages are in many cases the larger hamlets of the pre-Conquest period or hamlets which formed nucleating points for later growth.

Late hamlets, i.e. of post-medieval date and some of medieval origin, have grown from a number of causes. These include estate hamlets typically at the gates of the great parks of manorial lords; clusters of squatters on the edge of common land; and small groups which sprang into being on the enclosure of common arable fields. All these arose directly from the old communities and the manorial system. A second group arose as a result of communication patterns and these included notably the bridge-head settlements; small ports and fishing communities; cross-road hamlets; riverside hamlets; turnpike, post-road, canal and railway hamlets – these last generally datable with ease. Modern conditions, largely social or economic, have seen the rise of quarrying and mining hamlets; residential hamlets (or the expansion of an old hamlet or village where one such provided a suitable nucleating point); chapel-hamlets and, principally in the dispersed areas, late church-hamlets. These not only provide no problem of origin – they can be stripped, as it were, from the hamlet map, leaving as a residue the earlier hamlets which existed at Domesday and the rise of which was unrelated to any of these last causes.

In the Welsh Borderland, these early hamlets form the majority. Hamlets appear on first glance at the complete settlement map (Fig. 3) to be widespread, but when they are separated out their distribution is seen, as in the case of the nucleated villages, to be more restricted. They are essentially small agricultural communities whose character and economic régimes have run surprisingly parallel to those of the larger communities. The main differences are of scale and size. The community, the open fields or sharelands, and the township area, were all smaller. Communal organisation on a minor scale meant, for example, that there might be only one or two common fields instead of three or more, and that would be of limited acreage. Communal arrangements were therefore liable to die out earlier, and this may well be the explanation of the survival of open arable fields in the nineteenth century mainly in the larger villages. The hamlets are further divisible into parochial and non-parochial. In Herefordshire and south-east Shropshire where the parochial hamlet is widespread, there are in many cases associated manor-houses and park-estates. Where the hamlets lie in dependent townships as in Cheshire and north Shropshire, this association is rarer. Where, as in these last two, there is neither manor house nor church, there may similarly be no other buildings apart from agricultural steadings; but where 'public' buildings are found they are most likely to be either inns or chapels.

The human motivation for early hamleting is by no means simple to trace, and their origin is easier to postulate than to prove. Do they represent nucleation in a sparsely populated area, with its equivalent causation? Or are they imperfectly evolved villages in a nucleated zone? The first would tend to link them with the Celtic people, the latter with the English, and the distributional pattern therefore becomes a vital clue.

The Distribution of Settlement Units

In the total picture of nucleation and dispersal, the primary facts which stand out from the 1830–60 distribution are:

(*a*) the almost unbroken expanse of dispersed dwellings in the Welsh counties,

(*b*) the mixed patterning of the four English counties (including western Gloucestershire),

(*c*) the absence on either side of the Border of any extensive areas of closely distributed nucleations of the mid-English type.

In other words, the Welsh Borderland includes a characteristically scattered Welsh area, a hybrid border zone, but no markedly English nucleated areas.

In most parts of the eastern Welsh counties, the dispersal is virtually total, the only exceptions being the small towns. In some parts of the three main English counties it is also total, but these are of limited area and untypical. Hamleting is relatively rare on the Welsh side of the border. It is widespread on the English side. Nucleations are nowhere closely spaced except in Wirral, but they extend in the shape of a Madonna lily from Cheshire and east Flintshire (the flower head), narrowing south across north Shropshire (the calyx), and thence the long narrow stem runs in a curving line across western Herefordshire and into eastern and southern Monmouthshire and the adjoining fringe of western Gloucestershire which might be compared with the tuberous root (Fig. 20). East of this, from north-east Shropshire to south-east Herefordshire, lies an area which is all but devoid of true village nucleations, the main exceptions being the few which lie in and near the Worfe valley in mid-eastern Shropshire, and the occasional ones along the north-eastern border of the same county.

As has been said earlier, few of the clustered border villages resemble the large, mid-English villages and most are difficult to put into plan-categories such as the cross-road village, the green village, and the street village. Nowhere, except perhaps in Wirral do they attain the density per square mile which is typical of counties such as Lincolnshire, Oxfordshire, or the main part of Gloucestershire. For the entire area of the Borderland counties it

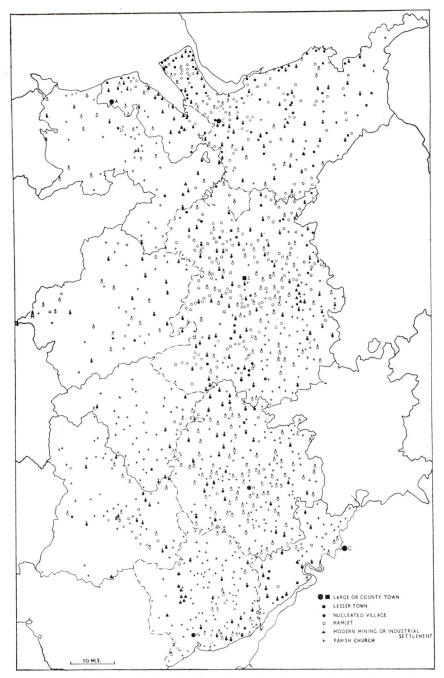

21. The Welsh Borderland: all nucleated settlements (mid-nineteenth century)

averages one village in 30·6 square miles (Table VIII). This average rises to one in 21 square miles in the nucleated counties (i.e. nucleated by Borderland standards), and falls to one in 98 square miles in the four non-nucleated Welsh border counties which between them boasted (in 1830–60) only 27 villages. In Radnorshire, the most completely dispersed of these four counties, there are only three nucleated villages apart from those with urban histories (five including lapsed towns) and the density is one in 94 square miles. Cheshire with one village every 12 square miles (a figure brought up sharply by Wirral in which lie 25 of the total of 80 Cheshire nucleated villages) has the highest density, and this falls eastward into Flintshire (one per 23 sq. miles) and south-ward into Shropshire (one per 24 sq. miles), continuing to fall southward into Herefordshire (one per 28 sq. miles) and Mon-mouthshire (one per 44 sq. miles). But the sharp distinction between even these last two low densities and those of the four mid-Welsh counties leaves no doubt that eastern Flintshire and eastern Monmouthshire must be classed in this respect with the English and not with the Welsh counties as regards nucleation.

The form of the nucleated villages area – the Madonna lily – makes the problems of causality less simple than might at first appear from the density figures which seem superficially to suggest a natural division between the Welsh dispersal and the English nucleation areas, the latter extending into Flintshire and Mon-mouthshire additionally. Were this division adequate, the hybrid settlement zone of the Borderland could be put squarely into the category of a transitional zone in which the English nucleated pattern had mixed with the underlying Celtic hamlets and dis-persed settlements. But the nucleations do not, as they should if this theory of origin obtained, increase in density eastwards. Instead they occur in a thinning density in eastern and central Cheshire, practically disappear from eastern Shropshire, and vanish almost totally from eastern Herefordshire. In other words, they are, in the Borderland, primarily a western distribution, with a blank, villageless area of very considerable size between them and the mid-English village lands, except in the north and south of the Borderland where they link up from Cheshire to Staffordshire, and in Monmouthshire where they are continuous with the Gloucestershire villages.

It is clear that the clustered village is not a feature of Welsh traditional life, for where villages are found in Wales they are either widely spaced or in areas of strong English contact. Granted that they are to be found predominantly on the English side of the border, what is the significance of their predominantly western distribution when what was to be expected would have been an eastern distribution thinning westward? Shropshire offers one of the clues to the riddle of western distribution, and it is the line which earlier has been called the 'parish line'[1] which divides Shropshire into two distinct parts. The entire west, together with a broad band of northern Shropshire and a strip on the north-eastern boundary of the county lies in that part of England which has large parishes. Here, and almost exclusively here, are Shropshire's nucleated villages. It will be further noted that 47 of the 56 nucleated villages in Shropshire are parochial. Fewer than ten of these lie in the single-township parish area, and among them are several which are the centres of the occasional multi-township parishes which occur south of the parish line, for example Worfield with its 30 townships and Claverley with 13. There is thus in Shropshire a strong correlation between the large parish and the growth of villages which offered the advantages of centrality to their numerous dependent townships. This being so, it would presuppose that their expansion as villages followed the establishment of parishes though they may have had an earlier existence as settlement sites. The number named -*burh* which elsewhere[2] has been suggested as having an Anglo-Saxon back reference to a number of Celtic or Early Iron Age sites becomes still more significant. It is highly possible that the Anglo-Saxons when they reached Shropshire and Cheshire took over the more important Celtic places, renamed them, and developed them as their main villages. In Cheshire, a high proportion of the large old parishes have at their centre a parochial village which is either the only village in the entire parish, or one of two. However, in Cheshire, although there are nearly as many parochial villages as in Shropshire (38 as compared with 47) there are more non-parochial than parochial (42 as compared with only 9 in Shropshire). An appreciable proportion of these are or were non-parochial villages, second centres in large parishes both in Cheshire

[1] Ch. 8, pp. 168–71.   [2] Ch. 4, p. 97.

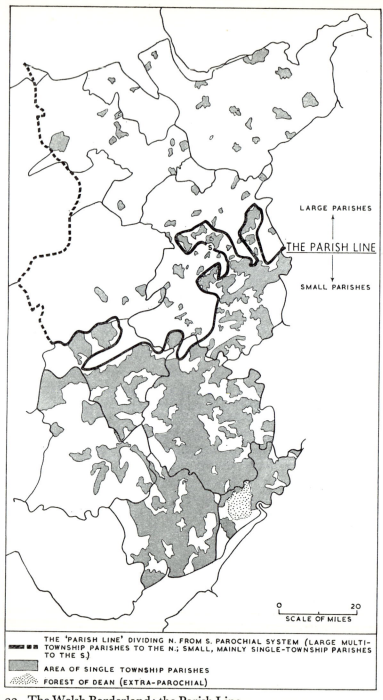

LARGE PARISHES

THE PARISH LINE

SMALL PARISHES

0   20
SCALE OF MILES

THE 'PARISH LINE' DIVIDING N. FROM S. PAROCHIAL SYSTEM (LARGE MULTI-
TOWNSHIP PARISHES TO THE N.; SMALL, MAINLY SINGLE-TOWNSHIP PARISHES
TO THE S.)

AREA OF SINGLE TOWNSHIP PARISHES

FOREST OF DEAN (EXTRA-PAROCHIAL)

22. The Welsh Borderland: the Parish Line

and Shropshire, e.g. Weston in Wybunbury, Helsby in Frodsham, Tiverton in Bunbury, Barnton in Great Budworth, Bollington in Prestbury, Tilstock in Whitchurch, and Little Stretton in Church Stretton. These suggest either a British retreat to and development of a nearby settlement on the arrival of the Anglo-Saxons, or an unfinished job on their part because of their small numbers, or a lapsed parish, or simply the later need of a second centre in a wide parish with a growing population and a developing economy. Of the 42 non-parochial villages in Cheshire, 17 occur in Wirral. In fact it is only in Wirral that their number exceeds that of the parochial villages (8). They occur in the Scandinavianised part of Wirral where, as in the rest of west Cheshire, parishes are appreciably smaller than in the centre and east. This may or may not be of major significance, for Celtic settlers were strongly entrenched there before the Scandinavians, and Mercians had also previously extended their colonies into Wirral, but the fact must be borne in mind.

On looking at Herefordshire, although 26 of the 29 nucleated villages are parochial, they can clearly not have arisen as in Shropshire and Cheshire for parochial reasons, for the majority of Herefordshire parishes are single townships. The same applies to Monmouthshire where the nucleations are in the east and south. But mid-Herefordshire is the area where Offa's Dyke swung away from the upland edge and from there continued east of the lower Wye. Here too, the main zone of Anglo-Norman defences, both the castle and the mottes (Fig. 14) swung away from the north–south line along the hill foot across to the valley of the lower Wye. On analysis, practically every village in the two counties of Herefordshire and Monmouthshire, proves to have had a defensive *raison d'être* in the Marcher period. This defensive line also extended north into western Shropshire, where centres of large parishes had this second reason for growth in the Middle Ages. In west Cheshire, however, the strategic element was a relatively minor one, for the Cheshire of the late Anglo-Saxon and early medieval phases had its western defences not along the Dee but along each edge of the Flintshire plateau and along the Clwyd, and it was there that defensive centres grew up. As in Shropshire, a number of Flintshire places could claim a double reason for expansion – parochial and military.

Dispersal in the Borderland seems to be of two main types: the secondary Celtic or Welsh dispersal which probably reached its full expression in the late Dark Ages or the early Middle Ages, and the sparse woodland settlement which simply failed to develop further in the medieval and later periods. This last type which is liberally peppered with Norman manorialism is common in the wooded country which so long survived as remnants of the great hunting forests such as Delamere, Macclesfield Forest, Wyre Forest and Brewood, and in large areas of Herefordshire. Far from all the dispersed settlement patches in the English border counties, however, are in this category. Looked at a second time, they emerge less as patches than as a general background in the areas of villages and hamlets. They may well be in part the Celtic basis persisting in this area where the Mercian settlement was so thin; in part the reflection of late enclosure.

Hamleting is perhaps the most difficult problem of all. There are few hamlets in modern Wales. They are most numerous (Fig. 21) in Shropshire and Herefordshire, plentiful but less numerous in Cheshire. They clearly belong to the English hybrid zone. But in Cheshire, the non-parochial villages are more numerous than in Shropshire and Herefordshire, and these may well represent expanded hamlets. Prior to the late Dark Ages or the early Middle Ages, Jones-Pierce has postulated that the Celts were not fully a dispersed settlement group. Yet their nucleations were not large and are thought to have been loose allodial clusters around an original *hendre* which began to break up from the later Middle Ages as compacting increased.[1] It would there-fore seem highly probable that in the tribal period the hamlet was a typical British settlement, and where the Borderland Britons were overtaken by the Mercian settlement their old hamlets became 'frozen' (as were many of their place-names). This is supported by the distribution of solitary and near-solitary churches which covers much of the English as well as the Welsh border counties.

Over the entire region, however, many tides have flowed, and the pattern, particularly in the English counties, is far from simple. No two places have an identical history, but many have parallel histories, and from the complexity certain major trends and pointers do emerge.

[1] J. Gareth Thomas, 'Rural Settlement', ch. v in *Wales*, ed. E. G. Bowen (1957), pp. 144–6.

TABLE VIII. *Statistics of Nucleated Settlements in the Welsh Border Counties*

Abbreviations: U small town (with urban status after 1894)
P parochial village
T non-parochial village

N.B. Nucleations are based on the maps of the period 1830–60

County	U	P	T	P+T	Total	County	U	P	T	P+T	Total
Denbighshire	7	5	–	5	12	Flintshire	7	8	3	11	18
Montgomery-						Cheshire	11	38	42	80	91
shire	5	8	1	9	14	Shropshire	13	47	9	56	69
Radnorshire	3	4	1	5	8	Hereford-					
Breconshire	5	7	1	8	13	shire	5	28	1	29	34
						Monmouth-					
						shire	3	11	1	12	15
TOTALS: non-nucleated counties	20	24	3	27	47	Nucleated counties	39	132	56	188	227

Average density of villages (based on area of administrative counties 1951)

Non-nucleated counties		*Nucleated counties*	
Denbighshire	1 in 133 sq. miles	Flintshire	1 in 23 sq. miles
Montgomeryshire	1 in 88 ,, ,,	Cheshire	1 in 12 ,, ,,
Radnorshire	1 in 94 ,, ,,	Shropshire	1 in 24 ,, ,,
Breconshire	1 in 90 ,, ,,	Herefordshire	1 in 28 ,, ,,
		Monmouthshire	1 in 44 ,, ,,

Average density non-nucleated counties   1 in 98 sq. miles
Average density nucleated counties   1 in 21 sq. miles
Average density all Welsh Border counties
(except west Glos.)   1 in 30·6 sq. miles

TABLE VIII (*contd.*)

List of Nucleations in the Welsh Borderland 1830–60

Abbreviations: U small town (with urban status after 1894)
P parochial village (or parish after U)
T non-parochial village (or township after P)
b motte and bailey
c castle or former castle
f fair or former fair
h religious house (prior to Dissolution)
m market or former market
l lordship

The date where necessary is indicated by C followed by the century number or numbers, e.g. C14, fourteenth century.

CHESHIRE   11U + 38P + 42T = 91

Name of place	Status	Other particulars
West Kirkby	P with 9T	
Heswall	P ,, 2T	
Bidston	P ,, 5T	
Lower Bebington	P ,, 5T	
Wallasey	U and P with 3T	
Bromborough	P with 2T	Medieval m
Eastham	P ,, 8T	
Great Neston	U and P with 8T	
Burton	P	
Thurstaston	P	
Hoylake	T	
Hoose	T	
Great Meols	T	Nucleation late and due to fishing industry
Moreton	T	
Saughall Massie	T	Not nucleated 1665 when only 7 houses
Greasby	T	
Liscard	T	
Ness	T	
Little Ness	T	
Brimstage	T	

Name of place	Status	Other particulars
Little Sutton	T	
Willaston	T	Head of the hundred
Little Neston	T	
Raby	T	
Poulton	T	
Seacombe	T	
Tranmere	T	
Ince	P	
Halton	T	*Caput* of lordship, c, former m
Helsby	T	
Dunham on the Hill	T	
Great Barrow	P	
Guilden Sutton	P	
Tarvin	P with 11T	Former m
Christleton	P with 5T	
Littleton	T	
Waverton	P with 3T	
Handbridge	T	
Dodleston	P with 2T	b
Saighton	T	
Aldford	P with 4T	b
Churton	T	
Farndon	P with 5T	
Frodsham	U and P with 12T	*Caput* of lordship, c, m
Weaverham	P with 8T	
Clotton Hoofield	T	
Eaton	T	
Tarporley	P with 4T	Medieval borough, former m
Bunbury	P with 12T	Former m and f
Tiverton	T	
Tattenhall	P with 3T	
Malpas	P with 24T	Former borough, former m, c
Wrenbury	P with 7T	
Audlem	P with 5T	Former m
Grappenhall	P	
Lymm	P	Former m

TABLE VIII (contd)

Name of place	Status	Other particulars
Upton by Chester	T	
Wilderspool	T	
Latchford	T	
Thelwall	T	
Mottram in Longdendale	P with 18T	
Ashton on Mersey	P with 2T	
Partington	T	
Carrington	T	
Cheadle	P with 3T	
Stockport Etchells	T	
Great Budworth	P with 35T	
Comberbach	T	
Barnton	T	
Hartford	T	
Northwich	U and T	Medieval salt wich, m
Spurstow	T	
Davenham	P with 12T	
Nether Knutsford	U and P with 5T	Medieval borough, m
Mobberley	P	
Ollerton	T	
Wilmslow	P with 4T	
Prestbury	P with 32T	
Macclesfield	U and chapelry	m, medieval borough
Bollington	T	
Holmes Chapel	P	
Middlewich	U and P with 15T	Early salt wich, m
Over	P with 3T	Medieval borough
Church Minshull	P	
Sandbach	U and P with 13T	m, Saxon crosses
Weston	T	
Haslington	T	

Nantwich	U and P with 5T	m, reputedly ancient
		  borough, chief medieval
		  salt wich

Wybunbury	P with 18T	
Astbury	P with 12T	
Congleton	U and chapelry	m, medieval borough

SHROPSHIRE 13U + 47P + 9T = 69

Name of place	Status	Other particulars
Welshampton	P	
Ellesmere	U and P with 24T	*Caput* of lordship, c
Colemere	T	
Whittington	P with 9T	c
Oswestry	U and P with 16T	*Caput* of lordship, c, m, early Iron Age camp
Cockshutt	T	
Wem	U and P with 13T	m, b
Myddle	P with 4T	*Caput* of l, c
West Felton	P with 5T	b
Ruyton XI Towns	P with 6T	*Caput* of l, c, former m
Kinnerley	P with 8T	
Baschurch	P with 13T	
Whitchurch	U and P with 14T	m, former c
Tilstock	T	
Prees	P with 10T	
Stanton on Hine Heath	P with 5T	
Shawbury	P with 7T	
Walton	T	
High Ercall or Ercall Magna	P with 14T	
Hodnet	P with 10T	Former m
Woore	P	
Norton in Hales	P	
Little Drayton	T	
Market Drayton	U and P with 6T	m
Bletchley	T	
Great Soundley	T	
Cheswardine	P with 6T	
Hinstock	P	
Newport	U and P	m
Edgmond	P with 11T	
Much Wenlock	U and P with 8T	Medieval borough, m, h
Great Hanwood	P	
Meole Brace	P with 4T	
Condover	P with 9T	

TABLE VIII (*contd*)

Name of place	Status	Other particulars
Church Stretton	U and P with 4T	m
Worthen	P with 19T	Small borough C14, m, f
Pontesbury	P with 20T	
Minsterley	P	
Shrawardine	P	
Ford	P	
Church Pulverbatch	P with 5T	m and f at Castle Pulverbatch C14
Acton Burnell	P with 2T	Medieval borough; c, m, f in Middle Ages
Woolstaston	P	Minor c
Chirbury	P with 14T	Small medieval borough with c, h; Anglo-Saxon fortification
Cardington	P with 10T	Medieval trading centre
Hope Bowdler	P with 3T	m
Wentnor	P with 5T	
Little Stretton	T	
Lydham	P	
Lydbury North	P with 7T	
Wistanstow	P with 6T	Former m and f
Hopton Castle	P	c
Bedstone	P	
Bucknell	P	
Culmington	P with 4T	Former m and f
Cleobury Mortimer	U and P	Medieval borough with m and f
Norbury	P with 3T	
Kempton	T	
Clun	U and P with 17T	Medieval borough with m and f, c
Bishop's Castle	U and P with 5T	*Caput* of marcher l, c, m, f
Stanton Lacy	P with 10T	C14 trading centre
Bitterley	P with 6T	
Albrighton nr. Shifnal	P	C14 trading centre
Beckbury	P	
Worfield	P with 30T	C14 trading centre
Claverley	P with 13T	Royal manor C14

Name of place	Status	Other particulars
Oldbury	P	c
Bridgnorth	U and 2P	Medieval borough, c, h, m, f; wool trade
Shifnal	U and P with 4T	m and f

HEREFORDSHIRE 5U + 28P + 1T = 34

Name of place	Status	Other particulars
Leintwardine	P with 12T	Roman Bravonium
Brampton Bryan	P with 3T	c
Leinthall Starkes	P	
Wigmore	P with 2T	*Caput* of marcher l, c, former h, m and f
Lingen	P	b
Orleton	P	
Brimfield	P	Small C14 trading centre
Luston	T	
Eardisland	P	c mount
Kingsland	P	c, b, former m and f
Shobdon	P	c, h
Pembridge	P	Medieval borough with m and f, ?keep
Dilwyn	P	Trading centre C14, c
Weobley	P	Medieval borough and trading centre, c, b
Eardisley	P	Medieval borough, b, c
Mansell Lacy	P	
Preston on Wye	P	Former m and f
Staunton on Wye	P	
Blakemere	P	
Monkland	P	h
Madley	P	Former m and f
Kingstone	P	Trading centre C14
Stoke Prior	P with 3T	
Bromyard	U and P with 5T	m and f
Ashperton	P	C13 c
Fownhope	P with 2T	
Weston under Penyard	P	Roman Ariconium, b, c, C14 trading centre

TABLE VIII (*contd*)

Name of place	Status	Other particulars
Longtown (Ewyas Lacy)	P with 6T	Medieval borough with m and f, c, b
Ewyas Harold	P	Medieval borough with m and f, c
Kington	U and P	b, m
Ledbury	U and P with 2T	Medieval borough, m and f
Leominster	U and P with 10T	Medieval borough, m and f, h
Ross on Wye	U and P	Medieval borough, m and f
Peterchurch	P	

MONMOUTHSHIRE $3U + 11P + 1T = 15$

Name of place	Status	Other particulars
Raglan	P	*Caput* of marcher l, medieval borough, c
Trelleck	P with 3T	Medieval borough, b, c, former m and f, l
St Arvans	P with 2T	
Shire Newton	P with 2T	
Caerwent	P with 2T	Roman Venta. Village within Roman walls. Former m
Caldicot	P	*Caput* of l, b, c
Undy	P	
Magor	P with 2T	Former market, l
Bishton (Llangad-walader)	P	c
Llangattock j. Caerleon (Caerleon)	P with 3T	Roman Isca, medieval borough, *caput* of marcher l; c, m and f, h
Llanfair Discoed	P with 2T	
Usk	U and P with 3T	Medieval borough, m and f, c, h
Abergavenny	U and P with 3T	Medieval borough, m and f, *caput* of l, c, h
Monmouth	U and P	Medieval borough, *caput* of l; m and f, c, h
Crick	T	

FLINTSHIRE 7U + 8P + 3T = 18

Name of place	Status	Other particulars
Northop	P with 6T	
Hawarden	U and P with 16T	*Caput* of marcher l, former m and f, c
Gwaenysgor	P with 2T	
Rhuddlan	U and P with 8T	Medieval borough, with m and f, b, c
Holywell	U and P	
Gronant	T	
Caerwys	U and P with 4T	Roman station, m
Halkyn	P with 4T	
Dyserth	P with 4T	c
Newmarket	T	Former m
Bretton	T	
Caergwrle	T	Roman station
Bangor on Dee (Bangor Is coed)	P with 6T	Site of Celtic monastery
Overton on Dee	P with 3T	Medieval borough with m, c
Flint	U and P with 2T	Medieval borough, c, m
Mold	U and P with 15T	*Caput* of marcher l, m, c
St Asaph (Llanelwy)	U and P with 11T	Cathedral city
Hanmer	P	

DENBIGHSHIRE 7U + 5P = 12

Name of place	Status	Other particulars
Henllan	P with 8T	
Gresford	P	
Ruabon	P with 4T	
Holt	U and P	Medieval borough, c
Llangollen	U and P with 9T	m, c
Wrexham	U and P	m
Ruthin	U and P	*Caput* of marcher l, c, m
Denbigh	U and P	*Caput* of marcher l, c, m and f
Llanfwrog	P with 5T	
Llanrwst	U and P with 7T	m
Eglwys-Fach	P with 5T	
Abergele	U and P	

TABLE VIII (*contd*)

MONTGOMERYSHIRE   5U + 8P + 1T = 14

Name of place	*Status*	*Other particulars*
Llanwddyn	P with 4T	
Meifod	P with 10T	*Clas* church, formerly 3 churches
Guilsfield	P with 11T	
Llanfair Caereinion	P with 15T	Unchartered m
Berriew	P with 15T	
Kerry (Ceri) or Llanfihangel	P with 19T	
Caersws	T	Roman station
Llanbrynmair	P with 5T	
Church Stoke	P with 11T	
Montgomery	U and P	*Caput* of marcher l, m and f, b, c
Welshpool (Trallwng)	U and P with 10T	Medieval borough, m and f, c, b
Newtown (Llanfair)	U and P with 2T	Medieval borough, m and f
Llanidloes	U and P with 8T	Medieval borough, m and f
Llanfyllin	U and P with 12T	

RADNORSHIRE   3U + 4P + 1T = 8

Name of place	*Status*	*Other particulars*
Gladestry (Llanfair Llethonw)	P with 4T	
Painscastle	T	Medieval borough, with m and f, c
New Radnor	P	Medieval borough with m and f, c, formerly county town of Radnorshire
Knighton	U and P with 2T	Medieval borough, m and f, c
Rhaeader	U and P	Medieval borough with m and f
Glasbury	P	
Clyro	P with 3T	
Presteigne	U and P	Medieval borough, m and f

BRECONSHIRE   5U + 7P + 1T = 13

Name of place	Status	Other particulars
Bronllys	P	c
Defynnog	P with 5T	Small borough C14
Llanfihangel Tal-y-llyn	P	
Llangorse	P with 2T	
Llangattock	P with 3T	
Crickhowell	U and P	Medieval borough with m and f, c
Trecastell	T	Medieval borough, c
Brecon	U and 2P	Medieval borough, m and f, c, h
Talgarth	U and P with 5T	Medieval borough with m and f
Builth (Llanfair)	U and P	Medieval borough, m and f, c
Llangammarch Wells	P with 2T	
Hay on Wye	U and P	Medieval borough with m and f, c
Llyswen	P	

10 Land Use and Field Systems

THE field systems of Wales and the Borderland have been the subject of enquiry and speculation for the better part of a century and, like nucleation and dispersal, have often been linked with the ethnic division between Celtic and Anglo-Saxon Britain. H. L. Gray's map, in which the Midland or two- and three-field system was shown as extending across middle England from the north-eastern coasts and the eastern Pennines, across the greater part of the Midlands and thence southwards into eastern Somerset, Dorset, Hampshire and the coastal belt of Sussex, has remained a classic on the subject and is still of considerable value in relation to the major areas it delineates. With regard to the Borderland, Gray showed Herefordshire and all Shropshire except for the western districts to be in his Midland System area; Cheshire, Monmouthshire and all Wales in the area of Celtic field systems.[1] Nearly a quarter of a century later C. S. and C. S. Orwin showed only 'a few scattered instances' of open field in Cumberland, Westmorland, Cheshire and Monmouthshire, and their views and conclusions have been followed by many economic historians until comparatively recently.[2] But during the last few years historians and historical geographers have traced the existence of open field husbandry from Cumberland and Lancashire to Devon as well as in various parts of Wales,[3] and the time is indeed ripe for the revision of old boundaries and interpretations of traditional systems of communal agriculture.

[1] *English Field Systems* (1915), frontispiece.
[2] *The Open Fields* (1938), p. 61. In a later edition Dr Orwin acknowledged the more extensive distribution of open fields in Cheshire and Monmouthshire based on the work of the present writer.
[3] See Bibliography.

Land Use

The physical contrast between highland and lowland, valley and upland, needs no stressing. It forms the perpetual backcloth of the history and economy of the Borderland. But the simplicity of a dual ethnic or cultural division has already been shown, however, to be falsely based, and no true assessment of the character of this broad zone can be made without recognising that the tides of Welsh and English movement have many times shifted the frontier between the two peoples and extended the hybrid Celtic–Anglian belts as, for example, is reflected in the place-name maps. The further superimposition of a feudal Anglo-Norman régime over all the English and extensive parts of the east Welsh districts, with an intensified marcher form of feudalism in the lordships of the border proper, confirmed and emphasised this intermediate zone and underlined the triple basis which is of such significance in relation to aspects of border history and culture. As might be expected, the Normans played a major role in relation to agronomical and tenurial systems also.

The proportional importance of pastoralism and the cultivation of crops has varied with the centuries as well as with place, but the preponderantly pastoral régime of hill farming has been necessarily a constant. Altitude, slope, poor soil conditions, rainfall and exposure have combined to make stock raising the only viable type of land use on hills of over 1000 feet above sea level, but areas of good, deep soil and favourable slope are found in comparative abundance up to 600 and even 800 feet in many parts of upland Montgomeryshire, Radnorshire and Breconshire. Where woodland flourishes, crops can be raised, slope permitting, and rich woods of deciduous trees are still abundant in these three counties as to the north of the Mynydd Epynt and in the hills of mid-Montgomeryshire.

The English lowlands, by contrast, are areas of convertible husbandry and have from time to time been noted now for their corn, now for their sheep and cattle. Their agricultural history, partly because of their climate, has shifted from one course to

23. The Welsh Borderland: distribu

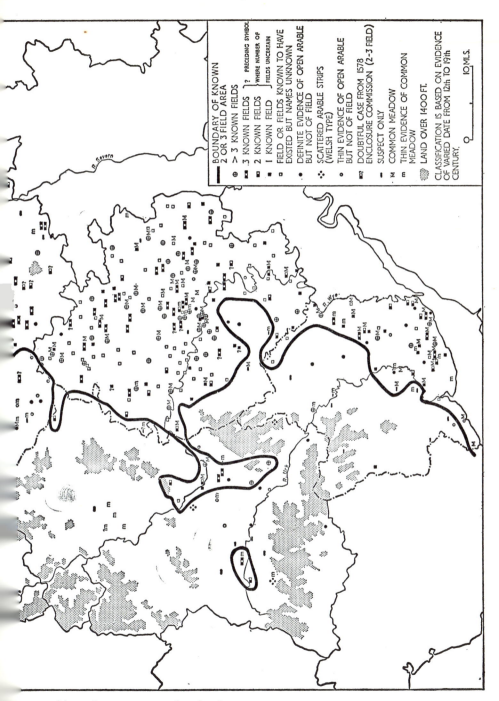

en arable and common meadow lands

another with comparative ease, especially in the warmer lands of Shropshire and Herefordshire.

NATIVE WELSH AGRICULTURE

Prior to the Union of England and Wales, native Welsh society and agriculture alike were based on communal arrangements in which the *cenedl* (literally and in modern usage, the nation, but until the Middle Ages the lesser nation or tribe) was divided into *trefydd* or townships, and these in turn consisted of family groups or *gwelyau* (*gwely* literally 'a bed'). There is considerable archaeological evidence to support the idea that, up to Roman times, the settlement pattern of the Celtic people in Wales included nucleated, hamleted and dispersed settlements, but at some time during the Dark Ages nucleation largely or entirely broke down, and allodial groupings, based on blood relationship to the fourth generation at least, developed round an original homestead or *tyddyn*, and inherited by the rule of gavelkind or equal division between all the sons.

Predominantly pastoral, both by tradition and by the physical limitations of the country, the tribes were perhaps originally semi-nomadic, but it is reasonably certain that by the early Middle Ages at latest, they were no more than transhumant, and that the old homestead or *hendre* formed the social and agronomical focus of each *gwely*, with *hafodau* or summer dairies on the hills serving the *gwely* or the entire township as the case might be. But although the basis of the economy was predominantly and necessarily pastoral, the arable land attached to the permanent homesteads, known as *tir priod* and carrying *priodolder* rights of occupancy which could only be lost after several generations of non-occupancy, was of tenurial significance. This land was not individually owned during the tribal phase but carried rights of occupancy. It was typically scattered in *erwau* or ploughing acres or strips, rather than lying in a single field, but the territorial arrangement shows every sign of having varied with the terrain and with the requirements and character of individual *gwelyau*. Around the family groups of *tyddynod* and dividing them from one another, were the open pastures, known as the *cytir*, on which the tribesmen enjoyed liberal grazing rights. In Anglesey,

G. R. J. Jones has shown that this arrangement of dwellings survived in the free townships until the late medieval or early Tudor period, but with the end of gavelkind and its replacement by primogeniture the loose pattern of clustered dwellings and their associated arable holdings broke down, giving place to patternless dispersal.[1] In the Borderland, where the terrain is very different, there was more rather than less reason for the township groups to become well defined because of the rarity of good arable land and the vast extent of intervening mountain land.

Only in the bond townships attached to the *llys* or 'palace' of the tribal chieftains, and distinguished from other *trefydd* by the name of *maerdref*, was cultivation usually of predominant importance, and arable strips intermingled in a field in an arrangement somewhat similar to the English open field. After Union, the breakdown in the tribal system advanced rapidly, while the bond communities had probably long since begun their slow decay. In the Borderland and South Wales, contact with the manorial system of the Anglo-Norman marcher lordships, however, influenced land use, and in the Englishries open field cultivation was introduced. To what extent this affected agronomy and field patterns in adjacent Welsh areas is one of the more interesting questions relating to medieval agriculture in the Borderland.

Field boundaries are subject to change from many causes including enclosure, compacting, division and abandonment as well as changes in modes of land use, but there is, despite this, a stronger tendency for traces of pattern to survive and this is especially true of the evenly ruled boundaries of former strip fields, arable, meadow or mossland. This pattern emerges even from below a superimposed pattern of enclosure and compacting in most townships, and where there is doubt it is usually possible to trace such old strip fields from aerial photographs. Thus, although eighteenth-century estate maps and nineteenth-century tithe, enclosure and Ordnance Survey maps may be (and in most cases usually are at best) the only plans available of the majority of Welsh upland townships, it is generally possible to deduce whether open field agriculture has had any place in the field

[1] 'Some Medieval Rural Settlements in North Wales', *Trans. Inst. Br. Geogr.*, 19 (1953), pp. 51–72. The maps of Llysddulas are based on T. Jones Pierce's translation of 'An Anglesey Crown Rental of the 16th Century', *Bull. Bd Celtic Stud.*, 1939–44, pp. 156–76.

pattern. When township after township in the uplands shows no such pattern and when adjacent valley townships do, it is clear that they provide the clue to the boundary between Anglo-Norman or Anglo-Saxon land use patterns on the one hand and Celtic or Welsh on the other.

The typical nineteenth-century field plan of Welsh townships in Radnorshire and Breconshire shows ribbons of cultivated land in valleys of varying width and slope with small fields on the valley floors and larger ones on the valley sides and higher ground, giving place to either the large, enclosed pastures of the higher uplands or the open waste or commons of the higher hills. Woodlands, by no means rare in the richer lands of north Breconshire and the fringes of Radnorshire, and once held in common, were enclosed long before 1800. Scattered farms form the characteristic settlement pattern, and are generally compacted now into units varying from small holdings of a few acres to the larger farms (usually only two or three in number) of over 200 acres. The habitation pattern is clearly derived from the *tyddynod*. Arable land is scarce, and the ploughing acres (*erwau*) are few and scattered. There is no evidence on the tithe maps of such townships of any strip fields, either in shapes or field-names. Examples of the Welsh type of township are Maes-car, Cray, Senny and Glyntawe in the broken hill country between the Vale of Brecon and the Brecon Beacons where the valleys are narrow and the hills reach 1100 to 1300 feet in height; Llananno in the narrow, winding Ithon valley of north Radnorshire where rounded hills occupy the greater part of the township; Llanbadarn Fawr on elevated but comparatively level land farther down the Ithon; and Llandeilo Graban in the steep hill land, deeply dissected by streams, to the north of the River Wye near Builth Wells. It can be repeated, with local variations, hundreds of times from Breconshire to Clun Forest and from the Radnorshire and mid-Montgomeryshire uplands northwards into the higher parts of the Flintshire and west Denbighshire plateaux. Once recognised, it is unmistakable, though the interpolation of occasional small strip-shaped fields is sometimes to be found and the cause is usually contact with manorialism, or the existence of medieval bond townships.

The massed map of open field (Fig. 23) shows with startling emphasis the western edge of open-field lands, and leaves no doubt that the line between them represents as distinctive a break between English and Welsh as is shown on the nucleation dispersal map (Fig. 3). Although by no means identical in detail, the boundary between nucleation and dispersal and that between open-field and strip-free areas is too similar in general course to leave any doubt as to their relatedness. Between them they define cartographically the area in which Welsh settlement predominates, modified by the centuries in which it has shared with England comparable economic ebbs and flows, but marked by the long, unbroken continuity which links it with its Celtic ancestry.

MEDIEVAL AGRICULTURE IN THE ENGLISH BORDERLAND

Anglo-Saxon agriculture is still a matter largely for speculation, yet it is a system which quite evidently holds the key to much of the character and distribution of early medieval field systems and agricultural practice. Archaeological evidence[1] as summarised by David M. Wilson is mainly from the south and east of England – from Northumberland (Yeavering) and Durham (Lanchester), East Anglia (Thetford), Oxford (Cassington), to Berkshire (Blewburton) and Wiltshire. In the Midlands there are finds from Leicestershire and Northamptonshire. Together, they supply evidence that the Anglo-Saxons used ploughs of some type, grew naked and hulled barley, wild oats, flax and woad, and raised domestic animals including oxen, sheep, pigs, horses, dogs and goats. Very little has so far been done as regards proving Anglo-Saxon fields archaeologically, but Wilson inclines to the view that many strip lynchets first began to be used in the Anglo-Saxon period.

H. L. Gray in 1915 enumerated eighteen late Anglo-Saxon charters which he considered gave evidence of open arable land.[2] All referred to places in the south Midlands, and four of these lie significantly near to the eastern edge of the English Borderland counties. Cofton (Wo.) is only some ten miles from the south-east corner of Shropshire; Barbourne in the County Borough of

[1] 'Anglo-Saxon Rural Economy', *Agric. Hist. Rev.*, x (ii) (1962), pp. 65–77.
[2] Op. cit. pp. 56–61.

Worcester is but eight miles from Herefordshire; and Clifford Chambers on the Warwick Avon and Dumbleton less than six miles from Tewkesbury near a tributary of the Severn are both on routes which lead quickly and easily into south Herefordshire and western Gloucestershire.

In 1957–8 H. P. R. Finberg followed in detail on the ground the boundaries of three Shropshire estates[1] from tenth-century charters previously translated by W. H. Stevenson and W. H. Duignan.[2] They were Church Aston with Chetwynd Aston (near Newport), Aston near Wellington, and Plaish in Cardington. The first two lie near the Roman road which leads into mid-eastern Shropshire and eventually to the middle Severn where lie the two Shropshire -ingahams.[3] It may also be of significance that Church Aston was in the seventeenth century still a three-field township, one of the most perfect examples in the county.[4]

The evidence of Domesday Book as regards agriculture must also be seen as reflecting late Anglo-Saxon conditions with the limited modification which alone can have taken place under the new Norman manorial lords in twenty years following the Conquest. The Domesday text contains no verbal proof of open field, but it does indicate the very extensive areas of ploughland which existed in Cheshire, Shropshire, Herefordshire and Gloucestershire in 1086. The plough teams were shared, together with the labour of villeins and cottars, and it is difficult to avoid the strong assumption that the greater part of the ploughing took place anywhere than in common fields. Strength is also given to this argument by the marked similarity of distribution in Cheshire of open arable fields of medieval and later dates.[5] By 1086, only the west-centre and the east of that county remained densely wooded, and although much of the eastern plains in particular was 'waste', cultivation survived to some degree, and in 1066 Wirral and west Cheshire were closely settled and cultivated, the Weaver valley only a little less so, and the plains of east Cheshire, suffering the aftermath of the Conqueror's depredations, somewhat thinly. In Shropshire, the distribution of arable land in Domesday was widespread except in the hills west of Oswestry,

[1] *Trans. Shrops. Archaeol. Soc.*, LVI, i (1957–8), pp. 28–33.
[2] Ibid. 4th series, I (1911), pp. 1–22.
[3] See pp. 94–5.   [4] See pp. 241–3.
[5] Sylvester and Nulty, op. cit., maps on pp. 19 and 29.

Clun Forest, and the higher uplands of south Shropshire. The comparative density of ploughlands in the middle belt of the county was despite, rather than because of, the extent of woodland clearing, and it was most remarkable that the south and the mid-Shropshire belt supported more arable land at that date than did the northern plains where, with a few notable exceptions, plough teams were recorded in comparatively modest numbers. Too much reliance cannot be placed on relatively blank patches on the map of later open field in this county (Fig. 23), for it seems certain that there is still much more evidence to come to hand, except perhaps for the Clun Forest area, but it may be noticed that in the northern plain the available documents for the extreme north-east and for the interior north-western plains suggest that the development of open fields, certainly on the two- and three-field systems, was not strong. Late woodland in the first case, extensive peat moss in the second may well have been effective deterrents to early ploughing. In Herefordshire, stands of timber were considerably more scattered in 1086 than in Shropshire, consisting with a few exceptions of small woodlands and patches of spinney and brushwood on the numerous hill slopes. As would be expected in view of this, Domesday ploughland was extensive but lay mainly to the east and north of a line drawn from Brampton Bryan to Ewyas Harold and thence across to Goodrich. In the western parts of the plain ploughs were scarce in the Domesday assessment except at the great stronghold of Clifford, newly built on the Wye where it emerges from the hills. They were absent from the Black Mountains except at the early Norman settlement of Ewyas Harold. In the Welsh district of Archenfield or Erging in the south-east they were also few in number except on the northern fringe. This may or may not be a reliable guide to the development of cultivation in those Welsh Border districts where the record was notably incomplete, but it was an index to the Old English area which was hidated, whereas the new territory added by the Normans was carucated. In Gloucestershire and Herefordshire plough teams were numerous in 1086 except in their western districts. In the border districts of Shropshire there was a similar reduction in arable land in the wasted border areas, but in Cheshire the central and eastern lowlands with their heavier woodland cover and suffering from extensive devastation by the Conqueror's armies were poorest and the Dee valley and Wirral the richest areas.

Both lay and ecclesiastical landholders advanced farming and landtaking during the Norman period and where their territories were wide the results in terms of the extension of manorial agriculture are most spectacular. Reclamation by assarting was carried out in Cheshire by the abbots of St Werburgh's (Chester), in Wirral and mid-Cheshire, and by the later Cistercian house of Vale Royal in Delamere Forest, especially on its eastern fringe,[1] only to be reduced or abandoned in many townships after the Black Death. In Herefordshire, the county most favoured by the Normans, church holdings were especially numerous in the central plain and spread far beyond that. *The Hereford Cathedral Muniments* beginning before the mid-twelfth century and calendared up to the seventeenth century afford a prolific source of documentation concerning the extent of the medieval and later open fields and common meadows together with a certain amount of information as to use and form, though less than one could wish. Numbering many hundred documents, a few illustrations must suffice to bring some light to the picture of medieval agriculture in lowland Herefordshire. The names of open fields and the furlongs into which many were sufficiently large to be divided were freely used, for example, a grant of $8\frac{1}{2}$ acres *circa* 1225–50 in Clehonger included '3 acres lying under one furrow' in the field called Burchehull, 2 acres in two different places in Clipstri field, 2 acres in two different places (and one a 'head acre') in Scrobinghal, and $1\frac{1}{2}$ in Kinewardin field.[2] The fields varied both in size and number and, like the common meadows, seem to have had ditches in many cases as their boundaries as at Stretton Sugwas which had a ditch on all sides of a croft and as a boundary between other lands referred to.[3] But hedges are mentioned from the mid-thirteenth century[4] as are assarts.[5] As land was brought into use, the church's resources were increased and there was

[1] Dorothy Sylvester, 'The Open Fields of Cheshire', *Trans. Hist. Soc. Lancs. and Ches.*, cviii (1956) interpreting, *inter alia*, the documents in *The Chartulary of the Abbey of St Werburgh, Chester*, Chetham Soc. (1920 and 1923), and *A Middlewich Chartulary*, ed. Joan Varley, Chetham Soc. (1941 and 1944).
[2] *Hereford Cathedral Muniments*, no. 947.
[3] Ibid. no. 2009 (1233).
[4] Ibid. nos 2180 (mid-thirteenth century), 1661 (same date), etc.
[5] Ibid. e.g. no. 882 (*circa* 1225–50).

evidently in some places a certain amount of oversight as at Madley where, in a release of 'all his grove in Medymor with ditches, hedges, plantations and boundaries . . . the said Richard de Medymor also grants full powers of digging trenches, enclosing, planting, and carrying out whatever seems necessary to the Dean and Chapter'.[1] They also had their mills, their shares in the meadows and rights in and over common pasture and woodlands used for swine pannage, all the subject of deeds in these *Muniments*. Two receipts detail farm implements and equipment. One dated 1332/3 lists one cart, four wagons hooped with iron, four ploughs and four harrows bought by the dean and chapter on taking Holme Lacy to farm;[2] the other, a receipt for a farmer's implements, was for one wagon hooped with iron, one plough with iron implements, one iron harrow, one winnowing fork, one bushel hooped with iron for measuring corn, one seedlip for sowing corn, one wooden *batellu* (presumably a beater or flail, cf. battledore), one spade and one iron shovel.[3] Both lists included oxen, the first specifying 24 oxen and 2 draught. Although grants and leases of customary lands in the common fields continued throughout the sixteenth century, they decreased in number markedly after 1350 while enclosures and severalty holding in turn became the subjects of more and more deeds.[4]

Lay lords similarly extended cultivation in common and cut out new fields from the waste until the Black Death halted progress and initiated an actual recession of the cultivated lands.[5] Except for the plain of Herefordshire and to a lesser degree the lowland of north Shropshire, the Welsh Borderland is more favourable to pastoralism than to the plough. In the hills this is normal, but in the lowlands and valleys the early enclosure of arable lands for grazing was partly on account of the gathering momentum of the wool trade and partly because climatically pasture was the more favoured agronomy. Only in Cheshire and north Shropshire was the wool trade unimportant, and in Cheshire the irregular open fields were reduced by attrition from

[1] Ibid. no. 1100 (first half thirteenth century).
[2] Ibid. no. 2507.
[3] Ibid. no. 2511 (1409).
[4] Ibid. e.g. no. 1146 (1400) leasing two parcels of land in the lordship of Wilton, one of which lay in the common field but the other was enclosed.
[5] See chapters in Part IV, especially those dealing with the Welsh counties.

the mid-fourteenth century. In Shropshire, I. S. Leadam listed seventy townships which, according to Wolsey's *Enclosure and Depopulation Commission of 1517*, had arable fields enclosed by that date.[1] In Cheshire and Shropshire and the normanised parts of eastern Wales, enclosure of open fields continued gradually from the time of the Black Death, and by the period of the Great Enclosures the principal remnants in use were single Town Fields. It was perhaps for these reasons that so many early authorities assumed that the open-field system had never taken root to any extent in the English border counties but, as is evidenced in Figure 23, this is now disproved, and in Herefordshire, where the system was most firmly established, there was the greatest residue of communal aration by the late eighteenth century for any part of the Borderland. The old fields can be traced in many townships by strips and quillets on the tithe maps, in many more by old field-names and shapes, but now also by aerial photographs and by an increasingly available body of early documents. The main work of the later Enclosure Commissioners in the Welsh Borderland was therefore concerned with the common pasture.[2]

Field and Land Use Patterns in Welsh Borderland Townships

The heterogeneity of settlement and field patterns in the Borderland is such that it is impossible to categorise them simply nor, from the angle of field patterns in particular, is it desirable even were it possible, to 'type' them beyond a point. It is rather the case that various elements occur and recur, sometimes in similar and sometimes in different combinations. As a basis for the local studies which follow, some of these patterns in the agricultural landscape are now picked out in selected townships where they are exceptionally clear. The main elements in the land pattern some of which have survived and some been overwritten or expunged may be summarised together with some later elements as:

---

[1] 'The Inquisition of 1517. Enclosures and Evictions. Edited from the Lansdowne MS. I, 153, part III', *Trans. R. Hist. Soc.*, N.S., viii (1894).
[2] See Chapter 2, and Tables II and III.

A. *Lands in the township or manor*

1. The open arable fields, cultivated in common and available for common grazing after the harvest.
2. The common meadows, grazed in common except before the hay harvests.
3. Open common pasture or waste, grazed in common and with certain rights in some cases to extract building stone.
4. Common woodlands with varying rights of taking lesser timber, small animals, fruits, berries; and varying rights of grazing and swine pannage. Most woods were eventually absorbed into demesne land.
5. Demesne lands including land adjacent to the manor-house (park-land, home farm, gardens, etc.), and shares in the common fields.
6. 'Toft and croft', land individually occupied by the villeins and cottars or customary tenants. The nearest Welsh equivalent of this formed the bulk of the township land in the free Welsh *trefs* under various nominations.
7. Church lands, typically the church, churchyard; parsonage and its gardens, crofts, and shares in the common fields, i.e. glebelands; in some places, the lands of a religious house.[1]
8. Land associated with secondary production: mills, workshops, yards, etc.
9. Later, land associated with inns and shops.
10. Later, land owned by trusts and companies such as railway companies, turnpike trusts, canal companies, Poor Law institutions, Nonconformist churches, mining companies, and more recently the Forestry Commission.

B. *Lands outside the townships*

11. Forests and chases for hunting and sport of the king and nobility.
12. Mountain and heath outside the bounds of both Forest and township. Some sea shores also fell into this category.

THE SUTTONS IN THE MANOR OF MARDEN
(Herefordshire)

Some of the principal open-field land in the border counties lies in and near the Lugg valley north of Hereford, and H. L. Gray has

---

[1] Lands owned by the cathedrals and some religious houses were extensive and included not only churches and glebe, but numerous manors and holdings in other manors and townships, town properties, etc.

made familiar the history of the arable fields of the great manor of Marden.[1] He did not, however, refer to a superb set of twenty parchment maps dated *circa* 1720[2] showing the layout of the manor and its members about a century before the Enclosure Awards of 1819 which, by enclosing a thousand acres in 46 fields, achieved the final breakdown of communal agriculture in its numerous townships.

The manor lies in the Lugg basin and includes some of the best agricultural land in Herefordshire. Its open fields, though some were small and irregular, displayed in the Suttons a close similarity to those of the Midland System. Figure 24 reproduces part of the 1720 plan covering the area of Sutton St Michael and Sutton St Nicholas, with Sutton Walls, the Iron Age fort just off the map to the north-west. The lack of compactness in the two hamlets is characteristic of the Borderland, but the three open arable fields – Upper Field, Middle Field and Lower Field – each divided into named furlongs, offer perhaps the best example not only in Herefordshire but in the entire Borderland of a regular and comparatively extensive three-field system. The earliest reference to it is probably a grant of *circa* 1300 of $1\frac{1}{2}$ acres of land in the field of Wynchord' of Sutton between the lands of (three others) and the walls of Walter of Monmouth.[3] There are four thirteenth-century references to the arable fields of Marden in the *Hereford Cathedral Muniments*,[4] and a fourteenth-century document mentions meadow, but later documentation is largely summarised by Gray.[5] The belt of doles in the common meadows of the Suttons is shown along a small tributary of the Lugg on the 1720 plan. The overall development of open common fields was sufficiently advanced to have reduced the open common pasture to a small proportion of the whole, but in addition to pastoral rights on the common fields each householder had his croft. The 'toft and croft' in some cases was so placed as to make clear that the original holding dated from and was taken out of the open arable fields. This piecemeal enclosure had been going on from the early seventeenth century at latest when the number of

[1] Op. cit. pp. 95–7, 147–50, and sketch of the 1819 Enclosure Map, p. 147.
[2] Hereford City Library.
[3] *Hereford Cathedral Muniments*, no. 307.
[4] Ibid. nos 1288, 664, 663 and 1112.
[5] Op. cit. pp. 95–7 and 150.

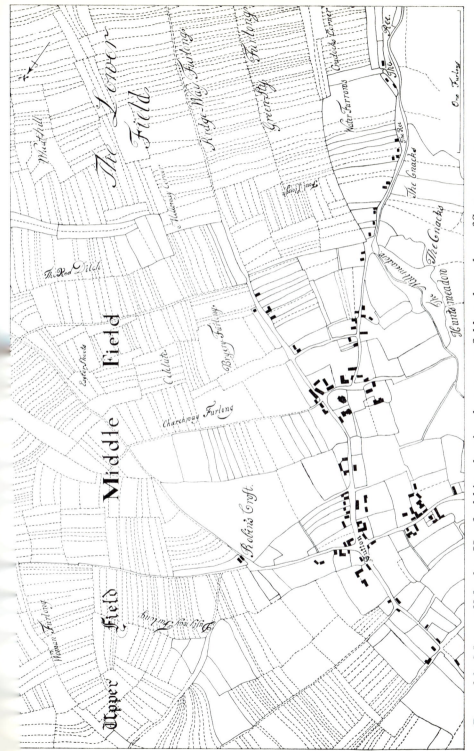

The Lower Field

The Middle Field

Middle Field

Upper Field

The Red Ditch

Easter Sheets

Cdlate

Briery Furlong

Churchway Furlong

Bolin's Croft

Woman Furlong

Yew Tree Furlong

Foul Plough

Ridge Way Furlong

Greenthy Furlong

Greenthy

Crackce's Corner

Water Furrows

The Gnacks

The Gnacks

Huntomeadow

Williamseng

The Ree

The Ree

One Furlong

Sutton

24. **Parts of the Manor of Marden, Herefordshire, showing the common fields and meadows of Sutton, *c.* 1720**

freeholders was 35 as compared with 141 copyholders in the manor of Marden as a whole.[1]

BECKBURY (Shropshire)

In the small Worfe valley near the mid-eastern margins of Shropshire, Beckbury is a compact village of moderate size, one of a group of such villages which appear to be related to the English lowlands rather than to the Welsh Border. Beckbury lies significantly only some four miles west of Pattingham and is likely to be a relatively early Anglo-Saxon settlement, i.e. early seventh century, and this is further supported in that its church is a Milburga foundation. The layout of its lands, despite the masking effect of wholesale enclosure, was clearly characteristic of English townships. Along its small valley was the belt of common meadows, succeeded eastward by probably three open arable fields, at the junction of which lay the village on well drained sands over Triassic sandstones. The Hall stands in the village and its demesne lands are only of small extent. Eastward of the village on a low ridge of between 300 and 350 feet above O.D., the land drops again to about 250 feet. Sandy soils predominate everywhere east of the Worfe and account for the high proportion of arable land in 1839 – 1012 acres out of a total of 1343. By that date, open fields and the wide heaths which occupied up to two-thirds of the township prior to enclosure, had alike given place to modern hedged fields and those on the former heathlands (Fig. 25) show the characteristic large rectangular shapes of late common enclosure. Those of the supposed three former open arable fields are more irregular and only reflect the old strips in occasional instances. On the eastern margins of the township, woodland may once have been held in common or, more probably after the Norman Conquest, have been part of the royal forests which covered a high proportion of these eastern lowlands of mid-Shropshire.

[1] *Jacobean Survey of 1608*, Land Rev., *M.B.*, 217 ff., pp. 194–292, qu. Gray, pp. 95–7.

BECKBURY
IN THE COUNTY OF
SHROPSHIRE

1839

BECKBURY
HALL

H

2

1

3

N

BROOK

HOUSES & GARDENS
PASTURE
FORMER COMMON MEADOW
AREAS 1-3 FORMER OPEN ARABLE
AREA H LATE ENCLOSED HEATH
WOODLAND

4 ML.

25. Beckbury, Shropshire: land use based on the tithe map of 1820

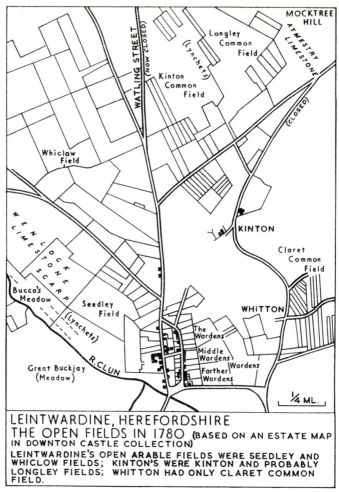

The map contains the following labels:

MOCKTREE HILL

WATLING STREET (NOW CLOSED)

AYMESTRY LIMESTONE

Longley Common Field

(Lynchets)

Kinton Common Field

(CLOSED)

Whiclow Field

WENLOCK LIMESTONE SCARP

KINTON

Claret Common Field

Bucca's Meadow

Seedley Field

(Lynchets)

WHITTON

The Wardens

Middle Wardens

Farther Wardens

Wardens

Great Buckjay (Meadow)

R. CLUN

¼ ML.

LEINTWARDINE, HEREFORDSHIRE
THE OPEN FIELDS IN 1780 (BASED ON AN ESTATE MAP
IN DOWNTON CASTLE COLLECTION)
LEINTWARDINE'S OPEN ARABLE FIELDS WERE SEEDLEY AND
WHICLOW FIELDS; KINTON'S WERE KINTON AND PROBABLY
LONGLEY FIELDS; WHITTON HAD ONLY CLARET COMMON
FIELD.

26. Leintwardine, Herefordshire: the open fields in 1780

LEINTWARDINE (Herefordshire)

This nucleated village, successor of the Roman Bravonium, lies near the confluence of the Clun and the Teme rivers and probably owes nothing to the Romans beyond its location on the Watling Street. Its Anglo-Saxon name and its medieval status as a marcher lord's demesne in the lordship of Wigmore are far more significant in relation to the origin of its field system. As late as 1780, Leintwardine's two arable fields were known as Seedley and Whiclow fields. Kinton, one of its twelve townships[1] also had two fields, but Whitton only one as shown on Figure 26. None of these was large, partly due to the broken relief of this Wenlock Limestone country, and they were enclosed in 1803.[2] Leintwardine also had common meadows along the valley of the river Clun as slopes permitted.[3]

MUCH WENLOCK (Shropshire)

Much Wenlock, at the northern end of Hope Dale between the two limestone scarps of Wenlock Edge, is the parochial township of an eight-township parish. Based on St Milburga's nunnery and a later Cluniac house, it became a small market town.[4] H. L. Gray points out the significance of the fact that, in the fourteenth century, it and the manors of two other abbeys in Shropshire, Shrewsbury and Lilleshall, 'were so tilled that one-third of the arable each year lay both fallow and in common'. While not conclusive, he considers this strong presumptive evidence of the existence of a three-field arable system.[5] Be this as it may, by the eighteenth century it worked a multi-field system, itemised in the index to a 1713 map (unfortunately of little use as a field plan), a 1714 survey, and a 1736 terrier.[6] The map which should have been of most use is unfortunately missing but with the help of field-names plotted on to the tithe map and some description of localities or boundaries in the surveys, it is possible to locate sixteen fields with a fair degree of certainty (Fig. 27). These are Edge field including the Sytch, Homer field, Whittle field, Bradley furlong and New Leasow north of the town, Spital field

---

[1] In the early nineteenth century, Leintwardine with twelve townships and Leominster with ten were the only Herefordshire parishes with more than six townships.

[2] H. L. Gray, op. cit. p. 140.

[3] This account is based on the map which was designed by D. G. Bayliss and used in illustration of his account of Leintwardine in an unpublished M.A. thesis entitled *The Leintwardine Area of Northern Herefordshire* (University of Manchester). His map was based on a plan in Downton Castle Collection in the possession of W. Kincaid Lennox, Esq.

[4] For a fuller description of the place itself see Ch. 14, pp. 339–40.

[5] Op. cit. p. 66, quoting Add. MS. 6165, ff. 37, 43 and 51.

[6] *Wynnstay MSS. and Documents*, nos. 2528–30.

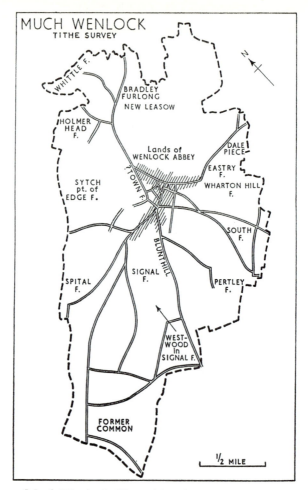

MUCH WENLOCK
TITHE SURVEY

BRADLEY
FURLONG
NEW LEASOW

WHITTLE F.

HOLMER
HEAD
F.

DALE
PIECE

Lands of
WENLOCK ABBEY

EASTRY
F.

SYTCH
pt. of
EDGE F.

TOWN F.

WHARTON HILL
F.

SOUTH
F.

BLUNTHILL

SPITAL
F.

SIGNAL
F.

PERTLEY
F.

WEST-
WOOD
in
SIGNAL F.

FORMER
COMMON

½ MILE

27. Much Wenlock, Shropshire: location of some of the
former open fields

and probably Town field to the west, Signal field including
Westwood, Blunthill, Pertley field and South field to the south,
and Dale Piece, Eastry field and Wharton Hill to the east. Some
of these, as their names imply, were furlongs within larger fields;
others appear to have been relatively late additions. A further five
fields were mentioned of which Ffaroly field may be Farley field
and have lain either on or across the northern boundary of Much

Wenlock township. By the eighteenth century, there had evidently been numerous enclosures and 'in Spittle field now three houses built thereon'. The 1714 survey lists rents for the holdings, averaging 3s per acre. A draft Bill was prepared in 1772, and the Enclosure Act passed in 1806. By the time of the tithe survey the open pasture of Westwood Common and all the open fields were enclosed, and only 1148 of the 2492 acres tithable were arable land.

REDWICK (Monmouthshire)

The extensive and highly developed common meadow system of Redwick is outstanding, though not untypical of the Monmouthshire Moors where the breadth of the coastal marshes makes possible a wider zone of water meadow than in any river valley. Its organisation resembles that of open arable fields, being divided into furlongs within large fields. In the tithe survey of 1844, the meadows were still unenclosed. The largest, Broad Mead, was divided into Ireland Length and Splots Length and lay nearest the sea coast. North-east and north of this were Longmoor Mead and five lesser quilleted fields, some of which may have been originally used as arable fields but later, on the mergence of Redwick with Magor, were converted to common meadow for which the land was far more suitable.[1] Dispersed acres in Chainesmeade were referred to as early as 1430 in a feoffment in the *Newport Collection*.[2] The tithe map (Fig. 28) and apportionment revealed that at that date there were still 130 doles or open meadow strips in Redwick, and of a total area of 2113 acres, 1994 were meadow or pasture. These doles, pegged for the hay harvests and opened out for the rest of the year for pasture, were far more valuable than arable strips. For example, at Bishton (Mon.) a 1788 survey quoted the value at 10s per acre as compared with 4s for the drier 'upland' on which the arable fields were located.[3]

[1] Dorothy Sylvester, 'The Common Fields of the Coastlands of Gwent', *Agric. Hist. Rev.*, VI, i (1958), pp. 18–20. See also Ch. 16, pp. 399–402.
[2] No. 4002.
[3] Ibid. (M 431) no. 3637.

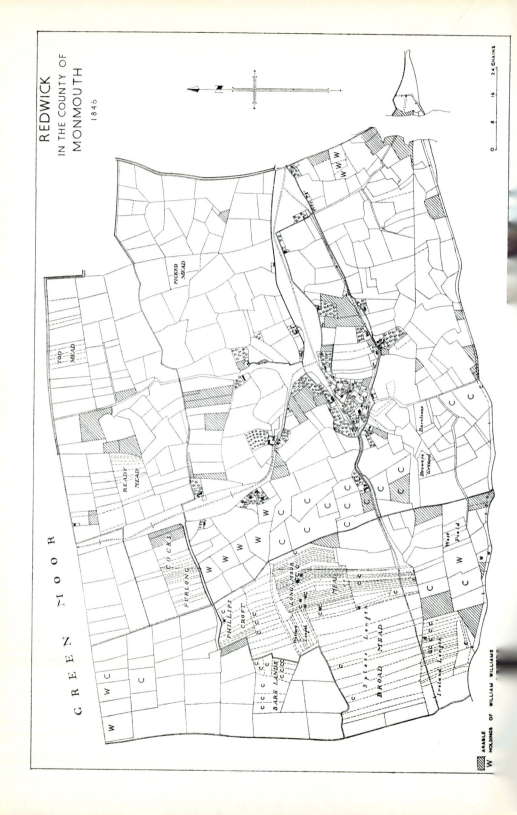

REDWICK
IN THE COUNTY OF
MONMOUTH
1846

GREEN MOOR

PICKED MEAD

TOD MEAD

READY MEAD

COCKS

FURLONG

PHILLIPS CROFT

BARE LANDS

LONG MOOR MEAD

BROAD MEAD

3 Plots Length

Ireland Length

Borleaze

Brewers Ground

West Field

0   8   16   24 CHAINS

ARABLE

W   HOLDINGS OF WILLIAM WILLIAMS

WYBUNBURY (Cheshire)

In south-east Cheshire very near the boundary of Staffordshire, Wybunbury was the parochial township of a large parish of eighteen townships in the early nineteenth century and, apart from Weston, was the only one in which there was a compact village. In 1240, it passed from the de Praers to the bishops of Coventry and Lichfield who, as lords of the manor made a number of entries concerning its open field and its (presumed) common meadow in the *Great Register of Lichfield Cathedral* about that time.[1] There was nothing in these records to suggest that there was more than one common field but surveys of *circa* 1297 in the *Anglesey Papers* listed arable holdings in twelve separate places in Wybunbury, one of which was named 'field' (Denesfeld) and several 'riddings' suggesting that they were comparatively recently cleared for cultivation. Others were crofts, and some simply acres. The significant point, however, is that both in this survey[2] and that of Tarvin,[3] also a nucleated parochial village where there were fourteen separate arable areas, a three-year arable course was practised which at least gives a strong suggestion that there had formerly been a three-field system here. As the tithe plan (Fig. 29) shows, by 1845 there was only one Town Field and that already enclosed. A further point of interest is the peat moss most of which was still held communally and in strips,[4] while relics of former common meadow were still traceable by the small stream in the south.

CHURCH ASTON AND LONGFORD (Shropshire)

Church Aston and Longford are adjacent townships near Newport, the former a small church hamlet, the latter dispersed. Their

---

[1] Nos 539, 547 and 531.

[2] *Anglesey Papers*, document no. D/1734/J.2268 f. 30d–31. William Salt Library, Stafford.

[3] Ibid. no. D1734/J.3268 ff. 29d–30d. Both these documents are reproduced *in extenso* in the writer's paper 'A Note on Medieval Three-Course Arable Systems in Cheshire', *Trans. Hist. Soc. Lancs. and Ches.*, cx (1958), pp. 183–6. There is a fuller discussion of the 1240 documents in 'The Open Fields of Cheshire', also by the present writer in ibid. xviii, pp. 9–10.

[4] Wynbunbury Moss is now a bird sanctuary. In many Cheshire mosses, the strips, pegged for peat-cutting, were known as moss rooms.

28 (*opposite*). Redwick, Monmouthshire:
the common meadows and other lands, from the tithe survey, 1846

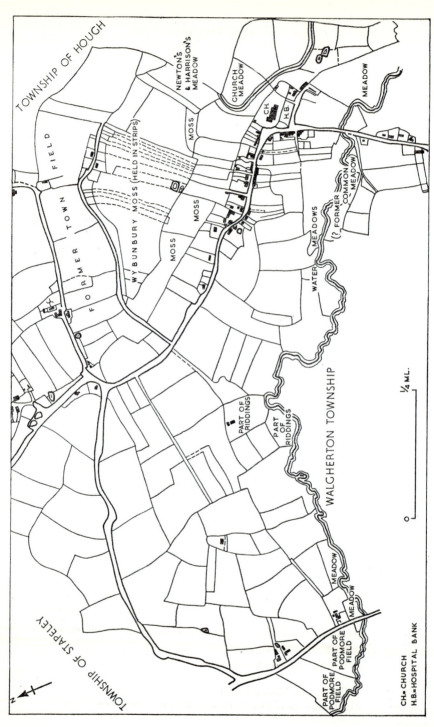

CH.=CHURCH
H.B.=HOSPITAL BANK

TOWNSHIP OF HOUGH

TOWNSHIP OF STAPELEY

FORMER TOWN FIELD

WYBUNBURY MOSS (HELD IN STRIPS)

MOSS

MOSS

MOSS

NEWTON'S & HARRISON'S MEADOW

CHURCH MEADOW

CH.

H.B.

MEADOW

WATER MEADOWS

(? FORMER COMMON MEADOW)

WALGHERTON TOWNSHIP

PART OF RIDDINGS

PART OF RIDDINGS

MEADOW

MEADOW

PART OF PODMORE FIELD

PART OF PODMORE FIELD

0   ¼ ML.

N

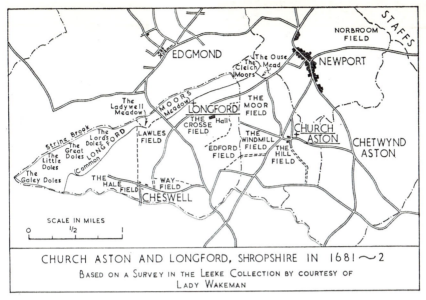

CHURCH ASTON AND LONGFORD, SHROPSHIRE IN 1681 ∼2
BASED ON A SURVEY IN THE LEEKE COLLECTION BY COURTESY OF
LADY WAKEMAN

30. Church Aston and Longford, Shropshire: in 1681–2

fields were the subject of maps in a 1681 Atlas[1] which included
both general maps of the two townships and their lands and
separate plans of Church Aston's three arable fields (Windmill
Field, Moor Field and Hill Field), of crofts in the north-west, and
of the common meadow doles in Cleich Moor. In Longford, there
were five small fields at that date and a very extensive system of
common meadows as compared with the open arable lands and
the size of the township. The open arable strips were variously
referred to in contemporary documents in the same *Collection* as
butts (equated with a day's work), selions, pikes and flatts in the
seventeenth century, and in 1736[2] occurred the first mention of a
copyhold – an enclosure in Mill Field (Fig. 30).

ASTON AND SHOTTON (Hawarden, Flintshire)

There was ploughland at Hawarden, Aston, Bretton and Broughton in 1086. A grant of selions was made in the thirteenth century

[1] *Maps of the Manors of Longford, Edgmond and Church Aston, Leeke Collection*, Shropshire Record Office.
[2] No. 53.

ASTON & SHOTTON
FLINTSHIRE
C.1650

at Bretton[1] and rentals of pepper and plough irons were paid for bovates of land in Hawarden in the same century.[2] A rental of 1464 listed 584 selions and their holders in Hawarden manor,[3] but otherwise, the first reliable indications of open fields at Aston and Shotton in the lordship of Hawarden are on a plan of *circa* 1651, one of five surviving of an original set of twelve in the *Glynne of Hawarden Collection*.[4] This is reproduced in part in Figure 31 and shows the Hom field and the Town field of Aston and the whole area is divided intricately into quillets. This was apparently a two-field township at that time, but a 1736 schedule with an associated map[5] listing the holdings in 'Aston Town Field' mentions not only the Town Field and the Hom Field but holdings in New Hey, Little Hom, Hall Flatt, Brook Field, Cowleys Field and 'a butt in Nangreaves headland,' as well as 'his Peg by Saltney' Wall meadow and two 'butts in grass ground'. Shotton shared Wall Meadow and, judging by the smaller area of the common field land on its division and enclosure in 1759, it probably shared its arable land also. The multi-field system of the eighteenth century in Aston would appear to result from the subdivision of the original two fields. Alternatively, the names indicated what were originally furlongs in the two fields. Here, as in the Monmouthshire Moors, the common meadow and open pastures were on the salt flats of the estuarine shoreland. In the early nineteenth century, the tithe map depicted a few open quillets and numerous parallel strip-shaped enclosures within the otherwise totally enclosed townships of Aston and Shotton.[6]

PENIARTH (Meifod, Montgomeryshire)

The parochial township of an eleven-township parish, Peniarth includes the nucleated village of Meifod[7] grouped around the northern arc of the great churchyard. This feature is exceptional, but the rest of the township is characteristic of hundreds of Welsh

[1] *Hawarden Deeds*, no. 5.
[2] *Writ of Extent*, Chan. Inq. P.M., file 10, no. 6.
[3] Qu. W. Bell Jones, in a *History of the Parish of Hawarden*, privately typed N.L.W.
[4] N.L.W. See an account of the dating in Dorothy Sylvester, 'Settlement Patterns in Rural Flintshire', *Trans. Fl. Hist. Soc.* (1954–5), pp. 25–6.
[5] Ibid. both map and schedule are reproduced.
[6] Ibid. the tithe map is reproduced as Fig. 6.   [7] See Ch. 18, pp. 448–9.

31 (*opposite*). Aston and
  Shotton, Flintshire

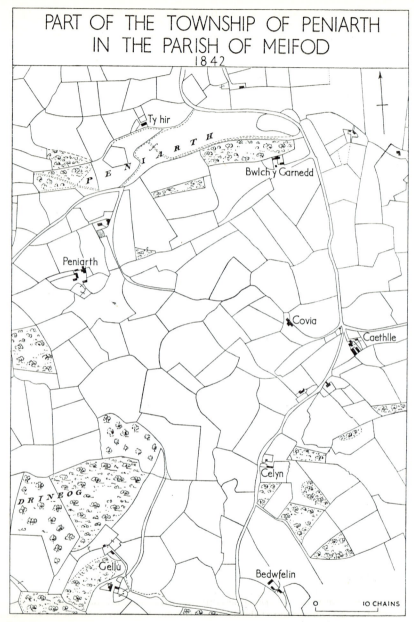

PART OF THE TOWNSHIP OF PENIARTH
IN THE PARISH OF MEIFOD
1842

Ty hir

PENIARTH

Bwlch y Garnedd

Peniarth

Covia

Caethlle

Celyn

DRINEOG

Gellu

Bedwfelin

0   10 CHAINS

32. Peniarth, Montgomeryshire: part of the tithe map of 1842

dispersed settlement areas. The portion illustrated (Fig. 32) shows the typically isolated farmsteads: Peniarth itself, Bwlch y Garnedd, Caethlle and Gellu among them. Small woods and plantations which do so much to beautify the landscape of eastern Montgomeryshire and which are found on part of almost every hill slope, are scattered over the township, and the rather fragmentary documentary evidence suggests that the compact farm is well established here,[1] and apart from sundry *erwau*,[2] there is no available evidence to indicate that co-aration took place in compact fields or even in small crofts. Indeed, the communal arrangements of the tribal period are wholly masked in the field patterns of the late eighteenth and early nineteenth centuries, but the pattern of dispersed steadings is almost entirely ancient. The irregularity of the field shapes is in sharp contrast to the large rectangular fields typical of common or waste enclosure.

RHIWLAS (Montgomeryshire)

The common pasture or waste in which all occupants, whether copyholders or otherwise, had rights of common pasturage both in England and Wales, forms part of many township plans in the pre-enclosure period. Maps depicting the open pasture in any detail or showing it as a separate feature are rare, but a number are to be found in the *Glansevern Collection* (N.L.W.) and one of these, near to Llangurig, is reproduced in Figure 33. The high point of these uplands is 1433 feet above O.D., and the plan includes several high moorland farmsteads, their limited small fields or in-land, and their extensive sheepwalks, most of which are part of the farm in the broad sense and the rights of pasture sold with it. Only in the north-east is there common pasture for two farms, but originally all rights were undoubtedly communal.

ORETON (Farlow, Shropshire)

The tithe map of Oreton (Fig. 34) on the slopes of Titterstone Clee reveals a large area of open common (300 acres in a total area of

---

[1] *Glansevern Collection*, plans of Peniarth and Capel farms, N.D. (late 18th or early 19th century).
[2] *Coleman Deeds*, p. 183, no. 701 (1719), 4 *erwau* mentioned in Nant y Mechiaid, a township of Meifod.

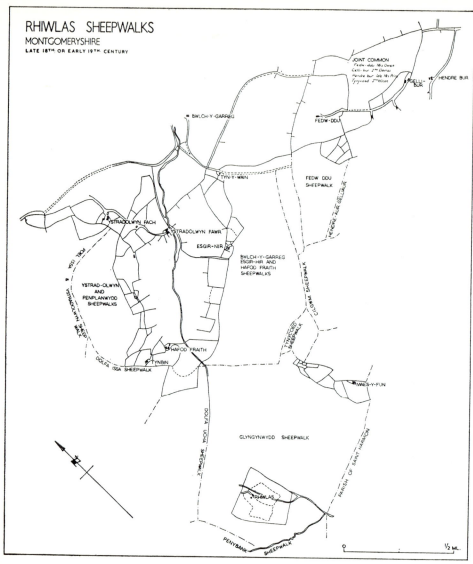

RHIWLAS SHEEPWALKS
MONTGOMERYSHIRE
LATE 18TH. OR EARLY 19TH. CENTURY

JOINT COMMON
Fedw-ddu Mrs Owen
Celli-bur Jno Davies
Hendre bur late Mrs Price
Tynycoed Jno Wilson

GELLI-BUR

HENDRE BUR

BWLCH-Y-GARREG

FEDW-DDU

TYN-Y-WAIN

FEDW DDU
SHEEPWALK

HENDRE-AIR GELLIAR

YSTRADOLWYN FACH

YSTRADOLWYN FAWR

ESGIR-NIR

BWLCH-Y-GARREG
ESGIR-HIR AND
HAFOD FRAITH
SHEEPWALKS

FOEL ISSA

YSTRAD-OLWYN
AND
PENPLANWYDD
SHEEPWALKS

YSTRADOLWYN SHEEP WALK

CILGWM SHEEPWALK

TYNYCOED SHEEPWALK

DOLFA ISSA SHEEPWALK

HAFOD FRAITH

TYNBIN

MAES-Y-FUN

DOLFA UCHA SHEEPWALK

GLYNGYNWYDD SHEEPWALK

PARISH OF SAINT HARMON

RHIWLAS

PENYBANK SHEEPWALK

½ ML.

33. Rhiwlas, Montgomeryshire: sheepwalks as shown on a map in the
Glansevern Collection of the late eighteenth or early nineteenth century

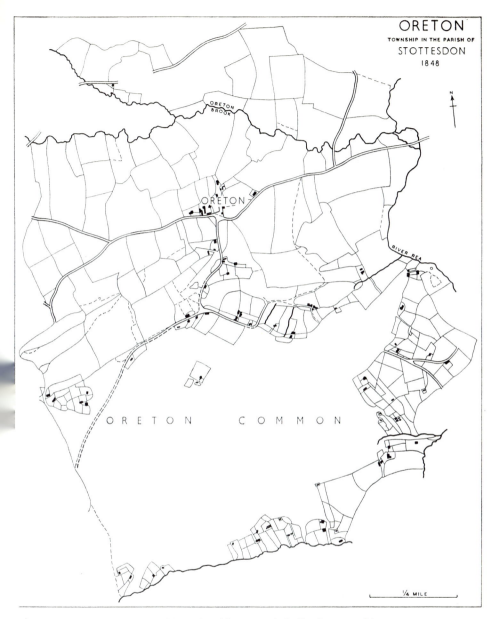

ORETON
TOWNSHIP IN THE PARISH OF
STOTTESDON
1848

ORETON
BROOK

ORETON

RIVER REA

O R E T O N   C O M M O N

¼ MILE

34. Oreton, Shropshire: the tithe map (1848) of a township on
Titterstone Clee showing squatting settlement around the common

843 acres) occupying the southern part of the township in 1844. The original settlement was the hamlet which lies centrally in the enclosed belt and the field pattern does not preclude its once having had an open arable field. By 1844, however, the majority of the cottages were those of (undated) squatters' holdings typically grouped around the fringe of the common moorland high on the Clee slopes, and one of these isolated towards the middle of the waste. This is a classic example of a squatting settlement in which the poor, simple dwellings were roughly thrown up overnight and a portion of land claimed with them. The small size of the 'crofts' and 'patches' listed in the tithe apportionment, and their irregular, patchwork pattern is quickly recognised either in plan or on the ground. Many of their occupants are now employed in the nearby dhustone quarries of Titterstone Clee.

SHELVOKE (Ruyton XI Towns, Shropshire)

The 'farm type of township' is found in numbers among the dependent townships of both Cheshire and north Shropshire and is characterised by a handful of compact farms or even by only one or two. Some at least of these are remnants of formerly rather larger communities and the history of their reduction to one or two or only a very small number of holdings is the history usually of the buying up of neighbouring farms or their compacting as the result of marriage or inheritance. Some, however, may represent the residue of a population reduced by plague or desertion. Lloyd Kenyon says that Shelvoke or Shelvock was a berewick of the manor of Wikey in pre-Conquest times, later supplanting it as the head of the manor and that in the fourteenth century the townsmen of Shelvoke claimed their immemorial right to pasturage on Wigmarsh Common.[1] This suggests that there was at any rate a hamlet-sized community. But by 1839 it consisted of one farm of 259 acres, a lesser holding of 63 acres, and Hanley Hall (in the north-west corner) with only an acre of its land in this township. This is an extreme example of a small farm-type township, but by no means unique. If this pattern is multiplied to include a fair number of farms, it can be seen as the

---

[1] R. Lloyd Keynon, 'The Domesday Manors of Ruyton, Wikey, and Felton', *Trans. Shrops. Archaeol. Soc.*, xii (1900).

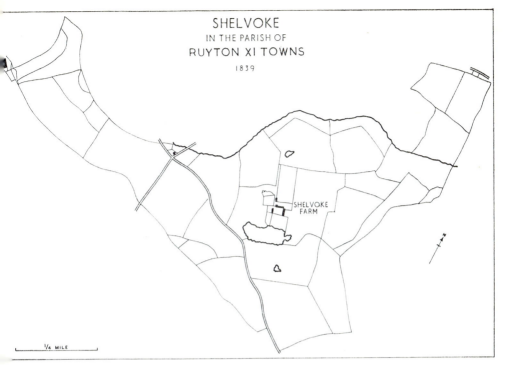

35. Shelvoke, Shropshire: a typical farm township.
The 1842 tithe map

characteristically dispersed township of many more of the dependent communities in the large parishes of Cheshire, Shropshire, and north-east and central Wales. Their generic relationship should not necessarily be inferred from their nineteenth-century pattern.

DODDINGTON (Wybunbury, Cheshire)

The expansion and frequently the isolation of the demesne lands from the time of the Norman Conquest resulted in the large park-estate type of township. In many cases, there was little else but a home farm, a mill, a lodge, perhaps a smithy and a few cottages for estate workers. In certain cases, the park absorbed parts of neighbouring townships and the former common fields, as was

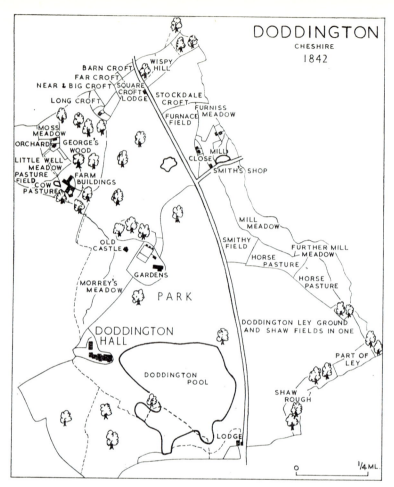

36. Doddington, Cheshire: A park-estate township.
   The 1842 tithe map

the case in Gwysaney (Flintshire) and Doddington. The manor
house or hall dominated the economy and the plan alike, as the
tithe map of Doddington (Fig. 36) shows. Its growth as an estate
can be traced century by century under the eventually united
Delves-Broughton family.[1]

   [1] It is described in greater detail in Ch. 10 and in the writer's paper 'Rural Settlement in Cheshire', *Trans. Hist. Soc. Lancs. and Ches.*, ci (1949).

The Distribution of Open Fields and Common Meadows
in the Borderland

The Great Enclosure period is a historical watershed of major importance in the history of the rural landscape. During the hundred years or so that it covered, many of the ancient field patterns became absorbed into the rectangular and sub-rectangular shapes which today characterise most lowland and valley townships. The habitation pattern, apart from easily recognised later additions, remained relatively little altered, especially in the Welsh Borderland where urban invasion of the countryside was in general very limited. But the ancient field boundaries which were widely erased are now traceable mainly through documentary sources, old maps and plans, old field names, aerial photographs, traces of ridge and furrow and of old field boundaries on the ground, and relict field shapes. The massive, but nevertheless incomplete, evidence of their former existence is presented in Figure 23. It would require a whole volume to describe it adequately, but as a summary, it serves as the second most important part of the rural pattern as it once was, and certain deductions can be made with confidence, others more tentatively.

The major feature of the map is the sharp contrast between the areas of native Welsh agriculture in the western parts and the wide distribution of open arable fields and common meadows in the east. There is no question that there is here a major cultural–economic boundary. A second striking feature of the map is the prime concentration of three-field townships in central and eastern Herefordshire and central and eastern Shropshire, supporting H. L. Gray's map of the extension of his Midland Field System westward into those parts of the Welsh Borderland.[1] There is also, however, a clear belt of open field townships, many of the two- and three-field types, to the west of Gray's western boundary. This occupies the lower Clwyd valley and adjacent coastlands, the lower Dee valley in Flintshire, Denbighshire, and Cheshire, north-west Shropshire, the Vale of Welshpool and mid-western Shropshire, parts of the Wye–Llynfi basin in southern

[1] Op. cit., frontispiece.

Radnorshire and northern Breconshire, and eastern and southern Monmouthshire. A glance at D. F. Renn's map of the distribution of mottes is sufficient to confirm the correspondence of this westerly extension of the two- and three-field system with the area of Anglo-Norman power in the Borderland. It leaves no doubt that this westerly belt is of Anglo-Norman origin and at the same time it raises the question of Norman influence in the remainder of the English border counties. There is direct evidence of the contribution of numerous lay lords and of the religious houses and the cathedral churches to the extension of open-field agriculture in their manors, as for instance in eastern Delamere Forest, in Wirral and Much Wenlock and we are therefore faced with the possibility that, in Cheshire at least, and perhaps also in Shropshire and Herefordshire, the two- and three-field townships may owe the full bloom of their medieval arable systems to the Normans.

The wide distribution of one-field townships in Cheshire, and their more restricted spread over a north–south belt in both mid-Shropshire and mid-Herefordshire poses the greatest problems, perhaps, in connection with this map. In some cases the existence of a one-field symbol on the map is a reflection of scanty evidence, and the total area may have to be reduced as further evidence comes in. The way must be kept clear, however, for the possibility that there is a genuine one-field belt and, if so, it may represent an area farther west than that covered by relatively close Anglian settlement, but insufficiently far west to have been included in the marcher belt where the Normans were undoubtedly influential in extending the two- and three-field system westward across the flanks of the Welsh hills, into the vales which cut across them, and in the adjacent piedmont. In other words, this belt may be one which fell between two stools and so retained an older Celtic arable system, or it may have lapsed for similar reasons from an original two-field system introduced by a weak Anglian settlement group. Whatever the cause, the Borderland again shows itself as a characteristic contact zone where, between the arable arrangements of the Welsh hill areas to the west and the two- and three-field system of Gray's Midland System in the English lowlands to the east, the Normans had created a third belt and there may have been a fourth immediately to the east of it.

PART FOUR

Local Studies

11 The Cheshire Plain

> The Cheshire folk differ from the rest of the English, partly better partly equal . . . . The Soil is fat, fruitfull and rich, yeelding abundantly both profit and pleasure to man. The Champion grounds make glad the hearts of their tillers; the Meadows imbrodered with divers sweet smelling flowers; and the Pastures makes the Kines udders to strout to the Paile, from whom and wherein the best Cheese of all Europe is made.
>
> John Speed in *The Theatre of the Empire of Great Britain*, 1611

THE greater part of Cheshire settlement is adjusted to an undulating, drift-covered lowland which extends from the Pennine hill-foot across the entire remaining width of the county, except where it gives place to the slim line of the Central Cheshire Ridge. There Triassic sandstones emerge from below the drift to form an interrupted north–south spine of upland nowhere more than three miles wide nor, except in the Bickerton hills, exceeding 600 feet in height. Comparatively minor though picturesque outcrops of Triassic sandstones also account for isolated low hills in Wirral and in some parts of south Cheshire, but the total extent of solid rock is negligible compared with the wide and deep blanket of glacial and post-glacial drift which mantles the plain. The value and workability of these deep-soil lowlands, however, was offset for early settlers by the fact that the greater part of the area bore surface deposits of heavy, sticky clays, and only comparatively limited patches of lighter loams and sands. In addition, the cool, moist northern climate combined with the clay soils, gave rise to dense damp oakwoods which offered a further deterrent to would-be settlers, especially to the Angles whose agronomy was arable rather than pastoral. The heavy forest cover and the relative remoteness of the Cheshire plain made colonisation slow and it is in parts incomplete to this day.

The Cheshire lowlands are divided into two major areas by the central Cheshire ridge. To the east, though no sharp physical

I

contrast exists, they can be further distinguished on the grounds of settlement geography into the broad area drained chiefly by the Weaver and the lower Dane, and the eastern plains which skirt the Pennine foothills. The Weaver valley always figured in the pre-industrial phase as the third sub-region of the county in order of prosperity and population, with its valley villages, market towns, rich meadowland and brine springs. The eastern plains are similar in that they are covered with mixed glacial clays and sands, but no major valleys dominate them and their late clearance from a heavy woodland cover and their devastation by William the Conqueror's armies after his mid-winter march across the Pennines long delayed their economic development. The western part of the plain falls naturally into two further divisions; the long peninsula of Wirral and the valleys of the lower Gowy and the lower Dee. By comparison with the second, Wirral is a low elevation of faulted Triassic sandstones which emerge patchily from under their cover of glacial drift to form hills of varying height up to 200 and, in the case of Heswall Hill, over 350 feet. The Dee–Gowy lowlands are, by contrast, the most level and include the most marshy stretches of the Cheshire plain. Their location and their general fertility favoured early development by both Celts and Romans, hence they ranked for centuries as the foremost, and Wirral as the second, most developed subdivision of Cheshire, and were among the first parts of the plain to be cleared for settlement.

The earliest settlers favoured the hills. The Central Cheshire Ridge and the Pennine Edge and its foothills were the principal lines of early movement. Seven Early Iron Age hill forts crown the Central Ridge. A prehistoric trackway followed the crest of the Ridge, but since the downhill movement of the Romano-British and sub-Roman phases it has remained virtually uninhabited over the greater part of its length and has functioned as a boundary rather than as an axis of settlement. To the east lies a spread of deltaic sands bearing much of the light woodland which formed part of the medieval Forest of Mara and Mondrem and this similarly, though for different reasons, limited settlement in the centre of the county. Beyond the sands lay wide stretches of damp oakwood on the boulder clays, forming a denser and more intractable woodland.

Although the heavy clays predominate, they bear patches of

glacial sands, narrow ribbons of alluvium, and pockets of moss-land. Throughout history, Cheshire's arable farming has been limited by the heavy and easily water-logged clays and the short, cool summers, so that cattle rather than sheep or wheat have long proved best suited to Cheshire, though corn was grown of necessity. Compared with the lighter loams and sands, the clays are resistant to the plough and expensive to cultivate, while cereals tend to be thin in the ear and long in the stalk in a typical Cheshire season. Nevertheless, bread being an essential item of diet, the common arable fields, though small, were an integral part of the land use pattern of most Cheshire townships.

The Progress of Settlement

The Celtic, the Mercian and the medieval phases saw the major shaping of the county's settlement pattern but with the influential addition of Roman roads, and some Scandinavian modifications in Wirral and east Cheshire. The Celtic foundations were of very great significance, the Anglian colonisation important but sparse, and Norman overlordship perhaps surprisingly universal and penetrating. These three main phases are reflected respectively in the wide distribution of early hamlets and dispersed settlement; the parochial villages and, in Wirral, the lesser villages; and the extraordinary prominence of the manor as an institution and the park-estate as an element in the settlement pattern.

The combined evidence of place-names, archaeology, woodland recession, and settlement features supports the conclusion that Cheshire west of the Central Ridge was closely settled and comparatively well developed during both the Celtic and Old English periods, but that beyond the longitude of Tarvin – the 'boundary settlement' – lay another province, still deeply wooded and thinly occupied in 1086 except along the Weaver and, to a lesser degree, some of the valleys of the eastern plain. The only exception to this broad division into a western and an eastern central province was the Mersey valley which has every appearance of having been settled at latest by the middle of the Mercian phase and perhaps before that, especially in the stretch up to Bowdon and Altrincham. Yet even during the Celtic period, there is evidence of not inconsiderable occupation of the eastern and central lowland. A significant line of Celtic place-names extends across it from west to east, and another along the foothills of the Pennines. This latter line is coincident with a string of early parochial villages including Prestbury, Astbury, Barthomley and Wybunbury, whence it swings round to Audlem on the edge of the Ellesmere moraine. Not far away are two other -*burh* villages with parochial status – Wrenbury and Marbury – and, turning north another -*burh* which is at the centre of a large parish, Bunbury. Most have elevated church-sites and could well have been pre-Anglian settlements, retrospectively named -*burh* as were so many Iron Age hill forts. They may, too, have been centres of Celtic Christianity, outliers of Bangor on Dee's great missionary community as was also, perhaps, Eccleshall in Staffordshire at no greater distance.

There can be no doubt that the depredations of William the Conqueror in eastern Cheshire obscured the picture of its earlier settlement geography to a marked extent. That its recovery was slow seems to be confirmed by the small size of its villages and hamlets for centuries afterwards. From Tarvin eastwards, only the Weaver valley was reasonably populated and cultivated in 1086. The dense oakwoods held sway to the west of it and in a wide belt below the Pennine foot. The central woodland became absorbed into the earl's Forest of Mara, which extended sufficiently far to include some areas of earlier Anglian cultivation, as did its southern portion, the Forest of Mondrem. The same was doubtless true of the Forest of Macclesfield which embraced the moorlands and slopes of the Cheshire Pennines and the woodlands at their foot. The overall density of population in Domesday Cheshire was probably about ten to the square mile, and about double that figure in 1300, representing an increase from some 11,000 to well over 20,000 people as compared with the present population of over one and a quarter million.[1] The average number of families in a Cheshire manor at Domesday was about six, and must therefore have been far smaller in the east and appreciably higher in the west, where numerous places could count ten or more households. Nor is it without interest to notice that after Eastham, then

[1] Dorothy Sylvester, 'Rural Settlement in Cheshire', *Trans. Hist. Soc. Lancs. and Ches.* (1949), pp. 7 and 10 summarising evidence from *Domesday Book*, J. Brownbill, 'Cheshire in Domesday Book', loc. cit. (1901), and H. J. Hewitt, *Mediæval Cheshire* (1929).

the second largest place in the county, Landican had the next largest population in Wirral.

The wide extent of woodlands and wastelands offered a clear field for Norman landtaking. Except in the Dee valley where defensive needs lent themselves to clustered villages, Norman settlement in Cheshire was not generally in rural nucleations but took one of two forms – the seignorial borough which became a market-town, or the park-estate based on the manor house. Practically every market-town in Cheshire of any consequence except Chester itself owed its urban status to medieval seignorial charters. Congleton, Over, Altrincham, Knutsford and Tarporley were created boroughs in this way in the thirteenth century.[1] The boroughs of Frodsham and Macclesfield were founded on the demesne lands of the earldom of Chester by earl Ranulf III. Stockport, Nantwich, Halton and Malpas had a similar origin at different times in the Middle Ages, and Northwich and Middlewich arose as dominial salt towns. Frodsham, Over, Tarporley, Malpas and Stockport had become parishes before 1291 but the rest remained, in some cases for centuries, in the parish of a neighbouring village: Altrincham in Bowdon, Macclesfield in Prestbury, Congleton in Astbury, Knutsford in Rostherne, Halton in Runcorn (the latter eventually becoming the market-town), and Nantwich in Acton. There thus developed the curious position that five of the Cheshire market-towns had no parochial status until late in their history, and the corresponding five villages had an abnormally swollen parochial population.

The intervening empty quarters of Domesday Cheshire offered ample room for the creation of new manors, and between 1066 and 1300 many were made by subinfeudation of the barons' holdings and by morcellation of lesser estates. In 1252, twenty-four holdings (totalling seventy-nine knights' fees) were listed in the *Red Book of the Exchequer* under Cheshire. In 1300, further lists were drawn up, in preparation for the Scottish wars of Edward I, of those who held from the king in chief by knight service in the county.[2] Together they add fifty-three to the Domesday total of 314 manors, yet it is doubtful whether even this figure represented anything approaching the real total at that date, the climax of

---

[1] James Tait, Introduction to the *Middlewich Chartulary*, II, pp. xxiv–xxix.
[2] Quoted in *Cheshire Sheaf*, 3rd series, v, nos 777 and 795.

manorial proliferation,[1] and it may be surmised that there were at least 400 to 450 manorial holdings at the end of the thirteenth century.

In this county as elsewhere, there have been innumerable changes in the overlordship of Cheshire manors. Many of the greater baronies broke up during the later Middle Ages, and the earl of Chester's estates passed via queen Isabella and the Black Prince to the Crown. Some manorial families, however, have held without a break from the Conquest, for example the Leghs of High Legh whose ancestors include Edward de Lega on whom was bestowed the vill of Lega in the eleventh century, Richard earl of Cornwall and brother of Henry III, and Hywel Dda and other Welsh princes.

By Tudor times the number of manors had been appreciably reduced, but the manorial lords, here as elsewhere, reached a new peak of prosperity after Union and the inclusion of Cheshire within the English realm. It was associated with a vast programme of re-building, usually in half-timber, and so important was it in this county that Cheshire earned the soubriquet of 'the seedplot of gentility'. As time went on, more manors disappeared, but the two major divisions of the county fared very differently in this respect. By Georgian times, there were comparatively few gentlemen's seats left in west Cheshire, apart from Eaton Hall, the magnificent mansion of the dukes of Westminster, but in the more thinly populated east with its late-surviving woodlands, ambitious lords had found every opportunity to expand their estates. By the late eighteenth and early nineteenth centuries their many great houses were surrounded by parks which were almost as wide as the townships in which they lay, and in some cases had absorbed lands from neighbouring townships. In many cases, neither village nor hamlet was to be found in the typical estate township, only a new (post-Conquest) type of dispersed settlement consisting of habitations for estate workers.[2]

---

[1] Architectural and place-name evidence, estate documents, and ancient moated sites are among the various facts supporting this assumption. In addition, the 1580 lists of armigerous families in the county include a number with seats not mentioned in D.B., or the thirteenth-century lists. Ref. *The Visitation of Cheshire in the year 1580 made by Robert Glover, Somerset Herald for Wm. Flower, Norroy King of Arms,* Harl. Soc. (1882).

[2] A map of the manors of Cheshire, according to the records, etc., of their origin and survival, was first published in *Trans. Lancs. and Ches. Antiq. Soc.,* lxx (1960):

Not only the manor-houses, but the cottages and farmhouses took on a new look as population and prosperity advanced in the Tudor age. The rude, barely habitable cottages of the Middle Ages were increasingly replaced by half-timbered, frame houses in the Cheshire Plain where timber was abundant or, as in the west, not far to seek. From the seventeenth century, bricks began to be used, especially away from the better forested lands, but many a brick farmhouse and cottage in Cheshire conceals the inner structure and old rooms of earlier frame houses.[1] Shortage of timber was only one reason for the change to brick, fear of fire an additional motive.[2]

The manor was perhaps the most potent influence in rural patterning from the eleventh to the seventeenth century, but its near-extinction in parts of west Cheshire was testimony to the strength of the community which had survived for so many centuries despite the power of the manorial concept. Although the park-estate was to blossom even more luxuriantly in the eighteenth century, the increasingly democratic temper of seventeenth-century England was quietly working like a slow ferment towards the eventual democratisation not only of society but of the rural complex as a whole. Nowhere in the Borderland was this more the case than in Cheshire where Nonconformity and industrialism were both symptomatic and causal. Enclosure of the Cheshire commons which covered the years from 1765 to 1898, the turnpiking of old and new roads, the rise of the new enclosure hamlets, the building of the very numerous Nonconformist chapels, the advancing prosperity of farmers and a further wave of farmhouse building, this time in brick, and of brick cottages for their farm labourers, spattered the county with more dispersed dwellings and more hamlets. The older villages in many cases expanded in the eighteenth century as travel and trade increased, but the real rural growth in nineteenth-century Cheshire was broadcast

---

Dorothy Sylvester, 'The Manor and the Cheshire Landscape'. In this paper the manor is discussed from its inception to the nineteenth century. Maps showing the distribution of Cheshire manors in the early Middle Ages and at 1673 are also included in this paper. Domesday, Tudor, and Georgian Seats are mapped in the *Historical Atlas of Cheshire*, op. cit. pp. 23, 31 and 33.

[1] W. A. Singleton, 'Traditional House Types in Lancashire and Cheshire', *Trans. Hist. Soc. Lancs. and Ches.*, civ (1952), pp. 75–91.

[2] The fires of Nantwich in 1438 and 1583, and the fire which destroyed most of Tarvin in 1752, exemplify its very real dangers where frame houses predominated.

over the entire plain, filling in the one-time commons and even many of the mosses with new fields, both large and small, with new cottages, hamlets and farmhouses, some along new roads, and extinguishing all but fragmentary evidences of the old town fields. Far from adding charm to the rural scene, the effect of the nineteenth century was to render much of it pedestrian and workaday, and where the industries of the new mechanical age arose the effect, as on the saltfields and in the Mersey belt, was all too often positively ugly. Fortunately the blight was restricted in area and it could happen, as around Crewe, that almost every township in the southern arc was affected by suburban influences, but in the northern arc the countryside remained happily remote and untouched.

West Cheshire

Although Wirral and the Dee–Gowy lowlands are clear sub-regions, many features of their rural geography proclaim them, nevertheless, to be parts of a larger division which enjoyed a long period of common history. It is these western lowlands rather than an overall distribution which give to Cheshire the highest density of nucleated settlements in any part of the Borderland. The majority of the townships of west Cheshire centre on villages or hamlets, and in a high proportion of these the siting is on low exposures of sandstone or on patches of glacial sands. Common arable fields were more numerous and the system of co-aration was more intensively developed here than in the centre and east. Correspondingly, woodland was negligible in extent even from the early period of Anglian colonisation, and open pasture less extensive. Dispersal was typical of many of the townships in which clays predominated, but the nucleated communities were a feature at least from early Anglian times, and this, combined with the scarcity of unoccupied land, served to bring about the comparatively early extinction of the manorial element in the greater part of the west. Both sub-regions were alike too in the smallness of their townships and, still more noticeably, their parishes. Woodchurch had ten, West Kirby nine, and Eastham and Neston each eight townships in their ancient parishes (early nineteenth century) but, apart from these four only eight others had as many as five townships, and one two, three, and four were more typical. Immediately to the east, the very large Cheshire parishes begin.

(i) WIRRAL

From the time of Hume[1] the site of ancient Meols on (and beyond) the present coastline of north Wirral has been recognised as being archaeologically the most important in the peninsula. More recently, J. D. Bu'Lock has brought up to date the occupational history of this remarkable site on which have been found evidences of continuous settlement from Neolithic times to the present day including Romano-British, early and late Anglo-Saxon and Irish–Norse material, much of it in abundance.[2] This site is unique not only in Cheshire, but in the entire Borderland and amply confirms the occupational succession in north Wirral.

Place-names and settlement alike reflect a fourfold series of habitation and land use patterns from Celtic to Norman together with later developments and modifications, mainly of the agronomy, prior to the present century when the large-scale invasion of Wirral from Merseyside began in earnest.

Dispersal is comparatively rare, dispersed townships at the time of the tithe survey including only Noctorum (a single farm township in 1844), Pensby (a two-farm township in 1846), Arrowe, Lea, Blacon, Little Saughall and Woodbank. Hamlets formed a cluster in mid-north Wirral around Landican, and a further group lay across the root of the peninsula north of Chester, continuing those of the lower Gowy valley. The rest of Wirral was characterised by a large number of closely situated small villages, some non-parochial, eight parochial. One of the more striking characteristics of Wirral rural settlement is its distribution on sandy sites on the low elevations which run parallel to its two estuarine coasts, while the median valley attracted only two valley villages – Barnston and Brimstage.

[1] A. Hume, *Ancient Meols, or Some Account of the Antiquities found near Dove Point on the Sea-Coast of Cheshire* (London, 1863).
[2] 'The Celtic, Saxon and Scandinavian Settlement at Meols in Wirral', *Trans. Hist. Soc. Lancs. and Ches.*, cxii (1960), pp. 1–28. A sketch map in this paper delineates the retreat of the coastline and the site of Dove Spit where many of the objects were found.

12

The typical Wirral pattern is that of a small township centred on a small to medium-sized village or hamlet occupying a hill or hillock, and with one or two formerly open arable fields adjacent to it, perhaps former common meadow also, and – by the nineteenth century – with any earlier open pasture generally enclosed in somewhat larger rectangular or sub-rectangular fields. The town field was still evident in the great proportion of the townships with its relict strips and the repetition of field-names such as *town field, town end, loon, loont, flat* and *shot* as well as the Scandinavian *dale*. With its consistently high population, arable land predominated and open pasture was scarce in most places.

Woodchurch is a parochial hamlet in mid-north Wirral whose church of Holy Cross is one of the oldest foundations in Cheshire. Woodchurch is a late name and was given to land taken out of the manor of *Landican* where there was a priest in 1086. As there was no church in what is now Landican, this must presumably have been the church of Woodchurch, situated within a circular church yard. The Rev. B. H. Turvey believes that this was an original Celtic *llan* associated with St Tecwyn or Degwyn, a contemporary of St Cadfan who died *circa* 616. He suggests in further support of this theory that the coincidence of the later dedication of Holy Cross, replacing an intermediate (Roman) dedication to St Peter, was conferred because the patronal festival on September 14th was the date of St Tecwyn's feast day. In other words that when the local people managed to get rid of the St Peter dedication they made the understandable mistake of thinking that the patronal date meant Holy Cross to be the original one whereas the probability seems strongly in favour of St Tecwyn.[1] Like the typical Wirral township, Woodchurch had remnants of both a town field and a town meadow in 1849.

The Norse-named villages or hamlets were very similar, for example Irby. Nor were those with Anglo-Saxon names very much different if at all, for it seems that the 'Wirral type' if such it may be called, was the result of an appreciable degree of fusion over the centuries succeeding the invasions. In south Wirral, however, the Norse element is lacking and two villages in particular have maintained a very English appearance. These are

[1] 'Was Woodchurch founded in the Sixth Century?', *Cheshire Historian*, 9 (1959), pp. 31–2.

Eastham and Burton. *Eastham*[1] was a large centre by the late Old English period, and remained throughout the centuries a compact sizeable nucleation around its church (which also lies within a circular churchyard) and a small green. Old sandstone and half-timbered cottages still survive in the centre, and at the tithe survey numerous town-field names and a Townfield Lane witnessed to the former existence of a town field, while strips in the south-west may have been remnants of a second arable field or of a common meadow. Former open heath completed the triple basis of the old agronomy.

At *Burton*, another compact and rather picturesque village consisting largely of old cottages, is given an Anglo-Norman touch by Burton Hall (now known as Burton Manor). The parish was anciently attached to the manor which, in the Middle Ages, was leased to the hospital of St Andrew in Denhall (Neston). Its size was partly due to its port and market functions during the Middle Ages, but it exemplified the stronger English element in south Wirral.

(ii) THE DEE–GOWY LOWLANDS

If the line dividing west from central Cheshire be drawn so as to exclude the large, multi-township parishes of Frodsham, Tarvin, Tarporley, Bunbury and Malpas, something like a true rural settlement region (i.e. West Cheshire) may be distinguished. The easterly part of this region includes the basin of the lower Gowy (except for parts in Tarvin parish) and the valley of the lower Dee within Cheshire. The Gowy lowlands include a considerable stretch of natural marsh below Stamford Bridge on the line of the Roman road from Manchester to Chester and this marshland recurves along the estuarine coast of the Mersey as far as the mouth of the Weaver. Island sites within it were occupied at an early date by Ince (Goidelic, *island*) and Elton, and sandstone outcrops around its edge provide low hill sites for the villages of Dunham on the Hill and Little and Great Barrow, the names of which last three similarly indicate a sub-Roman or earlier origin.

[1] For the account of Eastham and much of the descriptive material in this section on Wirral I am indebted to an unpublished B.A. thesis by Leonard Wharfe, 'Rural Settlement in Wirral', Univ. of Manchester, 1947, and to his article 'Norse Settlements in Wirral', *Cheshire Historian*, 8 (1958), pp. 29–33.

The marshes themselves provided valuable pastureland, as witness the place-name Thornton-le-Moors, and arable land was of necessity confined to the higher and firmer ground.

Dunham on the Hill is a small but perfect example of a community of Celtic origin adapted century by century to changing conditions. A small non-parochial street village of irregularly sited farmhouses and cottages, with a Methodist chapel (1843) towards its northern end, it occupies the crest of the low, mole-like hill. Much of the village street has rough exposures of sandstone along its course, but the hill slopes supported open arable land on either side, and the strips were traceable on the tithe map at a period when holdings were still disparate.

Except in the Gowy marshes, arable land predominates, and there is a higher proportion of open field land here than in any other part of the county. The lower Dee flows in broad meanders across a fertile flood plain to Chester, but on the Cheshire side, the land soon rises to firm ground. Low outcrops of Bunter Pebble Beds and occasional patches of sands provide, as in Wirral, favoured dry, well-drained sites for the somewhat numerous clustered settlements of this part of the Dee valley whereas, by contrast, most of the dispersal is on clays in the middle and southern parts of the area. Here too the parishes and townships are small and none except St Oswald (Chester) has more than five townships, while two, three and four are most typical. Small parochial and non-parochial villages and hamlets characterise the area but become less numerous in the south. Eccleston, Aldford and Farndon are the only true valley villages, and in Eccleston, despite its implicit pre-Anglian origin, the estate element now prevails. *Farndon* has a beautifully planned arcuate street village around a church and an old castle site. The river crossing, the defensive factor, and the one-time importance of Holt[1] immediately across the bridge largely account for its size. *Aldford*, with its extensive water meadows and former open field remains, therefore, the only typically English valley village in the sub-region. Farndon township nevertheless remained essentially rural, and in the seventeenth century it had a town field and in 1840 still lay, entirely nucleated, amid its strip-shaped fields. Aldford boasted two open arable fields – Grangefield and the Town

[1] See Chapter 19, pp. 492–3.

Field – and a Town Meadow by the Dee in 1638–9. In the tithe apportionment, eleven people had rights in one and twenty-one in another of five enclosures in Radley Meadow in a meander core. These rights still existed in the 1920s but as none was claimed, the boundary stones were removed and the meadow reclaimed.[1]

By far the greater number of the townships of this sub-region had open fields in the Middle Ages. It is significant that the majority were also occupied by nucleated settlements and that in most of the dispersed townships evidence of open field was weak or absent. 'Town field' and other open arable names persisted as did the strip shapes and even by the 1840s consolidation was only partial in most of the Dee and Gowy arable lands, disparate holdings dominating the tenurial patterns.[2] The pattern of parallel field boundaries of the old acre strip type can still be seen on either side of many of the roads in this part of the Dee valley both in Cheshire and Denbighshire.

The most notable feature of the rural history of the lower Dee and Gowy valleys in Cheshire is the way in which the villages have squeezed out the manorial element. At Domesday the manors of the Dee valley were the most numerous and the largest for any area of comparable size in the county. The use of the term 'manor' at Domesday does not, of course, pre-suppose the existence of a manor house in every place, for the Domesday manor was no more nor less in 1086 than the old Anglo-Saxon *tun* or *vill*. But the visitations of 1533[3] and 1580 showed a marked density in this area, as did the lists of nobility and gentry in 1673,[4] yet by the early nineteenth century there was hardly a gentleman's seat left in this part of the county, while in the east between the Weaver and the Bollin they were not only numerous but the estates were expanding. Today, there are remarkably few left, but there are numerous halls turned farmhouse, and the sites of the minor castles, mottes and baileys, and moats bear testimony to the once

[1] Vera Chapman, 'Open Fields in West Cheshire', *Trans. Hist. Soc. Lancs. and Ches.*, civ (1952), pp. 40 and 45.
[2] Loc. cit.
[3] *The Visitation of Lancashire and a part of Cheshire made in the year 1533 by a special commission of Thomas Benalt, Clarencieux,* Chetham Soc., xcviii (1876) and cx (1882), and Flower's *Visitation*, op. cit.
[4] Richard Blome, *Britannia* (1673), mapped in Dorothy Sylvester, *Trans. Lancs. and Ches. Antiq. Soc.*, loc. cit. (1960). The combined Tudor map is in *The Historical Atlas of Cheshire*, p. 31.

greater significance of the demesne element. No single cause lies behind this metamorphosis, but both the tightly-spaced nuclea- tions and the Civil Wars were influential. As a result, the estate township plays little part in parish structure in these small parishes of the Dee–Gowy lowlands, but a belt of names to which Norman surnames have been added from Chester eastwards to the Central Ridge, and which now are characteristically farm townships, bears witness to the nature of the change.[1]

Central and East Cheshire

The rest of Cheshire, despite a degree of physical and vegetational diversity, displays a number of features which give to its rural landscape an unmistakable, broad unity. Two of these have already been pointed out: the persistence of late woodland in vast stretches as contrasted with the early clearance of virtually the whole of west Cheshire, and the marked contrast of the very large parishes of east and central Cheshire with their characteristically satellite structure. Neither of these features occurs consistently over the entire area. The woodlands had significant breaks where both Celtic and early Anglian settlement was responsible for the clear- ing, and there is not absolute consistency (though nearly so) in the parish pattern. Nucleation in this part of the plain is again the mixed type including villages and hamlets, but both reach a far lower density than in the west, more nearly in line with that of north Shropshire, and non-parochial villages are very few in number except along the Mersey. The villages and hamlets and some dispersed settlements supported open arable fields in the Middle Ages, many of them persisting as town fields in whole or in relict form until comparatively late, but the dispersed township and the farm township in which there is no known evidence of one-time community arable land is in the majority whereas in west Cheshire it forms a small minority of the townships.

Other features compare with the west, for example the strong evidence of an underlying Celtic occupation in the form of place-names, ancient dispersal, hill- or mound-sited churches,

[1] E.g. Guilden Sutton, Cotton Edmunds, Cotton Abbots, Foulk Stapleford.

and the relative weakness of the valley-village tradition. In regard to valley siting the position is more mixed than in west Cheshire, and not dissimilar from that in north-west Shropshire. Along the Weaver, medieval and later urban settlement has given a deceptive suggestion of a strong valley tradition, but in fact the only rural valley villages are Audlem, Acton, Church Minshull, Davenham and Weaverham, and of these five Audlem has a Celtic name and a strikingly elevated church. Other ancient parochial centres in the Weaver valley area include Over on a ridge and with an isolated hill church, and Great Budworth some distance from the river, with a church so situated as to dominate the lowland to the south. In the Bollin valley Wilmslow appears to have been a village in the true valley tradition, but Bowdon and Lymm, both with Celtic names, are away from the river. In the Wheelock valley, Wheelock with a Celtic name was neither parochial nor a true village; Sandbach was an early village but its site and its church are elevated and away from the main stream, while Warmingham, a presumed early Anglian centre, is barely a hamlet.

(i) CENTRAL CHESHIRE

In terms of rural geography this subdivision begins with the change from the small parishes of the west to the large, multi-township parishes of the rest of the county. Its core is the long, scarped ridge formed by the emergence of Keuper Waterstones and Keuper Sandstones from under a broad sheet of Keuper Marls which infills the wide, shallow syncline of the eastern plain. To the west the land drops gently to Bunter sandstones for the most part overlain by glacial drift, and eastward to a spread of deltaic sands underlying much of Delamere Forest; farther south to glacial clays and then to a lowland of clays overlain with spreads of sand rising to the Ellesmere moraine on the Shropshire border. The seven hill forts which crowned the Central Ridge in the Early Iron Age, are believed to date back variously between 200 and 100 B.C. with later reconstruction work up to A.D. 50.[1] The date of their abandonment, no doubt a gradual and even a

[1] J. Forde-Johnston, 'The Iron Age Hill forts of Lancashire and Cheshire', *Trans. Lancs. and Ches. Antiq. Soc.*, lxxii (1962).

partial and repeated performance, is less easily determinable, but it may be supposed that the *pax Romana* eventually made this possible.

The Ridge which extends from Frodsham to Malpas is broken at several points but especially at the broad gap through which flows the Gowy. Known more familiarly as the Beeston Gap, it is occupied by the villages of Tarporley and Tiverton and a number of hamlets, by dispersed settlements, and two small park-estates. Around the northern half of the Ridge are the old hillside villages of Overton (Frodsham), Helsby, and Kelsall, and the lesser nucleation of Alvanley. Farther out on gently undulating lowland are Tarvin and its eastern hamlet townships; and to the east of the Ridge the late semi-hamleted settlement area of Kingsley, Oakmere and Cuddington, these last all within the bounds of the medieval Forest of Mara. The southern end of the Ridge, also surrounded until a late date by woodland, has only two nucleated villages within reasonable distance, Tattenhall on flat ground to the west, and Bunbury occupying a low but impressive hill site to the east. In the rest of the area around the Peckforton Ridge are hamlets, dispersed farmsteads, and park-estates. To the south, on a detached hill lies the impressive hill village, once the small market town, of Malpas. Thus, except for Tarvin and Tiverton, true valley settlement is lacking in this sub-region.

Tarvin (Plate IX) is in some ways typical, in others unique. As a valley village centrally placed in its large parish, and with an early open field system it compares with numerous other places in Cheshire. As the *terfyn* or boundary settlement, at the edge of cleared land and woodland, sited with regard to the Ridge, the Forest, and the cleared land and, moreover, on a Roman road junction, it is of unusual interest. It has already been suggested that it lay on the boundary of the well-developed Celtic province of west Cheshire and the contrasted area of the centre and east in which the watersheds of the lowland long lay wooded between cleared valleys in that same period. Apart from a mention in Domesday, the early history of Tarvin is inferential. No church or priest was there in 1086 if the Domesday record is to be believed, though it has one of the largest parish churches in Cheshire. From the thirteenth century, when the first mention of a church occurs, Tarvin was a manor of the bishop of Lichfield. In about 1297 a document in the *Anglesey Papers*[1] gave a description of the lands of this manor referring to fourteen separate arable areas, four of which were called fields, and in one of which reference was made to a three-year course of tillage. There was a new field in Horton, one of its ten dependent townships, and some arable land on *Brouneheth*, and the ploughed land was in turn used for pasture and for hay. Oscroft (later included in Tarvin township) also had a common field which lay amid the waste, and the bishop had a park here. The active colonisation of this century is witnessed by the note that 155 acres of the waste could be made fruitful if it were assarted. During the Middle Ages, Tarvin grew around its magnificent church, despite the fact that the vill was afforested and that it was not until the sixteenth century that it acquired a market charter. Both market and fairs became defunct in the nineteenth century. Although it stretched down to Tarvin Brook which turned its mill-wheel, the village itself grew up on the living sandstone of a low ridge, a fact which added considerably to the difficulty of bringing piped water to the village as late as 1961. The old village included not only a mill, but a manor-house, a school (adjoining the churchyard), a tithe-barn, two pinfolds, and a common pump which stood, until recently at the road junction.[2] In the nineteenth century, the dependent townships of Ashton and Kelsall were also nucleated, Burton had a small hamlet, Clotton Hoofield was semi-dispersed, and the remaining six townships were dispersed, some including so few dwellings that they ranked as farm townships. The existence of an ancient hall in several of these bears witness to the origin of numerous present-day farm townships as manors in which the park-estate either never fully developed or later, for varying reasons, fell back to farm status, its manorial rights lapsing. That this happened in ill-populated townships can be demonstrated on a small scale in the Dee valley, but it occurred on a much wider scale in central and east Cheshire.

Like Tarvin, *Bunbury* has both typical and atypical features. Not two miles east of the Central Ridge, its parish includes 17,000 as compared with Tarvin's 10,000 acres, and it has eleven depen-

[1] No. D1734/J. 2268 f. 29d–30d. Ref. Ch. 12, and the transcription and account in Dorothy Sylvester, *Trans. Hist. Soc. Lancs. and Ches.* (1958). Reference to this document by courtesy of the Most Hon. the Marquess of Anglesey.

[2] A fuller account of Tarvin village and church is contained in Dorothy Sylvester and Maurice Ridgway, 'Tarvin', *Cheshire Round*, i, 1 (Dec 1961).

dent townships. Only Bunbury township had a nucleated village. Most of the remainder included a few farms or at best a small hamlet, but in Beeston, its great scarped crag is the site of the superbly perched early thirteenth-century royal fortress, now a ruin, and in the neighbouring township of Peckforton lay the medieval royal park of this same castle, today the site of a mid-nineteenth-century castle. A third township, Calveley, is dominated by a more typical park-estate. It is suggested by Maurice Ridgway, a former vicar, that the accumulated evidence points to there having been a church on the present site from soon after A.D. 755 and the fact that the road turns three corners of an incomplete square to go round it and that it stands on a prominent natural bluff is certainly in line with the supposed antiquity of the site. The old village, Higher Bunbury or Churchtown, was laid out on the three sides of this encircling road until a land mine destroyed half of it in 1941. Apparently dating from the enclosure of its common fields, Lower Bunbury developed as a separate village nucleus which is now larger than the original Churchtown, and still later, Bunbury Heath grew up during the last and the present centuries on the enclosure of the old waste. Bunbury's townfields were slowly enclosed but some quillets remained open in 1840. Its location in relation to roads and place-names strongly suggests that it lay on the line of a sub-ridge road between the prehistoric ridgeway and the Roman road from Tarvin to Nantwich.[1]

It is significant that all the old nucleated villages and the older hamlets in central and east Cheshire lie within the areas which were cleared before the later Old English period associated with the *-leah* settlements, and that a high proportion of the numerous *-leah* townships either include at best a small hamlet or are dispersed. The successive phases of woodland clearance and settlement are thus well illustrated in Cheshire. Weaverham, for example, has a township – Cuddington – in which considerable additions were made to its plan of fields and houses by the enclosure of woodland under the Enclosure Award of 1760, and the parishes of Oakmere and Delamere were only carved out from the Forest under the provisions of the 1812 Enclosure Act referring

---

[1] A fuller account of the field systems is given in Dorothy Sylvester, *Trans. Hist. Soc. Lancs. and Ches.*, loc. cit. (1949); of the church in Maurice Ridgway, 'Bunbury Parish Church of St. Boniface', and of the village in Dorothy Sylvester, 'The Village of Bunbury', the last two both in *Cheshire Round*, 1, 4 (July 1964).

to Delamere Forest. Between the early and late colonisations of Delamere came the medieval extensions to the arable land of several manors on the eastern edge of the Forest belonging to the Abbey of Vale Royal.[1] In addition to the general absence of nucleations of any size in the later woodland townships, the field system was generally uneven in both shape and arrangement, and patches of woodland survived together with characteristic woodland names.[2]

(ii) EAST CHESHIRE

Like central Cheshire, this subdivision also includes two major landscape elements, the Weaver valley and the lowland to the east. The latter, like Delamere, bore a heavy woodland cover until late in its history, and numerous evidences remain to this day. Geologically, there is little to distinguish the two parts, boulder clays over Keuper Marl infilling the entire syncline except in the extreme north-east, peat occurring in numerous small hollows, alluvium in ribbons of differing width along the valleys, and glacial sands increasing in extent southward and eastward. There are, however, one or two more extensive patches of infertile sands within the main boulder clay plain, notably Rudheath which to this day is only thinly inhabited. Unbroken stretches of clays, as for example in the area of the one-time Crewe lake, are among the flattest land in the county, their soils cold and heavy to cultivate. The 'Crewe flats' continue northward to Northwich, particularly to the east of the Weaver and are sedulously avoided by early villages which, as in most of Cheshire, sought better drained and preferably sandy sites. The old villages occur where the flats cease – at Sandbach, Holmes Chapel and Wybunbury; where the river is flanked by high banks in the case of Church Minshull; or on the deeper, more varied, and dissected drift near the Pennine foot at Astbury and Prestbury. But the sizeable, clustered village is comparatively rare. Market-towns, by contrast, are closely spaced and may to some extent have taken the place of villages, for between Macclesfield and Congleton,

---

[1] See Ch. 10 and the fuller account in Dorothy Sylvester, 'The Open Fields of Cheshire', loc. cit. (1956).
[2] See the following section and examples in Ch. 13.

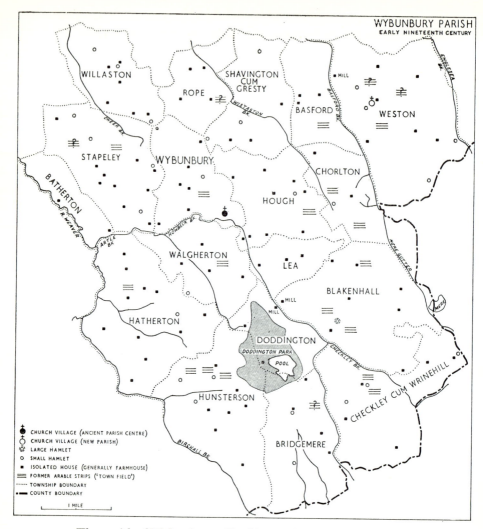

37. The parish of Wybunbury, Cheshire, and its townships at the time of the tithe survey

between Congleton and Sandbach, and between Sandbach and Middlewich, there is not a single village, while Haslington, the only village between Sandbach and Nantwich was, until recently, fairly small and non-parochial. Hamlets old and new, scattered farms of differing age, enclosure cottages on the fringes of former commons, heaths, and mosses complete a picture in which the overriding impression is of dispersal with hamlets, villages, and occasional market-towns. Park-estates and remnants of the old woodlands, rich pastures thickly hedged, little orchards and numerous minor stands of old timber trees, set with half-timbered farmhouses and old frame and brick cottages nevertheless combine to give the gently rolling parts of the eastern plain its particular individuality and elusive beauty.

The multi-township parish is all but universal, and where an occasional lesser one occurs it has usually been carved from an earlier and larger one, as in the case of Gawsworth and Wistaston where the church was almost isolated, but not in the case of Barthomley, a church hamlet of great charm and genuine antiquity. The satellite pattern is nowhere better demonstrated than in central and east Cheshire which boasts three of the four largest parishes in England on the basis of numbers of townships.[1] Prestbury, Great Budworth, Bunbury, Tarvin, Acton, Astbury all illustrate this structure perfectly – some of them so large that portions have 'hived off' as chapelries or as late-separated parishes with a resultant growth of the new ecclesiastical centre.

The parish of *Wybunbury* extends from the Weaver to the border of Staffordshire. This part of south-east Cheshire has extensive stretches of glacial sands overlying boulder clay, and is gently undulating with meandering streams, and with peat mosses in occasional ill-drained hollows. Wybunbury village, the parochial centre of eighteen townships in the 1840s and believed earlier to have been larger, is sited on running sand high above a minor stream, and the nave of the church has, in consequence had to be rebuilt at least three times, and the tower is considerably out of plumb. The entire parish at the time of the tithe survey measured some five miles by six, its area totalling 17,854 acres or nearly twenty-eight square miles. The structure of the parish at that time was as follows:

Type A. Nucleated village   (1) *Wybunbury*.[2] Ancient parochial, nucleated village with former open arable field or fields, common meadow, and peat moss held in strips.

[1] See Ch. 8.   [2] See Ch. 10, pp. 241–2 and Fig. 29.

| | (1) | *Weston*. Nucleated village with parochial status from the late nineteenth century, but according to Ormerod[1] a royal Saxon manor with berewicks. Evidence of common arable. |

Type B. Nucleated hamlet (1) *Blakenhall*. Nucleated hamlet with town field.

Types C and D. Semi-dispersed and dispersed (10) *Stapeley, Hough, Hunsterson, Checkley, Hatherton, Walgherton, Rope, Basford, Chorlton, Bridgemere*, semi-dispersed or dispersed townships with evidences of former common arable.

  (2) *Willaston* and *Shavington*, dispersed townships with no known common arable land.

Type E. Park-estate township (1) *Doddington*. Park-estate township.

Type F. Farm township (2) *Batherton* and *Lea*, townships with only two or three farms at the time of the tithe survey.

———

18 townships

In 1810 there were 76 inhabited houses in Wybunbury, 54 in Weston, 33 in Blakenhall and as few as eight in Basford and three in Batherton. Between the small farm townships and the townships with the major nucleations the population was by no means graded evenly at that date, for apart from some differences in area and the size of holdings which were part of the explanation, there were secondary intrusive elements of late date in a number of them. In Willaston and Shavington the dispersal of an earlier phase had been supplemented by loosely nucleated cottages associated with nineteenth-century enclosure of the common pasture, and Willaston in the latter half of the nineteenth century added a large street village as a result of railway employment both at Willaston station and in Crewe. Road hamlets also arose on the turnpiked roads in a number of areas, though they were negligible in Wybunbury parish except at Stapeley, the Hough and Wrinehill.

[1] Ormerod, G., *History of the County Palatine and City of Chester*, 2nd ed. (1882), iii, pp. 509–10.

Wybunbury was by no means unique in its inclusion of a graded series of satellite townships, but many parishes in Cheshire included only two to four of these types. In the case of Wybunbury, the parish and the manor of Doddington were practically coterminous at the time of the tithe survey, but this had not always been so, and several of the townships, as in Tarvin and Bunbury parishes, had at some time been separate manors and their old estates had either diminished with the loss of manorial rights, or had been down-graded to the status of farms. There is thus every gradation in pattern, size, population and status in the satellite townships, further varied by late intrusive settlement elements, and by differences in their individual histories, but the satellite relationship with the parochial township is a constant unless and until one or more acquires its own parish church or becomes a dependent chapelry, in which case the process of devolution sets in on a comparable pattern if it too has dependent townships.

Doddington[1] in 1842 was a typical park-estate township in which the park and two farms, both owned by the Delves Broughtons, occupied almost the entire township. Nor, probably, is its history untypical. The Delves originated at Delves Hall near Uttoxeter, and the Broughtons at Broughton Hall in north Staffordshire some twelve miles from Doddington. The original Doddington family was replaced by the Delves in 1353 when John de Delves acquired the estate. Knighted some years earlier in the French wars, Sir John was given the right in 1363 to fortify the house which he built at Doddington the following year. In the reign of Elizabeth I it was replaced by another house which has now disappeared, and the existing Doddington Hall was built in 1840. The estate was extended by purchases and in other ways. During the fourteenth century the Delves bought land in Chorlton and Checkley, followed by the purchase of the whole of Blakenhall. In the sixteenth century they acquired Walgherton, Weston and Rope, and in the seventeenth bought Lea and Batherton. Part of Hunsterson had been in their possession before 1365, and in 1762 the purchase of that township was completed by Sir Brian Broughton Delves (the two families having by that time been united by marriage) and the same Sir Brian bought Bridgemere. In 1817 Sir Thomas Broughton bought the Hough which in due

[1] For a short account of the layout of the township, see Ch. 10, pp. 251–2 and Fig. 36.

course passed to the Delves Broughtons, and at an unknown date the Broughtons and eventually therefore the Delves Broughtons, secured Basford and Gresty[1] (the latter not in Wybunbury parish). The greater part though not all this land was retained, but at the time of the tithe survey Doddington estate included some land in every one of Wybunbury's eighteen townships. The great park of Doddington was extended to include the greater part of Doddington township and eventually to take in parts of Walgherton, Bridgemere, and Hunsterson, including part of the old common fields in the last two. The extinction of lesser manorial rights was implicit where the Delves Broughtons acquired the whole township as they did in the cases of Walgherton and Hunsterson.[2] Comparable engrossments account for the de-grading of manors and manor houses to farm status or to minor residences in many other similar cases, and the estate township becomes, as a result, a type B, C or D settlement in the above grouping.

The typical park-estate township, like Doddington, was dissociated from anything but estate settlement – the manor house, the lodges, the home farm, the agent's house, the mill, the gamekeepers' cottages and those of other workers on the estate. This type of park-estate is one of the most characteristic settlement forms in Cheshire, and although it is found in many of the border counties, especially in north Shropshire and parts of Herefordshire, in no other does it reach the same proportional importance.

There is in fact no hard and fast line between B and C or C and D, but rather a gentle grading, but the common feature of B, C, D, E and F is that parochially and in the settlement scale they are dependants. From the eighteenth century this tended to be emphasised as improved communications and trade gave to the central village or sometimes to one of the dependent settlements on a main road a new focal value with growth following as new houses, workshops, shops and inns sprang up. Such developments in the one or two townships affected served only to emphasise further the remoteness of the rest in fully rural areas.

In 1291 single township parishes were rare in central and east Cheshire but by 1669 Gawsworth, Wistaston, Harthill and

---

[1] George Ormerod, op. cit., III, pp. 496–518.
[2] A fuller account and tabulated analysis of Wybunbury parish was first published in Dorothy Sylvester, *Trans. Hist. Soc. Lancs. and Ches.*, loc. cit. (1949).

Baddiley had been created parishes without dependent townships. All were dispersed settlements, though Harthill was to become a small estate village, and the estate element was prominent in both Gawsworth and Wistaston. Most of the single-township parishes in this part of Cheshire were late in origin. The other new parishes, mainly eighteenth and nineteenth century in date, were made to serve the growing market-towns, as in the cases of Nantwich and Congleton, which in so many instances had remained for centuries parochial dependants of a nearby village.

Great Budworth with thirty-five townships, Prestbury with thirty-two, Malpas with twenty-four and Acton with twenty-one, although larger than Wybunbury all had a similar satellite structure, but chapelries took some of the parochial burden from the mother churches of Great Budworth and Prestbury, and in Prestbury and Acton the towns of Nantwich and Macclesfield respectively both had ancient collegiate churches which eventually achieved parochial status. Apart from the inclusion of a market-town in these two and some other rural parishes, the hierarchical satellite structure was broadly comparable, but every township had a certain degree of individuality and this was even more true of the parishes as a whole. Nor was there any guarantee of a township remaining in the same category, for like all settlements they could advance or recede in the settlement scale.

Throughout the eastern plains, as in the Weaver valley area, these patterns can be repeated, but in the more easterly areas the remnant woodlands of Macclesfield Forest exercised a similar influence to that of Delamere Forest, and as late as the 1840s townships such as *Hurdsfield* typified the character and the changes taking place in many others in this belt. A small park-estate – in others frequently a much larger one – and one or two farms were gradually at that date enclosing more land from the woodland which otherwise lay uncleared around them and so dominant was the woodland environment as late as the nineteenth century that it must be associated with the township type W, Woodland.[1] The other distinguishing feature of the eastern plains, the large park-estates, resulted in there being a much higher proportion of this type of township (E) than in any comparable area elsewhere in the county. Nether Alderley, Capesthorne, Henbury, Birtles,

[1] Compare Cuddington, Oakmere and Delamere also of this type.

Chelford, Withington, all within a few miles between Knutsford and Macclesfield, and Somerford, Somerford Radnor, Moreton, Lawton and Rode in the Sandbach-Congleton area fall into this category to take only two small localities. True villages, apart from Newbold Astbury and Prestbury, are rare throughout the eastern plain, hamlets apart from a few of recent growth are almost non-existent, and dispersed settlement is characteristic of mile upon mile of this lowland portion of the old Macclesfield Forest.

Although the Danish element is represented by a small group of place-names, notably the Hulmes, and by numerous field-names, Danish influence on settlement forms is not in any sense conspicuous, and the occupation can at best have been sparse and brief. The Celtic, Anglian, medieval and modern phases account for the major settlement features.

Beyond this part of the plain lie the Pennine foothills and the ridged country of the Staffordshire border, and Welsh Border influences can have had no part to play so far west although it is claimed that the west tower of Astbury church at the edge of the plain was fortified to resist Welsh raiders.

Urban Influence on Rural Pattern

The alteration of settlement pattern which a single growing town can effect in a rural periphery may be illustrated by the influence of Crewe. In 1801, Nantwich with 3463 people and Sandbach with a total of 1844 lay at a characteristic ten-mile interval apart, two market towns in a moderately populated farming area. Only two other places had a population exceeding 600: Haslington with 677 and Odd Rode with 917. Most of the rural townships had fewer than 300, and many under 100. Few were even parochial centres in this multi-township district, and the pattern of occasional parochial villages with their hamleted or dispersed satellite townships prevailed.

The opening of the Grand Junction works in the thinly inhabited farming township of Monks Coppenhall followed the refusal of Nantwich to accommodate it and sparked off the growth of the new town of Crewe in 1842. Six important railway lines were to meet here and its growth was rapid, extending also into the adjoining township of Church Coppenhall, but only recently into Crewe township. By the turn of the century the population was some 40,000 drawn mainly from the nearby countryside but with considerable numbers from Wales, Scotland, Lancashire and Derbyshire.[1] Willaston, Shavington and Haslington were the first of the nearby country places to feel the effects of Crewe's growth, the first expanding partly on account of its own railway station and wharf. The three continued to show the largest growth rates until the garden city movement started in Wistaston just before the First World War and in fifty years its suburban expansion has given it a population of over 5000, the largest of any civil parish in south Cheshire, ousting Haslington from this position between the 1951 and 1961 Censuses. A few miles to the south-east, the population of Alsager, Odd Rode and Church Lawton has been influenced by both Crewe and the Potteries towns.

In a circle based on a Sandbach–Crewe–Nantwich diameter, there is a notable difference between the rates of increase in the northern and southern semi-circles. The northern, a less accessible area has remained a persistently agricultural district of widely spaced farms and some of its civil parishes have actually lost in numbers during the century and a half from 1801–1951 as farming families, in common with the national trend, have become smaller and farm work increasingly mechanised. By contrast, the southern semi-circle has concentrated all the major growth points and all the suburban expansion.

[1] Dorothy Sylvester, 'Whence come Cheshire Folk?', *Cheshire Historian* (1959).

12 Maelor Saesneg

MAELOR SAESNEG is unique in that it is the only part of Wales lying within the English Plain, and there is little now to remind the casual traveller that he is in Wales other than the road sign 'Croeso i Gymru'. But its physical location has resulted in its being tossed administratively between the two regions. Distinguished from Welsh Maelor or Maelor Gymraeg to the west of the Dee, it was formerly part of the kingdom of Powys, later of Mercia, and then became part of the earldom of Chester after the Norman Conquest, so remaining until its transference to Flintshire under the treaty of Rhuddlan in 1284. In 1086, it was in the Cheshire hundred of Dudestan (Broxton). Ecclesiastically it was in the diocese of Lichfield or of Chester until the middle of last century, though in the fifth and sixth centuries it had been within the area dominated by the British Church and by the great monastery of Bangor Is-coed.

Bounded by the Dee on the west, Maelor Saesneg is physically part of the morainic lowlands of the northern portion of the Border corridor and is divisible into five minor landscapes: the plains of the lowland Dee in the west and north-west, a gently undulating plain within this curve, a belt of hummocky morainic drift country, the narrow, incised valley of the Wych brook, and the peaty levels of Fenn's Moss. Though the terrain lacks strong contrasts lying wholly below 350 feet above O.D., these subdivisions are none the less distinctive. Today, Maelor is for the most part rich pastoral farming country, divided into large, prosperous farms interspersed by occasional villages and hamlets; well timbered, but almost wholly enclosed except for Fenn's Moss. It is also wholly rural for although Overton was a medieval borough and market-town it is now simply a large, quiet village, the centre of administration for its rural district.

Place-names afford a number of valuable clues as to the settle-

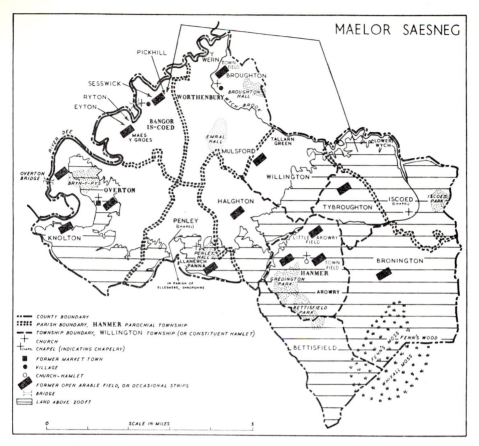

38. Maelor Saesneg: features of the rural landscape in the mid-
nineteenth century

ment history of Maelor and the mingling of peoples here. Three of
the four ancient parishes bear English names including an *inga* and
a *-burh* which must be assumed to date from the early period of
Mercian advance into the Borderland. Seven of the ten townships
have English names. Of the hamlet and locality names a number
are Welsh including Ywern (Worthenbury), Althrey (Bangor),
Arowry (Hanmer), Brynhovah (near the boundary of Bangor and
Overton), and Eglwys Cross (Tybroughton). The ending *-ington*
occurs in four place-names including three townships and the
hamlet of Wallington, and five more townships have the ending

-ton. As regards farm-names, the proportion is reversed, more being Welsh than English. Many of the English farm-names are recent, the documents revealing that in the Middle Ages and often into Tudor and later times they were nearly all Welsh.

The element *tref* is never encountered, but the medieval *vill* may well represent both *tref* and township. Welsh field-names and Welsh land measures are also persistent in early documents, and despite the importance of the Norman pattern reflected in powerful manorial families and their estates, the deeper and older current of Welsh life can be detected beneath manorialism. The complexity of the parish–township–hamlet relationship and the fluctuation of boundaries and entities of local administration is characteristic of north-east Wales.

In the early nineteenth century there were four ancient parochial centres. Bangor Is-coed included the two Flintshire townships of Bangor and Is-coed and four Denbighshire townships. Hanmer comprised the six townships of Bronington, Bettisfield, Hanmer, Halghton, Tybroughton and Willington, and the parish of Overton consisted of three – Overton Villa, Overton Foreign and Knolton. In Worthenbury there was no subdivision of the parish, but it numbered four hamlets in its area (Mulsford, Broughton, Ywern and Wallington) in addition to the parochial village itself. These four parishes accounted for all the Maelor townships except Penley which was a township and chapelry within the parish of Ellesmere, Shropshire.

Overton, Bangor and Worthenbury are valley villages of the lowland Dee comparable in situation with Shocklach, Churton and Aldford farther downstream in Cheshire. The site of Hanmer on the shore of its mere in a morainic hollow is a lesser settlement, but otherwise comparable in location with Ellesmere. Of these four parochial villages, Bangor is the only one built on the actual banks of the Dee, and on its site lay one of the largest Celtic monasteries of Wales in the Dark Ages, though there is no evidence of historical continuity with the present village. Overton one and a half miles from Overton bridge was the medieval centre for the temporalities, as Bangor was from early times for the spiritual life of Maelor. Overton had a castle, was a medieval borough, and had the market rights. Bangor was the mother church, and Overton was elevated from chapelry to parish under the Division of Parishes

Act in 1657 as was Worthenbury in the following year. Hanmer, by contrast, formed part of the estates of Haughmond Abbey, near Shrewsbury, and its vicarage and church are known to go back to 1291 at latest.[1]

Bangor Is-coed, known also as Bangor Monachorum and Bangor on Dee, and in Anglian times as Banchornabyrig is the only place in Maelor of more than local importance. Said to have been founded by Lucius, king of Britain, its community was described by Lewis in 1833 as 'the most ancient and extensive monastery founded in Britain.[2] Destroyed by the armies of Æthelfrith of Northumbria fresh from the battle of Chester, the site was deserted and was eventually reoccupied by a small parochial village, whose church was the mother church of Maelor Saesneg and perhaps of all ancient Maelor. In Edward Lhwyd's time the village consisted of only 26 houses, and although its bridge gave it some importance as a crossing point, the present village probably developed only in the eighteenth century. There are frequent references in the sixteenth and seventeenth centuries to intermixed lands in two or three parts of Bangor, especially in Maes mawr and Maes y groes,[3] while Althrey meadow was a dole field or common meadow.[4] References to open arable go back to the fifteenth century, and by the mid-sixteenth piecemeal enclosure had begun,[5] but nineteenth-century field-names give sufficient clues to locate both common arable and common meadow on the tithe map.

The plans and general layout of Worthenbury and Overton with their nucleated villages in the midst of Welsh-named fields in which traces of former common holdings can be traced are broadly similar to those of Bangor and call for no special mention. But *Hanmer* is quite different and merits attention. Like Bangor, it went unnoticed in Domesday Book: Bangor probably because it lay then in ruins; Hanmer because it may not have been in existence as an independent settlement. The first step seems to

---

[1] Thomas, *History of the Diocese of St Asaph* (1906–13), ii, pp. 429–31.
[2] S. Lewis, *Topographical Dictionary of Wales*. Said to have been a walled town with churches, libraries, etc., and to have housed over 2000 monks.
[3] *Plymouth Deeds*, 144 (1596), 784 (1625), etc.; *Bettisfield MSS.*, 437 (1462), 517 (1526), etc.
[4] *Plymouth Deeds*, 900 (1566), 143 (1576), etc.; *Bettisfield MSS.*, 517 (1526).
[5] *Plas Yolyn MSS.*, 225 (1531).

have been the granting of land to the Augustinian Abbey of Haughmond, and the church is listed as the 'Ecclesia de Hameme' in the *Lincoln Taxation*. On its dissolution, the abbey's rights and property here were bought by Sir Thomas Hanmer whose estate, first centred at Hanmer and later at Bettisfield, has been generally believed to be the second factor in its growth.[1] But when Hanmer was still perhaps largely waste in the thirteenth century, Gredington in the present township of Hanmer was referred to as a vill with houses, roads, intermixed holdings, mossland and waste.[2] It continued to be called a vill until the fifteenth century when three fields were mentioned in Gredington in which lay arable strips. The first reference to such strips in Hanmer is to two in Maes Hanmer in 1482.[3] In 1555 Gredington field in the parish of Hanmer was leased with the rectory of Hanmer and it is clear that the old vill had been submerged in the newer parish and township,[4] probably after the Dissolution, for in 1501–2 it was still the vill of Gredington.[5] Its name indicates its existence in the Mercian period, and does not exclude the possibility of an earlier Welsh community. In the Domesday Book the portion referring (under Cheshire) to Maelor Saesneg includes a *Radintone* which James Tait failed to identify and which he considered a lost name. Belonging to Earl Hugh and entered soon after Bettisfield and Worthenbury, it was waste but could maintain one plough. This was almost certainly Gredington, the original settlement in what became the parish and township of Hanmer, renamed by the Hanmer family when they acquired the Haughmond property. Gredington is now the site of a park, the seat of the Kenyons. In the south of the township is Bettisfield Park, the seat of the Hanmers, but in 1841 the tithe map showed it as an area largely of fields. At some intermediate date, the settlement may have transferred to the present Hanmer, or Hanmer is the old Gredington re-named.

[1] Thomas, ii, pp. 441–3.
[2] *Bettisfield MSS.*, 457 (N.D. C.13), 387 (C.13), 480 (N.D. C.13).
[3] Ibid. 424 (1486).
[4] *Bettisfield MSS.*, 265 (1555).   [5] Ibid. 413.

Land Use

FIELD PATTERNS

In the early Middle Ages, and perhaps earlier, there were open common fields in Overton and Worthenbury, Gredington and Bettisfield, and probably in Tybroughton and Broughton. A number of private collections of estate documents, notably the *Bettisfield MSS.*, the *Plymouth Deeds* and the *Plas Yolyn MSS.*, take the story of the open fields in a fragmentary manner to the period of the breakdown of community cultivation. In the thirteenth century, there was still waste and mossland in many of these fields suggesting that the system was comparatively undeveloped, the community small, or much of the ground partly unsuitable for cultivation. There were other references to open strips in the thirteenth and fourteenth centuries in Bangor, Althrey, Knolton and Penley, but the character of the evidence is such that no certainty exists as to the presence of well organised arable *fields*, and it is quite probable that small groups of ploughing strips or even scattered ploughlands were to be found in the Welsh tradition in the smaller or less well populated townships, only the major settlements having more regular and larger fields. The fields and strips alike generally bore Welsh names, and the following grant of 1526[1] illustrates the type of evidence, and the irregularity of the system:

Grant of lands in the vill of Bangor . . . two parcels of land lying in a place called *Dole Bangor*, one parcel called *Hafod vorvyddin* a place known as *y dangre*, seven butts of land in a place called *dan bryn y dangre*, land lying in a place called Cottnall, one butt of land in *ero y dangre*, lands in the above *Bryn y dangre* . . . one enclosure called *kaybrwyn* . . . two parcels in a place called *y maes mawr*, etc.

There is no evidence known of more than one open field in Worthenbury, but there were three (possibly more) in Bangor, Overton, and in Hanmer. In the early nineteenth century, Bangor had some 2000 acres of water meadow, and references to doles in Bangor meadows go back to the sixteenth century (see above). The lower Dee valley, like the Severn valley below Newtown, provided rich irrigation meadows, and it is not improbable

[1] *Bettisfield MSS.*, 517.

that, as in Montgomeryshire, they were areas of convertible husbandry – meadowland in a wet season and ploughland in a long dry spell.

In several cases, expanding estates absorbed the old open field land. For example, Llannerch Panna, now an estate in Penley township, was referred to in an exchange of lands as the vill of Llanerch bana, and open strips in various places in Llannerch Banna and Willington constituted the lands for exchange.[1]

WASTE AND WOODLAND

Coed and *-ley* place-names, frequent reference to waste and woodland in thirteenth- to fifteenth-century deeds, and surviving remnants of open moss and ancient woodland offer proof of the incompleteness of the medieval settlement of Maelor. The evidence builds up to a medieval landscape in which numerous small communities both Welsh and English in origin had carved out relatively limited areas of cultivated ground in a wide, undeveloped natural scene. Colonisation took place piecemeal through the Middle Ages, but at the time of the Great Enclosure movement in the late eighteenth and early nineteenth centuries much waste remained. This rough pasture had no doubt supplied the grazing on which was based Maelor's small woollen industry in the fifteenth to seventeenth centuries.[2]

Waste lands which were particularly extensive in the south-east in Penley and Hanmer were enclosed between 1775 and 1795, a period which saw the formation of many new farms, mainly with English names, and the rise of new enclosure hamlets on or at the edge of the old commons. These are the heath and green settlements such as Breadenheath, Lightwood Green, Tallarn Green and Threapwood Green. Of the last, Lewis said in 1833 that it had until recently been a tract of waste common and 'exempt from all local jurisdiction, was long a resort of abandoned characters of every description. . . .'[3]

The largest stretch of uncultivated land remaining is Fenn's Moss which, together with its Shropshire extension of Whixall

---

[1] *Bettisfield MSS.*, 476 (1476–7).
[2] There were fulling mills at Halghton and Tybroughton in the fifteenth century. *Bettisfield MSS.*, 364 and 929 (both 1425).
[3] S. Lewis, op. cit.

Moss forms the biggest unreclaimed stretch of peat in the Borderland. This moss is owned by the Hanmers and it has not been possible to trace early common rights which may long have been restricted. Drained by the Dutch in the seventeenth century, much of it is now an area of commercial development by peat-cutting firms but the mossmen still use tools of Dutch pattern and call them by Dutch names. It is a wide stretch of unenclosed land, its vegetation of birch, heather and cotton grass probably little different from the primitive cover of prehistoric times.

THE ESTATE ELEMENT

From the early Middle Ages large land-owning families have had an important influence on the territorial history of Maelor, notably the Hanmers, the Pulestons and the Lloyds. For its size, Maelor has a very large number of family seats, and mansions and parks are a striking feature of the Maelor landscape. This characteristically Norman feature, here as elsewhere, has resulted in many changes not only in land use but in settlement history, economy and administration.

More recently, their break-up has provided more land for new farms, and for building estates, for example at Overton Bridge, Emral and Penley.

The Dating of the Maelor Settlement Landscape

The comparatively abundant data for Maelor allows the reasonably accurate dating of the main settlement phases. These are:

Powysian Period	up to the seventh century. Scanty Welsh settlements. The monastic phase at Bangor Is-coed.
Mercian Period	seventh to tenth centuries. English settlements (-ington, -bury, -ton, etc.). Nucleated villages on the Dee.
Cheshire Period	tenth century to 1284. Disturbed by border warfare. Probable rise or expansion of some of the older hamlets. Origin of a number of open fields and expansion of cultivation.

Medieval Flintshire Period	1284 to 1536. Development of agriculture. Early break-up of open fields, growth of sheep farming and local woollen industry. Growing importance of large estates, notably of the post-Dissolution Hanmer estate.
Seventeenth century and early eighteenth century	Consolidation and enlargement of estates. Building of family seats. Increase of severalty farming and continued enclosure of open-field holdings. Piece-meal enclosure of commons continued.
Mid-eighteenth century to present day	Emparkment and rebuilding of family seats followed more recently by abandonment in some cases. Enclosure of commons. Rise of new farms and of heath and green settlements.

Finally, Maelor may be cited as an outstanding example of Anglo-Welsh hybrid settlement, unique because it remains administratively the only Welsh area wholly within the English Plain.

13 Shropshire
I *The Northern Plains*

> Shropshire is a county where the dignity and beauty of ancient things lingers long. . . .
>
> When antique things are also country things, they are easier to write about, for there is a permanence, a continuity in country life which makes the lapse of centuries of little moment.
>
> Mary Webb in *Precious Bane*

THE gently undulating, rich agricultural lowlands of north Shropshire are drained southwards by three main streams, the Perry, the Roden and the Tern. All three pour their waters into the Severn in the Shrewsbury Plain, the Perry near Fitz and the combined streams of the Roden and Tern just below Atcham. The shallow syncline which begins near Wilmslow in north Cheshire, extends SSW with a gently pitching axis, becoming deeper and narrower until it disappears south of Prees. Keuper Marls line the entire basin, but an outlier of Lower and Middle Lias extends from Audlem to just north of Wem, and Prees village surmounts a hill of Middle Liassic rocks towards the southern end. The upturned edges of the syncline are marked by exposures of Keuper Sandstones but, whereas in Cheshire they emerge only as a north–south line to the west of the syncline, in north Shropshire they curve round its southern end as a faulted crescentic line of escarpments. These escarpments occur as three main hill groups across the middle of the plain – Nesscliff, Grinshill and the Hawk-stone hills. Their vividly red rocks break sharply into the 250–300 foot level of the plain, rising to 450–650 feet O.D. Crowned with conifer and birch woods, mixed with heath and gorse, they form a distinctive micro-division within the drift-covered lowlands.

Although boulder clays predominate, the Shropshire drift is more diversified than that of Cheshire. Wide stretches of sands and gravels support extensive heaths where ling, gorse, bilberry and birch contrast with the richer loams and clays, now high quality farmland, but clothed originally with damp oakwood and mixed deciduous stands. Today, most of the heaths are enclosed and

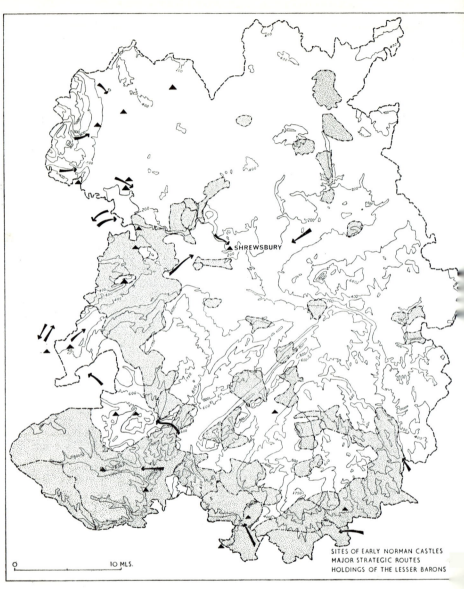

SHREWSBURY

SITES OF EARLY NORMAN CASTLES
MAJOR STRATEGIC ROUTES
HOLDINGS OF THE LESSER BARONS

0   10 MLS.

39. The strategic geography of early Norman Shropshire

farmed, but they formed the common open pasture of many north Shropshire townships in the Middle Ages. The drift also includes post-glacial alluvia which beribbon the stream courses, while extensive meres or former meres have produced peat mosses in the hollows of the drift. The largest of the mosses are the Wealdmoors, north of the Wrekin, and Whixall and Fenn's Moss on the border of Shropshire and Maelor Saesneg, but there are numerous lesser ones.

The southern flank of the lowland is the Shrewsbury Plain where the broadening waters of the middle Severn meander tortuously among their wide alluvial meadows. The British Pengwern, the Roman Viroconium, and the Mercian Scrobbesbyrig all made use of the natural centrality of this confluential riverine plain and its convergent routes, and for a thousand years Shrewsbury has continued to give unity to a county which, physically, consists of two strongly contrasted regions.

The northern belt of the Shropshire lowland is the deeply undulating ground of the Ellesmere moraine which, since the retreat of the last ice sheet, has divided the Cheshire–Shropshire lowland into two parts and caused the streams of mid-Cheshire to flow northward and those of north Shropshire southward. Although this post-glacial watershed is of negligible height, generally between 250 and 350 feet above O.D., but overtopping 500 feet at Wirswall, its effectiveness as a divide has been demonstrated throughout historic time, and the differences between Shropshire and Cheshire, especially from the Mercian period, are to no small extent dependent on the containing effect of the moraine on human movement. These differences, however, are more easily felt than defined. Shropshire is a more welcoming, more southerly land with a warmer aspect, Cheshire a cooler, more northerly one. Cheshire is deterred from making easy southern contact both by the moraine and the Midland Gate, but Shropshire lies open to the Midlands, and Stretton Dale and the Severn lead southward. The importance of this historically and culturally is unquestionable. On the other hand, the basic similarity of Cheshire and north Shropshire as drift-covered lowlands, their similar structure, and the comparability of their minor and major physical features and their soils is equally inescapable, hence the character of their rural geography is closely parallel in many ways.

The Salient Features of Rural Settlement

As in Cheshire, the Celtic, the Mercian, and the early medieval phases were the most important formative periods as regards the major elements in the rural landscape of the Shropshire lowlands. Consequently, the Celtic survival is strong, the Anglian village picture is clearly superimposed, while the mark of the early Middle Ages is evident in important manorial features. But in general contrast to Cheshire is the greater importance of the defensive element in north-west Shropshire which straddles the edge of the Cambrian uplands. For nearly five hundred years west Shropshire lay within the belt of marcher lordships in contradistinction from Cheshire's palatinate status and her lack of all but a few military works east of the river Dee.

The distribution of hill camps in north Shropshire is sparse, and the map of Celtic place-names gives a better overall picture of settlement in the pre-Mercian phase than do archaeological remains (Fig. 6). Shropshire and Herefordshire had no such closely developed and widely cleared district as west Cheshire. Instead, the whole of Shropshire, north and south, compared rather with central and east Cheshire, its valleys freed of woodland and the low watersheds still under primeval forest (Fig. 10). As in Cheshire, however, the line of the sandstone escarpments offered acceptable sites for Early Iron Age camps and there were larger stretches of open heath and peat moss to attract early settlement. All the three main streams of the northern plain were followed by belts of cleared and occupied territory, but the marshes of Baggymoor above the Ruyton XI Towns gorge evidently proved difficult, and the wide, level, deserted valley, now followed by the main road from Myddle to Ellesmere, was preferred. Near the Dee between Whittington and St Martin's and in most of Maelor Saesneg, was the most extensive stretch of cleared land in north Shropshire in the Dark Ages. Although no Roman road has been proved from Holt to Forden, there have been Roman finds along this line, there is a Street Dinas on B 5069 one mile north-north-west of St Martin's, and a series of possible *heol* names and of *ford* names (where there is no river) lead south from there towards a crossing of the Severn near Melverley where there was also a Roman find. This could indicate either a Celtic or a Roman road from Deva and Holt to link up near Stanford with the road from Viroconium to Lavobrinta (Forden Gaer). A Roman road from Aldford diverging from the Chester–Whitchurch road, though by no means known as a through route, is proved by an *agger* in the Aldford–Churton section.[1] It may be that it went, not to Viroconium but to the Viroconium–Lavobrinta road joining it near Stanford or Middletown, or that there was a second road diverging from the postulated loop between Holt and Viroconium. Old Oswestry and a group of hill-forts on the Breiddens immediately to the west of Middletown make a through Celtic route in this area a distinct possibility. At the northern end, the cleared and settled area near the Dee was an extension of the west Cheshire settlement province.[2] Comparable lines of *heol* and *ford* names lie along the Longford (a proved Roman road), up the Roden, its tributary Soulton Brook, and the road to Whitchurch and Tushingham, from near Stanford across the Severn to Walford and thence via Alford Farm, Whattall and Lyneal towards Ellesmere.

The distribution of Celtic and related names (Fig. 6) and that of mid-Anglian names is remarkably coincident here as in Cheshire, and although there are no *inga*, *-ingaham*, or *-ham* names in north Shropshire, Atcham (Attingham) and Uppington (Uppingham) in the mid-Severn valley, and the St Milburga nunnery at Much Wenlock point to an early occupation of that key region, from which the northern movement of the Wroecensaetan could have taken place up the clearways which the northern tributaries provided. There are only two or three doubtful *-ingatun* suffixes and one *-burh* (Shawbury), but a considerable number of *-tuns* mark out the advance of Anglian settlement in this area by the end of the middle phase, and confirm it as a valley and lowland settlement. Their distribution, as in Cheshire, means that many of these places were probably original Celtic sites over which was imposed a Mercian overlordship.

The *-leah*, *wood* and other late Anglian names are on the whole

[1] M. St J. Way, 'Watling Street south of Aldford', *Trans. Chester and N. Wales Archaeol. Soc.*, N.S. 48 (1961), pp. 15–23. Graham Webster, 'Roman Roads', *Cheshire Historian* (1953). S. O'Dwyer, *Roman Roads of Cheshire* (1935).
[2] Chs 4 and 11.

less numerous than in Cheshire, for the remnant woodlands were narrower, and by the time of the Domesday Survey the northern plain was largely denuded of woodland apart from isolated patches in the plain and a few denser and more extensive areas in some eastern townships. A high proportion of the townships were named in the Domesday Record. In fact only 56 of the present civil parishes of the county were omitted, and most of these were on the Welsh Border where raiding disturbed the tenor of life, or in the great forests of the south-east. Most of the old hamlets were in existence, and virtually all the villages. But wasting, though less devastating than it had been in Cheshire, had extended into north Shropshire during William's mid-winter raids of 1070-1, and the manors which lay untilled in this period between 1066 and 1086 were widely scattered over the northern and central belts of the plain. The Tern valley seems to have suffered most severely, no doubt because it lay on the route from north-east Cheshire which William's forces followed to Shrewsbury. North of the plain of Shrewsbury, this was the only area in north Shropshire to include a long string of barons' holdings in 1086 and it was clearly of strategic significance at that time.[1] As a result of the wasting by Norman armies and, in the west, by raiders from the hills, agricultural values were low over the entire lowland in 1086 except for the southern belt where they rose sharply towards the plain of Shrewsbury. The contrast between the numbers of ploughlands in the eastern plain, the plain of Shrewsbury, and the vales of the southern hill country at that date, and those of the northern manors is striking.[2]

The dislocation of economic life in the east was doubtless short-lived, for with the pacification of most of the country assured, the Normans turned to the Welsh Border. Mottes were fortified in great numbers in the west of the county, but it is significant that D. F. Renn shows an outlying group of them in the upper Tern valley, turning thence north-west towards the lower Dee valley, the route by which it was evidently thought that danger threatened (Fig. 14). In turn, stone castles were built in the *capita* of the marcher lordships in the west and centre of the

[1] Dorothy Sylvester, 'Rural Settlement in Domesday Shropshire', *Sociological Review* (1933), map of land values.
[2] Emrys J. Howell, *Shropshire*, The Land of Britain, part 66 (1941), fig. 21, p. 280.

plain (Fig. 39), and one lay outside this area – Red Castle in Hawkstone, defending the selfsame route from the north-east. The principal fortresses were Oswestry, Whittington, Ellesmere and Knockin, each the head of a lordship, but to the east were two lesser lordships, those of Myddle and Ruyton XI Towns.

Where freedom from Welsh raids was more certain, as it was in the eastern half of the plain, the Middle Ages saw a resurgence of prosperity, as is evinced by the spread of open arable fields, the rise of markets, and the building of churches and religious houses. Something like forty churches in the northern plain were founded in the early Norman period, and more were to follow during the later Middle Ages. The abbeys of Shrewsbury, Haughmond and Lilleshall in this region all helped to extend the open field system and to further agriculture. Though by no means absent from the west, there were more Norman churches built in the east and centre, and particularly along the line of the sandstone escarpments (Fig. 43).

The later history of the manors and their influence on settlement features was broadly similar to that of Cheshire, except that there was not the virgin woodland to offer comparable opportunities for expansion. Manor houses and, later, parks became numerous, but there was nothing to correspond with the great park belt of eastern Cheshire. They added, however, a similar element to the settlement pattern in the form of estate villages and estate townships, for example, Adderley with its estate village which had a market in the thirteenth century, Petton and Tedsmore.

By the modern period, the settlement picture was complete except for the 'green' and 'heath' hamlets which, like Whitchurch Heath, Hine Heath and Poynton Green, sprang up in appreciable numbers both before and during the period of parliamentary enclosure. This was to some extent further stimulated by the turnpike roads and by Nonconformity, but neither was outstandingly influential in north Shropshire. It is easier to enumerate the phases of growth than to answer the many questions as to the rise of individual settlements and settlement types. The hiatus in early Anglo-Saxon names in the plain and the re-advance of modern Welsh place-names in the west of the plain from the Welsh districts in the hills behind Oswestry both offer difficulties. The absence of early Anglo-Saxon names may well be due to later loss, and negative evidence cannot be regarded as final. The Welsh names which so freely spatter the western plains, e.g. Gadlas, Gwern y Brenin, and Argoed, and names such as Welsh Frankton which indicate Welsh settlers, are quite distinct from the older Celtic place-names farther east such as Prees and Hodnet, and they and the many Welsh farm-names compare with those in Maelor Saesneg. Welsh is still spoken by large numbers of people in the hills above Oswestry. Welsh modes of agronomy and Welsh customs were strong in this area in the fourteenth century, but the Domesday Book has few entries covering what was then a widely devastated district.

By the eighteenth century, arable land predominated in the eastern half of the plain, except on the richer clays, but in the western half a slightly higher average annual rainfall and, perhaps, the greater strength of the pastoral tradition in a semi-Welsh district served to keep the arable acreage lower. Rocque's map of *circa* 1750 shows that throughout the lowlands much boggy and heathy land still remained undeveloped and much of it was, in fact, unenclosed, for the early sixteenth century enclosures barely touched the north of the county. The period of parliamentary enclosure in Shropshire, from 1763–1891, brought about a wholesale transformation of the extensive heaths and peat mosses, and by 1900 comparatively little open land remained. The landscape of recent enclosure has appreciably modified the north Shropshire scene of, say, two hundred years ago, and converted it to a vast farmland with few breaks. As in Cheshire, brick three-storeyed farmhouses dating from the period of the Great Enclosures now occur in considerable numbers away from the villages, with their characteristically plain façades. By contrast, the older cottages are typically built of sandstone or are timber framed.

The resulting settlement complex in the northern plain of Shropshire, as would be expected from the analysis of physical and historical factors, is not one of clear regional or sub-regional contrasts but of gentler differences and the repetition of standard types with individual variations exaggerated by late intrusive elements. There are many parallels between the nucleation/dispersal pattern in north Shropshire and central and east Cheshire. Against a background of dispersal are set widely spaced villages, most but not all parochial, hamlets, a few of which are parochial, and solitary churches. In north-east Shropshire the density of villages and hamlets is closely comparable with that in Cheshire immediately across the border, but beyond Wem and Hodnet, the numbers of hamlets rise and they form a comparatively dense belt across the rest of the plain, resembling west rather than east Cheshire in this respect. Large, multi-township parishes characterise all the west and north but in the centre and south-east across the 'parish line' (Fig. 22), occurs the change to predominantly single-township parishes which continue throughout the rest of the English border counties. The major subdivision of the north Shropshire plain for the analysis of its settlement geography rests, therefore, on the distinction of the west with its long history of marcher lordships, and the south-east with its one-township parishes, from the north-east which has no such outstanding features to mark it out from Cheshire as a settlement region.

North-east Shropshire

No hard and fast boundaries can be laid down between the three sub-divisions of north Shropshire in respect of its rural landscape, but the north-eastern portion may be taken as extending westward to include the parish of Wem and southward to cover Shawbury, Stanton on Hine Heath, High Ercall, Stoke upon Tern and Cheswardine. It extends to the Hawkstone Hills and Grinshill but the rest of the area is typically drift-covered lowland in which settlement, with only rare exceptions, is on sandy sites, brown earths or sandstone, or on the margin of these with the clays and the gley soils. The strong parallelism between north Shropshire and Cheshire in this respect is evident equally in the numerous micro-physical units which repeat the familiar elements of the landscape again and again in a cellular distribution.

Comparable too, is the mingling of lowland, valley and hill-orientated sites, with valley sites in the minority. Market Drayton, Wem, Stoke upon Tern, Shawbury and Stanton on Hine Heath alone of the major nucleations are convincingly valley orientated. Lee Brockhurst is on a rise above the Roden. Prees is a hill-top village, and Hodnet, Clive and Grinshill are also hill-orientated. Others such as Woore, Ightfield, Moreton Say and Tilstock occupy positions of gentle elevation in the lowland as do many of the hamlets.

The now familiar satellite structure of the large, multi-township parish dominates the area. Wem with thirteen townships, Whitchurch with thirteen in Shropshire and one in Cheshire, Prees and Hodnet with ten each, Drayton with six, and Stanton and Moreton Say with five each account for the greater part of the total area, but like the Cheshire parishes the number of townships has altered with the centuries[1] and these mid-nineteenth-century figures need correction for both earlier and, in some cases, later dates. There is no doubt as to the ancient origin of the major parochial villages, and Prees, Hodnet, Wem and Ercall are Celtic names or include a Celtic element.

Wem (Lv Upml) in the Roden valley, although a market-town from 1205,[2] remained for centuries a typical country town with a strong agricultural background. Its three common arable fields were still open in the early seventeenth century, and lay on the drier soils to the north of the town. The marshy land to the west on the ill-drained bottoms of the Roden (including a 200-acre pool until 1586), was ditched and drained between 1553 and 1619, and converted into good farmland, though in the Middle Ages it had served as common pasture. The demesne element was important in the Middle Ages when, under the Pantulph family, it had been the head of a barony, but by the nineteenth century it had disappeared as had nearly all the once-numerous woodlands and coppices.[3] The market, the courts leet and baron, and its seventeenth-century grammar school led to the growth of this small market-town, but so too did its parochial status and its relationship to its twelve satellite townships. Of these, Tilley immediately to the south is a small village (type A), Cotton and Aston hamlets (B), Lacon, Lowe and Ditches, Horton, Newton (a chapelry from the seventeenth century), Edstaston (also a chapelry), Northwood, and Sleap dispersed or semi-dispersed townships (D or C), and Soulton and Wolverley farm townships (E). Of these, Aston, Cotton and Edstaston, had three common fields, Tilley four, and Sleap two.[4] Apart from the estate-type

---

[1] By subtraction and engrossment principally, but sometimes by re-definition.
[2] By 1951, the market had declined to a few stalls only.
[3] S. Garbet, *The History of Wem* (1818). [4] Ibid.

township, the hierarchy as it was found in Wybunbury was complete in Wem parish, but Wem itself is a parochial market-town.

In *Hodnet*, although both the village and the parish are smaller, the full range of the five township types was represented in the mid-nineteenth century. Of its ten townships Hodnet was of the parochial village type but with a strong estate element (Ap/E), Peplow and Wollerton non-parochial hamlets (B), Kenstone and Marchamley semi-dispersed (C), Bolas Parva, Hopton and Espley, and Lostford farm townships (F), and Hawkstone the park-estate type (E). Finally Weston and Redcastle township, the tenth, an old chapelry, was hamleted but included an appreciable part of Hawkstone Park (B/E). In 1841, Hodnet had a population of 596, Marchamley of 441, Weston of 348, and Peplow and Wollerton of 220 and 231 respectively – sufficient in each case to ensure that the community included a number of non-agricultural personnel such as blacksmiths, wheelwrights and shopkeepers, while both Wollerton and Weston had chapels and Independent ministers.[1]

Hodnet itself is of considerable interest. Now a compact village at a five-road junction, its plan is based on a long-disused small market-place set amid half-timbered houses.[2] The church stands behind it to the west on a steep rise, and Hodnet Hall and its park lie immediately adjacent to the south and west on the rising ground of the sandstone ridge. The village and estate elements are both strong. Some two miles to the west lies the Early Iron Age hill-fort of Bury Walls, second only to Old Oswestry in size and defences in the whole of north Shropshire. A line of Celtic and possible Celtic names runs approximately west–east from Nesscliff to the Longford three miles from Hodnet beyond Lostford. Unfortunately, the early history of Hodnet is shrouded with mystery, but its site and that of *Prees* (Lh/Ap) on its church-crowned hill less than five miles to the north-west, both with Celtic names, suggest an origin linked with the pre-Anglian period while the site and name of its neighbour, Stoke upon Tern, only a mile and a half to the east are alike typically Anglo-Saxon. *Stoke upon Tern* church is at the edge of the belt of water

[1] Samuel Bagshaw, *Gazetteer of Shropshire* (1851).
[2] There is no record of a market charter other than an indirect one. In 20 Edw. I a *Quo Warranto* was issued against William de Hodnet for holding a market. He produced his charter and was dismissed with honour.

meadows which lie along the Tern, with the houses scattered above it on firm ground. Having only four townships and an area of 5600 acres it ranks as a fairly small parish, and its population totalled only 1000 in 1841. (Compare Hodnet's parish acreage of 11,596 and population of 2185 at the same date and Wem's corresponding figures of 13,841 and 3919.) Its belted meadow-land, open arable fields, and former open common were typically those of the English valley village, though the nucleation itself is small.

Despite the high quality of much of the farmland in this part of Shropshire, the extensive spreads of droughty heaths broke up the pattern of fields and meadow land and provided open pasture for centuries prior to the late enclosure period. Some of the heathland, fortunately, remains open to this day giving a glimpse of the pre-enclosure landscape. Commons enclosure of lowland heaths was nowhere more important than in Shropshire and was associated with numerous privately commissioned surveys and maps as well as with parliamentary Enclosure Acts and Awards. It played a double role in the evolution of the rural landscape in that it resulted in the alteration of the farming map and farming methods by enclosure, drainage and land improvement, and the addition of a new scatter of farmhouses and cottages. The enclosure of Whitchurch Heath is shown on a map drawn by C. Grey in 1761 for the Duke of Bridgewater. The most extensive land was still that of the copyholders, though there was no indication of the location of individual holdings or of whether these were formerly open fields. Enclosed land, by that date transformed into farmland held in severalty, lay in two blocks across Black Park and between Twemlows Hall and Sandford, and in a belt from Upper Tilstock Park to Bubney. The remaining open heath was roughly as it was in the 1930s leaving Brown Moss, Whitchurch Heath and Prees Heath, but farm names incorporating 'Heath' give some indication of its former extent. Like numerous other enclosures, it tidied up and completed the process of piecemeal nibbling which had long continued; for example, the enclosing of 'the Lord's wast on houghton greene' in 1681, a presentment 'for maintayning of a cottage in Cockshutt upon my lord's land' in 1700, and an encroachment and the making of bricks on Braden-heath common in 1809. A plan of about 1600 entitled *A plott of Tilstock Park after its division into closes* provided the earliest record of the conversion of parkland on the Bridgewater estates into farm-land, and a William Fowler map of 1651 marked the enclosure of Bubney Forest.[1]

The open commons of north-east Shropshire were enclosed by Acts dating from 1795 to 1850, and most of this land was heath or peat.[2] The process of squatting and minor enclosure, however, had been going on, as in the manor of Whitchurch, for some time, and the settlement of Wistanswick Green in the parish of Stoke upon Tern was incipient in 1787[3] though the Act referring to Stoke upon Tern was not passed until 1800.

Only minor industries and occasional suburban extensions are to be found in this part of Shropshire, and the countryside mirrors centuries of change with little interference from modernity.

North-west Shropshire

The western half of the northern lowlands of Shropshire differs in two ways from the north-eastern area: first, Welsh influence increases progressively westwards, and secondly for nearly four hundred years the area was carved up into lordships which were part of the March. Both affected the rural pattern profoundly, but still failed to eradicate from the western lowland the evidences of an older British and a superimposed Anglian settlement. Its settlement geography is correspondingly complex.

Oswestry is the economic and cultural focus of north-west Shropshire, and has so effectively linked the upland and the plain that, despite marked contrasts, the history and the geography of the two are inseparable. The hills begin where the productive Coal Measures emerge from under the barren Coal Measures and the load of drift which covers the glaciated lowlands to the east. The hill edge forms a clear line from the Ceiriog to the Tanat, and Oswestry stands at the hill-foot midway between the two rivers. The county boundary lies some four to five miles to the west, and north of Oswestry this border upland is bounded by

[1] *Bridgwater Estate Collection*, N.L.W.
[2] W. E. Tate, 'A Hand List of English Enclosure Acts and Awards', *Trans. Shrops. Archaeol. Soc.*, LII, i (1947), pp. 31–7.
[3] *Adderley Estate Collection*, Shropshire Record Office.

Offa's Dyke on the Welsh side and by Wat's Dyke on the east. The highest points are only a little over 1300 feet, but it is none-theless an area of marked relief, deep valleys and upland soils.

Mercian control of the Border had extended to Oswestry by A.D. 641 and by the late eighth century under Offa English control had been pressed farther west into the hills. The Old English hundred of *Māersaete* with its caput at Maesbury was the mark of English political control and this has continued ever since, with only minor breaks.[1]

With the initiation of the Norman plan to conquer Wales, the lordships of Oswestry, Caus and Sai (Clun area) were among the first to be established in the middle Border, subsidiary to the palatine earldom of Shrewsbury. Although there were other lordships in north-west Shropshire, Oswestry remained its prin-cipal stronghold throughout the Marcher period. The lordship of Oswestry was divided into three parts. Its centre was Oswestry and its liberties – a comparatively small area; to the south, east and west lay the second part of the lordships, the Duparts; to the north of Whittington lordship, which cut that of Oswestry into two, lay the third part, the manor of Traian. The Duparts extended south to the river Vyrnwy, west to the border, and east to the lordships of Knockin and Ruyton. Twenty-two townships were included in its boundaries, and five more in the Traian.

The Domesday Book paints a picture of a wasted countryside, sparsely inhabited by Normans and English, but with 53 Welsh-men in 'Mersete' hundred – nearly four times as many as in all the remainder of the county. No place with a Welsh name was recorded, but this does not obviate the possibility of there having been minor Welsh place-names at that time. B. G. Charles, recognising the difficulties posed by the Domesday account, adds that when more information becomes available in the thirteenth and fourteenth centuries 'the area is Welsh to the core. The great Norman lordship of Oswestry had taken shape: a feudal super-structure on a Welsh base'. And by that time almost all the vills in the uplands had Welsh names.[2]

A number of surveys and rentals of the lordship of Oswestry

[1] B. G. Charles in O'Donnell Lectures (1962), p. 98. *Māersaete* means 'boundary people' and Maesbury is *Māeresburh* (O.E.) *not* derived from the Welsh *maes*.
[2] Ibid. pp. 99–100.

have been preserved and several of these have been transcribed and annotated by W. J. Slack, together with *Extenta Manerii*, 1393.[1] Further *Deeds Relating to Oswestry* in the Shrewsbury Public Reference Library were transcribed by the Rev. R. C. Purton,[2] and in addition there is a certain amount of documentary material contained in the *Brogyntyn Manuscripts*[3] and the Sweeney Hall deeds and documents[3] which, *inter alia*, provide a considerable body of data concerning this area.

The 1602 Survey gives a great deal of information as to the extent of wastes, forests and encroachments, and Slack computes the waste at that date as 5596 and the forests as 1473 acres, giving a total of 7069 acres or one-seventh of the whole lordship. He adds that some 3600 acres were still unenclosed in 1786.[4] Today it is a pastoral farming region, the greater part under grass, and with only small patches of ploughland.

Throughout the hills, Welsh place- and field-names form the overwhelming majority. The building of Offa's Dyke to the west of this area was little more than a military achievement, for there is not a single English village name in the hills. On the other hand, there is much to suggest that the coming of Norman rule brought about here, as elsewhere, many important economic changes. Open arable fields, and some common meadows are numerous, and although the nature of the land precluded the development of large open fields of the English type, there is evidence which suggests that small fields, rather than the scattered ploughing strips of the Welsh, were the rule by the fourteenth and fifteenth centuries.[5] One of the most striking instances of the spread of the English type of open field organisation is provided by a deed of 3 Hen. VI (*circa* 1425) which refers to '11 acres *minores et maiores*, 7 in the lower field of Cotton adjacent to the field of Weston; the 8th in the middle field; the 9th in the field above Cotton moor; the 10th and 11th in upper field between the ways which lead to the lord's mill'.[6]

[1] W. J. Slack, *The Lordship of Oswestry, 1393–1607* (1951).

[2] *Trans. Shrops. Archaeol. Soc.*, liii, pt. 1 (1949).

[3] In the National Library of Wales, the *Brogyntyn MSS.* deposited by the late the Rt Hon. Baron Harlech, the Sweeney Hall deeds by Major Parker Leighton.

[4] Slack, op. cit. pp. 19–20.

[5] R. C. Purton, *Deeds*, e.g. nos IX, XXXIII, LIII referring to the fields of Sweeney, Llanvorda and Upton in the liberties of Oswestry.

[6] R. C. Purton, loc. cit. LXI.

An interesting facet of the agronomic history of this district is the advance of cultivation into the higher and more remote uplands. A hint of this is given as early as 1340 when Jeyna' ap Madoc Pen of Sweeney gave to another Welshman and his wife an acre *in montana* between the arable and waste of Sweeney.[1] Similar deeds followed, and long lists of later encroachments are given in the sixteenth- and seventeenth-century surveys which show that colonisation of this type went on for many centuries. In certain cases this led to the creation of new settlements along the high, western margins of the lordship, and *Cynnion* is an example of this (Fig. 40). It is a small upland township west of Oswestry, in hilly land between the Morda and the Cynllaith rivers. A marginal note in the 1577 *Survey of Oswestry* says: 'Kyninion is the Lords and at the beginning was enclosed out of the commons which the township of Cricketh did clayme to be their common. The Lord did enter. Whereupon the tenants were contented to carry stone and lime to mayntayne the castle and walls of the towne and there upon they had fredom in towne and the Lord gave them the said land.'[2] The date of this 'begining' is a matter for surmise, but it was clearly within the period of Marcher feudalism, and perhaps quite soon afterwards Cynnion was invested with an open field system. In 1585 it had at least seven tenements, and to one of these were attached twenty-four parcels of open field-land or meadow.[3]

The establishment of a system of community agriculture is not remarkable in itself in these circumstances, although the entries taken together are significant in that they exemplify the process by which manorialism was extended in the Marches. The final touch is only given to the story when, with the help of the 1838 tithe map, it is seen not only that open fields were initiated, but that they persisted well into the nineteenth century and – even more remarkable – the arable fields are found to be situated in two separate areas both between 925 and 950 feet above sea level. The more northerly was known in the nineteenth century as the town field, and the southerly area – which may have been organised originally as one larger or two smaller fields – bore

---

[1] Ibid vi.
[2] F. 258a, qu. Slack, p. 121.
[3] Slack, op. cit. p. 115, Terrier of Lands and Tenements, etc., 1585, ff. 8a and 9a.

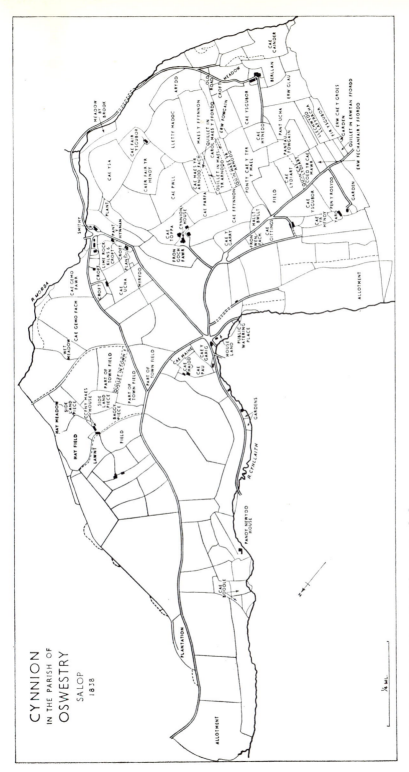

40. Cynnion, Shropshire: the tithe map, 1838

entirely Welsh names except for the use of the term quillet. Habitations were sparse and dispersed. This type of township differs from any in the lowland of Shropshire and Cheshire.

In the sixteenth and seventeenth centuries the greater part of the lordship of Oswestry was inhabited by Welshmen, as is clear from the old Welsh form of the personal names in the Surveys. Further, in all but four of the townships in the Duparts, rentals were made out by *gwelyau*. Welsh dues were paid throughout this Welshry, and Welsh customs persisted. It seems that the distinction between free and unfree townships, on the basis of Welsh tribal society, gradually faded as Anglo-Norman influence made itself felt. But habitations remained largely dispersed, and the countryside and the people retained much of their Welsh character.

Whittington and the lowland lordships to the east – Ellesmere, Ruyton, Knockin and Myddle – repeated many features of the Norman organisation of Oswestry lordship, but Welsh evidences gradually decreased eastwards, though they by no means disappeared. The period or periods during which they extended farther into the plain cannot be stated definitively, but Welsh field-names occur in a number of the tithe apportionment lists of Ruyton townships in the 1840s, and some at least may be comparatively modern. Far from breaking up the older satellite parish structure, the effect of administration in the marcher lordships was to strengthen it. *Ellesmere* (LUpmlc), for example, had twenty-three townships in the mid-nineteenth century though that number represented a decrease since Dudleston was compounded of five former townships including two with the Welsh names *Coed yr Allt* and *Pentrecoed*; the names of five others were dual, suggesting recent amalgamation, and one triple. Among this large number may be found the five main types traced in other north Shropshire lowland parishes, but the characteristically Welsh fluidity of boundary would seem to be implied in the complexity of the amalgamations. Like most *capita* of the lordships, Ellesmere was a market centre with fairs and a great church and, formerly, a castle on a mound near the church. In 1851, the area of the parish was 25,676 acres and its total population 7080. Knockin and Whittington near the Border were similarly organised, but Myddle well to the east had only a minor castle and less military importance (LAplc).

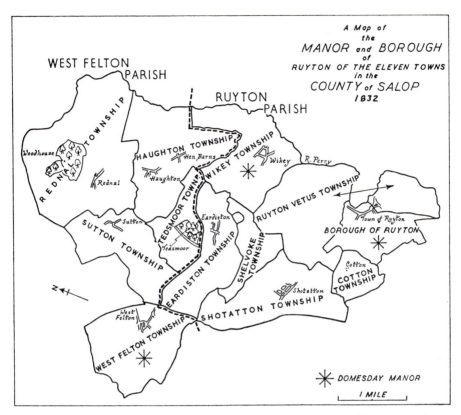

A Map of
the
MANOR and BOROUGH
of
RUYTON OF THE ELEVEN TOWNS
in the
COUNTY of SALOP
1832

WEST FELTON
PARISH

RUYTON
PARISH

REDNAL TOWNSHIP

Woodhouse

Rednal

HAUGHTON TOWNSHIP

Hen Barns

Haughton

WIKEY TOWNSHIP

Wikey

R. Perry

RUYTON VETUS TOWNSHIP

Town of Ruyton

BOROUGH OF RUYTON

SUTTON TOWNSHIP

Sutton

TEDSMOOR TOWNSHIP

Eardiston

Tedsmoor

EARDISTON TOWNSHIP

SHELVOKE TOWNSHIP

Cotton

COTTON TOWNSHIP

N

West Felton

SHOTATTON TOWNSHIP

Shotatton

WEST FELTON TOWNSHIP

✳ DOMESDAY MANOR

I MILE

41. The manor and borough (formerly the lordship) of Ruyton XI
Towns

The composition of the lordship of *Ruyton XI Towns,* though on
a smaller scale, was as complex as that of Oswestry.[1] Divided into
two parishes, its original eleven townships have also the satellite
structure of more easterly parishes (Fig. 41). Now a large village,
Ruyton was a medieval borough and market town, clustered
round its church and castle on the right bank of the River Perry,
but its castle was destroyed in 1212, and in 1407, it lost its market
to Oswestry. Records of its open fields go back to a Court Baron
Roll of 1332, and two open arable fields and two common
meadows were still worked as open common fields in 1839. The

[1] See Ch. 7, pp. 160–1.

tithe map shows Brown Hill Field as a large quilleted field south-east of the village, and nine tenants held land in it at that date. Three sets of quillets and strip-shaped fields lay to the south of the village and may originally have been part of one, two or three other fields. South-east of the village Bull Meadow Field was still held in open strips, and by the Perry were Mill Meadows in which some open strips also survived.

West Felton (LBp) is little more than a hamlet, but the settlement was nucleated at the time of the tithe survey, except for a few roadside cottages. Some quillets remained, and were no doubt relics of the open field which was mentioned in the time of Elizabeth I when there were a Lord's Field and a Lord's Meadow. Some moss strips existed in the east of the township and had perhaps been found at one time in the west also. Eardiston is a fairly large hamlet; Rednal, Haughton and Wykey small hamlets. Eardiston had two open arable fields in the sixteenth century; Rednal one or more. Wykey may have had an open field called Whytfield, but for Haughton there is no definitive evidence. Shotatton is a dispersed township, but may have had three open fields in the sixteenth century; Tedsmoor and Sutton, also dispersed, may each have had two. Shelvoke which included only two farms and two cottage holdings at the tithe survey had an open field in the sixteenth century, and in Cotton alone – a single farm township – there is no mention of one. Several of the townships included a hall, but they were without a park in Tedsmoor and Shotatton by the nineteenth century. Another feature of the land pattern at the tithe survey was the mossland, on which tenants had common rights including the depasturing of animals and the cutting of turves. Baggymoor in Wikey provides an example of parallel moss strips. Welsh field-names are numerous, especially in the four westerly townships of Rednal, Haughton, Sutton and Tedsmoor. In Haughton there is a field called Llanlleod near the hamlet, and Sutton and Tedsmoor both have fields called Maes. Haughton has a Towns Wood and there is every possibility that, although these townships bear English names they are and long have been Anglo-Welsh. Most of the Welsh field-names have disappeared from the more easterly townships and from Ruyton, West Felton, Wikey and Shelvoke – all heads of manors at one time.

The four hundred years since Union have converted the erstwhile castles into ruins and the *capita* of the lordships into quiet country market-towns or remote villages. The lowland soils are so rich that this is one of the more prosperous farming districts in the Borderland. Grazing herds in the peaceful meadows, widespaced farms, scattered brick and sandstone cottages, desolate mosslands and the unexpected beauty of lakes in the wooded hollows of the moraine country today compose this gentle countryside. But the rare nucleations which both parish and lordship combined to create, the occasional small hamlets, the wide areas with only scattered farms and occasional cottages are nonetheless evidence of the persistent satellite pattern of the large parish reinforced by the structure of the lordships. Welsh and English place- and farm-names are mingled. A number have alternative Welsh and English names. Others are anglicised Welsh[1] or cymricised English, some older Celtic and all contribute to the rural synthesis.

The Southern Margins of the Plain

The northern plain is flanked on the south by open alluvial vales. The middle Severn crosses the county boundary from Deuddwr, and before entering the Gorge receives the joint waters of the Tern and Roden, and the streams draining from the Wealdmoors into the Tern. Despite the frequent, and often disastrous flooding, these wide valleys are among the most fertile parts of the county and are characterised by valley settlement except on the Wealdmoors where Eyton, Preston and Kinnersley are on island sites safely above the once marshy peat flats. Otherwise the valley tradition is universal, sites varying from those actually on the alluvium such as Melverley's to those at the margin of the flood plain and the firm land as in the cases of Upton Magna and Eyton on Severn. The Severn is followed by parish boundaries throughout this stretch except at Atcham which lies on both sides of the river.

The only nucleated villages in the Severn valley section are Shrawardine, and Ford, the next nearest, Meole Brace and Great

---

[1] E.g. Baschurch, which was *Eglwysseu Bassa* in the *Canu Llywarch Hen*. (B. G. Charles, loc. cit. (1962), p. 87.)

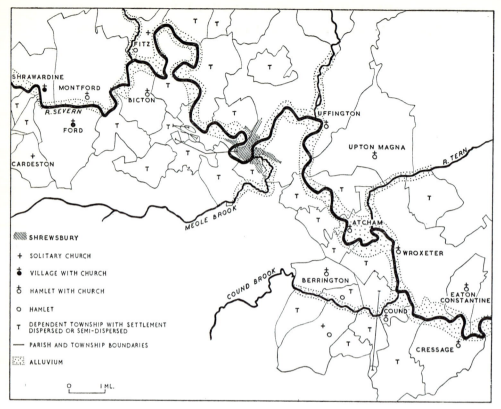

42. The Plain of Shrewsbury: settlement features, mid-nineteenth century

Hanwood being some distance to the south in the tributary valley of Rea Brook (Fig. 42). To the east of Shrewsbury there are no true old villages, only hamlets and dispersed settlement. The third distinctive feature is that this belt is just south of the parish line and is typified by single-township parishes, the multi-township parish with its satellite structure disappearing completely from the map in this stretch of wide alluvial and peaty lowlands. The transition is not gradual but abrupt, the exceptions for the most part having only two to six townships and occurring but rarely, with the single exception of Alberbury which in conformity with the northern and western areas of the county, had twelve townships within Shropshire and seven or eight in Montgomeryshire but has no parochial village.[1] Otherwise, Wroxeter with six is the largest, followed by Berrington and Upton Magna with five, while a further three have four townships, three have three, and three more have two. Something like thirty are single-township parishes, and this pattern dominates the belt.

Apart from its having no parochial village, Alberbury compares with the multi-township parishes of north-east and west Shropshire, but it is succeeded immediately downstream by the single-township parishes which prevail from here eastward and southward. Many gained population because of their position at fords and bridge points (Ford, Montford, Montford Bridge, Uffington, Atcham and Wroxeter are all at ancient crossing points of the Severn), but apart from this type of stimulus to growth most places are and have long been surprisingly small and slow to grow considering the natural fertility of these broad vales. The answer in part lies in their small geographical area, but the remarkable point is that each supported a church. Size and, consequently, to some extent, classification as settlement types naturally varies with the centuries, but past population figures were rarely large. In 1672 according to the Hearth Tax returns, none of these townships had more than 42 houses (Melverley). Uffington had 31, Ford 26, Withington (?) 23, and Sheinton and Bolas Magna each 20, no other place reaching that figure except Alberbury with 23 and Kinnersley and Preston on Wealdmoore each with 25.[2] Most supported only 10–20 households. In the Wealdmoors, growth was comparatively recent as each place probably had no more than three households in the late sixteenth century.[3] The disadvantages of inadequate drainage long delayed the growth of the Wealdmoors settlement but in 1086 the rich countryside of the mid-Shropshire valley lands stood out as the most extensive belt of developed crop farming in the county. Part of the area lay in the liberties of Shrewsbury and Shrewsbury burgesses held land and had pastoral rights there.[4] The Abbeys of Much Wenlock, Haughmond, Buildwas, Wombridge, White Abbey at Alberbury,

[1] R. W. Eyton, *The Antiquities of Shropshire* (12 vols, 1854–60), v, p. 83, says that in 1257 Alberbury was a capital manor with a Welshry pertaining to it. If so, it would seem to be a likely candidate for a lost village site.

[2] 'Shropshire Hearth Tax Roll of 1672', *Trans. Shrops. Archaeol. Soc.* (1949).

[3] Mary C. Hill, 'The Wealdmoors', *Trans. Shrops. Archaeol. Soc.*, LIV, ii (1953), p. 317.

[4] J. B. Blakeway, 'The History of Shrewsbury Liberties', *Trans. Shrops. Archaeol. Soc.* (1897).

and the abbey of Saints Peter and Paul at Shrewsbury all aided its medieval advancement. Haughmond, for example, had land in Sheinton, Rodington, Preston Boats and Wroxeter.[1] Churches were and are numerous and closely spaced. Emstrey (Eyminster) is significant. Eaton Constantine and Cressage may both have had Celtic churches.[2] In 1086 Wroxeter had a church and four priests and by 1291 most of the others were in existence.

The typical township of the middle Severn valley may be illustrated by *Sheinton*, a parochial hamlet built on a low shelf above the alluvial flood plain of the Severn at the opening of the trumpet-shaped plain which heralds the Gorge. Only two miles long and three-quarters of a mile wide, it has its northern boundary on the Severn near the point where it is joined by Harley Brook. The alluvial belt was the site of the old Town Meadow which, near a confluence, was doubly liable to flood, but the hamlet, which consisted of only twenty houses in 1672 and thirty-six in 1841, was safely built more than sixty feet higher amid its three former open common fields. These were Little Field, Middle Field and Townshend Field and were enclosed in 1813.[3] Melverley's open fields were enclosed in 1789, and those of Kinnersley a few miles to the north in the same year.[4] Sheinton is a one-township parish and in 1841 its total acreage was only 967, its population at that date 154.

The parishes of the lower Tern and Roden are comparable, but the area of the Wealdmoors and its continuation eastwards differ physically and economically from the valley settlements proper. The Wealdmoors, known in the past alternatively as the Wild Moors or the 'woody moors' are the remnant of glacial lakes formed in front of the retreating ice sheets and later drying out to form peat moss. Until they were drained, their use was limited, and they were described by the Rev. George Plaxton, rector of Kinnersley in 1706–7 as 'formerly overgrown by rubbish wood, such as

[1] W. A. Leighton, 'Extracts from the Cartulary of Haughmon Abbey', *Trans. Shrops. Archaeol. Soc.* (1878).

[2] B. G. Charles (1962) collates Llan Custenhin, former Welsh name of Welsh Bicknor in Herefordshire, with Constantine (see also Gould and Fisher, *Lives of the British Saints* (1907–13), iv, pp. 289–90). The church of Cressage is dedicated to St Sampson, a Welsh saint.

[3] Emrys J. Howell, *Shropshire*, Land Utilisation Survey Report (1941), p. 286. The 1813 map is redrawn and reproduced on p. 288.

[4] W. E. Tate, loc. cit. (1947), p. 30.

alders, willows, salleys, thorns and the like'.[1] Drainage was attempted on a small scale in the sixteenth century[2] when some enclosures were being made and this continued in the seventeenth century.[3] Islands of higher ground within the moors alone were habitable and on them were sited the tiny initial settlements of the historic period – Preston on Wealdmoors, Eyton on Weald-moors and Kinnersley, as well as minor ones such as Adney and fringe settlements like Longford, Brocton and Sleap.[4] A number of Bronze Age finds have been made in the Wealdmoors, and the Wall, a ramparted enclosure, 'would now be dated on analogy to the Early Iron Age, but it may yet prove that Hartshorne was right in assigning it to the Sub-Roman period'.[5] Yet, prior to the main enclosure carried out under the Acts of 1801–10, the area was a morass except in summer and only then could the moors be grazed.[6] Nevertheless, there was sufficient firm land to provide for cropping and Kinnersley and Sleap each had two open fields and Kinnersley may have had a third.[7]

In the sixteenth century, according to the Sutherland maps, Eyton was shown as having one or two houses and a church, Kinnersley two or three and a church, and Preston one or three houses. Their reliability is, of course, not great. But in the Hearth Tax Rolls the number of households in these three island settle-ments was respectively (?) 23, 25 and 25. Compared with the valley settlements these were very fair figures and the places were growing at no mean rate. In 1841, these same townships were recorded in the Census as having 82, 49 and 80 houses in the same order, but the central settlements still only rank as hamlets. The single-township parish characterises the Wealdmoors as it does the rest of the valley belt, except for the intrusion of the large parishes of Wellington and High Ercall, but neither of these is

---

[1] 'Some Natural Observations in the Parishes of Kinnardsey and Donnington in Shropshire', *Phil. Trans.*, xxv (1706–7).

[2] Mary C. Hill, loc. cit. p. 291.   [3] Ibid. pp. 315–16.

[4] Ibid. reproduction of a map of the Wealdmoors in 1580 from the Sutherland Collection, Shrops. Record Office, 38/1.

[5] Lily F. Chitty, 'Bronze Axe Hoard from Preston-on-the-Wealdmoors, Shropshire', *Trans. Shrops. Archaeol. Soc.*, LIV, ii (1953), p. 252.

[6] Emrys J. Howell, op. cit. p. 289. A map on the same page shows the Weald Moor Commons Improvement *circa* 1801.

[7] Mary C. Hill, loc. cit. pp. 302–4. Miss Hill includes in this paper a number of early estate maps from the Sutherland Collection showing fields, etc., mainly in the fringe settlements.

strictly within the valley settlement area of the Severn–Tern as here defined.

Celtic and Anglian settlement features are the main constituents of the pattern with some manorial and considerable later influence, but in other respects the area differs markedly from the other two major subdivisions of the northern plain.

14 Shropshire

II *The Southern Hill Country*

> Wenlock Edge was umbered
> And bright was Abdon Burf,
> And warm between them slumbered
> The smooth green miles of turf.
> from *Fancy's Knell*, A. E. Housman

WITHIN the curve of the Severn there lies another world. Here the great promontory of the south Shropshire hills thrusts out eastward into the English Plain, completely dividing the northern lowlands of the Borderland from the southern. One and all composed of Pre-Cambrian and Primary rocks, the south Shropshire hills rise ridge upon ridge from Long Mountain and the Breiddens, to Shelve, the Stiperstones, the Longmynd, the Stretton Hills and Wenlock Edge where, beyond the broad expanse of Corve Dale, ridge and dale give place to the great sub-circular platform which is crowned by the high, twin peaks of Brown Clee in the north and of Titterstone Clee in the south. Every ridge and dale in this unique succession is highly individual in both its structure and relief, as are the Clee Hills to the east and the mass of Clun Forest to the south-west. Innumerable *pays* here form perfect examples of the French concept of small sub-regions, and in no other part of the Borderland is the response of settlement to physical geography more sharply contrasted nor more beautifully demonstrated than in south Shropshire. Yet over and above the marked individualism, there are broader relationships which are important and inescapable.

This south Shropshire hill country includes both the highest and the most barren land in the English border counties. The Clees and the Stiperstones rise to well over 1700 feet; the Longmynd and Corndon Hill to within a few feet of that height; much of Clun Forest to over 1300 feet, with occasional hills over 1400; the hogbacks of the Stretton ridge vary up to more than 1500 feet; and the highest points of Wenlock Edge reach typically to something over 900 and 1000 feet above sea level. Around the main ridges and uplands many lesser groups and individual hills exceed 1000 feet and more, contributing still further to a country-side of endless variety and extraordinary interest and beauty, but one in which the natural poverty of the higher hills is perpetually set against the richness of the vales. Despite its nearness to the Cambrian massif, the south Shropshire hill country is in no way part of it, nor does it resemble it, except in height, in any part but Clun Forest.

Seen in relation to the Borderland as a whole, this broad hill promontory severs the predominantly low lying land of the English border country into two parts, acting, if not as a block to progress north or south, as a deterrent because it is an area of necessarily limited routeways. From Roman times, the major valleys have always been the chief lines of movement, lesser ways alone traversing the hills. Fortunately for ease of communication up and down the Border, the main grain of the country is within a few degrees of north–south. Stretton Dale from the Roman period has carried the main north–south road, and later the railway. By comparison, the Rea–Camlad is secondary and has functioned alternatively to the Vale of Welshpool as an access route between mid-Wales and Shrewsbury. Corvedale is of still less importance as a through route though of very considerable interest in settlement and in relation to the Severn valley below the Gorge, and the Worfe valley and the approach from Stafford-shire. Of the three east–west routes, the Severn in the plain of Shrewsbury is the easiest and has always been the least defensible. The Onny or, as Estyn Evans has called it, 'the road of the Castles', has been strategically the most important, and the Teme above Ludlow relatively minor, though below Ludlow it is of prime significance being part of the most direct route from London to mid-Wales.

To the geographer as to the strategist, this complex ground plan with its constant reiteration of the hill and vale theme is of outstanding interest. Agriculture, settlement siting, boundary drawing, access, communications, land tenure, tactics and history alike are to a remarkable degree related to and conditioned by this geographical patterning.

The Settlement Picture

South Shropshire is outstanding in the English border counties for the number of its Early Iron Age hill-forts, but it would be difficult to postulate that it retained this predominance in the settlement picture in the later Romano-British and sub-Roman phases. Celtic place-name elements survive in appreciable numbers in the south-eastern quadrant of the county and on the northern fringes of the hill country. In Clun, Brythonic names mingle with modern Welsh. In the ill-populated, wild moorlands from Longmynd to the Rea–Camlad valley, they are scarce, but so are settlements of any kind other than isolated farms and rare hamlets.

Of the Celtic names which remain, there are sufficient in the vales to substantiate the assumption of a valley-dwelling native Celtic population in the pre-Anglian phase. These names and the route of the *Hen Ffordd* from Droitwich and Bridgnorth, around the northern edge of the Clees into Corve Dale, and round the southern prolongation of the Wenlock Edge via Halford and the Onny valley to Forden, give each other mutual support.[1] This old route was one of many natural ways used by the British and, later, the Mercians when they occupied the valleys of south Shropshire.

The persistence of 'Shropshire Welsh' until the eighteenth century is proof of the long centuries during which Celtic influences – perpetuated no doubt by descendants of a British population – lingered actively in this county. Wenlock is a Brythonic name, but Much Wenlock bore the alternative name of Llan Meilien – the sacred enclosure of St Milburga – and this Welsh form cannot have been given before the late seventh century. Some fifty-four names of nineteenth-century parishes in Shropshire included either Celtic elements or early Anglo-Saxon elements indicating a fortified or a sacred place often of pre-Anglian date (*burh, stow, wig*, barrow). Of these about 37 are in the southern hill country including sixteen of the nineteen *burh*-barrow names. Two more of these last (Alberbury and Shrewsbury) lie in the middle Severn

---

[1] See Ch. 3, pp. 83–7.

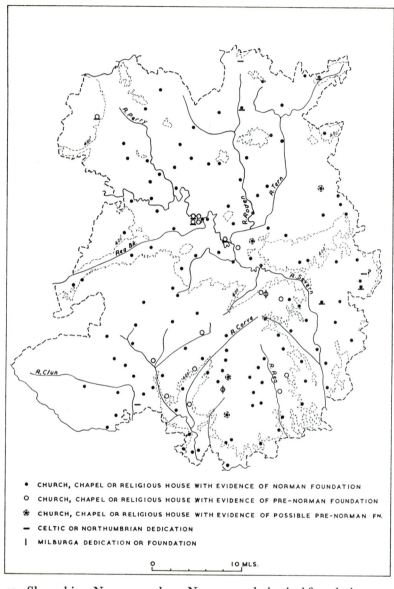

CHURCH, CHAPEL OR RELIGIOUS HOUSE WITH EVIDENCE OF NORMAN FOUNDATION

CHURCH, CHAPEL OR RELIGIOUS HOUSE WITH EVIDENCE OF PRE-NORMAN FOUNDATION

CHURCH, CHAPEL OR RELIGIOUS HOUSE WITH EVIDENCE OF POSSIBLE PRE-NORMAN FN.

CELTIC OR NORTHUMBRIAN DEDICATION

MILBURGA DEDICATION OR FOUNDATION

O   10 MLS.

43. Shropshire: Norman and pre-Norman ecclesiastical foundations

valley and only one (Shawbury) is in the northern plain. Many of these and of the Celtic-named parishes have elevated churches; some are hill villages – Wentnor, Burwarton, Cleobury North. Thirty-five Celtic parish names out of a total of 211 is a lower percentage than the 29 per cent British village names which Kenneth Jackson has reckoned for Cumberland,[1] but in Cumberland the *burh* element is almost absent from parish names and if, in fact, many of these are re-named British sites, then the proportion for Shropshire becomes almost the same as that in Cumberland. They occur both in the single-parish area and to the north and west of the 'parish line'. Six of the sixteen south Shropshire *burh*-barrow parish names are single-township parishes and all six lie east of the summit of the Clees (Beckbury, Oldbury, Barrow, Cleobury North, Burwarton, Sidbury). A number of the Celtic-named parishes and of the *burhs* are among the largest parishes in Shropshire, e.g. Pontesbury (hill church, 20 townships), Clun (17), Stottesdon (elevated site, 17), and Diddlebury (10), but the question of any significant link is not implicit.

It is characteristic of the zone crossed by the 'parish line' to find a mingling of small, medium- and even large-sized parishes and this is true of Shropshire. Four sizeable parishes with Celtic or related names occur on the edge of or within the small-parish zone – Stottesdon (17), Diddlebury (10), Much Wenlock (8) and Burford (8). Further east beyond the Severn, Worfield with 30 and Claverley with 13 townships (both English names) are nucleated villages, and, beyond them, Staffordshire in general shows this marginal character in relation to parish structure.

To a people whose settlements were based primarily on valleys, south Shropshire offered a clear basic pattern, and the three -*ham* suffixes, representing probably the earliest Mercian settlements amid groups of later -*tuns* are significantly placed on the old route north of Clee opposite the confluence of the Worfe with the Severn (Aldenham), in the Teme basin below Ludlow (Caynham), and in the Onny valley in the gap which leads from Halford to Montgomery (Lydham). Their valley distribution is striking and there are comparatively few early Anglo-Saxon names in the intervening uplands especially in the west, in the

---

[1] 'Angles and Britons in Northumbria and Cumbria', in the O'Donnell Lectures, *Angles and Britons*, pp. 74–7.

Shelve–Stiperstones ranges and Clun Forest. In the mid-Shropshire valleys Mercian advance would appear to have been from
the east and south, but the (eastern) Rea valley may well have
been colonised by them from the Aldenham area, just as, alternatively, the Rea–Camlad may have been approached from
either the middle Severn or from Lydham, or indeed from both.
Dating offers difficulties, but St Milburga's nunnery was established at Much Wenlock about A.D. 680, which presupposes
peaceful conditions to have been achieved by the Anglian settlers
at that date.

These same valley-ways were in turn exploited by the Normans
immediately after the Conquest as part of their plan to subdue
the Borderland and advance their political supremacy over
Wales but for the most part they took over existing settlements,
new *foci* being created only round the castles and manor houses
in the early phase. Richards Castle, foreshadowing the key
importance of Ludlow, was built before 1066 and very soon afterwards were built not only the strong line of castles along the
Border itself, but others related to the principal lines of access
from the English lowlands to the east and south-east. The castles
were focal points, and the lands of the greater barons, some of them
nuclei of later marcher lordships, were so arranged in 1086 that
they covered the major approaches to Wales. The Severn valley
between Bewdley and the Gorge was deeply wooded and difficult
to follow. Its defence was therefore less urgent. Bridgnorth Castle
was built only in 1101, but the angle between the Severn and the
Teme was held in 1086 by Ralph de Mortimer, who gave his
name to Cleobury Mortimer. A line of fortresses including the
great strongholds of Ludlow and Bishop's Castle, and beyond
them Montgomery, held the routes of the Teme and the Onny
with Clun and Hopton Castle on alternative and less vulnerable
roads to Wales. Roger de Say, Roger de Lacy and the bishop of
Hereford as well as Roger de Montgomery himself held lands
which completely covered south-western Shropshire including the
Rea–Camlad valley and the Long Mountain. These last, with
mighty Caus and Wattlesborough, were largely held by the
Corbets. The relatively minor attention paid to the Stretton area
is significant. Brockhurst Castle was a royal fortress in the thirteenth
century, but in 1086, though it may long have pre-dated that

period, it was not mentioned, nor was Stretton Dale, apart from its southern entrance, apportioned to the greater barons as were the more southerly and westerly routes. Rather surprisingly Holdgate in Corvedale was recorded in the Domesday Book though Corve Dale, like Stretton Dale, was then of lesser strategic significance (Fig. 39). When the marcher lordships took shape, Caus, Clun and Ludlow became their focal points in the south of the county. The valley pattern remained dominant, but over much of the hill country the *raison d'être* of settlement was primarily strategic. A distinction can nevertheless be made, as in north Shropshire and Herefordshire, between the Marcher lordships in the west and the lesser manors of the centre and east. The first were geared for defence and attack with a castle town at the apex of a typical hierarchy of settlements and landholders, but the last were single manors or small groupings of which the main purpose was the peaceful promotion of agriculture and trade, and the establishment of a lesser Norman seigneury. Norman affixes to place-names, and the numerous manor houses and churches of the centre and east, bear witness to the contrast between the two areas.

The south Shropshire hill country is to no small extent a region which is liable to be struck from time to time by disaster. Among these is the recurrent natural disaster of extensive flooding, especially of the broad vales which, in the west, are subject to the ponding back of flood waters from the Severn. In the Middle Ages, liability to invasion and war continued to take toll of the population, of stock and of agriculture in general. Shrewsbury and Ludlow in particular, and to a lesser extent Bridgnorth and the fortresses of the smaller towns and the rural areas, were subjected to Welsh raiding throughout the marcher period, and to the movements of troops in the Welsh Wars, the Wars of the Roses and later the Civil Wars. Strategic needs for a time created and supported settlements which later had no adequate economic basis. Others found themselves, at best, in reduced circumstances. The Black Death, a nation-wide scourge, added further to the causes of depopulation which, though far from being peculiar to south Shropshire, was more readily triggered off here in this economically marginal hill country than in most other parts of the English border counties. Thomas Auden noted that labour was scarce and that the number of vacancies for parish clergy in 1349 was approximately fifteen times greater in Shropshire in that year than in any one of the ten years before or after that date.[1] The task of tracing deserted medieval village sites has not advanced far in Shropshire, but among the number proved or suspected are several on remote hill and hill-foot sites in the south. The best authenticated, apart from Caus whose decline had set in by 1387, is probably that of Stitt, a township of Ratlinghope at the head of the East Onny between the moorlands of the Stiperstones and the Longmynd. Now consisting of two farms, an undated map in the MSS. of Thomas Farmer Dukes (vol. 3) shows a church and a hamlet of up to a dozen houses. Once a township belonging to Haughmond Abbey, a church was built here about 1180. The church failed to survive the Dissolution, and the settlement may have begun its decline as a result. By 1840, the date of the tithe survey, all trace of the hamlet had gone.[2]

Among other possible deserted or severely shrunken villages or hamlets in south Shropshire are Condover in the northern part of Stretton Dale, Pitchford three miles to the south-east, Heathway near Marton Pool (the source of the Rea and the Camlad), Sibberscot in Pontesbury parish, and two lost hamlets of 'Tornett' and 'Garway' in Stow parish on the southern edge of Clun Forest,[3] as well as a number in the Clee Hills.[4]

Agriculturally, south Shropshire has undergone several transformations. The opening up of the vales in the late Roman, sub-Roman, and Mercian periods set the scene for the predominant valley settlement phase which has dominated the rural geography of south Shropshire from then until now. Medieval assarting in vale and woodland extended the agricultural land of the vales and pioneered the clearing of the great forests which still clothed so much of the Midland Triangle in the early Middle Ages. More hill land was reclaimed also in the Middle Ages, and especially in the Tudor period when, partly on account of depopulation, partly as a result of the growing demand for wool, pasture was extended by the enclosure of both former common pasture and

---

[1] *Shropshire*, Oxford County Histories for Schools (1912).
[2] Ed. J. L. Hobbs, *Shropshire Newsletter*, 2 (Dec. 1957).
[3] Ibid.
[4] Information given verbally by Mr Trevor Rowley.

the old open arable fields.[1] The history of enclosure in Shropshire has been extensively treated by W. E. Tate, and his lists together with Rocque's map of *circa* 1750, and that of Greenwood (1826–7),[2] give a picture of the sweeping change brought about in the extent of open pasture between the mid-eighteenth century and the late nineteenth. This was naturally much more extensive in the southern hills than in the north, but there yet remained of necessity many square miles of intractable upland above the 1000 foot contour. Today, Longmynd, the Stiperstones, Corndon Hill, the higher parts of Clun Forest, and the high Clees remain open moorland from which earlier communities have fled, defeated by Nature's unequal forces.

Despite the changes which have taken place, the areas under the plough in the eleventh century in south Shropshire bore a remarkable resemblance to the cropped land of the eighteenth century, especially on the more level stretches of the Clee Platform which earned the name of the Wheatlands at that time.[3] Today, however, this is cattle and sheep country, for by the end of the nineteenth century arable land in the vales had shrunk to a small proportion only of the total farmed land. Nevertheless, there remains the inescapable response to differences in natural fertility. Vale land, if it is sufficiently drained, is always better and hill land at high altitudes poorer, and the reduction of arable land in the vales has been followed by the increase in good meadowland, maintaining the contrast with the thin pasture of the moors. Where better than from Major's Leap on the high ridge of Wenlock Edge can the patchwork of land use in the vales be seen as one looks down into the green, gold and brown carpet of Ape Dale?

With the reduction in crops and with population growth lagging, remoteness became the keyword in the geography of the south Shropshire hill country except for the route through

---

[1] I. S. Leadam, in *Trans. R. Hist. Soc.* (1894), listed enclosures from the 1517 Survey (Wolsey's *Enclosure and Depopulation Commission*). These covered the years 1496–1516 and were almost without exception in the south of the county where the wool trade was of greater importance. W. E. Tate, in *Trans. Shrops. Archaeol. Soc.* (1947), counts 71 places and says that the depopulation in these totalled 356.

[2] E. J. Howell, op. cit. pp. 281 and 283.

[3] Henry Tanner, 'Agriculture of Shropshire', *Jl R. Agric. Soc.*, xix (1858). J. Phillip Dodd, 'The State of Agriculture in Shropshire', *Trans. Shrops. Archaeol. Soc.*, lv (1954).

Stretton Dale and Ludlow. Forgotten markets, chartered in the thirteenth century when its importance was at its height, had decayed or were in rapid decline, and even the railway age failed to waken the more remote vales from the centuries-long slumber which had settled on them after the devastation of the Civil Wars, and the earlier loss of strategic importance after Union. Indeed, the railways, apart from the main West of England line, have themselves met defeat, and this in more than one case before the age of Beeching.

The foundation pattern of hill and vale remains, each unit having its individual geography, but the rural landscape of the hill country reveals wider sub-regions which are less evident to the eye, and which cannot be explained in physical terms. The primary division is that between the area with nucleated villages set at the focus of large parishes which dominates the western hill country east of Ape Dale. The second is the small-parish area of the eastern half, but this in turn can be further subdivided. In the lands west of Severn, hill and vale continue to dominate the scene and hamlets and dispersal are all but universal. Farther east, the narrow valley of the Severn from the Gorge downstream, itself difficult to settle, is near the fringe of the lower hills and the wider lowlands of the Staffordshire border and is distinguished by the late survival of the great woodlands of the Midland Triangle. Here, scattered late woodland communities prevail, but their distribution is interrupted by groups of nucleated villages, notably those of the Worfe. These, from the angle of the student of rural landscape, are the critical divisions of this complex countryside.

I. The Western Hill Country

(a) Clun Forest

The sweeping U-shaped curve of upland which can be broadly termed Clun Forest resembles the central Welsh plateau to which it is physically related, and in terms of place-names and culture it is more Welsh than any other part of south Shropshire. Its smoothed summits rise to 1300 to 1400 feet in the east and to over

1600 feet in the west near the Kerry Hills and the Montgomery-shire border. The river Clun, collecting the waters of all the northern side of the horseshoe and a few short tributaries from the south, is the topographical axis along which lie the main valley road to the Anchor Pass and a series of villages and hamlets – Newcastle, Clun itself, Clunton, Clunbury and Aston on Clun. The surrounding hills carry only a sparse population mainly in tiny hamlets and widely-spaced farmsteads, except for Bishop's Castle which belongs rather to the 'road of the castles' than to the Clun Forest uplands, and the now minor settlements of Hopesay and Hopton Castle on its eastern fringes. Clun and Kerry are famous for the breeds of sheep to which they have given their names. Hill pasture is the backbone of the economy, but woodland was comparatively abundant on the middle slopes until Tudor times. In the valleys most woodland was cleared by 1600 and a further 600 acres enclosed in the seventeenth century.[1]

The Anchor Pass and the Kerry Hills are by no means easy to negotiate, consequently the Clun valley road has always been of relatively minor importance in border campaigns, its role defensive rather than aggressive, and although Clun was the *caput* of a marcher lordship, and maintained a castle and a market, its long-term significance has been mainly as a natural focus for the broad pastoral uplands of which it is the centre, and as the head of a parish of nearly 20,000 acres.

Place-names alone would reveal it as an area of successive occupations. The group of 'Clun' names, and township names such as Treverward, Hobharris and Hobhendrid reflect a pre-Welsh Celtic occupation. More modern Welsh names such as Llanvair Waterdine, Bettws y Crwyn, and Bryn are mingled with large numbers of Welsh field-names, but Mercian elements are numerous, and there are occasional medieval elements and affixes as in Hopesay and Hopton Castle.

Characteristically Welsh dispersal in the western uplands gives place to mixed settlement patterns in the east and in the Clun valley which appear to be indebted in part to Anglian, in part to medieval origins. Parochially, the large parish of Clun with 17 townships accounts for the greater part of the upper basin. Medium-sized parishes with four to seven townships divide up

[1] *Ancient Documents of Clun, Concise Account* (1858).

most of the remaining part – Mainstone, Bishop's Castle, Lydbury North and Hopesay, on the northern side; Llanvair Waterdine, Clunbury and Clungunford on the southern. Llanvair dates back as a parish only to 1593, but the three single-township parishes of Bucknell, Hopton Castle and Edgton were all in existence in the early Middle Ages. Parochially, therefore, most of Clun Forest belongs to the multi-township zone, but its eastern fringe is just on the margin of the single-townships.

Clun itself (VUpclm) combines the most characteristic features of the settlement geography of the area (Plate XIV). At the time of the tithe survey the parish included the townships of Clun, Bicton, Berfield, Eddicliff, Guildendown, Hobharris, Menutton, Purlogue, Pentrehodre, Newcastle (which became a separate parish in 1849), Shadwell, Spoad, Treverward, Weston, Hobhendrid, Whitcott Evans and Whitcott Keysett. It has a typically satellite structure, but its economy is that of pastoral uplands dissected by deep valleys in which lie the occasional farmsteads and hamlets. The rarer steeper slopes are wooded, but the gentler are everywhere given over to permanent pasture. Occasional patches of ploughland with barley, swedes, or turnips occur on the lower slopes and in the valleys. On the higher hills, fields give place to open moorland which constitutes the common pasture and in the tithe period accounted for two-fifths of the total area of Clun parish, which was divided as follows as regards the principal types of land use:

Waste	39·9
Pasture	24·2
Arable	20·8
Meadow	9·9
Woodland	4·3
Houses, etc.	0·9
	100·0%

Total acreage titheable: 19,873

Welsh farm- and field-names are conspicuous in every township of Clun parish, except for the two tiny ones of Hobharris and Menutton to the south of Clun, and are especially numerous in

Newcastle and Whitcott Keysett in the north-west. Among them are numerous field-names which are typical of Welsh open arable such as *erw*, *maes*, *cefn* and *llain*. *Dolydd* in the meadows were also fairly numerous, and in both open arable fields and common meadows, English and Welsh names lay side by side. In Newcastle township for example at the time of the tithe survey, the higher hills, Caldy and the Fron, were open sheep-run, and between and around them lay pockets of fields which became a continuous ribbon only in the valleys of the Clun and of Forest (or Folly) Brook. Common meadow was to be found in the Clun valley above the small hamlet of Newcastle, and a small open field called variously *Maes Cannol* or *Maes y Bannol*, lay on an appreciable slope below Castle Idris at a height of 800 to 900 feet. A number of strip-shaped fields remained and names such as *Quillet in Maes Cannol*, *Quillet*, *Erw Fron* and *Maes y Bannol* also survived, together with a few open quillets. Up to a quarter of the field-names in the tithe survey were Welsh, rather more than half the surnames of tenants, and most of the farm-names.

Newcastle (VB) lies west of Offa's Dyke and it has been argued that this divides a predominantly Welsh area from a more English district to the east. It is difficult to support this from the evidence of Clun tithe maps. Bicton, Weston, Treverward, Pentrehodre and Hobhendrid all had a considerable proportion of Welsh field-names. The pattern of land use, the predominance of Welsh-type open strips, and Welsh surnames vary little west and east of the Dyke in Clun parish, nor is there much in the geography of the Clun area, except differences in distance and accessibility, to make it likely that the Dyke could have acted as a cultural divide during the last nine hundred years. The organisation of Clun as a border lordship in the Middle Ages served to override the earlier boundary and give the whole basin a new unity, except that within it Welsh and English both remained side by side. Clun was the natural focus of English culture, and hardly any of its field-names are now Welsh, but the Welsh language was spoken as late as the seventeenth century, and customs such as transpastoralism long persisted.

The marcher period left its mark in many elements in the landscape: in Clun Castle and Hopton Castle, and in fortified church towers. For example in Clun, the church, the vicarage and a meadow behind it were all defended by a deep ditch.[1] Yet feudalism was less deeply entrenched here than in most parts of south Shropshire. The park estate is rare with exceptions such as Walcot (E) and Hopton Castle (Ec), but at Hopton Castle there developed the most 'English' field system of the area round the most regular of its nucleated villages.

(b) The Western Ridges and Vales: From Long Mountain to the Stretton Hills

The Stretton Hills are a wild, tumbled belt of upland country rising from Ordovician sandstones, and craggy Cambrian hills to the remarkable line of hog's-backs composed of infertile Ordovician volcanics which terminate northward in the Wrekin. In the lower eastern part of these hills and in Ape Dale lie the multi-township parishes of Cardington, Rushbury and Hope Bowdler. To the east and north, the single-township parishes take their place. The central settlements of the three large parishes are nucleated villages. To the east and north, the hamlet and scattered habitations compose the greater part of the settlement picture.

In the west, the large parish is almost universal and, as in the northern plain and in Clun, villages are surrounded with hamleted and scattered townships. Few of the villages are large, nor do they have formal plans, but are typically ragged in arrangement, centred on parish churches many of which have fortified towers. The Rea–Camlad valley and Long Mountain in the west of this broad area were deeply defended and geared for the Welsh campaigns throughout the marcher period. The middle uplands – Shelve, Stiperstones and the Longmynd – unbroken by any vale of appreciable size, needed no such defence for they were barren and difficult of access, while beyond them Stretton Dale and the Stretton Hills were too far from the Border to be involved more than occasionally in border wars and raids. As the strategic characteristics fade out gradually eastwards, so do the evidences of Welsh culture, but throughout the western uplands and vales the British basis is strong, despite the widespread Anglian overlay.

[1] J. E. Auden, Shropshire, Methuen's Little Guides, (1926) p. 107.

LONG MOUNTAIN AND THE REA–CAMLAD VALLEY

The low sleek lines of the Long Mountain rise to a summit ridge of over 1250 feet. Together with the triple-peaked Breiddens, it is surrounded by an ovoid ring of lowland so vulnerable that both the Romans and the Normans were at pains to defend it, and yet so important as a gateway into Wales that some of their major advances were launched from this district. It has also functioned for century upon century as a border area, with the result that military and boundary works pepper the entire district, and in no part of the Borderland are there greater concentrations of strategic works than here. Hill-forts on the Breiddens and the Long Mountain, the Roman road from Viroconium to Caersws *via* Forden, Offa's Dyke passing over the Long Mountain, and a deep scatter of mottes, together with the stone castles of Caus, Wattlesborough and Montgomery, and many fortified church towers and moated sites make up the impressive proof of its constant involvement in border affairs.[1]

Yet today, it is a land of peaceful pastures and quiet villages, a still backwater of rural life where only the long memory recalls the battles and alarms of long ago, but a glorious countryside of wide panoramas and extraordinary historical interest. In no part of the Borderland does one feel more strongly the fascination of past and present welded into the subtle unity of regional personality.

The vale of the Rea–Camlad is so level that the watershed between the two divergent drainage systems is Marton Pool, and after periods of heavy rains the valley is converted into a vast lake stretching as far as Shrewsbury In normal times, like the Vale of Welshpool, it is valuable because of its rich water meadows on the broad alluvial flood plain, but there is general avoidance of streamside sites and most of the hamlets and villages are at or above the junction of the alluvium with firmer land.

Of the numerous factors which have influenced the character of settlement in this valley and the neighbouring hills, the strategic, though the most dramatic, has proved the least permanent. Castles and fortresses have fallen into disrepair and the

[1] See the lists in L. F. Chitty, *Trans. Shrops. Archaeol. Soc.*, liii (1949).

nearby settlements have declined or decayed with them. Not only Caus which was a walled market-town with gates as late as the Tudor period, but Wattlesborough, Westbury and Worthen which had markets in the early Middle Ages, had lost them before 1800. Yet the agricultural life, despite vicissitudes, has continued, and still provides the main support for the line of valley and hill-foot villages and hamlets which, from Westbury, are strung along the Rea–Camlad valley on the main road which follows its north-western side – Aston Rogers, Worthen, Brockton, Binweston, Marton – and each township has a slice of hill land, arable slopes and water meadow. In the hills on either side, dispersed settlement and irregularly shaped townships replace the villages and hamlets and the vale-orientated townships. Ancient hill ways such as the *Hen Ffordd* which runs from Pontesbury through Hemford (*Hen ffordd*) to Church Stoke, link up their sparse farm-steads and cottages, and sheep rearing is the main basis of the hill economy. Welsh names are rare in this part of the Borderland, and English parish names extend across into eastern Montgomery-shire.

Worthen (VAp(m)) is a characteristic village clustered irregu-larly along the main valley road. It is the head of a wide parish of over 18,000 acres which embraces townships in the Long Mountain, the vale, and in the hills to the south-west. In the tithe survey period it included nineteen of these townships, of which three were partly in Montgomeryshire, but its population was only a little over 3000 in 1851 when there were just under 600 houses. There has been sharp contrast between its component parts, some places like Binweston having remained virtually unchanged (ten houses in 1678, eleven in 1851), Walton declining from five to three, and Brockton growing from thirteen to seventy-two. A number of the townships in the southern hills grew considerably in the same period (e.g. Hope from eight to seventy-eight, Bromlow from fifteen to ninety-six, Meadowtown from six to twenty-seven), largely on account of the exploitation of lead ores. The satellite structure is clear, but the parallelism between the line of valley nucleations of Worthen, Binweston, Brockton, Aston Rogers and Aston Pigot is different from any patterning which can be found in Cheshire or north Shropshire, but it can be matched in other vale parishes of south Shropshire.

All these townships exemplify the agricultural belting typical of a south Shropshire hill-foot/vale township, extending from well up into the hill pastures through a gently sloping arable belt to the alluvial meadows of the vale. These represent the original open common pasture, the open arable land, and the common meadows, the last being economically dominant. The nucleated settlements are all situated at the junction of the belt of shaly clays and gravels which provided the ploughland and the irrigated water meadows, safe except in abnormal circumstances above the flood line.

On the tithe maps, the moors or wet meadows form wide belts, with indications of their former common status in names such as Lord's Meadow and Town Meadow. Remnants of former open arable fields were traceable in a small Town Field to the west of Worthen. The *Haughmond Abbey Cartulary*[1] takes 'the field of Aston' back to the early Middle Ages, but the most satisfactory early evidence is to be found in a 1540–1 *Account Roll of the Lordship of Cause*.[2] Several entries refer to Worthen and Brockton, mentioning a furlong called *Whitfurlonge*, short acres of meadow, 'langets' of meadow, selions, a parcel of meadow called *Merynge Ployke* (Plucks on the tithe map), 24 acres of demesne meadow called Worthyns Meadow, etc. Other acres of meadow were not rented at this date because 'they were held by the farmers of the demesne as parcel of their farm', implicit proof of disparate holding. At Brockton, Rowley Brook provided a sufficient head of water for a corn mill and a fulling mill at this date, which may be one of the reasons why it became incorporated with Worthen into a single township.

Of the Long Mountain townships, only *Caus* (type HU(m)cl) is known to have had common arable and meadow land, though rents from *Whitefeld* at Winnington, also in 1540, may have been from such a field. Caus probably had two arable fields, as there are separate mentions of a parcel in a field near the vill of Caus, and of a parcel of land in Bromehill field. In addition, there was a field in the Forest of Haia called *Wynstonfeld* which may or may not have been one of three worked by the men of Caus on a

[1] W. A. Leighton, 'Extracts from the Cartulary of Haughmon Abbey, Co. Salop', *Trans. Shrops. Archaeol. Soc.* (1878).
[2] J. R. Whitfield, *Trans. Shrops. Archaeol. Soc.*, LIV, i and ii (1951–3).

triennial system, and numerous free tenants at 'Muneton' near Caus, a lost place which may now be represented by Mundy Farm.[1] There can be little doubt that these fields were initiated by the Normans when Caus was created.

THE WEST-CENTRAL UPLANDS AND VALES

The wildest and most barren part of the country is the stretch of roughly parallel uplands which extend from the Shelve country to Stretton Dale unbroken except by high or narrow valleys. Ten miles wide and ten miles long, it has a core of almost unbroken high moorland culminating in the black crown of the Devil's Chair on Stiperstones, and in the high, round-backed moorland of Longmynd which has for centuries been intercommoned by the surrounding townships. Scattered settlement characterises the greater part of the moorlands, but small, compact villages are found in and above the valleys of the east and west Onny and on the spurs of the Longmynd. *Wentnor* (HAp), on a narrow spur-promontory west of Prolleymoor is one of the more impressive hill villages of Britain.[2] Norbury to the west, and Church Pulverbatch, Picklescott, Smethcott and Woolstaston on the Longmynd are other hill nucleations, and Ratlinghope (pron. Ratchup) is a remote valley hamlet for which H. L. Gray records 158 acres of open field arable and 45 days' math of meadow in the time of Henry VIII.[3] Such names as Townsend Meadow, Dale Acre, Furlong, Flat piece and Flat Meadow in Woolstaston at the tithe survey suggest that other places too, even in these remote hills, may once have worked some kind of open arable system.

Remoteness in these barren hills which have yielded little throughout their history but hill flocks and lead, is more real than in any other part of south Shropshire. Lead mining has scored the hillsides and left shining white spoil heaps near to Lordshill, and its extraction has brought limited and spasmodic employment for the people of the Shelve country from Roman times. Shelve in an old lead mining area is one of the numerous former markets of the southern hill country.

---

[1] Ibid.
[2] Dorothy Sylvester, 'The Hill Villages of England and Wales', *Geogrl J.*, cx (1947).
[3] Op. cit. p. 151.

To the north the hills fall to a gentler but still varied scene, in which larger settlements are to be found, notably *Pontesbury* (VAp), a large nucleated village trailing down from below the camp on Pontesford Hill to the central area clustered round a formerly collegiate church which in the mid-nineteenth century served a parish of over 10,000 acres and 20 townships, with a characteristic satellite structure. Woodland covered much of it in the early Middle Ages and new settlements such as Oaks, one of its southerly townships, had open arable land among its swine pasture in the woods from which more assarts were being taken in the fourteenth and almost certainly in the thirteenth century.[1] The adjacent village of Minsterley is now of considerable size, but despite the existence of an early minster (implicit in its name), it lost even parochial status and its recent growth from a handful of farmhouses only dates back to the closing years of the eighteenth century when lead mining was extended. Like Pontesbury it lay in the medieval lordship of Caus, and had open field in the sixteenth century, but its principal feature was then Minsterley Park which, with its pastures and cockshuts and bees, was a source of income to its lords.[2]

THE CENTRAL RANGES AND DALES

The faulted valley known as Stretton Dale (Plate XI) is the first of the series of rich farming vales in the middle hill country of south Shropshire. Here the Silurian is let down between water-bearing faults, above which Longmynd rises blunt and sheer to the west, and the striking hogback hills – Ragleth, Caer Caradoc, Lawley, etc. – of the Uriconian range lie to the east. From the building of the Roman Watling street this dale has carried the main west of England routes, and, like the Rea–Camlad valley, it is characterised by vale settlement, especially the Strettons (Plate XII), taking up the width of the valley from hill pasture to hill pasture.

The infertility of the Uriconian volcanics bears no relationship to their height but, as they give place eastward to the Cambrian

---

[1] R. C. Purton, 'Manor of Oakes in the Parish of Pontesbury', *Trans. Shrops. Archaeol. Soc.*, LIV, i (1951–2).
[2] J. R. Whitfield, loc. cit.

and then to a wide belt of Ordovician sandstones, the tumbled hill country, once deeply wooded, becomes the setting for occasional villages – Hope Bowdler, Cardington and Rushbury, each the centre of spreading parishes with satellite structure.

II. The Eastern Hill Country and the Eastern Woodlands

(a) The Eastern Hill Country

WENLOCK EDGE AND CORVEDALE

The ruled regularity of the scarps and vales of the Wenlock country is unique both in scale and character in the Welsh Borderland, its settlement geography is so clearly conditioned by physical belting that it is reminiscent of the south-east English scarplands (Fig. 44). Alternate shales and limestones are the basis of the parallel scarps of Wenlock Edge and View Edge, the first rising to 800, the second to summits of 800–1100 feet. Between them, Hope Dale in the Lower Ludlow Shales reaches an average height of 700 feet and on either side Silurian shales form the floor of Ape Dale and Corve Dale. Spring lines at the junction of limestones and shales, and the relief of scarped hill and valley are closely reflected in its settlement pattern. The unbroken ridge of Wenlock Edge forms a township boundary throughout its length except in Easthope. To the west, the townships stretch from the precipitous scarp across Ape Dale and in many cases beyond it, and Ape Dale itself lies across the parish line. Eastwards, they extend across Hope Dale from the summit of Wenlock Edge to the summit of View Edge, faithfully following this latter line where consequent valleys have cut back the Aymestrey Limestone, the township boundaries coinciding with the geological and relief edge of this scalloped escarpment. The third series of townships include the dip slopes of View Edge and a portion of Corve Dale, many having their eastern limit at the river Corve. The main road through Corve Dale, which follows the foot of the dip slope at the junction of the limestones and shales, links a line of hamlets – Bourton, Patton, Larden, Shipton, Broadstone, Hungerford, Munslow, Munslow Aston and so on. There seems every reason

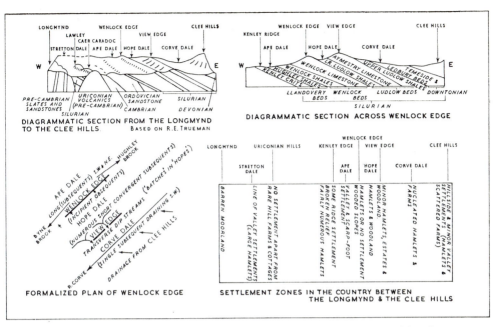

44. Wenlock Edge: sections and diagrams showing the relationship of settlement to physical features

to suppose that *Larden* (JD), a former manor of Shipton, which had common meadows by the stream and open arable fields called *Wyldesbysfeld*, *le Hardacr* and *Wodefeld* in the earliest fifteenth century,[1] was typical of these townships and that an open arable field system survived until the Enclosure Commission of 1578. The founding of the nunnery of St Milburga at Much Wenlock took place about A.D. 680. This first religious house in *Much Wenlock* (UVp(m)) was destroyed by the Danes in the ninth century, restored by Leofric of Mercia in the time of Edward the Confessor, decayed, and was replaced by a second, founded by Roger de Montgomery as a Cluniac Priory after the Norman Conquest. Much Wenlock is the central parochial settlement of a large parish with seven satellite hamleted and dispersed townships.

[1] R. C. Purton, 'Deeds relating to Larden', *Trans. Shrops. Archaeol. Soc.*, LIV, i (1953). Apart from the evidence of the Enclosure Commission which is not usually specific, data concerning open arable land in this area are not easily accessible, but there seems every reason to suppose that it was once widespread.

It has a former minster church, founded in the eleventh century, but the small town with its limestone and half-timbered houses and its former market failed to grow after the sixteenth century. It had several open fields and H. L. Gray presents evidence which suggests that it had three fields in the fourteenth century.[1] They were still open and the system flourishing in the early eighteenth century.[2]

THE COUND BASIN

The Stretton Hills and the north of Wenlock Edge give place to gently rolling country south of the Severn which is drained by small streams, Cound Brook and its tributaries, to the Severn at Cound. As a physical division it in no way ranks with those already described, but it is of interest as part of the area of single-township parishes and transitional in character between the hills and the plain of Shrewsbury. Hamlets and dispersed settlements are typical. Pitchford and Acton Pigot have records of open arable fields going back to the thirteenth century, Golding to the fourteenth, and Acton Burnell to the fifteenth preserved in the *Pitchford Hall Deeds and Documents* (deposited in the N.L.W. by General Sir Charles J. C. Grant, K.C.B.). The earliest of these is a thirteenth-century deed concerning a selion of land 'in the field of Acton Pigot' towards Golden (Golding), and the next a grant of 1273, of an assart containing 14 selions and a piece of meadow adjoining 'the vill of Pycheford' (Pitchford). The history of these fields can be traced through each century in one or other of the townships until the seventeenth when, certainly in the case of Pitchford, enclosure took place. The common fields of Pitchford were enclosed by covenants made between all the co-arators in 1633 (deed no. 905). Pitchford also had common meadow, open commons, and a park. In 1608–9 a fulling mill was leased near to the water corn mills in Pitchford, and this indication of a woollen industry seems to have some significance in relation to the enclosure of the common fields by agreement a quarter of a century later.

[1] Op. cit. p. 66.
[2] See Ch. 10, pp. 237–9 and fig. 27.

THE CLEE HILLS

The last subdivision of the south Shropshire uplands and the core of this area of single-township parishes is the Clee Hills – the wedge-shaped northerly terminus of the great triangle of Devonian rocks which extend from South Wales to south-east Shropshire. The Lower and Middle Devonian marls and some more resistant rocks are here folded into a gentle syncline whose marginal escarpments face over Corve Dale and the Severn below Bridgnorth. The Devonian rocks take the surface form of a broad, softly dissected platform 6–800 feet in height with a slight tilt to the south-east, and this rolling hill and plateau country forms the greater part of the Clees. The high, twin-breasted summit areas of the Brown and Titterstone Clees which rise dramatically above the Devonian base are formed of Carboniferous rocks capped and protected by resistant dolerites, to which the four peaks owe their altitude and preservation. Abdon Burf reaches a height of 1790 feet, and Titterstone Clee of 1749 feet. Hill forts crown Brown Clee (Abdon Burf) and Titterstone Clee, and a third (Nordy Bank) is situated to the west at 1100 feet. The greater part of the area is now one of dispersed and semi-dispersed settlement, but a line of small nucleated hamlets is found on the eastern slope of the high Clees, swinging round to terminate at Stottesdon. Both Brown Clee and Titterstone Clee have township boundaries radiating from their peaks, each township resembling a roughly cut slice of cake. Those of the Brown Clee meet in a north–south line which links Abdon and Clee Burfs, those of Titterstone in a central point on the summit of Titterstone.

The high Clees with their radial township boundaries are at the centre of hillside settlements, 650–850 feet above O.D. The steep slope to the summits begins at about 1000 feet and each township has a sector of open moorland above the enclosed farmlands. On Brown Clee, where little alteration has taken place in the agricultural settlements, *Cleobury North* (HBp) on the eastern slope is typical, a church-hamlet lying between the 650 and 700 foot contours. In 1841, this one-township parish included only 31 houses, of which eight were in the centre, another eight or so were scattered farmhouses, and the remainder tiny cottages of

LAND USE IN FOUR CLEE HILL TOWNSHIPS, *c.* 1840

All figures are %

Cleobury North	Burwarton	Farlow	Oreton	
30·2	27·0	4·9	35·6	Common
3·3	16·2	8·1		Woodland
31·6	33·0	76·8	32·2	Meadow and pasture
29·8	23·8	10·2	32·2	Arable
4·8				Glebe
0·3				Garden
100·0	100·0	100·0	100·0	

squatters on the edge of the moors, but these last have now disappeared. The township included a triangle of common moorland rising to Abdon Burf and below the 1000 foot contour was wholly enclosed in small squarish closes with only slim indications of possible former common fields in names such as Cleobury Field, Flatt Piece and Stony Furlong. Common and woodland (taken together), pasture or meadow, and arable were in approximately equal proportion in 1844. The gently shelving land below the hamlet is by no means unsuitable to the plough and there were four teams here at Domesday. Cleobury Brook draining from the village was the site of the mill. *Burwarton* (HB/Ep), lying 800 feet above sea level, at this date was remarkably similar, except that Burwarton Park altered the character of land use, giving a higher proportion of woodland, and preventing squatting on the moor edge.

At Abdon, near the solitary church just below 900 feet O.D., a survey carried out in March 1965 seems to have confirmed a deserted village site on the western slope of Abdon Burf. Four medieval sherds were found and part of the field near the vanished village was covered by ridge and furrow, the furrows approximately 20 feet in width.[1] The desertion of settlements at this height is not surprising, and raises interesting possibilities as regards their history in other parts of the Clees.

[1] R. T. Rowley in *Shropshire News Letter* (Dec. 1965).

On Titterstone, a considerable modification of the agricultural settlement pattern had been caused by 1840 by the extensive quarrying of dolerite or dhustone and by lime-quarrying and burning. Squatting took place on an extensive scale, the quarrymen taking advantage of the old custom of building between sunset and sunrise on the common to secure cheap houses. On the Carboniferous Limestone, *Oreton* (Fig. 34) in 1848 presented an all too typical picture of the ugly rash of squatting which was arising all round the quarries and kilns on Titterstone,[1] and they still, unfortunately, form a grievous blemish on this high upland with its sweeping views across the neighbouring counties.

Below these radial townships on what might be termed the outer circle of the Clees there lie parochial hamlets such as Stottesdon, Neenton, Ditton Priors, Heath, Cold Weston and Hopton Cangeford, occupying the outer flanks of the wide Clee platform where soils are deeper and more retentive. Their adaptability is illustrated by their wheat production in 1801, but now the characteristic appearance of this region is of gentle, maturely dissected plateau land green with meadows and occasional woodland. It is an area of dispersed and semi-dispersed settlement around church hamlets, where the solitary church or the church with only the parsonage and a house or two near to it is typical as at Monkhopton and Upton Cresset.

(b) The Woodland Zone of eastern Shropshire

This last sub-division cuts across geological and relief features and includes areas of large and small parishes, and nucleated and dispersed settlements, for the late survival of woodland has been of more significance than any other physical factors in giving character and a certain amount of similarity to the area. It is, however, predominantly an area of hamleted and dispersed settlement and of small parishes. The great woodlands clothed wide areas of eastern and southern Shropshire. Anglo-Saxon place nomenclature reveals something of the penetration of the Mercians, and the prevalence of *-leah* endings east of the high

[1] See Ch. 10, pp. 247–50.

Clees and their sparsity to the west indicates that they settled
Corve Dale and Wenlock Edge earlier and more thoroughly and
the eastern area later and more thinly (Fig. 10). With breaks of
varying width, the woodland extended west up the Severn,
through the Gorge, north across the Wrekin, and south over
Wenlock Edge in the Long Forest. In the south, Morfe and Wyre
were considered by Eyton to be part of the great woodland known
to the British as *Y Coed*.[1] Wyre Forest at one time covered south-
east Shropshire and most of Worcestershire to which it gave its
name. Clee Forest covered much of the Clees below 1000 feet
and extended to the Teme east of Ludlow, and numerous lesser
stretches were to be found as in Clun Forest, Hoggestow and the
Stiperstones Forest. The most important area of woodland in
relation to rural settlement in Shropshire was undoubtedly this
great eastern belt into which settlers were only beginning to
penetrate in late Mercian times, and which was still in the process
of active colonisation in the Middle Ages. The records of Domesday
woodlands show a further retreat eastward of the dense woodland
belt. By 1086, the eastern plains and the low hills across the
Severn were still covered by many leagues of woodland, especially
south of Shifnal and Badger, but on the eastern platform of the
Clees it thinned and stretched with varying density south of
Titterstone to the Teme valley almost as far as Ludlow. Woodland
was extensive in the east not only in the eleventh century but until
and after the great Perambulation of 1300. The Forests of Wrekin,
Brewood (much of it in Staffordshire), Shirlott, Morfe and Wyre
were wooded tracts which covered a high proportion of the eastern
plains from the Newport area to Bewdley and stretched beyond
that point into Worcestershire. Remnants of Wyre Forest still
cover many square miles of south-eastern Shropshire and today
throughout the orchard belt of the Teme valley, and over much
of the eastern Clee platform, the recency of a wide woodland
cover is evident in the richly timbered rural landscape.

There were already large Anglo-Saxon settlements in the
south-eastern plains when the Normans came – places like Worfield, Claverley and Alveley (LAp), which, with Nordley, formed
part of a continuous estate belonging to Algar, Earl of Mercia,
and in 1086, were still, according to Eyton[2] reputed to be in

[1] Op. cit., iii, p. 212.   [2] Ibid., iii, p. 214.

Staffordshire or Warwickshire. After 1066 all four manors were granted to Roger de Montgomery, and by the time of Henry II were certainly in Shropshire. Apart from Nordley, they form part of a group of comparatively large nucleated villages of which each must originally have been isolated in deep woodland. Numerous small hamlets were formed in some parts of the forest, notably around Worfield where, as H. L. Gray revealed, there was a marked development of open field, much of it three-field.[1] Yet large stretches of the forests remained virgin in Norman times. There were no Domesday manors recorded at all in the Severn valley between the upper side of the Gorge and Quatford except near Bridgnorth.[2] Similarly there was a gap between Morfe and Shirlott Forests and, as it is clear from the Perambulations of the thirteenth and fourteenth centuries that the area was still forested, it is reasonable to assume that some if not all of the Domesday omissions from this area were because the country was still unsettled primitive woodland. In the southern part in particular, dispersed habitations are the rule outside the occasional Anglo-Saxon nucleations, and late topographical names such as Four Ashes, Broad Oak and Nash are redolent of the woodland from which they emerged. Lying in the medieval forests, Claverley, Worfield and Alveley (Plate X) came into the hands of Henry II as manors of ancient demesne and although this status was short-lived they retained the manorial courts which, in Claverley and Alveley, were exempt from hundredal jurisdiction, responsible only to the county court and the King's justiciars.[3] Large parks, such as that of *Kinlet* (WD/Ep), with its great house, of which the chapel has become the parish church, and in which the woodland served as the common pasture with squatting on the edge, are a marked feature of the woodland belt. Dispersal is characteristic of the late-surviving woodlands and dates principally from the early Middle Ages onwards.

The last portion of the south-eastern woodland lies in the Teme basin between Ludlow and the county boundary, and is part of the extensive orchard belt which is continued into Herefordshire and Worcestershire. No definite proof of the former existence of

[1] Op. cit. pp. 64–6.
[2] Bridgnorth and its dependants also had, like the northern market towns, well developed and numerous open fields.
[3] Eyton, op. cit. iii, pp. 74 and 143.

community agriculture is yet known for this countryside, and if it existed it seems likely that, as in the adjacent woodland region, it may have been late established and early in breakdown. The tithe maps for Greet, Burford, Weston in Burford and Stoke in Burford give no hint of former open field, but Nash and Tilsop apportionment list includes fields called Butts, three Townsend Fields, one Townsend Meadow and two Nash Fields. From the eighteenth century, orchards became important here, and smallholdings with orchards forming much of their acreage added to the landscape yet another form of dispersed settlement (Do) which is characteristic also of much of Herefordshire. Solitary churches and ample timber, the brick houses of the smallholders, and a patchwork of orchards characterise the rural landscape of this southern slope of the Clee platform.

15 Herefordshire

> ... this country besides that it is most pleasant, is for yeelding
> of corne, and feeding of cattaile, in all places most fruitefull ...
> for three W.W.W. of wheat, woll, and water it yeeldeth to no
> shire in England. ... The hills that compasse it in, on both sides
> are clad with woods; under the woods lie corn fields on either
> side, and under those fields most gay and gallant meadowes.
> Camden's *Britannia*, 1694

> ... from the greatest person to the poorest cottager all
> habitations are encompassed with orchards and gardens.
> J. Beale, Hereford Orchards – *A Pattern for all England*, 1724

UNTIL the nineteenth century, Herefordshire was the English
equivalent of a land flowing with milk and honey. Today it has
one of the lowest population densities of English lowland agricultural counties, and from 1871 to 1939 it suffered progressive
decline in population in common with the mid-Welsh counties.
This implicit contradiction is characteristic of Herefordshire and
appears and reappears in its settlement geography. Although it
lies across the major north–south route along the border, its
approaches to the English Plain are relatively proscribed, and
the route of second importance is not eastward but westward up
the Wye valley into Wales. These facts have coloured its entire
history, and it is not perhaps surprising to find that its association
with the neighbouring Highland Zone has been closer than that of
either Cheshire or Shropshire. Even today, the claims of some
Herefordians to be part of *Gwalia Irredenta* if occasional are no less
vociferous from time to time.

In physical form it appears as a basin-shaped lowland all but
completely ringed by hills – the Black Mountains and the north-
western uplands both structurally related to the Cambrian
Uplands, Bringewood Chase, the Bromyard Plateau, the Woolhope Hills, the Malverns, the northern edge of the Forest of Dean
and the uplands of Archenfield. The Teme flows along much of
its northern boundary, the Monnow along its southern, but the
axis of the county is the middle Wye. This river leaves the Welsh
Hills at Whitney to pursue a slow meandering course across the

wide plain of Hereford, re-entering the hills in the south-east near
Goodrich. The northern lowlands span the north–south course of
the lower Lugg and a series of tributary brooks. Both lowlands lie
on the red marls of the Downtonian beds, level for the most part,
but broken by low sandstone hills whose closely wooded slopes
constantly diversify the scenery of these fertile plains. Eastwards,
low lying valleys and basins extend from Hereford across the river
Frome and its tributaries the Leddon and the Leadon.

The low Bromyard Plateau flanks the county in the north-
east – 6–700 feet in height – and is formed of Dittonian corn-
stones overlain with sandy soils, and of marls which give a heavy
loam soil. Farther south, the Malverns lie along part of the
eastern boundary of Herefordshire, an ancient north–south fold
forming a knife-edge ridge. The south-east is diversified by minor,
infertile uplands. The Woolhope anticline crosses Cambrian and
Silurian rocks which carry predominantly thin, poor, limey soils.
Farther south again, the Ross Plateau on the northern fringe of
the Forest of Dean consists largely of limestones through which the
lower Wye cuts its magnificent gorge in a sequence of incised
meanders, its valley almost devoid of bottom land. To the west of
the Wye lie the low uplands of Archenfield whose relatively good
soils overlie Old Red Sandstone strata. One of the two 'Welsh
Districts' of Herefordshire as defined from the early Middle Ages,
Archenfield is adjoined on the west by the second of these,
Ewyas, most of which lies in the dark impressive mass of the
Black Mountains. Sitting astride the Herefordshire–Breconshire
border its greatest heights exceed 2300 feet and present an abrupt
wall to the Wye valley. The long fingers of upland which point
south-eastward into Herefordshire are, by contrast, comparatively
gentle and the valleys between them provide the main lines of
settlement. Of these, the Golden Valley is, as its name implies,
highly favourable to settlement from Dorstone down its entire
length to Ewyas Harold. From the Brownstones and Dittonian
sandstones of the Black Mountains one passes across the Wye Gap
to the north-western uplands which are virtually extensions of the
Radnor Forest upland to the west. Predominantly Cambrian and
Silurian, the Silurian limestones break down, especially in the
most northerly parts of the county, into a varied and attractive
landscape of roughly parallel valleys and scarps related to

complex faulting, and distinguished by a number of important fortified Norman sites, notably Wigmore.

The central Herefordshire lowland is not one but a series of basins, divided sometimes by low watersheds but more typically by the minor picturesque ridges whose wooded slopes interrupt the broad acres of farmland. Despite the frequent interpolation of low uplands, it is these lowlands which concentrate the greater part of the population of Herefordshire. The Dinmore–Garnons Hill line breaks up the north-western lowland, extending from the Lugg to the Wye above Hereford, and smaller hills destroy the continuity of the more elevated and rolling lowland east of Leominster. South of Hereford are the similar detached heights of the Dinedor and Aconbury Hills near the northern fringe of Archenfield, but they afford only minor breaks in this wide stretch of fertile farmland.

Water supply in Herefordshire, as J. N. Jackson has pointed out,[1] offers few problems. Aquifers are abundant – Silurian limestones and sandstones, the Dittonian and Brownstone beds, and the Downtonian limestones and sandstones – and surface water is found on the Cambrian rocks, springs along the western boundary fault of the Malverns, while on many of the drift areas wells and surface supplies prove adequate. Drift deposits extend from the middle Lugg basin near Orleton south to the foot of the Black Mountains and thence from Kingstone to Hereford and the lower Lugg basin.

Geologically within the Highland Zone, in terms of relief Herefordshire appears as an enclave of the Lowland Zone. Seen from Dinmore Hill or from a high point on the Black Mountains in August, the Herefordshire lowlands extend at one's feet as a carpet of green and gold – the emerald of meadows, the deeper greens of woodland, and the rich gold of ripening cornfields. The temptation which led the hillsmen to raid the lowlands is seen in a single flash. Though not the best agricultural land, it is excellent corn, fruit, and grazing country. Corn was more important in the Middle Ages under the régime of subsistence economy than now, but it is still not unimportant. In the Middle Ages, the Ryeland sheep of north and central Herefordshire provided some of the

[1] 'Thoughts upon the distribution of the rural population in Herefordshire at the beginning of the nineteenth century', *Trans. Woolhope Nat. Fld Club*, xxxiv (1954), p. 14.

highest priced English wool. Today its good swards are mainly devoted to the rearing and fattening of one of the best beef breeds in the World – the white-faced Herefords. From the seventeenth century it became outstanding as a land of orchards and hop gardens and the pattern of the smallholdings which arose at that time, each with its separate cottage or small house, spatters much of the central lowland to this day. Yet its rural population density is now only 0·1 to the acre.

The total population, never large but increasing by almost 50 per cent in the first seventy years of the nineteenth century, reached 125,426 in 1871. After that, in common with the central Welsh counties, it suffered a steady decline to an estimated 108,767 in 1939. Since then the total has risen to 130,928 (1961), but over 18,000 of the 22,000 increase was recorded in the six towns. Nevertheless, a healthy if modest upward turn has been taken in the rural districts, especially in mid-county around Hereford.

Herefordshire's low population density and totals, its almost unrelieved agricultural basis, and its failure to make more spectacular progress in the modern period have been attributed to a number of causes. It should now be clear that few of these are physical, for its generally mild climate, long growing period, general freedom from May frosts, productive soils, good water supply and extensive lowlands offer a better basis for economic expansion than is enjoyed by many more prosperous and more densely peopled counties. Apart from Hereford with a 1961 population of 32,501, the entire county has only five country market towns: Leominster (6290), Ross on Wye (5399), Ledbury (3693), Kington (1890) and Bromyard (1697). Its sparse population and the lack of towns have been invoked as among the factors behind its largely dispersed settlement pattern. These may have served to keep scattered and sparse a habitation grouping already dispersed, but can only have been a minor contributory factor at most.

In settlement geography, Herefordshire is not only unique in the Borderland, but offers many puzzling features and many apparent contradictions. Largely dispersed or hamleted, it has nevertheless a belt of nucleated villages lying in the western half of the county (Figs 20 and 21). Apart from the three eastern market centres, there were only three nucleated villages in the entire eastern half of Herefordshire – Ashperton, Fownhope and Weston under

Penyard – in the mid-nineteenth century. The anomalous distribution of nucleations in the west and their general absence from the east, a feature found also in south Shropshire, has already been described (Chapter 9). Yet Herefordshire's open arable field system, though less regular and well developed than, for example, that of nearby Warwickshire and eastern Gloucestershire, was nevertheless far more regular and more persistent than in any other part of the Borderland (Chapter 10), and included a higher proportion of three-field townships than either of the other two English border counties. Open arable field cultivation was indubitably widespread in lowland Herefordshire in the Middle Ages, yet in the greater part of that area it was not apparently associated with the typically clustered English village as it was in the greater part of Gray's Midland belt. Like south-east Shropshire, but unlike the rest of that county and Cheshire, it lies largely south of the Parish Line and therefore almost entirely lacks the satellite settlement structure of the large parishes of its northern neighbours with the associated stimulus to the growth of the parochial centre.[1] The Welsh district of Archenfield is closely comparable in its settlement pattern with western and central Monmouthshire and with some parts of Wales to the west, but the comparison breaks down in the other Welsh district, Ewyas, as it does along the mid-Radnorshire border where villages extend right up to the hill edge and some, like Eardisley, are of remarkably English appearance and lack the characteristic irregularity of plan found in most border villages.

Herefordshire is also distinctive in that it sits broadly astride the cultural boundary of England and Wales rather than adjacent to it, as do Shropshire and Cheshire. Offa's Dyke, entering the county in the north-west, crosses the lowlands diagonally to take up its broken course just outside the extreme south-eastern corner of Herefordshire on the left bank of the Wye opposite Welsh Bicknor. Though not the western limit of Anglian settlement, the extent to which the Mercians established their *tuns* beyond it was limited. Indeed the Wye itself was long regarded as the boundary river between *Cymry* and *Saesneg* in the southern Borderland. So situated, Herefordshire has experienced centuries of war and raiding, not only across its boundaries but within them, a fact

---

[1] Leominster and a few other north-western Herefordshire parishes are exceptions.

which, prior to Union, militated against rising population, production and trade to an even greater extent than in the case of its northern neighbours. It is also far more truly Anglo-Welsh than either Shropshire or Cheshire. In north-west Shropshire, the Welsh place-names of the Oswestry district are believed to represent a re-invasion, but in Archenfield they replaced the older Celtic names without an intervening wave of Anglo-Saxon settlement, while in Ewyas most of its English place-names appear to be medieval.

Although in the Domesday entries Welshmen were recorded only in the manors west of Offa's Dyke, more recent centuries, especially since Union, have seen constant Welsh migration into Herefordshire and today Welshmen are found in large numbers in central as well as in west and south Herefordshire, so that Offa's Dyke has even less modern meaning than it has farther north. There are still some who would claim Hereford as Welsh and who call it by its cymricised name of *Henffordd*. Welsh was heard frequently in the city in Cromwell's day, and an Act of Parliament of 1563 nearly a century earlier charged the bishop of Hereford with the task of providing a Welsh bible in churches in his diocese where Welsh was spoken. Under the Act of Uniformity (1662) it was similarly insisted that Welsh prayer books should be made available. Many Welsh customs persisted in Archenfield until the twelfth century and later, and Duncumb says that gavelkind was the mode of inheritance there until his day.[1] J. N. Jackson alleges that no precise line delimits the present-day distribution of Welshmen in the county.[2] This long history of Welsh influence, grafted on to a people of Welsh ancestry who, until the seventh century experienced no intrusions other than the Roman, has left ineradicable traces even in present-day Herefordshire.

The Progress of Settlement

The four major periods which have shaped the border settlement landscape – Celtic, Anglo-Saxon, Anglo-Norman and postmedi-

[1] John Duncumb, *General View of the Agriculture of Herefordshire*, Board of Agriculture Report (1805).
[2] Loc. cit. p. 15.

eval – are reflected in Herefordshire in markedly individualised results.

Early Iron Age forts were built on many Herefordshire hills, occurring widely over the lowland amphitheatre especially across the north and in the south-east of the county. A further indication of the extent of the Celtic occupation is afforded by place-name elements and, from the sub-Roman phase, by ecclesiastical evidence. In Herefordshire, Celtic place-names and place-name elements are as widespread as in the two counties to the north, but whereas Welsh names are virtually absent from Cheshire and occur in Shropshire only in limited western areas, here they are closely packed and predominate over a high proportion of the country south of the Wye. In Archenfield they are scarcely interrupted by English names, and there is believed never to have been an effective English settlement. In the lowlands, however, the elements representing Celtic peoples are, as in Cheshire and the greater part of Shropshire, Brythonic, not Welsh. The basins of the Lugg and the Arrow between Leominster, Lynhales and Lingen have been named by Lord Rennell of Rodd 'the Land of Lene'. In these names and in Limebrook, Kingsland, Leen Farm, Eardisland, Lyonshall and Monkland he claims to trace the O.W. element *lion* or *lian* (pl *llieni*) derived from *lei*, to flow. Leominster bore the alternative of *Llanllieni*.[1] Celtic names occur in considerable clusters in the north-west, the north-eastern plateau, and the eastern lowlands, and no doubt preceded some of the modern Welsh names in Ewyas and Archenfield (Fig. 7). In the lowlands the *dun*, *din* group, as in Dinmore, and the retrospectively named *burhs* in hill-fort names such as Risbury camp and in old parish names such as Aconbury (which lies below a hill-fort) and Bosbury, survive in numbers. So do ancient road name elements. In the south, echoes of the age of Celtic saints are to be heard in Welsh ecclesiastical place-names: names in *llan* include Llangarren, Llanrothal and Llanwarne; saint names are exemplified in Dewchurch (*Dewi* or David), Bridstow (*Lan San Freit* from St Bridget or St Bride), Foy (*Lanntinoi* from St Tifoy or Tyfwy), and St Weonards (*Lann Santguainerth* or St Gwainerth).[2] *Church*

---

[1] 'The Land of Lene' in *Culture and Environment*, ed. I. Ll. Foster (1963).
[2] B. G. Charles, loc. cit. (1963), pp. 89–96. Bruce Dickins in *Celt and Saxon*, ed. Nora K. Chadwick (1963), p. 207.

and *stow* have replaced the *llan* element in a number of Herefordshire place-names, especially, but not exclusively, south of the
Wye, and the majority are associated with Celtic saints.[1]

There are sufficient Celtic place-names scattered over the plain
of Herefordshire to make clear the fact that from the hill camps
there was a movement down to the lowlands prior to the Anglian
occupation (Fig. 7). There are also patches where the Celtic
names are exceptionally sparse, and one such patch lies between
the Lugg and the Loddon, centred on Sutton Lakes, suggesting
that the absence of Celtic place-names may be the result of
deletion by later settlers. Lord Rennell has named this district
Magana, the land of Magonsaetan, an Anglo-Saxon people whose
prince was Merewald, son of Penda of Mercia. On his conversion
by Eadfrith of Northumbria, Merewald founded the church at
Leominster in A.D. 660 as well as the nunnery of Much Wenlock
of which his daughter, St Milburga, became abbess. Lord Rennell
claims that, prior to its occupation by the Magonsaetan, Magana
was dominated by the hill fort of Sutton Walls and that the
area was Celtic from the pre-Roman Iron Age until the fourth
century or later. It would seem reasonable to suppose that 'later'
might be interpreted as mid-seventh century when the Angles
reached this part. Further, Lord Rennell thinks that Leominster
may have been the ecclesiastical forerunner of Hereford and that
Putta, the first bishop in Herefordshire, may have had his seat
here. If so, it would suggest that it had early significance as a
regional metropolis prior to the rise of Hereford,[2] and the distribution of major Iron Age hill forts in this area certainly tends to
support this possibility.

The evidence relating to the early Celtic Church is concentrated
south of the River Wye. This may, however, be due to the
plains having since become areas of thin or negative evidence
rather than to the absence of Celtic influence here in the fifth and
sixth centuries. The names Eagleton in the Bromyard Plateau
and Eccles Green and Eccles Alley between Norton Canon and

---

[1] Dorothy Sylvester, 'The Church and the Geographer' in *Liverpool Essays in Geography: A Jubilee Collection* (1967).
[2] Lord Rennell further refers to St Milburga's *Testament* (B.M. Add. MS. 34633)
which throws light on the close association of Lene with Magana and Merewald's
link with both. He claims that the name Magana is perpetuated in *Maund* as in
Maund Bryan, Upper Maund Common, and Rosemaund. Loc. cit. pp. 312–13.

Almeley, well beyond the Wye in the mid-west, suggest an early extension of Christianity into the lowlands. Architecturally, it is not easy to distinguish Celtic from early Saxon, or late Saxon from Norman work in Herefordshire (and other) border churches. Nora K. Chadwick thinks the earliest Mercian Church was strongly Celtic. She suggests that Penda may have been of Welsh extraction and quotes Bede as having said that Penda, though himself a heathen, did not obstruct the spread of the Christian faith.[1] The association of the place-name element *stow* with the fringe of the *llan* area in south-east Herefordshire would not seem to be out of line with this, nor would the story of Merewald. Indeed, the ecclesiastical evidence as a whole, apart from the very probable disappearance of Celtic churches from the lowlands, suggests a degree of continuity in the history of the Church in Herefordshire. Joan and Harold Taylor similarly believe that there was co-operation between the Welsh and the Mercians not only during the time of Penda (632–54) but also in the eighth century when Offa's Dyke was built and the border adjusted and straightened by mutual agreement.[2] Among the surviving Borderland churches containing fragments of pre-Norman work are Hereford cathedral, Kilpeck, Peterstow, and Tedstone Delamere, and the Taylors add the churches of Edvin Loach (now in ruins) and Wigmore in both of which the herringbone masonry may be pre-Norman. The church at Wigmore occupies a spur of higher land,[3] very much in the tradition of the Celtic churches, and the element *wig* in the name is significant.

The resulting picture of Herefordshire prior to the Anglo-Saxon invasions of the seventh century is that of a widespread Celtic occupation. Some time before the Mercian settlement the Celts must have come down to the lower land, and no doubt some parts of the medieval Welsh Districts were used by them but these seem rather to have figured as fringe regions which, only later, became refuge areas when English pressure (Anglian and Anglo-Norman) mounted in the plains.

The map of woodland recession (Fig. 11)[4] indicates the likely Mercian inroads, and the distribution of early place-name

[1] 'The Celtic Background of early Anglo-Saxon England' in *Celt and Saxon*, pp. 336–7.
[2] 'Pre-Norman Churches of the Border', ibid. p. 226.
[3] Ibid. pp. 233–4.   [4] See also Ch. 4.

elements (on the same map) shows that, as in Shropshire and Cheshire, the Mercians pushed into the lowland valleys already cleared by the Celts, probably in a peaceful interpenetration. Their settlement was on a minor scale as compared with south-eastern England and thinner than in Shropshire and Cheshire. The middle Wye, the middle Lugg, and the eastern valleys appear to have been those most favoured by them and Lord Rennell's conclusions concerning Magana tie up with the cartographical evidence on the woodland recession map. Only slowly did the west become the scene of English settlement and the advance towards the hills was marked by a series of dykes from that which protected Leominster in the late seventh century to Offa's Dyke. The number of *leah* and related elements and the resulting woodland clearances on the western border between the Wye and the Teme show the extent of the advance made in this period, during or before the building of Offa's Dyke and, in the extreme west, perhaps in the years following. It is doubtful whether the Mercians ever made advances into Archenfield or Ewyas, and it can safely be concluded that theirs was an occupation largely confined to the lowland amphitheatre.

The Mercian takeover from the Celts seems to have been parallelled geographically by the early Norman takeover from the Anglo-Saxons. The Normans came armed and warlike and Herefordshire suffered wide devastation, yet they occupied the same area – the lowlands – and some cultural continuity is demonstrated by the Herefordshire school of carving described by Joan and Harold Taylor in connection with the early churches of the border. The style is not to be found in any other part of England. They follow G. Zarnicki,[1] who thinks that the inspiration derived from Parthenay-le-Vieux (*circa* 195 miles south-west of Paris) and in turn from Spain. But, although the period of workmanship was early Norman, the link with Anglo-Saxon crosses and Viking ornament is evident.[2]

When the Normans came to Herefordshire,[3] they found wide

[1] *Later English Romanesque Sculpture* (1953).

[2] Joan and Harold Taylor, loc. cit. The carvings include, typically, interlaced foliage, tall thin figures with pointed beards and quilted garments, and the churches listed by the Taylors in which this style of carving is to be found are Aston (near Ludlow), Brinsop, Castle Frome, Eardisley, Fownhope, Kilpeck, Leominster, Rowlstone, Shobdon and Stretton Sugwas (pp. 235–40).

[3] See Ch. 5.

stretches of woodland remaining, especially in the north-west and mid-west, and still more so south of the middle Wye. Compared with many south-eastern English and east Midland counties, the proportion of woodland was high, but compared with the greater part of the Midland Forest Triangle immediately to the east, it was only moderate. There remained, therefore, a considerable area of the county available for colonising, and even the better settled parts still carried populations sufficiently sparse to permit development. The mild climate and general air of fertility made this one of the Normans' most favoured counties and, to this day, the map and the landscape alike reflect their partiality.

They inherited, however, a troubled Borderland, and in 1066 the group of wasted manors in the mid-west was denser than was to be found in any other part of the Border. The contrast between the maps of named settlements and recorded population[1] in 1086 bears ample witness to the devastation of the western and southern belts thanks to the raids of the Welsh. As a result, Herefordshire was created a county palatine, and the west was carved into marcher lordships with the Mortimers in Wigmore and the Lacys in the mid-west (Clifford) and south-west (Ewyas). So began nearly five hundred years of contrasted development between the militarised west and the comparatively peaceful centre and east of the county.

By 1086, the belt of waste along the Welsh Border which then recurved south of the Wye along the edge of the Black Mountains, was already in process of reclamation and rehabilitation as is shown vividly by C. W. Atkin's two maps of 'Waste in 1066' and 'Plough Teams in 1086 on Former Waste'[2] and it is noticeable that this early recovery took place in the Wye valley rather than along the Radnor Forest border where the reclamation of arable land was then still negligible. The first move was made into Ewyas before the Conquest with the building of the castle at Ewyas Harold, and by 1086 ploughland had been extended southward from the Wye valley into the fringes of Archenfield. The similarity between the area of Norman occupation in 1086 and that of the Mercians is striking. Both occupied the lowland

---

[1] Figs 23 and 28 in ch. 2 by C. W. Atkin in *The Domesday Geography of Midland England*, ed. H. C. Darby and I. B. Terrett (1954).
[2] Ibid. figs 32 and 34.

amphitheatre primarily, but the Normans were to make a bolder
bid for the Welsh districts and to hold the border with infinitely
more determination.

The distribution of plough-teams in 1086 corresponds with
that of the recorded population but there is a significant difference
between them and the named settlements, these last extending
right up to the foothills in the west to include a belt of temporarily
deserted townships. Many new or revived settlements below or
beyond the hill edge were included in marcher lordships and
subject to the military organisation which prevailed in them. In
Wigmore in the north-west and in Ewyas in the south-west, the
Marches extended some six to eight miles into Herefordshire, but
in the mid-west, where they were backed by the lordship of Radnor,
the lesser lordships of Huntington and Stapleton were only two
to three miles wide. Between Huntington and Ewyas lay the
lordship of Clifford guarding the all-important route of the Wye
valley into Wales and its *caput Clifford* exemplified the temporary
character of some of the purely military settlements established
by the Normans along the Border. Centred on its castle on the
steep bank of the Wye, in 1086 this borough included 16 burgesses,
13 bordars, 4 oxmen, 5 Welshmen, 6 serfs and 4 bondwomen.[1]
Today, the fragmentary remains of the castle (mainly thirteenth-
century masonry) stand desolate and solitary and Clifford consists
of little more than an isolated church half a mile from the castle,
a farm occupying the site of a former priory, and a handful of
cottages.

During the later Middle Ages, a number of stone castles were
built along the Herefordshire border. A few relatively minor
strongholds lay in the east guarding routes from the English
Plain, otherwise all were in the western half of the county, and the
great majority in the north-west and south-western uplands.
The mottes had a not dissimilar distribution – more numerous,
and more widely scattered over the central areas, but still with a
predominantly western concentration, though Archenfield and the
plains of the middle Wye were by no means innocent of defensive
works. There is no hard and fast line to be drawn between the
militarised west and the peacefully manorial and agricultural
centre and east, yet the contrast between the two in medieval

[1] D.B., fo. 183 a.

Herefordshire is fundamental in relation to Herefordshire's rural landscape: its settlement forms, its place-names, and the general character of the rural scene. This duality was to some extent foreshadowed in the Mercian occupation, particularly in the mid-Herefordshire border, and – with differences – the two periods served to some extent to reinforce each other in their effects on the rural settlement picture. Both concentrated their major efforts on the development of the lowland amphitheatre. Both extended across the highland line, but the westward and south-westward expansion of Norman settlement was both more widespread and more purposeful than the Mercian, pressing into Ewyas and the borders of Radnor Forest in depth which was only rendered possible by the marcher lordships beyond.

Manorialisation, expressing itself in the park estate, the building of numerous churches and abbeys, in the extension of agriculture including open arable fields, and socially in the retention of a graded rural society, was stronger here than in any other part of the Borderland. Woodland which the Mercians had been laggard in clearing, fell to the Norman axe and a spate of new names appeared on the map from the twelfth to the fifteenth century. Many of these were Welsh names in the Welsh Districts, but there was a wide scatter of Anglo-Norman names and affixes in the lowlands as well as some few within the highland edge.[1]

Democratisation began only in the Tudor period, and then but slowly. More land changed hands. Inroads were made into the common fields. The wool trade increasingly commercialised agriculture, but changes in the land pattern were relatively slight and the manor remained the dominant element in the rural framework. Change accelerated in the seventeenth century when Herefordshire's natural fertility was matched by her rapid advancement in agricultural methods and in particular in the planting of orchards. Cider apples had been grown in the sixteenth century; pears for perry were grown in Ross on Wye in the seventeenth. Celia Fiennes, travelling in Herefordshire about 1696, described it as a county of gardens and orchards,[2] while

---

[1] C. W. Atkin, *The Evolution of Rural Settlement in Herefordshire*, unpublished M.A. thesis, University of Liverpool, Department of Geography (1951). Map showing distribution of place-names first recorded in each of these centuries.

[2] *Through England on a side saddle in the time of William and Mary, being the diary of Celia Fiennes*, ed. E. W. Griffiths (1888), p. 33.

Defoe claimed that the finest wool, the best hops and the richest cider were produced there.[1] The management of grassland and water-meadows improved. Selions were exchanged and compacted in the arable fields. New, small enclosures were made in common and and woodland to provide the fruit and hop growers with the square holdings so characteristic of the major fruit districts today, and on these arose their modest houses in a new form of dispersion.

The origin of Herefordshire's scattered settlement goes back to Celtic times and has since been added to by the Normans in many of whose manors dispersal was associated with the park estate, and later by the effects of enclosure as in other counties, but here also by orchard settlements which are more typical of Herefordshire than of any part of the Borderland. The strength of the Norman addition to nucleated settlement in the west is indubitable, but more problematic is the question of the Anglo-Saxon contribution to nucleation; whether the Norman defensive centres were grafted on to pre-existing Mercian villages or Celtic settlements; and why, with a widespread Anglian settlement and a more intensive development of the open arable system here than in most parts of the Borderland, there appears to have been in much of the county no associated village, or a village which knew early decay.

The Geography of Settlement: Welsh Herefordshire

The prime distinction in Herefordshire settlement is that between the Welsh Districts and the lowland bowl which centres on the middle Wye and Lugg valleys. In the first, the pattern of dispersed farms predominates, interspersed by occasional hamlets. The solitary parish church, the Welsh place- and farm-names, the ragged field pattern, and the comparative sparsity of ploughed land are all reminiscent of Wales. In Archenfield this pattern is only rarely broken by the introduction of alien elements, usually an Anglo-Norman defensive work or the moated house which succeeded it, a dovecot such as that at Garway, or the interpolation of English names in farm and field. In the Black

---

[1] *Daniel Defoe's Tour through England and Wales*, ed. G. D. H. Cole, II, p. 50. Defoe visited Herefordshire 1725.

Mountains (Plate II), conditions were different and the need to defend that part of the Borderland, more vulnerable because it was more westerly, brought the Normans very early to Ewyas, and saw them more or less permanently established in the valleys of the Monnow and the Dore which they named the Golden Valley, so much was it to their taste. The belt of villages and hamlets was extended across the eastern part of the Black Mountains as a result of the combined value for defence and agriculture of its valleys. Dorstone, Peterchurch and Vowchurch are strung along the length of the Golden Valley, with Ewyas Harold and its grim castle hill near the confluence of the Dore and the Dulas. None of the Golden Valley settlements is large, but Dorstone is a compact triangular green village, and today Peterchurch and Vowchurch have become swollen to village size. Solitary manor houses and the former abbeys of Ewyas Harold (Benedictine), and Abbey Dore,[1] with Llanthony not far across the border in Monmouthshire further infill the picture of partial Normanisation in Ewyas.

Ewyas Harold had many of the features of the *caput* of a lordship though it actually lay just outside the mountainous lordship of Ewyas Lacy whose *caput*, originally of the same name, is now known as Longtown. There, an even more formidable stronghold crowned the knoll whose summit supported the large cylindrical keep and on whose slopes curtain walls enclosed the bailey of this fortress of the de Lacys, the Norman lords of Ewyas. Both settlements had a market and developed the appearance of small towns, of which the present villages are the successors.

English Herefordshire: (1) Western Herefordshire

Dispersed, semi-dispersed and hamleted settlement are by no means absent from western Herefordshire, but the area is rendered distinctive by its inclusion of all but four of the clustered villages of the county. They lie in a broad strip from Leintwardine and

---

[1] Founded in 1147, it is said to be the only Cistercian house in England now functioning as a parish church. It stands solitary except for the parsonage and a farm in a parish of dispersed settlement.

Brimfield in the north to Ewyas Harold and Longtown in the south. They cross the boundaries of the marcher lordships, but an appreciable number are to the east of the true Marches. They occur in upland areas and in lowland, in areas of agricultural wealth and in others of comparative poverty, and no simple physical or economic causality can be invoked to explain their distribution. The most northerly are to be found in and near the two former lordships of Wigmore and Richards Castle, occupying in most cases the fringe of the north-western uplands or lying in or near one of its fertile basins. The modern map diverts attention from this area, for the main road and railway down the Borderland now go from Ludlow to Leominster and Hereford. But the Romans diverged from this route near Halford and took the Watling Street by the lower Clun across the Wigmore Basin and so south to Kenchester in the middle Wye valley. The location of hill forts suggests that this may well have been one of the British routes southwards, and it was certainly considered sufficiently vital by the Normans to become the most heavily and deeply defended stretch of the entire Borderland. Mottes extended in an unbroken belt across Radnor Forest and across the north-western and mid-western uplands of Herefordshire towards Hereford, only thinning out when they reached the lowlands of the centre. The distribution of the major stone castles was strongly concentrated in the same area, and motte or castle forms the core of many of these villages. The evidences of Norman occupation are still vivid and unmistakable. The triple signs – domestic, defensive and ecclesiastical – are writ large across this countryside in the form of manor-houses or courts, fishponds, dovecots, moats, mottes, castles, churches, chantries and abbeys. The castles of Wigmore and Brampton Bryan are still among the more considerable remains in the county and at Croft the house which succeeded the castle is one of the finer mansions of Herefordshire. *Wigmore* (HA/Jp(m)cl), the head of its lordship until Union, displays Norman trademarks. A once formidable fortress surmounts a steep bluff on the long ridge of which the lower part is occupied by the village. The castle is at 600 feet, the village between 450 and 500 feet, but the ridge overlooks the broad floor of the Wigmore Basin near the point where it narrows southwards to the gap across the Aymestrey–Leinthall ridge, so significant as an ancient Borderland route to

Celt, Roman and Norman in turn. Its military function was self-evident. The old church was a Norman structure, though the element *wig* suggests earlier religious significance.[1] In addition there was an Augustinian house here in the Middle Ages. The locational value of Wigmore is high and the Norman contribution to its growth indubitable. What we do not know is the extent to which it had pre-Norman importance or what was the Mercian, and perhaps the Romano-British history of the place. Hill-forts, Roman roads, Anglo-Saxon place-name elements (mainly *tuns*), and an overriding Anglo-Norman influence distinguish most of the villages in the north-western uplands, and some at least of the characteristics of Wigmore are repeated in Leintwardine, Brampton Bryan, Lingen, Leinthall Starkes and Orleton, all nucleated villages in this north-western part of Herefordshire (1961 population of Wigmore 315, Leintwardine 794, Brampton Bryan 217, Orleton 467).

Behind the nucleated villages lies a background pattern of hamleting and dispersal, less important here than in any other part of Herefordshire, but too significant to be omitted, and places like Elton and Yatton, and Lower and Upper Lye appear to spring from an earlier and less complex settlement stratum. Another example of such a minor settlement is *Rodd* in the half-mile wide valley of Summergill Brook just above its confluence, near Presteigne, with the river Arrow. Here the sixteenth-century manor house, with the earlier half-timbered fourteenth-century house alongside, is the major dwelling in a manor which includes two old cottages on the hillside and farm buildings on the valley floor. The demesne farm includes them all.[2] The domestic manor is less well represented than in central Herefordshire, but a notable exception is *Croft* (HEp) on the southern slopes of the Leinthall ridge which is a clear and unspoilt example of the park estate dating from Mercian times[3] and strengthened both in defensive and manorial character by the Normans. The township consists almost entirely of the park centred on the great house which retains some of its medieval walls and towers. The parish church for this township and its detached dependent township of

---

[1] See p. 321. [2] Lord Rennell of Rodd, *Valley of the March* (1958).
[3] Bernard de Croft was the holder of the estate T.R.E., and the Croft family have remained lords of the manor continuously except for an intermission of 170 years (from about 1750 until 1923). It is now National Trust property.

Newton in the Lugg valley is adjacent to the house, and the greater part of Croft is parkland and woodland extending up the ridge to the great Iron Age hill fort of Croft Ambrey which crowns it at nearly 1000 feet above sea level.

Eastward and southward the north-western uplands give place to the rich plains of the lower Lugg and the middle Wye or their tributaries. The country is rolling and diversified and generally favourable to settlement. No definable basis exists in physical or economic terms to distinguish the westerly lowlands from those of the centre and east, but beyond Yarpole, Kingsland, Weobley, Mansell Lacy and Kingstone nucleated villages suddenly disappear from the map except for the quite small village of Stoke Prior. The second group within the main western belt includes those which lay outside the marcher lordships – notably Kingsland, Pembridge and Weobley, all large and beautiful villages of strikingly English appearance. Their non-inclusion in a marcher lordship by no means implied the absence of the defensive aspect. Eardisland (Plate VIII), Weobley and Kingsland, all had mottes or castles. So too had Lyonshall, Pembridge and Dilwyn, but the markets were to become of greater importance, especially in the first two of these, and Pembridge, Lyonshall and Weobley ranked as boroughs in the Middle Ages. The reason for their nucleation may, therefore, be twofold here as in the north-west – defensive and economic – and the ex-market villages are usually recognisable by their form and layout. The multi-township parish cannot here be invoked as a cause of growth for a central settlement, for this is an area dominated by single-township parishes except in the north-west, where Leintwardine with twelve townships and Aymestrey with four may owe something to this factor.

Kingsland (LvAbp(m)) is an interesting and typical example of the larger villages of the middle of this belt of nucleations (1961 population 911). Between the Lugg and Pinsley brook, it is a lowland valley settlement aligned along a street parallel to the two streams. Merewald is said to have had a residence here and to be buried near the Glebe House, a fact which may be responsible for the first element in its name. If we can accept the *land* element as deriving from *lion* then Kingsland owes its existence to each of the three main early settlement periods. Only a little to the east of the Roman road which runs through Wigmore Gap, Kingsland had strategic importance probably from early times, and the battle of Mortimer's Cross in 1461 was fought only two miles to the north. There is a Norman motte and bailey here but no remains of masonry to indicate that it was the site of a later castle, and the motte, in Norman fashion, is adjacent to the church. Price[1] says that it was anciently a manor of the Crown, but it went to the Mortimers in 34 Edward I. Its medieval growth seems largely to have been on economic grounds, and during the fourteenth century it was a market centre and had a Michaelmas fair. The fair long continued, but the market has died out.

By the nineteenth century it was a single-township parish, but in the fourteenth century the manor of Kingsland included the townships of Longford, West Town, Aston and Lawton. The late fourteenth-century bailiff's accounts of the manor of Kingdon for 1389–90[2] reveal it as a large and rich agricultural unit worked by free men and *nativi*. There were 338½ acres of arable land in unnamed fields in the hands of 'divers tenants of the manor' at farm for 6d. per acre, and with a total value of £8 9s 3d. A mill newly built suggests the importance of the corn crops, and 213½ plough services arose from 30½ virgates of land every year. Each virgater had his customary work in the open fields, the woods and the meadows. The remarkable feature of the accounts is the wealth of differently named pastures, several of which were still marked on the 1709 map (Fig. 45). In addition there was reference to a parcel of meadow in *Brodemede*, 'an acre of land lying upon *Caldewallforlong*' (neither of these named in 1709), orchards, woods, a park, a dovecot, a barn, a sheepfold, and a barton, as well as a fulling mill, and a market and fair. The mills handled corn, malt and maslin.

The estate map of 1709 though essentially a demesne map, nevertheless gives a vivid picture of Kingsland as it was at that date. Moreover, by distinguishing arable land, meadow, pasture and woodland, and through the numerous field-names, it illuminates and extends the fourteenth-century accounts, so that between the two a clear picture of Kingsland emerges as a multi-field township, rich in water-meadows, common pastures, and

[1] John Price, op. cit. pp. 29–30.
[2] E. J. L. Cole, *Trans. Woolhope Nat. Fld Club*, xxxv, 2 (1956), pp. 168–75. The document was transcribed and published by courtesy of Major J. R. H. Harley.

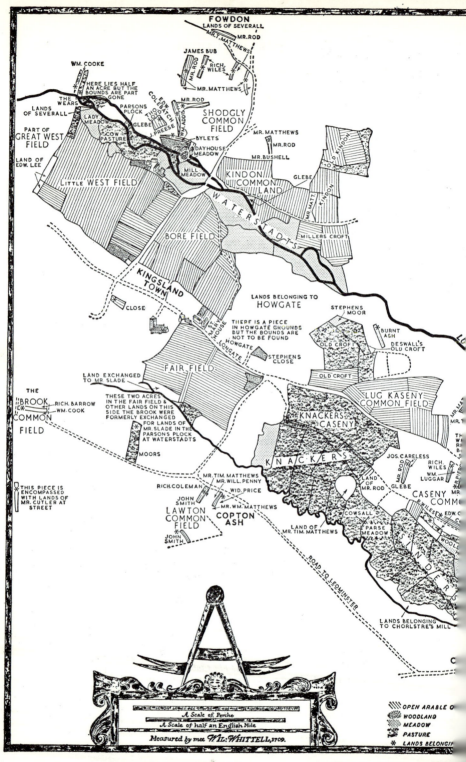

45. Kingsland, Herefordsh[ire]

OKER COPPICE

A Map of **KINGSLAND** in the *County of* HEREFORD, *Belonging to* the *RIGHT WORSHIPFUL* S.ᵗ *IAMES* BATEMAN, Knight, *And* ALDERMAN *of the* CITY *of* LONDON, 1709.

ORLINGS

HEWS

DS IN
ONE
PASTURE
NG TO THE
Y HOUSE, THE
DS NOT KNOWN

SHEERCROFT

THERE IS ONE
ACRE IN THIS
PIECE OF
THIS
LENGTH

ELD

CH

BURLANDS

LANDS

BELONGING TO

O L D   L A N D S

AYTON

ORDS
EADOW

MR.ROD
HEN
BUB
LORDS
ACRE

KINGSLAND GREAT
COMMON MEADOW

W E G N A L L

PART OF

LEOMINSTER

PARISH

MR.MATTHEWS
THO.TYLER
RICH. BARROW

IS ONE ACRE
D BELONGING
E ST. MARY'S HOUSE
S PIECE

CANTER FLU

STREE

PINSLY FLU

WILORE
SHEERS

WALLONS

HALF THIS PIECE
OF LAND BELONGS
TO ST. MARY'S HOUSE

PART   OF
LEOMINSTER
WEGNALL FIELD

R OPEN
RABLE FIELD

CURSNY HILL

ST. MARY HOUSE

ased on a map of 1709

still with some woodland. A certain amount of enclosure had gone on by 1709, but the main enclosure was to follow, and the picture of Kingsland as revealed in a nineteenth-century map (*Hanbury Collection* 896, Hereford Public Library) was one of a largely enclosed area, though some open strips remained in the Great West Field.

From the Middle Ages to the early eighteenth century the plan of Kingsland suffered comparatively little change other than that due to an expanding population. Kingsland 'town' lies along the road which is the north-west to south-west axis of the township, roughly parallel to its two streams. Today, it extends for a full mile lengthways, though the houses are scattered at each end. West Town, an undated extension lies to the south-west, linked by a cross road to the centre of Kingsland. East and south of this cross road are the church and the Norman motte and it was in the field near to them that the fair was held, hence its name on the 1709 map. Its arable fields, still ploughed in common in 1709, included Great and Little West Fields, Shodgly Common Field, Kindon Common Field, Bore Field, Fair Field, Lug Caseney Common Field, and Caseney Common Field on the interfluve to the north, and Brook and Lawton Common Fields to the south. In addition the township had its common meadows, though by 1709 they seem to have been largely enclosed as were various crofts and pastures, but the disparate nature of many of the holdings is evident, e.g. the scattered strips of Mr Matthews.

Kingsland is typical of the larger villages in this second part of the western nucleated belt. Many are sizeable and have been of considerable importance during the past, with extensive open arable lands. Weobley, for example, had three open fields in 1403 of 22, 30 and 23½ acres, and in 1599 of 99, 82 and 118 acres.[1]

On a different scale are the more agricultural villages near the middle Wye, that is villages in which the emphasis has been primarily (or over a very long period) on farming rather than on defence or market functions. One of the most interesting of these is Eardisley. It is situated two miles north of the Wye where that river emerges from the Black Mountains and is one of a group of small villages and hamlets in this lowland area of mid-west

[1] Harleian MS. 7366, p. 14.

Herefordshire which includes Whitney, Winforton, Kinnersley, Staunton on Wye, Mansell Lacy, Blakemere, Preston on Wye and Madley. All are lowland villages (or hamlets) well situated for crop raising and rich pasture, and many have land running down to the Wye. Like the previous group, they remained outside the marcher lordships though they were sufficiently near to their boundaries to be affected by marcher organisation. Almeley, Eardisley and Whitney, all very near to the lordship of Hunting-ton, had mottes. Trading privileges in the fourteenth century, when far too many market charters were given, were another feature of the area, and there were markets at Kinnersley, Winforton, Moccas, Preston on Wye, Madley at that period, and in addition Eardisley was a borough.[1]

Eardisley (LAcp), only some two or three miles from the foot-hills of Radnor Forest, is a street village in a single-township parish. Its name suggests that it existed in late Mercian times. In the church of St Mary Magdalen, the southern arcade of the nave is believed to be Norman but 'the chief treasure of the church is the splendid font' (to quote Methuen's *Little Guide to Herefordshire*, p. 132) and it is the carving on this font, depicting warriors in combat, a lion, a saint, and Christ which puts it into the Hereford-shire school of carving[2] and affords a link between the cultures of the late Anglo-Saxon and the Norman periods. To the west of the church is a motte and bailey or court now occupied by a farm, and the motte surrounded by a moat. Further courts to the west give some idea of the extent and importance of Eardisley in Norman times, as does the now enclosed park which lay behind. In 1086, mention was made in the Domesday Book of a *domus defensibilis* which belonged to Roger de Lacy. Three exceptionally large tithe barns lie north of the church, and, of these, two were converted to eight houses in 1965. A corn mill adjoins the nearby stream and this, together with the large tithe barns, leaves no doubt that it was an important corn growing manor. The tithe map shows open quillets and strip-shaped fields which suggest that its former open arable fields lay to the north-west and north-east of the village, and some of the farms are still disparate.

[1] William Rees, *South Wales and the Border in the Fourteenth Century*, a set of four maps on the scale of half an inch to the mile, together with a commentary. Published by the Ordnance Survey, 1932.
[2] Joan and Harold Taylor, loc. cit.

The village includes many fine stone and half-timbered cottages and, at the northern end of the village street, Upper House which is thought once to have had a private oratory. At least two of the cottages are cruck-built. Few modern houses have been added and Eardisley village street, of remarkably English appearance, is one of the most beautiful in Herefordshire.

Many of these villages worked their land in common and *Winforton* (VAp), adjoining Eardisley on the south, and situated in the Wye valley, is one for which records are ample. In a 1652 *Survey of Winforton* holdings are listed in six different common fields and in the common meadow of Hopton's Mead. There were pasture rights in several other meadows from Lammas to the following Candlemas and in Great Meadow 'after tithe and rake till the second of February following'. In addition it was laid down that 'one of the lord's fields was to be fallowed and ploughed yearly' and that there should be 'common of pasture thereon until the said field shall be sown and after sickle and sythe the same field to be common until Candlemas following'. The tenants also had common of pasture, pannage, and estovers in the wood of Winforton and on its wastes at all seasons, the right to fell the underwood, and to take a 'customs bough' every Christmas.[1] Some of the land in this parish was enclosed, however, under an Act of 1778, the first Parliamentary Enclosure for Herefordshire and the Award (1779) states that 379 acres of open arable land was enclosed, though certain rights of common were retained.[2]

English Herefordshire: (2) Central and Eastern Herefordshire

The second major subdivision within 'English' Herefordshire, i.e. the area which has here been called the lowland amphitheatre, is the extensive portion east of the belt of nucleated villages. It includes the central and eastern lowlands, the Bromyard plateau, and the various small upland districts which flank the eastern side of the county. The features which render it a distinctive

[1] Hereford City Library, L.C.D. 480.
[2] H. L. Gray, op. cit. p. 140.

settlement region are first, the almost complete absence of villages (as distinct from hamlets) and the wide distribution of open field, here more densely developed than in any other part of Herefordshire. This contradiction of the usually accepted dictum that the open field system and the village are associated makes it one of the more puzzling areas of the Borderland, and one of the most challenging in the study of rural settlement in Britain. The reasons why this part of the Borderland had a greater development of the open arable field system than any other included its relative accessibility from the English Lowlands where Gray's Midland Field System was mainly practised, its climate and fertility which combined to make it a rich corn growing region in the Middle Ages, and its comparatively fortunate position away from the major strategic routeways and away from the marcher lordships. The density of its open field development has already been established. The system was by no means confined to this part of Herefordshire, but a glance at the open field distribution map (Fig. 23) is sufficient to show that open fields were most numerous where nucleated villages are fewest in this county.

A One-Inch O.S. map of the present day or the tithe edition (on which the discussion of nucleation and dispersal in this study is principally based) offers for this major area of Herefordshire an almost unbroken pattern of hamleting and dispersal (Fig. 3). The hamlets occur generally, though not invariably, in the river valleys. The interfluves are widely associated with dispersed farms and cottages, with solitary churches and park estates. The solitary church is to be expected in and near the Welsh districts, but it extends in distribution far to the north: indeed, no major division of Herefordshire is without such churches. The strong Celtic basis, as evidenced in place-names, might well be invoked to explain the hamlets, some of the solitary churches, and some of the dispersal. The Norman manor, so characteristically developed into a park estate in this part of the Borderland, accounts for other elements in the dispersal pattern, e.g. in Stoke Edith, Bredenbury, Canon Frome, Bockleton, Pudleston, etc. The intensive orcharding and hop-growing which characterise the quadrangle between Leominster, Bromyard, Ledbury and Hereford account for a further element in this scatter. There are occasional squatting settlements, in the form of ragged hamlets or roughly ringing former commons, e.g. on Putley Common and Upper Maund Common, but squatting is extremely rare, perhaps because the pressure of population was not great, perhaps because the smallholding movement took its place. Such an analysis at first sight appears satisfactory, but the problem of the Mercian contribution is not provided for, and with the widely distributed Anglo-Saxon place-names, Mercian settlement there must have been.

The One-Inch tithe edition O.S. maps reveal only four concentrations in this area which seem to merit the description 'village': Stoke Prior on the edge of the western nucleated belt, Ashperton and Fownhope both near the foot of the Woolhope Hills, and Weston under Penyard two miles south-east of Ross. None of these is large; none is outstanding today; and the subjectively drawn line between village and hamlet is here so difficult to define as to be of little real significance. All nucleations are small. Many of the single-township parishes lack them altogether and travelling through this countryside one can go for miles with no indication that one has arrived at another 'place' apart from the fact that here is another parish church.

Although they are on an exceptional scale, Leominster's and Marden's open arable fields[1] are otherwise a fair sample of the field plans and disparate holdings which are to be found over the greater part of eastern and central Herefordshire. *Newton* (VD), a detached township of Croft parish, is situated in the Lugg valley immediately north of Dinmore Hill. A 1780 *Map of Gorwell and Whittington's Estates* (Hereford City Library, L.C.II) shows the two estates as largely disparate and holdings in a series of common fields and meadows as completely interlocked. Both had a hopyard; Whittington's included an orchard. An appreciable amount of each estate was in the form of enclosed strips, but the majority were still open quillets.

At *Ocle Pychard* (LCp), Hillhampton Estate, mapped in 1791 (Hereford City Library, L.C. II 24500), shows a more advanced stage in the compacting of holdings and the higher proportion of land given over to hopyards and orchards suggests the reason for this. Ocle Pychard, semi-dispersed and now with a large number of orchards and hopyards in the hands of large and smaller holders, is typical of a broad stretch of country around the west,

[1] See Ch. 10.

north and east of Hereford and these communities whose economy and land pattern changed during the sixteenth and seventeenth centuries add a distinctive element to the Herefordshire rural scene. A plan of a smaller estate in *Stretton Grandison* (VD) (Hereford City Library, LCD 4475) shows the same pattern on a smaller scale. The place-name reflects its Mercian and Norman history, and the two Egletons within the parish suggest its still earlier Celtic associations. This marriage of land patterns and traditions from contrasted periods, culminating with the super-imposition of a partial orchard–hopyard–smallholder economy is widespread in the quadrangle referred to.

There are easily detected regional differences in the settlement picture in this broad division of Herefordshire – differences of building material, of architectural style and above all of physical setting, but the basic similarities persist, even in the lower part of the Herefordshire Wye whose valley executes those magnificent incised meander curves across the northern approaches to the Forest of Dean.

In the extreme south-east of the county on the Gloucestershire border and on the eastern slopes of the Marcle Hills, lies *Much Marcle* (JBpb). Despite its comparatively distinguished history and magnificent parish church, the basic pattern is a repetition of that seen farther north – a loosely arranged central hamlet, an extensive former multi-field system (but a two-township parish), and the comparatively late addition of orcharding. Like a number of others, the parish included an estate element, in this case represented by Homme House the seat of the Money-Kyrles, and Hellens estate. The Anglo-Norman element is seen in these (Hellens also has an octagonal pigeon house though of 1641) and in the fortified motte which once existed near the church. In common with most of rural Herefordshire, Much Marcle reached its peak population figure in 1831 (1024). Decline became marked from 1871 (860) and reached its nadir in 1901 (654). It is com-paratively prosperous now as Herefordshire rural communities go, mainly on account of its farming but also because of a cider factory. An *Atlas of maps of Hellens Estate* of 1741[1] shows the now familiar pattern of disparate holding in a number of common fields together with occasional compacting and orchards, indicated

---

[1] Hereford City Library, *Ratcliffe Cooke Collection.*

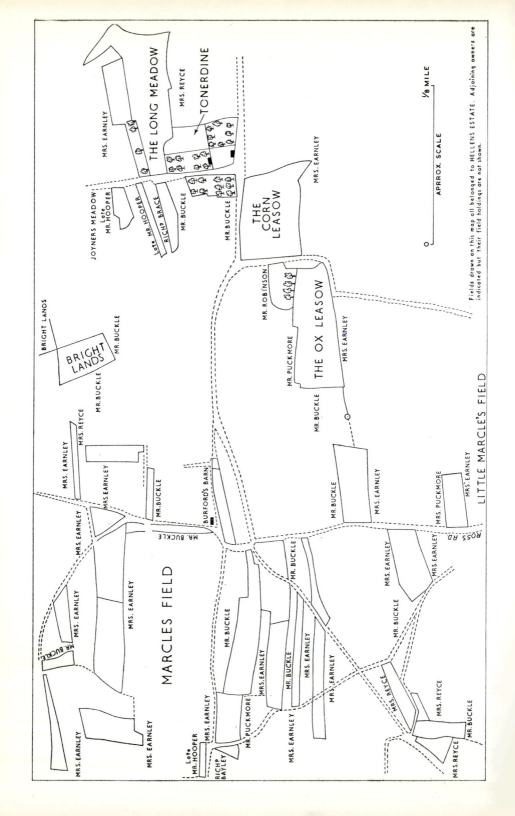

THE LONG MEADOW

MRS. EARNLEY

TONERDINE

MRS. REYCE

JOYNERS MEADOW

Late
MR. HOOPER

Late MR. HOOPER

RICHᴰ BRACE

MR. BUCKLE

MR. BUCKLE

MRS. EARNLEY

THE CORN LEASOW

MR. ROBINSON

⅛ MILE

APPROX. SCALE

Fields drawn on this map all belonged to HELLENS ESTATE. Adjoining owners are indicated but their field holdings are not shown.

BRIGHT LANDS

BRIGHT LANDS

MR. BUCKLE

MR. BUCKLE

MR. PUCKMORE

THE OX LEASOW

MRS. EARNLEY

MR. BUCKLE

MRS. REYCE

MRS. EARNLEY

MRS. EARNLEY

MRS. EARNLEY

MRS. EARNLEY

MRS. EARNLEY

MR. BUCKLE

MR. BUCKLE

BURFORD'S BARN

MR. BUCKLE

MRS. PUCKMORE

MRS. EARNLEY

LITTLE MARCLE'S FIELD

ROSS RD.

MARCLES FIELD

MRS. EARNLEY

MRS. EARNLEY

MR. BUCKLE

MR. BUCKLE

MRS. EARNLEY

MR. BUCKLE

MRS. EARNLEY

MRS. EARNLEY

MR. BUCKLE

MRS. EARNLEY

MRS. EARNLEY

MRS. REYCE

MRS. EARNLEY

MRS. REYCE

MR. BUCKLE

MRS. REYCE

Late
MR. HOOPER

RICHᴰ BAYLEY

MR. PUCKMORE

MR. BUCKLE

MRS. EARNLEY

MRS. EARNLEY

MRS. EARNLEY

by trees (Fig. 46). Among the numerous fields were Marcles Field, Hill Field, Upper Normandy and Lower Normandy. Under an Enclosure Award of 1797, over 620 acres of arable land and 304 acres of waste were enclosed.

H. L. Gray's plans of the Risbury Division of Stoke Prior and of Holmer,[1] the first between the Wye and the Lugg near Hereford and the second in the Lugg valley, repeat the pattern for the central valley lands and, with regional differences which are on the whole slight, the same may be said of the Bromyard plateau.

The evidence of rural pattern and evolution, only a small part of which has been cited here, remains the question of greatest interest as regards this region of dispersed and semi-dispersed settlement. It was partly with such questions in mind that S. C. Stanford excavated a deserted medieval site near Hampton Wafer Farm (some five miles from Bromyard) in the 1950s in the tiny parish of that name, but he was forced to admit that the lost settlement was only a hamlet and that 'the former possibility of the settlement reaching village proportions (had) disappeared'.[2] Open field strips were worked on at least one side of Hampton Wafer hamlet and in the published account of the excavation Stanford concluded a penetrating discussion of the problem of Herefordshire dispersal with the question relative to Hampton Wafer: 'Is it not more likely that it will provide us with a solution to fit many areas: the dispersion of farms from a nucleated village following the enclosure of its Open Fields?'[3] With the substitution of 'hamlet' for 'village', one would be inclined to agree, for here would be an obvious parallel with the Clee Hills position,[4] and the excavation at Hampton Wafer itself lends further support to the idea that if there were nucleations here in the Middle Ages they were probably small. The problem of Anglo-Saxon names in a dispersed settlement area, far from being insurmountable, seems most likely to be due to the thinness of the Anglian occupation, here reaching its outermost limits, and its superimposition over a pre-existing pattern of Celtic hamleting and dispersal. This is supported by parallel evidence from large areas of Shropshire and

[1] Op. cit. maps VIII and IX, pp. 144 and 146.
[2] Letter received from S. C. Stanford dated 9 May 1958.
[3] 'A Medieval Settlement at Hampton Wafer', *Trans. Woolhope Nat. Fld Club*, XXXV (1955–7), p. 340.
[4] See Ch. 13.

46 (*opposite*). Hellens Estate, Much Marcle, Herefordshire

Cheshire.[1] The absence of the village may also be attributable in part to the absence of the need for defence, and in part to the lack of large multi-township parishes. Sufficiently powerful to introduce an arable field system resembling the Midland type, the Mercians were followed by the Anglo-Normans under whose régime the open fields were extended and added to. The Celtic and Norman traditions are clearly dominant, and the extension of orchards and the enclosure movement did nothing to contribute to the idea of nucleation in communities so long devoid of the village tradition.

[1] See Chs. 9, 11, 12 and 13.

16 Monmouthshire

> The river Wye rises in the same mountains of Ellennith, and flows by the castles of Hay and Clifford, through the city of Hereford, by the castles of Wilton and Goodrich, through the forest of Dean, abounding with iron and deer, and proceeds to Strigul castle, below which it empties itself into the sea, and forms in modern times the boundary of England and Wales.
>
> Giraldus Cambrensis, *The Itinerary through Wales*, Everyman Edition, p. 160. The *Itinerary* was written *circa* 1188

THE eastern Welsh counties might each be compared with a Welsh head having a Norman brow, some additionally having Anglo-Saxon eyebrows. Monmouthshire is no exception, despite its equivocal political position for the past four hundred years. The greater part of the county is covered by topographical names which put it without question on the Welsh side of the cultural border, but the hand of the Normans was excessively heavy here. The entire area was absorbed into marcher lordships but it was in the eastern fringes, the Monnow and Wye valleys, and more especially in the coastlands that the Norman overprint was most marked. Elsewhere, the greater part of the countryside remained in Welshries, and only isolated *capita* became centres of Anglo-Norman settlement. Thus, over some three-quarters of the county's area, Welsh life and Welsh economy and culture continued with little disturbance throughout the Middle Ages, but the eastern and southern margins of Monmouthshire reflect the influence of Norman occupation in their settlement forms, their castles and manor houses, and in their ancient field and tenurial arrangements. Only after Union, was the entire area drawn together into the joint stream of British economic and political development.

The dominant fact of Monmouthshire geography is its position at the south-eastern corner of the Welsh Uplands, within the Highland Zone, at the southern terminus of the great Borderland corridor, and at the entrance to the South Wales coastal route. The significance of its location at the hinge of these two major land routes has been reiterated throughout its history. Celt,

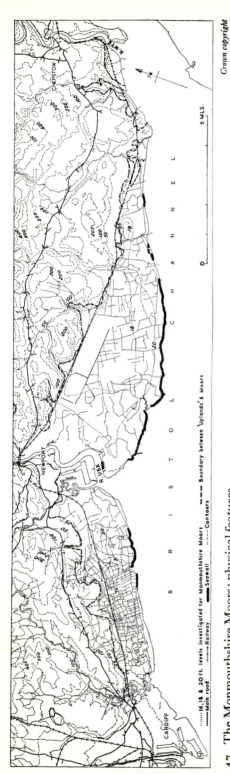

Crown copyright

16, 18 & 20 ft. levels investigated for Monmouthshire Moors
Main road
Railway
Boundary between 'Uplands'& Moors
Contours
Seawall

47. The Monmouthshire Moors: physical features

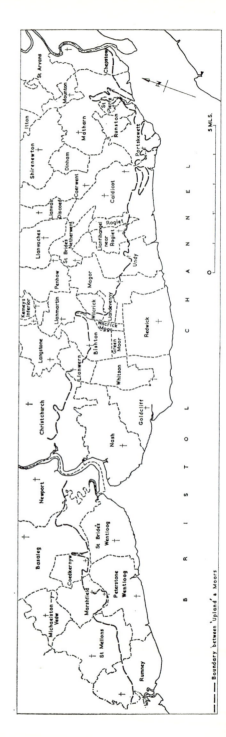

Boundary between 'Upland' & Moors

The Monmouthshire Moors: parish and township boundaries, tithe survey period

Roman and Norman in turn spread into South Wales using the broad ways across Gwent and Gwynllwg, and made use similarly of the corridor of lowland through the Borderland. In many ways, the positions of Chester and Caerleon were parallel and resulted in certain comparable developments in their history and the settlement of the surrounding districts, especially in Roman times and during the early Middle Ages. Both opened on to an estuary which in turn gave access to the western seas of Britain and although, in the Middle Ages, it was Bristol which ranked with Chester as a major western port, the sea trade of Monmouthshire was by no means insignificant and many of its minor ports long continued in use. In Roman times the parallel was clearer when Caerleon, then within the effective tidal limit of the Usk, was a port of some importance.

Physical geography offers a basis for a major threefold division into first, the high and largely inhospitable western mountains; secondly, the gentler, rolling uplands with their greater and lesser basins extending over most of the remainder of the county and rarely rising to as much as 1000 feet above sea level except for the higher hills of the north; and thirdly, the Wentloog and Caldicot Levels, known locally as the Monmouthshire Moors and forming an apron of coastal marsh only a few feet above sea level. In detail, far more subdivisions can be described within this county of varied relief and character, but for the purposes of settlement geography differentiation of lesser regions is most useful in the second division, that of the uplands which form the greater part of Monmouthshire and were the heart of ancient Gwent. There the Usk (Plate I) and the Wye, together with the mainstream of the Monnow which joins the Wye at Monmouth, break into the general relief to form fertile vales while, in the south and east, Wentwood and a continuous belt of higher upland overlooking the Wye have persisted as a characteristic settlement region less perhaps on the basis of morphology than of vegetation. The entire upland is an area of natural woodland, but in this reversed L-shaped belt a comparatively dense cover remained far longer than elsewhere, with the result that sparse, dispersed, and generally late woodland settlement distinguishes it from the rest of the upland in which older type Welsh settlements are widespread.

The basic triple subdivision of Monmouthshire is dependent on geological and structural contrasts, and both are in turn reflected in differences in soils and agricultural potential. The Black Mountains are so similar to the portions which lie in Herefordshire and Breconshire as to need no comment: apart from the valleys which in Monmouthshire are nowhere wide, these heights are for the most part barren and devoid of habitation. The western mountain belt south of the Abergavenny Gate is the eastern rim of the South Wales coalfield syncline and offered a not dissimilar basis for sparse settlement prior to the industrial development of the field. The soils of both are thin and poor and, together with the unfavourable slope, altitude and climate are unattractive to farmers. The rolling uplands of Gwent, by contrast, formed mainly on O.R.S. marls, conglomerates, and shales, though far from first-class agricultural land, are compensated by lower elevations, gentler slopes, and the most favourable climatic conditions of any part of the Borderland. Typical soils are freedraining loams, though on the marls they tend to be waterlogged in wet periods and are consequently most suited to cattle raising. Average annual temperatures are high (Newport 51·1° F, Usk 49·1° F). The summer heat is moderate, but the great advantage which Gwent and the Levels enjoy is that of mild winters thanks to the deep inlet of the Bristol Channel and the Severn estuary. The average temperature of the coldest month at Newport is 42·3° F (January) and at Usk 40·3° F (December and January). This feature is combined with an early spring and general freedom from May frosts.

The third division, the Moors or Levels, is unique in the Borderland though it compares closely with the opposite coasts of Somerset and, in physical character, with the Great Fens. A flat skirt of marshland, the present surface represents one phase of emergence in a series of coastal oscillations, and is the reduced relict plain of a much wider land surface which extended across to Somerset from Neolithic times to the Early Iron Age. It is believed that an appreciable marine transgression took place in the Romano-British period, since when there has been no major change in the extent of these coastal flats.[1] Its soils are a mixture of marine, riverine, and estuarine alluvium with inter-bedded

---

[1] H. Godwin, 'A Boreal Transgression in Swansea Bay', *New Phytologist*, xxxix (1940), and 'Coastal Peat Beds of the British Isles', *Jl Geol.* (1943).

peats, producing heavy blue clays, generally sour and deficient in lime. Avery[1] estimated that silty loams and clays on alluvium over peat are to be found on 900 acres, and mixed bottom-land soils on 300 acres in the Levels, the latter group especially on the back swamps of the Caldicot Levels which lie east of the Usk. A height of 20 feet above sea level is rarely exceeded, and the control both of land-flooding and of inundation from high spring tides is vital. A single low, but sharply defined step delimits the Moors on the landward side from the 'Uplands' where normal land conditions are resumed. On the seaward side beyond the sea wall, lie the saltings. Known also as the Welsh Grounds, they have long provided rough grazing for cattle and sheep, but are even more liable to inundation than the Levels. Recently, they have been invaded by *Spartina Townsendii* which aids consolidation as it colonises more and more of the salt marsh. Water levels are so critical, that excessive or long periods of rain can recreate swamp conditions and long periods of drought can reduce the naturally lush swards to hard-baked clay deserts. The annual average rainfall is 35 to 40 inches, but this may mean little as in 1954 when forty-nine successive rainless days impoverished pastures and ruined the hay crop, yet in September of the same year, after weeks of rain, the cattle on these pastures were sinking knee-deep in mud on the same fields.

The Progress of Settlement

In the southern Borderland, the river Wye has long been the accepted boundary of Welsh and English, and in its cultural and settlement features Monmouthshire is without question predominantly and basically Welsh. From the pre-Roman Iron Age, the greater part of the population of Gwent and Gwynllwg continued its unbroken evolution culturally and economically, and still by the time of the early Norman kings its rural society was largely based on agnatic groups. Princely families, free tribesmen, and bondsmen were the components of its tribal structure. Communal ownership took precedence over individual holding,

---

[1] B. W. Avery, Appendix on Soils in the *Monmouthshire Moors Draft Report*, published by the Welsh Agricultural Land Sub-Commission, Aberystwyth (1954).

and the Gwentian Code of laws regulated its customs. The economy was primarily pastoral, but cultivation had its place in the economy, co-aration generally being of more importance than the actual partition of a common field. With the change in language which resulted in the emergence of Welsh from its Brythonic roots, place-names took on their characteristic Welsh forms for the most part, and such common elements as *llan, aber* and *tref* are widespread over the mountains and uplands of Monmouthshire, as are the names of Celtic saints.

Two interruptions took place, however, in the long evolution from Celtic to Welsh society in this area. The first, the Roman occupation, made considerable impact. The second, the Anglo-Saxon, was so minor and so little is known of it, that it is of almost negligible importance as regards the settlement geography of the county.

Rome left its marks both in the form of roads and in the two important settlements of Caerleon and Caerwent. The late Dr V. E. Nash-Williams, in conversation at Caerleon in April 1955, estimated its peak population during the Roman period to have been *circa* 18,000. The civil settlement is now known to have been extensive, and by the time of the withdrawal from Britain the Romano-British population of Caerleon and Caerwent together must have been considerable enough to have spread over many of the existing Celtic units, if they did not additionally create new ones. To the Romans is attributed the first attempt to drain the Moors, and stones found three miles west of a Roman site at Redwick,[1] as well as the site itself, gave the first material support to Dr Nash-Williams' suggestion that the Second Augustan Legion, stationed at Caerleon, also attempted an occupation of part of the Moors. Caerwent itself lies near the edge of the Moors, and the present-day village lies within the very walls of the Roman settlement of Isca Silurum.

Of the Anglo-Saxon period, almost nothing is known apart from the building of the southernmost portion of Offa's Dyke on the steep high left bank of the Wye in sight of Gwent but entirely beyond its bounding river, and the traditional invasion of Gwent by Earl Harold in the eleventh century. A scatter of English place-names in the east and south may include a few early

[1] V. E. Nash-Williams, 'Note on a new Roman Site at Redwick, near Magor, Mon.', *Bull. Bd Celtic Stud.*, xiv (1951), pp. 254–5.

Anglo-Saxon ones, but the bulk are more probably medieval. There remain the great royal Saxon manor of Tidenham immediately across the mouth of the Wye and the name Chepstow[1] on the Monmouthshire bank to perpetuate the still unsolved problem of how far and for how long the Saxons advanced beyond that river prior to the eleventh century and what settlements they established, if any.

The Norman Conquest was of a very different order, bringing to eastern and southern Monmouthshire the second most important element in the rural settlement picture of today if one discounts recent industrialisation and urban spread. Normans had probably reached the lower Wye by 1067 when the castle of Strigoil or Chepstow is thought to have been built.[2] From this base on the right bank, they pressed rapidly westwards along the coastal route by Newport into Morganwg, and the carving out of marcher lordships, large and small, and the building of other castles proceeded with comparative rapidity. The occupation of Gwent and Gwynllwg was accomplished during the eleventh and early twelfth centuries, and most of the old Welsh commotes had been absorbed into the marcher lordships, whether as Englishry or Welshry, by the thirteenth century.[3] Strigoil lordship, which took over most of Gwent Iscoed (i.e. south of Wentwood), was strongly normalised, the lordship of Caerleon rather less so, but every lordship, however extensive the Welshry, had an Anglo-Norman core. Place-names were anglicised or Welsh names replaced by new English or Norman-French names. English settlers increased in number especially in the *capita*. They doubtless exceeded the Welsh in numbers in many of the lordly villages and small boroughs which were set up, though later the tide of Welsh in-migration was to run strongly again and by the seventeenth century English surnames were slightly fewer in number than Welsh in the manors of Gwent Iscoed held by the Duchy of Lancaster.[4] Elsewhere, Welshmen were markedly in the majority and in the greater part of the county as it is now there were few or no English outside the boroughs and the Englishries until after

[1] There are no known pre-Conquest records of this name.
[2] A. Morris, 'Chepstow Castle and the Barony of Strigoil', *Archaeol. Camb.*, 6th Series, ix (1909), pp. 407–32.
[3] William Rees, 'Medieval Gwent', *Jl Br. Archaeol. Assoc.*, new series, xxxv (1929), pp. 189–207.
[4] Ed. William Rees, *A Survey of the Duchy of Lancaster Lordships in Wales* (1953).

Union. Nearly every place originally had a Welsh name and the changes are etymologically of considerable interest. The proportionate importance of Welsh and English field-names is of similar significance. At the same time, the settlement picture was modified. Small towns, nucleated villages, park-estates, newly established markets and fairs, castles, and religious houses arose in this formerly dispersed, tribal land and the distinction between the two settlement patterns is clearer here than in any other part of the Borderland.

Four hundred years of union have failed to expunge the differences between Normanised and Welsh settlement geography in Monmouthshire, even though there has been a measure of convergence in economy resulting, notably, in enclosed field patterns which do not easily yield up to the inexperienced eye the original differences in field shapes and field systems. Yet the physical contrasts are so strong that they have never failed to assert themselves, and in 1815 Charles Hassall's[1] division of the county on the basis of the then agricultural régimes was broadly similar to the three basic subdivisions suggested above, but with the uplands divided into hills and vales. Overwhelmingly a grazing county, there are nonetheless marked differences between the poor mountain pastures of the west, the normally rich swards of the Levels and the intermediate animal farming of most of the uplands. In Hassall's day, arable land was far more important than now, especially in the Levels where enclosure of the open fields took place in many cases only after the middle of the nineteenth century. Of the Caldicot Levels, Hassall said the area lay 'convenient for exporting the produce across the Severn to Bristol in which several market vessels are employed in the ports of Monmouthshire'. He did not specify the type of produce but described both the Caldicot and Wentloog Levels as a region of mixed husbandry. The major vales, especially that of the Usk, he described as corn rather than grazing districts, with wheat on the clays and barley on the lighter soils.[2] Yet later he expatiated on the high quality of the natural grasses of the Levels, so rich that they provided 'green winter-keep for stock'.[3] Much of the Moors was still unenclosed in his day and he remarked on the benefits

[1] *General View of the Agriculture of the County of Monmouth,* Board of Agric. Report.
[2] Ibid. p. 36.   [3] Ibid. p. 55.

which might ensue on enclosure as compared with 'promiscuously depasturing the motley herds of six parishes' on Caldicot Moor.[1] Nevertheless, he granted that their pasture was excellent as contrasted with the 14–15,000 acres of waste which he estimated to exist on the mountains of western Monmouthshire, notably around Bedwellty, Aberystruth and Mynyddyslwyn.[2]

Although there are such marked differences between the three major types of region in Monmouthshire – mountains, uplands and Levels – the county is primarily natural pastureland. The lateness of enclosure on the Levels is surprising, and appears to reflect the depth to which the open arable field system had become entrenched there. Once it had begun to affect the arable lands, the enclosure movement gained speed rapidly and most arable was converted to pasture. From 81,205 acres in 1866, the total land under crops had fallen to 20,967 by 1938.[3] The eighteenth century saw the beginning of growing agricultural prosperity in this part of the country and the launching of numerous estate surveys which are invaluable both as records and for the maps and plans which generally accompanied them.

The improvement of the waste was slow until the early nineteenth century, and when it began it gave rise to the expulsion of many former squatters and cottagers on the one hand and to the making of new leaseholds on the other.[4] These last brought in large money rents to the lords of the appropriate manors, extended farming well up into the moorlands and wastes, and established here, as elsewhere, a new pattern of dispersed farmhouses set among their small or medium-sized holdings. Parishes which were particularly affected in these ways from the mid- and late-eighteenth century to the mid-nineteenth were Aberystruth, Abergavenny and Goytre, and in some, for example Llanfoist and Llanddewi Rhydderch, leases for new holdings date back to the late seventeenth century, and in Itton and Aberystruth to the late sixteenth.[5]

[1] Ibid. pp. 68–9. [2] Ibid. p. 68.
[3] A. Rhys Clarke and Emrys J. Howell, *Monmouthshire*, Land of Britain series, 38 (1943), p. 440.
[4] There are numerous examples of these in the *Abergavenny MSS*.
[5] Aberystruth: *Badminton Deeds*, I, e.g. no. 1518 (1753); Abergavenny: *Abergavenny MSS*. no. 840 (1732); Goytrey: ibid. nos 78 and 90 (1765 and 1773); Llanfoist: ibid. no. 910 (1689); Llanddewi Rhydderch, ibid. no. 683 (1693); Itton: *Badminton Deeds*, I, no. 71 (1547); Aberystruth: *Baker-Gabb Deeds*, no. 45 (1590).

It is surprising that on the Levels, where drainage schemes were initiated in medieval and even Roman times, enclosure did not make earlier progress on any great scale. Even the last major tracts of common were not enclosed until 1853 and 1858,[1] and there can be little doubt that it was because of the hold that traditional manorial methods of landholding and land use had obtained in this, the most intensively Normanised part of Monmouthshire. The land-use maps of the 1930s leave no question as to the widespread dominance of grazing over any other type of farming. In 1934–6 the average acreage of permanent grass occupied 89 per cent of the improved land and 54 per cent of the entire county (nearly 190,000 acres) and in addition there were 7670 acres under clover and over 56,000 acres of rough grazing.[2] Nevertheless, the woodland acreage is high also by British standards and increased from 29,800 acres in 1913 to 44,497 (12·8 per cent of the total area of the county) in 1924.[3] It provides a distinctive settlement environment over a considerable part of the southern and eastern uplands in particular.

In physique and in its settlement geography, Monmouthshire offers considerable contrasts with the English counties of the Borderland, except for the Welsh Districts of Herefordshire. For the most part an upland county, population and agriculture alike were affected by its only moderately rewarding environment prior to the development of the coalfield. Until the onset of the nineteenth century, the main wealth lay in the more fertile river valleys, especially the Usk, and in the Levels or such portions of them as had been drained. The strategic importance of the Wye and the Monnow, however, in the Middle Ages had resulted in the occupation and fortification of this vital route into Wales. The Usk was also defended, though thinly as were the Wye and the Monnow, and close occupation was confined to the far more vital and vulnerable route across the southern margins of the county into South Wales. All Gwent and Gwynllwg was carved up into marcher lordships, but the Englishries were of relatively small size in the western mountain belt, as for example at Abergavenny, and made only moderate impact in the uplands except around the castles themselves, for instance around Raglan and

---

[1] Clarke and Howell, op. cit. p. 489.
[2] Ibid. p. 445.   [3] Ibid. p. 451.

Usk. The triple physical division of Monmouthshire is, therefore, further differentiated in the settlement picture by a Norman overlay which is effective primarily in the south and in the Wye and Monnow valleys. In the west and centre the pattern has remained Welsh with the interpolation of Anglo-Norman villages and small towns or even near-solitary castles only in rare places. The fundamental contrast throughout Monmouthshire is between the intensively Normanised settlements, occurring especially along the southern and eastern margins, and the Welsh districts which account for the greater part of the area and where Normanisation is, at most, limited. Within these, physical geography imposes its own further subdivisions.

Settlement in the Normanised Areas

The effectiveness and permanency of the Norman overlay varies in part according to its original intensity and spread, with the favourableness of the environment from the Norman point of view, and with the opportunities for Welsh resurgence within the area of the lordship concerned. These factors are sufficiently variable within Monmouthshire to have resulted in marked differences between the rural patterns of the Levels and nearby areas on the one hand, and the rest of the county. Two contrasted districts illustrate this – the Monnow valley, and the Levels.

THE NORTH MONMOUTHSHIRE LORDSHIPS OF MONMOUTH AND THE THREE CASTLES

The whole of what is now Monmouthshire was divided into marcher lordships during the early Norman period, but the lordships were of very different size. Abergavenny, Usk and Wentloog were large, together taking up fully two-thirds of the county. Caerleon and Strigoil were medium-sized, and Caldicot very small. In the thirteenth century the north-eastern lordships of Monmouth and the Three Castles were of moderate size but the Three Castles had originally been three lesser lordships – Grosmont, Skenfrith and White Castle. Monmouth retained its importance sufficiently to remain the county town, and its status as such has only recently been challenged despite the fact that its population has long numbered only 5–6000. Lying on the fringe of Herefordshire and Gloucestershire, the town has retained much of its Anglo-Norman character, but the three neighbouring lordships have in each case become overwhelmingly Welsh as, indeed, has the countryside to the west of Monmouth town. Grosmont, Skenfrith and White Castle now barely merit the title 'village' and their ruined castles are but desolate and deserted reminders of long forgotten power.

Grosmont (H/VAlc(m)p) whose present population is something over 500, is a hamlet amidst dispersed and sizeable farmsteads (Plate XIII). It occupies the outer, precipitous cliffed bank of a meander of the river Monnow in the comparatively high upland country of north Monmouthshire, and under the shadow of Graig Syfryddin. This 1389-foot peak a mile to the south has provided part of Grosmont's common or waste from the early Middle Ages. The 200-foot drop below the castle is part of its natural defence, a moat fulfilling this function on the other side. It is possible, though by no means certain, that there was an earlier Welsh settlement, but the origin of the Grosmont of history was the medieval castle or a predecessor. Its Norman-French name – one of several in Monmouthshire – is justified by the site on which Hubert de Burgh built the existing castle (now in ruins) in the early thirteenth century. Like most *capita* of marcher lordships, it was a borough and had a weekly market and three fairs per annum. Its status as a borough has, in fact, only lapsed within the last eighty years. It experienced an actual increase in population during the nineteenth century until 1871, when the population numbered 742, but in common with Herefordshire and Central Wales, it has since declined.[1] The fairs decayed and the market became defunct, but it boasts a list of mayors who held office until 1852, and the corporation records are complete up to 1857.[2] Its nineteenth-century market hall still stands. There is also a church which, with the castle and old market hall forms the core

[1] J. A. Bradney, *A History of Monmouthshire*, 1 (1904), p. 69. Bradney records that Grosmont is reputed to have been the seat of Gwaethfod, prince of Cardigan in the eleventh century.
[2] Ibid. pp. 72–6. Bradney said that the corporation books were still in existence in 1904.

of this tiny settlement, but the borough has decayed in both the physical and the administrative sense.

The medieval manor of Grosmont included the parish of Llangua and part of Llanfihangel Crucorney. From the de Burghs, it passed to the Lancasters as a triple lordship with Skenfrith and White Castle, and it was bought by the sixth duke of Beaufort in 1825. As part of the Duchy of Lancaster lands in Wales, it was surveyed in the early seventeenth century, and from this a picture emerges of its social and agrarian character at that time. Grosmont was then a community of some seventy-odd families, of which 66 had freeholder status. There were nine copyholds, but of these it appeared that four were also on the freehold list. Even at that date, the castle was ruinous, for, the King being the lord of the manor, there was no resident lord but the demesne lands together took up some 200 acres. The market was held once every two weeks and there were three annual fairs. Common pasture was restricted to approximately 30 acres on Graig Syfryddin and some 16 acres on Graig Fawr, with pannage and herbage in the common wood known as Grosmont Wood, by that time only about 60 acres in extent. This lay on the slopes to the south-west and west of Graig Syfryddin, but it had been heavily depleted by 1613 thanks to encroachments. There were seven tenants who occupied cottages and gardens within the once-common area of the woods, four with cottages only, and six with gardens only, a record of particular interest in relation to Monmouthshire where the pattern of scattered clearings within the woodlands made by smallholders is one which is constantly met with. The commoners had further rights within the woods, being allowed one oak at a time for the maintenance and repair of their buildings and fences, and the right to collect windfalls, but the hunting and hawking were reserved for the king. Most of the free tenants held arable, pasture and meadow land, and a number had gardens and an orchard. Although one infers that the arable land was in common fields, there is no mention of any such field by name, but arable closes are specifically mentioned as such.[1]

[1] Ed. William Rees, *A Survey of the Duchy of Lancaster Lordships in Wales, 1609–1613* (1953). Transcription of *Duchy of Lancaster Misc. Books*, no. 122, P.R.O., on pp. 69–91.

It is evident that enclosure and encroachment were already considerably under way in Grosmont by 1613. By the time of the tithe survey, Grosmont parish consisted of dispersed farmsteads around a small castle-hamlet. There was no large landholder, but the farms were and are of appreciable size and in Bradney's day many of them were centred on substantial and ancient farm-houses and occupied by families with long pedigrees and each with their own coat of arms.[1] In the apportionment lists, English field-names predominated, and Welsh and English surnames were of roughly equal number.

The pictures that can be built up of *Skenfrith* (VAlc(m)p) and *White Castle* (HDcl(m)) from the 1613 Survey are very similar. In both, the castles were in ruins and the demesne lands parcelled out to tenants of the king. Similarly, there appear to have been both open and enclosed arable and meadow holdings,[2] common of pasture and extensive common woods. In these last, there were numerous encroachments by cottagers, and in the case of White Castle a list of 59 of these squatters is included in the survey. Not one of the three castles, however, remained important after the Middle Ages. Skenfrith had never been strategically significant, and although tolls were imposed on those who brought cattle and goods through the place, both it and White Castle had only minor burghal status and as they declined Monmouth and Grosmont secured the bulk of the local trade.[3] Today, Skenfrith is a small village; White Castle is no more than a once strongly defended castle on a lonely hill, and the very name has disappeared from the map of administrative units. Copyholders were entirely absent from Skenfrith and there were only two at White Castle. Rees believes that this reflects a strong Welsh element[4] which persists today in the settlement pattern of the three lordships where large dispersed farm-holdings typify the area, together with lesser holdings in former woodland which survive in varying numbers from the encroachments of the Tudor period. Anglicisation accounts for an increasing number of English field-names and

[1] Op. cit. I, p. 76 ff.
[2] A Tudor plan of Skenfrith shows considerable enclosure, but there were open fields west of the village including one named *Brodefelde*, P.R.O. Maps and Plans, MPC 69.
[3] William Rees, op. cit. (1953), Introduction, p. xii.
[4] Ibid. p. xxxii.

surnames, which is not surprising on this north-eastern border of the county.

Although adjoining the Three Castles, the case of *Monmouth* (VUmclp) is in some ways very different. At the confluence of the Monnow with the Wye, it remains today a junction of six main roads with a population of between 5000 and 6000. The Anglo-Norman borough which grew up in the eleventh and twelfth centuries was known to the Welsh as Abermynwy, and the name Chepingham or Chippenham which survived as the name of the common meadows south of the town within the confluential peninsula suggests possible Anglo-Saxon links. By the fourteenth century it was a walled town and a chartered borough, *caput* of the lordship of Monmouth, the most important of the Lancastrian lordships in the southern Marches and a market centre, and this important crossing point was and is distinguished by a medieval bridge carrying a fortified gatehouse of the latter half of the thirteenth century unique in Britain. A priory was founded here in 1075, and the Norman motte and bailey was still earlier, dating to before 1070, but the castle which replaced it was largely destroyed in the Civil Wars and the present castle goes back mainly to 1673. There is a twelfth-century church at Over Monnow, but the far older church of St Cadoc near the castle links it with the earlier Welsh or Celtic occupation, and the cathedral church of Llandaff had a mansion here in the sixth and seventh centuries. During the Norman period the lordship belonged to the FitzOsberns but passed to the Crown in 1256, subsequently becoming part of the Duchy of Lancaster estates. It was bought from the Duchy in the mid-seventeenth century by the duke of Beaufort, hence it is the subject of documentary evidence both in the *Duchy of Lancaster Miscellaneous Books* and the Badminton records. It is hardly surprising that Monmouth became and remained the county town or that it was created a county borough in 1888. Only comparatively recently has its status been challenged.

Its lordship, divided into the *villa* or Englishry and a Welshry, closely resembled the lordships of the Three Castles in its rural structure. The larger population of Monmouth, however, and the greater strength of Anglo-Norman administration there, resulted in a more widely developed system of open fields and common meadows and in their more extended survival. As in the typical small town of the Middle Ages, burghal rights covered shares in the open fields and grazing and other rights in the woods and pastures. In the fourteenth century reference was made to 'three parcels of land lying in the *Brodefelde* of Wycham in *le Netherende*[1] and in 1389 to a piece of land in 'a field called *Kynggesfeld*'[2] and an acre of land 'in a field below Castilgrove'[3] all in Monmouth, as well as to land in a field called *Polth Gwyn* in the fee of Hadnock,[4] a manor within the lordship. There is further reference to the Broad field in 1505/6[5] and 1510[6] in the *Milborne Papers* and in 1637 in the *Coleman Deeds*.[7] The *Marrysfeeld*[8] or *Marshefylde*[9] appears in documents of the Tudor period, as does a fifth arable field called *Williamffylde*,[10] but these were apparently only some of a numerous group of open fields in Monmouth drawn on a plan of 1654 in the *Milborne Collection* which showed about 15 open fields. The *Duchy of Lancaster Survey*[11] mentions Marrettes field, Margarettes field (?the same), Leviattes field, Castle field and Williams field. In addition there were common meadows, of far greater agricultural value than the arable fields and of these, Chepingham or Chippenham meadow was of outstanding size and importance, and lay at the confluence of the Wye and Monnow.[12] The *Duchy of Lancaster Survey* refers to another meadow, Humfreys meadow, also held in common.

There were three types of tenure in the borough of Monmouth – burgage hold, free socage hold, and free customary hold, and primogeniture was the mode of inheritance. The customary tenants were responsible for the cultivation of the demesne and, although by 1610 the medieval system was blurred by enclosures, encroachments, and compacting of holdings, theirs were still the majority of the holdings in the common fields. In the manor, gavelkind and Welsh customs prevailed and the holdings were consequently partible among all the sons. It was in the manor, not to the same degree in the borough, that the customary system of

---

[1] *Deeds and Documents deposited by His Grace the Duke of Beaufort, Badminton*, N.L.W., no. 1499 (1385).
[2] *Milborne Family Papers and Documents*, N.L.W., no. 110 (1389).
[3] Ibid. no. 161 (1443).   [4] Ibid. no. 114 (1442).   [5] Ibid. no. 159.
[6] Ibid. no. 166.   [7] Published N.L.W. (1921), no. 1413, p. 433.
[8] *Badminton Deeds*, no. 361 (1605).   [9] *Milborne Papers*, no. 252 (1578).
[10] Ibid. no. 506 (1597).   [11] *Misc. Books*, no. 121.
[12] *Badminton Estate Surveys*, N.L.W., 1765 Survey of Monmouth manor and Mitchell Troy Estate, folio 5, Chippenham field. It was still largely unenclosed at that date.

farming broke down most easily and, by the seventeenth century, the bond tenants had become free or leasehold tenants and much of the land was enclosed or compacted. By the nineteenth century, Monmouth lordship, beyond the borough, resembled the former area of the Three Castles with Welsh patterns of land-holding prevailing, and dispersed farms characteristic. In contrast with the defunct boroughs of the Three Castles, Monmouth fully maintained its urban character and size, and to this day is a fine example of an Anglo-Norman town planted in a Welsh country-side.

THE MONMOUTHSHIRE MOORS OR LEVELS

Apart from the town of Monmouth, no part of the county approached the Levels in the degree of normanisation. Physically and historically, they were and are unique, not only here but in the entire Borderland. Anglo-Norman occupation was both more extensive and more intensive, and the effects of manorialisation lasted longer. The resulting settlement map is of outstanding interest.

At the margin of upland and fen, the physical scene changes. The rolling, wooded uplands with pastoral farms, small stone-built hamlets and a predominantly Welsh pattern of settlement give place to fen so near to sea level and so dependent on the maintenance of an elaborate drainage system that an excessively high tide or prolonged rainfall may result in disastrous flooding such as that of 1606. In that year sea water swirled breast-high in the churches of Redwick and St Bride's Wentloog, many other churches and houses were inundated, and in the twenty-six parishes said to have been affected 2000 people were drowned in addition to large numbers of livestock. Commemorative tablets or inscriptions recording the height of these floods are to be found in a number of the Levels churches.

Drainage in the Levels is now almost entirely artificial and forms a predominantly rectangular pattern, especially in the more recently reclaimed lands. A series of lesser drainage lines lead to greater – grips to ditches, ditches to reens, reens to pills, and pills to the estuary. Grips and ditches drain the fields and the occupier is responsible for cleaning and maintaining them. The reens into

N2   S.R.L.W.B.

which they empty are the main artificial drainage lines of the Levels, some emptying direct into the estuary through the sea wall, others into the pills. The pills are embanked water courses which carry the upland streams direct across the marshes to the sea and, with one exception, receive the water discharged by the reens. Many pills flow within clay-lined embankments as high as 10–16 feet above the general ground level. At the seaward end of both reens and pills, penstocks or sluices are closed by the rising tide to keep sea water from the land drainage system, and re-opened by a rise in the outflow of fresh water so that this cannot flood back on to the land. At various points on the reens the water level is similarly controlled by boards slipped into stone piers to act as sluices by which the water level can be controlled below or above the board. Sewage disposal, drinking-water, building and agriculture are all problematic as in any fen country, and it is not uncommon to see great cracks in house and church walls, many of which are pinned, while others are clearly out of plumb.

Drainage and reclamation of the Levels has been piecemeal, as field and drainage patterns reveal. With the advance of settlement an elaborate and partially centralised control became essential. For centuries this was provided by the Court of Sewers and its commissioners appointed by the Crown and the Duchy of Lancaster, until they were replaced in this area under the Land Drainage Act of 1930 by the Caldicot and Wentloog Levels Drainage Board. In 1948 under the River Boards Act, the Usk River Board was created and became responsible for the sea defences and main rivers,[1] the Levels Drainage Board dealing with internal drains only.[2]

The prevailing heavy clays, deficient in lime and liable in any

[1] Under the 1963 Water Resources Act this became the Usk River Authority but its area was unchanged.

[2] W. T. Gustard, *Levels of the Hundreds of Caldicot and Wentllwg*, a bound vol. of typescript notes deposited in Newport Public Library, 1933. This paper also stated that the Caldicot Levels were 15,682 acres in extent with 22 miles of sea wall, 115 miles of reens and sewers, etc., and 475 miles of ditches. In 1884, the liabilities of owners for repair were commuted by Special Act of Parliament to a rent charge. This in turn has been changed to a levy on the Poor Rate, later to a levy based on a gross assessment to Schedule A, etc. In the *Monmouthshire Moors Investigation Draft Report*, 1954, far-reaching proposals for reform and improvement were made. Although the Court of Sewers was established by Statute 23 Henry VIII, ch. v, its records for this area date only from the 18th century. They include some extremely valuable material and maps and plans of the area. The *Court of Sewers surveys* were examined by courtesy of the Drainage Board.

season to become waterlogged, contrast sharply in terms of agricultural potential with the 'uplands' as the land is locally termed beyond the shallow step which divides the Moors from the shelf immediately to the north. There, drainage is normal and loams are the dominant soil type, albeit of differing quality, the best being found over sandstones or developed on mixed drifts. Large stretches of the 'uplands' above the fen margin have deep soils, easily worked and suitable for a wide range of crops, and they provide practically all the arable land in the coastal belt of Monmouthshire, though the proportion of cropped land to pasture has fallen during the last century.[1]

Ploughing is not impossible on the Levels but it is rarely rewarding and some nineteenth-century leases had a clause written in to restrict it, e.g. for Pillhouse Farm, Goldcliff, the 1824 lease included an agreement 'not to sow wheat, barley, oats, beans, peas, or vetches', and the 1831 lease for the same farm stated that 'the tenant was not to plough more than 5 acres in one piece and not in parcels'.[2] The chief agricultural output of the Levels is its haycrop and its pastoral products. In 1815, Hassall praised the natural grasses of the Wentloog Level – meadow soft grass, meadow fescue, cocksfoot, sweet vernal grass, foxtail, creeping trefoil, marsh bent and darnel – which he estimated as covering approximately 5000 acres of excellent fenland 'almost wholly occupied in pasture and meadow, the plough being very little used in this level'. Later, he referred to the summering of cattle, dairying and the raising of colts.[3] Today, the Levels are generally areas of good pasture with a high proportion of perennial rye grass and white clover, but *agrostis* pasture is found in poorer land south of the railway, and some of the back fen is still waterlogged peaty pasture bearing rushes, sedges, reeds and tussock grass.[4]

This natural division of pastoral and crop-raising activities between the 'upland' on the one hand and the Levels on the

[1] David Williams, 'The Acreage Returns of 1801 for Wales', *Bull. Bd Celtic Stud*, xiv (1950–1). In that year the 'upland' parishes returned far higher totals for the acreages under wheat, barley and oats than did those for the Levels. The acreages in some of the tithe apportionment lists show a similar situation some forty to fifty years later.
[2] *Newport Collection*, Mon. Co. Record Office, M 432, 4497 (1824); and 4512 (1831).
[3] Charles Hassall, op. cit. pp. 55, 72, 85 and 90.
[4] T. E. Williams and A. G. Davis, 'A Grassland Survey of the Monmouthshire Moors', *Jl. Br. Grassland Soc.*, i (1946), pp. 94–8.

other, and the physical environment which necessitates their different treatment and use, have influenced settlement in the southern belts of Gwent and Gwynllwg from the earliest period at which the plough was employed here, and notably from the Norman Conquest. The complementary character of the two zones is reflected in the fact that only six parishes lie wholly in the Levels: Peterstone Wentloog, St Bride's Wentloog, Nash, Whitson, Goldcliff and Redwick, and of these Redwick became interdependent agriculturally with Magor to compensate for its lack of good ploughland.

The settlement and drainage phases are only broadly known, but there is an unmistakable series of drainage and related field patterns ranging from the irregular early ones to the medieval strip patterns and the late enclosures with their large, rectangular layout. After the Roman period, it seems probable that the marshes long remained wild apart from the occasional hamlets established on more elevated portions of the fen by Celtic and Romano-British people, the last perhaps former inhabitants of Caerleon and Caerwent. A number of early Celtic church dedications suggest that in the fifth and sixth centuries the population here, though doubtless sparse, was at least sufficiently numerous to merit missionising. Religious houses were responsible for some medieval land drainage, and in the fourteenth century Goldcliff was a Benedictine manor, Peterstone church (said to be on the site of an earlier foundation) belonged to the canons of Bristol, and Redwick church to Tintern abbey. Field patterns and the very uneven information available on the progress of drainage suggest that the process spread from Goldcliff, Nash and Whitson in the south-west of the Caldicot Levels eastward. In the Wentloog Level, old enclosure patterns are fewer, but in both Levels the irregular type of field pattern and holding in severalty appear to be a reasonably reliable criterion for the selection of these as old nuclei. During the Middle Ages, the introduction of common holdings in arable field and meadows was associated with the *capita* and *sub-capita* of lordships and, in cases like Shirenewton, with dependent 'manors' in the Welshries.[1] Hamlets and villages grew up around manor-house or castle. Others were chartered

---

[1] Compare Hadnock in the lordship of Monmouth. Such manors served as granaries for the *capita*.

boroughs as in the cases of Chepstow and Newport. Between them lay the earlier dispersed and hamleted Celtic communities, administratively within the Welshries. The intervening wild fen remained as common pasture until the enclosure period, and enclosure in Monmouthshire both of common pasture and common fields was generally late. The last remnants of the commons were all allotted by 1870, and most of them by the tithe period, i.e. by 1840–50.[1] The broad greenways were the last to go. They are marked on many eighteenth and early nineteenth-century maps, but in the countryside today are best recognised by the long roadside intakes which finally reduced them to normal road width. Woodland as such has always been absent from the Levels, and common pasture has been confined to the natural inland marsh and the saltings or 'wharves' below the sea wall, and because of the value of the wharves township boundaries have long extended to mid-channel so defining the Welsh Grounds from the Somerset pastures or English Grounds on the far side.

In Monmouthshire, as in Herefordshire, nearly all parishes are conterminous with single townships, and on the Levels many of these in turn correspond with the old manors (Fig. 48). As the Normans spread westwards from the lower Wye to the Usk, they made a more intensive settlement here than in any other part of Monmouthshire. Even so, it was only partial, and Anglo-Norman influence dwindled markedly westward. The old Welsh commotes of Gwent Iscoed were carved up into the medieval lordships of Strigoil, Caldicot, Edlogan and Lebeneth; the name Gwynllwg became anglicised to Wentloog, and the lesser lordship of Machen north of Newport took in part of the old Gwynllwg. Anglo-Welsh hybridisation invaded every aspect of rural life and every element in the settlement pattern. This is very evident in the place-names. Prior to the Conquest most place-names were Welsh as they still are farther inland. Now the place-name map of the coastal belt is a patchwork of pure Welsh names such as Llanwern, Pencoed, Llanvair Discoed, Coedcernyw and Dyffryn; anglicised Welsh names such as Magor (from *Magwyr*), Mathern from *Merthyr Teyrn* or *Tewdrig*; hybrids like Michaelston-y-Vedw; English

[1] Among Enclosure Acts for the Levels parishes were those for Redwick, 1850 (7th Annual Report 15 Vict. c. 2); Whitson and the wastes of several manors including Redwick and Le Green Moor, Redwick, 1867 (2nd Annual Inclosure Act, 30 & 31 Vict. c. 71).

renderings like the two St Bride's, both of which were Llansant-ffraed on the tithe edition of the One-inch Ordnance Survey map; complete substitutions like Bishton, formerly Bishopston, replacing *Llangadwaladr*; and English names for which there is no known Welsh antecedent such as Castleton and Roggiett.

Whosoever the occupants, the strong physical controls imposed a certain patterning, if not on the actual field shapes, on the siting of village, hamlet and farm, and on the agronomy. In this coastal belt there are consequently three main choices for the location of settlements: elevated sites within the Levels, the actual fen margin, or the 'upland' proper. All offered relatively dry sites, but the shaping of township boundaries, that is of the terrain of the agricultural community, was a different problem. The Levels offered almost no arable land, but their pasture at best was excellent, at worst extensive. Only the 'upland' could be regarded as good arable land, but its pastures were by no means poor. Hence, the majority of the coastland parishes were so shaped as to include both 'upland' and Moor, and the fen-margin settlements had the best of both zones as in the cases of Bishton, Llandevenny, Magor and Caldicot. The Levels parishes were perforce primarily pastoral. The 'upland' parishes in many cases compromised by the inclusion of some Levels land.

Undy (JAp) neatly summarises the use made by a fen margin parish of the Levels and the 'upland'. Its six open arable fields lay immediately north of the village on the 'upland' at a height of 25–100 feet, open common on the slightly higher land beyond, the manor-house and a small park to the east of the village just above the fen margin, while below this step lay first a zone of open pasture on the Moors, next a belt of common meadows which extended to the sea wall, and below the sea wall open pasture on the saltings.[1]

At *Bishton* (JAp) three grades of land were distinguished in an eighteenth-century survey – hills, ridings and moors, the hills valued at five acres to the pound, and the moors at two acres. One of the smaller fen margin parishes, Bishton is sharply nucleated with only one farm outside the village. Its church stands solitary at the marsh edge and its single street curves with the

[1] Dorothy Sylvester, 'The Common Fields of the Coastlands of Gwent', *Agric. Hist. Rev.*, vi (1958), pp. 15–18 including a formalised plan.

25-foot contour round to Lanks Castle where the bishops of Llandaff occasionally resided.[1] The tithe map (1847) reveals that the site of its former open fields was similar to that of Undy's, and on the Levels lay its former common meadows and open marsh pasture. Documentary evidence of the existence of open arable fields is ample if not always specific, but in the sixteenth century one such field was named *Archdeconysfelde*.[2] The common meadows named included Chortemeade,[3] Aylwarrsmeade,[3] the short meadow and lord's meade,[3] and Great Meade.[3]

Magor (JAp(m)), one of the most amply documented of the Levels parishes, similarly exemplified the value of a fen margin site, and township lands on either side of this step between Levels and 'upland' (Fig. 49). The village itself, of remarkably English appearance, clusters round a square and bears witness to a once flourishing market which, until the building of the railway, also carried on a considerable trade in cattle, exporting them *via* Magor Pill to Somerset in exchange for corn. Its church, known locally as the cathedral of the Moors, was founded in the seventh century by Cadwaladr Fendigaid and stands, like many others in this area, immediately above the fen margin and the road to Aberwythel, Magor's long vanished port.[4] Its seventeenth-century name of *Magor Regis* bears witness to another reason for its growth, and at one time or another it has had a cider mill,[5] a smithy, a malthouse, a bakehouse and a corn-mill.[6] Today, the number of shops reflect the fact that it is one of the larger villages of the area, though they would hardly lead one to suspect its former burghal status.[7]

The tithe map of Magor is of unusual interest because, though drawn in 1847, it pre-dated the enclosure of the common fields. Three open arable fields – Lower, Middle and Upper Fields – lay immediately north of the village, and a fourth (Maes Bach) north of these. On the 'upland' beyond these were scattered farmsteads in the midst of compacted groups of fields, and more

[1] This was a manor of the diocese of Llandaff and was at some time also known as Lanks Cadwalader.
[2] *Badminton Deeds and Documents*, I, no. 115 (1562).
[3] Ibid. nos 113 (1557), 109 (1541), 912 and 913 (1575) and 914 (1575).
[4] *Badminton Deeds and Documents*, I, no. 163 (1546).
[5] *Newport Borough Collection*, Newport County Hall, M 436, no. 4425 (1763).
[6] Ibid. no. 3790 (1765).
[7] *Badminton Deeds and Documents*, I, no. 167 (1539).

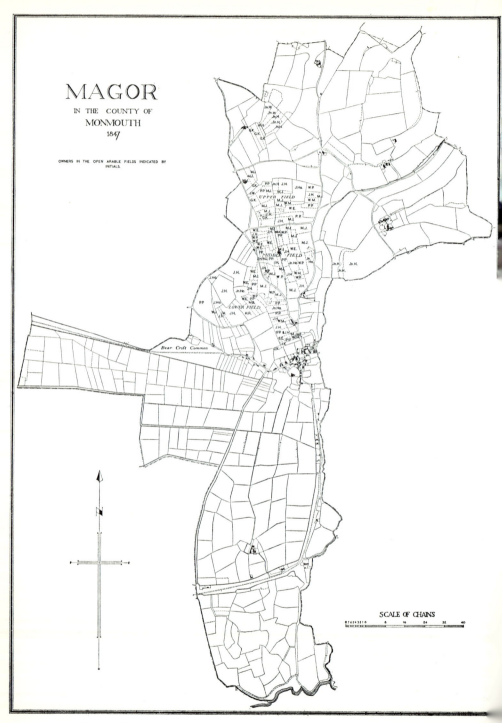

49. Magor, Monmouthshire: the tithe map, 1847

were situated on the Levels. The last surviving open pasture, Bearcroft Common, lay to the west of the village, but the rest of the Moors was enclosed by 1847 either in late rectangular enclosures or in the more irregular fields of an earlier period. Documentary evidence of its open arable fields goes back to 1392[1] and Bradney quotes a deed of 1448 in which is mentioned a disparate holding including '*duas acras terre arabilis . . . in campo de Magor*'.[2] In 1457/8, a grant was made of 4½ acres in 'a field called Calcrofte in Magor',[3] and from that date onwards a number of differently named fields appear in numerous deeds, but by the nineteenth century they had become simply Lower, Middle and Upper Fields. Although there had been some reduction in size by peripheral enclosure, the fields were otherwise little changed. Ownership was almost completely intermixed and compacting and enclosure had barely begun. Nothing is known of the small field (Maes Bach) to the north prior to the nineteenth century, but in 1847 it was used as an extension of Upper Field, so that there was a combined total of 38 holdings in these two as compared with 39 in Middle Field and 37 in Lower Field. With their enclosure in 1860, the last of Monmouthshire's open fields disappeared.

The last surviving open pasture was Bearcroft Common, west of the village. All the rest of the Moors was enclosed by the nineteenth century, some closes dating back to the sixteenth century, and probably around old farmsteads. No common meadows existed in Magor Levels in 1847, but there are one or two references to Avenellesmeade in the sixteenth century.[4] The mergence of Magor and Redwick into the single manor of Magor cum Redwick during the Middle Ages probably accounts for the later disappearance of this meadow, for Redwick lay wholly in the Levels whereas Magor had comparatively little land there. From the fifteenth century there are frequent references to the holdings of Magor tenants in the common meadow Broadmead in

[1] *Newport Borough Coll.*, M 436 no. 5808 (1392).

[2] Op. cit. IV, ii, p. 229.

[3] *Badminton Deeds*, I, no. 163 (1546). Lease of one close of pasture, 12 acres, in the parish of Magor . . . abutting towards the Grenemore wall. Ibid. no. 553 (1572). Grant referring to 6 acres lying together between le Blackewall and le Whytewall.

[4] *Badminton Deeds*, II, no. 1038 (1504). '12 acres of pasture lying together in Avenellesmeade.' References to a wall called Anneswall, *Badminton Deeds*, II, no. 170 (1569) and *Newport Coll.*, M 436, no. 3994 (1605/6) are probably the later Ynys Wall, and if so the former Avenellesmeade probably lay between Black Wall, Rush Wall and Ynys Wall, i.e. south-west of the village.

Redwick,[1] and after the seventeenth century all reference to open arable fields in Redwick ceases. An acceptable explanation would be that Redwick called off the struggle to maintain arable land on the ill-drained Levels and that Magor gratefully accepted rights in Redwick's common meadows in exchange for the allotment of strips to Redwick tenants in Magor's open arable fields.

Caldicot (AJLcp) is comparable geographically with other fen margin parishes although it is larger, but historically there are some differences. During the Anglo-Norman period, Caldicot was the greatest of the coastal manors and the head of a lordship which included the dependent manors of St Pierre, Portskewett, Crick, Caerwent and part of Rogiet, while Shirenewton was its detached Welshry. During the fifteenth century it passed from the Bohuns to the Duchy of Lancaster, yet despite its size and strategic siting the lords of Caldicot never made use of their right to create a borough there. Nevertheless it became the largest village in the area, clustered to the west of its great castle which was in ruins by the seventeenth century. It had a courthouse, a pound, several mills in various parts of the lordship, and a fulling mill later in Newton. The fen margin here is nearer to the coast and Caldicot proper consequently included a smaller proportion of Moor and a larger stretch of dry ground. Its numerous open fields, which were a distinguishing feature of the township, lay around the village especially to the north. Its common meadows were to the south and south-east, and its common pastures were on the wild fen, the saltings, and parts of Earlswood which was shared with its dependencies. At no time was Caldicot a self-contained economic unit, and as a result its tenurial arrangements were complex and tenants could hold land in any part of the lordship as well as inter-commoning on the wastes.

The open, arable fields were much larger and more numerous than those of Magor and their history can be traced back to the thirteenth century. One grant of that date refers to '$1\frac{1}{2}$ acres in a field called South field ... $\frac{1}{2}$ acre ... in the same field ... 1 acre at Neumedeshulle ... $\frac{1}{2}$ acre in a field called offeld ... 1 acre at brodelande ... 1 ferendell lies at le Cronciacre in the

---

[1] *Badminton Deeds*, I, no. 160 (1435), no. 1038 (1504), no. 166 (1555). *Newport Coll.*, M 436, no. 3994 (1605/6), no. 3996 (1672/3). *Evans and Evill Coll.*, no. 0230 (1716).

marsh of Caldecote towards pwlwrch . . . $\frac{1}{2}$ acre in a field called Shirfeld . . . $\frac{1}{2}$ acre in a field called he holes'.[1] It is evident from this that a multi-field system was no product of late expansion. Of the four or more which appear to have been arable fields, three were still known by the same names at the time of the 1609 Survey.[2] By the nineteenth century the open fields were Great Field, Church Field, Elm Field, Mill Field, Shire Field and Catbrain which was the northern part of Great Field. The tithe map also showed several groups of quillets which might have been remnants of other fields. Of the seventeenth-century names, a number remain to be identified, but some are traceable, like Brockholes, Dewstowes Field and the Sladd, from modern locality names. Others may have been names of furlongs for the fields were sufficiently large to have their furlongs identified by separate names. Despite their late survival, Caldicot's common fields had begun to break down by the seventeenth century as references to enclosures within them make clear.[3] Now, the expansion of Caldicot into a small town is rapidly obliterating ground evidence of their one-time existence.

Its common meadows were less numerous and less extensive, but these too can be traced back to the thirteenth century when a grant referred to pasture in Bieste-diche.[4] Another grant of similar date referred to $2\frac{3}{4}$ acres of meadow lying together in Wlputtes,[5] a name which was in use in the tithe survey though not then common meadow. The only common meadows then surviving were Bees Ditch and Little Bees Ditch. All were enclosed by 1858.

Of the six parishes which lie wholly in the Levels, Redwick has already been mentioned as having struggled to maintain arable fields until its union with Magor obviated that need. There are relatively dry years when meadow in the Moors is convertible to ploughland and this is probably what happened in Redwick. In Goldcliff, Nash and St Bride's Wentloog there is no evidence of open arable land, and throughout the Levels the prevailing

[1] *Newport Coll.*, M 421, 3, no. 6166 (n.d., latter half of the thirteenth century).
[2] Rees, *Survey of the Duchy of Lancaster Lordships in Wales*, Duchy of Lancaster Misc. Books, no. 123.
[3] Ibid. p. 161 where reference is made to '$\frac{1}{2}$ acre of pasture next Valleis House in a new close, recently part of the field called Westfield'.
[4] *Newport Coll.*, M 421.3, no. 5559 (n.d., late thirteenth century).
[5] Ibid., no. 5557 (equal date).

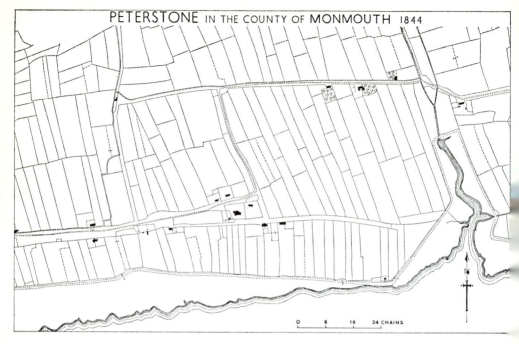

50. Peterstone, Monmouthshire: part of the tithe map, 1844, showing regular enclosure and drainage lines in the Wentloog Levels

economy has necessarily been based on meadows and animal farming. This gave rise during the Middle Ages to exceptionally well developed common meadow systems and to far larger units than are possible in the flood plains of rivers. Redwick's common meadows are outstanding in size and regularity in the Borderland, and at the tithe survey (1847) seven of them were still in existence, the largest, Broad Mead, so extensive that it was divided into 'lengths', the equivalent of furlongs in open arable fields. Around them, there long survived wide open pastures crossed by green-ways and between them on slightly elevated land and surrounded by irregular old enclosures were farms and farmlands of unknown date. Such old enclosures were also characteristic of Nash, Gold-cliff and St Bride's Wentloog but in Peterstone (Fig. 50) and in much of Whitson many of the field and drainage patterns indicate by their size and regularity the recency of enclosure, though the history of their settlement goes back to a far earlier period.[1] Disparate holdings were similarly a former feature of tenure, and some survived until 1828.[2]

The third settlement belt in the Normanised coastlands is the so-called 'upland', extending to Wentwood and Earlswood from the Caldicot Levels. The characteristic township is small with dispersed or semi-dispersed habitations and with the church standing either alone or near a small hamlet as at Llanvair Discoed. Most of this belt remained in the Welshries of the Anglo-Norman lordships and Welsh place- and farm-names predominate. Few were manorialised[3] and Welsh native economy continued with little interruption. There is good arable land but it was barely developed and open fields of the English type are generally absent. Pasture was the mainstay of life and pastoral rights were exercised in heath and woodland, for example 459 acres of 'wood undivided' (part of Wentwood) was entered under Penhow in a Survey of Chepstow Manor in 1763.[4] Woodlands large and small are found throughout the area, providing timber for building and fencing, wood for kindling, and many lesser perquisites such as birds and animals for the pot, together with nuts, berries and honey. The limited ploughland was worked under a system of co-aration in scattered strips or in a small bundle of strips in a tiny *maes*.

Penhow (HD(c)p) though predominantly Welsh in its habitation and field patterns, also included the manorial element in the shape of a castle built by the Norman Roger de St Maur, now largely replaced by Castle Farm. It surmounts an impressive eminence, but little else remains to indicate former manorial organisation. In 1447, however, there was a common field (Penhoysfeld)[5] and a lease of 1571 detailed a purchase of 24 acres by feoffment which included '4 acres called Whyteleyfeyld, 2 acres lying in the land of John Molgrey, 2½ acres in the lands of Thomas ap Hoskyn, ½ acre in a parcel of land called Pyscodlyn, 1 acre in the lands of Edmond ap Ievan, 6 acres together in a parcel called Mayse y

[1] In an atlas in the *Tredegar Collection*, N.L.W., are field plans of Peterstone and St Bride's Wentloog showing strip-shaped fields and some small irregular holdings (late eighteenth century).
[2] *Lockwood Coll.*, map no. 22, dated by watermark as 1828.
[3] With notable exceptions such as St Pierre.
[4] *Badminton Estate Survey* (1763).
[5] *Badminton Deeds*, I, no. 1443.

dree'[1] which reveals disparate holding, one or two common fields
and a mixture of Welsh and English tenants. The tithe map (1845)
shows little trace of such arrangements, revealing a largely wooded
northern area and to the south irregular fields around dispersed
farmsteads and a tiny hamlet near the castle, the whole interspersed with spinneys. The pattern indicates a reversion to the
Welsh type of settlement, or the submergence of manorial
arrangements by later enclosure and severalty holding – the two
are difficult to distinguish.

The farther one goes from the coastal belt the more typical does
the Welsh pattern become, but manorialisation showed itself in
numerous parishes in the south of the upland belt and in varying
ways, notably in the prevalence of small open arable fields and in
tell-tale remnants of intermixed holdings. *Shirenewton* (HAp) is a
special case. An attractive nucleated hill village, it was the centre
of the Welshry of Caldicot lordship, but it became increasingly
manorialised and by 1609 displayed a curious mixture of Welsh
and English tenure and land arrangements. Several open fields
were named in the Duchy of Lancaster Survey including Little
field, Westfield and Berfield. There was also 'le Courte' held by
William Blethin,[2] and to this day its successor, the Hall, gives it an
English air which is in fact shared by the village as a whole. But
the poorer soils contributed to an early break-up of the open
arable lands and they too lapsed into a field pattern which today
gives almost no indication of English influence.

Settlement in Welsh Monmouthshire

Apart from occasional Norman interpolations, the rest of Monmouthshire reveals three main settlement types: that of the
wooded uplands, that of the uplands where woodland is a minor
feature or virtually absent, and that of the mountain valleys in the
west. A feature common to them all is the absence of nucleated
villages (unless for some special reason and then usually of late
growth), the dispersal of farmsteads, the irregularity of field

---

[1] Ibid. no. 634.
[2] Rees, *Survey of the Duchy of Lancaster Lordships in Wales.*

shapes, the dominance of a pastoral régime, and the persistence of common rights especially in waste and woodland where the latter survived.

Ffwthog (Hv D) in the parish of Cwmyoy is a township in the Black Mountains occupying the eastern side of the valley of the Grwyne Fawr and the west-facing slopes of the high ridge which separates it from the valley of the Honddu. This ridge which rises to over 2000 feet forms an unoccupied barrier of waste land but the slightly gentler slopes below 1000 feet are occupied by farms whose fields form an unbroken belt flanking the Grwyne Fawr throughout the entire length of this characteristic high-mountain-valley township. Some of the farms are ancient, but in Cwmyoy the latter half of the eighteenth century saw both the decay of cottages and the enclosure of more of the waste to provide new smallholdings.[1]

Both the terrain and the lack of mineral wealth have imposed an almost unalterable pattern of settlement on the Black Mountain valleys, but in the South Wales coalfield, although physical limitations are important, the development of mining and industry at a sharply increased pace in the early nineteenth century saw the widespread development of urban and semi-urban settlements which were to wipe out or dominate most of the valleys from then on. The tithe maps are of particular interest for south-western Monmouthshire because they largely pre-date the industrial and mining phase. At the time of the tithe survey, *Bedwellty* (Hv Dp) was a large parish extending from the river Rhymney to the Ebbw and included the present-day administrative units of Ebbw Vale, Tredegar and Bedwellty. The first industrial undertakings were initiated in Tredegar and Black-wood, but the rest of the parish was largely mountain waste and woodland with occasional farmhouses in patches of discontinuous farmland in the valleys. In the neighbouring and not dissimilar parish of *Aberystruth* there are records of new allotments on the

---

[1] *Abergavenny MSS.*, e.g. nos 1375 (1775) and 1384 (1800) referring to decayed cottages and nos 1381 (1728/9), 1369 (1752), and 1380 (1797) referring to new allotments.

waste from 1590, but the greater number date from the late seventeenth century and continue through the eighteenth. After that, industrialisation began as in Bedwellty.[1]

SETTLEMENT IN THE UPLANDS OF GWENT

Between the western mountains and the Wye lies a countryside of low hills broken by minor valleys and basins and, towards the west, by the broad valley of the lower Usk and its tributary Olway Brook which flows from the Raglan area to Usk. The evidences of its former woodland cover are widespread and it is clear that the proportion of wooded land is in many cases a broad indication of the recency or otherwise of settlement. The major woodland belt extends from the neighbourhood of Monmouth southward along the Wye banks to Tintern Abbey, then swings south-west across Chepstow Park Wood, and, beyond a break at the once-wooded Earlswood Common, to Wentwood. Traditional and ancient Welsh communities are evidenced by the frequency of *llan* and *tref* as place-name elements and *Tregare* (correctly Tregaer) (HDp) is a typical example. Its church stands on a low hill some three miles north of Raglan, but the occasional cottages near to it can barely be considered a hamlet. In 1844, the entire parish (a single township) was enclosed and, apart from a few roadside intakes and a few squatters, gave every appearance of being an area of early enclosure around dispersed farms almost every one of which has a Welsh name. There is only a minor amount of woodland. Tregare is typical of the Welsh type of settlement in the open uplands and closely resembled by such parishes as Penrhos, Llanddewi Rhydderch, Llansoy, Llangwm Isaf, etc. Variations are produced by the presence of an estate element as at Llanarth, and by extensive squatting as at Llanishen. The influence of the Anglo-Norman settlement can also be detected in many of these upland settlements by the comparatively developed former open field system, though nowhere was this on the scale found in eastern and southern Monmouthshire. *Llangibby* (VB/Epc) is a sizeable hamlet situated on the western side of the Usk valley and combines an old Welsh community dispersed

[1] *Baker-Gabb Deeds and Documents*, no. 45 (1590) and *Abergavenny MSS.* nos 1136, 1137, 1154, 1160, 1179, 1518, 12, etc.

around the sixth-century church of St Cybi with a strong estate element dating originally from the building of the castle known as Tregrug to defend this part of the Marcher lordship of Usk. Tregrug has been succeeded by the seventeenth-century mansion of Llangibby Castle set in a park approached by the avenue known as Llangibby Walks. The majority of the field and farm-names are Welsh and there is nothing to suggest a former open field system other than a few *Kyvers* or *covers*. Woodland is still comparatively extensive.

As Wentwood and the Wye are approached, the woodland cover becomes more abundant and evidences of the recency of much of the settlement more numerous. Most of these late wood-land communities embody some indication of sparse early settle-ment in their names or in the existence of an early Celtic church, and many such churches are now ruined and deserted. Again the proportion of woodland acts as a rough guide to the recency or otherwise of settlement. *Tredunnock* (Hv Dp) is a dispersed com-munity around its church built on a low spur near the Usk less than two miles south of Llangibby, its beauty in part dependent on the prospect across the Usk, in part on the richness of its timber. *Itton* (W/FD) near the southern end of Chepstow Park Wood is a tiny township in which recent enclosure from the wood-land tends to predominate. *Kemeys Inferior* (H/WD) consists of little but a few dispersed farms on either side of the steep wooded ridge of Kemeys Graig which is the southern terminus of Went-wood. Overlooked by the hill fort of Great Caer Licyn, it is believed to be the Cemeis mentioned in the *Book of Llandaff* and given to the see of Llandaff in the seventh century.[1] During the early Middle Ages it was a manor in the lordship of Caerleon, and Kemeys House today represents the estate element, and the forsaken church in its overgrown but still gracious churchyard suggests all too vividly the forgotten place that it has now become.

The heights overlooking the left bank of the Monmouthshire Wye are, like Wentwood, peppered with townships in which the dominant pattern is provided by small settlements or single farms in clearings in deep woodland. Although Welsh place-names can still be found, the predominant place-names in this area are medieval or modern English names such as Whitebrook, Maryland

---

[1] C. J. O. Evans, *Monmouthshire: Its History and Topography* (1953), pp. 304–5.

and Parkhouse. In a number of parishes, old and new are mingled as in Llandogo and, notably, in *Trelleck* (HApb) the only nucleated village in this zone, in which and near to which are prehistoric remains, a church of Celtic (seventh century) foundation dedicated to St Trylec, and a Norman motte. It had open arable fields with Welsh names in 1436[1] and dispersed holdings were documented in 1567,[2] but it continued to lie in the heart of dense and extensive woodlands which still encircle it and which, from the Middle Ages onwards, have become dented by small clearings. These last typify the greater part of the parish.

With an overlay of recent enclosure and of compacting of fields which has gone on from the later Middle Ages, it is often difficult to distinguish between the elements which make up the pattern of a given township, but where documentation and cartographical evidence are reasonably ample as they are in Monmouthshire, a certain degree of reliability can be placed on the interpretation of the general picture. Monmouthshire offers one of the richest fields of the Borderland in this respect, and in the strength of the Norman stratum imposed on Welsh foundations, notably in the east and still more in the coastlands, it is unique.

[1] *Badminton Deeds,* I, no. 1597.   [2] Ibid. II, no. 876.

17 Breconshire and Radnorshire

> Brecknock is full of treason, and there is war in Ystrad Towy,
> In Ewias is found hatred and starvation,
> In Glynbwch are mangling and sharp words;
> In Talgarth robbery and shame, bribery and lawyers.
>
> Old quatrain, 1135

NO part of the Borderland demonstrates more forcibly than Breconshire and Radnorshire the significance of geography on the one hand and history on the other in the shaping of settlements. These two counties, incorporating the old Welsh divisions of Brycheiniog, Buellt, Elfael and Maelienydd include some of the wildest and grimmest uplands of mid-Wales, and the highest land in the Marches. Many of the most elevated tracts have remained virtually uninhabited since the Bronze Age, and having become herdsmen and cultivators, men were forced to seek the more rewarding valley lands and the fringe of the English lowlands. The vulnerability of the valleys from the east further moulded the character of settlement as, following on the valleyward movement during the Early Iron Age, came the succession of peoples and cultures from the flanking lowlands. The basis of its rural geography even today is the contrast between the Welsh settlement of the hills and the higher valleys, and the patterns of the lowland borders and the richer and wider vales, so markedly influenced by the Mercians and Anglo-Normans.

Along the line of the Rhaeader syncline, the high plateaux of the Central Welsh Uplands rise to heights of from 1700 to over 2000 feet on the north-western edge of both Radnorshire and Breconshire. The Mynydd Eppynt in northern Breconshire has a dissected plateau surface of between 1400 and 1500 feet, but in south-western Breconshire the peaks of Fforest Fawr are consistently over 2000 feet and Fan Fawr over 2400, while to the south and south-east of the Breconshire Usk rise the bare jagged rocky cwms of the Brecon Beacons, their highest points little short of 3000 feet. This western and southern flank of the Breconshire–

Radnorshire uplands is either uninhabited or carries only the sparsest population. Largely covered by poor mountain grasses such as *nardus* and *molinia*, by bracken and gorse, in stretches by mountain bog (even at lower elevations), it offers at best grazing of very low carrying capacity for mountain sheep. All the western and southerly parts of these areas belong properly not to the Borderland but to central Wales, for the influence of the Norman was negligible except in times of war, and place-names, people, and settlement patterns lack all evidence of the hybridisation of the border districts.

In the more easterly and central portions of the two counties rise Radnor Forest (over 1200 feet), Colwyn Forest (over 1700), and the Breconshire section of the Black Mountains, the most rugged and magnificent part of this mountain mass, crowned by Waun Fach and Pen y Gader Fawr, both over 2600 feet. These, and the central and eastern reaches of the Mynydd Eppynt constitute the greater proportion of the Brecon–Radnor uplands which have been influenced by their nearness to the Anglo–Welsh border. Below 1000 feet, apart from the Black Mountains, these hill masses offer appreciable stretches of land which is by no means infertile, and hill farms basing their economy on extensive sheep and poor cattle pasture extend well up towards the natural edge of the high moorlands. It is in many cases the deeply incised valleys rather than the upland surfaces which prohibit farming, but settlements, at most forming tiny hamlets, seek high ledges or the streamside where there is sufficient bottom land. Pasture on the better soils is fair, typically *agrostis*, but patches of plough land used for oats and roots or for pastoral crops are by no means rare up to heights of well over 600 feet. Today, Hereford beefstock and sheep of various mountain breeds such as Clun and Kerry are reared on these hills, the last often on the higher, open sheep runs of the commons, and the larger solitary farmstead is the typical settlement unit. Pastoralism has always and necessarily dominated the hill economy, for not only altitude and slope but soils and natural vegetation indicate the narrow agronomic limitations of this environment. Peaty podsols and gley soils typical of the higher uplands give place to varied sedentary and colluvial soils on the intermediate uplands as, for example, on the Downton Beds of the Mynydd Eppynt, with drift soils in parts.[1] Mountain bog on the peats and heather moor on many of the higher uplands offer little or no basis for a livelihood, and these vegetational types occupy much of the core of Radnor Forest, Colwyn Forest, the Radnorshire slopes of the Kerry Hills, and Maelienydd and other parts of the north-eastern heights. Below 1000 feet, grass moorland, mainly fescue and *agrostis*, covers wide stretches, with bracken, fern and gorse breaking into it on poorer land and inaccessible slopes, but with improved hill pasture now extending in the enclosures attached to the better farms.[2] The type and quality of grassland vary markedly with the micro-geography.[3] Some of the higher moorlands were formerly wooded in parts, even as late, it is claimed, as the Middle Ages. Today, hawthorn and mountain ash are signs of deterioration, but sessile oak, elm and ash are found in limited stands over much of southern Radnorshire and northern Breconshire, and on some of the limestone outcrops along the Radnorshire border,[4] and there are Forestry Commission plantations on the northern slopes of Radnor Forest, parts of the Mynydd Eppynt, and the southern slopes of the Brecon Beacons, though none of these is of major extent.

Only in the rare, favourable valleys or on more fertile shelves in these intermediate hill lands, can crop farming play anything but the most minor role, and the crop returns for the Llandovery Poor Law Union for 1854 illustrate just such an area. Lying across the upper Irfon valley and part of the western slopes of the Mynydd Eppynt, 75 per cent of the total area was rough grazing, permanent grass was returned as 16 per cent, while arable land accounted for less than 6 per cent and over half this acreage was under oats. In the Builth P.L.U. which covered part also of the Mynydd Eppynt, sheep were fewer but cattle were grazed in greater numbers on the better watered valley lands. One of the poorest areas of Breconshire was the south-west where sheep were depastured at the figure of only 1–3 per acre, and rough grazing accounted for 67 per cent of the total area.[5] None of these

---

[1] H. T. Davies, soil map of Breconshire in *Brycheiniog*, vi (1960), pp. 53–4.

[2] O. Gibbin, 'The Flora of Radnorshire', *Trans. Rad. Soc.*, vii (1937), p. 51.

[3] See the map of grassland types in G. Stapledon and W. Davies, *Survey of the Agricultural and Wastelands of Wales*.

[4] O. Gibbin, loc. cit.

[5] J. Phillip Dodd, 'The Brecknockshire Crop Returns for 1854', *Brycheiniog*, vi (1960), pp. 87–90.

was a natural geographical unit, but the averages are not un-representative of these intermediate uplands.

As the small, deep upland valleys widen, they sweep out into the broad, fertile vales of the Wye and the Usk and the Wye's major tributary, the Llynfi. The Ithon and Irfon valleys are of lesser importance both on account of their narrow width and their more remote location, but the Wye–Llynfi–Usk belt is both the fertile heart of the Brecon–Radnor area in terms of geography and economy, and the key, historically, to the history of invasion and occupation by the Normans. The greater part of this lowland and valley belt is floored by rocks of the Old Red Sandstone Series – red marls, Senni Beds and brownstones – and these, especially prominent in the Usk–Llynfi sector, give rise to richer soils, partly sedentary, partly drift of local derivation, with alluvial soils along the valley bottoms supporting rich meadow land.[1] So good are soils on the O.R.S. that cultivation was carried on at over 1000 feet above sea level near Llangorse in the eighteenth century.[2] Lying from 200–500 feet above sea level, the emerald ribbons of fat farmland in the vales break through the mountains like long oases or, as the invaders saw them, like fingers of the English lowland pointing and leading up into the hills. Better pasture of *agrostis* with ryegrass, deeper soils bearing heavier crops, and a richer natural woodland replace the thin economic environment of the hills – not gradually, but in most instances sharply and cleanly. Farms become more numerous, population densities here alone approach the norm for agricultural lowlands across the border, and climatically they are sheltered and warmer and escape many of the deep snows which isolate and bedevil movement in the hills in winter. Cattle become more important including milch cows; wheat and barley replace oats; and the returns per acre of farmland rise impressively. In the mid-nineteenth century these vales were the granaries of the two counties, and on their fine rich loams the percentage of land under the plough rose at the time of the tithe survey to 30 per cent in parishes like Bronllys and Llyswen and to well over 40 per cent in Clyro.

In Breconshire there is no 'border', for the contact zone with

[1] H. T. Davies, loc. cit.
[2] J. C. Grove, 'Eighteenth Century Land Use Records in Breconshire', *Brycheiniog*, viii (1962), p. 88.

the lowlands is blocked by the Black Mountains. There are, however, two most significant natural gateways, that of the Wye which is common to both counties, and of the Usk which, from Abergavenny, leads to Crickhowell and the vale of Brecon. In eastern Radnorshire the border lies across broken hill and vale country below the slopes of Radnor and Colwyn Forests. A generally lower altitude contributes to better farming conditions, but the amount of lowland and vale is still comparatively small, consisting principally of the Lugg valley around the Presteigne enclave and minor valleys drained by a group of streams which flow into the Lugg from the south-west. These open up above Knill into the Radnor–Evenjobb triangle, a faulted area of lowland some four miles wide into which open minor valleys from the south, occupied by Burlingjobb and Gladestry. This small but significant belt of lower country closely resembles the neighbouring west Herefordshire border country, as do its settlements and agriculture. The lower parts are areas of deeper soils and good pasture as well as corn land. Presteigne, a parish of 13 townships in 1620, had 241 acres under barley at that date, 417 under rye, and 1115 under oats out of a total of 1788 acres of arable land at that date. In 1845 there were 3535 acres of arable and 5075 acres of meadow and pasture land in the same area. It is notable that the only land producing a wheat crop in 1620 was in Stapleton[1] and that only totalled five acres.[2] Howse considered that rye bread must have been a staple food.

The Evolving Picture of Settlement

The distribution of settlements in the main phases of the history of Breconshire and Radnorshire reflects a progressive desertion of the higher lands and a growing predilection for the vales and the lower land. The Bronze Age saw the end of widespread occupation of the high uplands, and the Bronze Age remains in Breconshire show that the Usk–Llynfi basin was beginning to be

[1] A Herefordshire township which at that time was in Presteigne parish.
[2] W. H. Howse, 'Crops grown in the parish of Presteigne, 1620', *Trans Rad. Soc.*, xxvi (1956), pp. 46–7.

favoured. In the pre-Roman Iron Age, which H. N. Savory dates as approximately 400 B.C. to A.D. 100, the occupational remains are to be found almost entirely in that area. The higher upland was largely deserted, woodlands began to be extensively cleared in the lowland, and hill settlements were mainly in the form of forts on high points bordering the vales, and earthworks on hill slopes which, like Pendre (Talgarth) and Caerau (Llanfrynach), were not true hill camps. The 'crannog' or lake settlement of Llangorse is one of a small number known in Wales though common in Ireland.[1] Most of the larger hill forts both in Breconshire and Radnorshire are on sites overlooking adjoining lowland; most of the lesser ones more remotely located in the hills. There has been little excavation in the two counties but Pen y Crug north-west of Brecon with three large inner ramparts and two weak outer ones compares with the larger hill forts of Shropshire and Herefordshire.

The Roman occupation further emphasised the importance of the Usk–Llynfi area as a routeway, and the neighbourhood of the Pen y Crug and Slwch hill forts as focal, for here was the Roman cross road on the site of which Aberhonddu or Brecon was later to arise, and three miles above it the Romans built the fortress of Y Gaer. The road which crossed the Via Julia Montana went north up the river Honddu and across the Wye to the Ithon valley and Castell Collen. G. Arborn Stephens sees in Castell Collen a focal point of Celtic roads used by the Romans and in many cases improved by them and linked with the mineral trade from North and South Wales.[2] The continued use of early roads, whether Roman, Celtic or earlier trackways, by the Celtic saints has been stressed by E. G. Bowen who has used the Roman road links of Brecon with other parts of South and Central Wales to illustrate this thesis in connection with a number of saints, notably Brychan, Brynach and Padarn.[3] The distribution of dedications to the saints of the fifth to the seventh centuries is to some considerable degree a reflection of the then distribution of the Celtic population, and to this day it has influenced Welsh settlement

[1] H. N. Savory, 'Prehistoric Breconshire', *Brycheiniog*, i (1955), pp. 116–24. This paper includes maps of Neolithic, Bronze Age and Early Iron Age distributions.
[2] *Trans. Rad. Soc.*, xiv (1944), p. 52. See also Leslie Alcock's accounts of the Castell Collen excavations in *Trans. Rad. Soc.*, xxiv–xxvii (1954–7).
[3] *The Settlements of the Celtic Saints in Wales*, pp. 26, 28 and 54.

location and place-nomenclature. It further reflected the continuing valleyward movement of population, although the old love of the hills was equally clear in the siting of many of the Celtic churches.[1]

The evolution of the Welsh kingdoms and their subdivisions, the commotes and cantrefs, continued in the centuries up to and after the Mercian advance into the Borderland. In Brycheiniog which remained a fairly stable unit, and in the area of Elfael and Maelienydd, sometimes part of Powys, but later described somewhat indeterminately as *Rhwng Gwy a Hafren* (between the Wye and the Severn), there developed a predominantly pastoral Welsh society. The wide open uplands were grazed in common and the benefits of woodland were similarly communal, only arable land being measured and heritable together with shares in the *tyddynod*. Theophilus Jones writing in 1805 said that the *cyfair* or *cyfar* was still the usual unit of land measurement in Breconshire and was approximately two-thirds of an English acre, whereas the *erw* was an acre. He traced back many customs to the laws of Hywel Dda. The farms in Jones's day were generally small, and mainly pastoral with grazing rights on the sheep walks.[2] Farming remained equally traditional in Welsh areas of Radnorshire last century. Butter and cheese were among the chief produce of the cattle raising areas because of distance from markets, and ewes were milked for three weeks after the lambs were weaned. Most of the townships were economically independent and many of the farms made their own candles, baskets, brooms, mats and ropes.[3] Villages were and are almost unknown in the Welsh areas, and the dispersed farmsteads have long been the units which make up the loosely grouped Welsh *trefydd*.

Slowly evolving from their Celtic roots, Welsh life and Welsh forms of settlement went on with remarkably little change through the centuries, and the ancient patterns are still widely traceable today over the more westerly and the higher areas of occupation in Breconshire and Radnorshire. The Mercian impact, apart from Earl Harold's one or two earlier campaigns into the interior, was mainly around the eastern frontiers of what is now Radnorshire.

[1] The Breconshire distribution is shown in *Atlas Brycheiniog*, plate 8 (*Y Seintiau Celtaidd*).
[2] *A History of the County of Brecknock* (1898 ed.), pp. 153–6. (1st ed. 1805.)
[3] W. H. Howse, *Radnorshire* (1949), p. 88.

On both sides of Offa's Dyke, English place-names date from the advanced Mercian settlement of the seventh and eighth centuries – Cascob, Burlingjobb, Knill, Little Brampton, Shobdon, Titley, Stanage, Knighton, Norton and Kinnerton, all mentioned in Domesday Book. In addition in the same frontier district occur the names Walton, Gladestry, Whitton, Evenjobb, Downton and Harpton. There are few English names elsewhere in the two counties and those which today read like English names are in a large number of cases either very late introductions such as Crossgates near Llandrindod Wells, English replacements of Welsh names like Knighton which was Tref-ar-Clawdd, or anglicisations which are the most numerous of the so-seeming English names. There is much dissension and argument about these, for in Radnorshire, where Welsh speech has now all but died out, there has been progressive anglicisation even during the last hundred years with some exceptionally odd results, notably in locality, farm and field-names. Fairly straightforward examples of anglicised place-names are Glasbury (pronounced 'Glazebury') from Clas-ar-Wy, Clyro from Cleirwy, Erwood from Yr Rhyd, and Builth from Llanfair-ym-Muallt, all in the Wye valley. In Breconshire, Brecon is a replacement of Aberhonddu and Crickhowell an anglicisation of Crucywel, but examples are fewer from this county.

Incomparably the more important invasion of this part of Wales was the Norman and in no other part of the Borderland can the technique of conquest by valley penetration be seen better than in Breconshire and Radnorshire, especially the former where almost every motte and castle was located in the Usk–Llynfi basin or along the course of the Wye. In Radnorshire, the eastern border zone was thick with defensive works of this period and from between Knucklas on the Teme and New Radnor, numerous mottes are found on routes across Maelienydd which link up with a group in the Ithon valley and with another along the Severn near Newtown (Fig. 14). D. F. Renn has stressed his conviction that the mottes were built over a period of several centuries, and if so, it would seem that the persistence of Welsh campaigning in this part of Wales may explain the need to provide adequate strong points and lockouts.

The conquest of Breconshire and Radnorshire by the Normans

was comparatively late. Their claims were based on earl Harold's defeat of the Welsh in 1063, and the devastation that these wars against the Welsh had wrought from 1052 onwards probably rendered Norman ingress all the easier. But recovery was slow and a wasted hill country was of less importance to the Normans than the Severn valley and Gwent. It was about 1090 when de Breos began his conquest of Maelienydd and Buellt and at about the same time Bernard Newmarch advancing *via* the Wye valley and the Llynfi, reached the old hub of the Roman roads near Y Gaer. Brecon castle and town were founded about 1093 after the defeat of the last native prince of Brycheiniog. The de Breos family retained Elfael and Buellt for over a hundred years and replaced Newmarch in Brycheiniog. The more northerly and central districts of Radnorshire were won by the Mortimers of Wigmore, and the Lacys and later the Bohuns held the adjoining border country. With the Welsh kingdoms of Powys and Gwynedd adjoining these marcher lordships to the north, and Ceridigion to the west, the Brecon–Radnor area became a vital frontier region and, as such, was far more heavily defended than the northern borderland. It was under constant attack and threat of attack until the end of the thirteenth century and spasmodically after that in Edward III's campaign of 1322, in the Glyn Dwr rebellion and in the Wars of the Roses. Active castle building and rebuilding went on throughout the first two hundred years of the marcher period and, as in Herefordshire and Monmouthshire, some of the castles became the nuclei of small towns and villages.

The tradition of nucleation had by this time been abandoned by the Welsh, and the nucleated villages of the Wye–Llynfi–Usk lowlands and the frontier districts stand out in sharp contrast with the almost universal dispersal of the purely Welsh settlement areas (Fig. 3). This distinction has survived and, until the rise of Llandrindod Wells and Llangammarch Wells as spas and the growth of mining and industrial centres on the southern fringe of Breconshire during the nineteenth century, it had remained virtually unaltered throughout the intervening centuries. At the time of the tithe survey, the nucleated settlements of Radnorshire consisted of the small urban centres of Rhaeadr, Knighton, New Radnor and Presteigne, the decayed borough of Painscastle sunk to village status, and the three villages of Gladestry on the border

and Glasbury and Clyro in the Wye valley. In Breconshire, the
tally at that time was the five market towns (all ancient boroughs)
of Brecon, Talgarth, Hay, Builth and Crickhowell, Llangammarch
Wells newly grown as a spa, and the villages of Llyswen in the
Wye valley and Bronllys, Llanfihangel Tal y Llyn, Llangorse,
Llangattock, Defynog and Trecastell all in the Usk–Llynfi basin.
The totals of eight in Radnorshire and thirteen in Breconshire are
the lowest for any county in the Borderland.

Many factors have contributed to the growth of the nucleated
settlements and, as in the case of Painscastle, to their decay. The
period of growth cannot easily be determined, but Mercian and
Anglo-Norman development of the eastern border of Radnorshire and of the Wye–Llynfi–Usk vales, created conditions which
favoured them. Castles might be a factor in their growth, but
every castle by no means became associated with a sizeable
settlement and some that did were later to be the core only of a
decaying community as in the case of Painscastle (Castle Maud)
and Clifford just beyond the Brecon–Radnor border.[1] Single-
township parishes predominate in both counties but Presteigne,
which had thirteen townships in 1620 (some of these in Herefordshire), was a single-township parish in 1811,[2] and Welsh townships
were notably fluid in area.

Two hundred years of war and the threat of war did little to
advance the economy of Radnorshire or to increase its population.
The fourteenth century also brought difficult years such as that
of 1317 when the harvests failed. Everything, however, was not on
the debit side. The Black Death hardly touched the interior of
Radnorshire and had but little effect in Breconshire, though 1349
and 1363 were bad years of plague on the eastern borders of
Radnorshire. The fourteenth century saw a boom in the wool
trade and markets and fairs, some old-established, some new,
gave a fillip to local farming. In Radnorshire, St Harmon,
Rhaeadr, Knucklas, Knighton, Glascwm and Boughrood had
both markets and fairs. Cefnllys had a market and two fairs a
year were held at New Radnor, Presteigne, Michaelchurch and

---

[1] The castles of Breconshire are mapped in *Atlas Brycheiniog*, plate 9 and described in
D. J. Cathcart King, 'The Castles of Breconshire', *Brycheiniog*, vii (1961). Those of
Radnorshire are listed by W. H. Howse in *Trans. Rad. Soc.*, xxiv (1954).

[2] W. H. Howse, 'Crops grown in the parish of Presteigne', *Trans. Rad. Soc.*, xxvi
(1956).

Painscastle.[1] Some of these were held by royal charter, some by prescription of the church or the lords marcher and others were unchartered.[2] The proliferation of markets and fairs was due in part to the poor communications which necessitated exchange points at short intervals, but also to the improvement in sheep farming and the increase in fulling. Fulling mills in the fourteenth century existed at Aberedw, Llanbadarn Fynydd, Beguildy, Pennant, Llanbister, Llananno, Doldowlod, Llanbadarn Fawr, Cefnllys, Knighton, Whitton, New Radnor, Cregrina, Llansanffraid, Bryngwyn, Boughrood and Glasbury, while Nantmel had four.[3] In Breconshire similarly there was a rise in trade and in markets and fairs. A few of these were in the hills, but the majority were in the Usk–Llynfi lowland.[4] There seems also to have been a slow increase in the amount of corn grown for there were more corn mills as well as fulling mills, many of which survived until the eighteenth century, but by the mid-nineteenth Howse says there was not a fulling mill left in Radnorshire and corn mills were rapidly going out of use.[5]

Many of the markets were little more than convenient central points of exchange and the places where they were held benefited even less than places on the English side of the border which were only temporarily associated with market trade. Others experienced a modest growth as a result, but many Welsh families entered on a period of prosperity and consequent social advancement as a result of the wool trade and later the drovers' trade. Lewis Dwn observed in 1597[6] that many Radnorshire families can be traced back to the fourteenth century, and of the forty 'manorial' families in the county at that date thirty-four were Welsh. D. Stedman Davies adds that among them only one was Norman and the remaining five non-Welsh families came into Radnorshire after the fourteenth century.[7] Their status and that of many lesser farming families is reflected in the good manor houses and farmhouses built from the later Middle Ages onwards.

[1] D. Stedman Davies, 'Notes on Radnorshire, 1066 to 1400', *Trans. Rad. Soc.*, x (1940), p. 62.
[2] W. H. Howse, 'The Old Fairs of Radnorshire and its Borders', ibid. xvii (1947), p. 52.
[3] D. Stedman Davies, loc. cit.
[4] *Atlas Brycheiniog*. Plate 25 (*Ffeiriau*) shows Norman markets.
[5] *Radnorshire*, p. 97.
[6] *Heraldic Visitations of Wales*, ed. Sir S. Rush Meyrick.   [7] Loc. cit. p. 63.

It is also evident that long before the union of the two countries, Welsh and Anglo-Welsh families predominated over English, and if this was true of the more prosperous class it was certainly true of the people as a whole. The population of both counties has remained predominantly Welsh, but Radnorshire, more open to English influence, has become from the mid-nineteenth century an almost wholly English speaking area while in Breconshire the extreme west has over 75 per cent Welsh speakers, and even in the middle belt it claims from 10 to 60 per cent.

Until the 1861 Census, the population of both counties increased, that of Breconshire having almost doubled since the 1801 returns were made (from 31,000 to 61,000), due largely to the development of mining and industrial activities on the northern fringe of the coalfield. The more modest Radnorshire increase in the same period (from 19,000 to 25,000) is probably a truer reflection of the rural and small town position in both counties. From 1871 onwards, Radnorshire with its higher proportion of hill land has experienced a progressive population recession until, in 1961, the total for the county stood at only 18,471. In Breconshire, there was a second peak in 1921 (61,000) but decline set in during the depression years which severely affected the coalfield, and the decline in total population has since been progressive until, in 1961, the total was only 55,185. Nevertheless, this still represents a population density of double that of Radnorshire. Part of this higher density is accounted for by the industrial settlements of the south, but part too is a reflection of the far greater area of lowland in the Usk–Llynfi basin than exists anywhere in Radnorshire. It is not the lowland population which is decreasing seriously, though there is some drift from many rural areas, so much as the hill lands where even hill farming grants are insufficient to prevent the flight from the uplands. This is reflected in the rural habitation map by 'gone down' houses, to use the local expression, but these are by no means commensurate with the loss in population and family size and the decrease in farm servants and farm labourers living in the farmhouses explains a much bigger proportion of the total loss. On the rural settlement map, it means more widely spaced dispersal than at the tithe survey when the rural population was just about at its peak, especially in the hill lands, but a relatively smaller loss or a slight increase in the small towns and the larger villages. It is also associated with the compacting of farm holdings and the introduction of more mechanical aids to farming for, although population has decreased, agricultural production in most areas has actually risen. Many of these factors apply to Central Wales as a whole, including Montgomeryshire, but Radnorshire shared with Merioneth the highest rate of loss between 1951 and 1961 (7·6 per cent).[1]

Settlement in the Uplands

Because the uplands of Breconshire, Radnorshire, Montgomeryshire and Denbighshire are far more extensive than those of Monmouthshire (or Flintshire), their tiny remote settlements are more numerous. They are situated in locations which, though they give maximum advantage in the immediate area, are by any other standards little short of fantastic. The highest uplands are uninhabited, but farmhouses built at over 1000 feet are by no means rare in north Radnorshire and north Breconshire. Hill top and high hillside locations are not uncommon for the ancient parish churches and the associated settlements. Llansanffraed yn Elfael, for example, is on a steep hillside at almost 900 feet on the west of Colwyn Forest with only a minor access road. Patrishow in the Grwyne Fawr valley in the south-western Black Mountains is a scattered farming township with its highest farms on steep slopes at altitudes of up to 1000 feet. Talachddu and Llanddew in the Mynydd Eppynt are both at high points of over 700 feet, and such examples are not rare but typical of the Radnor–Brecon uplands. Many are near Early Iron Age forts; some, like Llanwrthwl (Brec.) are near to still older prehistoric sites, Llanwrthwl claiming that a stone in its churchyard is a menhir, while nearby is a stone circle. A high proportion of the upland parishes have churches founded by Celtic saints of the fifth to seventh centuries, many in Breconshire dedicated to saints of the family of Brychan. Few can claim features of recent origin, and for the most part they represent extremely ancient settlement patterns. Even small hamlets were

[1] The problem of depopulation in mid-Wales was the subject of a Committee Report under that title (H.M.S.O., 1964).

rare and such as there were could generally be explained by special locations, such as nearness to a major valley (e.g. Crickadarn above the high south bank of the Wye) or to the survival or introduction of a local industry.

Sites near the broader vales or in narrow valleys are on the whole those most frequently occupied by the solitary parish churches of high Radnorshire and Breconshire. Two such settlements are Cregrina and Llanbadarn y Garreg in the Edw valley on the west side of Colwyn Forest.

Cregrina (Hv Cpb) lies at 600 feet above sea level in a portion of the Edw valley with rather gentler slopes on the left bank near its junction with Clas brook, but the right bank rises steeply to the peak of Wylfre (1346 feet). Cregrina parish lies on the steep western bank and much of its area is open common pasture on which were occasional intakes in 1839, the date of the tithe map. It is said that one of the last wolves in Wales was killed in this wild area in late Tudor times. It is a small township of under 2000 acres based on the parish church of St David which Howse thought might be a sixth-century foundation.[1] In the days of the drovers, it lay on one of the drovers' roads across Colwyn Forest and had a forge where cattle were shod with iron 'cues'. Howse said that there was a small cloth factory there in the early nineteenth century but that it had disappeared by 1850.[2] A smithy was marked on the tithe map but no other building which seems likely to have been a mill. This is of special interest because the total dispersal of 1839 was broken down in the 1850s by the building of a few cottages. These constitute a small hamlet above the bridge which the county council built across the Edw in 1894. If Howse's date for the cloth factory is correct then the figure of 133 inhabitants[1] in 1801 is reasonable, but the population had fallen by 1851 to 109. In 1861 it rose to 124 which seems to be related to the rise of the hamlet, but since then it has dropped steadily to 76 in 1901 and 45 in 1961.

Llanbadarn y Garreg (Hv Cp) is three miles farther down the Edw along the difficult, winding lane which links the farms of this part of the valley. Its church, one of the three Padarn churches in Radnorshire, now stands almost solitary among scattered farmsteads in a parish which is based like Cregrina on the limited

---

[1] *Radnorshire*, p. 254.   [2] Ibid. p. 97.

resources of a valley which here is even more restricted than farther upstream, yet the fields climb to over 1000 feet before they give place to the bare moorland heights on either side of this deep mountain valley. At the centre and around the church were half a dozen houses which, although they were labelled 'village' on the tithe map of 1839, barely deserve the name of hamlet. The rest of the parish, as in all these upland townships is made up of scattered farmsteads among their irregular, compact fields on the hillsides.

The vast majority of the field and farm-names in the hill settlements are Welsh. The farms are dispersed, the holdings for the most part compact and sharing the common pasture of the open moorland above. The fields are irregular in shape, and evidences of former open arable strips are scanty but by no means absent. In Llanfihangel Nant Melan in 1839 four fields were named dole, and another Maes dan y coed, but these slim indications of former common fields are typically inconclusive in the absence of earlier documentation. Llanfihangel Nant Melan, however, lies at 1000 feet above sea level in the bleak, exposed Van Pass south of Radnor Forest and at best, the chance of cultivation there must have been slight. At lower altitudes, it was not unusual for the hill settlements to maintain small arable fields or scattered ploughing strips as at Llandefalle situated at 650 feet in a minor, but comparatively gentle valley two miles south of Llyswen in the Wye valley. It is in gently rolling green upland country and as far back as 1541 there was reference to 'four acres in Maysey Park',[1] while in the early seventeenth century a deed poll enumerated the names dole 'r velin, maes y velin, y saith kyver, pedwar kyver issa, 2 acres of land in a close called keven tredieni, maes y llan issa, maes y llan ucha, and pimp kyver ucha.[2] In the far west there are few or negligible signs of Norman influence, and all the evidence points to an unbroken tradition of Welsh life and Welsh farming methods.

As one moves eastwards, the mottes, castles, and courts make their appearance even in the hills, and in Radnorshire the mottes and baileys of the hills are remarkably numerous. In most cases, their effect on settlement was temporary and slight, but in a few

---

[1] *The Quaritch Deeds*, N.L.W. no. 674.
[2] Ibid. no. 309 (1614).

cases the Norman imprint was firm and longer lasting. *Cefnllys* (HD(c)(m)lp) bears comparison with Caus in Shropshire in that this great castle of the Mortimers erected on a hill promontory surrounded on three sides by the river Ithon was once the core of a borough which is reputed to have stretched two miles north-east to south-west and half a mile across, yet now is totally deserted except for the small church of St Michael restored in 1895. Once the seat of the Silurian lords of Maelienydd and Elfael, it was taken over by the Normans, and the Mortimer castle was built in about 1242, to be taken and re-taken by Welsh and Normans. A borough by prescription, in the Middle Ages it boasted a corporation of bailiff, recorder, and nearly two hundred burgesses.[1] In 1558, Camden described it as in ruins. At 1000 feet above sea level, it was one of the strongest points in mid-Radnorshire, and it is thought probable that an Early Iron Age fort preceded the hill-top castle. Today it is a lonely hill site in a parish of typically dispersed Welsh farms, of which the field names suggest not Anglo-Norman, but almost purely Welsh antecedents.[2]

Painscastle (Hv Ac(m)l) in the Middle Ages was the *caput* of the de Breos lordship of Painscastle, and has been variously known as Pain's Castle, Castle Matilda, and Castle Maud. Its immensely strong castle, now ruined but with substantial remains, is believed to have been built over an earlier fort. It became the focus of a borough after its erection in 1130, by Thomas de Paganus or Pain, and a weekly market and three annual fairs were held there, the market house surviving until the late nineteenth century. Lying in the gentle valley of Bach Howey, a tributary of the Edw in the middle of Colwyn Forest, it is, despite its height above sea level of 850–900 feet, a comparatively good pastoral farming area. It is a centre of upland roads and was an important clearing-house for the drover trade with its half-dozen inns (one of which was the Black Ox) and a shoeing forge. Today, its roads are minor and, lying high and remote above the main arteries of modern traffic, it has declined progressively since Union and is now a raggedly nucleated village around a triangular green. Many of the houses in the village are farmhouses and there is still a well on the green for the watering of cattle, and a smithy. The great

[1] 'Cefn Llys-Castell Glan Ithon', *Trans. Rad. Soc.*. xv (1945), pp. 50–1.
[2] T. P. Davies, 'Cefnllys Parish', *Trans. Rad. Soc.*, ii (1932), pp. 31–8.

motte on which stand the castle ruins, and the park[1] which once formed part of its demesne, are now partly built over by houses including Castle farm. Its significance in the settlement picture of Radnorshire is that it is the only nucleated village in the uplands, though it has no parish church and is a township of Llanbedr two miles to the west. Its Norman origin is indisputable.

The Vales of Wye, Usk and Llynfi

The sharp change of scene from the hills to the great central vales of Radnor and Brecon is associated with comparable changes in the settlement geography. Here are the principal nucleated villages, here are the best farmlands and the principal lines of movement and trade, and here the evidences of Norman occupation are strongest. These last, however, are far from being proofs of origin and the character and growth periods of the nucleated villages require critical analysis.

In the Wye valley, and on the hills overlooking it the majority of the townships are Welsh in pattern as in name. From Rhaeadr, which was a medieval borough with a minor castle and marcher lord's demesne, Welsh settlement is continuous in the deep, winding valley and its narrow offshoots, until Builth is reached, though Newbridge on Wye, a late nucleation at the point where the drovers crossed the river, disturbs the otherwise universal dispersal. Builth, the second of the medieval boroughs on the Wye has, like Rhaeadr, survived as a small country town with its ancient markets. Around Builth, *llan* settlements are found both on the flood plain or just above it (Llanelwedd, Llanfaredd) and in side valleys or on the nearby hills (Llanddewi'r Cwm, Llandeilo Graban), and other Welsh settlements, less easily dated, are found in similar positions (Alltmawr, Aberedw, Gwenddwr, Crickadarn, Erwood, Llanstephan). This pattern of distribution continues to the English border, though the flood plain widens and the hills become lower and, as a result, changes have taken place in the settlements themselves. The three most noticeable changes down-

---

[1] E. A. Lewis and J. Conway Davies, *Records of the Court of Augmentations relating to Wales and Monmouthshire* (1954), p. 518, no. 12 (1588).

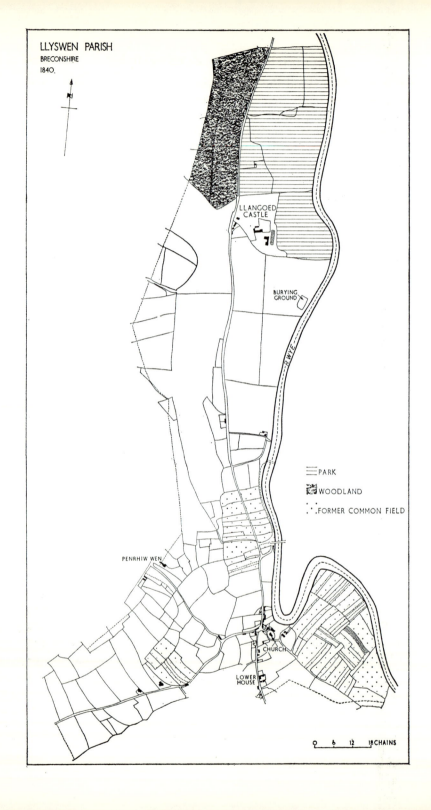

LLYSWEN PARISH
BRECONSHIRE
1840.

N

LLANGOED
CASTLE

BURYING
GROUND

R.WYE

PARK
WOODLAND
FORMER COMMON FIELD

PENRHIW WEN

CHURCH

LOWER
HOUSE

0   6   12   18 CHAINS

river are the increasing population, the existence of villages and
hamlets, and the evidence of Anglo-Norman occupation. The more
obvious examples of the last are the place-names and the remains
of mottes and castles, but there is also an increasingly English
atmosphere which it is hard to define. Castle sites and mottes
occur in and near the valley from Court Llechrhyd (Builth Road)
downwards, for example at Aberedw, Crickadarn, Boughrood,
Llyswen and Aberllynfi. Thence, they are found on each side of
the recurring river to the Herefordshire border. Rees's map of
'South Wales and the Border in the Fourteenth Century' distinguishes marcher lords' demesnes at Builth, Llanerchcoedlan
(Crickadarn) and Llangoed (Llyswen), and English knights' fees
at Pipton, Aberllynfi, Glasbury and Llanthomas. In addition,
Boughrood was the name-place of a small lordship but almost
nothing is known of the original castle or of that of Aberedw six
miles above it, but Rees shows Boughrood as having had a market
and fair in the fourteenth century. Its Welsh name is believed to
have been Bwlch rhyd.

Interest centres on the three villages of the Wye bend and the
section below it: Llyswen on the Breconshire bank, Glasbury once
on both banks of the river but now largely in Radnorshire, and
Clyro also on the left bank. *Llyswen* (VApc) believed literally to
have been the site of a 'fair palace' of a Welsh prince, became the
site of a Norman castle after the conquest. The present Llangoed
Castle, built in 1633, is in the same place and its small park and
woodlands occupy the northern end of this long, single-township
parish, in one of the most beautiful parts of the Wye valley. The
village lies nearly two miles away near a sharp U-bend in the
river which gives the township a broad section of the flood plain.
In 1840, the tithe map shows it to have been a sizeable, compact
village, as it is today, cross-road in plan, and with only half a
dozen houses outside the village and a motte to the south (Fig. 51).
The tithe map and the apportionment (1839) depict it with a
large common field on the flood plain. Forty-three separate
holdings were enumerated in the apportionment as being in 'the
common field' and the map shows many of these to have been still
unfenced at that date. Two lesser groups of strips indicate the
existence of a second and a third field, one of which was called
Maeslan cafan. Earlier documentary evidence refers to land

51 (*opposite*). Llyswen, Breconshire, in the
    Anglo-Norman settlement area of the Wye valley

measurement in both Llyswen and Llandefalle. This is in a final concord presented at the Great Sessions at Brecon in 1569 which acknowledged 5 messuages, 120 acres of land, 20 acres of meadow, 40 acres of pasture, 60 acres of wood, and 100 acres of furze and heath. The relative importance of arable land in this list suggests that the bulk of this holding was in Llyswen.[1] At the tithe survey the land use figures for the parish were arable *circa* 300 acres, meadow or pasture 530, woodland 150, and open common *circa* 1000. Its advantageous position on main roads in a rich valley and perhaps the attraction of a compact village, have resulted in a growth which is most untypical of this part of Wales. Its population almost doubled during the first half of the nineteenth century (from 137 to 225). In 1901, the population, following a small recession, again reached 226, and between 1801 and 1901 the number of houses increased from 28 to 53, effecting greater compactness in the village proper.

The largest and perhaps the most interesting of the Wye valley villages is *Glasbury* (VAplb).[2] The main centre and what appears to be the original core of the nucleation lies to the north of the river, but a considerable string of houses and St Peter's church lie on the Breconshire bank. Its Welsh name of Clas ar Wy links it with what Howse believes was the earliest of four churches, a fifth-century foundation of St Cynidr (Kenidr de Glesbiri).[3] It is thought that the *clâs* was a Celtic monastery, probably on what is now known as Ffynnon Cynydd Common. The Norman church of St Peter and a small castle were originally both on the Radnorshire bank, but the shift of the river's course during the sixteenth century left the castle on the Radnorshire bank but the church on the Breconshire side. The old church fell into ruins and the present church of St Peter which replaced it was built nearby in 1838. When Glasbury became a minor Norman lordship, it would seem that the village became a small Englishry and the northern part of what is now the parish, a Welshry.[4] The origin of the settlement would thus appear to be Celtic, and the origin of the compact

---

[1] *Quaritch Deeds*, nos 575 and 378 (1569).

[2] Dorothy Sylvester, 'Glasbury, Norton, and the Problem of the Nucleated Village in Radnorshire', *Trans. Rad. Soc.*, xxxvii (1967).

[3] W. H. Howse, 'Notes on the History of Glasbury', *Trans. Rad. Soc.*, xviii (1948), pp. 30–1.

[4] 'Map of South Wales and the Borderland in the Fourteenth Century', by William Rees.

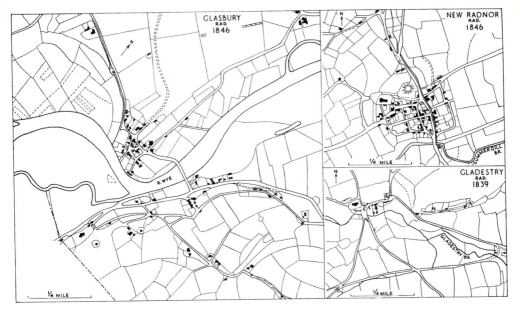

52. Glasbury, New Radnor, and Gladestry, Radnorshire

village may date from the founding of the four churches.[1] It could just possibly be Mercian, and is unlikely to be later than the Norman period though it no doubt continued to grow long after that. It was evidently a community of some size by the seventeenth century when numerous documents give the names of a series of common fields. These included an open arable field called Brodfilde mawr,[2] others called Ynys y Dommen (presumably the site of the Norman motte or tomen), Yr Erow Hir, Maes y Ddoy lwyn,[3] Maes y Pentre,[4] maes y llan issa, maes y llan ucha,[5] and maes y Gover[6] which was either in Boughrood or shared by the tenants of Boughrood. There were also doles in the common meadow as one would expect with this superb water meadowland at hand.[7] Enclosure was piecemeal, but the enclosure of the commons took place in the eighteenth century,[8] and by 1846, as the tithe map

[1] Cf. Meifod (Mont.). See pp. 448–9. [2] *Quaritch Deeds*, no. 412 (1642).
[3] Ibid. no. 182 (1644). [4] Ibid. no. 129 (1649). [5] Ibid. no. 289 (1666).
[6] Ibid. no. 268 (1670). [7] Ibid. no. 289 (1666), etc.
[8] *Tredegar Park MSS and Documents*, N.L.W. An undated eighteenth-century petition to Parliament was presented by 15 parishes in the lordship of Dinas, of which one was Glasbury, complaining on the leasing of large parts of the commons.

shows, there were only a few strips still open. There is little evidence to show the extent to which the village became anglicised. The church ceased to be a *clâs* on becoming the property of the abbey church of St Peter in Gloucester. Welsh custom is indicated by a payment in 1305 of 'iiijs.de Leirwyt' in respect of four daughters deemed incontinent,[1] and by the seventeenth century at latest almost all field-names were Welsh. It seems to have had a stormy history, its progress having been interrupted by the battle of 'Clastbirig' in 1056, by the war with Llywelyn in 1265, and by the 1403 rising of Owain Glyndwr when it was 'burnt, devastated and destroyed' by the Welsh.[2] Today, it is a quiet and beautiful village clustered along narrow lanes, and its layout and its houses look remarkably English.

In the Breconshire vales of Llynfi and Usk, many of the features which are characteristic of settlement in the Wye valley are repeated. *Llan* settlements are numerous on the hill fringes and on the lower lands, and the scatter of Norman mottes, castles, and seignorial towns and villages follows the belt of rich lowland, though thinner in the adjoining hills than in Radnorshire. Between Hay (from the Norman French name *La Haie* = the enclosure) on the Wye to Brecon on the Usk and down river to Crickhowell, were established the medieval seignorial boroughs – Brecon, Talgarth, Mara (Llangorse), Blaenllynfi and Tretower – and of these, only Hay, Talgarth, Brecon and Crickhowell have survived until today as small towns. Llangorse is a compact village, Tretower remains on the map as the name of a dispersed settlement, and Blaenllynfi is nothing more than an archaeological site. In addition, there were major castles at Bronllys, Dinas, Peytin, Llanddew and Pencelli. Bronllys is a nucleated village, Dinas a deserted ruin sharing a 1200 foot peak on the scarp edge of the Black Mountains with an Early Iron Age fort, Peytin the site of a farmhouse, Llanddew a hamlet, and Pencelli barely that. Numerous other seats of the lords marcher and many more knights' fees met similar fates, most of them mere names of no more than archaeological interest. Decline was due in part to the relative demerits of some locations, in part to the fact that the

[1] Entered in the Accounts of the Duchy of Lancaster.
[2] Valuation quoted by Mrs M. L. Dawson in 'Notes on the History of Glasbury', *Archaeol. Camb.* (1918).

centres, like the thirteenth-century markets, were too numerous for all to survive, territorial arrangements were complex, and, in a mesne lordship, the dependencies were of very unequal status, as has been illustrated in the case of Tretower, Cwmgu and Crickhowell (Chapter 7, Fig. 17).

Bronllys (VApcl) is an open, pleasant village in rolling, fertile, pastoral country in the lower Llynfi valley half a mile from the ruined tower which now represents the once strong medieval castle. In this part of Breconshire, deep, rich soils overlie Old Red Sandstone rocks and cultivation is possible up to great elevations. The area is noted for its progressive farming and its eighteenth-century associations with Howel Harris and Trefecca. Until 1860, it remained an open field parish. Minfield lay about a mile to the north of the village, Colebrook field to the north-east where Coldbrook stands today, and one or more open arable fields with the names Maes y bach, Maes Waldish, and Maes dan Derwad adjoined the village on the west. The layout and relative sizes of the three areas as shown on the tithe map of 1839 look remarkably like an original three-field system. In 1839 there were still approximately 70 separate holdings in the two northerly fields, and the lateness of their survival compares with that of the south Monmouthshire fields. A map in an *Ashburnham Estate Atlas*[1] of *circa* 1770 shows open strips and there are many English field-names. An earlier re-lease suggests a more complicated set of arrangements in fields with English and Welsh names: Muddy ffurlong, Lanffield, Maes mawre, kay dan yr hayrne, Mays bechan, Broadfield and Boundri phield.[2] An undated Survey of the Ashburnham Brecknockshire estates of the second half of the seventeenth century[3] includes a far more detailed account of the holdings in the Talgarth and Cantref Seliffe estates. Farm Vowr at that time included intermixed lands in Minsfield. John Mellor held in Maes Isa and Minsfield, and in nearby Porthamel, once a separate lordship, there was 'one field of arable land adjoining called ye 40 acres', also holdings in Red field (presumably in Talgarth) and in Thorney field (? in Porthamel) and Briery field (Talgarth). It is evident that agriculturally Porthamel and Talgarth, if not Bronllys, were interdependent.

[1] *Ashburnham Welsh Estates Muniments*, N.L.W.
[2] *Quaritch Deeds*, no. 688 (1618).   [3] No. 335.

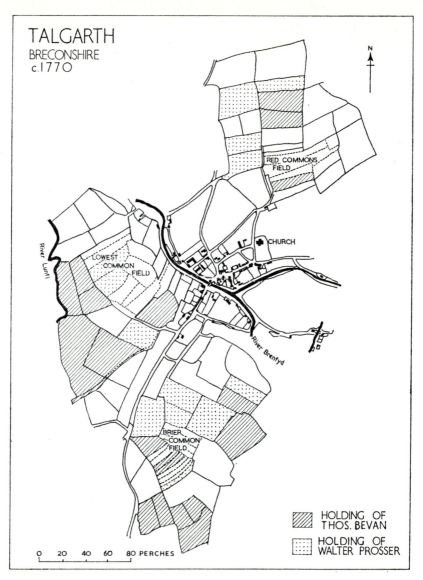

53. Talgarth, Breconshire, and its common fields, *c.* 1770

Talgarth (VUpclm) survives as a small town on the little river Enig just below the point at which it emerges from the Black Mountains. A separate mesne lordship within the marcher lordship of Blaenllynfi, it had only minor defences, but it had burghal status and a weekly market and two fairs, though Theophilus Jones described it as 'a borough by prescription, without privilege, jurisdiction or municipal officers'.[1] As a border lordship it consisted of an Englishry and a Welshry. Its church, dedicated to St Gwendolen, a descendant of Brychan, has records of incumbents from 1152 and is surmounted by an embattled tower, typical of the fortified churches of the Borderland. It is claimed that it was the royal seat of Brychan, and its position as a road centre may be responsible for its survival as a small town. There are many and valuable records, surveys, and rentals of Talgarth, and it is clear from these that it maintained an extensive open arable field system, much of the southern part of which is now covered by modern housing. It also has the distinction, as this implies, of having increased its population appreciably during and since the early nineteenth century (1801, 1059; 1871, 1408 following the extension of the Mid Wales railway; 1911, 1761; 1961, 1876). The most straightforward picture of its field arrangements is afforded by three plans in the *Ashburnham Atlas*. The first of these has been re-drawn[2] to show the holdings of Thomas Bevan and Walter Prosser at that time (*circa* 1770) in Talgarth's three common fields known as Red field, Briarfield and Lowest Common field (Fig. 53). They were fairly evenly distributed among the three fields, were intermixed, and many strips in all three fields were still unfenced. Numerous surveys, rentals[3] and field plans confirm the Talgarth triple field system, though it is also clear that there was considerable sharing between the neighbouring manors.

The broad area of fertile land in the Llynfi basin offered the best conditions for agriculture and therefore the most favourable for settlement in the pre-industrial age, and two more nucleated villages are to be found there. Of these, Llangorse is the former borough of Mara, but Llanfihangel tal y Llyn had no place in the

[1] Op. cit. p. 331.   [2] No. VI.
[3] *Ashburnham Muniments*, Survey no. 2 (1695–1708), no. 3 (N.D. mid-eighteenth century or later), no. 6 (1757), and no. 335 (N.D. latter half of seventeenth century).

seignorial scheme of things. In 1673, it had a total population of only 103.[1] The narrower valley of the Usk had very few nucleations in the mid-nineteenth century, and still has. Of these, Brecon is the chief, and recent administrative, industrial and tourist activities have brought about a modest expansion during the past quarter century. Above it, Defynog and Trecastell (the latter formerly Llywel, an outpost of Brecon borough and both minor lordships in the Middle Ages), are the sole villages, and below there is none nearer than Llangattock and Crickhowell. Crickhowell was a medieval borough with a market and fairs, and its position on the major route into southern Breconshire from Roman times onwards and behind the vital Abergavenny Gate, ensured its survival. Llangattock appears to have developed because of its adjacency to Crickhowell, and because of the Llangattwg Park estate.

The Radnorshire Borderland

This small but interesting area is a stretch of broken hill country covered by something over a dozen parishes. Its significance in the geography of settlement stems from its being the only part of the two counties in which Mercian influence can have been to any degree effective. It has had, as a result, like the neighbouring English areas, a full succession of Celtic, Mercian and Anglo-Norman settlers and the similarity to the nearby border district of Herefordshire is marked. The drainage is predominantly eastward from the slopes of Colwyn and Radnor Forests and habitation is mainly concentrated in the valleys. It is basically an area of dispersed dwellings in the Welsh tradition, but there are a number of hamlets – Norton, Whitton (both parochial), Evenjobb, Kinnerton and Walton (this last very minor) – and one nucleated village, Gladestry. In addition, there are three ancient boroughs. Of these, Presteigne and Knighton are still small towns, but New Radnor has declined to village status. The place-names are a

[1] As shown in App. 1 in Theophilus Jones, *History of the County of Brecknock*. The table records the population of most places in the county according to the Returns made by a Commission of the Archbishop of Canterbury in that year. Many of the figures are difficult to credit.

mixture of Welsh and English. By no means all the English names are associated with nucleations, though it is noticeable that each nucleated village has an English name, or includes an Anglo-Saxon place-name element. Offa's Dyke traverses the hills from Knighton southward before turning east across Rushock Hill north of Knighton, and it is clear that it merely indicates one stage in the Mercian advance and retreat along the Welsh border, and that the entire area was at some time subject to Mercian penetration. A number of the places are recorded in the Domesday Survey, for example, Cascob, Burlingjobb, Discoed, Knighton and Norton. Norman control of the area was strengthened by a large number of mottes which are liberally scattered over the whole of this border country.

Norton (Hv Bpb) with its Anglo-Saxon name and Norman motte and bailey is a nucleated hamlet east of Offa's Dyke in a narrow valley.[1] Norton Manor provides an important estate element and its court rolls have been discussed by W. H. Howse.[2] In a 1680 entry there is reference in a surrender to common meadow strips and to arable holdings in Chesell field, Crawlings field, Lower field, Longland field and Brook furlong field. The tithe map (N.D.) showed Colebrook meadow along the Lugg, and a series of open arable fields adjoining the village with the names Chissell field, Minn field, Longlands, Furlongs and Longfield. The whole pattern of this township is similar to that of the lesser nucleations of north-west Herefordshire.

Gladestry (Hv Ap) is a small, roughly nucleated and remote village of a type reminiscent of the Clun area, and situated in a small valley with poor access roads (Fig. 52). Its earlier Welsh name was Llanfair Llethonw, and its three other townships retain their Welsh names of Wainwen, Hencoed and Gwithel. Each is a small, dispersed township of Welsh type. The Anglo-Norman element is represented by Gladestry Court, originally fortified, and together with Colva, Gladestry was formerly a bailiwick under the paramount manor or lordship of Cantref Maelienydd. Its courts leet and baron were still held at the beginning of the nineteenth century. In a Parliamentary Survey of 1649 there is mention of a water corn grist mill and of arable land at Colva

---

[1] Dorothy Sylvester, *Trans. Rad. Soc.*, loc. cit.
[2] 'Court Rolls of the Manor of Norton', *Trans. Rad. Soc.*, xiv (1944), p. 47.

but not at Gladestry,[1] and there are no reliable indications of open arable on the tithe map of 1839.

South of Norton, unity was given to this border district in the Middle Ages by its inclusion in the lordship of Radnor, in which the principal settlement was the *caput*, New Radnor. Its core was the triangular plain with New Radnor, Kinnerton and Womaston at its apices and hill lands to west and south. *Old Radnor* (Lh Dpb) centres on an all but solitary hill-top church. Its Welsh names were Maesyfed Hên and Pen y Craig, the latter clearly referring to the site of the church which surmounts an impressively precipitous slope. Much is claimed for it; it has tumuli, possible Roman connections and two castle sites or mottes. Yet today its glory is past, and except for its fine church, it is a dispersed farming township of no particular note.

The place which took its name and is known as *New Radnor* (JUp(c)(m)l) stands under a shoulder of Radnor Forest where Summergill brook leaves the hills (Fig. 52). The ancient town, its burghal status lost, its former functions decayed, is now a large village but every inch of it reflects its origin and history. The settlement is on low ground, but the site of the castle is a massive hill-top immediately behind it (Plate XVII). It was a walled town of Norman origin, admirably placed for strategic purposes for it controlled the difficult but important pass between Colwyn and Radnor Forests on the one side, and a major route from Leominster on the other. As a borough and the head of a marcher lordship, it had a weekly market and two annual fairs. Under the 1562 Charter of Incorporation it had a recorder, coroner, receiver, sergeants-at-mace, and a corporation of 25 capital burgesses, and governed an area approximately ten miles by seven corresponding broadly with the old lordship of Radnor except for the exclusion of Gladestry. Speed's plan[2] shows it as a grid-plan town within roughly square walls, three main west-east streets crossing four north–south. A plan of 1800[3] depicts it as little altered, and the modern aerial photograph displays only relatively minor changes.[4] As early as 1482, Presteigne became a serious rival.

[1] D. Stedman Davies, 'The Parliamentary Surveys of the Manors of Radnorshire in 1649', *Trans. Rad. Soc.*, ix (1941), pp. 47–8.

[2] *Theatre of the Empire of Great Britain* (1611).

[3] Jonathon Williams, *A General History of the County of Radnor* (1905), plan opp. p. 188.

[4] M. W. Beresford and M. K. S. St Joseph, *Medieval England* (1958), p. 210.

Leland described the castle as partly in ruins, and the destruction was completed during the civil wars. The town from which the county took its name, it remained the county town until many of its functions were increasingly taken over by Presteigne and in 1884 Llandrindod Wells became the county town. It had a town hall and a gaol (closed in 1861), remained a borough until 1883, and sent a member to Westminster until 1884. Its market had already failed by 1778, Kington seizing and keeping its former trade. So another village was made from yet another Anglo-Norman borough.[1]

[1] As well as from Williams's account, some of the material for this description of New Radnor has been taken from W. H. Howse, 'New Radnor', *Trans. Rad. Soc.*, xviii (1948) and 'New Radnor Castle', ibid. xxviii (1958).

Note. Throughout this chapter use has been made of the information incorporated in William Rees's *Map of South Wales and the Border in the Fourteenth Century*.

18 Eastern Montgomeryshire

'Powys paradwys Cymry', ed. Owen Jones, *The Myvyrian Archaiology of Wales* (1870), I, p. 114

POWYS WENWYNWYN, of which the modern representative is Montgomeryshire, stretched across the entire width of Central Wales from the middle Severn to the mouth of the Dyfi, and with its western *cantrefi* of Arwystli and Cyfeiliog, border influence had no concern. Its eastern divisions were variously affected, especially Deuddwr, Gorddwr, Swydd Stradmarchell and Swydd Llanerchudol which lay on either side of the Severn in the Vale of Welshpool. In the hills farther west (i.e. in middle Montgomeryshire), Mochnant, Mechain, Caereinion and Cydewain were part of a belt in which border evidences were sometimes clear, sometimes faint, and it is in this belt that, as in mid-Radnorshire and mid-Breconshire, Welsh patterns gradually begin to predominate and English to disappear as one travels westward.

Except for the Dyfi, all the main streams of Montgomeryshire flow east toward the master stream of the Severn. In the west, the wild, majestic heights of Arwystli and Cyfeiliog dominate and make barren a high proportion of the land. In the middle belt, these mountains give place to gentler pastoral uplands broken by deep but not wholly infertile valleys, eventually breaking down into the low but distinctive hills of the east and the broad vales of Tanat, Cain, Vyrnwy and Severn. The flat bottomed Vale of Welshpool between Garthmyl and Llandrinio is one of the most favoured vales of the Borderland, yet for centuries it was a battleground between the British and the Mercians, and later between Welsh and Norman.

From the point of view of the student of rural settlement there is much that is similar in the uplands of Radnorshire and

Montgomeryshire as a physical setting. In both, the upper Ordovician and the Wenlock and Ludlow beds of the Silurian form the lithological basis of gently folded and glacially smoothed uplands, but in Montgomeryshire the elevation of the middle belt is less, ranging up to 1500 feet, and with an appreciably higher proportion of the surface below 1000 feet, so giving a wider theatre for human occupation, and resulting in somewhat higher population densities. The most significant difference between this and the area farther south, is that of layout. While in Breconshire and Radnorshire the eastern margin is hill country with the major valleys pointing westward into the hills from only narrow gateways, in Montgomeryshire the eastern margin is itself a broad complex of riverine lowland except only for the six to eight mile long ridge of the Long Mountain and the sharp intrusive triple peaks of the Breidden. Strategically, this is a region of self-evident weakness, and, far from offering protection, the Long Mountain is of value rather as a look-out than as a defence. The ends of the short ridge are easily turned either by Deuddwr or the Montgomery Gate, and it is not therefore surprising that throughout the Middle Ages the Severn itself was the boundary between Shropshire and Powys. What is, perhaps, more remarkable is that, after its initial swift conquest by Roger de Montgomery, Powys regained and, for the greater part of the marcher period, kept its independence, at least nominally, from the end of the eleventh century.

Early Iron Age hill forts are distributed with marked liberality over the hill-tops and hillsides of Mochnant, Mechain, Caereinion, and Cydewain, i.e. in the belt west of the Severn and between the Tanat and Newtown. A general distribution map shows them to be part of an area of comparative density extending eastward across south Shropshire. Neither to north nor to south in an area of comparable size was there anything approaching the number of hill forts that were to be found here, the second important concentration (including south Shropshire) in Wales and the Borderland, the Pembrokeshire peninsula being the first. It would seem, therefore, that already this part of Powys was earning its later title of 'Powys paradwys Cymry'. Its acceptability for human habitation was further underlined when, following the downhill movement of population in the Roman and sub-Roman periods, it proved the most popular part of Powys Wenwynwyn for the founding of Celtic churches, but the predilection of the Celtic saints for these hills and valleys bore no comparison with their evident preference for northern, western, and southern parts of the country of comparable altitude – or has the erosion of original Celtic dedications in this border district undermined the value of their distribution as a reliable guide?[1] In fact, in the early nineteenth century, 31 of the 52 known dedications of Montgomeryshire parishes were Celtic, 21 dedications from the Roman Calendar. Of the 23 *llan* parishes, 19 had retained their Celtic dedications.

Mercian and Anglo-Norman advances gave rise to a belt of non-Welsh place-names across the Long Mountain and the Vale of Welshpool, but the names die out sharply at the western edge of the Vale, hardly any English place-names being found in the hills and those for the most part minor and modern. Even in the Vale, however, there are an appreciable number of Welsh place-names, especially on the left bank of the Severn, and some survive on Long Mountain.

After the Norman Conquest and Montgomery's brief initial occupation of the hill country beyond the Severn, the river remained a fairly permanent boundary until Union, and no marcher lordship was established beyond it. The great lordship of Caus occupied most of what is now the Shropshire–Montgomeryshire border. The lordship of Montgomery covered the gap to the south, and beyond this, where the valley of the Severn narrows markedly upstream, it flowed almost wholly in Welsh territory, the lordship of Maelienydd lying south of the river by a mile or so. In sharp contrast with the border areas both to south and north, Montgomeryshire included only one Anglo-Norman borough, Montgomery itself. By the time of the Union, there were numerous Anglo-Welsh families, and the relations of Powys and the English realm, though fluctuating, were generally friendly. Territorial conquest shifted to and fro across the Severn. For the greater part of the marcher period Powys retained its independence or came under the overlordship of Gwynedd, but during the brief periods of Anglo-Norman supremacy some of the Montgomeryshire

[1] E. G. Bowen, *The Settlements of the Celtic Saints in Wales*, fn. on p. 104, map on p. 105.

mottes were raised. In the *Inventory of Ancient Monuments* for Montgomeryshire, the writers insist that although some of the mottes were Norman, many were Welsh or Anglo-Welsh and were simply built to control the estates of the Welsh lords. Their general conclusion on this matter is that 'The governing chieftains of Powys were more amenable to Norman influence than those of other divisions of Wales, and the study of mound castles corroborates the conclusions of history'.[1] The Anglo-Normans influenced castle building but, except for that of Montgomery, the major castles of the county were the seats of Welsh chieftains. Powys Castle, for example was Castell Coch ym Mhowys, the original fortress having been built by Cadogan ap Bleddyn in 1109, and Castell Caereinion, first mentioned at that date, was built by Iorwerth ap Bleddyn.

The map of English place-name distribution in Montgomeryshire marks out a strongly anglicised strip of country mainly between the eastern county boundary and the Severn. It has its parallel in eastern Radnorshire, but the density of English names in Montgomeryshire is incomparably greater and the nature of the physical features entirely different. Beyond the Severn, Welsh names occur almost without a break, and the overall Welshness of the hill country and the vales which pierce it is not in doubt. But no such simple division can be detected in other elements of rural settlement which have elsewhere been considered of importance. There is no belt of nucleated settlements in the east of Montgomeryshire such as exists in the Anglo-Norman parts of Monmouthshire, Breconshire and Radnorshire. The parish structure corresponds throughout, with only five exceptions in the early nineteenth century, with the multi-township pattern of the northern Borderland. Only in the distribution of common field patterns is there any parallel to the belt of English place-names, but these on present information give denser distributions west of the Severn than to the east, and Welsh forms spread across the middle belt of the county. The major nucleations are related to locations of maximum advantage for trade and exchange and

[1] Royal Commission on Ancient and Historical Monuments and Constructions in Wales and Monmouthshire, *An Inventory of the Ancient Monuments in Wales and Monmouthshire, I, County of Montgomery* (1911), p. xix. The map in this volume which shows their distribution is significantly entitled 'Norman-Welsh Castle Mounts'.

many are undoubtedly medieval or later growth points, such as market centres which flourished notably after Union. The parish structure links Montgomeryshire, as does all its early history, with a Powysian kingdom which embraced all north-east Wales, central Wales, and much of Cheshire and Shropshire. As regards the open field patterns, we can only presume extensive hybridisation as a result of the wide diffusion and ready acceptance of English ideas, but whether of Mercian or medieval date is less readily determined.

During its later history, eastern Montgomeryshire continued to show a convergence of Welsh and English features. Many of the manorial families had a mixed inheritance and the social distinctions found in other parts of the Principality were here faint or absent. Every advantage was taken of advances in agricultural economy. Estate management was ahead of that in many upland areas, and the compacting of holdings went rapidly forward. House building in the Tudor period was vigorous, and to this day the manor houses and the larger farmhouses are characteristically Tudor – half-timbered or stone – or date from the late enclosure period. During the late eighteenth and the nineteenth centuries, enclosure of the waste was carried on over most of the middle and eastern belts, and the land which was once the haunt of wild creatures was converted into rich pastoral farmland. Slowly, the disparate holdings of the common fields were also brought into the compacted farmlands, but relics of open strips lingered until comparatively late dates as they did in Monmouthshire.

The Uplands and Vales of Central Montgomeryshire

To the south-east and east of the Berwyns and the mountainous country of western Montgomeryshire, a line of small settlements marks the beginning of the 'middle country'. The line can be traced through Llanrhaeadr-ym-Mochnant, Llanfihangel-yng-Ngwynfa, Llanerfyl, Llanllugan and Aberhafesp. This broken plateau averages 800 to 1000 feet at summit level and, since the enclosure period, comparatively little remains as rough grazing. Most of it bears thin soil suitable for *agrostis* pasture or, at lower levels and on the richer drift soils of the lower slopes, *lolium-agrostis*. In the valleys, deeper drift soils predominate and towards the east, the proportion of arable land rises though nowhere is it of more than local importance in farming.

The Tanat, the Vyrnwy and its tributary the Cain drain the greater part of the northern and middle portion of these uplands, and the Rhiw most of the southern part, only minor streams running south to the Severn between Aberhafesp and Abermule. The small dispersed townships of this middle country are characterised by farmhouses and cottages perched well up on the slopes of the valley rather than in the valley bottoms, with a thinner scatter of hill farms between the vales. Llanrhaeadr, Llanfyllin, Meifod and Llanfair Caereinion occupy streamside sites and are the only nucleated settlements in the area. Llanrhaeadr, partly in Denbighshire, arose as a small market centre. Llanfyllin has had municipal privileges from the thirteenth century. Llanfair Caereinion grew as an unchartered market, and Meifod alone of all these owed its size not to trade, but to its early importance as the ecclesiastical capital of Powys Wenwynwyn. This middle hill country is the area which the dwellers in the hill forts found most desirable, and there is a broad and perhaps not accidental coincidence with the distributional field of the Anglo-Welsh mottes of Montgomeryshire's upland country. Primarily and predominantly Welsh, it has nevertheless admitted English, and especially Anglo-Norman influences particularly via the major valleys.

Its relief makes possible a certain grading of settlement features from the (now rarer) hill farms based on upland sheepwalks, through the thinly populated dispersed communities in the higher parts of the inhabited hills, to the lesser and then the larger valley townships. Dispersal is almost total and although the old *tref* or township boundaries encircled communities based on well established blood ties, many had little relationship to geographical realities. As a result there was here, as in much of upland Wales, a degree of fluidity both in their area and in the parishes to which they adhered, many townships being divided between two parishes, others coalescing as it became convenient. There is a broad similarity between upland townships in particular and the features of one are characteristic of a widespread number of such communities and their land use patterns, field-names and tenurial arrangements.

Although they are mainly in the higher mountains, some of the extremely interesting maps of sheepwalks in the *Glansevern Collection* (N.L.W.) serve to illustrate the pattern of the predominantly open waste prior to enclosure. A typical example is the plan of Rhiwlas.[1] This pattern still prevails in the higher hills, not only of Montgomeryshire, but of most of the inhabited mountain land above 1000 feet in Wales.

Llwydiarth (HD/E) is a hill township situated at a height of between 700 and 900 feet immediately adjoining Nant Llwydiarth, whose waters join those of the upper Vyrnwy. It is a township of the parish of Llanfihangel-yng-Ngwynfa and consists of a group of farms and the estate of Llwydiarth Hall, once the seat of the powerful Vaughans. Such an estate element is not typical, neither is it exceptional. An 1817 plan is one in a volume of surveys and illustrates a township made up of different sized farms based on dispersed dwellings. The township in 1817 was divided between twenty-two separate holdings of which ten were the principal farms, some cottagers', and some were fields belonging to tenants in other townships. The farms were for the most part compact and varied from 154 acres (Bryn Glas) downwards. Llwydiarth Hall farm extended over 639 acres. At this date there was little to remind one of formal communal ploughing arrangements, but names such as Cefn Cannol and two field-names Hir dir survived as did cefn ddol and two 'parts of ddol'. Practically all the field-names were Welsh.[2]

Llanerfyl (Hv Cp) in the Banwy valley is a spreading parish of six townships, some in the valley, some in the hills. In Cefnllys Issa the hills rise to over 1300 feet, and this is near the westward limit of the Early Iron Age hill forts and the Anglo-Welsh mottes. There are both within the parish. The two hill forts lie on hillsides a mile to the north and two to three miles to the southwest of the tiny central settlement of Llanerfyl, and the Llyssin

---

[1] See, Ch. 10, p. 247, and Fig. 33.
[2] *Wynnstay Miscellaneous Volumes*, 8, *A Survey and Particulars of Estates in the Parish of Llanfihangel, county of Montgomery, belonging to Sir William Watkin Wynn, Bart.* (N.L.W.), map of Llwydiarth township. A detailed analysis of *Llanfihangel yng Gwynfa parish* especially from the sociological angle was made by Alwyn D. Rees in *Life in a Welsh Countryside* (1950).

motte and bailey (near to Llanerfyl in the township of Llyssin), which, according to the *Inventory of Ancient Monuments for Montgomeryshire* is twelfth-century, is on ground which was unquestionably Welsh at that time. Llyssin was once the residence of the Herberts of Chirbury.[1] The parish church is dedicated to a sixth-century Breton saint, St Erfyl.[2] According to returns made in 1868–74 there still remained 1675 acres of common field land in the parish at that date,[3] and although the tithe map shows no open strips the tithe apportionment (1849) offers firm evidence of such fields in names like Lawnt Farm, Maes Gelynog Farm, Open field under house (Coed Talog township), Cefn faes, quillet in Cefn faes, etc. (Crane, the parochial township), while in Cefn Llys Issa in addition to Cefn Faes there were six separately named quillets in Rhos y Drinki, one in Rhos Nessa, one in Rhos fawr, a quillet in part of yr Hendre meadow, a dryll bach, and open strips on a turbary which was apparently shared by several townships. These names clearly indicate common arable and meadow strips, possibly strips on the open waste (cf. Garthbeibio tithe map, 1841), and strips still open on the common peat moss. There is nothing to suggest that they were used on an English system, nor is there anything to rule out English influence.

Some five miles farther downstream in a narrower part of the Banwy valley, *Llanfair Caereinion* (Hv Apm) is located at the junction of five roads. There is a Roman fort a mile to the south, and Owen suggests that the St Tysilio church at Llanoddian (now vanished) preceded the St Mary church which was probably a twelfth-century foundation. But Llanfair's modest growth seems to relate to more modern factors. A local flannel industry and the nodal position of the place combined by the early eighteenth century to give rise to an unchartered market despite the fact that it was not one of the early chartered boroughs. The market grew under the protection of the Herberts and because of the demand of local farmers and traders, so that by 1708–18 according to the municipal records 'ye weekly market or unlawful assembly on every Saturday in ye yeare held at Llanvaire contrary to ye known established laws of this Realm' had become an institution.[4]

[1] Op. cit. pp. 78–9.
[2] Robert Owen, *In the Heart of Powysland* (1930), ch. viii.
[3] Quoted in *Mont. Coll.*, xii, p. 289.   [4] Owen, op. cit. ch. vi.

In the early nineteenth century Llanfair had fifteen townships, a number only equalled by Berriew and exceeded by Kerry (which had nineteen). Settlement and field patterns are typical of the middle country except for the central nucleation. The rest of the parish is a dispersed habitation area and the tithe map offers considerable suggestions of open field strips of the scattered Welsh type.

Three miles to the north and near the junction of the Banwy and the Vyrnwy in one of the fairest vales and on one of the most impressive sites in Wales stood the now deserted site of the ancient *Mathrafal*. Four hill forts overlook it, and it commands a wide prospect of the most fertile vale land in Montgomeryshire save only for the Severn valley, and lies where the waters of three rivers meet. Yet today, only a mound marks the site of its castle, and this seat of the Welsh princes of Powys Wenwynwyn is on the way to being further destroyed by the ravages of river erosion.

Rees shows four *clas* churches in Montgomeryshire: Llandinam, Llangurig, Meifod and a minor one at Llanrhaeadr.[1] Of these, *Meifod* (VApb(m)) appears to have been the most important (Fig. 54). It is termed by Owen 'the old ecclesiastical capital of Powysland' and is deemed the burial place of many of its princes. In the part of the Vyrnwy known as Dyffryn Meifod, St Tysilio is said to have established a school.[2] Two churches on the site of the present one, that of Tysilio and the church of St Mary founded about 1137 by Madoc, prince of Powys, gave the combined dedication to the existing parish church. A third, Eglwys Gwyddvarch, disappeared in Tudor times but its floor was found under that of the present Congregational church which is built near the north-western corner of the churchyard which was once of vast extent.[3] Surrounded by hill forts, there seems little question that Meifod arose as a place of significance in the time of the early Celtic church, while the motte and bailey out of sight in a concealed valley and ploughed down for centuries[4] seems to have little relevance. In 1817, Meifod's plan was still that of a semi-circle to the north of the churchyard.[5] By 1847 (Fig. 54) it had extended in straighter lines to east and west, and the present village, pleasant

[1] *Historical Atlas of Wales*, plate 27.
[2] Owen, op. cit. ch. 6.
[3] *Inventory of Ancient Monuments for Montgomeryshire*, pp. 148–50.
[4] Ibid. p. 148.   [5] *Wynnstay Misc. Vols*, 6, plan of Meifod village, 1817.

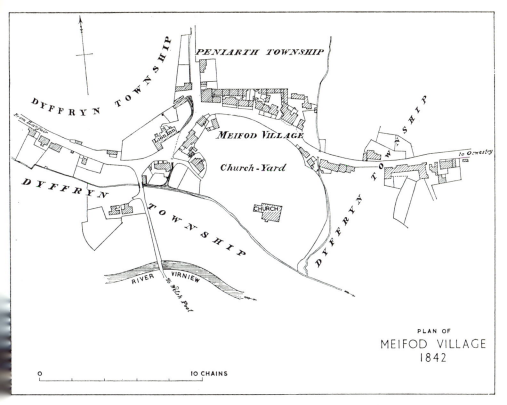

PLAN OF
MEIFOD VILLAGE
1842

54. Meifod village, Montgomeryshire, at the time of the tithe survey, 1842

though in a mixture of styles and periods, is an extension of this plan.[1] It is said at one time to have had a market, but this has died out and a few local shops have replaced it and at the same time converted it into a local service centre. Apart from the village of Meifod at the extremity of Peniarth township, its remaining ten townships were all dispersed.

The case of *Llanfyllin* (VUp(m)b) is different from any of the succession of settlements just examined in the Vyrnwy–Banwy basin. Its growth began, no doubt, like many of the others', as a parochial centre within a hill fort region but about 1290 Owain Cyfeiliog's grandson is said to have given the place its first

[1] For a description of Peniarth township see Ch. 10, pp. 245–7 and Fig. 32.

charter.[1] Other charters followed from the *Inspeximus Charter* of 6 Eliz. I to that of 29 Geo. III in which it was stated that, the market house being ruinous, it was taken down in 1775. In Elizabeth I's time, this free borough had numerous burghal rights including housebote and haybote in the common woods, and common of pasture in all common grounds of Mechain Uwchcoed. It also had a guild[2] and no doubt this and its market accounted for the growth of this small market-town in the narrow valley of the river Cain.

The Hill Margins

The Montgomeryshire plateau meets the Vale of Welshpool in a steep and almost unbroken slope, albeit of only moderate altitude. It affords little opportunity for settlement apart from the hillside farmhouses and cottages at moderate intervals, so characteristic of Montgomeryshire valley sides. But at two places this wall is breached by streams and the advantages that the two offer have been made use of by Berriew at the entrance to the narrow valley of the Rhiw (Berriew = Aber Rhiw) and by Guilsfield (the Welsh Cegidfa) two or three miles back from the hill edge in the comparatively wide vale of Guilsfield brook. Both belong to the hills rather than to the Vale of Welshpool but are sufficiently near to the Vale to have been well within the sphere of English influences from the Mercian period. Both are nucleated villages. Both are at the centre of multi-township parishes, Berriew having fifteen townships, Guilsfield eleven. In all the dependent townships there is dispersed settlement, and the field-names and patterns are closely comparable with those of other dependent townships in the plateau country of middle Montgomeryshire, except in those townships of Berriew which are partly or wholly in the Vale of Welshpool.

On the tithe map of the three townships of *Gungrog Fechan*, *Trelydan* and *Garth* in Guilsfield in low hill country to the south of the village and adjoining Welshpool, there are numerous evidences

---

[1] Owen, op. cit. ch. VIII.
[2] Robert Williams, 'History of the parish of Llanfyllin', *Mont. Coll.*, III (1870), 91–108.

of former open arable of the Welsh type – fields named maes in which were several strips, and portions of meadow indicating former sharing. There were, however, a very considerable number of English field-names including Common field and Headland field in the 1840 apportionment lists. The 1845 tithe map of Llan (the parochial township), Hendrehen and Trawscoed, covers the inner hills west of Guilsfield valley. There was considerable woodland in the last two of these townships, Welsh field-names were proportionately more numerous, but the evidences of open arable were thin except for two fields called 'part of Maes y Llan' and another named Maes y Garreg. *Guilsfield* (VAp) is a sizeable nucleated village of open plan, swollen in the eighteenth century by a flannel factory and by trade brought by river and a branch of the Shropshire Union Canal.

Berriew (Hv JAbp) is at the junction of the hills and the Vale, an attractive 'hidden' village built in stone and half-timber. There is an abundance of evidence about its field plan in the *Glansevern* and the *Powis Collections* (N.L.W.). The most useful map is a fragmentary plan, undated, and with many erasures and much overwriting, inaccurately surveyed and far from easy to decipher, but it shows beyond any manner of doubt three, and possibly five, open fields. Three of these are named on the map, which is pre-1748; they are Upper Berriew field, Lower Berriew field and Maes y Cenfes (presumably the field which in nineteenth-century documents was called Maes y henfes). Two further areas on either side of a road may have been open field land, but there is a strong suggestion of there having been a three-field system here at some date. Enclosure had as yet only nibbled the fields. For the most part the strips still lay open and adjacent, and intermixed ownership was widespread over the entire area.[1] Although documentary evidence is sparse, there is no doubt that English tenurial systems had affected Berriew township, and the same is true, though on a lesser scale, of some of the Berriew townships which ran down to the Severn, notably Trustywelyn for which a pair of maps, pre- and post-enclosure was made by the Enclosure Commissioners in 1799 (Fig. 55) and 1800. Many of the open

[1] The map was photographed for publication in the present writer's paper 'The Rural Landscape of Eastern Montgomeryshire', *Mont. Coll.*, liv (1955), opp. p. 18.

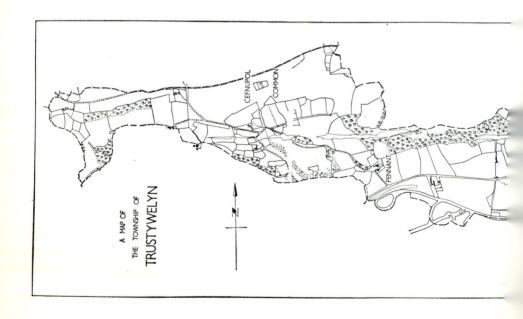

A MAP OF
THE TOWNSHIP OF
TRUSTYWELYN

CEFNUPOL
COMMON

PENNANT

N

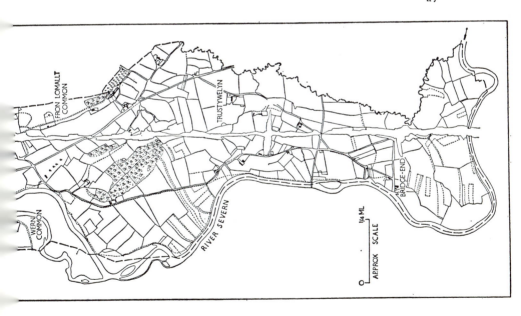

FRON LOMALLT COMMON

WERN COMMON

TRUSTYWELYN

RIVER SEVERN

BRIDGE-END

APPROX SCALE

0   ¼ ML

55. Trustywelyn, Montgomeryshire, 1799 (pre-enclosure)

fields in the flood plain must have been convertible to arable or pasture according to the weather and the height of the river.[1]

Deuddwr and the Vale of Welshpool

The Vale of Welshpool and Deuddwr, where the waters of the Severn and the Vyrnwy share a confluential plain, is the richest land in the entire county. Its meadows spread like a green carpet between the hills of the plateau to the west and Long Mountain and the Breidden to the east, and constitute some of the finest grazing in the Borderland. Here, if anywhere, is a true border zone. For centuries Shropshire was included in the Welsh kingdom of Powys; for still more, the Severn was the boundary line between England and Wales, shifting eastward only in 1536. The settlement features reflect this in the number of defensive works, but they show it too in the mingling of Welsh and English characteristics. Here are no nucleated villages with the single exception of the boundary village of Llanymynech, partly in Shropshire, which grew near its great quarries and around its one-time market. The dispersal pattern is almost universal. In terms of place-names, however, this is the heart of the belt in which English names are densely distributed, and the map of open field shows a comparable massing of symbols. This is genuine hybridisation.

The Inclosure Act for the manor of Tiertref (pre-1801) referred to 'certain open and common fields, commonable and waste grounds' totalling about 1200 acres, in the hamlets of Cofronydd, Gungrog Fawr, Trewern and Cletterwood.[2] Using the tithe map of 1845 and earlier evidence, E. G. Bowen pointed out in the early 1930s the significance of the open field arrangements in Trehelig, a small township on the flood plain of the Severn between Berriew and Welshpool.[3] A great wealth of material, especially in the form of estate plans, has now become available for this area and it shows that larger open fields and common meadows of the English rather than the Welsh type, though by no means comparable with the large, regular fields of the Midlands, were

[1] Ibid. p. 16.   [2] *Mont. Coll.*, XII, p. 272.
[3] 'A Map of the Trehelig Common Fields', *Mont. Coll.*, XLI–XLII, pp. 163–7.

widespread in eastern Montgomeryshire and especially in the
broad vales which were the most suitable land for ploughing.
As far up the Vyrnwy as Llansantffraid, Thomas Griffiths Jones
wrote that 'the hills (are) easy of cultivation and produce wheat
and barley that cannot be excelled, and in the lowland, pasture
of the best quality is found . . . the meadows have yielded two
crops of hay, and very good aftermath in addition'.[1] For one of
its townships, Melyniog Vechan, a series of deeds dated from
1588–1703/4 sketch an open field township with at least two open
arable fields in full use until the seventeenth century when, from
1613/4, they began to break up.[2] There was also common meadow
as in the vale townships of Berriew. An undated map, probably
late eighteenth century, in the *Glansevern Collection* shows unfenced
riverside meadow doles in intermixed tenancies in Garthmill and
Vaynor Issa, and a large piece of floodland to the north labelled
common and without any indication of division.[3] One strip of
arable is also shown as still open and is named 'one furlong in
Efal fach'. Similar evidence could be repeated many times both
for open arable and common meadow land, much of it no doubt
convertible in these particular physical conditions.[4]

The resulting settlement pattern in the Vale and Deuddwr is a
series of small dispersed townships, occasional tiny hamlets (some
of modern road, rail, and canalside growth), based on the flat
lands which formerly included what, for Wales, were quite sizeable open fields and series of meadow doles by the rivers. As
enclosure got under way in the late eighteenth and early nineteenth century, and in some cases well before that, compacting
took place, but disparate holdings were numerous still in the early
and middle nineteenth century, as in the case of two farms in
Allt Ucha (Berriew). A plan of *circa* 1800–14 delineated Cefn yr
Allt farm as largely compacted but with some open strips among
its fields and two outlying pieces of land. Cappel farm, adjoining
it on the south had a high proportion of its land still in the form

[1] 'History of the Parish of Llansantffraid ym Mechain', *Mont. Coll.*, IV (1871), p. 79.
[2] *Coleman Deeds* (N.L.W.), nos 477 (1594), 487 (1597), 489 (1608/9), 501 (1628),
547 (1613/4), 554 (1624) referring to 6 acres in an open field called Kae Ievan
chwith 'now divided by a hedge', 588 (1653/4), 621 (1610/11), and 677 (1703/4).
[3] Map no. PA 7427, with schedule. A comparable plan of Llivior is no. 8 in the
same Collection.
[4] See Ch. 10 and Dorothy Sylvester, *Mont. Coll.*, LIV, pp. 13–17.

of open strips with a resultant set of awkward boundaries and a detached close.[1] Examples could be repeated many times.

Llandysilio (VD/Bp) is a typical example of a parochial township in this part of Montgomeryshire. With a St Tysilio church of Celtic foundation, it lies across the line of Offa's Dyke, and was dispersed until the growth of Four Crosses, a cross-road hamlet of the turnpike period and later. On the hill to the west is Bryn Mawr hill fort, but most of its land lies between the Vyrnwy and the Severn on low ground. In 1759, a survey of Wttra-glas in this parish included a plan of this disparate estate, made up of a few compact fields and a number of detached strips: portions of Upper Field, Llanismaes (two), and of Great Meadow.[2]

Llandrinio (VD(m)p) also in Deuddwr is remarkably similar with a hill-fort, a St Trinio church which it is claimed contains relics of the 'early Welsh-Mercian period',[3] a location immediately east of Offa's Dyke, and a motte and bailey. It lacks a hamlet, but a 1309 charter granted by Edward II gave it the right to hold a weekly market and two annual fairs.[4] Whether this was ever associated with a settlement of any size is not clear, but if so, it has vanished completely. Its open fields and common meadows are documented in the *Barnard Collection*.[5]

The only nucleated settlement of any size in the Vale is *Welshpool* (VUmpcb) a chartered borough from 1263. According to Owen, it arose on the site of Pwll y Lleden, an undrained backwater of the Severn, and so became Y Pwll, Pool, La Pola, or Pola. The nucleus of the old Welsh town was the church of St Llewelyn, which had disappeared by the mid-eighteenth century. On its southern margins, Powis Castle replaces the original Welsh fortress of Castell Coch ym Mhowys, built in the early twelfth century by Cadogan ap Bleddyn. Near to the eastern edge of the town is a motte and bailey, and there are two others in the great park of Powis castle, probably all Welsh or Anglo-Welsh, rather than Norman. It was also an assize town and today is the chief

---

[1] *Glansevern Collection.*

[2] N.L.W. MS. Maps, vol. 12, *Survey of several Estates in Montgomeryshire and Shropshire now in the possession of the Revd. D. James Halifax.*

[3] *Inventory of Ancient Monuments*, p. 74.

[4] *Mont. Coll.*, XXVIII (1895). *Archaeol. Camb.*, 5th series, II (1885).

[5] (Shropshire Record Office), John Rocque's Survey of the Manor of Deythur situated in the county of Montgomery, 1747. This survey lists field-names in some 13 Deuddwr townships, and almost all are open field or common meadow names.

county administrative centre but is not officially the county town. Like other medieval boroughs, this Welsh town had its communal lands, and the tithe map of Welshpool and those of its dependent townships with land in the Vale give ample evidence in retrospect of the once extensive common fields and meadows. There is reason to suspect however that Welshpool itself had a multiplicity of small Welsh fields rather than an English open arable system, though there was at least one fair-sized field near the river in 1663.[1]

The Montgomery Gate and the Eastern Hills

The last and most easterly belt of Montgomeryshire extends from the Breidden in the north across the Middleton Gap and southward to include the greater part of the Long Mountain and all its western slopes. South of that it embraces the western part of the Montgomery Gate where the river Camlad debouches into the Severn and extends south-west into the low plateau country which is on the northern flanks of Clun Forest. During the Middle Ages, it lay wholly in the Marches, mainly in the lordships of Caus and Montgomery, but the Kerry area was part of Maelienydd. It is the perfect example of border country, and was seen as such in turn by Romans, Mercians and Anglo-Normans. In terms of settlement geography this is equally true, with its mixed habitation patterns and field systems, and its confusion of Welsh and English place-names.

For over four hundred years it lay in marcher territory, the Welsh commote of Gorddwr being absorbed into the great lordship of Caus, and that of Ceri into Maelienydd. Between them was thrust the lordship of Montgomery which, despite its relatively small size, held one of the most important gaps into Central Wales. As such, its *caput* Montgomery which later gave its Norman name to this Welsh county, was the only Anglo-Norman borough in Montgomeryshire as it was constituted in 1536. In the rest of this area, there is only one settlement which can claim to be a nucleated village: Churchstoke. The remaining townships can boast only dispersed settlement, except for Llandyssil a mile

[1] See under Hope and Leighton, p. 459.

S.R.L.W.B.

south-west of Montgomery which is a fair sized hamlet. The comparative remoteness of the area between the major routeways of modern times has meant little change in population, and that principally on the side of decline.

In 1086 a number of places now in eastern Montgomeryshire were entered in the Shropshire portion of the Domesday Book. Churchstoke (Cirestoc) is said to have had land for seven ploughs but T.R.W. there was only one Welshman there with one plough. In a total of eight places (Thornbury, Hem, Edderton, Wropton, Forden and Ackley, together with two 'lost' places), there were eight ploughs in demesne and a further 12½ held by 14 bordars, 3 radmen and 8 serfs. At Leighton there was one plough in demesne and, as one would expect, it was at Montgomery that the greatest number of ploughs were in use, the earl (Roger de Montgomery) having four and Roger Corbet two.[1] It seems reasonable to suppose that the Normans, taking over townships held by the Mercians, continued the development of their cultivated land as far as conditions then allowed and it would seem that we have here, as in so many places, the first record of ploughlands worked in common. It also underlines the association of the Normans in this early phase with places with English names, and it proves that their inhabitants came from different ethnic groups. Perhaps most significant of all is the fact that neither English place-names nor English settlement forms have succeeded in advancing farther west since the eleventh century, and that English-influenced forms of community agriculture moved effectively no farther than the hill edge of the Vale of Welshpool. Such is the conservatism of rural geography that its principal patterns date back centuries in this remote countryside.

Much of the eastern belt consisted of upland, some of it too high or too rugged to be cultivable, some above the habitation line. The Breidden and Corndon Hill came into this latter class, Breidden in the 'Forest of Haia and Brethen' in 1540,[2] Corndon a forest in the thirteenth century but rented as mountain land in the sixteenth century 'there having been no deer there this long time'.[3] Similarly, much of the Long Mountain and the Kerry Hills lay

---

[1] D.B., fo. 259 b 1.
[2] John R. Whitfield, 'The Lordship of Cause, 1540–1541', loc. cit. p. 331.
[3] *Cardiff Collection*, N.D., *Court of Augmentations*, op. cit. p. 463, N.D.

above the limit of, or was too steep for, cultivation. Emphasis thus fell on the lowlands of the Severn and the Montgomery Gate where most of the best land lay and, in consequence, many of the townships included portions of both upland and vale.

Hope, Leighton and Forden shared the greater part of the Montgomeryshire slopes of the Long Mountain, and this area was largely covered by William Fowler's map of the manor of Leighton of 1663.[1] By that time, enclosure and consolidation had begun, but the remnants of open field land and common meadow were traceable in Hope (and Welshpool). *Hope* (H/VD) anciently in the parish of Welshpool, later in Buttington, extended from near the summit of the Long Mountain to the river Severn. A sixteenth-century claim for unlimited pasture in the lordship of Gorddwr which was part of Caus and embraced the western slopes of the Long Mountain, suggests that it had been open waste from time immemorial, and it was so on William Fowler's map and on the tithe map. Offa's Dyke follows the western foot of the Long Mountain and on either side of the dyke in 1663 were the open arable fields named Upper Goppa and Lower Goppa, a third called Hope Field adjoining Lower Goppa towards the Severn. All included a number of open strips in 1663, but enclosure had begun in each and in Lower Goppa in particular, there were compacted and enclosed freehold properties. By 1841, evidences of the Hope Field remained and of numerous lesser *maes* names but the name Goppa did not appear in connection with possible open field holdings. In Leighton and Forden there were left only hints of former arable in the largely enclosed fields and compacted tenements, though some intermixed lands and meadow shares remained in Leighton and some strip-shaped closes in Forden.

The most fertile area of any extent was in the lordship of Montgomery. Because of its strategic importance its *caput*, the borough of Montgomery, was the site of the castle which crowned its Town Hill, and the whole district was peppered with mottes. Here the Camlad and the Caebitra flow through low lying land, sufficiently deep-soiled and well drained to afford opportunities for crop raising on a larger scale than to the west of the Long Mountain, and full advantage was taken by *Montgomery*

---

[1] 'A map of the Manor of Leighton with other lands and tenements in Welchpoole, Hope and Forden, etc.' (N.L.W.).

itself (UVcbmp). It had a castle by 1086, though the present ruins
date from 1223, and Eyton thinks that the two were erected on
different sites.[1] The town was constantly involved in wars and
skirmishes between the Welsh and the English, but the site of the
thirteenth-century castle must have been such as to render it
almost impregnable, whatever the fate of the town below. Before
1230, the town was a free borough with a market and two annual
fairs. The burgesses were given the right to enclose it with a wall,
and to have a gild and 'to have sac, soc, tol, theam, and infran-
ganthef, and to be quit of tolls, lastage, passage, pontage, stallage,
lene, and Danegeld'. By this time, and no doubt long before, there
were also mills and a church and a well organised system of land
use such as was associated with other Anglo-Norman boroughs
whose privileges were modelled on those enjoyed by the citizens
of Hereford.[2] Possibly in the thirteenth century[3] and certainly in
the fourteenth,[4] the burgesses were working the open arable fields
of Montgomery. It had already been well cultivated by 1086, and
it seems that the open fields remained for many centuries. By the
time of the tithe survey (1839) they had been enclosed, but field-
name evidence from the apportionment lists reveals that there had
been, prior to enclosure, two major and two lesser fields. Horse
field was situated north-east of the town, Mill field east of it,
while to the north was the very tiny field called Verlon in which
some open strips still remained, and to the south Maes Kerry.
Farther north, in the Sarkley area were two further fields which
had evidently formerly been shared – Horsewell and Sarkley
field – but these seem to suggest that Sarkley operated as an
independent hamlet (? perhaps the Horseford of D.B. which
Eyton regarded as a lost name). Though nominally still the county
town, Montgomery sleeps below the Iron Age hill-fort and the
medieval castle which overlook it from the hill above. The market
hall no longer functions as such, and the only relics of its former
trade are its shops and its cattle market.

　　The only other nucleation in the eastern belt apart from the
hamlet of Llandyssil is the loosely clustered village of *Churchstoke*

[1] Op. cit., xi, p. 132.　　　　　　　　　[2] Ibid. pp. 132–41.
[3] *Cardiff Collection*, N.D., probably thirteenth-century, grant of 'an acre of land called
Fountain Acre in the fields of Montgomery'.
[4] Ibid. (1356), grant of 'a plot of land and buildings and all other lands . . . in
the town and field of Montgomery'.

(VAbp). Apart from the fact that it is on the strategically important road which runs north of Clun Forest into Wales, its location and general character would put it into the line of villages which are strung along the Rea–Camlad valley and of which it is the most southerly. Like Chirbury, it lies under the shadow of the Corndon–Shelve uplands in an area where hill forts and mottes are alike numerous. It is also similar to the Rea–Camlad villages in that it is the head of a spreading parish of eight townships including two in Shropshire, and they display an interesting mixture of Welsh and English place-names. The western boundary of the parish is Offa's Dyke (also the county boundary), and in the Middle Ages Churchstoke was included in the lordship of Montgomery. The parochial township extends over Todleth Hill and, having combined with Hurdley, the joint township embraces the Hurdley and Broadway areas. The first time a farm was mentioned in the modern sense in the *Coleman Deeds* was in 1735 at Hurdley.[1] Most of the early plans available for Churchstoke parish show relics of common meadows or open fields, for they generally pre-date 1761, when the first private enclosure Act was passed for Montgomeryshire. The most interesting of these is for Millington, a township centred on Millington Hall to the south of Churchstoke. Its western boundary and that of the former open field called Millington fields and a second one called Coom Grounds to the south, is Offa's Dyke. Common meadow, still partially open, occupied the eastern corner of the triangular plan.[2] The *Coleman Deeds* include details of holdings in two common meadows in Hurdley: Chelmick's meadow and Hurdleys meadow,[3] and a small plan of the farm called Broadway delineates meadow doles by the Camlad. All the Churchstoke townships have dispersed habitations, and this is true of the increasingly Welsh district over towards Kerry which forms the tail of this eastern belt.

Kerry (Hv Bp) earlier known as Llanfihangel yn Gheri, is a diminishing centre of a nineteen-township parish. Once the centre of a considerable cloth industry and now only of the Kerry sheep rearing district on which it was based, it is no more than a hamlet.

[1] No. 669 (Blackland Farm and Sunny Bank Farm).
[2] *Pitchford Deposit Collection* (N.L.W.). Map by T. Bateman.
[3] No. 693 (1717).

Every one of its townships has a Welsh name, and there are few English names, either of fields or of farms despite the fact that it lay on a minor Norman route into Wales and had mottes to north and to south. For all practical purposes this area ranks as Welsh in the study of border settlement.

19 The Flintshire – Denbighshire Borderland

A land of mountains which forms the character of those who come to it . . . that is the abiding fact in the history of Wales. The inhabitants of the mountains feel, amid all their differences, that they are one nation because their land is unlike other lands. Eastwards they look on a plain which they believe they once possessed and ruled.

Sir Owen G. Edwards, *Wales*, 1903

THE role of the mountains as a refuge for the Welsh, and of the valleys and lowlands as highways for the invading Mercians and Normans, has been demonstrated time and again in the history of war and conquest in the Welsh Borderland. The Anglo-Saxon fringe settlement and the deeper Norman penetration up the broad vales of the Usk, the Wye, and the Severn and around the Welsh upland areas have laid the broad outlines of the settlement geography of the southern and middle Borderland. The theme is repeated in the northern Borderland and is basic to the interpretation of rural patterns. There, however, the physical ground plan though it can offer parallels to features farther south, as in the wall-like character of the junction of the hills with the English lowlands and the significance of the coastal lowlands as a routeway, also shows significant differences. Among these are the narrowness of the valleys opening eastwards to the lowlands – neither the Dee nor the Ceiriog, the principal valleys concerned, has proved sufficiently wide to attract English settlement above its emergence point into the plain. The approximately south–north direction of the lower Clwyd is unique in Borderland rivers west of the hill edge and its valley served in more than one phase of the English campaigns in Wales as an important frontier. It became, as a result, the site of three major Anglo-Norman castles – Rhuddlan, Denbigh and Ruthin – but because of its distance from the eastern edge of the Welsh uplands the degree of anglicisation which took place in the rural settlements, though traceable, was limited, not only in amount but in its extent southward.

Denbighshire and Flintshire consist fundamentally of Silurian and Carboniferous uplands in which Hercynian folding and faulting, superimposed on earlier Caledonian trends, tend to dominate the structural plan. This is notably the case in the Clwydian Heights, which are a slightly curving anticlinal range with a predominantly north–south axis, and in the broad box-faulted Vale of Clwyd. In this latter, the long Vale of Clwyd fault is responsible for the magnificent steepness of the slope from the Clwydian peaks, crowned by Moel Fama at 1820 feet above sea level, to the flat vale floor where Bunter is faulted in to form the underlying rock base of the broadest interior valley in North Wales of comparable length – three miles by twenty. It is delimited on the west by a series of short north–south faults which give to its junction with the plateau lands of Rhos and Rhufoniog an irregularity notably absent on the eastern side. Southwards the broad vale terminates abruptly against the Llanelidan fault, above which are the high folded and faulted plateaux of south Denbighshire traversed by the deeply entrenched course of the river Dee between Carrog and the Vale of Llangollen. In these southern heights the Caledonian trend again becomes dominant, and their altitude and relief are such as to render wide areas uninhabitable, and to obstruct movement between Dyffryn Clwyd and the upland course of the Dee. The plateaux of Rhos and Rhufoniog to the west of the Clwyd, consisting largely of Wenlock and Ludlow Beds flanked by Carboniferous Limestones, offer fairly good pasture on their northern and western flanks but the interior Moors are wide tracts of rough moorland over 1000 feet in height. This is for the most part well beyond the area which in terms of settlement can justifiably be designated Borderland, except for some townships on its fringe.

The Flintshire plateau is based on a shallow syncline in a broad Carboniferous belt behind the Silurian rocks of the Clwydian Range. It is everywhere below 1000 feet in height and large areas average only 6–800 feet. By contrast with the rest of the Flintshire–Denbighshire uplands, it is eminently habitable, and has been made the more so by the mineral deposits of the Carboniferous Limestone and, more recently, of coal.

On the eastern side of both Flintshire and Denbighshire, there occurs a belt of lowland which, except for a short stretch near

Chester, comes down to the river Dee. The old Welsh *cantref* of Maelor embraced both sides of the valley above Shocklach, but the 'English' side, Maelor Saesneg, was detached from Maelor Cymraeg when, in 1284, it became part of the newly constituted county of Flint under the Statute of Rhuddlan. From the time of Union, Maelor Gymraeg became part of Denbighshire. From the thirteenth century until Union, it had been included in the marcher lordship of Bromfield and Yale which extended beyond Wrexham to the Clwydian Heights. Its lowland portion, consisting of the flood plain of the Dee, together with the Flintshire portions of this riverine lowland, offers an example unique in the Borderland of such a physical area under Welsh occupation.

Beyond Chester, the flood plain soon gives place to an estuarine shelf, almost entirely above flood level and offering comparatively good cultivable land. From the lordship of Hawarden to the Point of Air and beyond it on the open sea coast, conditions are such as to have encouraged a fair density of population from comparatively early times and to have offered one of the two most favoured invasion routes used by the Anglo-Normans to reach North Wales beyond the Clwyd. The other was the Wheeler–Alyn route which crosses the plateau by Mold emerging into the Clwyd valley nearly opposite Denbigh. A third, but more difficult route, took advantage of the high pass above Llanfair Dyffryn Clwyd at Bwlch y Parc, cutting through to the Vale of Clwyd opposite Ruthin. In this way, arose the major strategic sites of the Middle Ages in this area.

Anglicisation depended to a high degree here, as elsewhere on the Welsh side of the border, on access, and access for the Anglo-Normans was clearly and closely linked with low lying land or land of easy gradient. Hence in north-eastern Wales, hybridisation in settlement features occurs in a broken ovoid ring of land of low and intermediate height beginning near Chirk, following the Dee and the open coast, and recurving up the Clwyd valley to the lordship of Ruthin. Within this ring and southward to the Montgomeryshire boundary, the hills are Welsh.

The Flintshire plateau, especially in the areas of intermediate height, has yielded abundant evidence of occupation during the Bronze Age, especially in the form of tumuli.[1] During the Iron

---

[1] Ed. C. R. Williams, *The History of Flintshire*, i (1961), ch. 2 by Peter Hayes, 'Prehistoric Flintshire', including a distribution map, p. 29.

Age, the pattern of occupation appears to have altered, relatively few finds having been made on the lower parts of the plateau apart from the north. Along the Clwydian Heights six large British hill forts were occupied during the Roman period (including Moel y Gaer in Denbighshire) and three more on the eastern side, including Moel y Gaer near Rhosesmor and the two near and in Caergwrle. These hill-top sites were intended and used as true hill forts in the military sense, and their builders lived in the valley below. There is as yet, however, little to suggest the close settlement of Iron Age people in north-east Wales that occurred in north-east Montgomeryshire nor is the density of *llan* settlements or of early Celtic church dedications notable. On these last two points, however, caution is needed, as both may have been eroded by later settlements – the *llan* names by Mercians and Normans, the dedications because of the known custom of replacement by Roman Calendar dedications under Norman rule.

A comparable line of three hill forts crowns the higher points of the northern edge of the north Denbighshire Moors, including Dinorben above St George. All make use of the Carboniferous Limestone outcrop. Over the rest of north-east Wales they are relatively sparse. Evidence for the descent to the lower ground during Roman or sub-Roman times is mainly in the form of place-names and Celtic dedications, and it may again be assumed that by the seventh century at latest Celtic settlement bore a close distributional relationship to Welsh settlements today, except for replacement and additions during the Mercian and Norman periods and, of course, later mining and industrial settlements.

The Mercian occupation is marked, not only by Offa's and Wat's Dykes, but by appreciable numbers of Anglo-Saxon place-names which, between them, delimit the main areas of Mercian settlement in the north-east of Wales. These occur, first, in the Dee valley below Farndon and along the estuarine shores of Flintshire as far as Whitford; and secondly, after a break in the Wrexham area, they extend up-river on the low ground and across the Dee into Maelor Saesneg (Fig. 12). It is clear that they are more closely related in distribution to Wat's than to Offa's Dyke. The distribution of mottes follows the place-name distribution in part, notably along the estuarine shores of Flintshire, but it also marks out the trans-upland routes which were evidently of value to the Anglo-Normans. One of these lines of mottes followed the Wheeler–Alyn route and then crossed the Denbigh Moors aiming at Deganwy and Conway. Others followed the Dee valley above Fron Cysyllte, but there is little basis for assuming that they had anything more than strategic significance, especially with regard to rural settlement. Except in the Borderland proper, it would seem that English influence on rural communities was exercised, if at all, from the boroughs.

These, as was usual in the Marches, were the *capita* of lordships, and in the matter of the setting up of lordships north-east Wales differed from the southern and middle Borderland. A few were established in the early Norman period. At the time the Domesday Book was compiled, Flintshire and Maelor were part of 'Cestres-cire' and the Domesday record gives a useful and fairly full picture of the manors and berewicks of this part of the Borderland. There were over a hundred in Flintshire, but only six Denbighshire manors were mentioned in the Cheshire portion of the Domesday Book. Those in Flintshire extended into all parts of the present county, though they were far more numerous in the lower lands than in the area of the Clwydian Heights. In Denbighshire, apart from a generalised mention of the *cantrefydd* of Rhos and Rhufoniog, the five manors recorded – Allington, Gresford, Sutton, Eyton and Erbistock – were all in the eastern lowland sector which, in 1282, became part of the lordship of Bromfield and Iâl (Yale). In 1086, Hawarden and Rhuddlan were held by earl Hugh of Chester, Robert of Rhuddlan sharing the lordship of Rhuddlan with the earl, and a castle and borough were already there when the Domesday record was made. Mold is not recorded in the 1086 Survey, but the mention of a priest at Quisnan, thought to be Gwysaney which adjoins Mold, suggests that this foundation may have been the forerunner of Mold church.[1] During early Norman times, Mold was fortified to serve as a flanking defence for Hawarden and Chester against the Welsh, but it fell into Welsh hands in 1199, was restored to the de Montalts and, with occasional periods of re-capture by the Welsh, remained under their overlordship until 1327.

Although a small part of Rhos and Rhufoniog were in the earl of Chester's hands in 1086, the real limit of effective power remained the Clwyd and its marshy deltaic mouth until the period

[1] D.B., fo. 269.

of the Edwardian campaign. Three of the four *cantrefs* of Perfedd-wlad, Rhos, Rhufoniog and Dyffryn Clwyd, had remained under Welsh law although nominally in Cheshire, only Englefield or Tegeingl having come.into the Anglo-Norman sphere of influence. In 1282, the lordship of Denbigh was created from Rhos and Rhufoniog, that of Ruthin from Dyffryn Clwyd, and Bromfield and Iâl from Maelor Gymraeg. Hence, Anglo-Norman influence on settlement features and on agriculture in most of what is now Denbighshire only began at the latter end of the thirteenth century, more than two hundred years later than in the Englefield lord-ships, and its phase of influence was correspondingly abbreviated. In the extreme south-east, the first mention of the lordship of Chirk was in 1202.

The boundaries of the new county of Flint created in 1284 are by no means certain. According to the Statute of Rhuddlan it included the *cantref* of Englefield, the land of Maelor Saesneg, the land of Hope, and 'the land joined to our castle and town of Rhuddlan unto the town of Chester'. The precise meaning of this statement is obscure. Professor Goronwy Edwards believes that from Cilcen the boundary turned north to exclude the lordships of Mold and Hawarden, but its course is uncertain.[1]

In each of the lordships of north-east Wales, the settlement pattern resembled that in other parts of the Borderland. A central borough based on a castle with a market and other privileges, exercised direct control of convenient adjoining townships, but the rest remained in the Welshries, and their inhabitants followed Welsh custom. In this part of the Borderland, however, close contact was maintained with adjoining districts of Cheshire and north-west Shropshire and it is difficult to avoid the assumption that there was mutual influence. Fortunately, the documentary evidence is remarkably rich for many parts of Flintshire and Denbighshire. The Domesday record is fuller for Flintshire than for any other Welsh county, and the *First Extent of Bromfeld and Yale* was made in 1315,[2] the *Survey of the Honour of Denbigh* in 1334.[3]

---

[1] J. Goronwy Edwards, 'Notes on the Boundaries of Medieval Flintshire', *Fl. Hist. Soc. Pub.*, viii (1922), pp. 52–9.

[2] T. P. Ellis, *The First Extent of Bromfeld and Yale, A.D. 1315*, Cymmrodorion Record Series (1924).

[3] Ed. Paul Vinogradoff and Frank Morgan, *The Survey of the Honour of Denbigh A.D. 1334* (London, 1914).

From that time onwards, surveys and private estate documents become increasingly numerous and it is possible to build up for many places a comparatively detailed picture of the patterns and evolution of land use and other aspects of settlements.[1] With the Union of the two countries, the close relationships between the Welsh and English sides of the border became even more effective and an increasing parallelism is detectable in the progress of enclosure and the related breakdown of the open field system on the two sides of the Dee valley. Palmer and Owen maintain that the breakdown of the Welsh system of tenure and inheritance occurred between the dates of the two surveys of Bromfield and Yale made in 1507 and towards the end of the reign of Henry VIII, and that by 1562 when a further survey was carried out, all trace of tenure by *gwely* and *gafael* had vanished as had inheritance by gavelkind.[2]

Despite the differences, there is an element of continuity between Cheshire and Shropshire on the English side of the border and Flintshire and south-east Denbighshire on the Welsh. This is seen not only in the communications link, but in the distribution of mottes and castles where a common strategy was the fundamental element especially in the case of Flintshire, south-east Denbighshire and Cheshire, which during the early Middle Ages were united in the earldom and the county of Chester. A diocesan link with St Asaph united all north-east Wales, but an earlier related ecclesiastical history had produced a shared pattern of large multi-township parishes, and the tendency for the central parochial settlement to grow as a focal point of satellite townships with only hamleted or dispersed settlement which is so marked a feature of Cheshire and north Shropshire, can be detected also in the lowland rim of east and north Flintshire and of south-east Denbighshire. It is notably absent from much of Dyffryn Clwyd and from the greater part, though not all, of the hill country, but in this last the probability is that the growth of hamlets was recent and only in two cases probably in the whole of west Denbighshire – Eglwys-Fach and Henllan – did the central

---

[1] Dorothy Sylvester, 'Settlement Patterns in Rural Flintshire', *Trans. Fl. Hist. Soc.* (1954–5).
[2] A. Neobard Palmer and Edward Owen, *A History of Ancient Tenures of Land in North Wales and the Marches* (1910), p. vii.

settlement achieve small-village rather than hamlet size prior to the nineteenth century.

The overall distribution of nucleated villages in Flintshire and Denbighshire undoubtedly reflects English influence, occurring mainly in the broken ovoid ring of lowland with only isolated examples elsewhere. In the greater part of the hill country the only nucleated settlements are small country markets or former markets. In most of the higher land, the dispersed pattern of habitations predominates, but farther east total dispersal is varied by patches of semi-dispersal. Hamlets further diversify the nucleation dispersal pattern in north Flintshire where the map (Fig. 3) looks strikingly similar to that of west Cheshire.

The open field evidence does not fully coincide with the distribution of nucleated settlements, but very clearly reflects the influence of the marcher lordships, being concentrated mainly in the districts around Hawarden, Rhuddlan and Denbigh, and in Bromfield. One conclusion is inescapable, and that is that by comparison with any of the more southerly Welsh border counties open fields were far more numerous, and that the Clwyd valley, whether because of physical advantage or on account of English influence or both, carries the most westerly extension of open fields in any appreciable numbers to be found in the entire Welsh Borderland.

Welsh Settlement Patterns in the Higher Uplands

(a) THE WEST DENBIGHSHIRE PLATEAU

The greater part of the Denbighshire Moors west of the Clwyd lay beyond English influence with the exception only of its eastern fringe. Welsh settlement characteristics are widespread and certain patterns are repeated in the greater part of the upland. Habitations are almost wholly dispersed, and the only nucleations are the fringing market centres of Llanrwst, Abergele (until recently little more than a hamlet), Denbigh and Ruthin; the small villages of Eglwys-Fach in a minor right-bank tributary of the Conway, and of Henllan near to Denbigh; and a few hamlets mainly in the commote of Rhos in the northern part of the plateau –

Betws-yn-Rhos, Llanfair Talhaiarn, Llansannan and Llanefydd. On John Evans's map of 1795,[1] Abergele was shown as a hamlet, but during the nineteenth century, especially after the coming of the railway and of better roads, the status of many places in North Wales changed. This applies not only to the resorts but to lesser places such as Abergele which has grown around a market on the main coast road, and Llanfair Talhaiarn which has experienced a far more modest growth as a minor inland service centre. The same is to a slight extent true also of *Eglwys-Fach* (VA/Dp) which is the parochial centre for one Caernarvonshire and four Denbighshire townships. John Evans mapped it as a distinctly nucleated hamlet in 1795, and today it ranks as a small village, but is essentially the centre of a district of typically scattered Welsh farms. An atlas consisting of maps of the last decade of the eighteenth century[2] depicts most of the holdings as consisting of irregular fields semi-compacted, but in the village itself houses were backed by long gardens rather suggestively called *drylliau*, and at Pennant Canol in the same parish were strip-shaped enclosures called *dryll* and *llainia*, relics presumably of a medieval semi-scattered Welsh system of ploughing strips. All the field-names were Welsh. Pastoral farming dominates the economy now to an even greater extent than in the days of subsistence farming and restricted marketing, and a limited portion of the higher hills is still open common. The valley sides offer a varied pattern of land use, cultivated and ploughed where the slope is kind, enclosed for pasture where it is moderate, and on the steeper parts given over to woodland and coppice. This pattern is repeated constantly over the Denbighshire Moors, but with almost total dispersal more usual than hamleting, though in the last century or so a number of parochial hamlets have expanded from the tiny former church/*ty'n llan* centres. So, at the extreme southeastern end of the western Moors, *Derwen* (HCp) on a steep hillside at 800 feet above the upper Clwyd, displays a similar pattern of land use and might be compared with Llanelidan, Clocaenog, Gwyddelwern and other elevated upland centres in the area, except that woodland is more widespread. For example, in 1779,

---

[1] *Maps of the six counties of North Wales*, by John Evans (Llwyngroes, 1795). Scale, 1·32 inches to 1 mile.
[2] *N.L.W. MS. Maps*, vol. 34, dated 1795–8.

Fforest y Glyn half a mile to the west of Derwen was described as
'a spot very proper for coppice of oak'.[1] Today Clocaenog Forest
covers many square miles of the higher upland between the village
of that name and Llanfihangel glyn Myfyr in the upper Alwen
valley, and although much of that area is Forestry Commission
plantation the nucleus evidently existed earlier, as names such as
Ty yn y Fforest, Fforest Maenion and Fforest bach testify.[1] The
names survived in the 1842 apportionment list, and on the
accompanying tithe map were traceable a Maes y llan, south of
the church, quillets immediately east of the church, and quillets
and doles by the stream. The surprising extent of arable land at
that date (2314 out of a total of 3912 acres) lends credence to the
possibility of there having been a number of small open fields as
well as streamside common meadow holdings. At the same time,
there is nothing in their names or arrangement to suggest English
influence. Another feature typical of many Denbighshire townships is the complexity of the road system. Four roads in 1842
centred on Derwen church, but some at least seem to have been
green roads. The largest extent of common was an elongated
patch to the east of the village, which is surprising in a township
at this altitude, but the suggestion conveyed by the 1779 maps is
that field nuclei around the farms had been eating up the common
and had been gradually coalescing for some time.[2]

(b) THE EAST DENBIGHSHIRE UPLANDS

Between Wrexham and the Llanelidan faults, lies some of the most
spectacular scenery in Denbighshire. Llantysilio Mountain,
Cyrn y Brain and Eglwyseg Mountain continue the trend line of
the Berwyns and are dissected by the deeply entrenched meanders
of the river Dee. Though little higher than the more elevated
parts of the Denbighshire Moors, they are more mountainous and
rugged, and the townships of Eglwysegle and Maes yr Ychain,
situated the one to the east and the other to the west of the
Eglwyseg river, show an expected relationship to this harsh

---

[1] *N.L.W. MS. Maps*, vol. 20, A Survey of Lands enclosed from the Waste in the
Lordship of Ruthin, 1779, by S. Minshull, nos. 71–3.
[2] No date is given in Ivor Bowen, *The Great Enclosures of Common Lands in Wales*
(1914), for Enclosure Acts relating to Derwen.

environment. *Maes yr Ychain* (Hv D) is depicted in part in an unusually interesting map of roads, wastes and encroachments of approximately 1819 (Fig. 56). The eastern boundary is the river Eglwyseg, and the 'new road to Ruthin' is the road through the Horseshoe Pass (Plates III and IV). Gribin Oernant and Foel Faen are peaks at the northern end of Llantysilio Mountain, the former rising to almost 1900 feet. This barren upland is open pasture today above the 1300 foot contour, but the plan shows that in the early nineteenth century eleven of the inhabitants of this township encroached on the waste to the height of at least 1000 feet on slopes so precipitous that the rewards of enclosure can at best have been meagre. Quarries and sheep-walks on the mountains indicate the desolation of the higher land and its uselessness for farming.

On the opposite side of the Eglwyseg valley, the township of *Eglwysegle* (Hv D) offers very similar conditions, though its highest point is only 1239 feet. Both townships share the deep, narrow vale which in 1200 became the site of Valle Crucis Abbey, Maes yr Ychain township being bestowed on the Abbey in 1200–2 by Madog ap Gruffydd Maelor. In Norden's Survey of 1620, the poverty of the environment was underlined by his series of negatives – no demesnes, no fee farmers, no park (and never was), no encroachments, no copyhold lands, no town, no customary mill, no decayed houses, no fishing and no market or fair. Leasehold tenants intercommoned with the neighbouring townships, and the only woods were on the freeholds, while 'upon the high moore, peats, turfs, furse, and ffearne' alone would grow.[1] Yet there were *hafodau* on the hills in the sixteenth century,[2] and on the lower land in the seventeenth century were closes with names such as *erw* and *dol*,[3] no doubt on the limited bottom land of the valley. The name *hafod* survived in two fields in the tithe apportionment list, so did *maes* (6), *cefn* (4), *llwyn* (5), and *ddol* (6), and inumerable fields were named *erw*. Of necessity, they were found on the lower slopes and in the valleys.

[1] Harleian MS. 3696, fos 223 et seq.
[2] *Court of Augmentations*, Denb., pp. 320 (1581) and 385 (1562/3).
[3] *Kinmel MSS. and Documents*, Univ. Coll., N. Wales, no. 553 (1627).

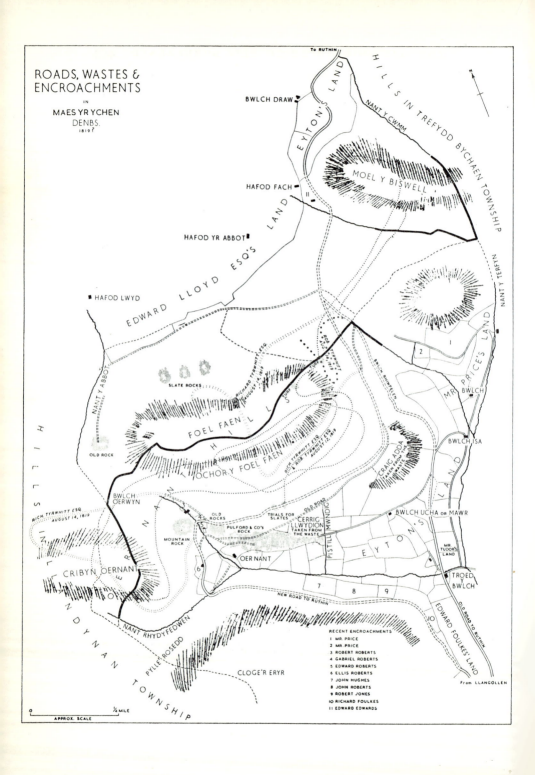

ROADS, WASTES &
ENCROACHMENTS

IN

MAES YR YCHEN
DENBS.
1819?

To RUTHIN

BWLCH DRAW

EYTON'S LAND

HILLS IN TREFYDD BYCHAEN TOWNSHIP

NANT Y CWMM

HAFOD FACH

MOEL Y BISWELL

HAFOD YR ABBOT

EDWARD LLOYD ESQ'S LAND

NANT Y TERFYN

HAFOD LWYD

NANT Y ABBOT

MR PRICE'S LAND

2

BWLCH

SLATE ROCKS

RICHARD TYRWHITT ESQ
AUGUST 14, 1819

BWLCH ISA

FOEL FAEN HILLS

OLD ROCK

OCHOR Y FOEL FAEN

RICH TYRWHITT ESQ
OLD ROAD TYRWHITT ESQ
AUGUST 14, 1819

CRAIG ADDA
NEW ROAD FROM THE
WASTE

BWLCH ISA

BWLCH
OERWYN

OLD ROCKS

TRIALS FOR
SLATES

OLD ROAD

BWLCH UCHA OR MAWR

RICH. TYRWHITT ESQ
AUGUST 14, 1819

PULFORD & CO'S
ROCK

CERRIG
LLWYDION
TAKEN FROM
THE WASTE

PISTILL MWNDIG

EYTON'S LAND

MR
TUDOR'S
LAND

MOUNTAIN
ROCK

TROED
BWLCH

CRIBYN OERNANT

OER NANT

6

7

8

9

NEW ROAD TO RUTHIN

EDWARD FOULKES' LAND

OLD ROAD TO RUTHIN

10

NANT RHYDYFEDWEN

HILLS IN LLANDYNAN TOWNSHIP

PYLLE'R ROSEDD

CLOGE'R ERYR

RECENT ENCROACHMENTS
1 MR. PRICE
2 MR. PRICE
3 ROBERT ROBERTS
4 GABRIEL ROBERTS
5 EDWARD ROBERTS
6 ELLIS ROBERTS
7 JOHN HUGHES
8 JOHN ROBERTS
9 ROBERT JONES
10 RICHARD FOULKES
11 EDWARD EDWARDS

From LLANGOLLEN

0   ¼ MILE
APPROX. SCALE

(c) THE FLINTSHIRE–DENBIGHSHIRE PLATEAU AND THE CLWYDIAN HEIGHTS

The thin soil and the steepness and considerable altitude of the Clwydian Heights are in general such as to preclude settlement or active farming, apart from the hill grazing of sheep, but to the east of the belt of Silurian rocks, the Carboniferous Limestone and the Millstone Grit series are more favourable in every way, and the townships of this side of the Clwydian Heights reach up to meet the hillfoot townships of the western side in the barren peaks of this magnificent range. Quarrying and mining have long supplemented farming in the Carboniferous Limestone belt, and have helped to build up a not inconsiderable density of population for country of this type. Much of the population is found in the Wheeler valley, partly on account of its long history as a major routeway, in small dispersed communities such as Nannerch and Ysceifiog. An exceptional case is that of Caerwys, a former market centre at 600 feet on open plateau land, the plan of the small town still coinciding closely with that of the Roman fortress which preceded it. From Holywell southward, the low Halkyn Mountain is peppered with disused mine workings and abandoned quarries, but the old Welsh pattern of the earlier rural communities is still discernible beneath the thin veneer of industrialisation. The upper Alyn valley above Rhyd-y-mwyn is another axis of settlement though, in this belt too, mineral wealth has helped to build up the population on the higher land of the Carboniferous Limestone to the east. The Welsh pattern of settlement may be demonstrated by *Llanferres* (Hv Dp), a scattered farming community astride the upper Alyn, between the peak of Moel Fama and the eastern slopes of the Flintshire–Denbighshire plateau above Nercwys (Plate V). A map of 1793 showed a broad belt of open waste on the Clwydian Heights, and marked the Bathafarn sheep-walks on the slopes of Foel Eithinen.[1] By 1838, the lower slopes of these high pastures were enclosed in the typically large rectangular fields of late enclosure, but the higher land remained open and the only other commons surviving in this single-township parish were comparatively small patches in the south-east. The

[1] *Goronwy Williams Purchase Collection*, N.L.W. (1927), map. 4.

56 (*opposite*). Maes yr Ychen, Denbighshire:
roads, wastes, and encroachments

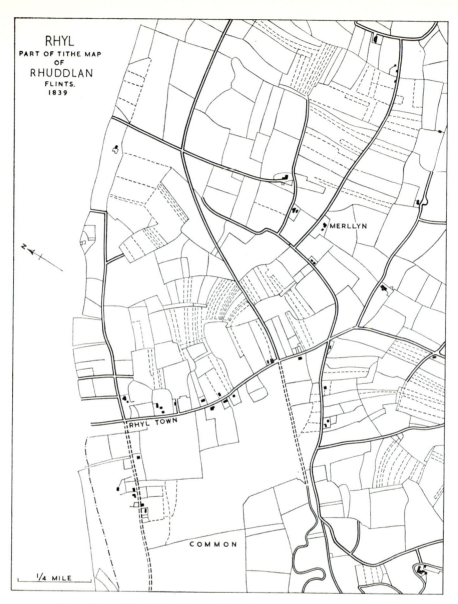

RHYL
PART OF TITHE MAP
OF
RHUDDLAN
FLINTS.
1839

MERLLYN

RHYL TOWN

COMMON

¼ MILE

57. Rhuddlan, Flintshire: Part of the tithe map of 1839, showing a well-developed arable strip system

rest of the area was and is divided into little sub-rectangular fields centred on the numerous homesteads which constitute this semi-dispersed group. Field-names such as quillet, *dryll, cefn, ddol* and *maes* survive in considerable numbers, but overwhelmingly the most numerous are the *erwau*, which occur significantly on every holding, suggesting by their distribution that they may represent the former scattered ploughing strips of a community which practised co-aration rather than true open field agriculture. In 1838, the holdings varied greatly in acreage, twenty-nine being under 50 acres, five over 100, and one of these over 300, but the fields were remarkably even in size, conforming to the pattern which was once considered to be typically Welsh. The road pattern was the complex maze characteristic of dispersed communities, most of the field and personal names were Welsh, and evidence of English influence at that date was exceptionally thin.

The Vale of Clwyd

Cradled among these uplands lies the Vale of Clwyd, its Bunter floor let down between faults, and much of its flood plain covered by fertile glacial and post-glacial deposits. Its settlement geography is related to its history of early Welsh settlement, to the early Norman occupation of Rhuddlan and the Clwyd mouth, and the later, thirteenth-century creation of marcher lordships under Denbigh and Ruthin in the old Welsh *cantrefydd* of Rhufoniog and Dyffryn Clwyd.

The Roman route into North Wales used the Llanelwy or St Asaph crossing, but the Normans developed the route through Newmarket and established their lowest crossing of the Clwyd at *Rhuddlan* (LUp(m)cb) (Plate XVIII). Traditionally on the site of Gruffydd ap Llewelyn's palace, the motte and bailey known as Twt Hill, which lies on the south side of the castle, was thrown up in the time of Robert de Rhuddlan, the kinsman whom earl Hugh of Chester established there as joint lord from as early as 1073. A small borough had been founded here by 1086, centred on Twt Hill, but the defences were still of wood in the mid-thirteenth century, and the present castle was only built between 1277 and

1286 when the borough was extended northward and north-westward. Neither the earlier nor the extended borough was defended by more than a ditch and bank. Like all the Edwardian castle towns of North Wales, it was so situated that it could not be cut off on the seaward side. To create the medieval port, the Clwyd was canalised and straightened for two miles to its sea outlet, and at Rhuddlan, the dock was connected to the castle moat. The main streets of the thirteenth-century town are the main streets of today, but its parliament house, in which the Statute of Rhuddlan was drawn up, is now only a relic indicative of its former status, and the old priory is part of a farmhouse.

Much of the delta-shaped area of the Clwyd mouth was marsh which, when high spring tides met an unusual volume of river water, was liable to the sort of inundation which occurred in 1636,[1] and which could pond back as far as St Asaph.[2] An 'exact survey' was made of the marsh in 1664, perhaps with a view to controlling this flooding,[3] but it was only in 1794 that the first Bill was obtained for embanking the coast and enclosing the marsh, and further Acts in 1807 and 1813 enlarged these powers. The more serious and successful control of the sea coast came only with the building of the railway, and the reclamation of the shore and the river banks for the planning of the new town of Rhyl.

In this environment grew the small borough of Rhuddlan. Its charter was granted in 1284 by Edward I, and from then on it was a free borough with free burgesses, a constable of the castle and a mayor. It had a market and fairs, corn mills and a fulling mill, and a prison. Like the other Edwardian boroughs in North Wales, the numbers of English in the borough increased, as did their wealth, and the surnames in the 1428 *Extent of Rhuddlan* are not only predominantly English but in many cases are topographical names and so give an indication of their origin, e.g. Henry de Oxford, William de Frodsham and Richard de Wyredale (Wirral).[4] The *Ministers' Accounts* of 1303–4 refer frequently to the value of hay crops from the meadows, and those of 'Carghanan' and 'Fiuyen' are mentioned in numerous parts of the *Accounts*. They produced two crops a year and after Michaelmas

[1] *Bettisfield MSS.*, no. 1638 (1636).   [2] Ibid. no. 1639 (1636).
[3] *Kinmel MSS.*, no. 1475 (1664).
[4] Arthur Jones, 'A Fifteenth Century Document of Rhuddlan', including a translation of the original Extent, *Jl Fl. Hist. Soc.*, v (1914–5), pp. 45–90.

were available for pasture.[1] In the 1428 Extent, a list setting out the allotment of the assize rents, enumerates the acreages of the burgages and the 'lands', i.e. the arable holdings. Although it has not proved possible to identify all the names of areas where these arable acres lay, it is clear that there were nine or ten such localities. Criccin, Pentre, Bryn and Spittal are still to be found on the modern Ordnance Survey map. 'Hempedich', 'Oldetown', 'le More', 'le Holme', 'le Heefeld', 'le Heys', 'le Molehull' and 'Drynsogh', are problematical, but the tithe map of 1839 proves how deeply entrenched the large English type of open field had been in this township (Fig. 57). The more problematical names have vanished even as field-names, but in the north and east of the map, a fine set of open strip fields still survived in 1839. Pentre and Bryn account for the more southerly ones, but no known name fits those nearer Rhyl and Rhydorddwy, and it seems likely that the lost names were in that part.

The extent to which Rhuddlan influenced the rural pattern of nearby areas is another question. The antagonism engendered in the thirteenth century between Welsh and English especially after the Statute of Rhuddlan was hardly likely to provide a climate favourable to imitation of English methods. As it died down – and D. L. Evans believes that this happened at least for the time being during and after the Black Death[2] – there was probably an increasing tendency to substitute adjacent for scattered ploughing strips in the Welsh townships. There were, further, many scattered English settlers who had been encouraged to take up land in North Wales, especially in Flintshire which was still administered for many purposes from Chester. Many of the local lords were similarly replaced by English or Normans and wielded their influence on the local agricultural régime. It is less easy to arrive at the area in which such influence was likely to be operative. Assuming that from Rhuddlan it began in early Norman times, then the list of berewicks held in the two portions of the lordship of Rhuddlan should have relevance. Though by no means all are identifiable, it seems that the part held by earl Hugh lay mainly in an arc looping southward from Rhuddlan,

[1] Ed. Arthur Jones, *Flintshire Ministers' Accounts, 1301–28*, ibid. iii (1913).
[2] *Flintshire Ministers' Accounts, 1328–53*, Fl. Hist. Soc. Record Series, no. 2, Introduction, p. lxxv.

through St Asaph and across to Ysceïfiog, Halkyn and Greenfield, and that Robert de Rhuddlan held the area north of this (though with a share in Brynford and Halkyn) as far as the Point of Air. Between them, they covered about two-thirds of Englefield including what later became Rhuddlan Hundred, Prestatyn Hundred and half of Coleshill Hundred.

Originally intended to be the administrative centre for Perfeddwlad after its conquest, Rhuddlan found itself after Llewelyn's campaigns merely at the remote end of Flintshire, for the four *cantrefydd* were taken over by the new lordships of Denbigh, Ruthin, and Bromfield and Yale. Flint was planned and created as a new town and replaced Rhuddlan in the administration of the recently formed county. But in Rhufoniog, English influence had at last become established and with the building of Denbigh castle and the founding of the borough and lordship the pattern of Anglo-Norman borough and Anglo-Norman 'manorial' agriculture in the heart of the Welsh area became a reality beyond the Clwyd.

The fourteenth-century organisation of the *Honour of Denbigh* has been superbly illuminated for posterity by the great *Survey*, and its value further increased by the introduction written by Paul Vinogradoff and Frank Morgan.[1] The interpretation of this *Survey* in relation to the rural geography of the ancient Honour could in itself prove a massive task, and there is occasion here to summarise only some of the more significant features in relation to regional and ethnic relationships and the associated rural patterns. After being granted the lordship of Denbigh, by 1284 Henry de Lacy was emparking land in which to preserve deer from the royal forest of Delamere, and by 1290 had granted a charter to the burgesses of Denbigh. Although after his death in 1311 he was succeeded by a number of lords in swift succession, a similar policy seems to have been pursued with regard to the development and organisation of the lands of this new lordship. By this date, Vinogradoff argued, experience in South Wales had shown that manorial methods were not popular with the Welsh and he thinks, therefore, that manorialisation in the new lordships

---

[1] Ed. Paul Vinogradoff and Frank Morgan, *The Survey of the Honour of Denbigh, A.D. 1334* (1914). The account of the Honour which follows is based on the Survey and the introduction.

of Perfeddwlad was carried out in more modified form.[1] Neverthe-less, the *Survey* reveals sufficient to show how the marcher lords went to work when they conquered or were allotted conquered territory. Escheat, and confiscation for misdemeanours on the part of the tribesmen, were the means of acquiring land from the local inhabitants, and on this land they established their new manors. There were four manors in the lordship of Denbigh in the fourteenth century – Denbigh, Kilford (Kilforn in the *Survey*), Ystrad Owain (Astret Oweyn) and Dinorben Fawr (Dynorben Vaur). Not surprisingly, the first three lay in or adjacent to the rich lands of the Vale of Clwyd; Dinorben on the limestone upland and the neighbouring lowland of the coastal plain. Vinogradoff thinks that there were also some embryo manors, but as some of the Welsh were 'quasi-feudal anyway',[2] this may or may not reflect English influence.

The significance of this *Survey* in relation to the study of rural settlement is enormous. It makes possible a remarkably precise estimate of the effects of marcher overlordship, at this late date, on the agriculture, land tenure and social classes of a Welsh district and, to a lesser degree, on the form of settlement. Prior to its annexation by the English in the Edwardian campaigns, the area had consisted of the *cantrefydd* of Rhos and Rhufoniog divided respectively into the commotes of Uwch Dulas and Is Dulas; Uwch Aled, Is Aled, and Cynmeirch in order from the north-west to the south-east. Apart from its limited strip of coastal lowland and its narrow valleys southern Rhos and southern Rhufoniog were, on the whole, the poorest land, and opportunities for the English policy of extending cultivation were at best slight. In northern Rhos and eastern Rhufoniog, where the greater part of the land is below 1000 feet, the rewards both of pastoralism and cultivation are richer, though the latter is limited except on the coastal and riverine lowland rim. Milch cattle were kept on the richer pastures even in Is Dulas, sheep were general, and it seems likely that pigs were afforded pannage in the extensive woodlands (there is one reference to pannage in Uwch Dulas). Oats were raised in all five commotes but, unless it was grown in some of the four manors, wheat was restricted to the lower land, especially between the river Elwy and the sea. A clear distinction

---

[1] Introduction, p. xcviii.   [2] Ibid.

was made in some parts of the *Survey* between 'dry pasture' and meadowland, the latter being by far the more valuable. Its importance in the economy and the method of dividing it into strips were no doubt due to the English, but their concern was to extend the area under the plough. This was possible in the direct sense only in the manors, and it was in these that an English-type open arable field system was introduced without delay. The fields varied in number – six are distinguished in Denbigh, seven in Kilford, and two or three in Ystrad Owain (it seems that much of the field land was used as required for crops, hay, or pasture) – but the three-course system was in general use for cropping. The ordered strip field and three-course method of cultivation must have contrasted sharply with the prevalent co-aration of the Welsh practised under the Welsh tribal system and, as there were many evidences of both social and economic change and of the beginnings of the break-up of the tribal structure, it is possible that English methods were imitated, at least for a time, in the Welsh *vills* of which some 80 were recorded in the *Survey*.

Other changes in land use and tenure brought about by the new lords included the increasing hold which they established on the common pasture and the rights of the coparceners, and in the setting up of parks as part of their demesne lands. Under the Welsh tribal system, all lands were held communally, even where rights of *priodolder* occupancy applied. This meant that the lands of an individual could not be seized for misdemeanours but, instead, the lords took a proportion of the land of the *gwely* concerned. This was one of several ways in which change was brought about in Rhos and Rhufoniog not only in landholding but in the movement of communities and in their social structure and numbers. Like the *Domesday Book*, the *Survey of the Honour of Denbigh* in certain parts refers to the situation as it was prior to 1284, i.e. *tempore principium*. For example, in the commote of Cynmeirch (Kaymergh) in which Denbigh lay, in the time of the Princes 3200 acres were held by *liberi* or free tribesmen, and about 6030 by *nativi* (unfree or *taeogion*). In 1334, their shares had dropped to 1730 and 2800 acres respectively, the lord holding 4700 out of the total area of 9230 acres. In Uwch Aled he escheated 5800 acres, and in Is Dulas 4900 out of totals of 15,800 and of over 13,000.[1]

[1] Introduction, p. xvi.

Although there was undoubtedly widespread reversion, especially in the Denbighshire lordships which had a lifetime of less than three hundred years, the effects of anglicisation, mainly in the manors, but extending in certain ways over the entire lordship, become clear. The taking of land by escheat and compulsory forfeiture made possible the planting of English-type manors and boroughs, the emparking of land in the Norman style, the development of ploughland and meadow on the open field pattern, the extension of crop growing, the improvement of herds, and the rise of a limited number of nucleated settlements, though these last were rare and the boroughs are the principal examples remaining. In the Welsh districts, English influence was most effective in the encouragement of cultivation and extension of sharelands in the Welshries, both meadow and arable, and in the consequent increase in production of all types of food. In particular, this relieved the monotony of a diet which, for the tribesmen in the time of the Princes, had been largely one of flesh meat, milk, butter and cheese with little or no bread. Ploughing devolved in Welsh tribal society on the bondsmen or *nativi*, and there is recorded the case of Brenbagl (Brynbach, some five miles south-south-west of Denbigh) where the settlement was divided into eight shares like the bovates of an English field system. Presumably nucleated, the medieval hamlet has disappeared. That this greater predilection for cultivation took hold is amply borne out by the records of arable strips in the *Kinmel MSS. and Documents*[1] in numerous townships in north Denbighshire and north Flintshire from the late fifteenth to the eighteenth century, notably in the several townships of Abergele where settlement patterns were characteristically Welsh. If nucleated settlements were indeed set up by the lords of Denbigh, they failed to survive in a rural setting. The loss of population during the plague years no doubt contributed to the lapse of any embryo nucleations, but more important may be considered the weakening of English influence both before and after Union. It is doubtful whether the so-called boroughs mentioned in the *Survey* other than Denbigh (i.e. Abergele, Llanrwst and Erethlyn[2]) were ever more than boroughs in name.[3]

---

[1] U.C.N.W. Library, Bangor.
[2] Thought to be Pennant Erethlyn, south of Eglwys Fach.
[3] E. A. Lewis, *The Mediaeval Boroughs of Snowdonia* (1912), p. 16.

Later, Abergele and Llanrwst were to experience modest growth, but the first causes of their real growth were their markets and ecclesiastical status. The latter also aided the rise at varying periods of the rare villages and hamlets of this Middle Country such as Eglwys-Fach and Henllan. Elsewhere, the overwhelmingly most important and prevailing pattern in the rural areas of western Denbighshire is that of the dispersed or semi-dispersed farm units which date back in many cases to medieval origins, both as units and as part of a dispersal pattern.[1] These generalisations seem to apply to wide areas of north Flintshire and western Denbighshire away from the *capita* of the medieval lordships, i.e. the habitation pattern, if it was altered at all, tended to revert to the traditional spread of the *tyddyn* which for so long was both an economic unit yet interdependent with other *tyddynod* within the *tref*. The increase in ploughing strips, some scattered, some in small crofts, some in small fields, persisted at least into the enclosure period. Interdependence was further demonstrated in the intermixed lands which long persisted here as in Montgomeryshire and elsewhere. Compacting came comparatively late and is still not wholly achieved.

The other bequest made by the marcher lords to the rural landscape of Denbighshire, though this element had its basis in the *maerdref* and the *llys* of the time of the Princes, is the great house and the park which characteristically surrounds it. There are a number of these estates such as Eriviat and Plas Heaton, both of which are within two miles of Denbigh, but perhaps the most interesting is that of Kinmel Park in the township and parish of *St George* (JC/Ep). Lying partly on Rhuddlan Marsh and partly on the limestone upland to the south, St George is dominated by the great park of Kinmel with its military camp, Lowther College and Clarendon School. Its history, however, is as ancient as that of any settlement in this part of Wales. A Roman road from across the Flintshire plateau runs from Varae (supposedly near St Asaph) to Betws yn Rhos and thence by a less certain route to Caerhun (Conovium) on the Conway. Just to the north in the parish of St George, is the great Early Iron Age hill fort of Dinorben or

---

[1] G. R. J. Jones, 'Some Medieval Rural Settlements in North Wales', *Trans. Inst. Brit. Geogr.* (1953), especially pp. 62–5, in which the present and earlier patterns of Hendregyda (Abergele) and Llanynys are analysed.

Parc y Meirch and near to this was the princely estate of Dinorben Fawr which, in 1334 became a manor of the honour of Denbigh. According to the *Survey* it had a grange, granary, bovary, barn, a ruined columbarium, arable lands held in common and sown on a 3-course rotation (though there appear only to have been two named fields, Spital field and Vaugh cleit, with old pastures newly brought into cultivation called le Maordern), meadow land and various pastures.[1] Y Faerdref was the nucleus of the estate, together with the tiny centre of St George. Kinmel House was built by the grandson of Robin Holland who supported Glyn Dŵr, and in 1647 the estate included the two capital messuages of Faerdref and Kinmel. Under a number of manorial families, the estate grew by the purchase of lands, especially in the nearby parishes of Abergele and Rhuddlan, but also as far away as Llewenni, and even in 1649, John Carter acknowledged in a Final Concord the ownership of over 2000 acres, 100 messuages, 50 cottages, 3 mills, 3 dovecotes, 200 gardens, etc.[2] Kinmel Park was mentioned as such in a marriage settlement of 1709[3] at a time when parkland was being extended everywhere around great houses, but it is clear that the estate had roots which went back not only to the fourteenth century but earlier. By 1839, it was dominated by the estate element rather than by the typical farm units of most Welsh townships, and only faint traces of the one-time open arable fields could be detected on the tithe map. It is, in fact, the park estate element and the boroughs which now remain as the principal settlement features inherited from the period of English occupation. The old field patterns may be traceable from the air, but on the modern map nearly all evidences of the old strip fields have vanished except to the seeing eye of the expert.

Eastern Flintshire

The effect of English occupation in the Flintshire–Denbighshire Borderland is most evident in the eastern part of that ovoid ring which is the prime belt of hybridisation. Nearness to the English

[1] *Survey of the Honour of Denbigh*, fo. 213.
[2] *Kinmel MSS.*, no. 700.   [3] Ibid. no. 724.

lowlands of which much of eastern Flintshire and Denbighshire is part, together with the fact that here alone was the Mercian settlement to any degree permanent, has resulted in the planting and survival of early and some medieval English place-names, and in widespread arable arrangements which long reflected English influence and, for some centuries, became deeply entrenched.

In the Flintshire portion of this belt, particular interest attaches to the physical setting. Because of the marshy character of the estuarine shores immediately below Chester, Hawarden as the first point on comparatively dry land commanded both the coast road and the Wheeler–Alyn route into North Wales until the nineteenth century. Its Norman shell keep, its medieval castle, and perhaps a wooden castle which earl Edwin of Mercia is thought to have built, had fine strategic siting both in relation to routes and as the most northerly fortification along the hill edge commanding a sweeping view across the Cheshire plains and the Dee estuary. Until the fifteenth century, the whole estuary was a broad sheet of water at high tide, with the main course of the river at low water lying under the north bank for some distance below Chester. Saxton showed the estuary as open water in 1577, but silting had begun actively long before that date. Outports came into use progressively on the Wirral shore as the upper reaches became blocked by the smothering sands, and when, after 1740, the New Cut was begun, the course of the main stream was diverted to the south side leaving part of the Saltney marshes on the north bank. At Hawarden, the Coal Measures emerge from beneath the Trias to rise gently to a low plateau which, within the lordship, nowhere exceeds 500 feet in height. The estuarine shores also become firmer westward, and good land becomes available for cultivation both on the low ground and on the drift soils of the plateau.

From Caergwrle, Wat's Dyke runs parallel to the plateau edge about two to three miles in, and it is within this line that the main spread of English names occurs. Superimposed over a scatter of Welsh pastoral settlement in what was probably largely wooded country, the Mercian names are mingled with Welsh of varying dates, and in the lordship of Hawarden which lies wholly within the line of Wat's Dyke are medieval names such as Manor, Moor and Rake in addition. One of the interesting features of Welsh place-names in eastern Flintshire and Denbighshire is the lack of ecclesiastical elements. There are no major *llan*, *eglwys*, or *betws* names in either, though a few minor *llan* names survive in the Wrexham area; nor are any Celtic saints' names incorporated in place-names except for rare examples like Daniel's Ash in Hawarden. This is not due to the absence of early Celtic church dedications in the area, as is shown in E. G. Bowen's distribution map,[1] and can no doubt be attributed to the erosion of such names during the Anglo-Norman period. Instead, numerous comparatively late Welsh place-names are abundant, such as *ffordd*, *stryt* and *parc*, and topographical names predominate. Place-names of Anglo-Saxon origin are numerous, and become proportionately more important eastward and, in the Hawarden area, northward. These include a number of *tuns* – Aston, Shotton, Bretton, Broughton in Hawarden parish (which is coterminous with the lordship or manor), Kinnerton to the south, and more in eastern Denbighshire. Names such as Manor and Rake are probably medieval, and later elements such as 'green' and 'wood' are numerous, for example Tallwrn Green, Ewloe Green, Ewloe Wood, Broughton Green and Padeswood. Farm and locality names, like surnames, are both Welsh and English in this extraordinarily heterogeneous border district.

This heterogeneity became evident comparatively early in relation to open field names. The first open field record goes back in Bretton to an undetermined date before 1300 when a grant was made of sixty selions of land.[2] During the sixteenth century open field records became abundant and the selions of the early Latin deeds reappear as virgates, lands, lounds and butts; in the seventeenth century as lounds, butts, pikes, 'hadlandes' and hardlands (i.e. headlands), yokings, acres, *erwau* (in Leeswood), and as balks in Kinnerton and errows in Hope to the south of the lordship. Beyond its bounds, Welsh names occurred more frequently, for example *Erw dau cyfar* (a two-*cyfar* strip) in Gwysaney two miles beyond Ewloe.[3] Cheshire influence is reflected in the references to the Cheshire acre in the *Hawarden Deeds*, and Palmer and Owen maintain that the Flintshire *cyfar* was a quarter

---

[1] *Settlements of the Celtic Saints in Wales*, p. 105.
[2] *Hawarden Deeds*, no. 5.
[3] Tithe schedule, 1837.

of a Cheshire acre, i.e. the equivalent of a Cheshire rood.[1] Open arable fields with English names were to be found in all the sixteen townships of Hawarden except Pentrobin and Bannel, both of which lie in the Welsh settlement area on the higher part of the plateau, and Saltney which was unreclaimed marsh used as common pasture until the late enclosure period.[2]

Hawarden (JUlc(m)p) first emerged into the light of history as a result of the missionary journey of Deiniol from Bangor on Dee *circa* A.D. 550, and his building of a simple church, probably on the site known as Daniel's Ash in Penarth-halagh, now Hawarden. At Domesday there was a church with half a carucate of land. Formerly held by earl Edwin, it had four ploughs and half an acre of meadow.[3] By 1093 if not before, Hawarden church had come under the control of St Werburgh's (Chester) and so remained until it became attached in 1258 to the diocese of Lichfield.[4]

The medieval manor was based on Edwin's Mercian holding at Hawarden and on the manor of Ewloe, the site of a second Norman castle and more Welsh than the Hawarden portion of the combined lordship. After the Conquest, it became the property of earl Hugh of Chester. In 1338, it passed to the Montacutes, and in the early fifteenth century to the Stanleys who held it until James Stanley, the seventh earl of Derby, was executed for treason in 1651. His estate at Hawarden became forfeit to the crown and was purchased by the Glynnes of Glynllivon. After their acquisition of the estate, the survey was made which includes the fragile and valuable plans of Hawarden, Aston and Shotton (Fig. 31), Bretton and Bannel.[5] Eleanor Glynne, sister of the last baronet, by her marriage in 1839 to W. E. Gladstone, brought the estate to that family who are the present owners. The Norman shell keep on the steep bluff was succeeded by the thirteenth-century castle on the hill slope below it and in 1731 the first Glynne to reside on the estate went to Broad Lane Hall. Completed in 1755, the house now known as Hawarden Castle replaced the dilapidated old Broad Lane Hall a

---

[1] Op. cit. pp. 6–24. The Flintshire *cyfar* was 2560 sq. yards; the Cheshire acre 10,240 sq. yards.

[2] For a fuller account, see pp. 243–5 and 490.

[3] D.B., fo. 268b.

[4] W. Bell Jones, *A History of the Parish of Hawarden*, 4 vols, privately typed, N.L.W., vol. i, pp. 3–8.

[5] *Hawarden Estate Maps*, N.L.W.

hundred yards or so below the medieval ruins.[1] The deer park in which all are situated, partly in Broad Lane and partly in Hawarden townships, was shown on the seventeenth-century estate map.[2] Certainly from the thirteenth century the lordship was run on lines similar to those adopted in other marcher lordships, with extensive open fields and common meadows in nearly every township, all linked to the lord and his demesne. In the 1464 rental, 584 selions were listed allotted between the demesne, 44 free tenants and over 50 tenants at will. Of these holdings, 12 were burgages, presumably in Hawarden. Beyond the town was the great park, and beyond the arable fields the lot meadows.[3] The layout of the land was a determining factor in the selection of areas of meadow which were largely on the low ground near the coast, while the arable land lay in a broad band on the better drained coastlands, notably in Aston and Shotton, and on the gentler slopes and, in some cases, on fairly level upland of the higher plateau. Farther inland were the pastoral lands of the Welsh in which cultivation was negligible, and common pastures were distributed both on the upland and on the broad marshes flanking the Dee towards Chester.

Hawarden as the *caput* of the manor was a borough with a market and it remained, much as in the cases of Rhuddlan and Denbigh, the sole nucleation of any size in the area of the former lordship, except that, in the case of Hawarden, industrial and mining activities during the industrial period have now transformed some of the erstwhile townships which were long dispersed into nucleated modern settlements. During the period of traditional settlement, Bretton was the only other place which could boast a small village, and it appeared as such on one of the seventeenth-century Hawarden Estate maps. Broughton and Rake were semi-dispersed in the earlier nineteenth century with small hamlets, and not one of the other townships could boast even a minor nucleation. In this respect perhaps more than in any other facet of its settlement, the pattern had remained predominantly Welsh, except for Hawarden and Bretton.

Of the once wide pastures held in common, little now remains.

[1] Bell Jones, ii, pp. 27, 44, 79–91 and 117–20.
[2] *Hawarden Estate Maps.*
[3] Quoted at length by W. Bell Jones, op. cit. pp. 47–59. The originals are in the care of Liverpool Corporation.

Saltney Marsh was enclosed in 1778, the open lands of Broughton and Pentrobin in 1798.[1] Drainage and enclosure followed the diversion of the Dee and the enclosure of White Sands in 1733,[2] and this land, which now lay across the river from the rest of the parish, became the new township of Sealand. By the time of the tithe survey it consisted of large regular enclosures cultivated by a few widely spaced farms, and the church of St Bartholomew was built at a lonely road junction in 1887.

The Lowlands of the Denbighshire Dee

Below the edge of the Coal Measure uplands of eastern Denbighshire the lowland Dee winds its meandering course across a wide riverine plain which it shares with Cheshire and Maelor Saesneg. In this last of the local studies of rural landscape, the return to the borders of the first two county divisions brings up points of peculiar interest and significance. All three areas – south-west Cheshire, Maelor Saesneg and east Denbighshire – have an almost identical physical setting and for several centuries their farming economy has been closely related. Passing from one to the other today, the same type of large dairy farms, the same rich grazing land, and a not dissimilar pattern of habitations tend to make one unaware of the historic importance of the Dee as the boundary of Cymru during certain periods. Yet this same river once drained the middle of Maelor and the mid-west of Cheshire and to this day the eastern part of Maelor forms the detached area of Flintshire. Here is unquestionably a key area offering some and withholding others of the solutions to the problems which rural settlement poses in the Borderland.

In the Denbighshire section of the lowland Dee there are both characteristic and contradictory features. Like nearby parts of Cheshire and Maelor Saesneg, following the early Celtic period it became the scene of a Mercian settlement still evidenced by the line of early Anglo-Saxon place-names, especially near the river. Some, like Allington, are anglicisations (the Welsh name is

---

[1] Statute 19 Geo. III, c. 90, and 39 Geo. III, c. 25.
[2] 7 Geo. II.

Trefalyn). Others appear to be straight examples of early English names planted in a conquered territory by contemporary settlers from the east – Burton, Eyton, Gourton, Dutton, Sutton, Bersham – their suffixes probably related to the foundation of these English settlements and matching comparable names across the river. Others are etymologically mixed names such as Gresford and Dutton Diffeth, but westward and southward Welsh place-names replace English and hybrid names as the riverine plain gives place to higher land.

This Mercian-settled lowland, like Flintshire and Maelor Saesneg was part of Cheshire in the Old English and early Norman periods, and in 1086, apart from the commotes of Rhos and Rhufoniog nominally attached to Rhuddlan, the only places now in Denbighshire which were mentioned in the Cheshire portion of the Domesday Book were five manors in this area – Allington, Gresford, Sutton, Eyton and Erbistock, though Eyton was recorded as two manors. This suggests that there had been Mercian settlements here continuously from the ninth century or earlier, and that English settlements and field systems were probably well established. It became part of the new marcher lordship of Bromfield and Yale in 1282, and so remained until the county of Denbigh was created in 1536. Today, this is indisputably a Welsh district, an area of Welsh speech as contrasted with most of the eastern lowlands of Flintshire, and one of dispersed habitation. Yet its field arrangements long reflected English influence and part at least of the explanation appears to lie in the late thirteenth or early fourteenth century.

There are certain parallel features in this and the Denbigh area, in that both were created marcher lordships during the Edwardian period, and the shorter duration of this form of administration meant that the hold of English customs was less successfully imposed than in those of early Norman origin. Until 1282, these lowlands were part of the territory of Powys Fadog and of the cantref of Maelor, eventually to be distinguished from Maelor Saesneg by the name Maelor Gymraeg or Welsh Maelor. The commotes of Cynmeirch and Iâl, both within Maelor, were combined in 1282 to form the lordship of Bromfield and Yale with Holt as the *caput*, manors at Marford and Hoseley and Wrexham, and demesnes on certain escheated lands in a few other vills.

The earliest of the Welsh medieval *Extents*[1] covers this area and, although it is less detailed in its account of landholding and cultivation than the *Survey of the Honour of Denbigh*, it has some extremely illuminating information to offer and throws light not only on contemporary conditions but on rural and urban patterns of the present day. In 1315, *Holt* or *Lyons* was the only borough, but Wrexham was growing actively and its bi-annual fairs were already associated with a flourishing trade. The population of Holt was almost exclusively English, and burgage holdings, of which there were 203 and three half-tenements, were held by 159 burgesses of whom only some four were Welshmen. In Wrexham there were only eight Englishmen, and elsewhere virtually the entire population was Welsh. In his introduction to the *Extent*, Ellis has shown that the record can be interpreted in such a way as to show that from Trefydd Bychain in the hills west of Esclusham, cognate groups of the progeny of Ken were in process of moving eastward, establishing themselves in clusters of small vills or *trefydd* in the plain. It may be that this was part and parcel of the uprooting of earlier English settlers who, in turn, may have been forced back into the English lowland or into Maelor Saesneg. The significant point is that, without wholly gallicising the place-names, they firmly re-planted the country-side as settlers, and, despite the English overlordship, here they remained.

Norden's Survey of 1620[2] lists the manors of the lordship of Bromfield and their constituent vills, and they bear a very close resemblance to the parishes and their townships of the early nineteenth century. The townships are for the most part tiny, but there are a few larger ones such as Burton, Allington, Holt and Marchwiel, and they tend to group into concentric arcs, the outer arc along the Dee, others farther west away from the river. Like many other Welsh areas, their parochial arrangements seem to have had a degree of fluidity, but the ancient parishes were for the most part large with numerous townships as in the adjoining areas of north-east Wales, Cheshire and Shropshire. The small townships closely resemble those of west Cheshire.

As in the lordships of Denbigh and Rhuddlan, one major

---

[1] T. P. Ellis, *The First Extent of Bromfield and Yale, A.D. 1315* (1924).
[2] *Harl. MS.* 3696.

urban unit represented English power, but the borough of Holt, though it alone had burghal status in the Middle Ages, had a vigorous rival in Wrexham, and even in 1315, as was recorded under numerous townships, the inhabitants were helping to build the houses of Wrexham.[1] Not only today as a considerable mining and industrial centre, but for some centuries prior to the development of the coalfield, Wrexham has ranked as a town, whereas Holt has declined to a large village. The rest of the riverine lowland of eastern Denbighshire is characterised by dispersed and semi-dispersed habitations, the only exceptions being Gresford, a nucleated village, and Ruabon, now a village but in the early nineteenth century nothing more than an estate hamlet and small parochial centre at the gates of Wynnstay.

In the fourteenth century, according to the *Extent* of 1315, the farming was rich and varied, its produce including wheat, winter wheat, oats, swine for which pannage was provided in the woods, and nuts which were gathered at Michaelmas for renders unique in Wales to this lordship of Bromfield and Yale. Hens were part of the traditional Christmas render, and the numerous references to meadowland pasture presuppose important pastoralism, though butter is only mentioned once as a render from the vill of Dutton y Brain. Although there is nothing comparable in this *Extent* to the specific description of open fields in the *Survey of the Honour of Denbigh*, manorialisation may be presumed to have either introduced or continued open field agriculture and lot meadows, and certainly by the time of Union the field patterns of many of these more easterly townships were characteristically those of strip holding. As in the Cheshire townships across the river, the rich Dee water meadows provided the most valuable land and were doled out in strips for the hay harvest.[2] The communal arable arrangements accounted for wide quilleted areas in many of these townships and A. N. Palmer's descriptions of the fields of Wrexham,[3] Gresford and its townships,[4] and the chapelry of Is-y-coed[5] rank now as classical analyses of open

[1] *Extent*, e.g. p. 105 under Dutton y Brain: 'Each helps for his own part to make the houses of Wrexham as his neighbours do.'

[2] Palmer and Owen, op. cit. plan of the lot meadows of Allington, opp. p. 70.

[3] *The Town Fields of Wrexham in the time of James I* (1883).

[4] 'A History of the Old Parish of Gresford', *Archaeol. Camb.*, 6th series, iii (1903), pp. 189–204.

[5] 'Isycoed', ibid. x (1910), pp. 229–372.

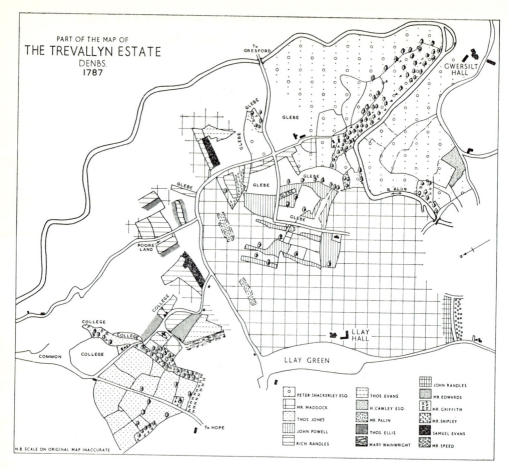

PART OF THE MAP OF
THE TREVALLYN ESTATE
DENBS.
1787

To GRESFORD

GWERSILT HALL

GLEBE

GLEBE

GLEBE

GLEBE

GLEBE

R. ALUN

POORS LAND

COLLEGE

COLLEGE

COLLEGE

COMMON

COLLEGE

To HOPE

LLAY HALL

LLAY GREEN

N.B. SCALE ON ORIGINAL MAP INACCURATE

PETER SHACKERLEY ESQ.
MR. MADDOCK
THOS. JONES
JOHN POWELL
RICH. RANDLES
THOS. EVANS
H. CAWLEY ESQ.
MR. PALIN
THOS. ELLIS
MARY WAINWRIGHT
JOHN RANDLES
MR. EDWARDS
MR. GRIFFITH
MR. SHIPLEY
SAMUEL EVANS
MR. SPEED

58. Part of the Trevallyn estate map, Denbighshire, 1787

fields and meadows in the Borderland. *Allington* (DL) is an example of a township in which landholding interests were numerous and complex and in which disparate holding persisted until a late date (Fig. 58). *Burton* (DL), its nearest neighbour and, like Allington, a township of the old parish of Gresford, experienced enclosure at an earlier date. In 1620, Burton included a sizeable area of quilleted closes, variously named Maes Croes Howel, Kae Kymisk (Cae Cymmysg or mixed field), and Burton field or Maes Burton. By the time Richard Norwood[1] was drawing his map of Burton in 1631 only a few field shapes, field-names, and an occasional open quillet remained as evidence of the old open strips, though disparate holding passed somewhat less quickly. The landscape of enclosure is typical today of the entire area, but long, strip-shaped fields persist in a number of townships and can be seen, for example, along the Holt–Wrexham road as clear evidences of the former existence of open arable fields, and ridge and furrow are clearly traceable on aerial photographs.

These features can in large part be matched across the Dee in west Cheshire, and there is little today which can be traced in the visible rural landscape which distinguishes one side from the other. The same comfortable brick farmhouses and large farms, similar field patterns, and a similarly successful strawberry culture distinguish both sides. But the gaps in rural history are tantalising. It is certain that at some periods their history was divergent, though in the Dark Ages, the early Middle Ages, and again after Union, common agents were at work to produce many of the shared characteristics of this river lowland and the adjacent plains.

[1] Harleian MS. 3696 and A. N. Palmer, *Archaeol. Camb.* (1903), pp. 99–101.

Conclusion

THE dictum that geography is a synthesis is fully borne out in the study of rural landscape, in which so many elements combine to compose a complex whole. Nor could one perhaps demonstrate better than in the geography of rural areas that interpretation depends also on invisible and visible cultural elements, on their ethnic associations, and on the changing balance and inter-relationships of all the contributory elements and factors with the passage of time. In the Welsh Borderland, Nature, Man and Time have surely combined to offer a wide and fascinating range of contrasted conditions.

The alterations in rural pattern are rarely either swift or whole-sale and, when they do take place, older features remain to a greater or lesser degree, readable below the newer as in a palimp-sest. The stronger certain emotive forces such as culture-group adherence, of conservatism as an expression of traditionalism, or of attachment to an ancient religion, the less likely is change to take place. Similarly, remoteness in the geographical sense and isolation in the ethnic sense foster the preservation of traditional forms. In the Welsh Borderland, it is the upland areas and some remote heaths and woodlands which have contributed most to conservative settlement patterns and to the survival of early strata of the population; the richer lowlands and valleys which have attracted the invaders and whose inhabitants have eventually embraced new ways of life and thought, and reshaped their economy on that of the newcomers. The relative homogeneity of the Welsh of the uplands ethnically and culturally stands out in every aspect of its rural geography, and hybridisation is equally a feature of the lowlands and vales. The hill edge from the head of the Dee estuary to the mouth of the Usk, and the valleys which are pushed like thrusting spears from the lowlands up into the hills are the critical areas in the distribution of innumerable features which make up the rural geography of the Borderland.

As there are critical areas, so there are critical periods – periods of vital change due to ethnic movement, war and strategic needs, the extension of early Christianity and church organisation, and economic innovations such as the Great Enclosure movement. The interplay of region, period, and cultural and ethnic groups is the basis of the study of the changing rural landscape in its widest connotation, but change has been on the whole so slow that two millennia span the history of the field patterns and a far longer period has seen the evolution of the habitation pattern. Nevertheless, the most significant elements in the present landscape have arisen within the Christian era, while the most important available body of evidence as regards patterns of land uses dates from the Norman Conquest. As time goes on, archaeology adds increasingly vital clues to the history both of medieval and earlier land and habitation patterns, and recent work on place-names is among the most valuable contributions to the unravelling of early ethnic distributions and movements. In combination, mounting data from various branches of knowledge make clear the importance of the Celtic foundation, the partial and varied overlay of Anglo-Saxon settlement, the somewhat wider Anglo-Norman occupation, and the tendency to follow similar paths, especially in economic matters, since Union. This gives the division into the four major periods under which rural history can most conveniently be treated if it is to afford some explanation of the present landscape features and the character of the rural communities. But few things are simple, and it seems more than possible that in the parts where the Celtic settlement was succeeded by an Anglian occupation and in turn by an Anglo-Norman, certain archaic elements such as the older forms of place-names and habitation patterns have survived from the Celtic period, whereas in the purely Welsh areas most of these older forms have been lost in the slow evolution to the predominantly 'modern' Welsh place-names and the dispersion of habitations. Thus, the English border counties offer clues to the earlier Celtic settlement geography which Wales itself cannot.

In some parts of the Borderland ethnic movement has been further complicated by the see-saw of advance and retreat and the Welsh districts of north-west Shropshire and southern Herefordshire are thought to represent a Welsh re-invasion. With the uneven recession of the Welsh language during the past hundred years or so and the in-migration of so many Welsh to England, it is not surprising that Offa's Dyke and the political boundary of the Principality have tended increasingly to become the axes of a broad zone, or that west–east links are often more real in daily life than the cultural associations which originally would have suggested northward and southward ties. Such Anglo-Welsh links go back in the northern border even in recorded history to the alliance of Cadwallon with Penda of Mercia in the seventh century, and to the close association of St Asaph with the northern archdiocese over many centuries. Very significant too in relation to rural settlement is the 'parish line' which has been shown to associate north-eastern Wales in parish structure with the west Midland area and northern England and to differentiate all of these from southern and west Wales and southern England. The relationship between parochial structure and settlement pattern, here investigated for the first time, has been shown to be a very real factor in village growth and in the local differentiation of rural settlements over a long period.

It is not easy to date the rise of nucleated settlements, but the rural settlement geography of the Welsh Borderland reveals that, unlike many parts of the English lowlands, a straightforward Anglo-Saxon origin is not only rare but exceptional and it is doubtful whether any villages other than those in the more easterly parts of the English border counties can be fitted into this category, unless – and this seems far from likely – the church villages of Cheshire, north Shropshire and some similar examples in north-eastern Wales belong here. Not only do many of them have earlier historical associations: another difficulty is that they are central, unlike those of southern England, to satellite townships having only hamleted or dispersed settlements, and the period of the rise of the central settlements is open to question. Some may be British; some may be genuine early English villages. Many were at best large hamlets until the period of modern expansion, that is until about the sixteenth or even in some cases the eighteenth and nineteenth centuries. It seems preferable to put these parochial villages in a class of their own. In the southern half of Shropshire and in Herefordshire, many of the places which were compact villages in the early nineteenth century may have had an Anglo-Saxon origin as settlement points – indeed, their place-names in most instances proclaim that this or a still earlier Celtic origin was implicit. But all the historical evidence supports the conclusion that their growth as compact villages dated from their defensive role in the early Middle Ages, and this assumption has been seen to be still further strengthened by the fact that they form a westerly belt in the two more southerly English border counties divided from the main village region of the English lowlands by a broad stretch of country in which the only nucleations are small country market towns, ex-market villages or the larger centres of Hereford and Ludlow.

The distribution of habitation groupings in the Borderland also sheds light on the problem of hamleting and dispersal. It is the latter which is now typical of Welsh areas, while the hamlet is a characteristic form of the English side of the border, and although some of these minor nucleations have a recognisably modern origin, the older hamlets, known to have been in existence before 1086, must be at latest Anglo-Saxon, and may either represent lesser nuclei near the sparse western limits of that occupation or be Celtic hamlets which became subject to Anglian overlordship and were in many cases therefore renamed by their new lords. There seems much to support the latter assumption.

Although distributional maps and local studies shed new light on rural settlement problems in this challenging and difficult border zone, many questions remain, for hybridisation has cast together strange partners in a complex patchwork. Perhaps the most curious association is that of the most intensive two- and three-field area – central and eastern Herefordshire – with a village-less landscape. But the distribution of this type of field system has been shown to extend in a belt within and near the marcher lordships, well to the west of H. L. Gray's Midland area and must unquestionably be associated with the Normans. For many reasons, it is difficult to assess their contribution and that of their Anglo-Saxon predecessors to the field arrangements in many Borderland townships. Further, the field systems, varying from the 'standard' two- and three-field pattern to multi-field on the one side and to co-aration in scattered ploughing strips on the other, show every degree of variation.

Far from complexity and hybridisation presenting only a confused picture, however, certain associations emerge, a number of geographical sub-regions are clearly distinguishable, and many parts of the puzzle fall into place when the nature of the rural landscape and its communities and culture are interpreted with the help of distribution maps and examined in the round. The first and major conclusion is that the Welsh settlement landscape has distinctive character where it remained beyond the direct influence of Anglian or Anglo-Norman economy, and this includes not only the areas beyond the marches but some of the Welshries. This prime division is underlined equally strongly by the place-name, the open field, and the nucleation/dispersal maps. Secondly, the greater part of the English border areas are seen as a mixed settlement belt in which hamleting and dispersal predominate except in Cheshire and north Shropshire where compact villages, parochial centres in almost every case, are added to the mixture, and in south-west Shropshire, western Herefordshire and eastern Monmouthshire where compact villages of strategic growth form a long narrow belt. The third significant division is in part implicit in the distinction between these two types of village; the division made by the parish line between the satellite settlement structure of the northern Borderland and the single-parish which dominates the southern Borderland. The link between settlement forms and ecclesiastical organisation, whether one or the other or both in turn operated as cause, cuts not only the Borderland but the whole of southern Britain into two parts. Other facets of local administrative geography have remained fundamental, especially the township which was sufficiently vigorous to re-establish itself after the Norman imposition of the manor as the universal unit of territorial division. Nor should the manor for this reason be played down unduly. It had widespread and important effects on the settlement landscape of all the normanised parts of the border counties: on towns, markets, some villages, field systems, the clearance of woodland and, of course, on the enhanced status of the lord and his great house and park, and the many other features such as mills, dovecots and artificial waters that went with them.

On balance, it seems that all three peoples – Celts, Angles and Normans – played a remarkably equal part in shaping the settlement landscape and the cultural character of the English side of the Welsh Borderland. The survival of the Celtic foundation in place-names, settlement patterns, and certainly in the matter of the physical character of its population, has been greater than many Teutonists in the past cared to allow. Equally, the tendency to play down the Anglo-Saxon invasion here can go too far. There is no doubt that their numbers were sparser than in either the Midlands or south-eastern England, but place-names and the spread of ploughland by 1086 suggest that they had at least exercised an effective overlordship and brought about a minor economic revolution. Yet one cannot avoid the conclusion that Norman influence was nowhere greater than in Herefordshire, one of their two favourite counties, and in the Marcher lordships to which they undoubtedly extended the two- and three-field system. Cheshire, as the longest lived of the three palatine counties of the Borderland, also reflected Norman influence in its widespread park-estates and in certain extensions of the open field system, but these last were relatively minor and it was mainly as 'the seed plot of gentility' that it became the mirror of Norman land planning and social change.

Behind all the detail of Man's settlement and his consequent modification of the land surface are the inescapable facts of the physical environment. Where these are generally favourable, the range within which they can be adapted to the basic needs of the individual and the community are considerable, but there is often a 'best' use and the choice between crop raising and pastoralism as the dominant feature of the economy is closely related to climate, altitude, slope, soil and subsoil. Beyond this broad choice, preference, technique, capital, market demand and other factors now operate, but even in the Dark Ages the distinction was present between the Celtic and the Anglo-Saxon modes of land use. As the natural environment becomes poorer the choice is reduced and it is at a minimum in the Highland Zone. The natural beauty of the Welsh hills meant little to those who were forced to win a thin living from its steep slopes and barren, windswept heights and the division between the two worlds of the hillmen and the plainsmen is for ever drawn as the geographer's basic physical contrast between the Highland and Lowland Zones.

So much is undeniable. But the second major element in the shaping of the rural landscape and the determination of geographical regions – Man – has, through the centuries, imposed his patterns of town and village, of hamlet and lonely farmstead, of *tir priodolder* and open field, of parkland and common allotments, of cultivation and pastoralism, of roads and boundaries, over the natural heathlands and woodlands, the hills, the vales, and the lowlands. The over-simplified concept of a Highland and Lowland Zone, useful though it has been and, as a physical springboard, still is, must give place in the determination of broad regional divisions to the overriding factors in human, economic, and historical geography which have been reshaping the landscape in an extended sense during the centuries. There is no question that the Borderland offers a third region astride the highland–lowland line, or that this has been beaten out on the anvil of Time by the Anglo-Saxons, and perhaps still more by the Normans, both of whom have 'frozen' in the older Celtic culture, and produced a newer, hybrid settlement landscape, with its own distinctive character and culture.

What we have inherited from the past in the countryside is still writ large across it. It poses numerous problems not only to the geographer and the historian but to the sociologist and the planner. The twentieth century like its predecessor the nineteenth has seen many changes, some for the better, many for the worse, and the moving finger having writ constantly moves on. The preservation of this great heritage becomes more difficult and more necessary as the town and the commuter move outwards, and it grows ever more urgent that its intricate history and geography should be interpreted both to guide the planners and to add to the understanding of Britain and the British people.

Glossary

abaty (W.), abbey

aber (W.), mouth of a river, confluence point

accar, acker, accr, Welsh variants of the adopted word *acre*

acre (i) a measure of land varying in extent according to district and period, e.g. the statute acre today is 4840 sq. yards, the traditional Cheshire acre was 10,240 sq. yards
    (ii) a strip in an open arable field

afon (W.), river

aratral curve, the inverted S-bend often found in medieval ridge and furrow, a device to check downhill drainage

aratrum (Lat.), *aradr* (W.), plough

ardal (W.), district

allotment, land allotted, especially used by enclosure commissioners when parcelling out the former open pasture

allt (W.), hill, hillside, slope, wood

anticline, a geological upfold

assart, a medieval term for enclosure from forest or waste

bach (W.), (i) n., nook, corner, bend
    (ii) adj., small, lesser

bailiwick, a medieval term denoting the area under the jurisdiction of a bailiff and associated with the *bailey* of a castle

balk, a boundary strip between selions or furlongs in an open field

ban, pl. *bannau* (W.), peak, crest, bare hill, beacon

bangor (W.), consecrated land, monastery within a wattle fence

banke (O.Dan.), *bank* (ME.), *banc* (W.), bank, slope, river bank

batch, bache (ME.), stream, brook, small valley

bedd, pl. *beddau* (W.), grave

bedellary, see *ringild*

berewick, a wick in which barley was grown. In practice, a detached part of a manor and semi-independent

betws (W.), a chapel of ease

blaen, pl. *blaenau* (W.), head, end, source of river, upland *bod* (W.), abode, dwelling

bote as in *haybote, hedgebote, housebote, ploughbote*, etc., the common right to take timber from the woods or waste to repair fences, houses, ploughs, etc.

bovate, an oxgang (q.v.), one-eighth of a ploughland or yardland

braich (W.), ridge, spur, arm

bro (W.), region, vale, lowland

bron (W.), breast, thus the breast or slope of a hill, hillside

brown earth or *brown forest soil*, soil type characteristic of deciduous woodland in temperate humid lands and formed in large part from the decay of leaves. Dark brown and relatively rich in organic matter

bryn, pl. *bryniau* (W.), hill

burh (OE.), a defended settlement, whence *burg* and *borough* and the place-name element *bury*

buth (ON.), *both* (O.Dan.), *booth*, shelter, temporary dwelling

butt(s), (i) in open field usage a strip, especially one abutting at right angles on another group of selions

　　　(ii) archery butts. By a Statute of Edward IV, such butts were to be erected near every village and each Englishman must shoot there every feast day under penalty of being mulcted one penny

bwlch (W.), pass, gap

bwrd eisdref (W.), a borough

bwrd sirol (W.), a county borough or shire town

bychan (W.), little, small, lesser

cadair, cader (W.), seat, stronghold

cae, pl. *caeau* (W.), field, enclosure, close. Not generally used in association with an open arable field

caer, pl. *caerau* (W.), fort, stronghold, camp

Cambrian, (i) a general term applicable to Wales and things Welsh;

　　　(ii) the oldest geological period of the Primary era and represented in the Borderland in small areas adjacent to the Uriconian hills in Shropshire

cantref, pl. *cantrefydd* (W.), literally a hundred townships; a major administrative division in Wales prior to the setting up of shires. Cf. the English *hundred*

capel (W.), *chapel*, meeting-house, religious building dependent on a parish church, Nonconformist church, private chapel in a castle or manor-house

caput (Lat.), head, head place (as of a marcher lordship)

Carboniferous, the most recent period of the Primary era to be represented in the rocks of the Borderland, and so named from its coal deposits. Its three series are: Carboniferous Limestone, Millstone Grit, Coal Measures. They occur on the flanks of the north-east Welsh uplands, in the Shropshire and South Wales coalfields, and in the Forest of Dean

carn, pl. *carnau* (W.), cairn, rock, mountain

carnedd, pl. *carneddau* (W.), cairn, barrow, tumulus, mountain

carreg, pl. *cerrig* (W.), stone, rock

carucate (from *caruca* (Lat.), a plough), a ploughland. Used in the Danish areas in the Middle Ages and earlier as a basis of taxation as was the *hide* (q.v.) in non-Danish areas, and of variable extent

cas (W.), a castle

castell (W.), castle, stronghold

castrum (Lat.), *caster, cester, chester*, fortress

cēap (OE.), *cieping, chip, chep, chipping*, a market (of pre-Norman date)

cefn (W.), ridge, whether a topographical feature or a ridge or strip in an open arable field

celli (W.), grove, copse

cemais (W.), bend of a river

ceunant (W.), ravine, gorge, brook

chapel, see *capel*

chapelry, a subdivision of a large parish consisting of one or more townships the spiritual needs of which are served by a dependent chapel

Charter Rolls, records of the foundation of monastic and other institutions; grants of land, liberties and fairs. Calendared to the time of Henry VIII

chartulary or *cartulary*, the register or record book of a monastery

chase, as a locality name indicates land formerly reserved for an earl's hunting

cil, pl. *ciliau* (W.), corner, retreat, nook

clâs or *clâs* church (W.), a monastic or collegiate religious foundation of the Celtic Church. Many clâs churches later became mother churches

clawdd (W.), dyke, hedge, ditch

clogwyn (W.), cliff, precipice

close, a small patch of land enclosed for agricultural purposes. See meaning (ii) of *field*

clun (W.), meadow, moor, brake, thicket, hip

coaration, communal ploughing

coch (W.), red

coed (W.), trees, wood, forest

coetre (W.), woodland dwelling or farm

comin (W.), common

common (i) adjective, pertaining to that which is held by a community
(ii) noun, waste or open pasture on which communal rights are exercised

common field, (i) usually an open arable field held in strips by the customary tenants but (ii) the name may be applied to an enclosure from the common

common meadow, meadow held in common and divided for the purposes of harvesting the hay crop into strips known as doles or lots

commote, see *cwmwd*

compacting, the act of making compact formerly disparate lands by exchange, purchase, etc. See *disparate* for the opposite meaning

cors (W.), bog, marsh, fen

cot (OE.), *cote, cottage*, the homestead of a cottar or cottager

cottar (ME.), *cottager*, tenant of a tenement with a small area of land not usually more than 8–10 acres. See *toft and croft*

court, (i) the seat of a manorial lord, a manor house
(ii) a judicial assembly. See below. There were and are numerous courts, national, ecclesiastical, etc.

court baron, a manorial court

court leet, a court of record attended by freeholders and tenants of a manor

Court of Augmentations, court set up by Henry VIII to deal with the seizing and redistribution of monastic lands and property at the time of the Dissolution of the Monasteries

craig, pl. *creigiau* (W.), rock

crib (W.), summit

croes (W.), cross, cross-road

croesffordd, croeslon (W.), cross-road

curtilage, a dwelling, usually of superior type, and the land adjoining it

cwm (W.), valley, combe; used now by geomorphologists to signify a glacial hollow or *corrie* on a hillside

cwmwd, pl. *cwmydau* (W.), *commote*, subdivision of a *cantref* (q.v.)

cwrt (W.), court, yard

cyd (W.), common

cyfair, pl. *cyfeiriau* (W.), *kyver, cover*, a customary acre, a day's ploughing, of varying size in different parts of Wales, e.g. in Flintshire the *cyfair* was 2560 sq. yards, in Gwynedd 4320 sq. yards

cyffredin (W.), common

Cymru (W.), Wales

Cymry (W.), the Welsh

dālen (O.Sc.), *dale*, (i) a narrow valley enclosed by hills
(ii), a strip in an open field

demesne, domain, literally dominial land or the land of a lord. In the Middle Ages this included the land attached to the manor house or castle and shares in the common arable fields and meadow. At varying dates, woodland was usually taken over also

denu (OE.), *den,* (i) lair of wild beast

    (ii) woodland pasture for swine

denu (OE.), *dene,* valley

Devonian, the geological period succeeding the Silurian and particularly associated with the Old Red Sandstone. Devonian rocks outcrop over a huge triangle in South Wales and the Borderland from the Clee Hills south to Monmouthshire, west to Glamorgan (and into Carmarthen and Pembroke), and north-east across Breconshire. Sandstones and shales predominate

din (W.), hill-fortress

dinas (W.), hill-fortress, city

diserth (W.), hermitage, wilderness

disparate holding, a landholding consisting of scattered pieces and in most cases, though not necessarily, an indication of open arable or former open arable land

dol, pl. *dolau, dolydd* (W.), meadow, water-meadow

dole, (i) portions or strips held in common meadow

    (ii) a share, a charitable donation

drift, geologically, unconsolidated 'rocks' of Quaternary and Recent date. In Britain it includes glacial and post-glacial deposits

drift map, map published by the Geological Survey in the One-Inch to the mile series of Drift Maps of England and Wales to show solid rocks only when they emerge at the surface and elsewhere the drift deposits which cover them

drws (W.), narrow pass, gap

dryll, pl. *drylliau* (W.), ridge or strip in open arable field

du (W.), black

dun (Br.), a defensive site, usually Celtic or with Celtic connections

dwr, dwfr (W.), water

dyffryn (W.), vale, valley

eccles, place-name element from *ecclesia* (Lat.) and related to *eglwys* (W.) from the same root. Generally considered to indicate a very early church

ēg, īeg (OE.), *ey* (ON.), *ey,* island, dry land in marshy area

eglwys (W.), from Latin *ecclesia,* a church

Englishry, the part of a marcher lordship administered by English law and custom *engrossment*, the drawing of two or more holdings into one

-ergh (O.Sc.), originally denoted a shieling or summer dwelling

erw, pl. *erwau* (W.), *errow, errowe, arrowe*, a Welsh measure of land, in some cases a ploughing strip which might or might not be in an open field. Three or four *erwau* might make up a customary acre, e.g., the Venedotian *erw* was 1440 sq. yards (30 × 3 rods of 16 feet), and three of these = 1 cyfair (4320 sq. yards)

esgair (W.), long ridge

ferendell, a quarter-acre

ffald (W.), enclosure or pound for strayed animals

ffin (W.), boundary

ffordd (W.), road

ffos (W.), ditch, trench

ffridd, pl. *ffriddoedd* (W.), sheepwalk, rough grazing enclosed from the mountain, woodland

ffrwd, pl. *ffrydiau* (W.), stream, torrent

ffwrn (W.), oven; in Radnorshire a place for drying corn

ffynnon, pl. *ffynhonnau* (W.), spring, well

field, cf. *campus* (Lat.), (i) originally an unenclosed area of communal cultivation, sometimes referred to as *champion* from the Norm. Fr. (ii) later an enclosed area used for any type of farmland – arable, pasture or meadow

flat, flatt (ON., ME., loan word), level ground, a strip in an open field

flax field, witness to futile legislation of 24 Henry VIII to foster flax growing in England

ford, (i) the crossing-place of a stream
(ii) a road in certain place- and road-names, e.g. the Longford in Shropshire

forest, land preserved in the Middle Ages for the royal hunt and subject to forest laws. It could cover woodland, heath, moor and even cultivated land

furlong, literally 'a furrow long'
(i) originally the length of a ploughing strip, eventually standardised as 220 yards
(ii) a group of aligned strips in an open arable field totalling 220 yards in width as well as length

gafael (W.), the land in which the *gwely* (q.v.) had individual or communal rights

gallt (W.), hill, slope, woodland

gardd, pl. *gerddi* (W.), garden, croft, occasionally a strip in an open field *garth* (W.), height, hill, enclosure

gavelkind, inheritance by equal division among all the sons (and in some cases daughters)

gefail (W.), smithy

glan (W.), river-bank

glas (W.), green, blue

glas, glais (W.), as in Dulas, Dulais, brook, stream

gley soils, waterlogged soils rich in organic matter, airless, also rich in carbon compounds

glyn (W.), deep valley, glen

gore, irregular, usually triangular patch in open arable field

gwaun (W.), moor, mountain pasture, meadow

gwely (W.), literally 'a bed', hence family group which became a settlement unit

gwern (W.), swamp, place where alders grow

gwlad (W.), country

gwyn (W.), white, fair, holy

hafod, pl. *hafodau*, *hafoty* (W.), summer dwelling, shieling, hill dairy used in summer

ham (OE.), homestead, village community

hamlet, a minor group of homesteads

hardwick, literally a 'wick' or settlement of herdsmen. A pastoral township attached to a manor or castle

headland, in an open arable field this was land at the head of a furlong on which the plough could turn

hen (W.), old

hendref (W.), the old *tref* or township; the permanent and, therefore, the winter settlement

heol, hewl (W.), a road. The word may be related to the anglicised place-name elements *hale, hal, hall*, etc. in certain cases

heriot, customary render of the best beast on death of a tenant

hide, medieval land unit used as a basis of assessment for taxation as in Domesday Book, and of variable extent. See *carucate*

hir (W.), long

holmr (ON.), *holme*; *hulm* (O.Dan.), *hulme*, lowlying land, isolated ground

Honour, a lordship, a group of manors under a single lordship

hop (OE.), *hope*, small valley, dingle

hryding (OE.), *ridding*, cleared land

hundred, from the Old English period until the Local Government Act of 1894, the hundreds were the major subdivisions of the counties.

They may have originated, like the *cantref* in Wales, from a hundred townships

hyrst (OE.), *hurst*, hillock, woodland, copse

ing, ingas (OE.),
ingaham (OE.), *-ingham* } place-name elements indicative of early
ingatun (OE.), *-ington* } Anglo-Saxon settlement

Inquisition Post Mortem, returns made by local juries concerning the lands and other property of deceased tenants in chief, etc. Calendared to the seventeenth century

intack, intake, enclosed piece of land, usually taken illegally from common land or from a road

is (W.), below, under

isaf (W.), lower, lowest

isel (W.), low

Jurassic, the middle period of the Secondary Era. Represented in the Borderland by an inlier of Lias in the Prees area of north Shropshire

kirkja (ON.), *kirk*, church

Lammas lands, meadows which provided common pasture after Lammas Day (1 August; Old Lammas Day, 12 August)

land (OE. and ON.), land, earth, estate, strip in an open field

-land, a place-name element. Where of Norse origin, probably represents the permanent winter seat or settlement

leah (OE.), *-ley,* woodland clearing

Liberty, an area outside a borough or lordship in which freemen and burghers had certain rights of pasture, pannage, etc.

Little London, a field set aside for cattle drovers en route for London

llain, pl. *lleiniau* (W.), strip in an open arable field, a quillet

llan (W.), originally an enclosure, but its association with the church finally stabilised its meaning as a church-place or church

llanerch (W.), glade, clearing

llathen, pl. *llathenni* (W.), yard or yardland. See *virgate.* In NE. Wales this measured 607½ sq. yards

llawr (W.), floor, flat valley bottom

llech (W.), slab, slate, stone, rock

llechwedd (W.), hillside, slope

llethr (W.), slope

llety (W.), small house, shelter, lodging

lluest (W.), cabin or hut

llwch, pl. *llychau* (W.), lake

llwyd (W.), grey, brown

llwyn (W.), grove, bush, a strip in an open field

llyn (W.), lake

llys (W.), a palace, the house of a chief or prince, court, hall

loam, a mixed soil of light texture characteristic of the margins of sand and clay, e.g. in drift-covered plains of Cheshire and Shropshire. Fertile and easily ploughed

loon, loont, lound, variants of *land* used in the sense of a *selion* or strip in an open arable field

lot meadow, a meadow in which strips or doles were allotted for the hay harvest, a common meadow

lynchet, a level terrace artificially cut out for cultivation on a hill slope

maen, pl. *meini* (W.), stone

maenol, maenor (W.), residence of a district chief

maer (W.), steward

maerdref (W.), hamlet attached to chief's court, lord's demesne

maes, pl. *meysydd* (W.), an open field, a plain

maes y dref (W.), town field, the open arable field of the township

manor, from the Latin *manerium,* the holding of a lord. Cf. Welsh *maenor*

March, Merse, a boundary or boundary zone, hence the Marches, Mercia, Mersey

math, mowing, hence *aftermath* on which stock were depastured

mawr (W.), big, great

mear, meer, a boundary mark in a common field. Cf. *balk*

melin (W.), mill

melyn (W.), yellow

merthyr (W.), burial-place, church

messuage, a dwelling and the land adjoining it

mign, pl. *mignoedd, mignedd* (W.), bog, quagmire

moel (W.), bald, bare hill

moor, rough open pasture hence (i) an upland area of rough pasture, e.g. heather moor, grass moor, (ii) common meadow, generally water meadow. This use of the word is obsolescent but survives in field-names and in the name Monmouthshire Moors

morfa (W.), marsh, sea-fen, saltings

moss rooms, strips or segments of a peat moss held in common (Cheshire)

motte, mount, a mound, natural or artificial, used by the Anglo-Normans and sometimes by Welsh lords as a defensive point or lookout

motte and bailey, the same plus a bailey or area in which the lord's retainers were housed

mur, pl. *muriau* (W.), wall
mwyn (W.), ore, mine
mynachlog (W.), monastery
mynydd (W.), mountain

nant (W.), stream, brook
nativi, bondsmen, the unfree, *taeogion*
neuadd (W.), hall
newydd (W.), new

odyn (W.), kiln, place for drying corn (Breconshire)
Ordovician, the geological period succeeding the Cambrian. Represented
    in the Borderland by the slates, shales, etc., of the Stiperstones, the
    sandstones of Apedale, and by extensive areas where rocks of this
    period are exposed in Denbighshire, Montgomeryshire and the west
    of Radnorshire and Breconshire
oxgang, bovate (q.v.)

pandy, pl. *pandau* (W.), fulling-mill
pant (W.), hollow, valley
parc (W.), park, field
parish, (i) ecclesiastical. The smallest unit of church administration,
    characteristically coterminous with one or more townships
            (ii) civil. Created by the Local Government Act of 1894,
    generally coincident with an old township, but adjusted as required
park, land attached to a manor house or castle as part of the demesne
    not held in common. Land used for ornamental purposes, grazing,
    protection of game
Patent Rolls, Chancery records *re* grants of land, offices, privileges,
    creation of peers, etc., compiled from the early thirteenth century.
    Fully calendared to the early part of the reign of Elizabeth I
peat, a post-glacial deposit consisting principally of decayed vegetation.
    There are two beds, a lower and an upper. Occurring in former
    marshy hollows and lake basins, peat mosses are found in many
    parts of Cheshire and north Shropshire, in the Monmouthshire
    Moors, and on the Welsh uplands
pen (W.), head, top, end
pentref (W.), village, hamlet, head or end of a settlement
perfedd (W.), middle
pike, *pyke*, a gore or triangular piece of land as in a common field
pill, a waterway, especially near the coast as in Monmouthshire
pingle, *pightle*, irregularly shaped portion of common arable field

Pipe Rolls, annual summaries of accounts returned by sheriffs and other royal officers to the Exchequer from the time of Henry II

plas (W.), hall, mansion

plwyf (W.), parish

pont (W.), bridge

port (OE.), from Latin *portus*, gate, road, harbour, town with market or mint

pound, (i) a measure of weight, (ii) money, including the Welsh *twnc* pound, (iii) a place for the impounding of animals, a pinfold

Pre-Cambrian, the era preceding the Primary of Palaeozoic. Represented in the Borderland by the Pre-Cambrian slates and sandstones of the Longmynd, by the volcanic rocks of the Uriconian Hills, and by the gneisses of the Malverns

Primary or *Palaeozoic*, geological era in which the oldest recognisable forms of life were considered to have been found. Extends from the Cambrian to the Permian period

priodolder (W.) *rights*, rights of exclusive occupancy of land and certain other rights in it accorded to the descendants of a common great-grandfather (i.e. fourth generation)

pwll (W.), pit, pool

pystyll (W.), spout, waterfall

Quaternary or *Cainozoic*, geologically recent era broadly coincident with the last glacial epoch and the post-glacial period in Britain. The deposits of this era are known as 'drift' (q.v.) and occur over most of Cheshire and north Shropshire, in numerous upland vales and on the fringe of the Border uplands

quillet, an unfenced strip of land associated with communal aration

rector, originally one who could claim the greater or rectorial tithes of a parish, whether the incumbent or a layman

reen, a major field drain collecting from lesser drains and, in Monmouthshire, tributary to the pills

rhaeadr (W.), waterfall

rhiw (W.), hill, slope

rhos, pl. *rhosydd* (W.), moorland

rhostir (W.), moorland

rhyd (W.), ford

ridding, see *hryding*

ridge, *rigg*, (i) a long narrow hill

(ii) a strip in an open arable field

R

ringild (OE.), *rhingyll* (W.), beadle, hence bedellary, the area in a beadle's care

rood, cf. *rhwd* (W.), in standard measure 40 sq. poles or a quarter of an acre

rundale or *runrig*, a form of common field cultivation found in Celtic Britain, especially in Scotland and the west of Ireland

saint, pl. *sant*; *san*, pl. *sain* (W.), saint

sake, matter in dispute between litigants

sarn, pl. *sarnau* (W.), causeway

Secondary or *Mesozoic*, geologically the 'middle' era and includes the Triassic, Jurassic and Cretaceous periods

selion from Lat. *seliones*, a strip in an open field

-sett (O.Sc.), in some place-names a former shieling or *saeter*

severalty holding, individually owned or farmed land; the opposite of common holding

Silurian, the geological period succeeding the Ordovician. Its varied sedimentary rocks cover large areas of western and south-eastern Denbighshire, Montgomeryshire and Breconshire. The Wenlock and Aymestrey limestones and shales form the scarp and vale country of Wenlock Edge and much of north-west Herefordshire

sir (W.), shire, county

soke, seeking or sueing. Also used as a term for a division of land

squatting, taking possession of land by occupancy. Associated with *ty un nos* (house in a night) and a feature of periods of land pressure when squatters settled on the commons

stint, to limit, especially as applied to pastoral rights on the waste

stocc (OE.), *stock*, *stoke*, trunk, stockade, stockaded place

stocking (ME.), cleared place, pasture

stow (OE.), a place, a holy place, frequently Christian

strata (Lat.), *street*, *stret*, *strat*, road

stratum, pl. *strata* (Lat.), a bed or layer of rock

sych (W.), dry

syncline, a geological downfold

synclinorium, a major and complex downfold

taeog, pl. *taeogion* (W.), bondman, unfree member of Welsh tribe

tal (W.), end

tan (W.), end, below

terfyn (W.), boundary

terrier, ecclesiastical document concerning church lands

tir (W.), land, territory

tir cynefin (W.), stinted pasture

tithe, literally 'a tenth', the portion of their produce given to the church by all landholders and tenants. Originally given in kind, tithes were all commuted to a money payment under the Tithe Act of 1836

tithe maps and apportionment lists, these twin documents were executed by the tithe commissioners appointed under the 1836 Act for all parishes except the small number exempt from tithe. They form an invaluable survey and are the only documents which provide field plans and corresponding lists of field-names for the entire country

toft and croft from toft (ON.) and croft (OE.). Where the joint term is used, the croft (a small field or paddock) is understood to adjoin the toft (homestead)

tomen (W.), mound, usually a motte

ton (W.), grassland, lea

town field, the one or principal open field of a township. Cf. *maes y dref*

town meadow, the common meadow of a township

township, the land associated with a *tun* (q.v.); the smallest administrative unit prior to the Local Government Act of 1894

traeth (W.), strand, beach, shore

trallwng (W.), wet bottom land, quagmire

transhumance, the practice of moving herds and herdsmen to summer hill pastures. Practised in early times by the Norse and the Welsh

traws (W.), transverse, cross; direction, district

tref (W.), homestead, hamlet, township, town

-trey, *-try*, place-name element which in some cases in the Borderland is derived from *tref*

Triassic, the oldest geological period of the Secondary era. Trias or Triassic rocks include principally sandstones known as the New Red Sandstones, but also include the Keuper Marl, salt-bearing beds found mainly in east Cheshire

troed (W.), foot

tros (W.), over

trum (W.), ridge

trwyn (W.), literally nose, hence hillock, cape

tun (OE.), the village or basic agricultural community of Anglo-Saxon society, cf. Welsh *tref*

turbary rights, the right of cutting peat or turf usually from a common mossland or waste

twyn (W.), hillock, knoll

ty, pl. *tai* (W.), house

ty un nos (W.), house in one night (as built by squatters)

tyddyn, pl. *tyddynnod* (W.), a small farm, a holding

ty'n llan (W.), the rectory or vicarage

uchaf (W.), upper, higher, highest
uchel (W.), high
uwch (W.), above, over

vicar, originally one who could claim the lesser or vicarial tithes of a parish whether the incumbent or a layman
village, a sizeable cluster of houses without urban status
villata (Lat.), *ville* (Norm. Fr.), *vill*, a township, a settlement
villein, the man of the vill or township, a medieval term used for tenants whose holding was a virgate or yardland (q.v.)
virgate, a yardland (q.v.), a medieval land measurement which varied with the district. The holding of a villein

wald, weald (OE.), wooded land
wealh, pl. *weala* (OE.), foreigner; often applied to the Welsh, hence used in place-names such as Walton
Welshman's leasow, field set aside for cattle drovers from Wales
Welshry, that part of a marcher lordship where the Welsh lived according to their own laws and customs
wic (OE.), *wick, wich, wig*, dwelling-place, settlement, salt town; wig is sometimes a sacred place
worth, worthy, worthen, wardine, place, enclosure, cleared land, estate

yardland, see *virgate*
ynys (W.), island
ysbyty (W.), hospitium, hospital
ystad (W.), estate
ystrad (W.), valley floor, strath
ystum (W.), bend

Bibliography

The bibliography and list of original sources which follow include those items which have been directly used in the preparation of text and maps. The many other books, papers, etc., which have been consulted are omitted to avoid making the lists unduly cumbersome.

Original Sources Published and Unpublished

The Abergavenny MSS. and Documents presented, and *Three Manorial Court Books* deposited by the Marquess of Abergavenny. N.L.W.

Acton Reynald Estate Documents (The Corbet Family). Sa.R.O.

Adderley Estate Documents (The Corbet Family) Sa.R.O.

Ancient Documents of Clun, Concise Account, 1858

The Arley Charters, Calendar of Ancient Family Charters preserved at Arley Hall, Cheshire, the seat of R. E. Egerton-Warburton Esq., with notes by William Beamont.

Badminton Deeds and Documents and *Badminton Estate Surveys*, deposited by the Duke of Beaufort, Badminton. N.L.W.

The Baker-Gabb MSS., deposited by Miss Blanche Baker-Gabb, the Chain, Abergavenny. N.L.W.

The Barnard Collection (Vane Family). The Lord Barnard. Sa.R.O.

Baron Hill MSS., deposited by Sir Richard Williams Bulkeley of Baron Hill, Beaumaris. U.C.N.W.

Bettisfield MSS. and Documents, deposited by Sir Edward Hanmer. N.L.W.

Birch, W. de G. (ed.). *Cartularium Saxonicum*, London, 1885.

The Bodorgan MSS., deposited by Sir George Meyrick. U.C.N.W.

The Bodrhyddan MSS., deposited by Lieut.-Col. the Lord Langford of Bodrhyddan, near Rhuddlan. N.L.W.

The Bosanquet Collection. Mon. County Archives.

The Bridgwater Estates Collection, deposited by Lord Brownlow. Sa.R.O.

The Brogyntyn MSS. and Documents, deposited by Lord Harlech. N.L.W.

Brownbill, John (ed.). *The Ledger Book of Vale Royal Abbey*, Record Soc. Lancs. and Ches., **68**, 1914.

Browne, R. Stewart (ed.). *Cheshire Inquisitions Post-Mortem, Stuart Period 1603–60,* Record Soc. Lancs and Ches., vols. **84, 86** and **91,** 1934–8.

Capes, W. W. *Charters and Records of Hereford Cathedral,* Hereford, 1908.

Chancery Rolls, including the Welsh. P.R.O.

The Coleman Deeds, compiled by Francis Green, Aberystwyth (N.L.W.), 1921.

Court of Sewers Surveys of the Monmouthshire Moors. Drainage Board.

Court Rolls, Rentals, Surveys, and analogous documents in John Rylands Library, Manchester. Calendared by F. Taylor, *Bull. John Rylands Lib.* **31** (2), 1948.

The Courtfield Muniments, deposited by Maj. H. Vaughan, Courtfield, Ross on Wye. N.L.W.

Crawter, H. and Garling, H. *Perambulations of Manors in Herefordshire,* MS. vol. 1824, MSS. Coll. 914. 244, Hereford City Lib.

Davis, F. N. (ed.). *Diocese of Hereford: Registrum Johannis de Trillek, Episcopi Herefordensis, 1344–61,* Canterbury and York Series, **8.**

Deeds, Documents and Maps, deposited by the *British Records Association.* N.L.W.

Deeds of the Marchioness of Crewe, Hist. MSS. Commission.

Deeds purchased from J. Kyrle Fletcher. N.L.W.

Dolforgan Deeds, deposited by John Bancroft Willans Esq., Dolforgan, Kerry. N.L.W.

The Dolman Collection, Mon. County Archives.

The Domesday Book.

Edwards, J. G. *Calendar of Ancient Correspondence concerning Wales.*

Ellis, T. P. *The First Extent of Bromfield and Yale, A.D. 1315,* Cymmrodorion Record Series, **11,** London, 1924.

The Eriviat Estate Deeds and Documents, deposited by the trustees, Messrs. Peckover-Burrill and Owen, Denbigh. N.L.W.

The Evans & Evill Collection (Solicitors, Chepstow), Mon. County Archives.

Evans, J. Gwenogvryn and Rhys, John. *The Text of the Book of Llan Dav (Liber Landavensis or Llyfr Teilo)* reproduced from the Gwysaney MS., Oxford, 1893.

Ewenny Priory MSS and Documents, deposited by Charles Grenville Turberville Esq., Ewenny Priory, Glamorgan. Glam.R.O.

Farm Accounts of Holme Lacy, Book C, 1708–9, L.C. MSS., 631, 16. Her. City Lib.

Flenley, Ralph. *A Calendar of the Register of the Queen's Majesty's Council in the Dominion and Principality of Wales and the Marches of the same, (1535), 1569–1591,* from the Bodley MS. no. 904. Cymmrodorion Record Series, **8,** London, 1916.

Garmonsway, G. N. (ed.). *The Anglo-Saxon Chronicle*, Everyman ed., 1953.

The Garthewin MSS., deposited by R. O. F. Wynne Esq., of Garthewin, Llanfair Talhaearn. U.C.N.W.

Giraldus Cambrensis. *The Itinerary through Wales*, Everyman ed., 1908.

Glynne of Hawarden Family Papers and Documents, deposited by the late Lord Gladstone of Hawarden. N.L.W.

The Gwysaney Collection of Deeds and Documents, deposited by Philip Tatton Davies-Cooke Esq., of Gwysaney, Mold. N.L.W.

Hall, James (ed.). *The Book of the Abbot of Combermere*, Record. Soc. L. and C., **31**, 1896.

The Hanbury Collection. Her. City Lib.

Haughmond Abbey Chartulary. Boro. Lib., Shrewsbury.

The Hawarden Deeds, compiled by Francis Green, Aberystwyth (N.L.W.), 1931.

Hereford Cathedral Muniments. Her. Cath. Lib.

Hereford Charters. Bodleian Lib.

Herefordshire Enclosure Acts. Her. City Lib.

Howard, Duchess of Norfolk. *Perambulations of Manors and Parishes in Herefordshire*, 9 vols. MSS. fol. 1894. Hereford City Lib.

Hulton, W. A. *The Coucher Book of Whalley Abbey*, Chetham Soc., vols **10, 11, 16** and **20**, 1867–77.

Hunter, Joseph. *An Introduction to the Valor Ecclesiasticus of Henry VIII*, P.R.O., 1834.

The John Capel Hanbury Collection, Pontypool Park Estate. Mon. County Archives.

Jones, Arthur. 'A Fifteenth Century Document of Rhuddlan' (including a translation of the original Extent), *Jl Fl. Hist. Soc.*, **5**, 1914–15.

Jones, Arthur (ed.). 'Flintshire Ministers' Accounts, 1301–28', *Jl Fl. Hist. Soc.*, *3*, 1913.

The Kinmel MSS. and Documents, deposited by Capt. D. E. Featherstone-haugh, Kinmel Manor, Abergele. U.C.N.W.

Leaton Knolls Estate Documents (Lloyd Family). Sa.R.O.

Lee of Alveley Collection: Survey of the Manors of Nordley, Romsley and Alveley in the parish of Alveley, Shropshire, by T. Slater, 1770. Sa.R.O.

The Leeke Family Records, deposited by Lady Wakeman and Miss Leeke. Sa.R.O.

Leominster Cartulary, Cottonian MS. Domit., AIII.

Lewis, E. A. and Conway Davies, J. *Records of the Court of Augmentations relating to Wales and Monmouthshire*, B.C.S., Univ. of Wales Hist. and Law Series, no. 13, Cardiff, 1934.

Lilleshall Estates Documents (Leveson Family). The Duke of Sutherland. Sa.R.O.

List of Special Commissions and Returns (Exchequer), Lists and Indexes 37. P.R.O.

Llanarth Court Collection. Mon. County Archives.

Llanelidan Manorial Records: MSS. and Papers deposited by Miss F. M. Jones, Ruthin. N.L.W.

Llanerfrochwel Estate Deeds and Documents, deposited by O. Gilbert Davies Esq., Welshpool. N.L.W.

Llangibby Castle Collection: MSS., Letters and Manorial Records from the Library of the late Maj. Albert Addams-Williams, Llangibby Castle, Mon. N.L.W.

Lloyd Estates (Leaton Knolls) Deposit: 1780 Survey of Estates. Sa.R.O.

Local Collection of Deeds, Hopton Collection. Hereford City Lib.

Local Collection of Deeds and Documents. Her. City Lib.

Lockwood Deposit Collection of Documents and Estate Plans, deposited by J. C. Lockwood Esq., Bishops Hall, Lambourne, Essex. N.L.W.

Ludlow Corporation Records. Sa.R.O.

Morris, George. *Abstract of the Grants and Charters contained in the Chartulary of Wombridge Priory, Co. Salop*. Shrewsbury Boro. Lib.

MS. Vols., Special Commissions and Depositions, Exqur. Qr., vol. 7. P.R.O.

Newman Paynter Deeds and Documents, deposited by Messrs. Newman Paynter and Co. of Hendford, Yeovil. N.L.W.

The Newport Collection. Mon. County Archives.

Oakly Park Documents (Fox and Clive Families). The Earl of Plymouth. Sa.R.O.

Peele and Aris Deeds and Papers. Sa.R.O.

Pentre Mawr MSS., deposited by J. Rigby Esq., Pentre Mawr, Llandyrnog. U.C.N.W.

Pitchford Hall Deeds and Documents, donated by Gen. Sir Charles J. C. Grant, Pitchford Hall, Sa. N.L.W.

Plas Coch MSS. U.C.N.W.

Plas Heaton Deeds and Documents, deposited by W. J. Heaton Esq., Plas Heaton. N.L.W.

Plas Yolyn Collection of MSS. and Documents. N.L.W.

The Plymouth Deeds and Documents, deposited by the Earl of Plymouth. N.L.W.

Porth yr Aur MSS., deposited by the Corporation of Caernarvon. U.C.N.W.

Puleston Deeds, deposited by Crawshay Wellington Puleston Esq., of Emral Worthenbury. N.L.W.

Purton, R. C. 'Deeds relating to Larden', *Trans. Shrops. Archaeol, Soc.*, **54** (i), 1953.

Purton, R. C. 'Deeds relating to Oswestry', *Trans. Shrops. Archaeol. Soc.*, **53** (i), 1949.

The Quaritch Deeds. N.L.W.

The Radcliffe Deeds, deposited by D. C. Radcliffe Esq. of Rhyl. N.L.W.

The Ratcliffe Cooke Collection. Her. City Lib.

Rees, William (ed.). *A Survey of the Duchy of Lancaster Lordships in Wales*, Cardiff, 1953.

Register of Edward the Black Prince, part III: Palatinate of Chester 1351–65, H.M.S.O.

Rentals, Surveys and other Analogous Documents (Lists and Indexes no. xxv). P.R.O.

Rhual MSS. and Documents, deposited by Mrs G. M. Heaton. N.L.W.

Roderick, A. J. and Rees, William. 'Lordships of Abergavenny, Grosmont, Skenfrith and White Castle, Ministers' Accounts 1256–7', *South Wales and Mon. Record Soc. Publications*, **3**, 1950, pp. 69–128.

The Rudge Hall Collection, deposited by Mrs Arkwright. Sa.R.O.

St Pierre Collection of Deeds and Documents. N.L.W.

Savage, H. E. (ed.). *The Great Register of Lichfield Cathedral known as Magnum Registrum Album*, William Salt Archaeol. Soc., Stafford, 1926.

Shrewsbury Abbey Chartulary. N.L.W. MS. 7851.

Shropshire Hearth Tax Roll of 1672, Shrops. Archaeol. Soc., 1949.

Sweeney Hall MSS. and Documents, deposited by Maj. E. B. Parker Leighton, Sweeney Hall, Oswestry. N.L.W.

Tabley House Collection, Hist. MSS. Collection, Nat. Register of Archives.

Tait, James (ed.). *The Chartulary or Register of the Abbey of St Werburgh, Chester*, Chetham Soc., new series, 1920 and 1923.

Taxatio Ecclesiastica Angliae et Walliae, auctoritate P. Nicholai IV, circa 1291, Record Commission, 1802.

Taxation of Pope Innocent IV or *Vetus Valor* or *The Norwich Taxation, 1254*, Cottonian Coll., Vitellius, **110**.

Taylor, F. 'Handlist of the Legh of Booths Charters in the John Rylands Library', *Bull. John Rylands Lib.*, **32**, 1949–50.

Thornton Rental, Cheshire Sheaf, Jun., 1896, p. 53.

Tilley Albert Deeds and Documents relating to lands in mid-Breconshire. N.L.W.

Valor Ecclesiasticus of Henry VIII, 6 vols, Record Commission.

Varley, Joan (ed.). *A Middlewich Chartulary compiled by William Vernon in the seventeenth century*, 2 vols, Chetham Society, 1941 and 1944.

Vinogradoff, Paul and Morgan, Frank (eds). *The Survey of the Honour of Denbigh, A.D. 1334*, London, 1914.

The Welsh Assize Roll.

Whitfield, John R. 'The Lordship of Cause, 1540–1', *Trans. Shrops. Archaeol. Soc.*, **54**, 1951–3.

Williams and Tweedy Collection, Solicitors, Monmouth. Mon. County Archives.

Wolryche-Whitmore MSS. Nat. Register Archives.

Wombridge Abbey Chartulary. Brit. Museum.

Wrottesley, Maj.-Gen. the Hon. George (ed.). *Chartulary of Dieulacres Abbey*, Staffs. Hist. Collections, new series, **9**, 1906.

Wynnstay MSS. and Documents, deposited by Sir Herbert Lloyd Watkin Williams Wynn. N.L.W.

*Selected Cartographical Sources Additional to
Those Included in the Above*

Adderley Estate Maps. Sa.R.O.

Atlas Brycheiniog, Llandysul, 1960.

Bryant, A. *Map of the County Palatine of Chester* from actual survey in the years 1829, 1830 and 1831, London, 1831. Scale: $1\frac{1}{4}$ inches = 1 mile.

Davies, Margaret. *Wales in Maps*, Cardiff, 1951.

Enclosure Awards and Maps, various.

Evans, John. *Maps of the Six Counties of North Wales*, Llwyngroes, 1795. Scale: 1.32 inches = 1 mile.

Hereford City Library Collection of Maps and Plans.

Maps and Plans *circa* 1430–1603. P.R.O.

Ordnance Survey of England and Wales, various, but mention may be made of:
The 1st, 2nd and 3rd editions of the One-Inch maps
Map of Roman Britain, 3rd edition, 1956. Scale: 16 miles to one inch.

Rees, William. *An Historical Atlas of Wales*, Cardiff, 1951.

Rees, William. *Map of South Wales and the Border in the Fourteenth Century*, Ordnance Survey, 1932. Scale: two miles to one inch.

Tithe maps and apportionment lists.

Secondary Sources

I. GENERAL, i.e. referring to the whole area and its relationships and so to Parts I, II and III.

Addleshaw, G. W. O. *The Beginnings of the Parochial System*, St Anthony's Hall Publications, London, 1953.

Agricultural Statistics, annual publication of the Ministry of Agriculture and Fisheries, H.M.S.O.

Arnold-Foster, Francis. *Studies in Church Dedications*, 3 vols, Oxford, 1899.

Ashley, A. W. and Evans, I. L. *Agriculture of Wales and Monmouthshire*, Cardiff, 1944.

Hunter Blair, P. *An Introduction to Anglo-Saxon England*, Cambridge, 1959.

Bowcock, E. W. *Shropshire Place-Names*, Shrewsbury, 1923.

Bowen, E. G. 'A Study of Rural Settlements in South-West Wales', *Geog.*, **13**, 1926.

Bowen, E. G. *The Settlements of the Celtic Saints in Wales*, Cardiff, 1954.

Bowen, E. G. (ed.). *Wales*, London, 1957.

Bowen, Ivor, *The Great Enclosures of Common Lands in Wales*, London, 1914.

Cambrian Archaeological Association Centenary volume, *A Hundred Years of Welsh Archaeology*, ed. V. E. Nash-Williams, Gloucester, 1946.

Cameron, Kenneth, *English Place-Names*, London, 1961.

Census of Population of England and Wales, H.M.S.O., 1801 to 1961.

Chadwick, N. K. (ed.). *Celt and Saxon*, Cambridge, 1963.

Chadwick, N. K. (ed.). *Studies in Early British History*, Cambridge, 1954.

Chadwick, N. K. (ed.). *Studies in the Early British Church*, Cambridge, 1958.

Charles, B. G. *Non-Celtic Place-Names in Wales*, London, 1938.

Church, Leslie F. *The Early Methodist People*, London, 1948.

Cobbett, William. *Rural Rides*, London, 1830.

Cole, G. D. H. (ed.). *Daniel Defoe's Tour through England and Wales*, 2 vols, London, 1927.

Collingwood, R. G. and Myres, J. N. L. *Roman Britain and the English Settlements*, Oxford, 1936, 2nd ed. 1937.

Darby, H. C. (ed.). *An Historical Geography of England before 1800*, Cambridge, 1936.

Darby, H. C. and Terrett, I. B. *The Domesday Geography of Midland England*, Cambridge, 1954.

R3

Davies, Elwyn. *Gazetteer of Welsh Place-Names*, Cardiff, 1957.

Davies, John. 'The Celtic Elements in the dialects of the counties adjoining Lancashire', *Archaeol. Camb.*, 5th series, **1**, 1884.

Davies, Margaret. 'Field Patterns in the Vale of Glamorgan', *Trans. Cardiff Nat. Soc.*, **84**, 1955–6.

Davies, Margaret. 'Rhosili Open Field and related South Wales Field Patterns', *Agric. Hist. Rev.*, **4** (ii), 1956.

Davies, Margaret. 'The Open Fields of Laugharne', *Geog.*, **40**, 1955.

Depopulation in Mid-Wales, H.M.S.O., 1964.

Dodd, A. H. *The Industrial Revolution in North Wales*, Cardiff, 2nd ed., 1951.

Dwnn, Lewys, *Heraldic Visitations of Wales and part of the Marches between the years 1586 and 1613*, ed. by Sir Samuel Rush Meyrick, 2 vols, Welsh MSS. Soc., Llandovery, 1846.

Ekwall, Eilert, *A Concise Oxford Dictionary of English Place-Names*, 4th ed. 1960.

Emanuel, Hywel D. 'Dissent in the Counties of Glamorgan and Monmouth', *N. L. W. Jl*, 1954 and 1955.

Finberg, H. P. R. *Lucerna*, London, 1964.

Finberg, H. P. R. 'Three Anglo-Saxon Boundaries', *Trans. Shrops. Archaeol. Soc.*, **56** (i), 1957–8.

Fisher, J. 'Welsh Church Dedications', *Trans. Hon. Soc. Cymmrod.*, **15**, 1906–7.

Förster, Max. 'Celtisches Wortgut im Englischen' in *Texte und Forschungen zur Englischen Kulturgeschichte. Festgabe für Felix Liebermann*, 1921.

Foster, I. Ll. and Alcock, L. *Culture and Environment*, London, 1963.

Foster, I. Lloyd and Daniel, Glyn. *Prehistoric and Early Wales*, London, 1965.

Fox, Sir Cyril. 'A Find of the Early Iron Age from Llyn Cerrig Bach, Anglesey', Nat. Mus. Wales, 1946.

Fox, Sir Cyril, *Offa's Dyke*, London, 1955.

Fox, Sir Cyril. 'The Boundary Line of Cymru', Sir John Rhys Memorial Lecture, British Academy, 1940.

Fox, Sir Cyril. 'Wat's Dyke: A Field Survey', *Archaeol. Camb.*, *89*, 1934.

Gray, H. L. *English Field Systems*, Harvard and Oxford, 1915.

Griffiths, E. W. (ed.). *Through England on a Side Saddle in the time of William and Mary, being the diary of Celia Fiennes*, 1888.

Grimes, W. F. *The Prehistory of Wales*, Nat. Mus. Wales, 2nd ed., 1939.

Harden, D. B. (ed.). *Dark Age Britain*, London, 1956.

Hartley, Galland T. (ed.). Hall's *Circuits and Ministers*, 1765 to 1912, London, 1912.

Hill, Geoffrey, *English Dioceses*, London, 1900.

Hodgkin, R. H. *A History of the Anglo-Saxons*, 2 vols, Oxford, 1935, 3rd ed. 1953.

Hogg, A. H. A. 'The Date of Cunedda', *Antiquity*, **19**, 1945.

Hogg, A. H. A. and King, D. J. C. 'Early Castles in Wales and the Marches: a preliminary list', *Archaeol. Camb.*, **112**, 1963.

Jackson, Kenneth. *Language and History in Early Britain*, Edinburgh, 1953.

Jackson, W. Eric. *Local Government in England and Wales*, Pelican Books, 1945.

Jones, G. R. J. 'Some Medieval Rural Settlements in North Wales', *Trans. Inst. Brit. Geogr.*, 1953.

Jones, H. R. 'A Study of Rural Migration in Central Wales', *Trans. Inst. Brit. Geogr.*, 1965.

Jones, O. T. 'Aspects of the Geological History of the Bristol Channel Region', *Report Brit. Assoc.*, 1930, p. 57.

Jones Pierce, T. 'A Note on Ancient Welsh Measurements of Land', *Archaeol. Camb.*, **97**, 1943.

Knowles, David and Hadcock, R. Neville. *Medieval Religious Houses of England and Wales*, London, 1953.

Leadam, I. S. *The Domesday of Inclosures, 1517–18*, London, 1897.

Leeds, E. T. *The Archaeology of the Anglo-Saxon Settlement*, Oxford, 1913.

Lewis, E. A. *The Mediaeval Boroughs of Snowdonia*, Cardiff, 1912.

Lewis, S. *Topographical Dictionary of England*, 4 vols and atlas, 1831.

Lewis, S. *Topographical Dictionary of Wales*, 2 vols, 1833.

Lhwyd, Edward. 'Parochialia', ed. Rupert H. Morris, *Archaeol. Camb.*, 2 vols, 1909–11.

Lloyd, J. E. *A History of Wales*, 2 vols, London, 1911.

Maitland, F. W. *Domesday Book and Beyond*, Cambridge, 1897.

Margary, I. D. *Roman Roads in Britain*, 2 vols, London, 1957.

Nash-Williams, V. E. *The Early Christian Monuments of Wales*, Cardiff, 1950.

Nash-Williams, V. E. *The Roman Frontier in Wales*, Cardiff, 1954.

Nash-Williams, V. E. and Savory, H. N. 'The Distribution of Hill-Forts', *Bull. Bd. Celtic Stud.*, 1949.

North, F. J. *The Evolution of the Bristol Channel*, Cardiff, 1929.

North, F. J. 'The Geological History of Brecknock', *Brycheiniog*, **1**, 1955.

O'Donnell Lectures, *Angles and Britons*, Cardiff, 1963.

Orwin, C. S. and C. S. *The Open Fields*, Oxford, 1938 (2nd ed. 1954).

Owen, G. Dyfnallt. *Elizabethan Wales*, Cardiff, 1962.

Palmer, A. N. and Owen, E. *History of Ancient Tenures of Land in North Wales and the Marches*, Wrexham, 1910.

Parry-Williams, T. H. *The English Element in Welsh*, 1923.

Pocock, R. W. and Whitehead, T. H. *The Welsh Borderland*, Regional Geology, 1935.

Poole, A. L. *From Domesday Book to Magna Carta*, 1087–1216, Oxford, 1951, 2nd ed. 1954.

Pringle, J. and Whitehead, T. Neville. *South Wales*, Regional Geology, 1948.

Rees, William. *South Wales and the March, 1284–1415*, Cardiff, 1924.

Rees, William. *The Union of England and Wales*, Cardiff, 1948.

Renn, D. F. 'Mottes: A Classification', *Antiquity*, **33**, 1959.

Report of the Royal Commission on Common Land, 1955–8, H.M.S.O., 1958.

Richards, Melville. 'The Irish Settlements in South-west Wales', *Jl R. Soc. Antiquaries of Ireland*, **90** (ii), 1960.

Roderick, A. J. (ed.). *Wales through the Ages*, 2 vols, Aberystwyth, 1959.

Royal Commission on Ancient and Historical Monuments in Wales and Monmouthshire: Denbighshire, 1914; *Flintshire*, 1912; *Montgomeryshire*, 1911; *Radnorshire*, 1913.

Ditto on *England: Herefordshire*, **1**, 1931; **2**, 1932; **3**, 1934.

Savory, H. N. 'Some Sub-Romano–British Brooches from South Wales', in *Dark Age Britain*, ed. D. B. Harden, 1956.

Sayce, R. U. 'The Old Summer Pastures', *Mont. Coll.* **54** (ii) and **55** (i), 1956 and 1957.

Skeel, Caroline J. *The Council in the Marches of Wales*, London, 1904.

Slater, Gilbert. *The English Peasantry and the Enclosure of the Common Fields*, London, 1907.

Smith, Bernard and George, T. Neville. *North Wales*, Regional Geol., Geol. Survey, 1948.

Smith, L. T. (ed.). *The Itinerary of John Leland in or about the years 1535–1543*, 5 vols, London, 1906–10.

Stamp, L. Dudley. 'The Common Lands and Village Greens of England and Wales', *Geogrl J.*, **130**, 1964.

Stapledon, R. G. (ed.). *A Survey of the Agricultural and Waste Lands of Wales*, 1936.

Stenton, F. M. *Anglo-Saxon England*, Oxford, 1943, 2nd ed. 1947.

Strahan, Aubrey. *The Country around Newport*, Geol. Survey Memoir, sheet 249, 1909.

Sylvester, Dorothy. 'The Hill Villages of England and Wales', *Geogrl J.*, **110**, 1947.

Tate, W. E. *The Parish Chest*, Cambridge, 1946, 2nd ed. 1951.

Thomas, Brinley. *The Welsh Economy*, Cardiff, 1962.

Thomas, David. *Cau'r Tiroedd Comin*, Liverpool, N.D.

Thomas, D. R. *St. Asaph*, Diocesan History Series, London, 1888.

Thomas, D. R. *The History of the Diocese of St. Asaph*, 3 vols, Oswestry, 1906–13.

Thomas, Trevor M. 'The Geomorphology of Brecknock', *Brycheiniog*, 5, 1959.

Tupling, G. H. 'The Pre-Reformation Parishes and Chapelries of Lancashire', *Trans. Lancs. and Ches. Antiq. Soc.*, 67, 1957.

Vince, S. W. E. 'Reflections on the Structure and Distribution of Rural Population in England and Wales, 1921–31', *Trans. Inst. Br. Geogr.*, 1952.

Wainwright, F. T. 'North-West Mercia', *Trans. Hist. Soc. Lancs. and Ches.*, 94, 1942.

Watkin, I. Morgan. 'English and Welsh Racial Elements in Western Shropshire and the adjacent Welsh Borderland: ABO Blood Group Evidence', *Jl R. Anthrop. Inst.*, 94, 1963.

Wedd, C. B., Smith, B., King, W. B. R., and Wray, D. A. *The Country around Oswestry*, Geol. Survey Memoir, sheet 137, 1929.

Williams, A. H. *An Introduction to the History of Wales*, 1, 1941; 2, 1948.

Williams, D. Trevor. 'A Linguistic Map of Wales according to the 1931 Census', *Geogrl J.*, 89, 1937.

Williams, David. 'A Note on the Population of Wales, 1536–1801', *Bull. Bd Celtic Stud.*, 8, 1937.

Williams, David. 'The Acreage Returns of 1801 for Wales', *Bull. Bd Celtic Stud.*, 14, 1950–1.

Williams, Sir Ifor. 'When did British become Welsh?', *Trans. Angelsey Antiq. Soc.*, 1939.

Williams, Penry. *The Council in the Marches of Wales under Elizabeth I*, Cardiff, 1958.

Wilson, David M. 'Anglo-Saxon Rural Economy', *Agric. Hist. Rev.*, 10 (ii), 1962.

Wray, D. A. *The Pennines and Adjacent Areas*, Regional Geology, Geol. Survey, 1948.

II. CHESHIRE

Bagshaw, S. *History and Directory of Cheshire*, 1850.

Boon, E. P. *Cheshire*, L.U.S. Report, London, 1941.

Bu'Lock, J. D. 'The Celtic, Saxon, and Scandinavian Settlement at Meols in Wirral', *Trans. Hist. Soc. Lancs. and Ches.*, 112, 1960.

Chapman, Vera. 'Open Fields in West Cheshire', *Trans. Hist. Soc. Lancs. and Ches.*, 104, 1952.

Crossley, F. H. *Cheshire*, London, 1949.

Crump, W. B. 'Saltways from the Cheshire Wiches', *Trans. Lancs. and Ches. Antiq. Soc.*, **54**, 1939.

Earwaker, J. P. *East Cheshire*, 2 vols, London, 1887–8.

Hewitt, J. *Mediaeval Cheshire*, Chetham Soc., **88**, 1929.

Holland, H. *General View of the Agriculture of Cheshire*, London, 1813.

Leycester, Sir Peter. *Historical Antiquities*, Book II, Particular Remarks Concerning Cheshire, London, 1673.

Lysons, D. and S. *Magna Britannia*, **2** (ii), *Cheshire*, London, 1810.

Nulty, Geoffrey. *Shavington, the story of a South Cheshire Village*, 1959.

Ormerod, George. *The History of the County Palatine and City of Chester*, 3 vols, Ed. Thos Helsby, 2nd ed., London, 1882.

Potter, Simeon. 'Cheshire Place-Names', *Trans. Hist. Soc. Lancs. and Ches.*, **106**, 1954.

Richards, Raymond. *Old Cheshire Churches*, London, 1947.

Rideout, E. H. 'Sites of Ancient Villages in Wirral', *Trans. Hist. Soc. Lancs. and Ches.*, **29**, 1926.

Sylvester, Dorothy. 'A Note on Medieval Three-Course Arable Systems in Cheshire', *Trans. Hist. Soc. Lancs. and Ches.*, **110**, 1958.

Sylvester, Dorothy. 'Cheshire in the Dark Ages', *Trans. Hist. Soc. Lancs. and Ches.*, **114**, 1962.

Sylvester, Dorothy. 'Rural Settlement in Cheshire', *Trans. Hist. Soc. Lancs. and Ches.*, **101**, 1949.

Sylvester, Dorothy. 'The Manor and the Cheshire Landscape', *Trans. Lancs. and Ches. Antiq. Soc.*, **70**, 1960.

Sylvester, Dorothy. 'The Open Fields of Cheshire', *Trans. Hist. Soc. Lancs. and Ches.*, **108**, 1956.

Sylvester, Dorothy and Nulty, Geoffrey. *The Historical Atlas of Cheshire*, Chester, 1958, rev. ed. 1966.

Thompson, F. H. *Roman Cheshire*, Chester, 1964.

Varley, W. J., Jackson, J. W., and Chitty, L. F. *Prehistoric Cheshire*, Chester, 1940.

III. SHROPSHIRE

Auden, J. E. *Shropshire*, Methuen's Little Guides, 1926, 2nd ed., 1932.

Bagshaw, S. *Gazetteer of Shropshire*, 1851.

Blakeway, J. B. *The History of Shrewsbury Liberties*, Shrops. Archaeol. Soc., 1897.

Chitty, Lily F. 'Bronze Axe Hoard from Preston-on-the-Wealdmoors, Shropshire', *Trans. Shrops. Archaeol. Soc.*, **54** (ii), 1953.

Chitty, Lily F. 'Interim Notes on Subsidiary Castle Sites west of Shrewsbury', *Trans. Shrops. Archaeol. Soc.*, **53**, 1949.

Chitty, Lily F. Paragraphs on the Prehistory of Shropshire in the Report of the 1954 Annual Meeting of the Cambrian Arch. Assoc. held at Shrewsbury. *Archaeol. Camb.*, **114**, 1955.

Cranage, D. H. S. *The Churches of Shropshire*, 2 vols, 1901.

Dodd, J. Phillip. 'The State of Agriculture in Shropshire 1775–1825', *Trans. Shrops. Archaeol. Soc.*, **55** (i), 1954.

Eyton, R. W. *The Antiquities of Shropshire*, 12 vols, 1854–60.

Garbet, S. *The History of Wem*, 1818.

Hill, Mary C. 'The Wealdmoors', *Trans. Shrops. Archaeol. Soc.*, **54** (ii), 1953.

Houghton, A. W. J. 'A Roman Road from Ashton, North Herefordshire to Marshbrook, Salop', *Trans. Shrops. Archaeol. Soc.*, **57** (iii), 1964.

Houghton, A. W. J. 'The Roman Road from Greensforge through the Central Welsh March', *Trans. Shrops. Archaeol. Soc.*, **56**, 1960.

Howell, Emrys J. *Shropshire*, L.U.S. Report, 1941.

Kenyon, R. Lloyd. 'The Domesday Manors of Ruyton, Wikey, and Felton', *Trans. Shrops. Archaeol. Soc.*, **12**, 1900, pp. 64–83.

Leadam, I. S. 'The Inquisition of 1517. Inclosures and Evictions. Edited from the Lansdowne MS. I, 153, part III', *Trans. R. Hist. Soc.*, N.S., **8**, 1894.

Peele, E. C. and Clease, R. S. *Shropshire Parish Documents*, Shrewsbury, 1903.

Plymley, Joseph. *General View of the Agriculture of Shropshire*, London, 1803.

Purton, R. C. 'The Manor of Oakes in the parish of Pontesbury', *Trans. Shrops. Archaeol. Soc.*, **54** (i), 1951–2.

Rowley, N. and S. V. *Market Drayton*, Market Drayton, 1966.

Slack, W. J. *The Lordship of Oswestry, 1393–1607*, Shrops. Archaeol. Soc., 1951.

Sylvester, Dorothy, 'Rural Settlement in Domesday Shropshire', *Soc. Rev.*, **25**, 1933.

Tanner, Henry, 'The Agriculture of Shropshire', *Jl R. Agric. Soc.* **19**, 1858.

Tate, W. E. 'A Hand List of English Enclosure Acts and Awards', *Trans. Shrops. Archaeol. Soc.*, **52** (i), 1947.

Thompson, Gladys Howard. *The King's Ley*, Shrewsbury, 1951.

Victoria County History. *Shropshire*, vol. i, London, 1908.

IV. HEREFORDSHIRE

Atkin, C. W. *The Evolution of Rural Settlement in Herefordshire*, unpublished M.A. thesis, University of Liverpool, 1951.

Bannister, A. T. *Place-Names of Herefordshire*, Hereford, 1916.

Bayliss, D. G. 'The Lordship of Wigmore in the Fourteenth Century', *Trans. Woolhope Nat. Fld Club*, **36** (i), 1958.

Beale, J. *Hereford Orchards: a pattern for all England*, London, 1657.

Beddoe, C. 'Manorial Customs in the County of Hereford', *Trans. Woolhope Nat. Fld Club*, 1900.

Cole, E. J. L. 'Fourteenth Century Bailiffs' Accounts of the manor of Kingsland', *Trans. Woolhope Nat. Fld Club*, **35** (ii), 1956.

Cole, E. J. L. 'Kingsland, a Caroline Court Record', *Trans. Woolhope Nat. Fld Club*, **36** (ii), 1959.

Duncumb, John. *General View of the Agriculture of Herefordshire*, Board of Agriculture Report, London, 1805.

Easton, Harold. 'The Manor of Kingsland', *Trans. Woolhope Nat. Fld Club*, 1923.

Humfrys, W. J. 'Lammas Lands', *Trans. Woolhope Nat. Fld Club*, 1899.

Jackson, J. N. 'Some Observations on the Herefordshire Environment of the seventeenth and eighteenth centuries', *Trans. Woolhope Nat. Fld Club*, **34** (iii), 1958.

Jackson, J. N. 'Thoughts upon the Distribution of the rural population in Herefordshire at the beginning of the nineteenth century', *Trans. Woolhope Nat. Fld Club*, 1954.

Jones, E. L. 'Agricultural Conditions and Changes in Herefordshire, 1660–1815', *Trans. Woolhope Nat. Fld Club*, **37** (i) 1961.

Price, John. *An Historical and Topographical Account of Leominster and its Vicinity*, Ludlow, 1795.

Lord Rennell of Rodd. *Valley on the March*, Oxford, 1958.

Robinson, Stewart. 'The Forest and Woodland Areas of Herefordshire', *Trans. Woolhope Nat. Fld Club*, 1923.

Stanford, S. C. 'A Medieval Settlement at Hampton Wafer', *Trans. Woolhope Nat. Fld Club*, **35**, 1957.

Tate, W. E. 'A Handlist of English Enclosure Acts and Awards, part 15, Herefordshire', *Trans. Woolhope Nat. Fld Club*, 1941.

Victoria County History. *Herefordshire*, vol. **1**, 1908.

V. MONMOUTHSHIRE

Bradney, J. A. *A History of Monmouthshire from the coming of the Normans into Wales to the present time*, 4 vols, 1904–33.

Clarke, A. Rhys and Howell, Emrys J. *Monmouthshire*, L.U.S. Report, 1943.

Davies, Margaret. 'Common Lands in south-east Monmouthshire', *Trans. Cardiff Nat. Soc.*, **85**, 1955–6.

Evans, C. J. O. *Monmouthshire: Its History and Topography*, Cardiff, 1953.

Gustard, W. T. *Levels of the Hundreds of Caldicot and Wentllwg*, bound vol. of typescript notes, Newport Pub. Lib., 1933.

Hassall, Charles. *General View of the Agriculture of the County of Monmouth*, London, 1815.

Matthews, John Hobson. 'Old Monmouth', *Archaeol. Camb.*, 6th series, **9**, 1909.

Monmouthshire Moors, Draft Report, Welsh Agricultural Land Sub-Commission, Aberystwyth, 1954.

Morris, A. 'Chepstow Castle and the Barony of Strigoil', *Archaeol. Camb.*, 6th series, 1909.

Nash-Williams, V. E. 'An Early Iron Age Coastal Camp at Sudbrook, Mon.', *Archaeol. Camb.*, **94**, 1939.

Nash-Williams, V. E. 'An Early Iron Age Hill-Fort at Llanmelin, near Caerwent, Mon.', *Archaeol. Camb.*, **88**, 1933.

Nash-Williams, V. E. 'Note on a new Roman site at Redwick, near Magor, Mon.', *Bull. Bd Celtic Stud.*, **14**, 1951.

Nash-Williams, V. E. *The Roman Legionary Fortress at Caerleon, Mon.*, Nat. Mus. Wales, 1952.

Rees, William, 'Medieval Gwent', *Jl Br. Archaeol. Assoc.*, N.S. **35**,, 1929.

Sylvester, Dorothy. 'The Common Fields of the Coastlands of Gwent', *Agric. Hist. Rev.*, 1958.

Williams, T. E. and Davis, A. G. 'A Grassland Survey of the Monmouthshire Moors', *Jl Br. Grassland Soc.*, **1**, 1946.

VI. BRECONSHIRE

Davies, H. T. 'The Soils of Brecknock', *Brycheiniog*, **6**, 1960.

Dodd, J. Phillip. 'The Brecknockshire Crop Returns for 1854', *Brycheiniog*, **6**, 1960.

Evans, Christopher J. *Breconshire*, Cambridge County Geographies, 1912.

Grove, J. C. 'Eighteenth Century Land Use Records in Breconshire', *Brycheiniog*, **8**, 1962.

Jones, S. R. and Smith, J. T. 'The Houses of Breconshire', *Brycheiniog*, **9** and **10**, 1963 and 1964.

Jones, Theophilus. *A History of the County of Brecknock*, 2 vols, Brecknock, 1805–9, 2nd ed. 1898.

Kay, Richard E. 'Castell Dinas', *Brycheiniog*, **10**, 1964.

King, J. Cathcart. 'The Castles of Breconshire', *Brycheiniog*, **7**, 1961.

'Llangattock Parish Scrap Book'. *Brycheiniog*, **7**, **8** and **9**, 1961, 1962 and 1963.

Phillips, Thomas R. (ed.). *The Breconshire Border*, Talgarth, 1926.

Savory, H. N. 'The Hill-Forts of Brecknockshire', *Bull. Bd Celtic Stud.*, **14**, 1950.

Savory, H. N. 'Prehistoric Brecknock', *Brycheiniog*, **1**, 1955.

Watkins, Tudor E. 'Special Problems of the Mid-Wales Area', *Brycheiniog*, **4**, 1958.

VII. RADNORSHIRE

Cole, E. J. L. 'The Castles of Maelienydd', *Trans. Rad. Soc.*, **16**, 1946.

Davies, D. Stedman. 'How Old is this Church?', *Trans. Rad. Soc.*, **15**, 1945.

Davies, D. Stedman. 'Notes on Radnorshire 1066 to 1400', *Trans. Rad. Soc.*, **10**, 1940.

Davies, D. Stedman. 'The Parliamentary Surveys of the Manors of Radnorshire in 1649', *Trans. Rad. Soc.*, **11**, 1941.

Dawson, Mrs M. L. 'Notes on the History of Glasbury', *Archaeol. Camb.*, 6th series, **18**, 1918.

Fox, Sir. C. and Aileen. 'Platform House-sites of the South Wales type in Swydd Buddugre, Maelienydd', *Archaeol. Camb.*, **100**, 1948, reprinted *Trans. Rad. Soc.*, **19**, 1949.

Gibbin, O. 'The Flora of Radnorshire', *Trans. Rad. Soc.*, **7**, 1937.

Howse, W. H. 'A Short Account of Wigmore Castle', *Trans. Rad. Soc.*, **20**, 1950.

Howse, W. H. 'Crops grown in the parish of Presteigne, 1620', *Trans. Rad. Soc.*, **26**, 1956.

Howse, W. H. 'Encroachments on the King's Wastes in Cantref Maelienydd as recorded in 1734', *Trans. Rad. Soc.*, **25**, 1955.

Howse, W. H. *Radnorshire*, Hereford, 1949.

Howse, W. H. 'Scheduled Ancient Monuments in Radnorshire', *Trans. Rad. Soc.*, **24**, 1954.

Howse, W. H. 'The Old Fairs of Radnorshire and its Borders', *Trans. Rad. Soc.*, **17**, 1947.

Jerman, H. Noel. 'The Bronze Age in Radnorshire', *Trans. Rad. Soc.*, **6** and **7**, 1936 and 1937.

Parry, Owen. 'The Welsh Cattle Trade in the Eighteenth Century', *Trans. Rad. Soc.*, **16**, 1946.

Perfect, L. C. 'The Mortimers of Wigmore', *Trans. Rad. Soc.*, **9**, 1939.

Stephens, G. Arborn. 'Castell Collen and the Metal Routes of Wales', *Trans. Rad. Soc.*, **14**, 1944.

Stevens, M. R. A. 'Geographical Survey of the Sheep Rearing Industry of Knighton and Neighbourhood', *Trans. Rad. Soc.*, **18**, 1948.

VIII. MONTGOMERYSHIRE

Bowen, E. G. 'Plan of the Trehelig Common Fields', *Mont. Coll.*, **41**, 1930.

Jones, Morris C. 'Enclosure of Common Lands in Montgomeryshire', *Mont. Coll.*, **12**, 1879.

Jones, Thomas Griffiths. 'History of the Parish of Llansantffraid ym Mechain', *Mont. Coll.*, **5**, 1871.

King, D. J. Cathcart and Spurgeon, C. J. 'The Mottes in the Vale of Montgomery', *Archaeol. Camb.*, **114**, 1965.

May, J. and Wells, S. F. *Montgomeryshire*, L.U.S. Report, London, 1942.

Owen, Robert. *In the Heart of Powysland*, Welshpool, 1930.

Rees, Alwyn D. *Life in a Welsh Countryside*, Cardiff, 1951.

Roberts, J. E. and Owen, Robert. *The Story of Montgomeryshire*, Cardiff, 1916.

Sylvester, Dorothy. 'The Rural Landscape of Eastern Montgomery-shire', *Mont. Coll.*, **54**, 1955.

Thomas, J. Gareth. 'Some Enclosure Patterns in Central Wales', *Geog.*, **42**, 1957.

Thomas, J. Gareth, 'The Distribution of the Commons in part of Arwystli at the time of Enclosure', *Mont. Coll.* **54**, 1955.

Williams, Robert. 'History of the Parish of Llanfyllin', *Mont Coll*, **3**, 1870.

IX. DENBIGHSHIRE

Davies, Ellis. *Prehistoric and Roman Remains of Denbighshire*, Cardiff, 1929.

Davies, Walter. *General View of the Agriculture of North Wales*, London, 1810.

Davies, W. Lloyd. 'Enclosure Award of Henllan Common Lands and Denbigh Green', *Bull. Bd Celtic Stud.*, **9**, 1814.

Dodd, A. H. 'The Enclosure Movement in North Wales', *Bull. Bd Celtic Stud.*, 1926.

Dodd, A. H. 'Welsh and English in East Denbighshire', *Trans. Cymmrod. Soc.*, 1940.

Evans, Hugh. *The Gorse Glen*, Liverpool, 1948.

Hemp, W. J. and Ralegh Radford, C. A. *Denbigh Castle and Town Walls*, London, 1932.

Jones, J. Idwal. *An Atlas of Denbighshire*, Wrexham, 1951.

Lloyd, J. Y. W. *The History of the Princes, the Lords Marcher and the Ancient Nobility of Powys Fadog*, 6 vols, London, 1881–7.

Neaverson, Ernest. *Medieval Castles in North Wales*, Liverpool, 1947.

Palmer, A. N. 'A History of the Old Parish of Gresford', *Archaeol. Camb.*, 6th series, **3**, 1903.

Palmer, A. N. 'Isycoed', *Archaeol. Camb.*, 6th series, **10**, 1910.

Palmer, A. N. *The Town Fields of Wrexham in the time of James I*, Manchester, 1883.

Palmer, A. N. 'The Town of Holt in the County of Denbigh', *Archaeol. Camb.*, 6th series, **6–10**, 1906–10.

Palmer, A. N. 'Welsh Settlements east of Offa's Dyke during the Eleventh Century', *Trans. Cymmrod. Soc.*, 1889.

Thomas, D. R. *The History of the Diocese of St. Asaph*, 3 vols, Oswestry, 1906–13.

Williams, A. H. *The Early History of Denbighshire*, Cardiff, 1950.

X. FLINTSHIRE (see also under Denbighshire)

Davies, Ellis. *Prehistoric and Roman Remains of Flintshire*, Cardiff, 1949.

Edwards, J. Goronwy. 'Notes on the Boundaries of Medieval Flintshire', *Fl. Hist. Soc. Pub.*, **8**, 1922.

Forde-Johnstone, J. 'Fieldwork on the Hillforts of North Wales', *Trans. Fl. Hist. Soc.*, **21**, 1964.

Forde-Johnstone, J. 'The Hill Forts of the Clwyds', *Archaeol. Camb.*, **114**, 1965.

Jones, G. R. J. 'Some Medieval Rural Settlements in North Wales', *Trans. Inst. Br. Geogr.*, 1953.

Jones, W. Bell. *A History of the Parish of Hawarden*, 4 vols typescript, N.L.W.

Palmer, A. N. 'Bangor Is y Coed', *Trans. Cymmrod. Soc.*, **10**, 1889.

Sylvester, Dorothy. 'Settlement Patterns in Rural Flintshire', *Trans. Fl. Hist. Soc.*, 1954–5.

Williams, C. R. (ed.). *The History of Flintshire*, **1**, Denbigh, 1961.

Index